English Wall Painting
of the Fourteenth Century

ENGLISH MEDIEVAL PAINTING
Tancred Borenius and
E. W. Tristram, Paris, 1927

ENGLISH MEDIEVAL WALL PAINTING
The Twelfth Century, Oxford, 1944
E. W. Tristram

ENGLISH MEDIEVAL WALL PAINTING
The Thirteenth Century, 1950
E. W. Tristram

ENGLISH

WALL PAINTING

of the Fourteenth Century

by

E. W. TRISTRAM

Edited by Eileen Tristram with a Catalogue
by E. W. Tristram compiled in collaboration
with Monica Bardswell

ROUTLEDGE & KEGAN PAUL
London

First published in 1955
by Routledge & Kegan Paul Ltd
Broadway House, 68–74 Carter Lane
London E.C.4
Printed in Great Britain
by Butler & Tanner Ltd
Frome and London

Preface

THIS volume contains material collected by my husband, the late Professor E. W. Tristram, for a full history of English wall-paintings of the fourteenth century, and also a Catalogue of such paintings, compiled in collaboration with Mrs. Monica Bardswell, and completed some three or four years before his death.

The volume has also a secondary purpose to fulfil, as a memorial to my husband and his devoted and selfless work over a period of some fifty years. With this work some of us were privileged to have the closest possible connexion. Thus we learnt, as we worked beside him day after day, whether on the recovery and treatment of paintings or on recording them, to appreciate to the full his remarkable ability, accuracy and thoroughness, on all sides. This was particularly noticeable in his drawings, which we saw in course of execution, when the paintings from which they were made had just been freed, whether from lime-wash, superimposed oil paint, or layers of accumulated dirt, and were, after treatment, at their clearest. A constant increase in power is observable in the drawings, made as they were throughout his life, even from his days as a student under W. R. Lethaby, to whom he was greatly indebted.

In the List of Plates acknowledgements will be found to those who have allowed the use of photographs, or the taking of photographs. The Director of the Courtauld Institute has permitted the reproduction of some by Mr. Kersting, which are now at the Institute and were taken four years ago or more under the general direction of my husband, Mrs. Bardswell, and myself. Although the value of really good photographs of ancient wall-paintings is generally recognized, comparatively few of the first quality have as yet been secured or published in this country. This is a fact very much to be regretted, but easily accounted for by the unusual difficulties of the enterprise. One or two of these difficulties may receive brief mention here. If scaffolding is not available on account of expense, a photographer may be forced to work from planks laid across high trestles, and then every movement causes vibration; and if an entire painting on a large scale is photographed, one part of the ancient, irregular wall on which it lies may be at a not inconsiderably greater distance from his lens than the rest. In consequence, such a part is in some degree out of focus. A section may even 'lie back', and then slight distortion is unavoidable.

While editing the material contained in the first part of this book I have received the most generous help of my brother-in-law, the Rev. Henry Tristram, of the Birmingham Oratory; of Mrs. Monica Bardswell; and of my two undergraduate daughters, Mary and Philippa. I should like to acknowledge as well the very great kindness and sympathy shown to me and to my daughters during the past two years, and formerly

PREFACE

to my husband, by Dr. Bell, Lord Bishop of Chichester; Miss Margaret Babington, O.B.E.; the Lord Abbot of Buckfast, and the Rev. Charles Norris, O.S.B.; Mr. Thomas Derrick and Mr. Michael Derrick; and my husband's chief assistant for over twenty years, Mr. Lewis Mobley. I would also wish to mention in particular, the consideration shown to me by the Rev. T. Corbishley, Master of Campion Hall, Oxford; by authorities connected with the Ministry of Works; and by Mr. Howgrave-Graham, F.S.A.

EILEEN TRISTRAM

June, 1954

Contents

Illustrations

at End of Book

The plates marked with an asterisk (*) are from drawings that combine evidence afforded by remaining traces on wall-surfaces (when such traces were at their clearest after cleaning and treatment) with evidence drawn from earlier pictorial records. Plates marked with a dagger (†) are from paintings made from earlier pictorial records only, the originals having perished.

1. The Destruction of Job's Children. The Messengers of Misfortune. Wall-paintings formerly in St. Stephen's Chapel, Westminster, and now in the British Museum. Photo: courtesy of the Trustees of the British Museum.

2.† The Adoration of the Magi; St. George, and Edward III with his sons: St. Stephen's Chapel, Westminster; from paintings by E. W. Tristram in the Houses of Parliament.

3.† The Presentation in the Temple, the Nativity, the Annunciation to the Shepherds and the Adoration of the Shepherds; Queen Philippa and her daughters; St. Stephen's Chapel, Westminster; from paintings by E. W. Tristram in the Houses of Parliament.

4.† King and Attendants; detail from the Adoration of the Magi, as above; from a painting by E. W. Tristram in the Houses of Parliament.

5.† St. George, Edward III and his sons, as above; from a painting by E. W. Tristram in the Houses of Parliament.

6.† *a.* Two of the Daughters of Queen Philippa, as above; *b.* Two Warrior Saints, as above; from paintings by E. W. Tristram in the Houses of Parliament.

7. *a.* ? Henry III; *b.* ? Edward 1st: paintings on the Sedilia, Westminster Abbey. Photo: courtesy of R. P. Howgrave-Graham Esq., F.S.A.

8. *a.* Head of a Seraph, from the Majesty in the Chapter House, Westminster Abbey; from a drawing by E. W. Tristram, in the Victoria & Albert Museum; *b.* The Blessed Virgin, from a painting in the Byward Tower of the Tower of London. Photos: R. B. Fleming & Co.

9. *a.* Head of the Blessed Virgin; *b.* Head of St. Michael the Archangel; from a painting in the Tower of London, as above. Photo: R. B. Fleming & Co.; courtesy of the Ministry of Works.

10. St. Michael the Archangel (part of figure); from a painting in the Tower of London, as above. Photo: R. B. Fleming & Co.; courtesy of the Ministry of Works.

11. *a.* Apostle, Ante-Reliquary Chapel, Norwich Cathedral; *b.* St. William of York, Presbytery, St. Alban's Cathedral; from drawings by E. W. Tristram.

12. *a.* Head of St. Nicholas; *b.* Head of St. Richard of Chichester: Ante-Reliquary Chapel, Norwich Cathedral; from drawings by E. W. Tristram.

13.* Tester over the Tomb of the Black Prince, Canterbury Cathedral; from a drawing by E. W. Tristram; courtesy of the Governors of Campion Hall, Oxford.

14. One of the Signs of the Evangelists, from the Tester, as above; from a drawing by E. W. Tristram.

15. *a* and *b*, details from the Tester, as above. Photos: courtesy of the Courtauld Institute.

16. South Newington, Oxfordshire. *a.* The Blessed Virgin and Child; *b.* St. Margaret of Antioch; from drawings by E. W. Tristram in the Victoria & Albert Museum. Photos: R. B. Fleming & Co.

17. As above: Martyrdom of St. Thomas of Canterbury; from a drawing by E. W. Tristram in the Victoria & Albert Museum. Photo: R. B. Fleming & Co.

18. As above: Execution of Blessed Thomas Earl of Lancaster near Pontefract Castle, Yorkshire; subject

Taught by her Nurse; from drawings by E. W. Tristram.

51. Selling, Kent: *a*. St. Peter; *b*. St. John the Evangelist: from drawings by E. W. Tristram.

52. *a*. Christ Church, Oxford: musician, on vaulting of the south choir aisle; *b*. Selling, Kent: St. Bartholomew; from drawings by E. W. Tristram.

53. Selling, Kent: *a*. Head of St. John the Evangelist; *b*. Head of St. Paul; from drawings by E. W. Tristram.

54. Abbots Langley, Hertfordshire: *a*. St. Thomas of Canterbury; *b*. St. Laurence; from drawings by E. W. Tristram.

55. Sanderstead, Surrey: *a*. St. Edmund, King and Martyr; Heacham, Norfolk; *b*. St. John Baptist; Photos: courtesy of the Courtauld Institute.

56. *a*. Starston, Norfolk: Burial Scene, formerly in tomb recess; from a drawing by E. W. Tristram, after one by C. J. Winter, *c*. 1872; Inglesham, Wilts; *b* and *c*, consecration crosses; from drawings by E. W. Tristram.

57. Clifton Campville, Staffordshire: Majesty, with donors, within tomb recess; from a drawing by E. W. Tristram.

58. Ducklington, Oxfordshire: The Trinity; from a drawing by E. W. Tristram.

59. Chalgrave, Bedfordshire: *a–c*, examples of heraldic and other decoration; Inglesham, Wiltshire; *d*, ornament.

60. *a*. Inglesham, Wiltshire: drapery; *b*. and *c*. Broughton, Buckinghamshire: stencilled pattern; painted hanging.

61. Inglesham, Wiltshire: *a*. Masonry Pattern, enriched with cinquefoils; Chalgrave, Bedfordshire; *b*. Masonry Pattern, enriched with cinquefoils and foliated ornament; from drawings by E. W. Tristram: Selling, Kent: similar Masonry Pattern to that just described. Photo: courtesy of the Courtauld Institute.

62. Paston, Norfolk: St. Christopher; from a drawing by E. W. Tristram.

63. As above: *a*. A King, with Attendant, from *Les Trois Vifs*; *b*. Head of the same King; from drawings by E. W. Tristram.

64. Potter Heigham, Norfolk: *a*. The Works of Mercy—Visiting the Sick; Longthorpe Tower, near Peterborough, Northamptonshire; *b*. The Wheel of the Senses; Photos: courtesy of the Courtauld Institute.

Note. It has of course been impossible to visit all the widely separated places listed above, to ascertain the present condition of the various works illustrated. Those shown in the first 20 plates, and in plates 22–25, 28, 30–45, 54, and 61–63 seem to have suffered little, if at all, over periods ranging from some 45 years (e.g. the paintings on the Sedilia at Westminster, though at that time they were in a poor state before treatment) to ten or fifteen years. However, in some instances, as in the south choir aisle of Oxford Cathedral and at Croughton in Northamptonshire, paintings have been obscured by dirt carried upward on currents of air rising from heating apparatus, with pipes covered only by a grating. Elsewhere, dirt has been deposited on surfaces in other ways. Small detail, often not very clearly decipherable, may have been lost in the course of years, or may merely be obscured by dirt. Where paintings have been left for long periods after discovery and exposure, with no protection from any preservative, much has naturally been lost. Penetration of water, one result of the enforced neglect of many ancient buildings during the recent war, has been an obvious and potent cause of damage.

Unless otherwise stated, all the drawings by E. W. Tristram here reproduced are in the possession of Mrs. E. W. Tristram; and all those by him that are mentioned throughout are her copyright.

PART ONE

Chapter One

★───────────────────────────────────★

GENERAL CONSIDERATIONS
AND THE ICONOGRAPHIC SCHEME

★───────────────────────────────────★

ENGLISH wall-painting of the fourteenth century, when compared with that of the preceding period, shows on the whole a steady increase both in technical accomplishment and in iconographic complexity. It should be borne in mind, however, that although this is true alike of schemes executed in the main centres and in lesser places before 1350, some change is noticeable after the Black Death had swept the land; for then in the poorer churches and more remote areas a decline is evident in quality. However, after the Plague, there was no diminution in the richness and brilliance of the best work, but rather the reverse. The magnificent decoration of St. Stephen's Chapel in the Palace of Westminster was in fact begun with the pestilence at its height, and though the work had been substantially completed by 1351 it was elaborated at intervals over a period of some years. Moreover, there is evidence to show that this was not an isolated or an exceptional case, for 'nobles and men of religion' evidently had schemes in view for their own buildings. Edward III complained in 1361 that craftsmen were being drawn away from the royal service by offers of better remuneration than he himself felt able to give.[1] In ordinary country churches, after 1350, comparatively few extensive schemes were put in hand, as they had been earlier, at, for instance, South Newington and Chalgrove in Oxfordshire, and Croughton in Northamptonshire. Painting was now no longer regarded[2] as the necessary and inevitable completion of a building and gradually became merely a desirable addition. Quite large expanses of wall were still painted, but more often with separate scenes and subjects than with long sequences. As time went on, and very large windows filled with stained glass occupied increasingly great areas, isolated paintings and purely decorative work accounted for more and more of the remaining space. When the general development

---

[1] See chap. II, *Westminster; the Abbey and Palace*, p. 31.
[2] Tristram, *English Medieval Wall Painting*, vol. II, Oxford, 1950, p. 1.

reached its height, at a much later date in England than in France, theme-paintings were, as in Eton College Chapel and the Lady Chapel of Winchester Cathedral, largely relegated to the length of wall below the great windows. Moreover, so far as may be judged from the few survivals of the kind in this country, they were sometimes carried out in monochrome. There is no doubt that this was done with deliberate intention, in order that there should be no conflict between the almost blinding brilliance of stained glass above and the bright colour and gilding below. In brilliance alone painting can, of course, never compete in effect with stained glass. Evidently in the fifteenth century there persisted the sure aesthetic judgment which had led Henry III, in 1236, to order that an elaborate Bestiary in the Painted Chamber of Westminster Palace should be abandoned in favour of a simple painted curtain, so that the effect of a 'great history' higher on the walls should be unimpaired.[1]

After 1350, painting took on a rather morbid cast. Allegories and Moralities achieved an intensified popularity, and those most frequently represented were the Seven Deadly Sins, the Three Living and the Three Dead, and the Seven Corporal Works of Mercy. Even in small country churches these subjects were normally depicted competently enough; but the majority of the later examples—far more numerous than those dating from the first half of the century—have suffered even more severely than have most wall-paintings from the effects of time and rough usage. The grimmer scenes were very liable to misinterpretation by their nineteenth-century discoverers, who normally misunderstood and disliked them. This dislike was in many ways not surprising, for sometimes such paintings resembled certain of Chaucer's more pungent passages. It is remarkable that so many of them have survived, even in a defaced condition; for the medieval painter, like the medieval preacher, was direct and realistic to a startling degree. Disagreeable features, of which the mildest are the tempting or else tormenting demons of the Seven Deadly Sins or the Last Judgment, have perhaps been intentionally defaced more often and more thoroughly than anything in our wall-painting.

THE CHARACTERISTICS OF FOURTEENTH-CENTURY PAINTING

The painted church of the first half of the fourteenth century differed but little in general appearance from that of 1200–1300.[2] Subjects arranged in tiers often covered large areas, just as they had earlier, and they comprised 'histories' (Plates 30–8) drawn from the life of Christ, and, increasingly, from legends of the Blessed Virgin and of Saints. After 1350, however, the arrangement in tiers is seldom found, and scenes were frequently framed in large 'panels' between windows and other features. In the country churches the tendency to abandon 'histories' in sequence was increasingly marked. Painted arches, or arcading, as a setting for subjects, thus became progressively less popular; but occasional examples are to be found late in the period, e.g. Moulton in Norfolk (c. 1400), where the new art of perspective was employed.[3] In England the first recorded instance of this new art occurs at Westminster some fifty years earlier

---

[1] Tristram, *Eng. Medieval Wall Painting*, 1950, pp. 73, 92.
[2] ibid., pp. 8–13, 18–42.   [3] See chap. II, pp. 51–3.

4

(c. 1350), but, so far as the available evidence goes, it seems never to have become popular for country church schemes. These had to be executed with speed and therefore quite simply if the painter was to meet his patron's wishes as to cost; perspective, because it was not yet fully mastered and was also at variance with the strong native liking for patterned and linear representation, was no doubt partly responsible for the abandonment of architectural settings. It is noticeable that after 1350 interest declines in building forms as components of painted decoration, and even the common 'masonry pattern', composed of outlined blocks of masonry, enriched in various ways, gradually disappears.

The painters' finest work between 1300 and 1400 became ever richer and more accomplished. No doubt this was partly a result of the increased wealth of patrons after the country's successes in war. In both wall-paintings and panel paintings of the best type, such as those of St. Stephen's Chapel, Thornham Parva, and Norwich Cathedral, an extraordinary degree of skill and variety was attained. An astonishing number of different technical methods were in use, not only for wall-paintings but for architectural features generally, and especially on the shrines of Saints. There are very few relics of the latter, though traces of decoration on the shrine of St. Alban may be mentioned. Their original beauty may be imagined from survivals on those tombs where remains of rich and vivid colour, of gilding, glazing, 'marbling', 'prints' and raised gesso-work are found. The tombs of the period often have considerable traces of elaborate 'marbling'; and sometimes it was undoubtedly the intention to simulate red and green porphyry. Work in raised gesso was sometimes used to represent chain-mail on effigies, e.g. the tomb of Sir Oliver de Ingham (c. 1344) at Ingham in Norfolk. As well as gesso, 'prints' produced in various ways, often with the help of tin-leaf, were in evidence throughout the period. They were used on columns, walls, effigies and altar-pieces alike.[1] 'Imitation enamels', a combination of painting, gilding and glass, enriched objects as diverse as the famous Norwich Retable (c. 1380), the Coronation Chair (1300–1), and the slightly earlier tomb in Westminster Abbey[2] of Edmund Crouchback, Earl of Lancaster. The ground of a wall-painting, as in St. Stephen's Chapel,[3] might be stamped with small patterns by means of heated 'dies'. The 'printing of the painting with impressions' is in fact mentioned in the accounts for the decoration of this Chapel.[4] On the vaulting of the Chapel of Our Lady Undercroft in Canterbury Cathedral, suns and stars, in relief, have convex centres with 'mirrors' laid over them which are made of talc backed by silver leaf. The ground is now black, but this was probably an underpainting to a rich blue that has disappeared. The 'mirrors', reflecting as they must have done the light of many candles burning below, would have given the effect of a firmament glittering with stars. On the vault, immediately above a niche that is known to have housed a famous statue, there are disks of some composition that may be the remains of 'prints', but were more probably bedding for jewels, whether real or imitation. In St.

---

[1] e.g. the Thornham Parva Retable, the Cluny Panel, the effigy of Sir Roger de Bois, at Ingham in Norfolk, and formerly in St. Stephen's Chapel.

[2] Tristram, *Eng. Med. Wall Painting*, 1950, pp. 130, 154, 405–7.   [3] ibid., p. 408.

[4] J. T. Smith, *Antiquities of Westminster*, 1807, 220. 'Stupis' in this entry must mean tow; see *Cennino Cennini*, chap. 128.

Mary's Church, Bury St. Edmunds, there were formerly on a roof, stars of cast lead, each having in the centre a convex piece of glass blackened at the back so as to form a mirror. This was surrounded by wavy clouds, silvered, and from these issued four groups of golden rays.[1] Such decorated vaulting as this recalls a passage in the *Romance of Arthur of Little Britain* where a roof is described ornamented with 'all the seven planettes wrought with fine gold and sylver and all the situacyons of the hevens wherein were pyght many carbuncles and other precious stones'. Above the chancel arch at Grendon Underwood in Buckinghamshire was formerly the Sacred Monogram, with 'the representation of the firmament'.[2] Ideas concerning the 'Firmament of Faith' and the sun, the moon and the planets are set forth at some length in Deguilville's *Pilgrimage*[3] and at the base of the Wheel of Life at Leominster (*c.* 1275) David, as perhaps also on the vaulting of Longthorpe Tower, symbolizes music and stands as an interpreter of the universal harmony.[4] The 'music of the spheres' was borne in mind; and the Zodiac was regarded as an image of Time. Lydgate says that there are two opposite rotations of the firmament, from East to West and West to East, the former betokening spiritual and the latter sensual things.

Extreme richness of surface quality, very great delicacy and an extraordinary power of technical invention characterize the finest work of the time. Its superlative skill is reflected, though faintly and at a remove, at least before 1350, by a higher general level of accomplishment in the productions of the itinerant wall-painter in the countryside churches. Their decoration varied in quality, however, with the wealth or otherwise of patrons in the neighbourhood. Thus buildings that are not of exceptional size, nor near any great centre, are sometimes found to be treated in a surprisingly lavish way. Even when a scheme has been virtually ruined owing to the vicissitudes it has suffered, traces showing what its original quality must have been may be recognized by the experienced eye. At Fring in Norfolk, for example, there was evidently painting equal to that of the Ante-Reliquary Chapel in Norwich Cathedral, since there are still slight fragments in the south-east corner of the nave to indicate what must formerly have existed.

The pigments used in the fourteenth century remained, on the whole, much as they had been earlier, although vermilion, after the discovery of an easier method of making it,[5] became more common and was in fairly general use by the close of the period. A freer use of such a brilliant pigment since more vivid blues, greens and yellows were of course employed with it, had the result, that colour schemes were 'pitched' in a higher 'key'. However, the earth colours—the ochres—and lime white, remained in evidence for a considerable time wherever less expensive work was carried out. Black was used more often than it had been, doubtless by way of contrast. Dark red and black were

---

[1] *Associated Architectural Societies Reports*, X, 90–1: Blackburne, *Decorative Painting*, 44: 'Ther was a royal rooffe—Hyt was bushed (burnished) above with besauntes ful brygth.'

[2] Keyser, *Mural Decorations*, 1883.

[3] Lydgate, *The Pilgrimage of the Life of Man*, 1426, from Guillaume de Deguilville, 1330, 1355; E.E.T.S., 1899, 1901, 1904, 341–4. *Reson and Sensuallyte*, E.E.T.S., 1901, 90.

[4] Émile Mâle, *L'Art Religieux du XIIe siécle en France*, 1922, 316–17, 319, 321.

[5] D. V. Thompson, *The Materials of Medieval Painting*, London, 1936, 106.

freely employed for outlining figures and heads; patterns, too, were often executed in black, and underpainting in black is not infrequently found. 'Grisaille' painting developed, but more slowly, side by side with the brilliant colour schemes already mentioned. In its fully-developed form it is first seen in the work of St. Stephen's Chapel. The origin may be found in the custom first traceable as early as 1305, on the screens of Prior Henry of Eastry at Canterbury and c. 1335 on the Octagon at Ely, where stone-work is simulated [1] in paint. Our best-known examples of 'grisaille' painting are of the late fifteenth century and are to be seen in Eton College Chapel.

There was a great burst of activity during the first half of the fourteenth century and works were produced in large numbers. The majority are now lost, or badly defaced; but where they are well, or fairly well preserved, the dexterity of the handling, the sureness with which folds of drapery and other features are delineated with long, sweeping strokes of the brush, and the lively rendering of figures and faces are all remarkable. When we consider the many examples of skilled workmanship that remain from this time, it seems far from surprising that, when painters were conscripted for execution of the superb decoration of St. Stephen's Chapel, it should have been possible to draw them from no less than fourteen counties. When we attempt to assess the works we still possess, the vast destruction wrought by time and iconoclasm must of course be borne in mind. Even so, there are not very many examples of the fourteenth century that equal in pure inspiration such masterpieces of the earlier period as the Chichester Roundel, the paintings of the Holy Sepulchre Chapel, the Chapel of the Guardian Angels in Winchester Cathedral, and the superb decoration of Henry III's Painted Chamber.[2] However, for sheer technical mastery the best fourteenth-century work surpasses all these, but the scheme in St. Stephen's Chapel, the wall-paintings at South Newington in Oxfordshire, panel paintings like the Thornham Parva Retable, the Cluny Panel, the Wilton Diptych, and the portrait of Richard II are in every way superlative productions.

Even the comparatively simple of the wall-paintings in countryside churches show remarkable power and dexterity in handling, though they hardly can have been the work of outstanding men brought from one of the greater centres [3] by some unusually generous patron. Good examples of this type are those at Idsworth in Hampshire, Chalfont St. Giles and Little Kimble in Buckinghamshire, Chalgrove in Oxfordshire, and Paston and Heacham in Norfolk. All these are of a quality to stand comparison with the better, though perhaps hardly the very best illuminations of the time. The lively handling apparent in them, together with a strong sense of pattern and line, and a sweeping vigour, are all remarkable. The last quality, though proper to wall-painting, is not normal in book illumination; but the miniatures of the Holkham Hall Bible have it in some degree, and it seems very likely that their author may also have practised as a painter of walls.[4] In wall-paintings small areas of pure decoration not infrequently survive in good condition, though subject-paintings have either been destroyed

---

[1] G. E. Street, *Associated Architectural Societies Reports*, 1855, III, 361.
[2] Tristram, *Eng. Med. Wall Painting*, 1950, 89–111.
[3] As, for example, at South Newington in Oxfordshire and Weston Longville in Norfolk.
[4] See also Tristram, *Eng. Med. Wall Painting*, 1950, pp. 191–2, 279, 379–82, re William de Brailes.

or have suffered severely. Where these areas have so survived, the eye concentrates the more easily upon them through lack of distraction; therefore the certainty in execution, the strong vitality and sense of good pattern and line that are also familiar in Hispano-Moresque or Persian painted pottery become apparent.

A change in the character of figure-painting is evident in the closing years of the thirteenth century and becomes more pronounced as time goes on. Grace, elegance and sweetness replace the more virile qualities which were in evidence earlier, but some vigour as well as grace still informs the best work, as may be seen in the series at South Newington and in the miniature of St. Michael at Berlin.[1] Though the works just mentioned are widely different in scale yet in style and in feeling they have much in common. Their date is about the same, the St. Michael being perhaps a little later than the wall-paintings. By degrees effeminate characteristics and even some insipidity developed at the expense of virility. Throughout the first half of the century, the pose of figures follows an undulating line; heads are less stiffly poised than before; feet are not so firmly planted, and their action and the sway of the body above suggest an approach to a dancing movement. Falling drapery, which may be said to cascade downward, is designed with a remarkable feeling for rhythm and sequence of line in the complexity of its folds. Thus, about the year 1270 a formula was evolved for delineating the drapery of mantles—as first seen in the St. Faith in Westminster Abbey [2]—which was continued in use, with ever-increasing elaboration, well into the fourteenth century. The garment is slung in a wide festoon across the front of the body and hangs from the arms at either side in involved and sinuous folds that are often excellently designed and are drawn with consummate skill. There is sometimes a marked use of gradation in rendering the folds of drapery, as on the mantle of St. John in the panel painting of St. Edward and the Pilgrim at Forthampton Court, near Tewkesbury (Plate 25). Other examples of this use of gradation may be found in the subjects from St. Stephen's Chapel that are now in the British Museum (Plate 1), and also on the Thornham Parva Retable, the Cluny Panel, and the illuminations of the East Anglian Psalters. This gradation is also noticeable in certain other wall-paintings, e.g. South Newington, executed in oil colour on plaster—a new development and one that is unusual from the technical point of view (Plates 16–20). Gradation would be the more readily remarked there, had the surface finish survived to the same extent as it has on panel paintings.

The conventions employed for delineation of features and hair were generally though not always rigidly followed in the fourteenth century; and it may be useful at this point to dwell on their development from earlier times. During the twelfth century, in the drawing of eyes, the upper and lower lids were shown as of equal curvature; in the next century the lower lid was straightened considerably; and in the fourteenth century it was often quite straight, while the upper lid was arched markedly and was lifted slightly above the iris so as to give an oddly alert expression to the face. Again, for the greater part of the thirteenth century, hair had been represented in the main by parallel wavy or curved lines, but before its close painters had discovered how

[1] Bernath, *Burlington Magazine*, vol. LII, 159: Oakeshott, *The Sequence of English Medieval Art*, London, 1950, 48, pl. 35.　　　　　　[2] Tristram, *Eng. Med. Wall Painting*, 1950, 121–3.

to draw the 'under and over' sides of a curl and thenceforward took a great delight in doing this. The hands depicted in fourteenth-century work are extremely expressive. The painter seems to have been sure of the position that each finger should take and even of the angles at which knuckles and wrist should be bent to give emphasis in the expression of various meanings or emotions. So uniform are the resulting formulae that through observation of large numbers of examples and constant practice in copying them, one may have the experience of 'completing' a half-visible fragment, in the imagination, and then, on further search of the wall-surfaces and removal of obliterating lime-wash, of finding the remainder in the expected position. Conventions such as those that we have just been discussing, when they were used by a painter who was merely competent, were helpful to him in practice; but the brush of a master informed them with a degree of life and expression that lies beyond the compass of all formulae in themselves. Some at least of the prevalent formulae derived from the sign-speech common in monasteries during hours of silence. At Syon Abbey, for example, the sign for sleep was 'to put the right hand under thy cheek and forthwith close thine eyes'—a gesture often seen in paintings of Sloth as one of the Deadly Sins.[1] To signify 'red colour' it was usual to 'put thy forefinger to the red place of thy cheek'; and this 'red place' was shown in thirteenth-century paintings as a 'roundel' of colour that varied in intensity of tint and also in position, but later was represented by tinting in red as a step towards naturalism. A constant striving for greater naturalism is evident in many changes like this. How conscious and intense the effort was is shown by the well-known extract from the Chronicle of the Abbey of Meaux in Yorkshire, to the effect that the carver of a crucifix for Abbot Hugh (1339–49) 'had a naked man before him . . . that he might learn from his shapely form and carve the crucifix all the fairer'.

An instance of the light-hearted charm evident in the earlier half of the century—a charm and gaiety with an underlying seriousness—may be noted in the Dancing Angels of Christchurch, Oxford (Plate 27), as well as in some marginal illustrations of psalters. We are told that St. Basil wished that his disciples should dance,[2] so that they might prepare for a likely occupation of the Angels in heaven. The theme recurs in the poetry of our period, as in Lydgate's *A Kalendare*, where 'this holy daunce' for which 'mynstralcy is good' is frequently mentioned in the refrain; in this dance 'God reulith both angel and man In right true loue withouten variaunce'.[3] Saints are appealed to thus— 'Bring me to that merry daunsing so swete, A, gentyl mayden, O, seynt Margarete!' Below the Dancing Angels on the Christ Church vaulting there is a musician, playing for the dance. It may be recalled that in the *Ayenbite of Inwyt* [4] the Lord's Prayer is compared to 'the prelude of the fiddle'. In Queen Mary's Psalter a marginal illumination, often misunderstood, shows two nuns and two friars dancing,[5] and yet another friar

---

[1] Coulton, *Life in the Middle Ages*, 1928, 322.

[2] Summers, *The History of Witchcraft and Demonology*, London, 1926, 140; re the ceremonial dance in churches and its survival in Seville Cathedral.

[3] *The Minor Poems of John Lydgate*, ed. MacCracken, E.E.T.S., 1911, 363, lines 8–10, 152–3, 200, 244–5, 285–6, 304, 316, 329, 332.

[4] Dan Michel, *Ayenbite of Inwyt*, 1340, E.E.T.S., 23, 1866, ed. Morris, 105.

[5] Evans, *English Art*, Oxford, 1949, 16; the meaning of this marginal drawing is here completely misunderstood.

and minoress playing respectively a psalterion and a mandolin. The former recalls a Christmas song that occurs in a series of outlines for sermons (*c.* 1350) by a Franciscan. Its refrain runs: 'Hound by hound we schulle ous take and ioye and blisse sculle we make.'[1]

Pure ornament followed the general trend of the time, as might be expected, and became ever more varied. One of the designs used around subjects, or to decorate the divisions between tiers of paintings was the 'waved' border, carried out in two colours, counter-changed and often elaborated with small roundels. Like this design, the 'bent-riband' pattern continued for some time after 1300, but was gradually superseded, much sooner than the other, by scroll-work. Scroll decoration was ever more freely executed as time went on, since brush-work became 'swifter' in character and more masterly. To enrich the scroll floral and leaf forms of very varied and increasingly delicate kinds were developed. A scroll pattern, difficult to describe but perhaps best called a 'stem and small leaf arabesque', for the 'leaves' were little more than flourishes of the brush, appeared in the first half of the century (*c.* 1330), and was used as an all-over design for backgrounds. A notable example may be seen at South Newington, on the Virgin and Child (Plate 16*a*) which may be dated *c.* 1330–40. 'Arabesque' backgrounds like this have been called, quite mistakenly, a 'mid-fourteenth-century innovation into English illumination, presumably from France'.[2] There is from this time onward a greater profusion of ornament of a more realistic type than before. Small 'repeat' patterns also increase, especially on backgrounds, where we find various floral and other diapers, and even, towards 1400, heraldic ermine. 'Masonry pattern' (Plate 61), at first elaborated chiefly with sexfoils, cinquefoils or 'roses', and simple scrolls, later has the Sacred Monogram, the letter M crowned, and, from the end of the previous century, an increasing number of fleur-de-lis and many-petalled flowers like daisies. Bluebells and hyacinths, recognizable[3] as such, are to be seen both on the vaulting of the Chapel of the Guardian Angels at Winchester, and elsewhere, and their date must be *c.* 1280 or soon after; in carving identifiable leaf and floral forms are found even earlier than this. After 1350, however, there is in wall-painting a reversion to conventionalized patterns, which, apart from scroll borders, become consistently stiffer in character, and, towards the close of the century, much broader both in design and in execution. The rather coarse and mechanical device of the stencil then comes into its own (Plate 60*b*); and even the later background 'prints', like those on Westminster work forming part of renovations of *c.* 1390,[4] are coarser in quality than the earlier type.

The draperies often painted during the twelfth and thirteenth centuries to fill the lowest division of the wall-space were gradually replaced by masonry pattern,[5] and, sometimes later still, by heraldry. After 1400 all three types of decoration were aban-

[1] *Religious Lyrics of the Fourteenth Century*, ed. Brown, 1924, no. 88.

[2] Wormald, *Journal of the Warburg & Courtauld Institutes*, 1943, VI, 73.

[3] Tristram, *Eng. Med. Wall Painting*, 1950, 170–1.

[4] See chap. II, 42.

[5] Perhaps our earliest example of masonry pattern used in this way is to be found at Stowell in Gloucestershire—Tristram, *Eng. Med. Wall Painting*, I, 1944, 44–6, 147–8, pls. 67, 68. Painted drapery (? *c.* 1125) was found behind wainscoting at Hardham in Sussex in 1950; it is executed in black on cream, somewhat coarsely, and seems to be a medieval renovation.

doned in favour of boldly designed and executed 'repeat' patterns, or else diapers, on a fairly large scale.

The use of stencilling is rare for the greater part of our period, the earliest surviving example being perhaps that in Malmesbury Abbey. A stencilled diaper of crowned Ms in black may be noted at Cranford in Middlesex, of *c.* 1400 or later. Since the four-teenth-century painter was clearly capable of far greater technical feats than the use of stencils, it may be deduced from the rarity of stencilling at this time that although the process was not unknown it was not liked. Some examples that have been assigned to our period are in fact, like that at Pickworth in Lincolnshire, fifteenth-century 'renova-tions', and are markedly 'out of character' with the paintings on which they are found. Our earliest example of a medieval 'renovation' is to be seen in the Chapel of the Guardian Angels in Winchester Cathedral, referred to above; there quite elaborate work was added, *c.* 1280, around the earlier medallions that frame heads of Angels.

Hangings depicted on walls are in the fourteenth century far from unusual (Plate 60c).[1] Their popularity, so evident earlier, when they were used to fill the lower part of the wall-space, continued unabated. They were now most frequent about altars, e.g. at Little Melton in Norfolk and Newington in Kent; but traces of these painted versions of actual altar-hangings are often fragmentary and difficult to identify. At Headington, near Oxford, there was once an elaborately striped and bordered hanging finished by a fringe, with masonry pattern below it at the base of the wall, forming part of a scheme of *c.* 1310–25; and at Horley, not far away, part of another still sur-vives, decorated with black fleurs-de-lis in alternation with quatrefoils, and having hooks at the upper edge. A third, elaborately patterned in black and grey on cream, and also finished with a fringe, is on the flat face of a massive pier opposite the south door at Lakenheath in Suffolk. At Martley-with-Hillhampton, in Worcestershire, the delight in animals and fantasies, so characteristic of the time, finds expression in a painted curtain suspended from loops, that frame various creatures, including a rabbit, a hart and a dragon, and also a grotesque.

Actual hangings, ornamented by means of painting,[2] became increasingly common, but although there is an almost overwhelming amount of evidence for them, especially in fifteenth-century wills and inventories, very few if any examples, known to be of English origin, have survived. The 'imitation' hangings, as found on wall-surfaces near altars, would seem to illustrate one at least of the uses for actual 'painted cloths' bequeathed to churches; for example, 'iij stayne cloths for iij autres' left to the church of Northfleet in Kent in 1499.[3] Inventories made after the Dissolution of the monas-teries include such items as 'a paynted hanging for an altar with a fringe for the same'. At Long Melford in Suffolk there were three long cloths hanging before the rood loft stained or painted 'with the Dance of Powlis'—they were evidently inspired by the famous wall-painting of the 'Dance of Death' at Old St. Paul's. There was also a cloth for Lent painted with 'whips and Angels'. The continued popularity, well beyond the medieval period, of paintings on walls as against hangings or tapestries, is indicated

[1] Tristram, *Eng. Med. Wall Painting*, 1944, 75–6; 1950, 388–92.
[2] Tristram, ibid., 1950, 119–20, 373.
[3] *Archaeologia Cantiana*, 1898, XXIII, 134–49.

by the words Shakespeare puts into the mouth of Falstaff: [1] 'And for thy walls,—a slight drollery, or the story of the Prodigal, or the German hunting in water-work, is worth a thousand of these bed-hangings, and these fly-bitten tapestries.' 'Water-work' was doubtless painting in size on plaster; and in the fourteenth century paintings on linen in water-colour mixed with lime were often used as substitutes for tapestries.

Heraldry is almost as commonly found in church decoration as in the illuminated manuscripts of the time, and particularly in the decoration of tombs, or tomb recesses, for instance, at Dodford in Northamptonshire, Northmoor in Oxfordshire, and Clifton Campville in Staffordshire. Sometimes it forms a very prominent feature of an entire scheme, as at Hayles in Gloucestershire and Chalgrave in Bedfordshire. At most of these places the work was carried out in ochres, and, as often happened when this was so, true heraldic tinctures were necessarily disregarded. At Chalgrave, where the scheme is of *c.* 1310, shields-of-arms outlined in black and suspended by 'guiges', also in black, have on either side of them sprays of foliated ornament in red. They are to be seen in the nave and aisles, in the spandrels above the wall-arcade. At Hayles (*c.* 1330) large areas of wall-space are covered with shields framed by barbed quatrefoils, or a large diamond pattern. One of the coats-of-arms is—*Argent a lion gules within a bordure sable bezanty*, for Richard of Cornwall, brother of Henry III and the founder of the adjacent Cistercian Abbey. Two interesting examples of extensive heraldic decoration in association with elaborate theme-paintings formerly existed in the north transept of Worcester Cathedral and in the nearby Guesten Hall. In the crypt of the former, filling the spandrels above an arcade, were 'many shields'; one at the centre was charged with three lions passant 'for England',[2] while others were identified as those of Beauchamp and Clare. At the upper end of the Hall, near the site of the dais, there was a diaper of star-shapes that covered 'the whole of the north wall to the height of about twelve feet' and framed small shields. An even more interesting scheme was once to be found about a Norman arch in Hereford Cathedral, where there were not only numerous shields of arms,[3] but intricate patterns in almost bewildering variety, and also animals or grotesques within roundels. On the flat facets of the capitals, devoid, as in Norman work they so often are, of any carving, occurred large floral forms resembling half-roses. Often, indeed, heraldry enriched 'the fair polished and painted stone' of noble tombs; and, also, 'the gay pawmentis for mennes feet and the peyntid roofis above'. An Abbot's 'carriage' might show the arms of his Abbey church,[4] and even the courier bore a box painted with the arms and insignia of his lord. Chests were enriched with painted heraldry. Thus, on the lid of one, formerly in the Chancery Court at Durham, there are four shields, two of them charged respectively with the arms of Sir Richard d'Aungerville and England and France quarterly. Around them against a ground of green diaper are painted a centaur fighting a dragon, a lion and a griffin. This is a com-

---

[1] *Henry IV*, Pt. 2, Act 2, Scene 1.

[2] This seems to be a slight error in the account; for the lions-leopardy of England, if this is what they were, would of course have been lions *passant gardant*.

[3] A few of these were of the fifteenth century.

[4] *Historia et Cartularium Monasterii S. Petri Gloucestriae*, ed. W. H. Hart, R.S., vol. I, 44; Owst, *Literature and Pulpit in Medieval England*, Cambridge, 1933, 30.

bination of heraldry and 'babwyns' (or grotesques) like that once adorning a frieze in St. Stephen's Chapel in the Palace of Westminster. Another chest, still preserved in the church at Eye in Suffolk, originally had on its front a knight, his shield emblazoned with a wyvern and his surcoat ornamented by 'an elegant flowing pattern in red'. On the 'peyntid roof' of St. Helen's church at Norwich are as many as 252 spread eagles; shields-of-arms, whether painted or both carved and painted as in the Abbot's Hall at Westminster, are quite frequently found on ceilings and their supporting corbels. A curious development of the period is what may be called 'sacred heraldry'; it comprises shields of the Five Wounds, of the Angelic Salutation, and many others. There can be no doubt that heraldry played a very great part in the decoration of noble houses, not only in carving but in the form of wall-painting; however, very little survives, and even records almost fail us. At Ingham Old Hall in Norfolk a continuous band of shields, one with the arms of Stapleton, was discovered early in the present century; large shields-of-arms, and a heraldic diaper, are still to be seen at Longthorpe Tower near Peterborough. Nevertheless, for a fairly adequate picture of heraldic decoration in a great house, whether of our period or rather later, we must turn to Stowe, who has this passage:

'Basinghall Ward . . . the arms of the family were of old time abundantly placed in sundry parts of the house, even in the stone-work, but more especially on the walls of the hall which carried a continual painting of them on every side so close together as one escutcheon could be placed by another . . . these arms were gyronny of twelve points, gold and azure.'

As we shall see, on special occasions of all kinds from Christmas revels to funerals, notable Court painters supplied from their shops quantities of painted banners and so forth. It is certain that a nobleman's house, like his richly-wrought garments, was 'Y-painted all with amorettes, and with losenges and scochons,[1] with briddes, libardes, and lyuons, and other bestes wrought ful wel' just as:

> Al hir meyne, oon by oon,
> Wern y-armed euverychoon
> With sheldys on her shuldres square . . .
> Ymages thereupon depeynt
> With freshe colours no thing feynt.[2]

The medieval passion for vivid colour is apparent in the last line, as in many others that might be quoted; but unfortunately the brilliance and intensity of true 'Gothic' colour is even now but little realized, surviving as it does only on areas of wall-painting protected accidentally, on coloured sculpture, or on panel paintings like the Wilton Diptych which is undimmed by the dirt and discoloured varnish still obscuring many. The protagonists of 'Revival Gothic', in their use of colour, imitated remains broken by time and partially concealed by layers of dirt; such remains bear roughly the same relation to authentic schemes as do the tints of a pressed flower to those of a fresh one. However, even supposing that some Gothic Revivalists had realized this, they would

[1] Chaucer, ed. Skeat, Oxford, 1915. *Romaunt of the Rose*, 10: amorettes—love-knots; scochouns—escutcheons; libardes—leopards.　　[2] Lydgate, *Reson and Sensuallyte*, I, 1901, 160; sheldys—shields.

hardly have dared to outrage current taste by making use of their knowledge; and thus, primarily by its comparative absence of colour, their work betrays its origin.

We cannot give much space here to a consideration of the coloured sculpture of our period, and so will dwell only upon two examples. The 'Tumbler' corbel at Exeter has a vermilion ground, and the foliage is gilt, with some green on the stems; the cote-hardie of the Tumbler himself is blue, patterned with small roundels in yellow and red, and the gipon of the musician who plays for him is white, sown with leaves of gold outlined in black. There is bright red on lips and cheeks, and eyebrows are emphasized with black. As often with colour in high or otherwise protected positions, the remains of the scheme when cleaned were found to be quite well preserved. Very considerable traces, however, may sometimes be found lower down than this, as at Harty, Isle of Sheppey, where in the chancel there is, or was some years ago, a carved and painted niche of mid-fourteenth-century date, with its carving gilt, its mouldings picked out in bright blue and vermilion, and some small carved heads realistically painted. One, not more than two inches in height, has the cheeks painted in gradated flesh colour, the lips in vermilion, and the iris of the eyes blue, while the pupil of the eye, the eyebrows and the headgear are all in black. Niches that have been blocked and later reopened, and carving found built into walls, often yield specimens of sculpture with paint in a remarkably good condition. It may be noted here that in Lydgate's *Pilgrimage of the Life of Man* [1] Avarice is said to steal images out of Abbeys and 'paynt them newe, and make them seme fresh of hewe, with colours bothe whit and redd'. Legacies are given expressly for the repainting of statues, as when in 1500 Gilbert Carleton, vicar of Farningham in Kent, left directions 'to newe paynte and burnysshe with golde' images of the Blessed Virgin, and of St. Peter and St. Paul. [2]

EXTERIOR PAINTING

Exterior painting, of which there are but the scantiest survivals in this country from any period, seems in the fourteenth century to have been confined in the main to accentuation with colour of architectural forms. Sculpture and areas devoid of carving alike were enriched with some painted pattern. Diapers comprising lozenges and circles in red are still discernible on the exterior of the Lady Chapel at Ely, and it is recorded that on the outside of the west door of Salisbury Cathedral traces of a Virgin and Child were found *c.* 1890. A small carved head, fully painted, was discovered some years ago high on the west front of Exeter Cathedral where it had long ago become detached. When considered in conjunction with records, this discovery indicates that the façade was once painted and gilt, just as the earlier façade of Wells had been. St. John Hope and Lethaby have left the following description of the latter:

'The whole of the doorway, with its sculptures and mouldings, was painted and gilt. In the tier above several of the niches in which the statues stood showed evidence of

---

[1] Lydgate, *Pilgrimage of the Life of Man*, 492.
[2] Leland Duncan, *Archaeologia Cantiana*, 1898, 134–49.

having had a full red background. Nearly all the statues retain some part of at least the ground coat of colouring, especially on their heads, which have been protected by the niches, and in the folds of the drapery. This ground coat of ochre had been carried over the whole of the front, sculptures and plain surfaces alike. Many of the statues showed further traces of colour, red on the lips and black on the eyes and hair.'

Traces of painted pattern, of gilding, and, around the central group of the Coronation of the Virgin, of 'some applied decoration, probably gilt stars' are also mentioned.

Two interesting examples of subjects painted on exteriors may be mentioned here, although either, since they are not dated with certainty, may have belonged to a period slightly later than the fourteenth century. In 1865 what were evidently representations of the Works of Mercy were discovered 'all round the outside of the walls' of a church at High Wycombe; and at Modiford in Herefordshire a dragon,[1] with an explanatory inscription, was visible until 1811 on the outside of the tower. In 1799 it was described as 'a large green dragon, 12 feet long . . . red mouth and forked tongue . . . the wings elevated and expanded and the feet webbed'. Green and gold are mentioned in another account of it. The church belonged to the Priory of St. Guthlac, whose armorial bearings in the fourteenth century included a wyvern, a species of dragon. It is uncertain how the painting came to survive, apparently in quite good condition, in such an exposed place; but, if the tower was originally plastered, survival may have been due to layers of superimposed whitewash, and the 'dragon' may have been lost when the plaster was stripped from the walls, as too often happened in the nineteenth century.

SECULAR PAINTING

The evidence for secular painting, though sparse by comparison with that which we have for decoration in churches and cathedrals, is not negligible. The most remarkable and extensive survival is found at Longthorpe Tower, near Peterborough, where almost an entire scheme of c. 1330 still exists. It will be discussed in some detail later. The Chapel in Berkeley Castle would seem to have been enriched with subjects from the Apocalypse, but only inscriptions now exist on walls and roof-timbers. A fine panel painting of St. Edward and the Pilgrim of c. 1360, at Forthampton Court near Tewkesbury, should be noted (Plate 25). Little is known of its history, however, and it may not have belonged originally to the house, which was once a grange for the Abbots of Tewkesbury. Technically, it is of some excellence, the colour has considerable charm and the drapery on the figure of the Pilgrim is very well designed. In the Great Hall of Luddesdown Court, near Rochester, a representation of a ship survives and may be dated c. 1320. Masonry pattern near it comes within the previous century,[2] but another example, enriched with roses, was of the early fourteenth century. This still survived c. 1870 at Moor Hall near Uxbridge in Middlesex, a building that belonged to the Knights Hospitallers of St. John of Jerusalem. Another such pattern, once on the south

---

[1] *The Church Builder*, 1865, 168 and footnote; *Woolhope Club*, 1886-9, 59, and 1939-41, lxxii.
[2] Tristram, *Eng. Med. Wall Painting*, 1950, 13, 289, 390, 578.

wall of the demolished Sub-Chantry House at Salisbury, was more elaborate than that just mentioned; and there was on another wall a heraldic diaper, mainly in blue, white and red. On the oaken ceiling of a room in the Bishop's Palace at Exeter traces of colour were noted in 1848 [1] on two well-carved bosses of a Bishop and a hooded woman, both surrounded by foliage. On the adjacent cross-beams were the arms of Grandisson and Montacute. Records show that the Bishop's Palace at Lichfield and that of the Archbishop of York in London, as well as Westminster Palace, were extensively decorated during our period, but all these will be considered later in connexion with our study of Westminster. It may be noted here that the Dominican John de Bromyard mentions in his sermons both rude paintings, discoloured by smoke, on the walls of modest houses, and the 'royal banqueting hall with its painted figures'.[2] One of the miniatures in the well-known Luttrell Psalter shows a banqueting scene in a hall, whose walls have paintings on them; another shows signs hung out from houses. They are too small in scale, however, to serve as illustrations of painted signs, and again we must turn to Stowe. He says:

'St. Laurence Lane . . . there is one large inn for receipt of travellers called Blossoms inn . . . and hath to sign St. Laurence the Deacon, in a border of blossoms or flowers.'

He also mentions the decoration of another inn:

'The Three Cranes lane was of old time, to wit, the 9th of Richard II, called the Painted Tavern Lane, of the tavern being painted.'

A few examples of painted decoration have been discovered on the fronts of taverns, but they are later in date than the fourteenth century. Lydgate gives a good description of painted signs: [3]

'Maystres of divers crafftys hang out, on polys . . . dyuers synys high and lowe wherby that men ther crafft may know; as some of hem hang out lyuons, somme Eglys and gryffouns, peynted on boards . . . Dyuers Armys and ymages.'

It is evident that painters were employed to make designs for embroidery; since there are records to show that Robert Asshcombe, 'king's broderer', and Peter Swan, who held the same office, impressed from the city of London, not only 'broderers' and tailors, but painters.

Interesting references in medieval sermons show how conscious the painter's practices were and how far some of his contemporaries were aware of them. Thus, Bromyard notes the advantage of a white ground in the painter's colour schemes—and grounds of white or cream are of course common in the wall-paintings of our country churches.[4] He notes, further, that the craftsman 'strives to combine in one master-piece the various features of beauty' revealed to him by his study 'of the master-pieces of

[1] Keyser, *Mural Decorations*, 1883.   [2] Owst, *Literature and Pulpit*, 1933, 27, 28.
[3] Lydgate, *Pilgrimage of the Life of Man*, 544. For embroidery and painters see *Patent Rolls*, 1396–9, 40; and 1399–1401, 400.   [4] Owst, *Literature and Pulpit*, 1933, 51.

others'. The importance of painting for purposes of edification is well brought out in Myrc's *Festial*:

'I say boldly that ther ben many thousand of pepull that couth not ymagen in her hert how Christ was don on the rood, but as thei lerne hit by sight of images and payntours.'

As in the previous century an important purpose of country church wall-paintings was didactic;[1] and this purpose was still served, by means of clarity in composition and vigour in execution. The average wall-painting, like the 'current literature of religion',[2] might be described as 'crude, but instinct with life and significance', though few wall-paintings can be justly described as 'crude'. It is unfortunate that, with a marked lack of discrimination, they have been so termed by some who have mistakenly sought in them the very aesthetic qualities that they neither do nor should possess. Such have failed to appreciate their proper qualities which they exhibit despite the injuries and defacements suffered in the course of centuries. To disparage our simpler wall-paintings, as is sometimes done, through a lack of capacity to 'read' and appreciate them when injured, or, on the other hand, to criticize them for the absence of qualities inappropriate to them, is of course equally ill-judged. Condemnation for inappropriate reasons of the average medieval wall-painting is roughly equivalent to condemnation of really good modern 'poster' design, on the ground that the latter lacks the 'finish' peculiar to a portrait miniature on ivory. Each has its own qualities, and each would be the worse for any attempt to combine with them the special characteristics of the other. The 'obvious pictorial sense' in a medieval preacher's 'handling of his narrative' has received appreciative comment;[3] and it may be remarked here that that 'pictorial sense' owed something to the preacher's surroundings, with their painted schemes. A similar sense is noticeable in Chaucer, who might justly be termed a 'painter's poet', and also in Langland.

Despite its mainly didactic purpose, gaiety of spirit, as has been noted, not infrequently informs the art of the times, at least until *c.* 1350 and in some degree even later than this. It finds expression in many ways, for instance, in the 'babwyns' or grotesques. They are characteristically English, and are now mainly found in the margins of manuscripts, or in stained glass or carving. Yet they were also once common enough in our wall-painting:

'the figures called babewyns which artists depict upon walls; for some of them they draw with a man's face and a lion's body; . . . and yet others with the head of a man and the hindquarters of a bear, and so forth.'[4]

A few survive, as at Christchurch Priory, Hants, on a fine wooden roof now hidden from view by later vaulting, at St. David's Cathedral, Fairstead in Essex, Hayles in Gloucestershire, Martley-with-Hillhampton in Worcestershire, and at Westminster on the Coronation Chair. There can be no doubt that they were often enough iconomatic, even though in general they had perhaps no serious purpose, and represent

---

[1] Myrc's *Festial*, E.E.T.S., XCVI, 1905, 171.   [2] Owst, *Literature and Pulpit*, 1933, 217.
[3] Owst, ibid., 155.   [4] Owst, *Liverpool Review*, ix (May 1934), 150.

merely the 'subtil compassinges . . . babewinnes and pinnacles' in which the creative urge of the times found expression. Yet, when we read in other writers than Chaucer, or in sermons, of Venus, like a Chimera, with serpent's tail and goat's belly, full of lust;[1] of the Minstrel, Worldly Gladness, man above and bird below,[2] of Avarice, who has the paws of a griffon and with her six hands holds all things fast,[3] of the popinjay or parakeet that, saluting by instinct alone the 'Emperor of Rome', stood for reverence,[4] or of the Ass and the lyre it could not play, an image that symbolized a good beyond the comprehension of fools;[5] it is easy to realize that often enough 'babwyns' were more than mere decorative drolleries. They may incidentally have diverted those who depicted them, or such passers-by as admired the ingenuity shown in designing them, but they evidently formed a kind of pictorial 'shorthand' in which a great variety of ideas could be expressed, and many derived ultimately from the Bestiaries, where both real and imaginary beasts and birds were 'moralized'.

THE ICONOGRAPHIC SCHEME

In the twelfth and thirteenth centuries a definite iconographic scheme prevailed for the arrangement [6] and disposition of subjects, but in the thirteenth some variations appeared. These, in the fourteenth century, increased as iconography became more complex. Nevertheless, some features, and one subject of importance the *Coelum*, virtually vanished. The Majesty, an abbreviated form of it, is less often found in wall-painting than it had been earlier; only five examples, some of them doubtful, may be quoted, in contrast with almost three times as many for the previous century. It was apparently transferred by degrees to the decoration of altar frontals, so far as may be inferred from the sparse information available.

The Christ of the Apocalypse, closely related to the Majesty, is at Widford in Hertfordshire on the north wall of the chancel, but it has been practically repainted. There is another from the Apocalypse series in the Westminster Chapter House, and a third of later date [7] formerly existed in St. Michael's church at St. Albans. The subject of course occurs in miniatures, and in a fine drawing, made by Brother William the Englishman, a companion of St. Francis.[8] There may have been other wall-paintings of the Christ of the Apocalypse that were destroyed without adequate records, which described them merely as a 'Majesty', or even more vaguely, as a 'figure with swords thrust into the head'.

By contrast with the *Coelum*, the Doom, in which Christ appears 'as chefe-justice, sittyng

[1] Lydgate, *Reson and Sensuallyte*, I, 1901, 89.

[2] Lydgate, *Pilgrimage of the Life of Man*, 573, 574: see Millar, *English Illuminated Manuscripts*, 1928, pl. 55 (Luttrell Psalter); Saunders, *English Illumination*, II, 1928, 108 (Arundel Psalter).

[3] Lydgate, ibid., 460–1, 492.

[4] *Middle English Sermons*, ed. Woodburn, O. Ross, E.E.T.S., 1940, S.51, 332.

[5] Owst, *Preaching in Medieval England*, Cambridge, 1926, 192, n.1.

[6] Tristram, *Eng. Med. Wall Painting*, 1944, 8–10; 1950, 42–3.

[7] Aymer Vallance, *English Church Screens*, 1936, 21, repr.

[8] Tristram, *Eng. Med. Wall Painting*, 1950, 321–3.

in His mageste all this world demyng', was more frequent in the fourteenth century than it had been before. On the whole, variations from the earlier type are not great, but the Blessed Virgin and St. John in intercession are more often found, while paintings of the Apostles as Assessors are less frequent. In the fourteenth and fifteenth centuries the normal position for the Doom was above the chancel arch, since it symbolized the division between this world and the next. At Pickworth in Lincolnshire St. John the Baptist takes the place of St. John the Evangelist, as he does also in the fifteenth-century Doom in the Guild Chapel at Stratford-on-Avon. St. Michael Weighing Souls is seen fairly often both in the Doom and as a separate subject. As a separate subject, it represented the judgment of the individual Soul at the moment of death, and not the General Judgment. However, it served also in some degree as an 'abbreviation' [1] for the Doom. The Weighing of Souls, which is of extremely ancient origin, was represented in the Near East in early times, and derived ultimately from pre-Christian sources. In ancient Egypt Anubis, weighing the heart of the deceased before Osiris and his assessors, was represented. For the Doom itself, as seen in wall-painting, there could be no better brief description than that afforded incidentally by Myrc, in his *Instructions for Parish Priests*:

> And [He] shall come with woundes rede
> To deme the quyke and the dede
> And we each one as we ben here
> In body and sowle both I-fere,
> Shall ryse at the day of dome
> And be redy at Hys come,
> And take thenne for oure doynge
> As we have wrought here lyvinge,
> Who so has do wel schale go to blysse,
> Who so has do evel to peyne I-wysse.

The Heavenly City is always represented, and the painter delights in depicting it as it is described in contemporary religious literature and sermons.[2] St. Peter stands by the Gate of Heaven, as in Lydgate's *Pilgrimage of the Life of Man*, and all who enter are 'made naked'. Both the Blessed and the Accursed, being nude, are distinguished by their headgear, and Kings, Queens and Bishops are prominent among both. Members of the religious orders, who help men in various ways, are not seen in surviving works of our date, as they sometimes are earlier. For example, in the thirteenth-century Doom formerly in St. John's Church, Winchester, a Franciscan leads forward the Blessed. The Damned, who are often chained and dragged by demons to the Mouth of Hell, are not yet characterized individually, as sometimes happens later. In a Doom of the fifteenth century the Fraudulent Alewife, who in her time had cheated many, might be shown being carried off by a devil. Her type of dishonesty was prevalent in the later Middle Ages, and constant 'presentations' apparently had little or no effect. At Brooke in Norfolk an Alewife was depicted holding a vessel of flaming liquid and, too, the bung of the cask, also flaming. The Doom, with the Seven Deadly Sins, and the Seven

[1] ibid., 45–6, 620.　　　　[2] Lydgate, *Pilgrimage of the Life of Man*, 9–17.

Corporal Works of Mercy, all allied subjects, are more often found after *c.* 1350 than any others, except perhaps figures of Saints. Langland gives utterance to the feeling of the times:

> *Forthi I conseille alle cristene to crye God mercy,*
> *And Marie his moder be owre mene bitwene;*
> *That God give us grace here, ar we gone hennes,*
> *Such werkes to werche, while we ben here,*
> *That after owre deth-day Dowel reherce,*
> *At the Day of Dome, we dede as he hight.*

At Trotton in Sussex there is an abbreviated version of the Doom, *c.* 1380. It is painted on the west wall, and, together with the Sins and the Works of Mercy below it, it occupies almost the entire space. Two Angels, one on each side of Christ,[1] each bring a Soul into His presence and inscriptions read, respectively, VENITE BENEDICTI, and ITE MALEDICTI. The Accursed Soul and the Sins beneath are on the right of the Judge, and not, as would be normal, on His left. A bust of Moses, with the Tables of the Law, is placed centrally, just below this level. His presence here may be accounted for by passages in contemporary religious literature. In Lydgate's *Pilgrimage of the Life of Man*, Moses confirms the Pilgrim and also signs all men with the sign of Tau, in order that they may be good pilgrims:

> *In hys hond a staff he held*
> *Crooked before (I took good hed)*
> *Hys garnement, by gret delyt,*
> *Was of lyne cloth al whyt . . .*
> *Thyn hornys and pyk also*
> *Be yove to thee, bothe two*
> *Ffor Punysshyng and for chastysyng*
> *Off folkys Rebel in werchyng . . .*

Angels often lead the Blessed into the Heavenly City; 'Holy Archangel Michael, Saynt Gabriel and Raphael' guide them to the 'castel ther alle zaulen [souls] vareth wel'.[2] As to the gaping Jaws of Leviathan, on the other side of a Doom, the painter had little difficulty about his rendering of Hell within and about them; for the pains of Hell, *caligo, vinculum, flagellum, frigor, flamma, timor, vermis* and so on, were described quite frequently in medieval sermons. Preachers could point to the Doom and say: 'I consell all maner of men fully to thenke on this Dome . . . the angels' trompe sowneth . . . seyinge, ryse ye dede men, and com to the Dome.' Turning to a painting of the Works of Mercy on an adjacent wall, he might continue:

'The vii werkes of bodely mercy ben these: fede the hongry, give drynke to the thirsty, clothe the naked and nedye, herbowre the howslesse, comfort the seke, visite

---

[1] These two Angels are almost entirely defaced, as shown in an early photograph, taken not very long after P. M. Johnston's discovery and treatment of the paintings.
[2] Dan Michel, *Ayenbite of Inwyt*, 1340, E.E.T.S., ed. Morris, 1866, I (opening of Preface).

prisoners, and bury the dede. These seven werkes thou art bondon to fulfil. . . . For of these werkes of mercy Criste shall speke inspeciall at the Day of Dome.'

Many schemes of painting, until *c.* 1350, and some even later than this, comprised 'histories' of Christ, of the Blessed Virgin, and of Saints; and those of the Virgin and of Saints, and especially the former, became both more complex and more numerous as time went on. Two elaborate schemes, at Chalgrove in Oxfordshire (Plates 30–8) and Croughton in Northamptonshire (Plate 21), will be considered later. In them the life of the Blessed Virgin is depicted at length, in part from legendary or Apocryphal sources. Her life was naturally included to some extent in any 'history' of her Divine Son; but it is by the legendary or Apocryphal scenes that a cycle devoted specifically to her may be identified. 'Histories' of Saints, though they sometimes comprised numerous scenes, never appear to have filled both the north and south walls, or extended on to the east wall, as sometimes happened with the life of Christ. The west wall was normally excepted from such 'histories'. In the earlier centuries, and also later, it bore paintings of Hell and of the Torments of the Damned, as at Hardham in Sussex. It appears that the medieval Doctors connected 'occidens' with the verb 'occidere',[1] and thus the west for them became the region of death; and the conception evidently affected the disposition of paintings within a church.

The Life of Christ was in the fourteenth century represented much as it had been earlier, apart from the increased naturalism that marks all the work of the period. The Annunciation and the Crucifixion are often found as single subjects, not part of a series, and as such are more numerous than any others. There are some thirty-four representations of the former, though some of them are doubtfully identified, and thirty-five of the latter. The Nativity, the Virgin and Child, the Adoration of the Magi, and The Last Supper, all occur as separate subjects, but not nearly as often as the Annunciation and the Crucifixion. There is some variation here from what was usual in the previous century, for then paintings of the Virgin and Child out-numbered those of the Annunciation. From our period there are less than twenty paintings of the former. When 'histories' of Christ, or of the Blessed Virgin and the Saints are considered, it should be recalled that metrical lives of the latter, as well as expositions of the Gospel, were read in the vernacular in church on Sundays.[2] Further, sermons were usually drawn from the Gospel or Epistle for the day; and thus, in a painted church, a priest had before the eyes of his audience vivid illustrations of many familiar themes. A considerable number of those who entered the building for one purpose or another in the ordinary way would also understand, from sermons and books of devotion, the underlying symbolic significance of subjects depicted there. They would know that a painting of the Last Supper stood also for the Eucharist, and one of the Washing of Feet for the Sacrament of Penance;[3] or that Judas, receiving the bread from Christ at the Last Supper, represented sacrilegious communion.[4]

Like the religious poetry of the times paintings of the Crucifixion stressed the pain

---

[1] Mâle, *Religious Art in France of the Thirteenth Century*, 1913, 6.
[2] Owst, *Preaching in Medieval England*, 1926, 29, 235, 275.
[3] Mâle, *L'Art religieux du XIIe siècle en France*, 1922, 420.   [4] ibid., 113.

and pity of the theme. From the late thirteenth century until after 1350 the Body of Christ was contorted, and sagged in a double curve. Later, it was shown taut and straight, with the arms strained upward, and with blood flowing in streams from the Five Wounds. The representations illustrate vividly poems like the following:

Wit was his nakede brest and red of blod his side,
Blod was his fair face, his wounden depe and wide,
Starke weren his armes hi-spred op-on the rode;
In fif places an his bodi stremes ran of blode.

As has been said previously, the Annunciation is at this time found more often as a single subject than any other save the Crucifixion, there being an almost equal number of representations. The numerous paintings of the former as a single subject no doubt resulted partly from the increased devotion to the Blessed Virgin that characterizes the period. The jar of flowers, shown between the Archangel Gabriel and the Blessed Virgin, changes in character. Early in the century, as at South Newington (Plate 20) and in Coventry Cathedral, the flowers resembled the wild tulip rather than the lily, but with the growth of naturalism the species of flower became unmistakable. It is certain that it was usually intended for a lily. What its significance was is clear from passages such as that in the *Ayenbite of Inwyt* (1340), in which maidenhood is likened to a lily that has six leaves, namely, holiness and purity of body, purity of heart, meekness, fear of God, austerity of life, and steadfastness.[1] Further, the lily had a double significance, symbolizing at once the virtues of the Blessed Virgin and the Body of her Divine Son. This second significance is clear from the 'arms of Christ', 'borne' when He 'came on earth to fight the devil'.[2] These arms, according to the preachers, comprised 'a lilie of whyte, that was His owne precious body in all His bitter penaunce'. That the symbolic flower might also be regarded as the iris appears from the following passage:

'Goddes Sonne of heven . . . found a floure full swete smellynge of maydenhode that evermore shuld last. To that floure he drewe him . . . Wherefore she [the Blessed Virgin] may be lykened to the root . . . The iris is the root of the lilie of heven and some clerkes calleth it the floure-de-lys.'[3]

A contemporary lyric says:

'*The Angel tolde, of thee should spring the Flour-de-lys.*'[4]

Whether the flower were the lily or the iris, was a matter of indifference to preachers and painters alike, and the two flowers seem to have been considered almost identical. In wall and panel paintings of the more elaborate kind, where it was easy to represent the full form of the lily, by means of modelling, it becomes more popular as the power of naturalistic representation increases. Yet the fleur-de-lis, with its clear-cut shape resembling the iris seen in silhouette, holds its own in simple decoration. It is often found, for instance, in the centre of the blocks in 'masonry pattern'. Early versions of

[1] *Ayenbite of Inwyt*, 1340, ed. Morris, 1866, 230.
[2] *Middle English Sermons*, ed. Ross, 1940, S.8, 38.   [3] ibid., S.35, 188.
[4] *Religious Lyrics of the Fourteenth Century*, ed. Brown, 1924, no. 112, lines 39–40.

the lily in painting may resemble the wild tulip, but unless the tulip was at this time regarded as a kind of lily it is unlikely that the resemblance was intentional.[1]

The Annunciation is seen twice, in connexion with a painting of St. Anne teaching the Virgin, at Croughton and Slapton, both in Northamptonshire; another may once have existed at Headington near Oxford. There appeared beneath a painting of St. Anne and the Virgin what was almost certainly an Annunciation, since the Archangel was in the normal pose, with the right hand raised and a scroll in the left. This was still to be seen in 1864, though the rest of the scene was unfortunately defaced. At Hereford Cathedral, within a tomb recess, St. Anne was shown holding before her daughter not only the Book of Psalms but the symbolic Rose. On the Cluny Panel she points to the verses from Psalm XLIV (Vulgate):

'Hearken, O daughter, and see, and incline thine ear; and forget thy people and thy father's house. And the king shall greatly desire thy beauty; for He is the Lord thy God, and him shall they adore.'

The first verse is given in the *Byzantine Guide to Painting* as also suitable for use on representations of the Annunciation.[2] In wall-painting, the subject of St. Anne teaching the Virgin may sometimes form part of a 'history', but more frequently appears either singly or beside an Annunciation. The scenes that accompany it on the Cluny panel are as a set unusual, and point to some special association or use for this work.

The Assumption, as part of a series, is at Croughton, and also at Broughton and Chalgrove. In each case St. Thomas receives the Blessed Virgin's girdle from Heaven, in satisfaction for his doubts. The Coronation of the Virgin is, or was, to be seen at approximately a dozen places. At three it is associated with a tomb, e.g. at Clifton Campville in Staffordshire, Northmoor, near Oxford, and Westminster. At the two former places it is in each case within a recess, and at Westminster fills two panels of the tester above the tomb of Richard II, one of them formerly showing God the Father and the other the usual figures of Christ and the Blessed Virgin. In the le Despenser Chantry at Tewkesbury there is a Coronation that was once part of a series of the richest type. At Winchester the subject is to be seen on the lid of a reliquary chest, and at Canterbury it formerly decorated the back of the Prior's seat in the Chapter House. Broughton, near Banbury, has five subjects from a series of the Death of the Virgin, and one is a Coronation. In this, a small tonsured donor holds a scroll with a repainted inscription, now reading:

LEUEDY FOR PI JOYZES FYVE LED ME PE WEY OF CLENE LIVE

This may be compared with a fourteenth-century Prayer of the Five Joys, in which occur the lines:

Marie, for thine ioies V, Help me to leue in clene lyue.[3]

There are five, or perhaps six paintings of the Tree of Jesse from our period, if we

---

[1] See: *A Book of Lilies*, Stoker, 1943.   [2] Didron, II, 297.
[3] *Lyrics of the Fourteenth Century*, ed. Brown, 1924, no. 122, lines 9–10.

include that on the lower part of a ceiling in St. Helen's Church, Abingdon. It culminates in an Annunciation and a Lily Crucifix, and, apart from the Tree at Weston Longville in Norfolk, is the best example we possess. The latter is both earlier and finer than the other, though rather less interesting iconographically. At Chalfont St. Giles in Buckinghamshire a Tree of Jesse forms part of a full scheme comprising a St. Anne and the Virgin, Miracles of Our Lady, parts of a Passion series, a 'history' of St. John the Precursor, the Temptation of Eve, and the Expulsion from Eden. The two last-mentioned subjects have a symbolic connexion with those from the New Testament.[1] Almost the entire scheme centres on the Redemption, although at first sight its relation to some of the subjects seems to be remote or non-existent. A fourth Tree opens the extensive scheme at Chalgrove, and prefaces a cycle specifically devoted to the Blessed Virgin; there is a fifth, much defaced, at Corby in Lincolnshire. The examples at Abingdon and Weston Longville will be studied in detail later, and it only remains to make some brief remarks here on the Abingdon roof, with its Tree of Jesse, Annunciation, and Lily Crucifix. Of the last-named there are twelve known instances, all of them English and most of the fifteenth century; these have been closely studied. Half the number, as at Abingdon, are represented in connexion with the Annunciation,[2] and it has been noted that in medieval times there was a belief that the Annunciation and the Crucifixion had taken place on the same day of the year, that is, 25th March. A phrase has already been quoted here in connexion with the pot of lilies seen in paintings of the Annunciation, to the effect that 'a lilie of whyte'[3] was at this time symbolic of the Body of Christ 'in all His bitter penaunce'. It is clear that the development of the Lily Crucifix must have followed naturally from this idea, and thus it stands both for the Crucifixion and for Christ's Crucified Body. The connexion with the Annunciation is quite obvious. The Lily Crucifix may readily be understood as an attempt to combine in the same pictorial image beliefs that relate to the Incarnation, the Sacrifice of the Cross, and the Redemption. As a symbol, this Crucifix, when properly understood, shows all the love of duality and parallelism characteristic of the medieval mind. It is easy to understand its place as the culmination of a Tree of Jesse, like that on the Abingdon roof, where the Prophets, who foretold the Incarnation, and the Kings, who were ancestors of Christ, are ranked on either side. Another such ceiling once existed in the chancel of St. Leonard at Hythe, Colchester, but was 'removed' in 1815. Morant[4] says that it was 'of exquisite workmanship', and that the decoration comprised 'The patriarchs and Ancestors of Jesus Christ according to His genealogy in St. Matthew and St. Luke'.

There are but very few subjects from the Ministry and all of them of more or less doubtful identification.[5] The only one of interest is what may have been the Parable of the Prodigal, once seen at Brooke in Norfolk where it was appropriately associated with the Seven Deadly Sins. The head of Christ alone is sometimes found, as at Barton in Cambridgeshire and Kingston Lisle in Berkshire, at both places over the arches of

[1] Tristram, *Eng. Med. Wall Painting*, 1950, 58.

[2] Woodforde, *The Norwich School of Glass-painting*, Oxford, 1950, 77, 92, 117, 126, pl. XXII.

[3] See p. 22. [4] Morant, *History and Antiquities of Essex*, I, 129.

[5] Tristram, *Eng. Med. Wall Painting*, 1950, 46–7: Mâle, *Religious Art in France of the Thirteenth Century*, London, 1913, 177–9.

windows. In Coventry Cathedral there was a third, above a Virgin and Child on the north wall of the nave, but it has been destroyed. There is only one *Agnus Dei* from this date, on the soffit of a window arch at Bradwell in Essex. At Preston in Sussex there was once a representation of the Holy Child in a chalice set upon an altar, as part of a most unusual scene, which will be discussed in detail later. Cowley, near Oxford, once had a Christ as Creator, bearing the Orb of the Universe; this was situated on the east wall of the chancel just below a Trinity that was painted above the east window. The subject of Christ as Creator is one not commonly found, though an earlier instance exists on the Westminster Panel.[1] It is derived from the Epistle of St. Paul to the Colossians,[2] where the Son is described as 'the image of the invisible God, the first born of every creature; for in Him were all things created in heaven and on earth . . .' As a subject for wall-painting the Trinity is not found in England before the fourteenth century as far as our evidence goes; reasons for its comparative popularity at that time will be considered in connexion with our most famous medieval painting of the theme, that on the tester above the tomb of the Black Prince at Canterbury. At Dorchester, near Oxford, below a very large cross, set high above an altar, is a repainted Crucifixion, with the Virgin and St. John. Other wall-paintings of the Crucifixion that are above altars or their former sites are at Bishop's Cleeve in Gloucestershire and Milton Regis in Kent. Emblems of the Passion, held by Angels, are normally seen in the Doom; but at Smarden in Kent there are twelve large medallions in the chancel, each of them framing Emblems, and each surrounded with a border on which is painted in Lombardic capitals one of the Twelve Articles of the Creed.

It is no exaggeration to say that a flight of Angels seems to descend on our wall-painting in the fourteenth century; they were found earlier, but are now everywhere. They swing censers; hold richly-patterned draperies; bear shields of arms; revolve a Wheel of the Seven Corporal Works of Mercy; sit enthroned above arcading; dance and play musical instruments; in the Doom hold Instruments of the Passion, and scrolls or incense boats elsewhere. Above tombs, or within tomb recesses, they bear the parting Soul heavenward.[3] With the Angels, the Saints appear in increasingly great numbers. St. Christopher is by far the most popular, and paintings of him, a few of which are of doubtful identification, are recorded in nearly fifty different places. He is almost invariably shown as a single gigantic figure, bearing the Divine Child (Plate 62). No scenes from the legend survive from this date, though some may once have existed. Towards the end of the century however there are indications to show that certain associated features with an allegorical character were already becoming popular in paintings of him. These features will be considered later, in connexion with representations in countryside churches. St. Catherine of Alexandria apparently came next to St. Christopher in popular esteem, and she is depicted in some twenty-four churches, with 'histories' from her legend in twelve instances (Plates 47, 48). It may be suggested that the episode of her Dispute with the Philosophers assisted her reputation during a period of increased religious doubt and disturbance. St. Margaret of Antioch, her 'companion' Saint, almost equals her in the number of representations, and has some half-

---

[1] Tristram, *Eng. Med. Wall Painting*, 1950, 127-48.   [2] Chap. I, v. 15-16 (Vulgate).
[3] See also: Woodforde, *The Norwich School of Glass-painting in the Fifteenth Century*, 1950, 128-48.

dozen histories (Plates 49, 50*b*). St. Peter and St. Paul, also 'companion Saints', are frequently found (Plates 46, 51*a*, 53*b*,) and sometimes in a series of Apostles; but figures of the Apostles, each with a scroll, having on it a sentence from the Creed, survive only at Longthorpe Tower (Plates 11, 41*b*) and Norwich Cathedral. They were frequently represented in this way on the rood screens of East Anglia at a much later date. During the fourteenth century there is no 'history' of any individual Apostle.[1] St. Thomas of Canterbury appears most often in the scene of his Martyrdom, and this is found or recorded in some ten or twelve churches (Plate 17). It should be remembered that any figure of an Archbishop that is unidentified may very well have been intended for him (Plate 54*a*), and, further, that his representations were eventually destroyed with the greatest care. A very considerable increase in paintings of St. John Baptist is noticeable (Plate 55*b*), and his 'history' is found in six or seven places (Plate 42). St. George, like St. Christopher, gained in esteem during the fourteenth century, but appears far less often (Plate 5). He was hardly as yet the latter's 'companion' Saint, though in village churches at a later date the paintings most often seen, with the exception of the Doom, are those of St. Christopher and St. George. At Barton in Cambridgeshire, in a Weighing of Souls,[2] St. George strikes hard with his lance at a demon perched on the balance-beam; at seven other places he is shown fighting the Dragon, a creature that frequently symbolized evil. As the patron of English warriors and of the Order of the Garter, St. George stood for the ideal qualities of the knightly and noble 'estate'. Paintings of him are often placed on one wall of the nave contrasting with those of St. Christopher, which are opposite or nearly so; for the latter typified the 'third estate', that is, the common people, whom he sustained against weariness under their various toils and burdens. At Pakefield in Suffolk a painting of him has, or once had, the inscription:

Christophori Sancti speciem quicunque tuetur
Illa nempe die nullo languore gravetur.[3]

He was said by prayer to have obtained 'power to put away sickness and sores from them that remember his passion and figure',[4] and therefore was invoked against plague. It is noticeable that wall-paintings of him increased very greatly about and after 1350. They are usually on so large a scale that they are seldom preserved as a whole, and sometimes only the feet of the giant remain, with fish swimming in the water about them. St. Anthony Hermit, a protector against plague like St. Christopher, appears at only some five places, an unexpectedly small number, in view of the great pestilence. At Barton in Cambridgeshire and Kempley in Gloucestershire he has with him his pig, though it is barely recognizable as one and looks rather like a boar.

Subjects from the Old Testament are less often found in fourteenth-century wall-painting than they were earlier, though they were not omitted from elaborate schemes like that of St. Stephen's Chapel (Plate 1). It may be suspected, however, that at this date any unusual series from the Old Testament was chosen chiefly for its underlying

---

[1] See Tristram, *Eng. Med. Wall Painting*, 1950, 49–50.
[2] This painting has become much defaced (Eileen Tristram, 1953).
[3] James, *Suffolk & Norfolk*, 114.   [4] *The Golden Legend*, IV, 119.

symbolism, which was derived from the sermons and religious treatises of the time. The story of Job, set forth at length in St. Stephen's Chapel, illustrated true charity, the love of God and man, and so was an example to the proud and to courtiers. Thus regarded, it would indeed have seemed appropriate for a royal chapel. Scenes related to the Fall of Man appear in ordinary churches just as they had done in the previous century; in connexion with those from the New Testament treating of the Redemption, the relation between them was an obvious one. If Types and Antitypes continued at this time to play a part in decoration,[1] then they have been lost without record. Kings and Prophets are almost invariably depicted as part of the Jesse Tree (Plates 22–4), though there are exceptions such as David playing the harp on the vaulting of Longthorpe Tower and Moses holding the Ten Commandments at Trotton.

The Allegories and Moralities fill so large a place in the history of our wall-painting from 1350 onward, that those most frequently found will, with certain allied subjects, be considered in detail later.

The Seven Ages of Man exist at Longthorpe Tower, and also perhaps at Hoxne in Suffolk; the Labours of the Months are also to be seen at Longthorpe. There is a subject at Kentford in Suffolk which has been identified as the Seven Sacraments, or the Seven Virtues, although both identifications are doubtful. The Wheel of Fortune remains at Belchamp Walter in Essex and Old Weston in Huntingdonshire, but both are in a poor state of preservation and neither can compare with the fine thirteenth-century Wheel[2] at Rochester. Lady Fortune, clad in parti-coloured garments, with her 'whel dyverse and dowble'[3] and her 'double face', 'princesse of al worldly glorye' and of 'al joye that ys transitorye' was a favourite with fourteenth-century moralists, who repeated constantly that no one should trust her wheel:

> My whel . . . whiche turnyth evere round aboute,
> Ther may no man aloft abyde
> But if so be I be his guyde,
> It turneth evere to and ffro.

She must have appeared more frequently on church walls than would seem likely from the sparse evidence. Symbolic wheels of many kinds find mention in contemporary literature, from the Wheel of Heaven and its music, to the Wheel of Lust or Sensuality with a butterfly resting upon it. The latter symbolized the Spirit of Man moving contrary to the Wheel. The significance of Wheels such as those at Stoke Orchard in Gloucestershire and above the north door at Thornham Parva in Suffolk, or those forming a pattern in the chancel at Legerwood in Berwickshire, is quite elusive. The Seven Corporal Works of Mercy and the Seven Deadly Sins, although usually shown as the fruit of Trees, are sometimes represented within Wheels. A Wheel of Life, or of the Seven Ages of Man, exists at Leominster in Herefordshire, but it is of c. 1275,[4] and there is no surviving example of the fourteenth century, so that for a representation of our date we must turn to a miniature in the Psalter of Robert de Lisle.[5] The

[1] Tristram, *Eng. Med. Wall Painting*, 1950, 58.   [2] ibid., 286–8.
[3] Lydgate, *Pilgrimage of the Life of Man*, I, 519 et seq.
[4] Tristram, *Eng. Med. Wall Painting*, 1950, 261–2.   [5] British Museum, *Arundel MS.* 83, f. 126b.

symbolism of Wheels may best be understood from such a passage as the following taken from Lydgate's *Reson and Sensuallyte*:

'thy lyff... ys lyk a cercle that goth aboute, round and swyfft as any thouht, wych in hys course ne cesset nouht... tyl he kam to hys restyng place wych ys in God... [1]

According to Durandus wheels painted in the hands of Patriarchs and Prophets, by contrast with the open books held by Apostles, signified imperfect knowledge.[2] The complicated symbolism connected with them derived in part from the first chapter of Ezekiel, but in time it evidently gained much from classical sources and even perhaps from indirect contacts with the Far East. The Wheel, for example, was the earliest form of representation of the Buddha. There are various features in our wall-painting that derive ultimately from the East; even the custom of filling the lowest spaces on walls with drapery is traceable there in remote times.[3] To explain any Wheel found on church walls as necessarily that of St. Catherine's Martyrdom is a tendency that is prevalent but erroneous.

Decorative motifs with symbolic significance are very numerous in our fourteenth-century wall-painting. Some are associated with the devotion to the Passion that spread widely from this time onward; we may mention the Crown of Thorns about the Sacred Monogram, diapers of crosses, and of drops of blood, or tears. The meaning of patterns formed of the letters J or M, crowned, and of the Sacred Monogram, is easily understood. It has been noted that in sermons of the day each separate letter of the Sacred Names [4] served to introduce significant words, so here we may trace yet another link between sermons and wall-paintings. The symbolism of the fleur-de-lis and of the rose or cinquefoil, that so often enrich 'masonry pattern', usually relates either to Christ or to the Blessed Virgin. However, there are subsidiary meanings for both; for example, roses in red refer to Martyrdom, and are frequently found on the background of a Murder of St. Thomas of Canterbury. Even the common 'masonry pattern' and the rafter-like patterns of chevrons, the latter often seen on painted representations of roofs,[5] perhaps have their symbolism. This may be inferred from passages in sermons that relate to 'God's temple, the soul', with Charity as its foundation and all the 'rafters of the Virtues' supporting the roof. At Amney Crucis, in Gloucestershire, decoration in the north transept is now much defaced. It originally comprised: figures of Saints within canopied niches, the canopies being supported on slender shafts painted with chevrons; masonry pattern enriched with roses; some heraldry; scenes from the Life of Christ, executed on a small scale within barbed quatrefoils; and 'hangings', covered with fleurs-de-lis, below a painting of the Annunciation that filled both splays of an east window. A leaf, like that of the maple or the vine, is not infrequently found in scroll-work on borders, as at North Stoke, Oxfordshire. On similar scroll-work, that forms an 'all-over' pattern within a recess in the north choir transept of Rochester

---

[1] Lydgate, *Reson and Sensuallyte*, 1901, 94.　　　　[2] Durandus, 1843, pt. I, 63.

[3] See Andrews, *Wall Paintings from Shrines in Central Asia*.

[4] Owst, *Preaching in Medieval England*, 1926, 329: and see the *Pepysian Sketchbook*, Magdalen College, Cambridge, ed. James, pl. XXII.

[5] *Vices and Virtues*, E.E.T.S., ed. Holthausen, 1888, 92–3.

Cathedral, there are parakeets, or 'popinjays'. Even oak-leaves are sometimes found on scroll-work, as at West Chiltington in Sussex.

Consecration crosses,[1] at this time, are usually quite simple in design, and the plain cross paty, within a circle, is the normal type (Plate 56b, c). The containing circle, occasionally incised in the plaster, is sometimes ornamented with cusping and trefoils or with roundels. Both the circle and the cross itself may be painted in green instead of the red that is almost invariable earlier. At Sheering in Essex two containing circles about a cross are in red outlined in black, and in St. Mary-le-Crypt at Gloucester, there are three, respectively in black, green and white. A cross at Crostwight in Norfolk has foliated terminals and trefoils about the centre. There are crosses of a sexfoil pattern, which is reminiscent of flowers with pointed petals, at Cerne Abbas in Dorset and Colton in Norfolk. At Inglesham in Wiltshire and Preston in Sussex there are, or were, crosses of rather elaborate design. Two, once to be seen in the chancel of St. Saviour's Church, Norwich, had around them inscriptions reading: ET PORTA COELI: ET AULA VOCABITUR DEI. Examples of consecration crosses, whether surviving or recorded, are about as numerous for our period as for the thirteenth century. One very noticeable feature is that inscriptions in general rise from but a few in the thirteenth century to some sixty or so in the fourteenth.

It is clear beyond all doubt that wall-painting held a prominent place in our churches and other buildings in the fourteenth century, just as it had earlier. Not only the carvings and stained glass contributed to their beauty, but also the 'fair paintings and images', and the 'colours with the wiche holy houses beth y-peynted'.[2] Paintings and painted statues alike were valued, and were well cared for. For example, it was provided that members of the Guild of St. John at Spalding in Lincolnshire [3] should have particular care for the fine image painted in honour of St. John. Ideally, the House of Worship was to be 'worthily and splendidly furnished with paintings, gold, silver and precious stones', and so in fact it often was;[4] but an incalculable amount was either destroyed by iconoclasts or perished through neglect and ignorance. In his grief at the results of iconoclasm, Roger Martin of Long Melford in Suffolk wrote:[5]

'The state of Melford Church and of our Ladie's Chappell, as I did know it . . . There was in my Ile, called Jesus Ile, at the back of the Altar, a panel with a crucifix on it, with the two thieves hanging, on every side one, which is in my house decayed, and the same I hope my heires will repaire and restore again, one day. There was also two fair gilt tabernacles, from the ground up to the roofe, with a faire image of Jesus . . . holding a round bawle in His hand, signifying, I think, that He containeth the whole round world; and in the tabernacle at the south end there was a fair image of our Blessed Lady having the afflicted body of her dear Son in her lapp . . . named the Image of Our Lady of Pity.'

[1] See Tristram, *Eng. Med. Wall Painting*, 1950, 61–4.
[2] Owst, *Literature and Pulpit*, 51.
[3] *Norfolk & Norwich Arch. Inst.*, 1847, 143n (12th Richard II).
[4] Tristram, *Eng. Med. Wall Painting*, 1950, 119–20; Boase, *English Art*, Oxford, 1953, 8.
[5] *Gentlemen's Magazine*, 1830, 206; James, *Suffolk & Norfolk*, 46–7.

Chapter Two

WESTMINSTER: THE ABBEY AND PALACE

ALTHOUGH for the Westminster School we have far less documentary evidence in the fourteenth century than is available for the earlier period,[1] there is enough to show that schemes of painting, sometimes extensive, were carried out in the Palace of Westminster and in the Abbey. It is clear that men who were engaged by the King worked elsewhere in London, and farther afield. The Benedictines of Westminster were at this time active patrons of the arts, and they no doubt employed some of those who were working in the Palace. Most of them were not on a permanent footing, in contrast with those who were specifically termed King's Painters.[2] Many were Londoners; and indeed it would perhaps be more accurate, in a study of this period, to speak of the London rather than of the Westminster School.

From 1350 onwards, however, craftsmen were impressed over a wide area for work in St. Stephen's Chapel, and they came from no less than fourteen counties. In the March of that year warrants were issued to Hugh of St. Albans, Master of the painters, for impressment of men from Kent, Middlesex, Essex, Surrey and Sussex. John Athelard had a similar commission for Lincolnshire, Northamptonshire, Oxfordshire, Warwickshire and Leicestershire, and Benedict Nightingale for Cambridgeshire, Huntingdonshire, Norfolk and Suffolk. Two years after, Hugh of St. Albans was directed by Edward III to 'take painters for the King's works in the Palace of Westminster, and to arrest and commit to prison all those' who were 'contrariant or rebellious'. Still later, in 1363, William Walsingham impressed men from the city of London itself. There can be no doubt that the ranks of the painters, like those of other craftsmen, had been thinned by the Black Death, but it would appear that the royal service was less popular by this time than it had been in the days of Henry III. Edward III, in view of prevailing circumstances, no doubt felt that he as sovereign was bound to adhere to recent provisions of the law concerning the payment of craftsmen. In 1361 a command

[1] Tristram, *Eng. Med. Wall Painting*, 1950, see Catalogue, under Westminster Palace, etc.
[2] ibid., chap. XII.

was issued to the Sheriff of Kent 'as he would avoid the King's wrath', to forbid by proclamation that 'any prelate, noble, man of religion or other whatsoever' should, under pain of forfeiture, retain

'any craftsmen . . . who are or have been retained to serve the King on his works and have withdrawn or shall withdraw from them without his licence, or to pay any other wages than those contained in the ordinances made in the last Parliament concerning craftsmen . . . Great numbers of craftsmen . . . hired upon the King's works in divers places, finding their wages thereby diminished, and that they can take more in the service of men of religion and other masters than in the King's service, have eloigned themselves from the King's works and are drawing to divers parts to abide in the service of others, whereat the King is much moved.'

It is obvious from this entry, when it is considered with our general information, that 'men of religion' and 'nobles', like Walter de Langton, Bishop of Lichfield, Bishop Grandisson of Exeter, and John of Gaunt, Duke of Lancaster, were active and generous patrons of the arts. For an example of generosity to a craftsman, we may recall, that in 1348 Humphrey de Bohun, Earl of Hereford, made ample grants for life to 'his painter, Peter Peyntour', and also gave him supervision of various 'parks and warrens' including Great Waltham in Essex.[1] We should be on our guard against the assumption, too easily made, that the finest decoration was to be found in the royal residences and that the King himself was easily foremost among patrons, though this may well have been true in the days of Henry III.[2] There are still paintings in at least one countryside church, that of South Newington, which are of the first importance, and were commissioned by members of the families of Gifford and Mortayne. They would have had in their own houses works by equally competent hands. Mention has already been made of the scheme at Longthorpe Tower. At Tamworth Castle,[3] Staffordshire, there once survived in the Hall large paintings of Sir Lancelot of the Lake and Sir Tarquin. Their exact date is uncertain, but it is reasonable to suppose that they were executed during the reign of Edward III, for then, under the royal influence, the Arthurian legends were very popular. There may have been a re-decoration of the Castle under one of the de Freviles, possibly after a fire in 1345, but perhaps much later. Walter de Langton, Bishop of Lichfield from 1295-1321, commissioned for the Hall of his palace a scheme of secular type. Among the subjects depicted were 'the coronation, marriage, wars and funeral of Edward I'. The exploits of various 'earls and lords' against the Scots were 'very lively portrayed, with their banners of arms bravely before them'. The loss of such an interesting scheme as this is greatly to be regretted. It survived as late as the year 1844, when Erdeswick lamented that it was not restored 'before it be quite decayed'. In many ways it must have resembled the one in the great Painted Chamber of Henry III,[4] where also 'the meaning of the history' was explained by means of inscriptions. Such schemes as these followed a tradition so old that it was exemplified in the palaces of Charlemagne.

[1] *Patent Rolls*, Edward III, 1916, XVI, 1374-7.   [2] Tristram, *Eng. Med. Wall Painting*, 1950, chap. II.
[3] Dugdale's *Warwickshire*, 1730, II, p. 1138; Parker, *Domestic Architecture*, pt. I, 1859, 67.
[4] Tristram, *Eng. Med. Wall Painting*, 1950.

At Gloucester, in the Abbot's Hall, the Kings of England were depicted,[1] and the paintings attracted the attention of Edward II. Abbot John Wigmore (1329–37) not only patronized the arts, but was himself a practising craftsman, as appears from the following passage:

'... he took great pleasure in different arts, so much so that he often worked himself and excelled many different craftsmen in diverse arts both in mechanics and in building.'[2]

As a patron, he caused a panel at the prior's altar to be decorated at his own cost 'with exquisitely wrought and gilded paintings'. A Painted Chamber, once in the monastic buildings at Ely, is mentioned in a document of 1541, and may have been of the four-teenth century. From 1322–55 decoration was in progress in various parts of the Cathedral, and vaults and columns alike were painted. Among the craftsmen named in the accounts are a Master William Shank,[3] a John Painter, who was also employed at Tydbury (Turbutsey) and elsewhere, Nicholas Painter, and Walter Painter with his assistant Truboke. Walter is not termed 'Master', but this was perhaps by oversight, for he was evidently a man of repute, enjoying the patronage of members of the nobility.[4] Expensive colour, gold and silver leaf, tin leaf, and oil 'pro colore temperando' are all mentioned in the accounts, and the gold is described as 'goldfyn' and 'goldparti'. The last is evidently the same as Cennino Cennini's oro di meta.[5] Our own Painter's Guild, in 1466, provided that carving should be decorated only with fine gold 'and no party gold' unless 'whoever setteth the workmen awork would have it so done'.[6] It is probable from the description that an Adoration of the Magi, formerly in Ely Cathedral, and described in Barclay's Ecologues (c. 1514), dated from the fifteenth century. Barclay (1474–1552) a Dominican, evidently admired it, for he says:

> I sawe them myself, well paynted on the wall,
> Late gasing upon our churche cathedrall ...
> The thre Kinges with all their company,
> Their crownes glistening bright and oriently,
> With their presentes and gifts misticall,
> All this behelde I in picture on the wall.

This Adoration can hardly have been much inferior to that portrayed on the east wall of St. Stephen's Chapel in the Palace of Westminster. There was also a Nativity that much impressed Barclay, for he continues:

> Lately myselfe to se that pycture was,
> I sawe the manger, I sawe the oxe and asse ...
> Me thynke yet I se the herdes and the kynges,
> And in what maner were ordred theyr offrynges.

[1] Most probably as wall-paintings.   [2] Evans, English Art, Oxford, 1949, 67, n. 4.
[3] F. R. Chapman, Ely Sacrist Rolls, 1907, II, 169; a Thomas Shank was engaged in St. Stephen's Chapel in the Palace of Westminster in 1351.
[4] Tristram, Eng. Med. Wall Painting, 1950, 15.
[5] The Book of the Art of Cennino Cennini, trans. Herringham, chap. 151.
[6] Englefield, The History of the Painter-Stainers Company of London, London, 1923, 36.

At Thornton Abbey in Lincolnshire much decoration was carried out during the earlier years of the fourteenth century. In 1313 a painting of the Blessed Virgin was executed on a column. Craftsmen were employed in the choir in 1315, and again in 1328. A panel, probably an altar-piece, was provided for St. Augustine's altar in 1336, and another, with a tabernacle, for the high altar in 1341. Master John Bernetby (? or Barnaby) was paid the large sum of £15 for it. He seems to be the Master who was employed in St. Stephen's Chapel in 1354, at two shillings a day. This very high wage was double the normal amount, and may have been given to him on account of some special skill. However, he may have received it merely because he did not take subsidiary allowances, and preferred not to follow the custom, general at the time, of receiving remuneration partly in the form of meals, gifts of robes, and so forth.[1] There is a village named Barnetby in Lincolnshire, and it will be recalled that John Athelard was directed to impress painters from that county in 1350. Just as painters were brought under duress from considerable distances, for work in St. Stephen's Chapel, so it was not unknown for men to make long journeys voluntarily, even so far as Scotland, to fulfil commissions. In 1333, 'John le Peyntour of Wyggeton'[2] was engaged to paint an 'image' and to do other work for William de Karliolo, and for this purpose he crossed the border, remaining for a year. He eventually found himself under suspicion, it being supposed that he had joined the Scots, and, to recover confiscated property on his return had to show that he 'had always remained in the peace of the King'.

Returning to London, we may consider Old St. Paul's, destroyed in the Great Fire of 1666. This was as magnificent an edifice as Westminster Abbey, and no doubt as splendidly decorated, although the evidence is not extensive. According to Dugdale, a fine altarpiece was made in 1309 for the high altar, 'variously adorned with many precious stones and enamel'd work; as also with divers images of metal'. It had 'a frame of wood to cover it, richly set out with curious pictures, the charge whereof amounted to 200 marks'. Dugdale also says that in 1325 Roger de Waltham, a canon, founded an oratory on the south side of the choir,

'and adorned it with the images of Our Saviour, St. John the Baptist, St. Laurence and St. Mary Magdalene. So likewise with the pictures of the celestial Hierarchy, the Joys of the Blessed Virgin, and others, both in the roof about the altar, and other places ... neither was there any part of the said oratory or roof thereof but he caused it to be beautified with comely pictures and images.'

Dugdale's account of 'the picture of St. Paul'[3] richly painted and placed to the right of the high altar in 1348 is well known. In 1336 Stephen de Rokesle, cordwainer, left a legacy for the execution of decorative work 'about the representation of the Annunciation of the Virgin Mary in the new work of St. Paul's'. In 1380 John of Gaunt

---

[1] It is fairly well known that craftsmen received part of their remuneration in this way; but it should be noted that Squires did so too. In 1323 it was provided that the King's twelve squires should have sevenpence halfpenny a day, two robes, and certain food. See Rickert, *Chaucer's World*, 1950, 139, 144. There are instances, however, of other arrangements.

[2] *Close Rolls, Edward III*, 1333–7, 54.

[3] Most probably a statue.

33

commissioned 'noz chers et bien amez' Richard Burgate and Robert Davy,[1] painters and citizens of London, to decorate the tomb of his Duchess, including 'touz les aysshelers et touz les ymages'. A painting, or else a statue, of 'Thomas late Earl of Lancaster' caused some difficulties during the year 1323, since a belief arose that miracles had been wrought [2] in connexion with it, and this naturally aroused the royal anger. About the same date, as we shall see, a wall-painting of the Earl's 'Martyrdom' was carried out at South Newington (Plate 18), and was pointedly placed near another of the martyrdom of St. Thomas of Canterbury.

Evidence both actual and documentary relating to Westminster is quite extensive when contrasted with St. Paul's. In the Abbey church in both the north and south aisles of the nave painted shields survive, and there are carved and painted label stops. Very slight traces of colour indicate that subjects once existed within the bays of the wall arcade, like those of the thirteenth century in the south transept.[3] In the Abbot's Hall painted shields are held by Angels carved on the stone corbels that support the roof, the arms of Abbot Litlington and those of the Abbey still being visible. If there were once wall-paintings in this Hall, as existed in the hall of the Bishop's Palace at Lichfield, and in the Painted Chambers of St. Albans,[4] Ely and Maxstoke, no record of them is known. Still other remains of fourteenth-century heraldic decoration are to be seen in the Muniment Room, where a piece of fascia-board, patterned with foliage and bearing three shields of arms, is preserved. In the same place, a plastered partition bears a large but somewhat defaced representation of the White Hart of Richard II. The very small chapel of Our Lady of the Pew, that is formed in the thickness of the abutment between the chapels of St. John Baptist and Abbot Islip, shows extensive remains of pattern, and colouring in vermilion, blue, white and black. An unusual subject, 'the Grand Mysteries of the Philosopher's Stone', is recorded as having been represented upon an arch by order of Abbot Cremer. It was still visible in the days of Ashmole, but was later defaced by the Puritans.[5]

Of three tombs that were once splendidly painted and gilt, and that still retain much of their colour in the higher and more protected positions at least, two are late thirteenth century—those of Edmund Crouchback, Earl of Lancaster, and his wife Aveline,[6] but a third, that of Aymer de Valence, Earl of Pembroke, comes within our period. Its 'weepers' were once painted in red, green, blue and white, against backgrounds alternately in red and green and diapered with flowers in gold. There are still to be seen shields with painted charges. On horsemen carved in the gable of the canopy there are remains of a naturalistic treatment. The roof of the structure has a masonry pattern, large in scale; and on other architectural features there is 'marbling', executed by means of white brush-strokes on grounds of red, green and black.[7] Two more tombs may be mentioned here, on account of their former painted decoration. There is

---

[1] Probably son of one of the earliest known Wardens of the Painter's Guild (1328) and member of a well-known London family of painters; see Appendix D.

[2] Rymer's *Foedera*, I, 222.   [3] Tristram, *Eng. Med. Wall Painting*, 1950, 121-6.

[4] Walsingham, *Gesta Abbatum*, III, pp. 418, 462.

[5] Warton, *History of English Poetry*, 1870, quoting Elias Ashmole, *Theatrum Chemicum Britannicum*, 1652, 211, 465, 466, repr., 467.

[6] Tristram, *Eng. Med. Wall Painting*, 1950, 152-3, 564-5.   [7] See Ingham, Norfolk, in Catalogue.

little to be seen now on that of Philippa of Hainault, but it was formerly enriched with colour and gilding, the foliage being gilt, the coats-of-arms emblazoned, and the dresses of figures ornamented with patterns in gold. Further, their eyes were blue and their lips red. To make way for this tomb, a monument to some of Henry III's children was moved in 1395 to its present position in the south ambulatory, and was also redecorated. Dart says that in his time there was on the wall at the back of the recess containing the tomb a representation of four figures in prayer beneath 'a piece of church perspective'.

It is clear that the monastery of Westminster at this time extended generous patronage to the arts; Richard Merston, prior, who died in 1376, caused a crucifix to be placed in the cloisters, '*juxta sedem Magistri Noviciorum*', at a cost of 20 marks, a very large amount. Others gave considerable sums for work about the altar of St. Andrew, the tomb of Cardinal Langham, the altar of St. Paul, and in the cloisters. Keepe gives a good picture of decoration [1] still surviving in his day in the cloisters, and some of it may well have been of our period. He says:

'Leading out of the church into the adjoining Cloysters, which you are let into by two doors on the south side thereof; by that towards the west was the Picture of Our Saviour Christ nailed to the cross, the Blessed Virgin standing on one side, and St. John on the other, curiously painted and very pitiful to behold, and round about the sides of these Cloysters were other noble paintings with variety of verses alluding to the history of the foundation, and the figures thereon; on every side opposite to the walls (where now are only frames of wood) was fine glazed windows of tinctured glass of divers colours.'

Brother John of Northampton not only commissioned the Apocalypse series that still survives in the Chapter House, but also a painting of a Doom, and a calendar in the cloisters, besides unspecified painting '*ad hostium ecclesie*'. With another inmate of the monastery, he ordered a retable for the altar of St. John Baptist. Important wall and panel paintings, that are still to be seen in the Abbey church and the Chapter House, will be discussed in detail later.

With the exception of Windsor, the Tower of London and Westminster Palace, there are but the briefest glimpses of work that was carried out in the royal houses. In 1284, towards the close of the previous century, Edward I had had the hall and chamber of a manor at Woolmer in Hampshire plastered and painted, but no details are recorded. At Chester Castle the chapel of St. Mary de Castro, in Caesar's Tower, was decorated, and it seems that the subjects portrayed included a Martyrdom of St. Thomas of Canterbury,[2] by one William of Northampton. Little is known about this scheme, however, and relics of it still visible in 1937 comprised nothing more than traces of scroll ornament on the vaulting. It is abundantly clear that Windsor Castle received its share of attention. There was in St. George's Chapel an expensive altar-piece, painted 1353-4 by John, a canon of St. Catherine's by the Tower, who was at the time a King's Painter, though Master Hugh of St. Albans held the first place. About a year later, a reredos was purchased. William Burdon received the very large sum of £40

---

[1] H. Keepe, *Westminster Abbey*, 1682, pp. 177–8.
[2] T. Borenius, *Journ. Warburg & Courtauld Institutes*, 1943, VI, 43, 44, n. 17.

in 1355–6 for a panel painting 'in the great chapel of the canons' and a reredos 'for the upper chapel'. He was also employed, at the Master's wage of one shilling daily, on extensive but unspecified decoration in the Rose Tower, where he supervised twenty-one other painters. At this same time, and also about ten years earlier, there was great activity in the royal rooms of the High Tower. There, in 1363–5 John Peintour of Iver in Buckinghamshire, was 'painting the windows', presumably the window-splays, in the King's Chamber. In 1353–4 Gilbert Pokerig or Pokeritch, assisted by Thomas Rothwell and an apprentice, worked in the 'Treasury House'. Pokerig, in the same year, was also active in St. Stephen's at Westminster, as he had been previously, in 1350–1, and was to be again in 1356–7. The work in the Rose Tower was certainly of importance, for very large quantities of expensive colours were used, including verdigris, vermilion and blue, as well as gold leaf. We also obtain from these accounts a brief and unsatisfactory glimpse of a fourteenth-century painter engaged in technical experiment. His name was Richard Assheby, and he was evidently practising some special method that he had evolved, of painting woodwork 'with varnish and ochre', presumably an oil varnish, 'according to his own devising'. He was employed in the 'canon's chamber' in 1353 and in St. George's Chapel and elsewhere three years later.

At the Tower of London, in the Byward Tower, a discovery of the greatest importance was made in 1953. Both decorative painting and figure subjects were found, the former being earlier and chiefly of a heraldic kind, while the latter are superimposed upon it. There are lions-leopardy and popinjays with fleurs-de-lis, and some of the gilding remains, together with touches of the brightest vermilion. A fairly close comparison of the lions and fleurs-de-lis may be made with those seen in a late fourteenth-century Psalter of a member of the Bohun family, now at Vienna. The page on which they appear is illustrated in E. G. Millar's *English Illuminated Manuscripts*, as Plate 70. In another room in the Byward Tower, fourteenth-century slip-tiles are recorded, bearing the lions-leopardy of England, a hart, and other designs. The theme-paintings in the Tower, masterly in execution and beautiful both in drawing and colour, comprise St. John the Baptist, who bears the Agnus Dei; the Blessed Virgin (Plate 8*b*), with hands placed in a gesture of mourning associated with a Crucifixion ('*destreint ses meins*'); the head and upraised hand of a complementary figure of St. John the Evangelist, as normally seen on the opposite side of the Cross, though the latter is obliterated; and a painting of St. Michael Weighing Souls (Plate 10). Gold and the most costly colours were used freely by the painter responsible, who must have been one of the outstanding men of his day. The work, of *c.* 1400, is unequalled even by the finest contemporary illuminations; and though it is surpassed in feeling and delicacy by such a masterpiece as the Wilton Diptych, nevertheless, when we regard its scale, in technical accomplishment alone it is not greatly outdistanced. The figures are by comparison heavier in type, and less sensitively rendered, but they are handled with an almost equal mastery. Further, the drawing and design of the wings in the St. Michael of the Byward Tower have a pronounced resemblance to the Angels in the Diptych, though the colour of the wings differs widely, for in the former they are intense and brilliant. The heads of the various Saints, all markedly English in character, are firmly and finely drawn and modelled, as are the hands, feet and drapery. The work is throughout greatly superior to the almost contemporary Apocalypse series in the Chapter House at Westminster, hitherto perhaps our outstanding example of wall-paintings from the end of the fourteenth century. Some comparison may profitably be made with the screen paintings of the Orders of Angels at Barton Turf in Norfolk, which are also approximately contemporary, though these, while good, are less masterly.

It is idle to speculate on the identity of the artist, but it is greatly to be hoped that research may be undertaken into any likely documents preserved at the Tower of London, and that it may yield results. Gilbert Prince, chief King's Painter to Richard II as well as to his predecessor Edward III, had attained prominence as early as *c.* 1375, and had been employed in St. Stephen's Chapel, on the great scheme there, at a comparatively high wage, already in 1350. He died in 1396, and his successor as King's Painter, Thomas Litlington, alias Prince, was drawing payments of very large sums on his senior's behalf in 1393. The work in the Byward Tower is not that of a man already ageing. Litlington himself accompanied John, Duke of Exeter to Ireland, in 1399, on Richard II's last expedition there, and is named as a citizen of London, but after 1401 there are no records relating to him. Thomas Wryght, an associate of Litlington's, and Thomas Kent, were prominent in the service both of Henry IV and Henry V. They were paid considerable sums for banners 'ornamented with the arms of all the kings of Christendom and other nobles of different kingdoms of the world', and for 'valances, painted with images', to be placed about the hearse of Henry IV at Canterbury. Earlier, in 1403, Kent had decorated a chariot for the Princess Philippa; just as Walter of Durham, nearly a century before, had been responsible for the Coronation Chair. But there is a considerable number of names of painters who were evidently well known in London about the close of the fourteenth century and the opening years of the next. Richard Davy, 'of County Gloucester', one of a prominent family of painters, is recorded as having left the craft of the painters for that of the stainers in May, 1416, and with a certain William Gynore was sworn 'Master of the mistery of Steynours' in the following year. Further, in the same year, Thomas Richer and John Northfolk became Governors of the Painters' Guild.

There is no reason to suppose, from the nature of the subjects depicted in the Byward Tower, that the part of the building in which they exist must have been a chapel, though this may have been so. The extensive records available for the reign of Henry III show that sacred subjects were often depicted in ordinary rooms. This room in the Tower is surely an example of a chamber, such as the one described by Chaucer in the *Boke of the Duchess*:

> *And, sooth to seyn, my chambre was*
> *Ful wel depeynted, and with glas*
> *Were al the windowes wel y-glased . . .*
> *And alle the walls with colours fyne*
> *Were peynted, both text and glose . . .*
> *[Of] al the Romance of the Rose . . .*
> *And through the glas the sunne shone*
> *Upon my bed with brighte bemes,*
> *With many glade gilden stremes.*

Not only of churches might it be said: 'thou makest clad the walls of dead stone with painture of brightness, shining with gayness . . .'

Westminster Palace in the year 1307 saw Master Thomas of Westminster engaged in the Great and Little Halls, in the Marculph Chamber, and in a number of other chambers and chapels, on new paintings as well as on repairs and renovations. He was the son of Master Walter of Durham, who had been chief King's Painter in the latter years of Henry III [1] and also during the greater part of his successor's reign. The burst of activity in the Palace in 1307 was associated, as might be expected, with a great occasion, in this case a royal marriage. Master Thomas supervised the decoration of the ship in which Edward II crossed to France for the event. Activity in the Palace continued for some time. Among the men employed, four received wages equal to those of the Master, and a fifth, William of Sudbury, slightly more. It should be remembered, however, that Master Thomas almost without doubt had the advantage of his subordinates financially, and received as his father had done, many emoluments beside the daily wage. Some expensive colours as well as gold leaf are mentioned in the accounts. Interesting items are parchment strips for making size, 'pakthread' for use in setting-out paintings,[2] and the manufacture and mending of brushes. Peacocks' and swans' feathers, as well as squirrels' tails and hogs' bristles, are mentioned in connexion with brushes, and also thread to bind the latter. The feathers would have been wanted for their quills, since into these appropriately chosen hairs, from the squirrels' tails, would have been tied in order to form brushes for use on fine work. Cennino Cennini recommends 'the quill of a vulture, of a goose, of a hen, or of a dove'. The brushes of hog's bristles, according to him, normally took a pound of bristles, and were bound to a large stick. From a description of coloured and gilt stonework, of our date, that was found in the Painted Chamber after the disastrous fire of 1834, it would seem that some of the work resembled that in St. Stephen's Chapel of *c.* 1350. The gilding 'was laid upon a thick coat of *gesso* . . . modelled on the surface so as to break up the light, and so obtain a richer effect from the metal'. Also, one 'large convex moulding' had 'a row of roundels of gold' rather elaborately treated.

All surviving work of importance that is identifiable as that of the Westminster School is of course to be found in the Abbey church, with two probable exceptions, i.e. the well-known altar-panel in the Musée de Cluny and the Thornham Parva Retable. The earliest example in point of date is the decoration of the Coronation Chair, carried out *c.* 1300–1 by Master Walter of Durham.[3] On the obverse of the back are slight traces of the figure of a King enthroned, with his feet upon a lion. The arms bear exquisite patterns, executed with extraordinary delicacy and skill, by means of 'pouncing' [4] on a gilded ground of *gesso*, like those on the background of the Wilton

[1] Tristram, *Eng. Med. Wall Painting*, 1950, 84–6, 88–9, 113–15, 444–5, 450–3.

[2] British Museum, Add. MSS. 30, 263: fo. 1, fo. 2d, fo. 4 (John of Norfolk grinding colours and sizing walls), fo. 5d, fo. 7, fo. 7d, fo. 9, fo. 13, fo. 14, fo. 16. The mention of decoration of the ship suggests 1307 as the date of the earlier of these records.

[3] See Catalogue, under Westminster Abbey.

[4] 'Pouncing' is actually the method by which a design may be transferred to a panel, by pricking through the lines on a cartoon, and dusting powder against the 'pricking' (see Cennino Cennini, chaps. 141 and 142.) The word 'pouncing', however, is sometimes used also to signify the delicate 'pricking' or

Diptych. There are grotesques that appear to be rather later in date, since they resemble some in the Pepysian Sketchbook;[1] they may be part of a medieval renovation. Formerly, there were also vestiges of 'glass enamels', like those still to be seen on the Westminster Panel (*c.* 1269), the Prior's Seat in the Chapter House at Canterbury (*c.* 1304), and the much later Norwich Retable (*c.* 1380). The painting of a King, now almost vanished but recorded, has been tentatively identified as Edward the Confessor. However, as the Chair was made for the special purposes of housing the Stone of Scone, trophy of Edward I, and serving as a 'memorial in perpetuity' of him, it seems safe to conclude that Edward I, and not his saintly predecessor, was depicted here. There is a record of a chair painted for Henry III[2] in 1250 with 'an image of the King holding a sceptre in his hand'. The grotesques on the inner surface of the right arm call to mind yet another chair decorated for Henry, this one in 1256,[3] with 'an image with beasts'. This is a very early recorded example of the use of grotesques in our decorative painting. The birds, oak-leaves, and other foliage on the Chair are most beautifully designed, and like certain features in the earlier Douce Apocalypse,[4] are naturalistic in a high degree. The birds in particular are characteristically English in treatment, and may be compared with those on the Toledo Cope. The gilding and 'pouncing' are most remarkable. It has been observed that English miniatures offer more numerous and elaborate specimens of gilding and 'pouncing' than are to be found in foreign work, and that they are usually more delicate in execution.

The Sedilia were decorated in 1308, presumably by Master Thomas of Westminster, who at this time succeeded his father, Master Walter of Durham, as King's Painter. There are on the panels of the back figures more than life-size; the two that are best preserved, which occur on the north face, are almost certainly portrayals of Henry III and Edward I (Plates 7*a* and *b*). As with the Coronation Chair, the Sedilia recall earlier examples of seats painted with figures, as well as the almost contemporary Prior's Seat at Canterbury. It may be noted at this point that the portrait of Richard II was once at the back of a stall in the Abbey choir. After a period in the Jerusalem Chamber, it has been placed at the western end of the nave. About the year 1720 it sustained damage to the lower part, caused by the shoulders of those using a stall on the north side. It is mentioned by Weever as being in the choir as early as the year 1631. The comparative measurements of the portrait panel and those in the four bays of the Sedilia are, respectively, 7 ft. × 3 ft. 7 in. and about 8 ft. 11 in. × 2 ft. 7 in. There is a great development towards naturalism in the portrait, by comparison with the Sedilia paintings. Like Richard II in the Wilton Diptych, the former is a masterpiece of early portraiture. Nevertheless, certain changes in character that are evident in it may to some extent be regretted by comparison with the works on the Sedilia, for the latter are not only

stamping of a design into a gold ground laid on *gesso*. In his chap. 140 Cennino speaks of indenting haloes 'with small stamping tools so that they glitter like grains of millet'. He says, further, that the 'stamping' should be confined to the half-lights on drapery, and 'a good many in the lights; because this stamping, so to say, brightens the gold.' See the account of a chair of state made for Henry III at Windsor and ornamented with 'painting in gold'. Tristram, *Eng. Med. Wall Painting*, 1950, 71.

[1] M. R. James, *Walpole Society*, XIII, 1925, pls. II, IX, XIX. (The surmise was confirmed when the Chair was X-rayed in 1953; *The Coronation Chair*, London, 1953.)

[2] Tristram, *Eng. Med. Wall Painting*, 1950, 623 (1250). [3] ibid., 549 (1256). [4] ibid., 124.

powerful and dignified and also in one instance show a convincing portrait, but exhibit to a greater degree than the Richard II the characteristically English qualities of strong pattern and sinuous line. These qualities are to be found not only in illuminations, stained glass, and the finer wall and panel paintings, but also in almost all work in countryside churches. They are not absent even from the lesser productions of the itinerant painter in the fifteenth century. Unfortunately these special characteristics of English work have not always been appreciated fully by comparison with the more obvious qualities of 'naturalistic' representation, and so our medieval painting has seldom been valued at its true worth. The 'Henry III' on the Sedilia may, despite evident idealization, be identified with virtual certainty, through some resemblance to the equally idealized effigy on his tomb. Further, as rebuilder of the Abbey, he holds a 'founder's sceptre', with a head like a small spired building. The identification of the second King is less positive. On the background are the royal lions-leopardy in gold, and it is clear that an English sovereign is represented, but it is a debatable matter whether it is at this date Edward I or Edward II. The strong head, as already noted, is convincingly characterized and acceptable as a portrait. It bears no resemblance whatever to the head of Edward II at Gloucester, which is of a rather weak type, especially the mouth, and has moreover a short, curled beard. By contrast, the head on the Sedilia has an aquiline nose, a firm, even hard mouth, and a prominent chin. These features suggest emphatically all that is known of the character of Edward I. Further, a description of the figure as a whole might almost be paralleled by quoting the description of his body and the accessories, as they were revealed when the tomb was opened early in the nineteenth century.[1] The body was regarded in medieval times with some veneration, and was kept covered with cere-cloths that were renewed at intervals, so that it was well-preserved. Those who opened the tomb noted that (as in the painting) the lips were prominent, the dip between underlip and chin pronounced, and there was no beard. The portrait-head shows no more than stubble. On the Sedilia, the sceptre in the right hand is surmounted by three tiers of oak-leaves, like the one found in the left hand of the corpse, though in the case of the latter the oak-leaves were not gilt but enamelled in green and surmounted by a dove. Other details of costume, as given in the description of the body, agree with those in the painting. It is highly probable that the painting was inspired by the wax effigy that was used according to custom at the funeral, and later preserved in the Abbey. This seems all the more likely if it is recalled that Master Thomas, as chief King's Painter, would have been concerned with preparations for notable funerals, just as Gilbert Prince was some fifty years later.[2] Our early painters, and also our sculptors, at least from the thirteenth century onward, were not incapable of portraiture as we now conceive it.[3] In royal portraits, however, the manifest trend towards naturalism was evidently checked by a wish to preserve the royal dignity to the full by means of idealization. Edward I, unlike his father and his son, aroused general admiration and respect no less in his person than by his actions;

[1] Brayley and Neale, 1823, *Westminster Abbey*, II, 72–4n.
[2] Harvey, *Burlington Magazine*, No. 536, LXXXIX, 303–5; Tristram, *The Month*, July 1949, 34–5.
[3] Prior and Gardner, *Medieval Figure Sculpture in England*, Cambridge, 1912, figs, 225, 228 (*c.* 1225), 230, 234–6 (*c.* 1250–70).

and so Master Thomas, or any other painter, would have felt no hesitation about making portrayal as veracious as lay within his power. It seems significant that the head on the Sedilia should be so close in type to two others of the period as to be attributable, if not to the same hand, at least to the Westminster or London School of the day. These heads are to be seen on the Cluny Panel and the Thornham Parva Retable. In the former the head of the Magus on the extreme right of the Adoration should be noted, and in the latter, that of St. Edmund, King and Martyr.

On the south side of the Sedilia St. Edward the Confessor is depicted with the legendary Ring in his right hand. He no doubt formerly faced the Pilgrim, but this figure is destroyed and the panel is blank. There is also an Annunciation that once filled two panels, and was clearly a fine work, but only the lower part has escaped deliberate defacement. As on the Westminster Panel,[1] the handling suggests the use of an emulsion of oil and white of egg; but as in the case of other comparable works there has been subsequent saturation with an oil varnish, and this has made it difficult to reach absolute certainty about the medium. The oil varnish has to some extent altered the quality of the colour, though it remains rich and beautiful. The general evidence favours the theory that the paintings on the Panel, on the Sedilia, and on the tester over the tomb of Richard II were executed in oil or in an emulsion like that just mentioned above. Governor Pownall, who examined them all about the year 1775, evidently before varnish had been applied to any of them, found that all 'stood firm' against 'washing with plain water', a process that included 'a pretty strong rubbing with a wet hand-kerchief'.[2] Since fresh protective varnish had not then been applied, they would hardly have withstood such treatment if the medium had been size, or even ordinary egg tempera well hardened through the effects of time.

The general decoration of the Sedilia is a remarkable example of our early crafts-manship, and in this respect in no way inferior to that of the Westminster Panel. The following forms of enrichment are to be seen: coloured glass, laid over grounds of gold, or alternatively silver leaf; gilt *gesso* reliefs; painted chevrons and banding; a small masonry pattern elaborated with roses, and on the vaulting splendidly designed scroll ornament in red on white. The carved corbel-heads, realistically painted, are good specimens of coloured sculpture, and the whole forms the finest example of early painted woodwork that we still possess. It would be hard, indeed, to find its equal from this date elsewhere in north-western Europe. With other specimens, now almost all lost to us, it may be regarded as the prototype of our magnificent East Anglian fifteenth-century screens.

If we turn from the Sedilia to the two panel paintings mentioned above, those at Thornham Parva and in the Musée de Cluny, we find close resemblances, not only in the handling of the drapery, the modelling and drawing of heads and hands, and in the colour harmonies, but also in details of the decoration. For instance, the royal lions-leopardy, designed with close similarity, are seen not only on the background to Edward I on the Sedilia but also on the frame of the Cluny Panel, and on the back-ground there of St. Anne and the Virgin. Some of the 'prints' on the two altar paintings are astonishingly alike. The fleur-de-lis within a quatrefoil adorns the backgrounds of

---

[1] Tristram, *Eng. Med. Wall Painting*, 1950, 135–6, 403–5   [2] *Archaeologia*, 1789, IX, 145.

the Nativity and the Adoration of the Kings on the Cluny Panel, and those of the St. Catherine and the St. Edmund on the Retable. Addorsed birds, probably doves, framed by diamond shapes, enrich the Dormition of the Virgin and the St. Anne and the Virgin on the Panel, and the St. Peter on the Retable. Moreover, all these designs are almost identical to the least detail, and it can hardly be doubted that they were taken from pattern-books used in the same workshop. Other points of resemblance to be noted between the Panel and the Retable are the types chosen for heads of female Saints, and the sensitive quality displayed in rendering them. The management of the transparent veils over the hair of the Blessed Virgin and St. Margaret on the Retable is especially noteworthy, and at least equals in delicacy what is seen in various Italian works of later date.

The technical means employed to produce the 'prints' on the backgrounds are worthy of close study, and will be discussed later in connexion with the scheme carried out c. 1350 in St. Stephen's Chapel. Like the Sedilia Panels, the two retables are master-pieces of truly 'Gothic' painting, and as such should receive far greater appreciation than has so far been accorded to them. The Sedilia paintings are executed upon what is in effect a wooden partition wall between choir and ambulatory, and so may well serve as illustrations of such fine early fourteenth-century wall-paintings as are now lost to us. The medium in the case of the two retables would seem to have been either egg tempera or the emulsion of oil and white of egg mentioned above.

The portrait of Richard II is a magnificent work, and, apart from the representation in the Wilton Diptych is undoubtedly the finest medieval portrait to have survived from so early a date. As it stands, it is the fruit of careful restoration carried out by Richmond and Chance in 1866. It was recovered by them from beneath thick layers of repainting, and detailed notes were fortunately kept as work proceeded. From these it is evident that one serious blunder was made; but it is remarkable, in view of the con-temporary state of knowledge of our medieval painting, that no others were com-mitted. The background diaper, except for a very small section, was removed under the mistaken impression that it was an undesirable and very much later addition. This impression arose almost inevitably at the time, from the discovery that the surface of the panel had been everywhere lowered about a quarter of an inch to allow application of the raised diaper of 'prints', and further, that the 'prints' overlaid parts of the painting. It is clear, however, from the nature of the solitary remaining fragment, and a close study of the notes just mentioned, that a medieval renovation, of a type by no means unknown, had taken place, very probably c. 1395. At that date Master Peter, the Abbey sacrist, was paid for various activities that included the decoration of the tester destined for the royal tomb, then in course of erection under the supervision of Richard himself. This tester has a raised and highly ornamented ground, composed of 'prints', and it is very likely that it was decided to enrich the portrait in similar fashion. This is all the more probable because, as we shall see later, renovations of the kind were carried out in St. Stephen's Chapel. It is obvious from the King's appearance that the portrait must have been painted some years before 1395. Scharf surmised that the lowering of the sur-face to accommodate the 'prints' may have been carried out with the secondary object of effacing 'some deeply punctured ornaments already existing', because otherwise 'there would have been no very effective means of obliterating them'. This earlier decorated ground, fragments of which were discovered beneath the 'prints' in 1866, is described as of 'plain' gold, covered with 'undefined sprigs and scrolls'. This description obviously involves a complete contradiction, unless we are meant to infer that the gilded ground was not painted with a pattern in colour over the gold, but was delicately 'pounced' after the manner of that on the Wilton Diptych. Comparable 'pouncing' is seen in the robes on the effigies of Richard II and Anne of Bohemia. Moreover, the phrase 'undefined sprigs and scrolls' suggests that the pattern was probably the remains of 'stem and leaf scrollwork' something like that seen on many of our illuminations.[1] The original gesso-work of the crown, globe and sceptre on the portrait was revealed in 1866 from beneath later fourteenth-century renovations of these features, and was not destroyed, as has been erroneously stated.[2]

The rest of the portrait, except for the lower part, where there is considerable retouching,[3] evidently left the restorers' hands very much as it was when first completed, apart from some slight inevitable loss in sharpness and definition, consequent on the vicissitudes that it had undergone. It is most valuable to know from their notes that the face 'came out' (from beneath heavy repainting of the clumsiest kind) 'as now seen, saving an injury on the right temple, particle of the nose, and a spot below the mouth'. The eyes, too, having at some time been 'slightly rubbed' only 'required trifling repairs'. Apparently painted before 1395, the picture was 'at the upper end of the Quire' before 1631.

Shortly after the close of activities in 1866 Scharf described the portrait as 'a delicate pale picture, in carefully modelled forms . . . grey eyes . . . pale yellow eyebrows and golden-brown hair'. He commented, further, on its obvious points of resemblance to the head of Richard in the Wilton Diptych. That head, however, since it has never been painted over nor sustained other damage, remains virtually intact. The portrait on the other hand, must always have been 'broader' in handling than the small and precious Diptych.[4] It is also, at the time of writing, yellowed and obscured by darkened varnish, presumably applied in 1866, and can no longer be called 'a delicate pale picture'. After this study of its history, it is hardly necessary to point out that there is danger in the assumption sometimes made that, on account of what has been called its 'comparative breadth of handling' it is more probably a foreign than an English work. This apparent 'breadth' is at least in some degree fortuitous. Moreover, certain English wall-paintings, i.e. those from St. Stephen's Chapel now in the British Museum, despite their earlier date, show something at least of the same quality. Further, two

[1] See Millar, *English Illuminated Manuscripts*, II, pls. 10, 49, 54, 56, 58, 60, 62, 65.

[2] Evans, *English Art*, Oxford, 1949, 101–2.

[3] This was no doubt partly consequent on the damage sustained *c.* 1720, and perhaps partly the work of Richmond. J. Weever, *Ancient Funeral Monuments*, 1631, 473: 'That beautiful picture of a King . . . crowned in a chair of estate, at the upper end of the Quire in this church . . . witnesseth how goodly a creature he was in outer lineaments.' It had evidently not then suffered as seen in the engraving by Vertue of 1718.

[4] For the Diptych, see T. G. Nichols, *Archaeologia*, 1842, XXIX, 32–59: G. Scharf, *Arundel Society Pub.*, 1882: W. G. Constable, *Burlington Magazine*, LV, 1929, 36–45; Sir Martin Conway, ibid., 209–12; M. V. Clarke, ibid., LVIII, 1931, 283–94; W. A. Shaw, ibid., LXV, 1934, 171–84; V. H. Galbraith, *History*, March 1942, 237–8; T. Bodkin, *The Gallery Books*, No. 16.

significant stylistic points have escaped remark hitherto. One is that the closest parallel to the rendering of the hand holding the sceptre is to be seen, not as has been suggested, in French work,[1] but in the St. John of the Crucifixion on the Norwich Retable, an indubitably English painting of approximately the same date. The second point is that the arrangement of the drapery from the knees is closely similar to that which is found in one of our miniatures of *c.* 1375 or after, namely, the Christ Enthroned of the Fitzwarin Psalter.[2]

The background 'prints' formed in the interspaces crosses clechy (i.e. of mascles). This point is interesting if it is considered in relation to the mascles on the crown and morse, and that on the collar worn by Richard in the Wilton Diptych, and can further be connected with the controversy about his collars and the broomcod badge.[3] The assumption that the Diptych is of foreign origin is founded on no stronger evidence than is afforded by the superlative intrinsic excellence of the painting. This assumption now seems to be yielding to the belief that this is a most precious survival of English work of the most exquisite kind. If it be granted that the head of the young Richard in the left panel, with its poignant rendering of youthful innocence and hope, is the work of an English hand, then there is no valid reason for assigning the wistful, sensitive head in the great portrait to any foreign school. The idealism of both Diptych and portrait, lyrical in expression though it is in the first of these, keeps a quietly firm hold on factual truth, and in this is as characteristic of our art in some of its phases as it is of the finest poetical passages in Chaucer. Earlier examples of good portraiture may be found abroad, especially in Germany;[4] but none combines realism with idealism in the same way as the works we are considering here. In them the painter has seized upon, and has most beautifully expressed, the poetry inherent in his subject, nevertheless keeping in touch with actuality. By comparison with them, the well-known miniature in the *Belles Heures* of Jean, Duc de Berri, that is so often related to the Diptych, seems dull and obvious in the attempt at idealization after the Italian model, and also relatively weak in portraiture. When considering the question of English provenance for both portrait and Diptych, it should be borne in mind that while there is no direct evidence of origin for either, the attribution to any foreign school ignores the very strong evidence derived from records to show that Richard, like his predecessors on the throne of England, employed English painters almost to the exclusion of all others.[5]

The tester over Richard's tomb, now sadly defaced apart from the background 'prints', must once have been a work of quite exceptional beauty. The second panel from the west has usually been described as showing Christ Enthroned, but in fact it originally framed a representation of God the Father 'as a venerable old man'. This subject was complementary to the Coronation of the Virgin in the third panel, and

[1] Sir S. Cockerell, *Burlington Magazine*, X, 1906–7, 126–7.   [2] Paris, *Bib. Nat. lat*, 765, f. 21v.
[3] See publications noted above (n.4, p. 43).   [4] Harvey, *The Gothic World*, 1950, 90.
[5] From *c.* 1250 to *c.* 1425 only one Court painter of prominence can be named, who seems to have been a foreigner—Peter of Spain, and even this has lately been questioned. The notable names over a period of 175 years are: William of Westminster, Walter of Durham, Thomas of Westminster, Jack of St. Albans, Hugh of St. Albans, John Barnaby, Gilbert Prince, Thomas Litlington, Thomas Wryght, and Thomas Kent. Even among lesser men names of foreign origin are both rare and doubtful. See E. W. Tristram, *Eng. Med. Wall Painting*, II, 443–57, and Appendix.

formed with it one scene, even though this was divided into two sections owing to exigencies of space. In 1815 the head of Christ and that of the Blessed Virgin were described as 'still very beautiful'. This description indicates that they were then not only well-preserved, but possessed a degree of naturalism at least equal to that in the Diptych and the portrait. Had they lacked such naturalism they would not in the early nineteenth century have been considered 'beautiful'. The pose of the Angel on the dexter side of the shield in the first panel, so far as it is discernible from the surviving silhouette, has the slight bend and sway apparent in the Angel in the right foreground of the Diptych; further, the type of the figure would seem to have been very similar. Angels supporting shields are delineated on the wall at the eastern end of the late fourteenth-century monument to Bishop Hatfield [1] in Durham Cathedral. There are two more Angels, much defaced, but perhaps originally with shields, at the western end. It is probable that this arrangement appeared first in wall-painting and carving, and was later adopted for panels. Series of Angels with shields form a useful decorative motif for filling considerable spaces, but such sequences, though they are found also in illumination, do not seem nearly so natural in the latter.

The tester, as we have seen, is mentioned in a record of 1395 which shows that Master Peter, the Abbey sacrist, was paid about that time 'by the hands of John Haxey' for work which included 'painting the covering of the tomb of Anne, late Queen of England'. A painting of Richard II, apparently the great portrait, is referred to in the same entry. It has been assumed, perhaps first by Eastlake, that Master Peter received payment with the object of passing it on to some unidentified painter or painters. No reason, however, has been suggested for such an indirect and exceptional method of payment, by which money would have passed without apparent necessity through three people's hands. It seems more than likely that he was paid for work on the tester simply because he had in fact carried it out himself, or had, in the medieval fashion, in part executed and in part supervised it. In this connexion, it may be emphasized that in the records he is called 'Master'. This must have been so because he had attained mastership of an art, like Master William, monk of Westminster, who for the greater part of Henry III's reign was the latter's chief painter. In the fourteenth century there were still many artists who were members of one religious body or another.[2] If Master Peter was in fact a painter his experience would have been valuable to him in his capacity as sacrist. As is well known, the sacrist was generally concerned with the supervision of the fabric and its decoration and 'furniture'.[3] If it is supposed that Master Peter was a painter, then Richard II, like his predecessors Henry III and Edward III,[4] had a favourite artist who was also a cleric. Master Peter's name should then stand beside those of the foremost artists of the day, as a possible author of the superb and hieratic portrait, or the exquisite Wilton Diptych. The beautiful serenity of both these paintings brings to mind the sculptured Virgin and Child of the Outer Gate at Winchester College, and also the later masterpieces of Fra Angelico.

We may now turn to the wall-paintings in the Chapter House; namely, the Majesty

---

[1] Died 1381.   [2] Tristram, *The Wilton Diptych, The Month*, July 1949, 33.
[3] See, for example, H. W. Saunders, *An Introduction to the Obedientiary and Manor Rolls of Norwich Cathedral Priory*, 1930, 102–13.   [4] Tristram, *Eng. Med. Wall Painting*, 1950, 445–450.

(Plate 8) on the east side of the building and the Apocalypse series near its entrance on both sides. The former is the earlier, and may be dated 1350, or a little after. At that time Master Hugh of St. Albans was employed by Edward III on the great scheme in the royal Chapel of St. Stephen in Westminster Palace. When Eastlake studied and described the Majesty in 1847 it was at least partly in fair condition. The central figure of Christ, displaying the Wounds and surrounded by Angels with Instruments of the Passion, had behind it 'a deep blue diapered drapery', held in position by Angels. This feature at once recalls the drapery held by the Angels within the arcade at the base of the walls in St. Stephen's Chapel. Moreover, some of the Angels in the Majesty had wings with 'eyes' on them 'like those on the peacock's tail'. We know that those in St. Stephen's were feathered, as

> *Pokokes, that yaf a gret lyght*
> *Wyth her Aungelys fethers bryght.*[1]

J. T. Smith, who studied the scheme in the Chapel before its destruction, and whose judgment is quite reliable, found in it a strong resemblance, both in style and execution, to the Majesty in the Chapter House. Marked Italian influence is seen in some of the fine heads that survive from the latter. It may be recalled in this connexion that Master Hugh seems to have travelled abroad,[2] for not only did he provide vermilion from Montpellier for use in the Chapel, but mentioned in his will a valuable painting from Lombardy that he possessed. In 1348 he had been engaged in preparations for the King's voyage to Gascony, undertaking the decoration of ships, and of flags and pennons, both the latter with the 'arms' of St. George. Later, in 1355, he was active about similar preparations for the Black Prince's expedition. The mention in his will of a 'bacynett' and other armour does not, however, afford conclusive evidence that he actually embarked on some such adventure. It may mean nothing more than that he was in readiness to bear arms on the occasions when 'each alderman put his ward into array under his pennon' to 'lead his men whithersoever commanded for the defence of the city'.[3] Nevertheless, it seems highly probable that Master Hugh at some time left these shores. It is known not only that English masons were employed, one as early as 1336, when Clement VI's new palace at Avignon was in course of erection, but also that a Master Thomas, an English artist, was there in 1333.[4] This may be Master Thomas of Westminster, who had been Master Hugh's predecessor as Chief King's Painter. The scheme in St. Stephen's Chapel, known to have been supervised and in part executed by Master Hugh, comprised representations of an architecture that differed from 'anything that was ever practised in this country'. There can be no absolute certainty, however, that they were drawn from Master Hugh's own notes, and not from the sketch-book of some wandering English mason such as those who worked at Avignon.

[1] Lydgate, *Reson and Sensuallyte*, 1901, I, 38. See also *Wardrobe Accounts*, Ed. III, 1348: 'for Christmas celebrations at Guildford Castle, 14 heads of Angels, made with silver, . . . 14 white tunics wrought with heads and wings of peacocks . . . 14 tunics painted with eyes of peacocks'. See also panel of *Opus Anglicanum*, British Museum, given by A. W. Franks, 1884.

[2] Harvey, *Burlington Magazine*, LXXXIX, 303–5.

[3] E. Rickert, *Chaucer's World*, Oxford, 1948, 44–6, 62, 65.

[4] Harvey, *The Gothic World*, 1950, 103.

The Majesty in the Chapter House, when perfect, must have been a work of great beauty, as its remaining and most precious fragments show. Since there seems to be every reason to attribute it to Master Hugh, together with the almost contemporary scheme in St. Stephen's, he must undoubtedly be ranked as one of the greatest masters in north-western Europe at the time. Upon the wings of some of the Angels, or around the head, were inscribed the names of Virtues, some being decipherable as *Confessio*, *Satisfactio*,[1] and *Mundicia carnis*. The outermost arches on either side were filled with groups of Saints, gazing in adoration towards the central Figure. This subject as a whole has usually been called a Last Judgment, but would seem to be more accurately described as a Majesty, since it lacks most of the features normal in a Judgment, such as the Weighing of Souls, the division of the Just from the Lost, the Heavenly City, and the Torments of the Damned. A Majesty, whether carved or painted, or both, was a most suitable subject for a Chapter House, in view of the uses made of the building. At Syon Abbey, founded by Henry V in 1414, it was provided that the inmates 'when they come before their seats in the Chapter House . . . shall incline religiously towards the Majesty'.[2] The Chapter House at Westminster, as is well known, was used on occasion by Parliament, and the phrase 'Parlement-hous' is sometimes synonymous with 'Chapter House', as in *Piers the Plowman's Creed*—'a parlement-hous y-peynted about'.[3]

The Apocalypse series, in general idea related to the earlier Majesty, was the gift of John of Northampton, who was a monk at Westminster from *c*. 1372 to 1404. It would seem to have terminated with a Last Judgment, though if so it is now much defaced. As a work of art the series is inferior to the Majesty but far better preserved. Cleaning has shown that it possesses fairness of colour, skill and delicacy of execution, and good qualities of pattern and composition; hence, deprecatory opinions expressed while it was still obscured by dirt and discoloured varnish should now be revised. Within the central cusps of the arches, above the tiers of subjects, are small Angels with musical instruments, and they have considerable charm. There appear, from beneath the rather later Bestiary towards the base of the wall, remains of scroll-work in green, executed on a vermilion ground and enriched with white roses. The dogs that decorate some of the borders between the subjects are not without meaning, although we cannot 'read' them with certainty as symbols. Preachers, for instance, were sometimes called the hounds of God, in full chase with Christ, 'the wiche over al other lovithe the hunt-yng of soulis'. In the scene showing St. John before Domitian, a figure that leaps from the ground in a frenzy of vituperation strongly recalls another in the Flagellation on the Norwich Retable, a work of approximately the same date. The Chapter House series has been attributed on stylistic grounds to a foreign hand, and the view has been put forward that it may be of the school of Bertram von Minden. However, attribu-tions like this may be disregarded, since they rest solely on rather vague stylistic evi-dence and that for a period when products of the 'international school' are almost impossible to distinguish one from the other on such grounds alone. Further, these

[1] See *Vices & Virtues*, Stowe MS. 240, B.M., *c*. 1200, 1888, 120–5.
[2] G. G. Coulton, *Life in the Middle Ages*, 1928, 314.
[3] G. R. Owst, *Preaching in Medieval England*, Cambridge, 1926, 149.

attributions ignore overwhelming evidence for the presence and activities at Westminster of great numbers of English painters and by comparison very few foreigners.[1] The proportion, as established by the records, is in fact about forty or more Englishmen to two with names that are apparently Flemish, and who can be shown to have been employed only for a very short time. It should be noted that this occurs when the activity in St. Stephen's was at the peak, and the country had been scoured for men, who, as we know, were conscripted at the royal pleasure. It is not of course out of the question that among those who worked in the Chapter House, as elsewhere, there may have been some from overseas; but, on the evidence, the possibility that one of them painted the Apocalypse series can only be described as very slight. Finally, it should be remembered that strict Guild rules normally regulated the employment even of men from English cities other than London, quite apart from foreigners.

ST. STEPHEN'S CHAPEL

This superb building, erected in the main under the auspices of Edward III, was destroyed by fire in 1834, together with the greater part of Westminster Palace. The Chapel had been completed with a splendid scheme of painting that was begun in the Spring of 1350 and substantially completed, as indicated by an analysis of the evidence,[2] by the Summer of the following year. Large payments to painters ceased about the end of June 1351, but those for materials not until the September. The great scheme, that had been rediscovered c. 1795 behind much later fittings, was not left in existence to perish at last in flames as that of the Painted Chamber had been.[3] It was deliberately destroyed by James Wyatt, when he was commissioned to alter the edifice, then long in use by Parliament, for the accommodation of a hundred Irish members. He did this by cutting down on the inside, between the buttresses, the thickness of the walls, and so he ruthlessly destroyed their painted surfaces. John Topham, J. T. Smith, Robert Smirke and John Carter made either verbal or pictorial records, or both, of considerable areas of the scheme, often under the most difficult conditions. The last-named was almost overwhelmed by despair both as artist and antiquary at his helplessness in the face of vandalism. However, it is to the records these men made, and to the study of a few paintings saved from the general wreck and placed in the British Museum, that we owe such knowledge of it as we possess. Carter's impressions of the edifice and its decoration may be given in his own deeply-felt if rather stammering phrases:

'I solemnly declare . . . that this chapel, . . . must have been the first of all the architectural works of the land, where sublimity of design, grandeur of arrangement, richness of ornaments—where sculpture, painting and gilding dazzled the eyes of vision, to receive an emanation of those realms of light which await the blessed. No common

[1] See table, Appendix D.
[2] See Appendix C.
[3] Tristram, *Eng. Med. Wall Painting*, 1950, 89–111.

praise is now my theme; had I the eternal-catching comprehension of the inspired Milton, I could but faintly tell the wonders of this place.'

This was the impression made on a mind sensitive to beauty by one of our finest medieval buildings, when seen, not stripped, as too often of most of its painted decoration, but retaining large areas in a good state. It is not surprising that Carter should have thought that what he saw was unique; yet there is sufficient evidence to show that St. Stephen's Chapel once had equals in this country both in decorative and in architectural splendour. Topham speaks of the 'gilding and colours' as 'appearing extremely fresh'; of his impression of 'one universal blaze of splendour and magnificence'; and of 'the numerous paintings' on the walls, and 'the profusion of gilding and minute tracery and diaper'. All are characteristic of our finest fourteenth-century decoration, with its high degree of technical skill and its elaboration. Gesso-work, both raised and gilt, as well as 'prints', colour glazed over gold and silver leaf, imitation 'glass' enamels and 'marbling', were all used, almost as lavishly, in relation to the whole, as though the area to be treated had been no larger than that of the famous Westminster Panel of c. 1269.[1] On that Panel specimens of most of the technical methods just mentioned may be seen, and many of them occur in records of Henry III's Painted Chamber. Even the carving of a frieze in St. Stephen's, and that of brackets supporting statues, was inset with stained glass enriched with 'flowers and diapered ornaments of various colours'. There seems to have been reason to think that when the building was illuminated lights were so placed as to shine through this glass.[2] Like the Sainte Chapelle, St. Stephen's was decorated almost as richly and almost with the same lavish disregard for cost as if it had been a shrine or reliquary on a very large scale. There was, however, a greater reliance on painting and allied techniques, and less on the glazier's art, in which the French excelled. In a brief summary of the paintings are listed: 46 Angels and 40 servers, the latter described by Smith as 'youths', but illustrated accurately; 32 'knights', evidently militant Saints, since St. Mercurius and St. Demetrius were among them; 18 large subjects on the east wall, about the altar; and 80 smaller ones, 'on the walls under the windows', many of them containing 'ten or twelve figures'. There were also '12 statues of stone, at least six feet high, on brackets on the piers'. These statues were richly painted and gilt like the general features of the architecture, where a frieze was adorned by shields-of-arms interspersed with grotesques, the arches of the windows with gilt fleurs-de-lis and 'prints', and even the shafts of columns were similarly decorated.

The subjects at the eastern end were arranged in two tiers, the upper and deeper of these being filled with Holy Infancy scenes. They were: an Adoration of the Magi (Plates 2, 4), a Presentation in the Temple, a Nativity, and an Adoration of the Shepherds (Plate 3). In the lower tier, framed by the bays of a painted arcade, were 'donor' figures (Plates 2, 3, 5, 6a). On the north side, St. George knelt with left arm outstretched encouraging Edward III, who, with five sons, was behind him; on the south were complementary figures of Queen Philippa and four of her daughters.

---

[1] Tristram, *Eng. Med. Wall Painting*, 1950, 127-48.
[2] Smith, *Antiquities of Westminster*, 1807, 153.

Further to the south, beyond a wide recess, was another daughter, also kneeling, with hands clasped in prayer. As throughout the scheme, there were surprisingly successful attempts at rendering perspective; but we will return to this later.

The backgrounds to all the Infancy scenes were enriched by varied patterns composed of 'prints'. In the Presentation, as Smirke remarked, they were renovation work, of the kind with which we have become familiar in our study of the portrait of Richard II. As on the portrait, the surface had been lowered to receive the 'prints', and the original background had been 'chipped out with care'.[1] Although Smirke does not say so, it is clear from the character of the 'prints' as recorded in engravings, that those in the other scenes were also medieval renovations, carried out towards the close of the fourteenth century. The later 'prints' seen on the subjects in the British Museum should not be confused with some earlier ones on the same paintings, nor with ornamentation that has been stamped into the ground here and there by means of heated metal 'dies'.[2] All this earlier work is more delicate than the rest both in design and execution. The 'prints' used for the renovation are rather carelessly laid on, and do not follow angles, such as those of battlements. Further, it is clear that no attempt was made to level surfaces before application, so that the 'prints', except of course where they have sustained damage, stand out from the surfaces and the effect is in parts rather clumsy. In the scene showing the Archangel Raphael leaving Tobias, the oblong 'prints' are very clearly distinguished, and it may be seen that the sections are each roughly $2\frac{1}{2}$ in. $\times$ $3\frac{1}{4}$ in. in size. In the 'Job and Zophar', they are composed of 'border' strips, about an inch or a little over in width, laid one below the other. Since the process employed, except for the fact that the ground was not lowered,[3] was otherwise similar to that noted by Richmond and Chance on the great portrait, it seems reasonable to conclude that all these renovations were part of a general refurbishing, probably carried out at the time of Richard II's marriage with Isabella of France in 1395. Moreover, many of these later 'prints' are very similar both in design and quality to those on the tester over Richard's tomb, of approximately the same date. Finally, it is to be noted that the crown worn by the third of the Magi in the Adoration and that laid on the patterned floor in front of the kneeling Magus, are clearly renovations of the same period, for both crowns are high, and elaborately ornamented in late fourteenth-century fashion.[4] The general renovation at this time seems to have been confined to raised ornamentation in gold, for there is no sign either of partial repainting, or of over-painting, in the subjects that are now preserved in the British Museum. It may be recalled that in the thirteenth-century scheme in the Painted Chamber, a renovation of $c.$ 1294 was evidently confined to the gilded areas. For obvious reasons, gilded areas show signs of wear much sooner

[1] The word used by Smirke is 'floor', not ground; obviously a slip, since a painted representation of a floor, if in need of renewal, would not have required 'chipping out'.

[2] See p. 38, footnote 4.

[3] The areas to be renovated by the use of 'prints' were on these subjects too small to admit of any lowering of the ground.

[4] For the type of crown usual $c.$ 1380–1400, see the portrait of Richard II; the Madonna of the Outer Gate, Winchester College ($c.$ 1394); statues at the southern end of Westminster Hall ($c.$ 1385); the Flawford Madonna ($c.$ 1400); and the Virgin and Child, the latter holding a bird, Jesse Window, by Thomas Glazier of Oxford, 1393, Winchester College.

than do painted areas, and this even though medieval gold leaf is considerably thicker than the modern variety. The medieval renovator generally confined his activities to such features as were most in need of attention.

The point last mentioned is one of importance, for it has been surmised that those paintings from St. Stephen's Chapel, known through copies, which embody perspective, may only do so as a result of renovations, or alternatively through modifications made in their work by the copyists themselves.[1] Some reasons have already been indicated for disregarding the first of these suggestions. Further, it is obvious that any medieval renovation of the 'donor' scenes with a view to introducing perspective into them would necessarily have involved their painted setting, which is however no later in style than the architecture of the Chapel itself. The painted arches were in fact almost identical with the actual arcading that surrounded the walls and framed the Angels holding patterned draperies. It is certain that any medieval renovator, if faced with the task of altering the setting expressly in order to incorporate perspective, would also have modified the type of the painted architecture itself, in ruthless conformity to the taste of his own day.

The notion that perspective may have been introduced by the copyists of the late eighteenth century into their copies does not survive examination. It was clearly put forward in complete ignorance of the detailed verbal, as well as pictorial records given by Topham, who refers many times at some length to the 'incorrect' perspective that he had noticed in the scheme. When speaking of the 'donor' scenes, for example, he says:

'The lower division . . . exhibits a row of arches, seven in number, but which are divided into three compartments, each having its separate perspective of groins and windows, resembling in some degree small oratories or chapels . . . The perspective of the ornaments over the arches, particularly of the small row of battlements which terminate the design, is very inaccurate. Each arch is supposed to be viewed from a near point directly in its centre, and, in consequence, the flanks of the battlements next the centre on each hand are seen; but they are all equally seen, which is false from any assumed point of sight. The perspective of the interior building behind the figures is likewise very defective . . .'

In his description of the 'Destruction of Job's Children', now in the British Museum, he remarks:

'It may be observed that the perspective . . . is much better than is usually seen in works of this period, and evinces a degree of acquaintance with the principles of that art far beyond its first elements . . .'

—though of the Parting of the Archangel Raphael from Tobias he says that 'the building in the background is in very awkward perspective'. It cannot be supposed that any renovation of the scheme took place soon after the medieval period, for then it would have been altered out of all recognition. Subsequently it was lost to sight for centuries.

[1] M. S. Bunim, *Space in Medieval Painting & the Forerunners of Perspective*, New York, 1940, 162–9.

It is also quite impossible to visualize an extensive renovation in the closing years of the eighteenth century, after the re-discovery, before Topham and Smirke made their records. Destruction, to Wyatt's lasting disgrace, was then undertaken with a haste and vigour which would have been better applied to the preservation of so priceless a heritage. Finally, such a renovation would not have shown fumbling and incorrect perspective; indeed, it is only too easy to imagine what its painful accuracy and rigidity would have been.

The engravings in Topham's *Account of the Collegiate Chapel of St. Stephen*, as well as other pictorial records, agree in showing that there was throughout the entire scheme a conscious striving towards complete realization of a new system in pictorial representation. Such an endeavour was consistent with that development towards naturalism to which England so greatly contributed.[1] It is noticeable that Master Hugh, 'disposer of the works of the painters', showed so intense an interest in obtaining an effect of recession that he even made use of glazing with colour 'for the purpose of making the floor appear to recede'. It was treated, in the Adoration of the Magi, with 'a transparent brown' that deepened in strength 'as the floor' approached 'the diaper work', i.e. the 'prints' on the background.

It is also impossible to accept the claim that other English work of the second half of the century affords no evidence of an advance in the treatment of spatial problems equal to that of the scheme in St. Stephen's Chapel. The background to the Flagellation on the Norwich Retable (*c.* 1380) at least equals in this respect the Arrival of the Messengers to Job, in the British Museum, and so does the treatment of the throne in the portrait of Richard II. There is a much earlier, and naturally less successful attempt at rendering perspective to be seen in the throne of Christ, and those of the Evangelists, in the superb Majesty from the Psalter of Robert de Lisle, of *c.* 1325. Miniatures of a rather later period identified as English are not very numerous, but it should be recalled that some in the Fitzwarin Psalter, to name no others, show fairly good perspective. Finally, essays in the art are not unknown in our wall-paintings of the latter part of the century. They are seen or else recorded at the following places: Westminster Abbey, at the back of the recess covering the tomb of some of the children of Henry III (*c.* 1395); the chantry of Edward le Despenser (*d.* 1375) in Tewkesbury Abbey; and at Notgrove in Gloucestershire and Moulton (Plate 29*b*) and Wickhampton in Norfolk, towards the close of the period. It may well be argued that if the art was known and practised late in the century by some of the lesser men, like those who were employed at Moulton and Wickhampton, it must have become generally familiar, and therefore have been a commonplace in the main centres very much earlier. It may be remarked at this point that the development may more reasonably be attributed to the wall-painter than to the illuminator of books; for it is obvious that the former inclined more readily than the latter to the use in his compositions of architectural features. Moreover, his work, like the mason's, might involve him in extensive travel, as we have seen. Thus the painter had on the whole the advantage of the illuminator in the matter of direct contact with developments made abroad. This at least may be admitted by those who tend to assume that all developments are necessarily of foreign origin, and that nothing so revolution-

[1] Tristram, *Eng. Med. Wall Painting*, 1950, chap. I et seq.

ary as the adoption of the art of perspective can possibly have taken place here before it did in France, however strong the evidence may be to the contrary.[1]

If we turn to problems of chronology that arise from the history of the great scheme, we come to the conclusion that the eastern section, where perspective was most in evidence, must have been the first completed, apart, perhaps, from any decoration there may have been on the vaulting. It is in fact recorded that Gilbert Pokerig and John Elham were priming the east end of the Chapel in June, 1350. This section was of course that about the altar, and here the most important subjects were represented. Prominence was given to the Adoration of the Kings and to the 'donor' scenes below it. This had its significance, for since the French royal house did so, Edward III must have laid claim to 'descent' from the Magi.[2] Activity in the body of the Chapel began in the Spring of 1350, when the first order for impressment of painters, dated 18th March, occurs. The 'donor' figures, of Edward III, the Black Prince, Lionel Duke of Clarence, John of Gaunt, Duke of Lancaster, and Edmund of Langley, Duke of York, as well as those of Queen Philippa and her five daughters, were no doubt painted about that time. This was by far the most active period of work on the great scheme. The two remaining royal figures, of a son and a daughter, perhaps represent Thomas of Woodstock and Margaret Countess of Pembroke. They are on a smaller scale than are the rest, and rather awkwardly placed, in a way that gives the impression that they were later additions, perhaps even so late as c. 1356–7. It would certainly be unsafe to assume that because Thomas of Woodstock was not born until 1355, the eastern end of the Chapel cannot have been decorated before that date. As in the case of the Painted Chamber, additions and alterations were evidently made long after the scheme was substantially complete.[3] We cannot even be certain that the small figure in armour represents Thomas; for there were two other sons, born before him, who died very young, either of whom, following medieval custom, may have been depicted on a smaller scale than the rest, as of lesser importance.[4]

From the tabulation of items in the accounts of 1350–1, and those of 1354 and 1356–7, and a consideration of the general evidence they afford, certain conclusions emerge.[5] The first is that the scheme was substantially finished by the Summer of 1351, when the series of Angels depicted within the arcading, and also some carved 'Angels within tabernacles', were almost certainly painted. Then, it appears that activities undertaken from July to September 1354, when John Barnaby was the most prominent craftsman employed, were far from extensive, however costly. Only seven painters, two of them

---

[1] O. Pacht, *A Giottesque Episode in English Medieval Art*, Journal of the *Warburg & Courtauld Institutes*, VI, 1943, 53: 'The French selected quite different Italian elements and assimilated them in an entirely different way.' For the Majesty in the Psalter of Robert de Lisle, see Oakeshott, *The Sequence of Medieval Art*, London, 1950, pl. 8.

[2] Tristram, *The Wilton Diptych*, The Month, July 1949, 26–8. Mâle, *Religious Art in France of the Thirteenth Century*, 1913, 212.   [3] Tristram, *Eng. Med. Wall Painting*, 1950, 89–111.

[4] The figure that is perhaps that of Thomas of Woodstock was on a narrow section of wall at an angle with the rest; and the other, female figure, as we have seen, was beyond a wide recess, and cut off from the series of 'donor' figures. Had both been viewed from the first as part of the scheme, Master Hugh could easily have 'set out' his painted arcading so as to include them. For the priming of the walls at the east end see Smith, *Antiquities of Westminster*, 210.   [5] See Appendix C.

apprentices, were engaged, and comparatively few materials were bought. By contrast, at the height of activity in the Chapel in 1350, some forty men or more were at work from September to November. Several of them were highly paid, and they were supplied with a constant stream of materials of all kinds. Finally, it may be seen that the activities supervised by Master Hugh in 1356–7 cannot have been of the first importance to the scheme as a whole, and may not have involved much work, if any, upon it. It is true that William Maynard was employed for nearly a year, as well as six other men at different times; but it is highly probable from the general evidence that either the addition of isolated subjects, or else the rich and delicate decoration of fittings, was involved.[1] In 1356 timber was bought for stalls in the Chapel, which were evidently being extended at that time; and Master Edmund Canon, stone-cutter, was engaged on the stalls from June 1356 for nearly a year. A pulpit and cupboards for vestments are mentioned earlier. The former, even in country churches, might be richly painted.

The chief painters mentioned in the accounts are Master Hugh, John Cotton, John Barnaby, John Barnaby junior, William Maynard, and the apparently indispensable Gilbert Pokerig. Apart from them, the most interesting group in St. Stephen's at this time is that of eleven men who were employed for a few weeks in the period of greatest activity. They all received ninepence daily, a fee high enough to show that they were of good standing, since it was double the apprentices' wage. It is clear that they were engaged at a time of considerable pressure, when the execution of the great scheme had reached such a point as to call for the assistance, at least for a time, of a number of men of a skilled, but not the most highly skilled and generally experienced type. During the late September and the October of 1350 the group included William Walsingham, Roger Norwich, William Maynard,[2] John Exeter, Thomas Ruddok, Gilbert Prince, John Davy,[3] John Cambridge, Henry Blithe, Lowen Tassyn and Janyn Godmered. To judge from their names, the last two may have been Flemings. They left after about a month's work, as did most of the rest, for by the end of October only four of the eleven remained. The outstanding name is that of Gilbert Prince, who appears again in May 1351, with six others. Among the latter was John Athelard, who was also a glazier.[4] As we have seen, they were 'painting Angels for tabernacles' at this time.

It is interesting to think of Prince as a young man employed in St. Stephen's under Master Hugh during the execution of the great scheme. He was later head of London's chief 'painters' shop', and perhaps the foremost artist of the day. He was employed first by Edward III and then by Richard II as chief Court Painter. Further, he worked for many members of the royal family and also of the nobility. Among his employers were: John of Gaunt, Duke of Lancaster; the Princess of Wales, mother of Richard II, and her two daughters, the Duchess of Brittany and the Countess of St. Pol; Anne of Bohemia and her mother the Empress; Joan, Queen of Scotland; Ralph, Earl of

---

[1] Tristram, *Eng. Med. Wall Painting*, 1950, 93–4, 96–100; Smith, *Antiquities of Westminster*, 1807, 200, 201. Forty-four pieces of timber were bought, from 'the prior of the church of the Holy Trinity', and eleven images were also made for the stalls. For an instance of a richly decorated lectern, see *Eng. Med. Wall Painting*, 1950, 82, 427, 453, 459. For example of painted pulpit, South Burlingham, Norfolk, Brit. Mus., Dawson Turner Coll., 1845, III, 172 (fifteenth century).

[2] William Maynard, by 1354, received 1s. daily and by 1356–7 was chief painter under Master Hugh.

[3] One of a well-known family of London Painters.   [4] Tristram, *Eng. Med. Wall Painting*, 1950, 386–7.

Stafford; and Sir Simon Burley. By 1376 Prince was already a Warden of the Painters' Guild, and by 1384 a member of the Common Council of the City of London. To give an idea of his financial standing, it may be remarked that the Aldermen, to whom the Common Councillors were not much inferior, ranked for purposes of taxation as Barons.[1] He was a member of the Council again in the two following years, and also in 1388. Both in 1383 and 1393 he received grants of exemption from service on assizes or juries, that of 1393 being for life; and such grants as these were given only to the foremost craftsmen in royal employment. It was not unknown for him to receive for 'works of his art' sums that amounted to small fortunes. If he, or any close associate, painted one of the masterpieces of the age, whether the portrait of Richard II, or the Wilton Diptych, with its lovely Angels, its superb technical and decorative qualities, and its heraldry, then he could hardly have been trained in a better school than St. Stephen's when the noble series of wall-paintings was undertaken there.

The main argument against a date for the Diptych early in Richard's reign is drawn from its heraldic content, and has been much weakened by recent studies.[2] It is clear that the broom-cod emblem was not introduced from France by Richard's second Queen, as was thought previously. Indeed, a robe worn by Anne of Bohemia in 1392 was embroidered with it.[3] Further, general evidence drawn from costume, evidence that is so often invaluable when dating a work within narrow limits, strongly supports an early date, just before or soon after Richard's accession. There may be noted in this connexion: the comparatively low, unexaggerated and unexpanded collar of Richard's houppelande, by contrast with later collars that almost engulfed the head at the back; the length of the sleeves, for these, were he standing, would hardly reach to his knees, whereas, later, those of houppelandes of the rich ceremonial type trailed almost to the ground; [4] the absence, at both shoulder and hem, of the 'dagging' used in extraordinary profusion after 1380; and, finally, the quite low and comparatively simple crowns worn by Richard and his two royal sponsors.[5] It would seem unreasonable to ignore the clear evidence from costume, supported as it is by the slighter but by no means negligible evidence from style.[6] Again, the Diptych is without doubt a votive painting, and more-over one designed, by its qualities of freshness, charm and gaiety, to appeal to a child or youth. In sentiment nothing could well be further removed from a *memento mori*. This is one interpretation of the picture among the many that have been offered, and that cannot be sustained in face of the evidence both from costume and from the style of the work itself. In style, there is nothing very similar after 1390.

The unusual gesture of Richard's hands is unlike anything normally found in paintings of devotees, but it cannot be meaningless. It is not explained by the suggestion that they are placed as they are for reception of the standard held by the foremost of the eleven Angels, even though this suggestion would agree with a 'reading' both as a 'Coronation piece' and as a votive painting. The hands are held quite low and are

[1] Woodforde, *The Norwich School of Glass-Painting in the Fifteenth Century*, Oxford, 1950, 105. The Mayor ranked as an Earl (1379).   [2] Tristram, *The Wilton Diptych, The Month*, July 1949, 18–28.
[3] Hartshorne, *Archaeological Journal*, 1909, LXVI, 86.
[4] Kelly and Schwabe, *A Short History of Costume and Armour*, London, 1931, 26–7, pl. XIV.
[5] See p. 50, footnote 4.   [6] Tristram, *The Wilton Diptych, The Month*, July 1949, 28–32.

slightly 'cupped', not extended forward and upward as though to grasp a banner pole. No painter, when 'posing' a model, would place them so, in order to suggest the imminent grasping of such a pole, especially not one weighted by a banner floating above. Moreover, they would not be placed as they are for the imminent reception of any fairly large or heavy object. They might be so placed to show that the right foot of the Holy Child, that is held in a prominent position by the left hand of the Blessed Virgin, was about to be received by Richard that he might kiss it in a gesture of homage and fealty. Perhaps here we have the meaning of the picture, of the Crown of Thorns and the Nails that are seen on the nimbus of the Holy Child, and of the banner held by one of the eleven Angels. It may be recalled that devotion to the Passion was both widespread and increasing in the fourteenth century. It is evident that Richard's father, the Black Prince, was moved by it, for the 'colour' black that he is known to have affected signified mortification of the flesh, just as the white that was worn by Richard himself on the day of his coronation symbolized purity of life.[1] The Angels, eleven in number, one of them holding and pointing to the banner charged with a cross, are portrayed as of the same age as Richard himself. In a pageant prepared for his entry into London before his coronation, four girls of his own age appeared, dressed in white, and an 'Angel' offered him a golden crown. It is almost impossible not to believe that the number of Angels in the Diptych was chosen as representing the eleven years of his life. Further, eleven is an unusual number to find, when the mystical numbers three, or seven, or nine, might normally be expected. However, if the medieval view of numbers is borne in mind, it becomes possible to 'read' with some confidence the inner, as against the obvious significance of the number of Angels. Eleven is a combination of three, the number of the Trinity, which connotes all things spiritual, with eight, which is symbolic of the new life after Resurrection, and also of the anticipated Resurrection implied in Baptism. It is obvious that Richard, when he was knighted, and through the anointing at his coronation, had indeed begun a new and a dedicated life. He had been knighted not long before his accession. The Diptych, then, may reasonably be 'read' as a painting of the young Richard as Knight of Christ, and so as an expression in another medium of such sentiments as are found in a contemporary poem beginning with an invocation to the Trinity, that had been the object of the Black Prince's strong devotion. It continues thus:

> Ye fiend me tempteth day and nyght
> He wol me reve hevene bright . . .
> Sweet ihesu, I am thy knyght,
> Against him I take the fight,
> Stiffly him to abide . . .
> *The holy cross my banner biforn*
> *Myn helm thy garlond of sharpe thorn*
> *My plates shall thy nailes be.*[2]

[1] Durandus, *Rationale Divinorum Officiorum*, Neale & Webb, 1843, 77, par. 39.

[2] Brown, *Lyrics of the Fourteenth Century*, no. 125, lines 1, 5, 8–10, 14–17 (of the end of the century, slightly modernized above). Richard was knighted on St. George's day; Walsingham, *Ypodigma Neustriae*, R.S. 1876, 326.

After this digression, we may return to study of the scheme formerly in St. Stephen's Chapel, and consider its technical characteristics. 'Prints', as we have seen, were often enough used on the wall and panel paintings of our period. They should be carefully distinguished from work in raised *gesso*, which was executed freely with the brush. It is impossible, in default of actual experiment, to arrive at absolute certainty about methods employed in the making of different kinds of 'prints', but it is clear that they were not all produced by identical means. It has been said already that those of an earlier type are superior on the whole to those of later date. In considering the means used in their production, we may turn to such evidence as exists concerning technical methods common in the fourteenth century and later for the production of raised ornament, whether on walls or on panels. Here Cennino Cennini is invaluable. Much raised ornament, as is obvious from its comparatively free and flowing quality, was produced with the brush,[1] in *gesso sottile*; and there are also recipes for executing reliefs on walls with varnish, and with wax, by means of the brush. Good examples of reliefs in *gesso sottile* may be studied on the Norwich Retable, and also on the panel painted with the Arrest of Christ, from St. Michael at Plea, in Norwich. The method was used on panels and walls alike. Ornament produced by mechanical, or semi-mechanical means, is found in English work from *c.* 1270 at least, for it is to be seen on the Westminster Panel, side by side with raised ornamentation executed in *gesso* with the brush.[2] Tin-leaf, for making actual 'prints', is mentioned in accounts for materials that were bought for use in St. Stephen's. The leaf was most probably used after the manner described by Cennino,[3] who says that it should be laid on a stone that had been deeply engraved with a design, covered with a layer of moist tow and then beaten hard, through the 'cushion' of tow, with a mallet of willow wood, until the design was transferred to the leaf. The back of the latter was then filled with *gesso grosso*, and its front was gilt, the resulting 'print' being in due course attached to wall or panel with ship pitch. It is evident that some of the coarser 'prints' on the wall-paintings from St. Stephen's that are in the British Museum, or those on the tester over the tomb of Richard II, may have been made in this way. On the other hand, those on the Thornham Parva Retable or the Cluny Panel are so delicate that a different method must have been employed. These 'prints' present much the same general appearance as do medieval waxen seals, and were therefore probably produced by some means such as that described by Cennino [4] for obtaining 'very perfect' impressions of a seal or coin, 'or in general of anything of which you desire impressions'. These were made 'in a sort of plaster', of wood-ash and salt, and dried gradually 'without sun or fire'. 'Prints' made after this recipe would not only be delicate, to judge from the claim made by Cennino that this 'plaster' would take so fine an impression as would result from a seal or coin, but they would also be very strong; for he says that even molten metal might be poured on to the 'paste' if desired, since it was 'sufficiently tenacious to bear a great weight'. It is observable that the 'prints' on the two panels mentioned above have withstood the

[1] *The Book of the Art of Cennino Cennini*, trans. Herringham, London, 1899, chap. 124.
[2] Tristram, *Eng. Med. Wall Painting*, 1950, 408.
[3] *Cennino Cennini*, chap. 128.
[4] ibid., chap. 189.

effects of time and rough usage even better than is the rule with the work of the medieval craftsman.

The colour schemes in St. Stephen's, to judge from records and from the paintings that still exist, had considerable beauty. In the 'Destruction of Job's Children', and the companion painting, there is gold, vermilion, olive-green, grey, white, blue and rose-purple. Quite strong Italian influence is evident in the heads and hands, as might be expected from what is known of Master Hugh's history; but 'English Gothic' elements are nevertheless unmistakable, in many of the heads, as well as in the design and rendering of drapery. The Adoration of the Shepherds has in the foreground an attractive pastoral scene, in which two of the Shepherds guard sheep that are grazing a flowered pasture and others that are within an enclosure of wattle. The third plays his pipes, while the Angel appears in the golden sky above him. The lavish use of inscriptions recalls those once in the Painted Chamber. Good as the surviving works from St. Stephen's are, it should be borne in mind when assessing them as examples from which may be drawn some idea of the entire scheme, that they came from subsidiary parts. They were just below window-level, and higher than the arcading with its ranks of Angels. It may be concluded that they are without doubt in the main if not entirely, the work of assistants to Hugh of St. Albans. His own masterpieces we know only at a remove, through the hand and eye of Smirke and others, except, perhaps, for the fragments of the Majesty in the Abbey Chapter House. Even so, it is abundantly clear that Master Hugh was capable of grandeur of conception, as evinced in the general scheme for St. Stephen's. Further, the Angels within the arcading had most exceptional beauty of design. It is also clear that he possessed a wide knowledge of technical methods, and that he took a delight in experiment, for his essays in the new art of perspective are evidence enough of this. They show that he was not content merely to repeat lessons perhaps learnt, directly or indirectly, from Italian sources, but that he explored the possibilities of the new art with a lively and intense personal interest. In his work, too, may be seen the earliest known and fully-developed example of 'grisaille' painting (c. 1350).[1] This eventually became so popular that the entire scheme in Eton College Chapel, of over a century later, was carried out in 'grisaille', apart from very slight 'accents' in colour. A close examination of the 'Destruction of Job's Children' shows that at the side of a pilaster painted at the left of the scene there is a very small 'classical' figure, unmistakably painted in 'grisaille', and appearing almost as if carved in stone, while above it there are fragments of another.

[1] See chap. I, 7.

Chapter Three

★————————————————————————————★

FOURTEENTH-CENTURY WALL-PAINTINGS
OF THE MORE 'ELABORATE' TYPE

★————————————————————————————★

FOURTEENTH-CENTURY wall-paintings of the more 'elaborate' type—an unsatis-factory description adopted merely for the sake of convenience—are to be found most often in the main centres, as at Norwich and St. Albans. However, they are sometimes seen in smaller places such as South Newington in Oxfordshire. Recorded examples are numerous for cathedrals, castles and palaces; e.g. at York and Rochester, Windsor and the Palace of Westminster. It should be remembered, how-ever, that in country churches some of the survivals that can hardly be termed 'rich and elaborate', are in other ways most remarkable, and, further, possess aesthetic quali-ties of their own. It must be clearly understood that those here called 'elaborate' are so termed for two main reasons. In the first place, they either have a greater degree of finish than others, or if much defaced still bear signs that they once possessed it. Secondly, when they are lost, accounts indicate that they must have been works of the richest kind. Many extensive schemes, such as that at Chalgrove in Oxfordshire, have been excluded from this section because of their relatively unpretentious character and broad handling, but it does not follow that they are inferior as works of art, and still less that they are not of the greatest interest from the point of view of iconography.

We may first give our attention mainly to those paintings that though lost, or mainly so, are recorded. The most noteworthy of these is perhaps the scheme which existed on the destroyed wooden vaulting of the Chapter House at York. Only three figures survive, those of the Synagogue, St. Edmund King and Martyr, and an unidentified Archbishop. They are painted in oil colour, and strongly outlined in black, with the view of making the forms 'tell' as clearly as possible from a considerable distance, for they would have been seen from the floor below. Further, since these figures were designed as parts of a decorative ensemble on a great scale, they are less delicate in handling than are panel paintings intended for altars, or wall-paintings placed in comparatively low and accessible positions. It is not the least noteworthy characteristic of our wall-paintings that many of them are consciously designed and treated with the view of securing maximum visibility in given circumstances. In some schemes of the thirteenth century the tiers of paintings are deeper, and the figures in them therefore larger, as they recede upward from eye level.[1] This device was borrowed from Byzantine work, and our latest known instance, at Fairstead in Essex, dates from the latter years of that century. The general effect of the roof recorded at York must have been really beautiful, for it contained: borders of foliated ornament; cream ground patterned by medallions of different sizes; large figures of Saints, Bishops and Kings, about twelve feet in height; birds, and a variety of grotesques; knots of carved wood silvered —'knottes graven clere, depeynt'; and a colour scheme of bright red, green, gold, black and rose-pink. The figure of the Synagogue, graceful and long-haired, has the eyes bound by a transparent veil, through which they show faintly, and the colours of face, hands and tunic are all quite delicately shaded. The gallery over the seats in the Chapter House was described in 1736 as 'so richly gilt and painted as to be above description'. The wall above the doorway had within carved tracery two tiers of figures, against grounds enriched by delicately painted scroll-work, and geometrical ornament.   In the passage that leads from the north transept to the Chapter House there are remains which show that the mouldings were once coloured, chiefly in red, and that the vaulting ribs were outlined in red and patterned with lozenges in white. Wall-spaces free of carving were filled by coats-of-arms in alternation with rosettes. Engravings in Britton's *York* show figures on the vaulting, and below within quatrefoils and spandrels appear grotesques and scroll-work. From what we know of this decoration, as well as of the work in the Chapter House, it is possible to extend a little in our imaginations the brief and unsatisfactory glimpses which we find in the York Fabric Rolls of the decoration once to be seen in the Lady Chapel, where 'many traces', now lost, were still to be seen in 1859.

At Rochester, in the choir, on the wall-surfaces above the stalls, there is still elaborate work of the heraldic type, but it is in the main repainted. There are also considerable remains of decoration in the north choir transept about the site of the shrine of St. William of Perth. The effigy of Bishop John of Sheppey has a rich painted treatment that was recovered, so far as was possible, from beneath nineteenth-century repainting in fairly recent years. In the Lady Chapel and the crypt there are vestiges of rich and considerable schemes, now barely decipherable. At the east end of the Chapel, around the lofty arch over the former site of the altar, there is, or was, decoration of *c.* 1350 or a little earlier. In three tiers were subjects framed by an elaborate architectural setting in incised line, and the colours, so far as traceable, were in the main cream or light stone, with pink, or light red, and bright green. Amongst the subjects were an Annunciation, St. Catherine, St. Margaret, and two donors, one of them a woman in kirtle and veil. In 1322 there is record of a grant made to the altar of the Blessed Virgin, '*de novo constructa*'.[2]

The fragments in the crypt are in the bay beneath the altar of St. John Baptist in the

---

[1] Tristram, *Eng. Med. Wall Painting*, 1950, 101.
[2] St. John Hope, *Archaeologia Cantiana*, 1898, XXIII, 264.

upper church. They comprise, or once comprised, very varied decoration, with some heraldry, and on the quadripartite vaulting a series of scenes within medallions. On the broad soffit of an arch on the western side of the bay there were also subjects, framed within twelve square cusped panels. The 'history' of a Saint filled the medallions, and apparently also the panels, but has not hitherto been identified even with fair likelihood, though various suggestions have at different times been made. Altars dedicated to St. Catherine, St. Michael the Archangel, St. Edmund, St. Denis and also the Holy Trinity, once existed in the crypt. On careful consideration, however, the remains of painting do not agree with any of the legends of these four Saints; and by a process of elimination the conclusion may be reached that St. Mary Magdalen, who also had an altar here, is the most likely choice. Her story is related both in the *Golden Legend* [1] and in an *Early South-English Legendary*. According to these sources, the 'Prince of a Province', where St. Mary Magdalen was preaching, desired a child, and professed himself and his wife ready for conversion, if the wish were fulfilled. They eventually embarked on a pilgrimage to Rome, and on the voyage a son was born to them. However, the wife, who was invisibly tended during childbirth by the Saint, to all appearance died, and 'covered all about' with the Prince's mantle, was left with the living child on an island. The Prince, who continued his pilgrimage, received comfort and reassurance at its close from St. Peter, and on the return voyage again landed on the island and found his wife and child alive. Two medallions that were still decipherable many years ago contained, respectively, scenes in which St. Mary Magdalen blesses the Prince and his wife at the outset of their pilgrimage, and the Prince's discovery of his living wife and child on the return journey. There is an alternative explanation of the second scene, which might be from a legend of St. Michael, in which a woman on pilgrimage bore her child safely in the midst of the returning tide, by which she had been overwhelmed. This explanation does not seem at all likely, however, from the presence of a boat, for the woman was overtaken by the tide when on foot. The scenes in the other medallions were very much defaced some thirty years ago or more. If they may be 'read' in relation to the legend of St. Mary Magdalen, it seems at least possible from such traces as existed then, that originally they showed the Saint encouraging the Prince to undertake a pilgrimage, and appearing to a monk as he said mass in the course of his return from a similar adventure. Paintings which were even more damaged occurred on the soffit of the arch nearby and, as is evident from the fact that they included trees, were almost all of scenes in the open air. If they also related to the legend of St. Mary Magdalen, then they may have shown her life in the desert and her death, attended by Angels, in the presence of Bishop Maximus. [2]

In Winchester Cathedral, a building so rich in works of thirteenth-century date, there is very little from our period. In a chapel off the south transept slight traces exist of an altar-painting with scenes connected with the Benedictine Order, but they were in a very poor state many years ago and are now almost indecipherable. The lid of a reliquary chest of 1320–30 is preserved in the north choir aisle, and its decoration comprises a Majesty, a Coronation of the Virgin, a Virgin and Child, a Crucifixion, and

---

[1] *The Early South-English Legendary*, E.E.T.S., 1887, 462–80; *Golden Legend*, IV, 73–85.
[2] See Catalogue, under Rochester.

Angels with Instruments of the Passion. There are also figures of St. George and other Saints, and of the donors, Sir William de Lillebone and his wife Anastasia. Though this work is in many ways of considerable interest, it is not of the first quality, and equals but few wall-paintings of the same date. The drawing and handling may be compared with that seen in a 'history' of St. John Baptist at Idsworth in Hampshire, which shows some similarities but is distinctly superior.

Records afford little information about the original decoration of the great Abbey of Bury St. Edmunds.[1] Old St. Paul's, Thornton Abbey in Lincolnshire, Gloucester and also Ely have already been discussed. Lichfield was described as early as 1323 as being 'most gracious and of wondrous beauty, with very high stone [2] steeples and belfries, paintings and carvings, and excellent well enriched and adorned with other church furnishings'. At Ely there are remains of extensive schemes in the choir, and also in the Lady Chapel, but the work in the Octagon, though it was clearly visible about a century ago, was later repainted. Reference has previously been made to evidence afforded by the Sacrist Rolls. There are remains and records of fine work in a chantry chapel at Tewkesbury and on tombs at Hereford and Wells. Exeter Cathedral and Malmesbury Abbey are both rich in survivals of colour on carving; and the former possesses extensive records of the painting of corbels and bosses, the Bishop's Throne, Sedilia and pulpitum, and in these the names of many painters are given. The colour treatment of the Minstrels' Gallery and the fine drapery painted on the Sedilia are still in existence. The colour decoration of the West Front has already been discussed. On bosses at Malmesbury there are very extensive remains of brilliant colour, comprising vermilion, red lead, yellow ochre, azure, and a copper green, the dominant tint being a bright 'scarlet' vermilion. For our period, Durham is best described from the well-known account given by one of the monks at the Dissolution, even though much he mentions may have been somewhat later, or earlier, than the fourteenth century:

'All the nine altars [at the eastern end of the church] had their several screens and covers of wainscot over head, likewise between every altar a very fair and large partition of wainscot, all varnished over with fine branches and flowers and other imagery work, most finely and artificially pictured and gilded; . . . next to these nine altars was the goodly monument of St. Cuthbert . . . his sacred shrine was exalted with most curious workmanship, of fine and costly green marble, all limned and gilt with gold . . . [the cover of the shrine] on the outside was very finely and artificially gilded. And also on either side of the said cover were painted four lively images curiously wrought, and miraculous to all beholders thereof, and on the east end was painted the picture of Our Saviour sitting on the rainbow to give judgement . . . and on the west end of the cover was the picture of Our Lady and of Christ on her knee . . . Also within the same feretory . . . there were almeries of wainscot, varnished and finely painted, and gilt over with fine little images . . . [The Black Rood of Scotland was attached to wainscot] red varnished over very finely and all set full of stars of lead, gilt over with gold. [The 'Lady of Bolton' was very finely varnished within] with green varnish, and flowers of

---

[1] Tristram, *Eng. Med. Wall Painting*, 1950, 346–9, 515–18; and Catalogue, in this volume.
[2] Nasmith, *Symonis Simeonis, Itinerarium*, 1778, 46; Harvey, *The Gothic World*, 1950, 10.

gold. [On the Jesus altar there was] against the wall, a fine table with two leaves to open and shut, comprehending the Passion of Our Lord, richly set in fine colours, all like burnished gold . . . There was also in the height of the wall from pillar to pillar, the whole story of the Passion [in stone carving] gilt, and above the Passion, the Twelve Apostles, gilt, and above these . . . a carved border, with branches and flowers, coloured and gilt . . . Above the top of all, upon the wall stood the most famous Rood that was in all the land, with the picture of Mary on one side, of Our Saviour and that of St. John on the other, with two glittering Archangels . . . for the stateliness of the picture and the liveliness of the painting it was thought to be one of the grandest monuments in the church . . . And over the church door was all covered above head with wainscot very finely painted and varnished azure, and set out with stars of gold. And the fore part of the wainscot from pillar to pillar within the church was a brattishing . . . very curiously wrought and gilt with gold . . . and in the midst of the brattishing was a star of great compass, like the sun very curiously wrought with gold and enamelled. [In the Galilee] stood Our Lady's altar, wainscot work above the head, at the back and at each end . . . the wainscot being furnished with most heavenly pictures, in colours and gilding . . . On the north side of the Galilee Our Lady of Pity's altar . . . having above . . . on the wall a part of Our Saviour's Passion in large pictures.' [1]

At Castle Acre Priory, Ingham and Gorleston, all in Norfolk, there are, or were, interesting vestiges of schemes of various types. In the Prior's Chapel at Castle Acre may be seen relics of what was probably an Adoration of the Magi, and also slight traces of vermilion, green, gold and black. Further, there are on a corbel 'prints' that have generally been taken for carving. Three panels, painted in oil colour, were found in the Outer Parlour in 1939.[2] Panel paintings also existed at Ingham, where they illustrated the life of St. Nicholas and were executed in rich colours against a ground of red diapered [3] in gold. The tomb of Sir Oliver de Ingham, previously mentioned, has remains of delicately-painted scroll patterns in blue, and of minutely-worked 'marbling', and on the wall at the back of the recess that houses it there was formerly a 'hunting scene'—probably from the legend of St. Hubert or St. Eustace. The tomb of Sir Roger de Bois, nearby, has already been mentioned. At Gorleston the church of St. Andrew once possessed a number of wall-paintings, and, within an Easter Sepulchre, a Trinity painted in bright colours and enriched with gold.

In St. Mary-le-Crypt at Gloucester the Sedilia and an Easter Sepulchre once possessed decoration that was described c. 1845 as of exceptionally high quality, that of the latter comprising a Resurrection of Christ. Inglesham in Wiltshire has fragments of a reredos with paintings of four Saints upon them, together with traces of gold, brilliant colour, and delicate patterns. At Milton Regis, in Kent, remains of plaster found beneath the floor retained at the time of discovery painting minutely executed in brilliant colours, with gilding. The Fitzwilliam Museum at Cambridge possesses a stone taken from Chesterton church, painted with the figure of a girl, her hair flowing over her shoulders.

[1] Sanderson, *The Antiquities of the Abbey or Cathedral Church of Durham*, 1767, 5–10, 22–7, 32–3, 35–6, 40–1, 45–6.

[2] Borenius, *Antiquaries Journal*, XVII, 115, et seq., pl. XXIX.

[3] *Norfolk Archaeology*, VIII, 208; *Archaeological Journal*, XIV, 285.

She carries a pick or hammer, and a basket filled with small objects, that are unidentifiable. They have been thought to be roses, and in consequence it has been suggested that this is a representation of St. Dorothy. The suggestion, however, leaves the implement unexplained. The figure might be identified as St. Helena, and thus the hammer would be accounted for while the objects in the basket would no doubt be the nails; but St. Helena would not be represented with hair flowing loose, and as uncrowned. Deguilville indeed mentions Penance with her hammer Contrition, but nothing to account for the basket;[1] and therefore this figure must remain unidentified. The stone bearing it had been used as part of the filling of a blocked window. The drawing is sensitive, and the colour pleasant.

The painted ceiling at Abingdon and the St. Edward and the Pilgrim at Forthampton Court have already received brief mention. In some accounts the former has been dated c. 1390 because of a reference in an inscription upon it to an indulgence granted by Boniface IX in 1391. It is obvious, however, that this inscription may have been added some time later, perhaps when a medieval renovation took place. There are strong indications that there was such a renovation, for instance, the presence in the paintings of both a simple and a much more elaborate type of crown[2] on some of the figures of Kings. Further, in their costume neither dagging, nor the much expanded collars of c. 1390 are to be found. There is repainting of a very clumsy kind on the 'Josias', 'Jeremiah' and 'Jeconias', which must have been carried out during the 'restoration' of 1872, when a great deal of damage was done to the ceiling. Some of the figures now have ugly, unconvincing profiles. Within such a series of tall, narrow 'niches' as frame them all, figures with heads in full profile not only appear most awkwardly placed, but 'break', without adequate reason, a dignified sequence otherwise disposed. No competent medieval painter would have been guilty of such ineptitude in design, nor of the incompetent handling so painfully obvious on the 'Jeconias'.

In the Lady Chapel of Christ Church Cathedral, Oxford, there are some slight remains of a scheme carried out when the tomb of Lady Montacute was erected after her death in 1353. Traces of 'banding', in yellow, red and black, are to be found on the vaulting, and also of red, black and pale blue on the ribs and arch mouldings. Eight censing Angels, now very much defaced, are placed as if radiating from the centre, and it is evident that the colours were a deep orange, pale blue, and red, used with gold. The medium was oil, and the work was very solidly executed. This unusual technique will be studied later, when considering the remarkable scheme at South Newington, less than twenty miles away. Oil colour was employed also on the stone carvings on the tomb, but there it was only to be expected. There are quite extensive remains of a rich scheme both on the effigy and on the structure generally. Besides reliefs it comprises quatrefoil flowers, and leopards' masks in gold set amidst foliated and floral motifs in green on a vermilion ground. Coats-of-arms, minutely patterned in some parts, appear within the richly-coloured gilt tracery of the sides; and vermilion, red, a bright green, a deep blue, with purple, black and white, are to be found. On the earlier Sutton tomb nearby, traces are very slight, but include fragments of elaborate patterns, and 'prints'.

---

[1] Lydgate, *Pilgrimage of the Life of Man*, 106-22.
[2] See chap. II, 50, footnote 4.

THE MORE 'ELABORATE' TYPE

NORWICH CATHEDRAL

There are various interesting remains from our date in Norwich Cathedral, in the nave, the presbytery aisle, and the Bauchun Chapel. Records, moreover, afford brief glimpses of the 'decoration of images', the painting of panels, benches, tombs, and the shrine of St. William of Norwich. A crucifix, or, more probably, a Crucifixion, existed in the Refectory. The activities called for the use of precious colours, gold and silver leaf, and oil and varnish. In connexion with the shrine, there is a payment in 1325 to 'Simon the Painter' and his assistant. Earlier, in the closing years of the thirteenth century, several painters are mentioned in the Sacrist's Rolls,[1] together with expenditure for materials. Later, in 1427, a certain John Virley was employed, and his name, by a curious coincidence, recalls that of John Varley, the well-known water-colourist of the nineteenth century. The most important medieval survivals at Norwich are the famous Norwich Retable and the wall-paintings, that by a happy chance survive in the Ante-Reliquary Chapel (Plates 11a, 12a, b).

The wall-paintings, of c. 1325, are on the vaulting and the western transverse arch of the Chapel. The scheme on the former centres about a small medallion framing a figure of Christ, seated on the stem of a vine-branch that spreads into all sections of the ceiling and so makes a beautifully-designed background for four groups of Saints, each comprising three figures. The best-preserved of these figures are a Virgin and Child, flanked by the Virgin Saints, St. Catherine and St. Margaret, and also St. Peter, St. Paul and St. Andrew. The work is carried out in oil colour, or perhaps an emulsion of oil, against the ivory ground, while the vine-scroll is in bluish green, outlined in black. The colours seen on the drapery are blue, emerald green, reddish brown, and pink, with white, and the effect of the whole is fair and bright. The tints are gradated, and there is a considerable use both of outline in dark red and of underpainting.[2] The latter is employed in various parts; beneath flesh tints there is a greyish green, and beneath the coloured draperies a dark grey. Underpainting in black, outlining in dark red, and vestiges of colouring similar to that found in the works just discussed, are all discernible in the partly ruined scheme, of approximately the same date, at Fring, near Docking, about thirty-five miles from Norwich. On the transverse arch, previously mentioned, we find beneath elaborate architectural canopies, Apostles painted in pairs (Plate 11a), in a varied range of tints comprising blue, pink, purple and green, against a ground of ivory. The colour harmonies are somewhat 'cooler' than those on the vaulting. Inscriptions no doubt once discernible on the books and scrolls carried by the figures have unfortunately vanished; but titles over the Saints depicted on the vaulting survive in part, and are in well-designed and executed Lombardic capitals. The dignity and charm of the whole is remarkable, and its execution masterly.

The Norwich Retable, a much later work of c. 1380, is so well known as to call for

---

[1] *Norfolk & Norwich Archaeological Inst.*, 1847, 207–8.

[2] Instances of the use of underpainting, whether in black, dark grey, or greyish green, may be noted at the following places: Belton, Suffolk; Coombes, Sussex; Crostwight, Norfolk; Fring, Norfolk; Hales, Norfolk; Harbledown, Kent; Lambourne, Essex; and Slapton, Northants.

little detailed description. Like two contemporary panels, from St. Michael at Plea in Norwich, which are painted with the Crucifixion and the Betrayal, it has backgrounds most richly ornamented with raised *gesso*. The 'beading' upon them is the counterpart in reverse of the 'pouncing' on the Wilton Diptych and the effigies of Richard II and Anne of Bohemia, and on numerous English miniatures. The nimbi on the Retable and on the panels just mentioned are also very alike, and so, too, is the painting of the heads and hands. If these works are not from the same brush, they are almost certainly products of the same workshop. On the Retable, as has already been remarked in our discussion of St. Stephen's Chapel, there is a use of perspective, especially in the Flagellation scene. It is noticeable even in such a detail as the 'bowed' tops of the shields in the Resurrection, and in the vaulting depicted over the tomb, although the painter was defeated by the perspective of the tomb itself. It has already been remarked that the left hand of St. John in the Crucifixion closely resembles in treatment that of Richard II in the great portrait. The 'glass enamels' on the frame of the Retable follow a tradition that is traceable at Westminster as early as the late thirteenth century.[1] It may be noted, in passing, that Benedict Nightegale (or Nightingale) was commissioned to impress painters from Norfolk and Suffolk in 1363, for work in St. Stephen's, and that names such as Richard and Roger Norwich and William Walsingham are found in slightly earlier accounts. Both Norwich and Walsingham were rich centres at this date, and the latter as a place of pilgrimage was as famous as Canterbury. The colour scheme of the Retable, with its green, blue, and both light and deep greenish blue, its pale and dark purple and gold, white and 'accents' of vivid vermilion and black, is exceptionally beautiful. The scroll-work on the first and fifth sections is elaborated with vine-leaves and small bunches of grapes, and that on the second and third with oak-leaves and acorns. The vine-leaves and grapes, very similarly designed, are seen also on the Crucifixion from St. Michael at Plea. The long tunic worn by St. John in the Crucifixion is ornamented by bands of 'cufic' ornament, which appears from time to time in English work, not only in miniatures and glass but also on the Westminster Panel. Some frontals and vestments [2] that had been given to Westminster by Cardinal Langham (d. 1376) survived at the Dissolution, and are described in an inventory as 'of bawdekyn haveing in hit strypes of gold with Greke letters'. These borders, whether 'Greke' or 'cufic', evidently had a symbolic meaning. Chaucer, for instance, when describing the garments of Philosophy, which 'a dispysed elde hadde dusked . . . as it is wont to derken bismokede images' remarks that in their borders there was a Greek P, 'that signifyeth the lyf Actif', and a Greek T, 'that signifyeth the lyf Contemplatif'.[3] In the Carrying of the Cross, the sergeant-at-arms who drags Christ forward by means of a cord has in his mailed left hand what has been taken to be a mace, but is in fact a 'singing arrow', found also in some of our miniatures and wall-paintings. Its significance in this scene may be taken to be that while the world wastes its time in idle amusement, Christ bears the burden of its sins. The ground is sown with very small flowers that are painted with exquisite delicacy, and recall Chaucer's lines—'ful gay was al the ground and queynt, and poudred, as men had it peynt, with many a fresh and sondry flour'. It is

---

[1] Tristram, *Eng. Med. Wall Painting*, 1950, 405–6.   [2] *Archaeologia*, LVII, 229, 231, 252, 261.
[3] Chaucer, ed. Skeat, 131. For the 'singing arrow' see chap. V, under 'The Christ of the Trades'.

hardly necessary to remark that this is a feature often found in our miniatures. There is apparent in this altar-piece that combination of the characteristic qualities of an oil and of a 'water' medium, so noticeable in the Westminster Panel and other of our more remarkable paintings. The same explanation of it may be suggested as has been put forward in relation to the Panel, namely, that an emulsion of oil and white of egg was probably used.[1]

CANTERBURY CATHEDRAL

It is clear, from evidence afforded both by survivals and by records, that Canterbury Cathedral must once have been rich in fourteenth-century painting. What still exists, however, is in the main simple decoration. It includes, as has been noted before, imitations of stone tracery, and there are also on the screens of Prior Henry of Eastry patterns of heraldic type, and on the Prior's seat in the Chapter House vestiges of 'glass mosaic'. The remarkable relics in the Chapel of Our Lady Undercroft have already been discussed, and should not be forgotten. Records with their usual tantalizing brevity tell of painting in the Prior's Great Chamber, and in other chambers, and of paintings on panels, and perhaps wall paintings, that were executed for the altars of St. Martin, St. Stephen, St. John the Evangelist, and several others. A painter called Jordan is mentioned in 1310, another named Thomas about 1332, and a third, John, in 1390. By far the most notable surviving work is the representation of the Trinity on the tester above the tomb of the Black Prince, of c. 1376. On account of its scale and general character it may be taken as representative of contemporary wall-paintings of the finest type, which are now lost, but certainly existed in the Cathedral (Plates 13, 14, 15a, b).

The background on the tester is a deep, greenish blue, sown with small roses and stars in *gesso*, raised and gilt. Larger roses are placed at the points of the cusping that ornaments the aureole surrounding the figure of God the Father. They are in strong relief, and must have been made by a method similar to one described by Cennino.[2] The rainbow that forms the throne of the Almighty is executed in transparent colour over gold, by the *translucida*[3] method. The head, at some time deliberately defaced, is encircled by a cruciform nimbus, ornamented in a way very similar to the nimbus of Christ in the Majesty of the Westminster Chapter House, while the Signs of the Evangelists have nimbi of a pattern identical with that of the majority of the Angels there. Two of the Signs, namely, the Eagle and the Angel, are in a fair state of preservation. They are beautifully painted, as are also the borders and patterns on the robes of God the Father. The Crucified Christ has been largely defaced, and only almost indecipherable traces of the Dove remain; so slight are they, indeed, that they may easily escape notice. The colours, apart from the ground, are a deep green, enriched by delicate diapers in gold; pink, also much modified in appearance through the use of patterns in colour; and a bright red, with some grey, cream and black, the last being employed in the main for outlining.

[1] Tristram, *Eng. Med. Wall Painting*, 1950, 403–5. [2] *Cennino Cennini*, chap. 125.
[3] Tristram, *Eng. Med. Wall Painting*, 1950, 406–7.

The devotion to the Trinity characteristic of the Black Prince is well known, and it has naturally been held to account for the choice of subject for the tester over his tomb. It may be noted, further, that the Order of the Garter was dedicated to the Trinity, with the Blessed Virgin and St. George. There is however a deeper significance still in the choice. This becomes evident from the *Ayenbite of Inwyt*, for example, where a description of Heaven opens with a reference to the 'ineffable and indivisible majesty of the Holy Trinity', and the statement that the 'life of the Blessed is in the sight of the Trinity'. Thus, the effigy of the Black Prince has lain for nearly six hundred years facing upward toward a symbolic painting of the Vision of Heaven. The symbolism is carried into minute detail, moreover; for the pattern on the robe of God the Father consists of 'suns in splendour', charged each with the Sacred Monogram; and the Trinity was often likened to the sun, as in *Cursor Mundi*—'in the sune that schines clere es . . . a bodi rond, and hete, and light, this thre we find al at a sight'. It is not surprising that paintings of the Trinity are found in tomb recesses, chantry chapels, and Easter Sepulchres. Even the battlemented framework of the tester is not meaningless, for the battlements are those of the City of God, and the lion masks and fleurs-de-lis are set about them in alternation for the same reason and in just the same way as the fleurs-de-lis and wyverns on the Westminster Panel.[1] The cruciform nimbus about the head of God the Father will cause no surprise, in view of what has been said previously concerning figures of Christ as Creator.[2] In the Byzantine Guide to Painting it is stated that the cross should intersect the nimbus of each of the three Persons of the Trinity.[3] It was accepted in the Middle Ages that numbers were endowed with some occult power, and, following St. Augustine, it was claimed that every number has its divine significance. The number three, that of the Trinity, connoted all things spiritual, and in this idea may be traced the origin of the trefoils that appear so frequently in the decorative borders to wall-paintings.

Master Hugh of St. Albans can hardly have been responsible for the tester, since he died in 1368; nevertheless the conventions employed in parts mentioned above would appear to have derived from his atelier. There his most probable successor would seem to have been Gilbert Prince, who was closely associated with Master Hugh, at least from 1350 onwards. The association was continued by Master Hugh's widow, for whom Prince witnessed a deed in 1374, only some two years before the latest date for the execution of the Trinity on the tester.[4] Any attempt to attribute the painting to him, however, meets with many difficulties. If it was his, it would, like a wall-painting, have been a corporate production, the design and the figures being directly his own, and the rest carried out by assistants in the workshop.[5] But there are other possible claimants to authorship of this splendid work. Master Hugh himself received very considerable payments from the Black Prince in 1351, 1355, and 1361. A certain Simon de Coudrey obtained by instalments, paid over two years, and ending in 1359, the extremely large

[1] Tristram, *Eng. Med. Wall Painting*, 1950, 133.   [2] See chap. I, 25.

[3] See Didron, I, 46–7, II, 45–7; Rushforth, *Medieval Christian Imagery*, 1936, 29; *Middle English Sermons*, ed. Ross, 1940, S.48, 314; Millar, *English Illuminated Manuscripts*, II, pls. 49, 71.

[4] Harvey, *Burlington Magazine*, LXXXIX, 303–5.

[5] Tristram, *Eng. Med. Wall Painting*, 1950, 411–43.

sum of three hundred and eighty-seven pounds 'for divers things of his craft'.[1] He was a Londoner, and must have been of very high standing. Earlier, in 1347, a man named Stephen Doget had supplied 'two hundred standards and one hundred and forty-four pennons of the Prince's arms', which he may or may not have designed and executed, although in all likelihood he was responsible for them. On the whole, the probability would seem to be that the Trinity is a comparatively early work by Gilbert Prince, executed whilst he was still to some degree influenced by Hugh of St. Albans. It may be noted in passing that in 1392 the City of London presented Richard II and his consort with a 'Trinity' valued at eight hundred pounds, an enormous sum at that time. There are few miniatures with which the tester may profitably be compared. The Signs of the Four Evangelists show similarity with those in the Missal of Abbot Litlington (1383–4), and a Trinity in a book of Hours at Cambridge, in the Fitzwilliam Museum, may also be mentioned.

ST. ALBAN'S CATHEDRAL

From records concerning St. Alban's Abbey we learn of an extensive scheme in the Infirmary; its exact date is uncertain, but it was destroyed towards the close of the fourteenth century. Other works mentioned are: a painting of St. Thomas of Canterbury, ordered in 1380 by Robert of Trunch, keeper of the shrine of St. Alban; two representations of the Adoration of the Magi, formerly in the nave, where very slight traces of one of them still remain; and an elaborate decoration of heraldic type, also once in the nave, and still to be seen there in 1864. The few survivals consist mainly of decorative patterns, and colour on carving, but they also include a remarkably well-preserved figure of St. William of York, with a shield of the arms of Fitzwilliam below, and the inscription SCS WILLMUS. The drawing and handling are very good, and the colour, which includes blue, red and gold, with some yellow, black and white, is attractive. The work is early in style, and recalls the figures of Archbishops and Bishops in the great Coronation of St. Edward formerly in Westminster Palace,[2] although it is gentler in handling and less austere in conception. The same may be said of it by comparison with the fine pen drawing of an Archbishop which occurs among four drawings added to the Westminster Psalter.[3] At St. Albans, near the St. William, is a second and similar figure, surrounded by a pattern of roses, but it is very much defaced. Within niches on the pedestal that once bore the shrine of St. Alban are traces of leopards and fleurs-de-lis, on grounds of red and blue diapered by stars and small roundels, the sole remains, apart from the figures just mentioned, of a scheme of decoration once associated with the shrine (Plate 11b).

St. Albans was closely connected with Westminster[4] and was a centre of great importance. Master Thomas of Westminster seems to have lived here and also his father

---

[1] See Black Prince's Register, IV, 1933, 35, 47, 60, 151, 327–8, 389. For comparisons with miniatures see Millar, *English Illuminated Manuscripts*, II, pls. 49, 71.

[2] Tristram, *Eng. Med. Wall Painting*, 1950, 103, pl. 16, supp. pl. 13.

[3] ibid., 155–6, supp. pl. 11.   [4] ibid., 6–7, 137–9, 317–31.

Walter of Durham, both of them King's Painters of the first standing. Jack of St. Albans, of whom little is known beyond the fact that he amused Edward II by dancing before him, for which he was handsomely rewarded, and Master Hugh, whose work at West-minster we have studied here, continued a connexion with the town that lasted little less than a century, and terminated only with Master Hugh's death in 1368. His will shows him to have been a man of wealth for his times. He left to his wife his 'mansion-house', all vessels of silver and brass from the hall, chamber and kitchen, and also forty pounds and a valuable painting from Lombardy. He gave his implements and colours to be sold for the benefit of the poor, and to the church of St. Giles, which was associated with the Painters' Gild, he made bequests for the maintenance there of the painters' light, and other lights. Among many other legacies are some that are of particular interest, for instance sums to friends at St. Albans, to 'the hermit of the meadows beyond the Thames', and two other hermits, to inmates of religious houses, to hospitals and prisons, and for masses to be said and pilgrimages to be undertaken for the good of his own soul. The will of Gilbert Prince, his associate and successor as chief King's Painter, suggests even greater prosperity, for it mentions a number of servants and apprentices, and provides for legacies of one hundred pounds, a large sum in those days, to each of his three children, who were also to have distributed among them his 'three belts garnished with silver'. Evidently his house contained a chapel, a privilege only granted to persons of standing, since he bequeathed to the 'painters'' church of St. Giles 'my missal, chalice, and vestments'. In view of all this, it is far from surprising that 'men of craft', including 'peyntourys', are distinguished in *Jacob's Well* [1] from 'the comoun labourerys and alle servauntys'; or that, in discussing the 'four estates', the 'people' should sometimes be subdivided into clergy, nobles, craftsmen, merchants and peasants. Neither is it matter for astonishment that, at least in England, the craftsmen shared with kings and clerics a title of respect such as 'dan', as, for instance, 'daun Salamon', 'sir monk . . . damp Piers',[2] and 'a smyth . . . daun Gerveys'.

SOUTH NEWINGTON IN OXFORDSHIRE

At South Newington in Oxfordshire there is a scheme that possesses many remark-able features. The colour is exceptionally rich and beautiful, the design excellent, and the execution both sensitive and masterly. The technique is also unusual, for the work is carried out in oil, or an emulsion of oil, on lime plaster. It is perhaps easiest to appre-ciate the colour in the Virgin and Child (Plate 16a) on the north wall, since the other subjects, apart from a St. Margaret (Plate 16b), are at most times of the day in shadow. The Virgin is depicted against a background of pink, modified by the warm red of some delicate 'stem and leaf' scroll-work, that is rendered with remarkable freedom and certainty. The Blessed Virgin's tunic is also pink, the folds being delineated in red, and it is bordered at the neck with small roundels in white. Her mantle is drawn across the body and falls on either side in well-designed folds, following the formula seen in

[1] Owst, *Literature and Pulpit*, 1933, 362, n. 4.
[2] *Lay Folks Mass Book*, 1879, 169; Tristram, *Eng. Med. Wall Painting*, 1950, 427–31.

the earlier St. Faith at Westminster.[1] Its colour is a light green, shaded in a darker tint, and the folds are defined in black outline. She stands with a slight sway, bearing the Holy Child on her right arm and holding in her left hand a green rod, the 'rod of Jesse', with a fleur-de-lis at its head and a second below on the shaft. The Child holds a red apple in one hand, and with the other caresses his Mother in tender affection. Apart from the earlier Virgin and Child of the famous Chichester Roundel, there is little in north-western Europe to surpass this painting, whether in the feeling that informs it, its beauty of conception, or the charm of its colour. This fact would be even more obvious than it is had the work suffered less through the vicissitudes of time; however, for a wall-painting it is in quite good condition. Beneath the Blessed Virgin's feet is a shield charged with—*Gules, three lions passant argent*, for Gifford. The containing niche is painted for the most part in neutral tints, and has crockets outlined in black, cusping in red and white and black upon white, and single-light windows in alternation with quatrefoils. Windows like these are not infrequently represented on actual architectural features, e.g. on the lower, original part of richly carved canopies over the Sedilia in Exeter Cathedral. In this case they must have been painted before the stone sections were placed in position, for when preservative was to be applied some years ago it was found to be impossible to reach some of them. To the left of the Virgin and Child two donors kneel in prayer (Plate 19*a*), against backgrounds of red enriched by a rather broadly painted scroll and leaf pattern in a lighter tint of the same colour. Their garments are painted in red, and an intense, dark green, with some black and white, and are excellent and most interesting representations of the clothes of the period, *c.* 1330–40. The figures have been identified as those of Thomas Gifford and his wife Margaret Mortayne; and thus one reason for the representations of St. Thomas of Canterbury and of St. Margaret of Antioch elsewhere in the church becomes apparent.

An Annunciation nearby (Plate 20), with St. James the Great and a donor below it, must once have been the equal of the Virgin and Child, but it has suffered to a much greater extent, so that very close, careful and informed study is necessary before much of it can be deciphered. Given such study, it becomes evident that the head of the Archangel is delicate-featured, the hair, yellow and curling, bound by a fillet ornamented with roses, and the wing feathers coloured in red, yellow and green. The folds of the pale pink tunic are drawn in red, and the mantle, a very dark, rich green, edged in vermilion. In the left hand is a scroll, while the right is raised in an expressive gesture towards the Blessed Virgin, who bends her head in assent and holds a book in her left hand. Her robes are painted in cream, dark green, and red. The flowers in the vase placed as usual at the centre of the scene are shaped like the native wild tulip, rather than the lily. The vessel containing them is supported upon a shield charged with—*Ermine, a chief dancetty gules*, for Mortayne. The background is similar to that of the Virgin and Child. A third painting that possesses the grace and charm found in the Virgin and Child, also the Annunciation, even though the latter is much defaced, is that of St. Margaret, mentioned above. This is on the southern splay of a window in the adjacent east wall. Like the Blessed Virgin, the Saint stands with a graceful sway, being placed however not above a shield but on a painted corbel composed of two large green leaves with

[1] ibid., 121–3, pl. 7.

a shield of arms between them, again that of Gifford. Her green mantle is edged with vermilion and draped to fall in well-designed folds over the right arm and also,voluminously, from the left side. In her right hand she holds a cross-hilted spear which she thrusts into the jaws of the dragon beneath her feet. Her head recalls the head of St. Michael the Archangel in a fine miniature at Berlin,[1] and the dragon too is very like that upon which he tramples. Moreover, the treatment of drapery, and of some of the scroll-work on backgrounds in the paintings at South Newington, especially behind a figure of Margaret Mortayne, near the Virgin and Child, is reminiscent of the painting of St. Michael.

Two more fine paintings remain for consideration, both of them martyrdom scenes, the one of St. Thomas of Canterbury (Plate 17) and the other of Blessed Thomas of Lancaster (Plate 18). The former is without doubt the finest surviving representation of the subject in the entire range of our wall-painting; whoever the painter was, who was responsible for it, he was certainly not excelled, in technical accomplishment or general ability, by many of his contemporaries. The composition is that which had become traditional for the subject, but it is rendered with exceptional power. The head of the Saint is well painted, and shows considerable feeling, and the figures of the attacking knights, so far as they survive, are drawn with mastery. Patterns that are very well designed and delicately painted are to be seen on many parts, for instance, on the drapery of the altar, which is enriched with foliated patterns in white on green, black on yellow, and white on red. Fylfots are seen more than once, in particular on the super-frontal, where they are painted in white or black, and as ornament on squares of green, yellow and red. The second martyrdom, of Blessed Thomas, is much simpler than the other in composition, since only the figure of the executioner and that of his victim are seen, the former depicted in vigorous action. The head of the latter, though well drawn and of a fine type, hardly equals the head of St. Thomas of Canterbury. There is in it, however, some slight attempt at characterization, and this need cause no surprise, for the murder was still fresh in the minds of many when it was painted, and Blessed Thomas was almost undoubtedly known to the Giffords, who may well have had some close connexion with him. It is far from improbable that the painter himself may have seen so prominent a personality. Thomas Earl of Lancaster, a cousin of Edward II,[2] was executed in 1322 at Pontefract, and within a year pilgrimages to his tomb began as the result of reported miracles there. The cult spread rapidly, so that thousands of pilgrims are said to have collected in the neighbourhood. By the year 1327 petition was made in Parliament for an approach to Rome in respect of a possible canonization, since this had already been anticipated by popular acclaim. It is reasonable to suppose that the Giffords were supporters of the cause, and that they may have secured some relic of the 'Saint'. The presence of such a relic would explain the exceptionally rich scheme carried out in the north aisle of South Newington church, a scheme from which only parts now survive. Within a period of no more than some ten or at most twenty years after his death, to which the paintings may be assigned on

[1] Bernath, *Burlington Magazine*, LII, 1928, 159, repr.; Oakeshott, *The Sequence of English Medieval Art*, 1950, 48, pl. 35.

[2] Jusserand, *English Wayfaring Life*, trans. Toulmin Smith, 1891, 339–43; in 1338 a tankard was sold in London ornamented with an 'image of St. [*sic*] Thomas of Lancaster'.

stylistic and other grounds, many relics would still have been in the possession of relatives, friends and supporters of the cause for canonization, which, however, never took place. It is evident, too, from the costume of the donors of the scheme that it cannot have been executed after 1340, and was probably carried out earlier than this. Like the painting of Blessed Thomas, these figures show a distinct attempt at portraiture, and are not devoid of characterization.

It has already been remarked that the scheme is exceptional in its technical characteristics. A similar instance of painting in oil, or an emulsion of oil, on plaster, has been noted at Christ Church, Oxford, though there the work is much defaced and can only be examined profitably at close quarters, from scaffolding. Cennino Cennini [1] gives recipes for painting in oil on plastered walls, and begins with directions for treatment of the plaster surfaces by sizing them in order to counteract their absorbency. He continues with advice on the preparation of the oil, and on the grinding of colours in it, and also says how they should be applied when ground. He further recommends that the oil should be placed in the sun, in order to reduce and so thicken it, during what is still known in parts of Italy as the 'lion heat', or *caldo leone*. This recommendation can have been of but little use to any contemporary English painters who may perhaps have known of it. It is more than probable, however, that painting in oil reached Italy from northern Europe, rather than that the reverse occurred.[2]

CROUGHTON IN NORTHAMPTONSHIRE

At Croughton in Northamptonshire there is an extensive series of *c.* 1310, which was discovered in 1921. It covers the north and south walls of the nave to within a few feet of the floor, and terminates at the eastern end of the north aisle, where the Lady Chapel was situated, with an Annunciation and the subject of St. Anne Teaching the Blessed Virgin. The scheme as a whole is devoted to the Virgin, although in the parts devoted to the Holy Infancy and the Passion the theme of her life that is otherwise prominent throughout naturally takes a second place. On the south wall, however, there are only three scenes out of a total of twenty-two that are not intimately connected with her, and many of them are from Apocryphal or legendary sources. It is unfortunate, but inevitable, that many of the thirty-six surviving subjects are as usual damaged. The best-preserved are the Massacre of the Innocents, and the Flight into Egypt (Plate 21), the Last Supper and the Crucifixion. In technique and handling all are of the normal type for their period, except that they show traces of some more expensive colours than usual—that is, blue and vermilion in small quantities. There are signs, too, that they originally possessed more than the degree of finish common to country church schemes. It is clear from fragments still retaining such finish, that in this respect as well as in general design they equalled most contemporary illuminations. Although the loss of detail consequent upon centuries of accident and neglect is much to be regretted, at least it serves to bring out in some subjects a quality of design that is full of vitality. This is evident especially in the silhouettes of figures, such as those in the

[1] Chaps. 90–3.   [2] Tristram, *Eng. Med. Wall Painting*, 1950, 399–402.

73

Flight into Egypt.[1] The plaster ground was first treated with an ivory colour, and upon this were executed tentatively-drawn setting-out lines, from which the final painting diverges here and there. Then the craftsman laid in his subjects with long, sweeping strokes of the brush, and finally picked out parts in flat colour, while delicately tinting others. All this was done with a surprising sureness of hand, and great dexterity. The paintings possess those qualities of rhythm and sweetness, combined with strength and reserve, that result from a blend of the characteristics of late thirteenth and early fourteenth-century art. There is much in them, too, that is typical of a good drawing in line and wash; and, like such drawings, they would suffer through retouching a most serious loss in essential character, as would be the case with Chinese painting. This observation is true of all our medieval wall-painting. Some difference is noticeable at Croughton between the work on the north and south walls, and it is marked enough to suggest that two craftsmen were employed there, one of them, either the elder or trained in a slightly more archaic tradition, having been responsible for the paintings on the north wall.

The first scene, reading from the east on the south side, is the Rejection of Joachim's Offering, and is fragmentary, while the third, the Meeting of St. Joachim and St. Anne at the Golden Gate, is fairly well preserved, and has much feeling and charm. This scene was a customary way of representing the Immaculate Conception.[2] From the next, the Birth of the Virgin, little remains but part of a figure, perhaps of an attendant, and a cradle. This last is delightful, with its balustered sides, foliated terminals to the head and foot posts, and, attached to the side rails, three bands to keep the bedclothes in place. It is most unfortunate that the remainder of the scene should have been lost, for otherwise it would have afforded an attractive 'interior' of the early fourteenth century. The painter's ability to render a subject with considerable feeling, is not his least remarkable characteristic. He does so both by direct means, as in the embrace of St. Joachim and St. Anne, and her consolation of him upon the departure of the Blessed Virgin for the Temple, and by slight touches, such as the cradle set ready for the child, and the small dog disturbed by the vision of the Angel, in the Annunciation to the Shepherds. That such slight touches had by this time for the most part become traditional detracts not at all from the special ability he shows in making use of them. It may be granted that for his sympathetic understanding of the different scenes he no doubt owed much to preachers and miracle plays alike; but his notable capacity for expression in a medium other than theirs, and one with its own peculiar difficulties and opportunities was his own, and demands recognition. In spirit these paintings, and many others also, show much of the practical wisdom and the sensibility combined with naivety that is found in the utterances of the invaluable Cennino, who, incidentally, remarks that painting on walls 'is the most delightful and charming kind of work that there can be'. His observations on the spirit that should guide the painter would certainly have been appreciated by those who created the scheme at Croughton. He says that, after 'Science', a word which he understood in a different sense from ours

'comes an art . . . dependent on the operations of the hand, and this is called Painting,

---

[1] Paintings obscured by dirt (1954).
[2] Mâle, *Religious Art in France of the Thirteenth Century*, 1913, 241.

for which we must be endowed with both imagination and skill in the hand, to discover unseen things concealed beneath the obscurity of natural objects, and to arrest them with the hand, presenting to the sight that which did not before appear to exist.'

The rest of the scenes at Croughton, apart from the Passion series, follow closely the accounts given in the *Apochryphal Gospel of Pseudo-Matthew*, except that, as in certain miracle plays, the Blessed Virgin is shown leaving her home a second time, in obedience to the commands of the High Priest, for the Espousals. It is tacitly assumed that she had returned to her parents at some time, after her presentation in the Temple as a child. At Croughton, while St. Anne teaches her to read, her wrist is grasped by St. Joachim, who prepares to take her again to the Temple, and her slight and gentle figure is most sympathetically drawn, as it is on the Cluny Panel, where St. Anne is shown instructing her.

There is a strong general similarity between the series at Croughton and various contemporary miniatures. This is most marked in the Psalter of Robert de Lisle, especially in a miniature of the Last Supper, and in particular the treatment of its central group. In the drawing of hands and feet there are mannerisms to recall the Holkham Hall Bible; and, although the work in Queen Mary's Psalter is undoubtedly of later date, there are in its illuminations some features that are strongly reminiscent of the wall-paintings. One that should be noted is the flagon at the end of the table in the Last Supper, for this is placed in the same way in the Psalter and is of just the same type. The Annunciation recalls another Annunciation executed in embroidery on the Felbrigg book-cover. In conclusion, it may be said with some confidence that the painters who worked at Croughton were either from the London School, or else that they were very strongly influenced by its productions.

The Tree of Jesse at Weston Longville in Norfolk is one of our outstanding wall-paintings, even though it is carried out mainly in simple earth colours that are varied only by a little black and some green (Plates 22, 23*a* and *b*). However, it is excellent both in design and in execution, and the best-preserved among the figures, those of two Prophets and a King to the left of the centre, are exceptionally well drawn. One of them, the King, who is seated on a branch of the vine that forms the Tree, turns towards a Prophet beside him, and points with outstretched left arm to the Virgin and Child in the usual position above (Plate 24). His hair and beard are plaited, and the former hangs behind him to waist level. There is in his finely-rendered figure a curious, almost Egyptian quality, which is emphasized by the accident of time that has reduced his headgear to a silhouette resembling that seen in Egyptian paintings. The variety of attitude, type and costume throughout, as well as the vigour and certainty of the delineation, are very striking. There is nothing to surpass these figures for strong draughtsmanship and vitality of conception in any contemporary miniatures, and very little to rival them. The closest approximations to this Jesse Tree, perhaps, may be found in the Ormesby Psalter and the St. Omer Psalter, both of them of the early fourteenth century.[1] It is much to be deplored that the figure of Jesse once occupying the normal position at the base of the Tree is lost, and also several of the Prophets and Kings. The Virgin and Child, too, are seen only in vague silhouette, but nevertheless this suggests a tender sweetness contrasting strongly with the powerful treatment of the work as a whole. It may be affirmed without any hesitation that in this wall-painting we have not only one of the finest to have survived, but a most notable example from the East Anglian School. There is nothing else of equal date in the county of Norfolk which is quite like it, although some later works, and in particular the Doom at West Somerton, show equally vigorous and decided handling, although they are damaged in large areas.

Among prefigurations of the Blessed Virgin, for which the Fathers of the Church searched the Scriptures, were the three *virgae*, the *virga Moysi*, the *virga Aaron*, and the *virga Jesse*. The last-named is of course mentioned in Isaiah's prophecy of the rod that should come forth out of the stem of Jesse and the flower that should grow out of his roots. The rod, in medieval times, was usually regarded as symbolic of the Blessed Virgin and the flower of Christ. Further, painted Trees of Jesse are normally shown as rising from the recumbent figure of Jesse [2] himself, and are pictorial versions, whether more or less elaborate, of St. Matthew's record of the ancestry of Christ, in the first chapter of his gospel. They are however much more than this. In the branches are shown not only the Kings who were ancestors of Christ, but also the Prophets who foretold His coming, and this reflects ideas set forth, for instance, in the *Legenda Aurea*, concerning the Blessed Virgin. As in miniatures, so in wall-paintings, Virgil and the Sybil may sometimes have been included among the Prophets, but if so no instances of their inclusion are known. The Prophets, often in animated discussion, bear scrolls, either blank, or inscribed with suitable quotations from the Scriptures, and they frequently point, like the Kings, to the Blessed Virgin and the Holy Child above them. That the Tree of Jesse may be regarded as a Tree of Salvation is shown by its occasional connexion in iconography with the Tree of the Cross.[3] The vine branches that often compose it derive at least in part from Voragine's statement that on the night of the Nativity the vines flowered throughout Palestine. Dan Michel, in the *Ayenbite of Inwyt*, says that the devil can no more endure Mercy than the toad can abide the smell of the vine. The prominence almost invariably given to Our Lady in representations of the Tree of Jesse, has been associated with an increased devotion to the Immaculate Conception, as expressed in the *Golden Legend*.[4] At Chalgrove in Oxfordshire a 'Jesse' is the subject opening a long series devoted to the Blessed Virgin, and as we have seen this series, like that at Croughton, is drawn, apart from a Passion sequence, largely from the *Apochryphal Gospel of Pseudo-Matthew*. The other more notable Jesse Trees among our examples of the fourteenth century, are the elaborate version at Abingdon and the much simpler one at Chalfont St. Giles, the former associated with a Lily Crucifix.

[1] Millar, II, *English Illuminated Manuscripts*, pls. 1 and 19.

[2] In the fine Tree on the *Beatus* page of the Windmill Psalter, Jesse is seated; Millar, *English Illuminated Manuscripts*, I, pl. 99.

[3] Mâle, *Religious Art in France of the Thirteenth Century*, 1913, 208.

[4] *Golden Legend*, II, 122–9; Mâle, *Religious Art in France of the Thirteenth Century*, 1913, 241.

The largest and best-known Tree of Jesse is to be found on the Continent, at Hildesheim, and, like that at Abingdon, is on a ceiling. However, it has suffered far more from re-painting than the other, which has almost escaped such maltreatment. There are numer-ous very beautiful examples of 'Jesses' of various dates on the *Beatus* pages of English manuscripts, beside those already mentioned above. It was even made a subject of pageantry, as we learn from Lydgate's poem on the occasion of Henry VI's entry into London after his coronation in France:—

Upon this castelle unto thoder side
Ther whas a tree, wiche sprang out of Jessé,
Ordeyned of God ffulle long to abyde—
David crounyd ffirst for his humilité,
The braunchis conveyed, as men myght see,
Lyneally and in the genelogie,
To Crist Jhesu that whas born of Mary.

Chapter Four

★──★

FOURTEENTH-CENTURY
WALL-PAINTINGS OF THE 'SIMPLER' TYPE

★──★

THE 'simpler' wall-paintings have already been discussed in broad outline, and some variations from the work of the thirteenth century have been noted in them. It remains to consider some of these paintings in detail, and in relation to other examples, and also with reference to technical changes not yet mentioned. In iconography, the most interesting developments are to be found in renderings of the Allegories and Moralities, and are clearly connected with the sermons and the general literature of the times, so that they demand close study in a final chapter. Apart from these, some 'histories', either still in existence or only recorded, are to be noted in Kent, Sussex, Buckinghamshire, Oxfordshire, Northamptonshire, Worcestershire, and Norfolk. Short series that hardly constitute 'histories' are at various places, i.e. Selling in Kent and Soberton in Hampshire. Single works of an exceptional kind are at Heacham and Starston in Norfolk, and elsewhere.

It has already been said that there was at this date a marked increase in paintings of the Annunciation, and reasons for this have been indicated. Many are found on the splays of east windows, e.g. Little Melton in Norfolk, where the Archangel is depicted, as is normal, on the spectator's left and the Blessed Virgin on the opposite splay. Figures such as these, even though in a defaced condition, often retain some beauty of line and silhouette. An Annunciation on the splays of an east window would have been complementary to the Crucifixion without doubt incorporated in the carved or painted retable of the high altar, and often in that of the Lady Chapel.[1] However, since retables were almost everywhere destroyed and none remain *in situ* there is no actual example of such an arrangement, which would have had an iconographic relationship with the Lily Crucifix, when, as at Abingdon, this was associated with an Annunciation. Sometimes the Annunciation is placed at the side of the altar steps, or towards the entrance to the

[1] cf. the Thornham Parva Retable.

78

Sanctuary, as at Tarrant Crawford in Dorset, where little more than a silhouette remains incised in the plaster. Here the Archangel holds a sharply-pointed spear, so startling a feature that it cannot be genuine, but must have resulted from misapprehension and interference at some past time. Many of the lines incised on the wall are hard and doubtful in character and have not the appearance that results from 'softening' through superimposed painting and work with the brush. This subject, though later obliterated and rediscovered not so very long since, is first recorded, very briefly, some thirty or forty years ago. The herald's baton, for which the spear has in error been substituted, is, or was, to be seen at Stanley St. Leonard in Gloucestershire, where the Archangel is shown kneeling. It is found quite frequently in Byzantine paintings, mosaics, and even textiles. The position of the Tarrant Crawford Annunciation, at the entrance to the chancel, should also be noted in connexion with Byzantine work.[1] At Barton in Cambridgeshire the subject is painted on either side of the south door. The three 'lily' blooms in a vase placed between the figures in an Annunciation have a complicated significance, as we have seen earlier, and symbolize the immaculate virginity of the Blessed Virgin.

The altar-painting of the Crucifixion at Turvey in Bedfordshire is perhaps the most remarkable rendering to have survived from our period. It has in fact some claim to be classed as one of the 'richer' wall-paintings. Both the drawing of the figures and the colour are exceptional, and the dark green ground is ornamented by a delicate diaper of flowers. The attendant figure of St. John has been partially retouched at some time in the past and in consequence resembles that of a female Saint. At Dorchester near Oxford there is an entirely repainted Crucifixion, that to judge from its present appearance must have suffered in this way not many years after discovery, c. 1846. The repainting, however, was carried out in this instance with some knowledge and with evident attention to what had been found on the wall. Like that at Turvey, the work was of an early type, the Body of Christ being bent in a double curve and the feet fastened by a single nail, as in the small painting below the St. Faith in Westminster Abbey.[2] The curve of the Body at Westminster is slight, and not as pronounced, as it is in the two later works. In the representations at Turvey and Dorchester the blood does not flow in streams from the Five Wounds, as it does in representations of the second half of the century which bring to mind the lines in Lydgate's *Testament*: 'Myd of a cloyster, depicte upon a wall, I saugh a crucifyx, whose woundes were not smalle . . . with "*vide*" wrete ther besyde.'[3] Another quite early altar-painting at Grimston in Norfolk, though now almost lost, still has sufficient remains to show that it was painted on an exceptionally large scale, for the figures when complete must have been of slightly more than life-size. The whole was framed by a low, crocketed arch, and the painting once possessed delicate detail, which may be seen on the parts of the nimbi that are still distinguishable. At Faversham in Kent on an octagonal pillar of the eastern arcade, is a series of the Holy Infancy and Passion of c. 1300, which is arranged so that the Virgin and Child in the Adoration of the Magi come directly below the Crucified Christ, and both subjects face the spectator as he turns eastward in the direction of the

---

[1] See Mâle, *L'Art religieux du XII* siècle en France*, 1922, 54, 55, 58, fig. 42; Rushforth, *Medieval Christian Imagery*, 1936, 84.

[2] Tristram, *Eng. Med. Wall Painting*, 1950, 121-3, pl. 9.   [3] *Minor Poems*, no. 68, p. 365.

high altar. In this instance the Crucifixion has been connected deliberately, not with an Annunciation, as in some renderings of the Lily Crucifix, but with the Homage of the Kings. These paintings, like the Turvey Crucifixion, have some claim to be classed with work of the more 'elaborate' type, on account of their colour, and because, although little finish survives upon them, there is sufficient here and there to show what degree they once possessed. The Nativity, with the Virgin suckling the Holy Child, who is in swaddling clothes, and the Ox and Ass above them, still retains some charm; there is also a fine Angel, in the Annunciation to the Shepherds, who are themselves well drawn and not devoid of character. The Shepherd's 'crook', at this date, and for a considerable period after, resembles in shape the modern hockey stick. In wall-painting, the best fourteenth-century renderings of the Adoration of the Magi are to be found at Croughton and Chalgrove, with that at Faversham, and each forms part of a 'history'. The Adoration was sometimes represented as a solitary scene, as noted previously, e.g. at St. Albans, where there were formerly two representations quite close to each other in the nave, but almost indistinguishable fragments of only one remain.

The finest of all our *Mariolas* from this period is that at South Newington. In Coventry Cathedral the Blessed Virgin is represented below a head of Christ (now lost) supporting the Holy Child on her right arm and with three flowers in her left hand that resemble the wild tulip in shape. The painting is of quite early date, c. 1330. At Belchamp Walter, in Essex, the head of the Virgin has still some beauty, although it is reduced to little more than an outline. There is an unusual subject at Little Kimble, in Buckinghamshire, where a bearded man holds a triptych, the central panel of which is filled with a Virgin and Child, now much defaced, and the panel on the right with a Trinity. Since the church is dedicated to All Saints, and there are on its walls representations of no less than seven identified Saints, some of them in 'histories', and also of several that are unidentified, it is at least a reasonable suggestion that the bearded man is St. Luke, holding the picture of the Blessed Virgin that he is traditionally said to have painted. Lydgate says: 'Beholde and se this glorious fygure, Whiche Seynt Luke of Our Lady lyvinge After her lyknes made a picture.' [1] It is not in any way surprising that in the wall-painting of the triptych at Little Kimble the Virgin and Child should be associated with a Trinity. At Barton, near Cambridge, birds perch on the branches behind the Blessed Virgin, as she suckles the Holy Child. Birds were in the Middle Ages considered to be milder by nature than beasts.[2] and to be representative of the better sort of men. In the *Ancren Riwle* anchoresses that are worthy of their vocation are compared to them. In this village church at Barton, the 'boske of briddes', or 'bush of birds', may be regarded as singing to the beholder 'For thy sins amends make'. The same theme runs through Lydgate's *Make Amendes*: 'By a wylde wodes syde, As I walked myself alone A blysse of brydes me bad abyde.' At Weston Beggard, near Hereford, a *Mariola* with censing Angels on either side is recorded within a tomb recess, but it was lost long ago, and the account of it hardly seems quite reliable. There is yet another Virgin and Child, also within a tomb recess, and now almost indecipher-

---

[1] Lydgate, *Minor Poems*, 290.
[2] *Piers Plowman*, ed. Skeat, pt. IV, 354; *Lyrics of the Fourteenth Century*, ed. Brown, 1924, no. 117; Lydgate, *Minor Poems*, ed. Halliwell, 1831, 229.

able, at Northmoor near Oxford. Thornham Parva, in Suffolk, has on the south wall a puzzling scene that has been identified as another representation of the same subject, but the identification is a doubtful one. A crowned Queen holds a child, also crowned, on her knee, and has in her hands a book, while behind her there stands another figure, much defaced. If it is regarded as a Virgin and Child, there are three unusual features in this painting, at least for its period—the crown on the child's head; the book in the mother's hand; and the third figure, behind the chair or throne. The subject is in the lowest tier on the wall, and the only others surviving in the same tier, although on the opposite side of the small nave, are drawn from a 'history' of St. Edmund, King and Martyr. It may be suggested though with diffidence, that this is St. Edmund, as a child, learning the Psalter, and that the third figure is an attendant.[1] The book itself was said to have been preserved for centuries at the Abbey of Bury St. Edmunds.

The Jesse Tree has already been studied here in some detail, as has also the subject of St. Anne Teaching the Blessed Virgin. Among paintings of the 'simpler' type, the rendering of the latter at Corby in Lincolnshire is the most interesting. The Trinity, apart from that on the tester over the tomb of the Black Prince and another with censing Angels, found within an Easter Sepulchre at Gorleston in Norfolk, is depicted in four of the five remaining cases on the east wall, whether of a church or of a chantry chapel. At Bradwell in Essex, however, the subject is seen on a window-splay at the eastern end of the chancel, below an abbreviated Last Judgement on the soffit. At Catherington, in Hampshire, there are two censing Angels, and also an Angel with a harp. The Trinity at Gorleston, already mentioned, has on one side a shield of the Trinity and on the other side a shield charged with the Emblems of the Passion.

In the fourteenth century scenes from the life of Christ were still drawn from the Infancy and Passion, almost excluding the Ministry. It is hardly necessary to recall the reason for this, for the paintings were selected in conformity with the feasts of the Church, and therefore no attempt was made to present a strictly historical sequence. The increased concentration on the Passion that characterizes the period is reflected in wall-painting, for while there are fourteen sets of scenes from the Passion there are only very few from the Holy Infancy, two of them placed beside or near a Passion series. Apart from the general increase in naturalism, there are few fresh features in renderings of the Holy Infancy. The Child is no longer placed on an altar, as in earlier representations, at Winterbourne Dauntsey in Wiltshire and Ashampstead in Berkshire. The Shepherds are sometimes shown as playing [2] the bagpipes and are more strongly characterized than before. At Cocking in Sussex their dog barks vigorously at the Angel, and is a small, rough-coated animal, like a terrier. In representations of the Massacre of the Innocents, there are instances where, as in the later *Coventry Mysteries*, the following phrases are appropriate: 'upon my spear a gerle [3] I bear', and 'the boys sprawlyd at my sperys end'. It has been remarked that the oldest surviving homilies are almost invariably on the Gospels. In the fourteenth century there were homilies in metrical form for both the learned and the unlearned; [4] the latter would have found the metrical type fairly easy to memorize, at least in part, and could have pondered on what they

[1] James, *Suffolk and Norfolk*, 137. [2] Rushforth, *Medieval Christian Imagery*, 1936, 381.
[3] i.e. boy. [4] *The Lay Folks Mass Book*, ed. Simmons, 1879, xxxii, 212.

had learnt before the paintings on the walls of a church. There they might see, too, the Entry into Jerusalem, and be reminded of the Palm Sunday procession, which is accompanied by the hymn *Gloria Laus et Honor* to 'Christ that darly us bought, to whom cried osanna chyldren clene of thought'.[1] In scenes from the drama of the Passion are included executioners clad in 'raye', i.e. striped cloth, 'degised as turmentours that comen from clerks plei'.[2] Their heads are often rendered as hideous caricatures, as they had been earlier, and suggest the use of masks in the miracle plays.[3] Herod, seated cross-legged, has the bearing of a stage 'tyrant'. His posture is chosen to indicate direct contrast with contemporary ideas of sober behaviour, which was not, among other things, to 'sit tottering'[4] with a foot, nor 'throw the one over the other'. He is no longer armed, as earlier, with an ordinary sword, but with Wrath's falchion,[5] as described by Deguilville. The spear held by the centurion Longinus now has an inner meaning, for it is one of the 'two spears' in the eyes of Envy, which pierced Christ to the heart as did the weapon of Longinus. The wound in Christ's side is the earliest to be represented with streams of blood flowing from it, though late in the century and in the next, blood flows copiously from all the Five Wounds. In an early treatise on the Virtues and Vices, of *c.* 1200, occurs this phrase 'when the devil, or any evil man, will harm thee, creep into thy hole, into Christ's open side'. In the later *Ayenbite of Inwyt*, Our Lord is spoken of as the 'dove-cot wherein resteth the meek heart, who goes into the hole of the rock [Christ] as the dove into the dovecot'.[6] Holes, henceforward, have a significance in both paintings and illuminations, that is by no means obvious. The rabbit, among other creatures, is depicted beside a burrow not merely as one of Chaucer's 'litel conyes' that 'to hir pley gunne hye . . . sqerels, and bestes smale of gentil kinde', but as a soul in danger. Even foxes and hedgehogs, fleeing to their holes, do so in the character of sinners taking refuge.[7] Among the more notable Passion series are those existing, or formerly existing, at Cowley in Oxfordshire, Crostwight in Norfolk, Peakirk in Northamptonshire, and St. Brelade's, Jersey, in the Fishermen's Chapel. West Somerton in Norfolk has the remains of a fine series, but it is now much defaced. The majority are found in the nave, but in the chancel of North Cove, in Suffolk, a Passion sequence is to be found painted against a vine-scroll background, and associated with a Doom; unfortunately it is repainted. There is a series at Lakenheath in Suffolk on a massive pier facing the south door. It is confused with remains of an earlier painted hanging and a 'Tree' composed of scroll-work, and has in consequence been partially misinterpreted. The 'Tree' has a dove in its branches, and may have been intended for the 'peridexion tree' in whose branches doves, representative of the souls of men, are safe.[8] There are remains of a Passion series in the Beauchamp chantry at Flamstead in Hertfordshire. Near a tomb at Northmoor, in Oxfordshire, there is a Majesty that has

---

[1] *Piers Plowman*, ed. Skeat, pt. IV, 1885, 396; *Lyrics of the Fourteenth Century*, ed. Brown, 1924, no. 14.
[2] Lydgate, *Pilgrimage of the Life of Man*, 678.   [3] Tristram, *Eng. Med. Wall Painting*, 1950, 340–3.
[4] *Vices and Virtues*, ed. Holthausen, 1888, 132.
[5] Lydgate, *Pilgrimage of the Life of Man*, 417–18, 424.
[6] ed. Morris, 1866, 142; *Vices and Virtues*, ed. Holthausen, 1888, 100.
[7] Lydgate, *Pilgrimage of the Life of Man*, 449.
[8] Bestiary, Cambridge Univ. Lib., MS. I, lv, 26, f. 45v.; Mâle, *Religious Art in France of the Thirteenth Century*, 1913, 244.

been misinterpreted as a Resurrection, but is readily identifiable by reference to contemporary roof bosses. An early subject at Amberley in Sussex has been tentatively identified as an Adoration of the Cross, but is in fact a series of paintings of Saints.[1]

A sequence in the nave at Preston in the same county is well recorded, apart from some obvious errors, and this is fortunate, since it was almost entirely destroyed by fire in the year 1906. Extensive repainting had been carried out at some time before the disaster occurred, but it is evident that few mistakes were made, and those chiefly on a St. Michael Weighing Souls. This was near the chancel arch, and the figure of the Blessed Virgin, shown in intercession as is usual, was repainted as an Angel with wings upraised. Other subjects about the arch were an Incredulity of St. Thomas, a single figure of the same Saint, bearing the 'glaive' of his martyrdom, a *Noli Me Tangere*, a St. Catherine, a St. Margaret, and a Martyrdom of St. Thomas of Canterbury. Adjacent, at the eastern end of the north wall, there was a most remarkable set of paintings. The highest of three tiers was entirely filled by a Last Supper, the lowest by demi-figures of the Magi holding their gifts, painted against a background of scroll ornament, and the central section by a subject that is paralleled, but only in part, in only one other instance. This is found at Cold Overton in Leicestershire and dates from the previous century. At the centre of the scene was an altar, with a very large chalice upon it, and within the vessel was the Holy Child, wrapped in swaddling clothes. Immediately above appeared a star, and on either side were the Ox and the Ass, with the manger behind them. The midwives, Salome and Zelemie, were not depicted at Preston as they were at Cold Overton; instead, on one side of the altar were two figures, whose costume resembled that associated with the Shepherds, on the other a third, clad likewise, and a female Saint. One of the two Shepherds, if that is what they were, had a hood and cloak, and a T-headed staff, as is sometimes found, and the other a tunic and soft cap. In paintings of St. Christopher, the T-headed staff is associated with the idea of pilgrimage.[2] The second shepherd extended his arms over the *mensa* toward the chalice, and his folded hands just touched it. A high stool standing nearby bore an object not identifiable with certainty, on account of repainting, but possibly a basket or other vessel containing gifts. The gifts of the Shepherds, just as those of the Magi, took a prominent place in later miracle plays. At the opposite side of the altar the female Saint also extended her arms over the *mensa*, and with her right hand touched the nimbus of the Holy Child. Behind her stood a hooded figure holding a pendent scroll, probably the third of the Shepherds. Behind these two figures was a slanting bar, which, since it was partly defaced, had not been understood by the 'restorer' and had therefore been left untouched at the repainting. It was perhaps part of the cross associated with St. Helena, and if so the Saint is thereby identified.

This partial interpretation of such an obscure subject is in the main confirmed through reference to *The Three Kings of Cologne*,[3] by a Carmelite friar, John of Hildesheim, who wrote between 1364 and 1375, among his sources being an outline of a legend of the Magi known *c.* 1200. In brief, this legend, as expanded in *The Three Kings*

[1] See Catalogue, under Amberley.   [2] See chap. V, under St. Christopher.
[3] See *The Three Kings of Cologne*, 1886, ed. Horstmann; for the Star with the face of a child (an Angel) see *Golden Legend*, I, 45.

of Cologne is as follows: on the night of the Nativity a star arose, and above it was a figure of a child and the Sign of the Cross. The star led the Magi to Bethlehem, and on their journey they found the Shepherds, who told them of the appearance of the Angel who announced the birth of Christ. The Magi, after seeing the young Child, and presenting their gifts, returned home and there proclaimed all that they had seen and done, also setting up in their temples a star, with the figure of a child, and a cross. After the Ascension, St. Thomas preached the Gospel in India, and while doing so saw in the temples these emblems; also, on meeting the Magi he baptized them, and subsequently ordained them as priests. Centuries later, St. Helena found in Palestine, as well as the True Cross, many other treasures, and further obtained from Prester John the bodies of the Magi or Kings, Jaspar, Melchior and Balthasar. Medieval preachers [1] often said that, like the Magi, the faithful should offer to Christ the gold of good belief, the incense of prayer, and myrrh represented by mortification of the flesh. The tradition that St. Thomas the Apostle preached in India, and was martyred there, is a very ancient one. It seems virtually beyond doubt that the wall-paintings formerly at Preston in Sussex were inspired by these medieval legends of the Magi.

The life of the Blessed Virgin, when illustrated fully in wall-painting, is arranged in four parts:—her own childhood and death, both of them derived from legendary and Apochryphal sources; and the Holy Infancy and Passion, rendered without any special emphasis to differentiate portrayals of the scenes from those normally found in a series of the life of Christ. If there is any such emphasis, it is not in the Nativity and Passion scenes themselves, but in the presence of a Jesse Tree, as at Chalgrove, or the repetition of subjects like the Annunciation and St. Anne teaching the Virgin, as at Croughton. The scheme at Chalgrove (Plates 30–40) first discovered *c.* 1860, seems to have been in a fairly good state when described and illustrated by J. C. Wall, but by 1927 had deteriorated considerably, though many features might be deciphered on close inspection. Apart from that at Croughton, already discussed, it is the most complete of its kind to have survived, and in fact possesses features that are absent elsewhere. As with all paintings of the 'simpler' type, the work is carried out in earth colours, and so no special descriptions of the colour schemes are necessary in each case. The warm, varied reds and yellows, on a ground of cream, often combined, at our date, with touches of black and, occasionally, green, have a beauty of their own. The pigments used were much the same as those mentioned by Pliny, who regretted the abandonment of standards of simplicity set by Apelles and other famous painters of the ancient world, 'a single one of whose pictures the wealth of a city could hardly suffice to buy'.[2] Late in the fourteenth century, even in the countryside churches, for reasons indicated earlier, there was a great change in the pigments used, a change that would not seem to have been wholly desirable in its results.

At Chalgrove, where the scheme may be dated *c.* 1350, the subjects, arranged in three tiers, are not divided by the usual bands of ornament. Foliated scroll-work fills spaces above the windows, and sexfoil flowers in red are scattered over the mouldings of window-arches. This 'scattering' of the flowers, together with the general character of the scheme, recall paintings of the legend of St. Catherine in the chancel at Eynsham

---

[1] *Piers Plowman*, ed. Skeat, 1885, pt. IV, 429, 430–1.   [2] Herringham, *Cennino Cennini*, 1899, 253.

in the same county, and similarities, in particular in the handling of drapery, may be found further afield, at Nassington in Northamptonshire. The Jesse Tree that opens the series at Chalgrove is placed next to an Annunciation filling adjacent window-splays. Like all the figures seen here on the window-splays, those of the Archangel and the Blessed Virgin stand with a graceful sway and are exceptionally tall, with a view to filling the allotted space. There are no scenes from the childhood of the Blessed Virgin, as there are at Croughton, but those from the account of her death are rendered in exceptional detail. At the western end of the wall there is a Last Judgment, and this seems unexpected, until it is recalled that one of the Five Joys of the Virgin was sometimes represented as her presence at the 'dreadful day of Doom', and her intercession then for mankind. The Doom at Chalgrove fills three tiers on the wall, and in the second and third of these the dead are seen rising from their graves; among them are bishops and monks, and their grave-clothes are in some cases patterned with crosses. The sequence of the Death of the Virgin follows almost exactly the account given in the *Golden Legend*, which may be quoted here in brief: [1]

'An Angel came tofore her, with great light, saying: All Hail, blessed Mary, lo! here a bough of palm of paradise, Lady, which I have brought to thee, which thou shalt command to be borne tofore thy bier . . . Lady, wherefore desirest thou to know my name? which is great and marvellous. All the Apostles shall assemble this day to thee and shall make the noble exequies at thy passing . . . And wherefore doubtest thou to see the wicked spirit, sith thou hast broken utterly his head, and hast despoiled him from the empire of his power? Nevertheless thy will be done, that thou see not the fiend. And this said, the Angel mounted into heaven with great light, and the palm shone by right great clearness, and was like to a green rod whose leaves shone like to the morrow star . . . And when the blessed Virgin Mary saw all the Apostles assembled, she blessed our Lord, and sat in the midst of them where the lamps, tapers and lights burned . . . And about the third hour of the night Jesu Christ came with sweet melody and song, with the Orders of Angels . . . And then all the people was moved with that sweet melody . . . and the prince of priests was all abashed and full of anger and laid hands on the bier willing to turn it, and both his hands waxed dry and cleaved to the bier, so that he hung by the hands on the bier, and was sore tormented and wept and brayed.'

The sequence at Chalgrove is placed between two windows in the south wall, and the first decipherable subject is that of the Blessed Virgin praying to be preserved from the sight of the Evil One. Drapery hangs behind her, and may represent the 'vestments' brought for her by the Angel, from whom she receives the palm in the next scene. In the tier above, the Assembling of the Apostles is combined with a Gathering of the Neighbours (Plate 35), for the former kneel on one side and the latter on the other. Of the group of six women, one has her hair braided and two others wear barbettes and crespines. The burial scene is damaged, but that of the Miracle of the Jews is in a better state (Plate 36). Beyond it, the penitent 'Prince of priests' is sprinkled with an aspergillum by St. Peter, who in another scene advances to cure his temporarily blinded followers through the touch of the heavenly palm. The series is concluded on the east

[1] *Golden Legend*, IV, 234-41.

wall with a representation of St. Thomas receiving the Blessed Virgin's girdle from heaven, her Assumption, with an Angel on either side, and her Coronation (Plate 37). The Angel's message with the palm of Paradise is also depicted at Broughton in Oxfordshire, but it has been misread as an Annunciation; and we also find there the Gathering of the Apostles, the Burial of the Virgin, and her Assumption and Coronation, as well as an inscription having reference to the Five Joys, quoted earlier.[1] No paintings of the Joys, however, are known to have survived from our period, although there are some of later date, e.g. at Seething in Norfolk. It is evident that the scheme at Chalgrove, which is completed by series of the Nativity and the Passion, was of considerable merit, as may be seen from such sections as are still in fair condition. The drawing and handling are vigorous, and the subjects are composed with skill. Points of resemblance may be found in illuminations in a Missal of the Sarum use, now in the Pierpont Morgan collection, where figures of St. John Baptist and St. John the Evangelist are much like those in the wall-paintings. The work in the Missal was executed before 1332 for John Fitz-Roger of Clavering, and has been considered to be of the East Anglian school. At Chalfont St. Giles in Buckinghamshire two miracles of Our Lady are represented, namely, her rescue of the Jewish boy from the Baker's Oven, and the miracle of the Youth Betrothed to the Virgin. The handling in these instances is slighter than that seen at Chalgrove, where the treatment is less markedly linear, and where there is a considerable use of white, with the view of making the forms 'tell' against the general background of deep cream. There is no underpainting there, however, as there is at Eynsham. An early and most interesting scheme, of c. 1310–25, once existed in the south aisle (often the site of the Lady Chapel) at Headington near Oxford; it opened with the subject of St. Anne Teaching the Blessed Virgin, and with what was almost undoubtedly an Annunciation. Tracings from the series are preserved in the Bodleian Library.

It has been noted previously that at Longthorpe Tower are found the earliest representations in our wall-painting of the Twelve Apostles holding scrolls, with sentences upon them from the Creed. Each Apostle was believed to have composed [2] a sentence of the Creed after Pentecost, and although the sentences were not always ascribed to the same Saint, the first was always given to St. Peter and the eleventh, CARNIS RESURRECTIONEM, almost invariably to St. Jude. Also the Signs of the Four Evangelists were evidently depicted at Longthorpe, in this case on the vaulting, though only three of them remain and are much defaced; they are also seen on vaulting over a tomb in St. David's Cathedral. At Whaddon in Buckinghamshire they are placed on either side of the east window in the chancel; and since they were also symbols of Christ, their position there is easily understood.[3] As has been noted previously, a position above an east window was one chosen for representations of the Trinity.

At many places St. John the Evangelist is painted as a single figure, although there are no identified representations of the other three Evangelists from our period, apart from those in the series of Apostles at Longthorpe (Plate 41b). At Chalgrove he is seen on a window-splay, bearing the Palm, and at Selling in Kent there is a very good

[1] See chap. I, p. 23.   [2] e.g. *Ayenbite of Inwyt*, 1866, ed. Morris, 5.
[3] Tristram, *Eng. Med. Wall Painting*, 1950, 50–1.

figure of him, with the Eagle at his feet (Plates 51*b*, 53*a*). At Idsworth in Hampshire on either side of the east window, are St. Peter [1] and St. Paul, the former with a conical tiara, and holding the Keys of Heaven and Hell (Plate 46). At Selling, only the head of St. Paul remains but it is strongly characterized, with high, bald forehead, and hair only from the level of the ears, as a 'portrait' in the traditional manner (Plate 53*b*); however that at Idsworth is not as vividly drawn or as well-preserved. A special significance is traceable in the representations of St. Peter and St. Paul at Idsworth, if they are considered in connexion with the rest of the scheme there, which is a most remarkable one from many points of view, and calls for close study. In the higher of two tiers of paintings on the north wall a 'history' of St. John Baptist opens with the arrest of the Saint, and continues in the lower tier with his imprisonment (Plates 42, 45). In the former scene his chasuble-shaped short cloak is clearly seen, and in the second, although little of the figure is visible in the half-opened door of the building, the shaggy fur of the garment may be made out, as the Saint is thrust into prison by a gaoler armed with a club, and wearing fantastic winged headgear. It is evident, from the details of this garment of skin, as shown here and in other representations of it, how closely painters followed such accounts as that given in the *Golden Legend*, where it is said that St. John Baptist [2] 'ware the skin of a camel, in which he had made a hole to put his head'. The Feast of Herod follows, with Herodias to the left of a long table, Herod on the right, and animated groups of courtiers and attendant squires between them. One of the latter has a feather in his hair, and holds a charger with the head of the Saint upon it. In front of this Squire, and of the table, Salome executes a sword dance, with body bent in a curve and head almost touching the ground. In the sermons it was said that 'Herod's doughter was a tumbestere and tumblede byfore him and other grete lordes of that contre'. [3] Above and to the left of the banqueting scene, in the upper tier of paintings, a hunt is shown, in which horsemen approach from the left, a huntsman winds his horn, with numerous lively dogs about his feet, and on the right a figure in a cloak ornamented with large roundels grasps the right hand, not paw, of a most strange creature. It has a human head surrounded by a nimbus, long hair and beard, and shaggy coat, while its remaining limbs are those of an animal and terminate normally in paws. It emerges through the writhing boughs of an oak tree, over which it steps, and its hind legs are between the legs of the Baptist (Plates 42, 43).

Different explanations of this extraordinary painting have been suggested. It has been identified as St. Hubert's conversion of the lycanthrope, but this identification [4] has been rejected on the ground that no such legend is connected with the Saint. A much more likely suggestion has also been made, that the painting illustrates the Legend of the Hairy Anchorite, who seduced the daughter of a king [5] and then murdered her. He performed the penance of eating grass, and walking on all fours, became shaggy like a beast, and was eventually discovered by hunters, to whom he confessed his crime.

---

[1] There are many figures of both these Saints: see Iconographic list, Appendix F.

[2] *Golden Legend*, III, 259. [3] Owst, *Literature and Pulpit*, 1933, 118.

[4] *Victoria County Hist., Hants*, III, 109.

[5] *Journ. Warburg and Courtauld Institute*, 1937–8, I, 183; Wormald, *Antiquaries Journal*, 1945, XXV, 43 *et seq.*

There is an engraving by Durer, in which the central figure in the story is shown crawling on hands and knees, and has a nimbus. In the wall-painting, however, there is no woman with a child, as there is in the engraving, and, moreover, the figure winding a horn cannot be that of the king in the legend, since there is no crown. The headgear is somewhat defaced, but the general silhouette can be made out and is that of a slouch hat, similar to one to be seen, for instance, in a miniature in the Luttrell Psalter.[1] In order to arrive at an explanation, it is necessary to consider with care all the features in the wall-paintings, including those on the east wall, when it may be suggested that the motif running throughout is that of diabolical possession and its cure at the intercession of St. Hübert. His name is found in *graffiti* of the fifteenth and sixteenth centuries on the lower part of the wall-space; and the small chapel is like one of those that were often erected in or near the forest, so that huntsmen might make their devotions before the day's hunting began.[2] St. Hubert, patron Saint of the chase, was also patron of dogs, and they are often introduced into pictures of him. Further, bread blessed at his shrine was considered to be efficacious against hydrophobia, and the same affliction was also cured by means of a horse-shoe, first blessed in a chapel dedicated to him, and then applied red-hot to the wound.[3] It was related of him that he had cured a woman 'possessed of an evil spirit', by the sign of the cross.[4] No doubt many afflictions thought in the Middle Ages to be the result of possession were due to natural causes, among them epilepsy and hydrophobia. It has been remarked that Luther held the prevalent belief in possession, even in regard to the dumb and the idiot, and especially the raving maniac.[5] This belief in possession may be studied in the late fifteenth-century *Malleus Maleficarum*, together with the belief in the witch-queen Herodias, whose followers claimed the power of changing human beings 'into some other semblance or shape'. Such changes were accepted as occurring, but it was claimed by the less credulous that, though due to Satanic art, they were not actual but only apparent. The nimbus around the head of the weird creature depicted at Idsworth is undoubtedly that of evil, as seen in some miniatures of the Beast of the Apocalypse,[6] and signifies possession. The human head and hand, the thumb of the latter being clearly decipherable, indicate that by the help of the man grasping the solitary hand, the 'animal' is returning to its human shape and condition. The figure of the man in question may or may not be intended for that of St. Hubert; and on the whole it seems more likely that the scene records some 'cure' believed to have been effected in his name. It is a minor point of interest that the beast steps over and through the low-growing boughs of an oak; for in the *Discovery of Witchcraft*, of 1665, it is said 'that never hunters or their dogs may be bewitched, they cleave an oaken branch, and both they and their dogs pass over

---

[1] Millar, *English Illuminated Manuscripts*, II, pl. 59 (*b*). [2] Jameson, *Sacred and Legendary Art*, II, 734.
[3] Mâle, *Religious Art in France of the Thirteenth Century*, 1913, 270; horseshoes were also used against witchcraft, Brand, *Popular Antiquities*, 1813, 12. [4] Butler, *Lives of the Saints*, XI, 64–8.
[5] Summers, *The History of Witchcraft and Demonology*, London, 1926, 231; it may be remarked that those responsible for the decoration of the chapel at Idsworth would have had reason for interest in a cure thought to have been miraculous, but the legend of the Hairy Anchorite, or anything similar, would have had little importance for them. Wall-paintings fulfilled some vital need, and the fact that they now sometimes puzzle antiquaries is incidental. On the whole, an exceptional explanation is not likely to be the right one. [6] See, for example Saunders, *English Illumination*, II, pls. 90, 98.

it'.[1] There is no sign of a tail on the animal, and this may be intentional, for one distinctive mark, for example, of a werwolf was that it had no tail.[2]

We may now turn to the sequence from the life of St. John Baptist. The way in which it opens seems significant, for the first scene, of the Arrest, is inextricably intermingled with that representing 'possession', as already observed. Mention has previously been made also of strange ideas concerning Herodias, ideas that date from the twelfth century, if not earlier. Further, the vigil of the Feast of St. John Baptist, on 23rd June, when the St. John's Fires were lit, had some indirect association with witchcraft, since it was also one of the chief Sabbats. Finally, the other paintings in the church, apart from figures of two Angels, are of St. Peter and St. Paul, in connexion with whom the story of Simon Magus should be remembered. The Feast of Herod, with Salome's Sword Dance, is made very prominent. The dance is also found in other wall-paintings, at Chalfont St. Giles in Buckinghamshire, and Kingston Lisle in Berkshire, where St. Peter and St. Paul are again on the splays of the east window. It was formerly to be seen at Elsing in Norfolk, and is not infrequent in illuminations.[3]

These paintings at Idsworth are most exceptional no less for their design, drawing and handling than for their subject-matter. The figures in Herod's Feast, and the group of two huntsmen with hounds are lively, and vigorously drawn. The latter is strongly reminiscent of the best contemporary tile design. A good single figure of St. John Baptist, very different in style, is to be found at Heacham in Norfolk (Plate 55b); and at Bishop's Cleeve, in Gloucestershire, he was once to be seen in attendance on the Crucifixion, which is exceptional.

We may now consider representations of the 'companion' Saints, Saint Catherine (Plates 47, 48) and St. Margaret (Plates 49, 50b). There are at Sporle in Norfolk as many as twenty-four scenes, of c. 1390, from the legend of St. Catherine, but although in 1872 they were clearly visible, and retained details such as jewels, chaplets of flowers, forked beards and 'piked shoon', they are now much defaced. As well as the usual subjects, which are the Saint before the Emperor; the dispute with the philosophers, who were later converted and burnt, and the Saint's imprisonment, torture on the Wheel, and execution, there are others that are rarely found. These are connected with the subsidiary 'history' of Porphyry, the 'prince of knights', who was converted with two hundred followers, later slaughtered with him. Before his death, he had buried the body of the Empress, who had likewise suffered death as the result of conversion. There is a scene, difficult to understand, which is placed just before that in which St. Catherine is lead away to be beheaded; in the centre of it, as drawn by Winter, is a small nude soul surrounded by devils, which may be the tormented soul of the tyrant Maxentius, or Maximinus.[4] In scenes from the Passion, or from the martyrdom of Saints, executioners are not infrequently shown with tongue protruding in mockery.

---

[1] Brand, *Popular Antiquities*, 1813; for a comparable woodland scene, with oak-leaves, hounds, etc., see Millar, *English Illuminated Manuscripts*, I, pl. 100.

[2] *William of Palerne*, 1867, ed. Skeat, Preface, xx, xxix; see also for possession and nimbus of evil, *Malleus Maleficarum*, ed. Summers, 1928, 3n., 31, 47, 62, 63, 65, 129; Didron, I, 158-63, fig. 47.

[3] Jusserand, *English Wayfaring Life*, 1891, 214-16. For St. Peter and St. Paul, and Simon Magus, see *Golden Legend*, IV, 14-20.   [4] *Golden Legend*, VI, 25.

There are other meanings, however, for heads with protruding tongues, as found, for instance, on bosses. They are sometimes those of backbiters, since the backbiter's tongue was said to be 'wavering in ys hede', with a venomous worm, the devil,[1] under it. Alternatively, protruding tongues are those of the Damned, who 'gnaw their tongues for pain'.[2] Robert of Brunne mentions a backbiting monk who had to gnaw his burning tongue in Hell.[3]

There are six or seven 'histories' of St. Margaret, but unfortunately the most interesting, that at Limpenhoe in Norfolk, is lost, and the longest, at Tarrant Crawford in Dorset, is much defaced. The former, and also a sequence at Charlwood in Surrey, have features derived from *Seinte Marherete*, or some analogous work. Thus, after the Saint's emergence from the dragon, a dove appears,[4] welcoming her to Paradise; it also delivers her from a vessel of boiling water. It again descends, when before her execution she prays for a blessing on all who cherish her memory, and for women in childbirth, whose patroness she later became. The Dove is also mentioned in the *Golden Legend*, where, after the torment of water, it set a golden crown upon St. Margaret's head.[5] In the *Pilgrimage of the Life of Man* a white dove rescues the Pilgrim from Sloth, and appears later to encourage him. The story of Theochimus or Theotimus, who while the Saint was in prison, fed her with bread and water, and later buried her body at Antioch, is found only in some versions of her life; it is not seen at Tarrant Crawford, but the long series there may once have been continued on the west wall. Her name first appears in English litanies of the seventh century, and there are three renderings of her life in the vernacular, which date back to the eleventh century.[6] Her day was included among the great feasts after 1222. In a series at Wendens Ambo in Essex there is an attractive rendering of the Instruction of St. Margaret (Plate 50*b*), where she is shown, with other small girls, being taught by her nurse, as if in a 'dame's school', of the early fourteenth century. It is a work in which naturalism is exceptionally strong, so that there is some reason to regard it, with certain scenes already noted at Croughton in Northamptonshire, as an astonishingly early 'genre' painting. In another scene at the same place, she holds a distaff, and awaits the approach of the Prefect's servant, who bears a large ring (Plate 49). She appears, with St. Catherine, on the Thornham Parva Retable where her figure is beautifully rendered, and also, again with St. Catherine, at Soberton in Hampshire, where she spears the dragon and St. Catherine tramples on the Emperor Maximinus. At Tarrant Crawford, in the last surviving scene, she scourges devils, as she does in the series in Queen Mary's Psalter.[7] The wall-painting sequence follows that given in *Seinte Marherete*, except for the eighth to the eleventh scenes, which when decipherable are apparently from the *Golden Legend*. The alternation of red and white grounds makes for legibility as is frequently the case. At Limpenhoe was a curious feature, for one of the executioners had hair standing in

[1] *Middle English Sermons*, ed. Ross, 1940, S.35, 195.

[2] *Revelations*, VIII, 10–11; *Douce Apocalypse*, 25, 66; Cave, *Roof Bosses in Medieval Churches*, Cambridge, 1948, 25, pls. 9, 35.

[3] *Handlyng Synne*, 1303, 1901, 119, 123–4.   [4] *Seinte Marherete*, ed. Mack, 1934, 28, 44, 48.

[5] IV, 70; Deguileville, *Pilgrimage of the Life of Man*, 378, 526.

[6] *Seinte Marherete*, ed. Mack, x.   [7] pls. 307–314.

upright tufts upon his head. Men possessed by demons, or the demons themselves, are sometimes shown in English and French art of the twelfth century,[1] with their 'hair on end' in this strange fashion, but it is surprising that the mode of representation should be found in the Limpenhoe paintings, which are of a date towards the end of the fourteenth century.

St. Martin of Tours and St. Nicholas of Myra are often found together, e.g. a former painting at Halesowen in Worcestershire, for they were regarded as the greatest miracle workers, the one of the West and the other of the East. The former almost always appears in the Raising to Life of the Three Boys, who had been killed and pickled in a tub by an avaricious innkeeper in time of famine, an episode that has been traced to its sole source in the popular imagination. At Halesowen, however, St. Nicholas was shown dealing with 'the evil and foul Diana',[2] while St. Martin was saving a man from death by hanging, whereas, as an example of charity, he is normally depicted with the beggar to whom he gave part of his cloak. In the chancel of St. Martin's church, at Birmingham, there was formerly a 'history' of the Saint which included the episode of the beggar, what was perhaps the Translation of the Relics, and either the story of St. Martin and the Robbers, or that of the Tree Hewn Down.[3]

The chapel at Halesowen in which appeared the paintings mentioned above, possessed a very full scheme. It was dedicated to St. Kenelm, who became King as a child of seven years of age:

'and his sister Dornemilde loved him much . . . But Quendred, that other sister turned her to wickedness, because she would be Queen, and reign after him . . . and she laboured to Askeberd, who was chief ruler about the King . . . if he would slay this young King her brother . . . This young holy King was asleep and dreamed a marvellous dream. For him seemed that he saw a tree stand by his bedside, and that the height thereof touched heaven, and it shined as bright as gold, and had fair branches full of blossoms and fruit . . . And Askeberd stood beneath and hewed down this tree . . . and this young King was heavy and sorrowful, and him thought there came a fair bird which flew up to Heaven with great joy.'

The story goes on to relate that Askeberd killed Kenelm, and a poor widow who pastured her cow on the site of the grave found that it ate nothing, but nevertheless 'was ever in so good point'. In due course, when the body was raised by Angels from the grave, and borne to Winchcombe Abbey, the bells rang of their own accord, and, when Quendred scoffed, her eyes fell from her head upon the Psalter she was reading. The greater part of the story was illustrated in the paintings, which, to judge from the tracings which have been preserved, must have been an unusually good series, as well as the only known sequence from the story of St. Kenelm. They were lost early in the last century, but dated from c. 1380, and so had been executed not long after the accession of the young Richard II, whose coronation took place, as Walsingham expressly states, on the eve of the feast of St. Kenelm.[4]

---

[1] Mâle, *L'Art religieux du XIIe siècle en France*, Paris, 1922, 199, figs. 145, 161, 213.
[2] *Golden Legend*, II, 113–14; VI, 145. [3] ibid., 147.
[4] Tristram, *The Month*, NS. II, July 1949, *The Wilton Diptych*, 22.

St. James the Great is not often depicted at our period, and there is no representation of him like that of the previous century above an altar at Wisborough Green in Sussex,[1] where he is seen welcoming pilgrims to his shrine at Compostella. There is, however, an interesting record of such a pilgrimage, undertaken about the year 1365, and of a vow made when in danger at sea, to erect an altar in his honour upon the pilgrims' safe return to Lincolnshire.[2] It is hardly necessary to remark that no such altar would have been complete without some representation of the Saint.

The fine panel painting of St. Edward the Confessor and the Pilgrim at Forthampton Court has already been mentioned more than once; and the same subject, partially lost, has been noted at Westminster. An exceptionally good wall-painting of it was discovered at Faversham in Kent in 1851; although it was then in a good state of preservation, it has since been allowed to perish almost entirely. The two figures were seven feet in height, and St. John, in the guise of a pilgrim as he is described in the legend,[3] held the bourdon with a palm attached to it by thongs. Nearby was a painted tabernacle of very elaborate design within which knelt the donor, Robert Dod of Faversham. An inscription indicated that St. Edmund the King and the Martyrdom of St. Thomas of Canterbury, were also represented in the same chapel, which is dedicated to the latter Saint. The paintings were earlier than the panel at Forthampton Court, and may be dated c. 1340. Nearly a century later, in 1429, a bequest was made 'to the light of St. Edmund in St. Thomas' Chapel', namely, 'one Cowe'. The finest representation of St. Edmund from our period is that on the Thornham Parva Retable, but two others may be noted, at Sanderstead in Surrey (Plate 55) and Lakenheath in Suffolk, as well as four wall-paintings of his martyrdom, and the 'history' at Thornham Parva, already discussed. St. Francis, preaching to the birds, is found only at Little Kimble in Buckinghamshire, and St. Thomas of Cantelupe at Barton in Cambridgeshire. St. Helena, who was believed to have been a daughter of King Coel, which made her popular in this country, is represented at four places, among them Chalgrove, but two of the paintings have been lost. One was at Amney Crucis, in Gloucestershire, where there was formerly the only known instance of a wall-painter's signature—'Thomas ye paynter of Malmesbury'. It was given in black letters, on a St. Christopher, and seems to have been of later date than our period.[4] It should be remembered, in connexion with the numerous figures and 'histories' of Saints from the fourteenth century, that metrical lives of the Saints were read or recited on their feast days, or on Sundays.[5]

At Starston in Norfolk, in 1872, a unique painting of a funeral scene was found and almost immediately destroyed (Plate 56a). It was of a date early in our period, and was rendered with so much feeling that it remains poignant in effect even though known only at second hand through a drawing fortunately made at the time of discovery. Then, 'the colours were exceedingly bright and perfect', and 'the painting of parts very beautiful'; especially a small crucifixion, which 'was a perfect miniature and would bear looking into with a magnifying glass'.

Many of the wall-paintings at Longthorpe Tower, and in particular that of the

[1] Tristram, *Eng. Med. Wall Painting*, 1950, 311.   [2] Rickert, *Chaucer's World*, 1950, 269.
[3] See: *Golden Legend*, II, 175–6; VI, 26–8; Tristram, *Eng. Med. Wall Painting*, 106–8.
[4] Keyser, *Mural Decorations*, 1883.   [5] Owst, *Preaching in Medieval England*, 1926, 275.

Wheel of the Five Senses, have already been discussed or referred to, but it remains to consider some that have not, and in particular the subjects on the west wall. Of these the most interesting is that on the higher part of the wall-space, where a barefooted figure, clad in a hooded cloak and a tunic, stands with a staff resting idly between his arms. Behind him is a tree with birds in its branches, and opposite a seated figure, with another standing behind him. Both are shod, and clad in long tunics and hoods, and the former is making something from fenland withies. It is most unusual to find any figure, apart from those of Apostles and St. Francis, represented at this date with bare feet. The birds in the tree call St. Francis to mind, but since he is not facing them, this is clearly not a representation of the Preaching to the Birds. He has turned away from them, towards his disciples, and a reasonable interpretation of the scene is that he has stilled their singing, in order that his followers might say their Office, as related in the *Golden Legend* (Plate 41a).[1] His own arms, between which his staff rests, are raised as if he were about to pray, with the hands placed palm to palm. The standing figure opposite holds something too defaced for identification, and at first sight the other, busy with the withies and a small hammer, would seem in part to belie the reading of the subject that has just been suggested. However, there is an explanation to be found in the withies or osiers that are being used to make what is evidently a receptacle, and probably a basket. In the *Pilgrimage of the Life of Man*[2] the Ship of Religion is represented as bound with osiers, and these stand for the observances that may be neglected by young folk, when the 'osiers' break and the 'ship' founders. Further, basket-making was evidently at our period considered as being in itself meritorious, and characteristic of the Apostles.[3] Finally, it should be recalled that it was an occupation favoured by hermits, and that St. Francis and his early friars themselves lived as hermits, at least until 1220. The two 'companions' of St. Francis, in the wall-painting, are clad as one is in the painting of St. Francis Preaching to the Birds, at Wiston in Suffolk, where he is seated at the Saint's feet with a book, presumably saying his Office.[4] The rabbit at the foot of the tree near which St. Francis stands, is beside its hole, and this has a significance that has been noted previously.

On the lower part of the same wall are two figures of which only the setting-out lines remain. They appear to be in discussion, and are in medieval Doctor's habit, so that they doubtless represent philosophers. There are numerous references to philosophers in contemporary and slightly later literature, so numerous, in fact, that it is impossible to identify those depicted at Longthorpe; though Virgil is an obvious choice, since he was mentioned in a sermon attributed to St. Augustin that was read in churches at Christmas[5] and he sometimes appeared, as we have seen, in the Jesse Tree. Virgil was also considered in the Middle Ages as a great Magus, who had been responsible for certain magical statues at Rome. Aristotle is perhaps the most likely identification of the other figure.

---

[1] V, 227.   [2] 558–9; 627.

[3] *The Pardonere's Tale*: 'I wol nat do no labour with my hondes, Ne make baskettes, and lyve therby . . . I wol non of the Apostles counterfete.'

[4] Tristram, *Eng. Med. Wall Painting*, 352, pl. 190.

[5] Mâle, *L'Art religieux du XII* siècle en France*, 1922, 142, 169. *Piers Plowman*, ed. Skeat, IV, 285.

In both the east and west walls of the chamber are recesses with subjects in them that seem to be connected with the teaching of youth. In one a bearded figure holds a scroll, and points to it as though instructing a group of three youths who stand before him, and in the other a female figure also bears a scroll and points to a child in front of her. On the scroll in this last instance are some letters from an inscription which read ME . . . VS ASOVDR . . . DEL, so that possibly there was once here a phrase in Anglo-Norman French relating to absolution. Children, besides the Creed, the *Pater-noster* and *Ave Maria*, were taught the *Confiteor* and *Misereatur*.[1] On the south wall, above a band ornamented with a wyvern, birds and flowers, are two enthroned Kings, each flanked by a shield of arms; the less defaced of these shields being that of England. Below them is a rich heraldic diaper of diamond design, with several repetitions of the arms of the family then owning the Tower, that is, a fess between six fleurs-de-lis, for Thorpe.

[1] *The Lay Folks Mass Book*, ed. Simmons, 1879, 181; Myrc, *Instructions for Parish Priests*, 13, 14; *Middle English Sermons*, ed. Ross, S.9, 48.

Chapter Five

★——————————————————————————————★

THE ALLEGORIES AND MORALITIES

★——————————————————————————————★

WALL-PAINTINGS that are classifiable as 'Moralities' are obviously didactic in intention to a greater degree than the majority. They include representations of the Seven Corporal Works of Mercy, the Seven Deadly Sins, and the Three Living and the Three Dead. Even allowing in many cases for a very defaced condition it cannot be claimed that, aesthetically, any of them reach the highest level, although there are some of average quality. It has already been noted that they have suffered more than most through deliberate defacement, and reasons for this have been suggested.[1] Until quite recent years, the aversion they inspired was apparently strong enough even to deceive the eye, for they have been described as 'gaudy'. Since they are almost always painted in ordinary earth colours with some black, it is rarely, if ever, possible for them to be so. In historical interest they stand high. In the first place, they are the pictorial equivalents of medieval sermons and treatises, and served to some extent as illustrations of them, as has been remarked before. Secondly, they are at least the equals in quality of the ordinary writing of the day, writing that is unpolished, but often vital and vigorous. While the more 'elaborate' wall-paintings, like those of South Newington, may be ranked, roughly with Chaucer, or much contemporary lyric poetry, the 'Moralities' are on a somewhat lower plane. With them, we leave 'Al other love is lych the mone' or 'Quia Amore Langueo', for 'The Four Foes of Mankind' or 'An Old Man's Prayer'.[2] Nevertheless, when forming a general estimate of them, the claim may be recalled that has justly been made on behalf of medieval preaching— that while the dilettante [3] may spurn it, the true historian of letters will never do so; and neither should the serious student of our art spurn the 'Moralities'.

If a really good example had survived in fair condition of a wall-painting of the Seven Deadly Sins, it would no doubt have shown the characteristically English power in caricature. There are signs of this in the Wheel formerly at Ingatestone in Essex,

---

[1] See chap. I, 4.   [2] Brown, *Lyrics of the Fourteenth Century*, 1924, nos. 6, 27, 49, 132.
[3] Owst, *Literature and Pulpit*, 1933, 469.

95

which is only known through a copy; and still earlier instances are to be noted in some thirteenth-century 'histories' of Saints, with their torturers and executioners.[1] A full development of this power may be seen in some paintings of *c.* 1590 in the Hastings Chantry of St. George's Chapel at Windsor. In them there are heads, among the executioners stoning St. Stephen, that might almost have come from the brush of a Rowlandson or a Hogarth. Lydgate has a passage which shows that caricature in wall-paintings was keenly appreciated in his day:

> Vpon the wallys environ
> Many wonderful ymages,
> *Ful ougly of ther vysages,*
> Purtreyed high upon the wal . . .
> I saugh first Hate and Felonye . . .
> And in order Covetyse
> And hir suster Auvarice;
> And after I sawgh Envye . . .
> *And al the whiles I there stood,*
> *Me thought, yt dyde me gret good*
> *To be-holde the purtreytures*
> *And the wonderful figures*
> *With ther ougly countenances . . .*
> *Bothe in shappe and portrayture . . .*
> *They wer by craft made ful sotyle,*
> *As I behelde aryght grete while.*[2]

It is evident from this quotation that Lydgate, and no doubt many of his contemporaries also, appreciated force in a painting at least as much as other qualities. However, for a good idea of the medieval craftsman's ability to portray the sensual or the terrible, we must turn to bosses such as those in the aisles of the Angel Choir in Lincoln Cathedral. Some of these bosses, although a few have not previously been identified, clearly represent the Seven Deadly Sins. The 'Wrestlers', for instance, stand for Wrath, and 'a man and woman kissing' for Lechery. The latter [3] is striking and quite unmistakable, even though the sculptor through exigencies of space, was forced to carve little more than three heads, the third, with its tormented frown, being that of Satan the Tempter. There is also at Lincoln, in the south walk of the cloisters, one of the so-called 'toothache' bosses, in which a bloated and wide-mouthed head has a finger thrust between distorted lips, as though vomiting. This, and others like it, may be identified from the wall-

---

[1] Tristram, *Eng. Med. Wall Painting*, 1950, 340–2.

[2] Lydgate, *Reson and Sensuallyte*, I, 1901, 130 (pictures on the walls of the Garden of Pleasure).

[3] Owst, *The Times*, 19th December 1935; Cave, *The Roof Bosses of Lincoln Cathedral, Archaeologia*, 1936, vol. 85. Angel Choir. It has not been observed that these bosses, taken together, form a Jesse Tree, with some of the Deadly Sins. In the first bay is a King and a Prophet; in the second, Jesse at the base and David with a harp above, and also a Coronation of the Virgin, in place of the normal Virgin and Child; in the third bay, two Prophets; in the fifth bay are the Wrestlers, for Wrath; in the first bay of the North aisle, heads of two women, for ?Pride; in the third bay, a Naked Man fighting a Merman, ? for Worldly Gladness; in the fourth bay, Luxuria (as identified by G. R. Owst).

painting at Ingatestone mentioned above, where Gluttony is shown vomiting into a bowl.[1] The likeness in the painting to the heads on the bosses is most striking. One of the questions that might be put to a penitent by a priest in confession was this—'Hast thou eaten so greedily that thou hast vomited?'[2] It may be noted in passing that even the Lollards allowed that 'Virtues and Vices' as well as 'truths of the Gospel' were suitable 'matter to preach to the people'.[3]

It is not necessary to point out that general ideas relative to the Virtues and Vices may be traced to the Bible; but the pictorial symbolism that was associated with them was much elaborated in course of time, and it is not always easily understood. The pictorial conception of a conflict between armed knights, the forces of Evil being on one side and those of Good on the other, is drawn from the *Psychomachia* of Prudentius, and is embodied in one of our earlier wall-paintings, of *c.* 1200, at Claverley in Shropshire.[4] Late in the thirteenth century noble figures of Virtues, each an armed maiden shown trampling on an opposing Vice, filled the window-splays of Henry III's great Painted Chamber at Westminster.[5] In the fourteenth century, however, there is a marked alteration in the manner of representing Virtues and Vices. The paintings we still have, or of which we have adequate records, are of the latter half of the period, and they show no link either with the vigorous, chivalric rendering at Claverley, or the noble and idealistic version at Westminster. The idea of conflict lapses, and the artists, or their patrons, no longer turn to early allegories like the *Hortus deliciarum* of Herrade of Hohenburg (1175–95) but to contemporary sermons or moral treatises. Of the latter it was said by a contemporary that:

'Ther beth so manye bokes and tretees of vyces and vertues . . . that this schort lyfe schalle rathere have an ende of anye manne, thanne he may owthere studye hem or rede hem.'[6]

For example, Bishop Hamo when he died in 1346 left to Rochester Priory 'one little book of the Vices and Virtues'.[7]

There had been tracts of the kind in English from as early as *c.* 1200,[8] but they only became numerous a little later, and so far as the evidence goes, do not seem to have influenced painters to any great extent before the middle of the fourteenth century. There was apparently a lapse of time, and often enough a considerable one, between the earliest appearance of ideas in literature, whether homiletic or otherwise, and their frequent embodiment in pictorial form on the walls of churches. This seems natural, since new pictorial themes, or new versions of old themes, would have to become generally known before they became popular with patrons. However, the Works of Mercy are recorded at the great Abbey of Bury St. Edmunds *c.* 1300 at latest, and were

---

[1] Lydgate, *Pilgrimage of the Life of Man*, 1899, 349, 354; *Middle English Sermons*, ed. Ross, 1940, 56 (Gluttony in the form of Drunkenness). [2] Myrc, *Instructions for Parish Priests*, 1868, 33–46.
[3] Owst, *Preaching in Medieval England*, 1926, 133, n.1.
[4] Tristram, *Eng. Med. Wall Painting*, 1944, 48–49, pls. 72, 73. [5] ibid., 1950, 105–6, pls. 19, 20, 21.
[6] Owst, *Preaching in Medieval England*, 1926, 277.
[7] Coulton, *Life in the Middle Ages*, 1928, 112, 118.
[8] Owst, *Preaching in Medieval England*, 1926, 282, 286, 288, 290.

perhaps painted a good deal earlier than this. Further, subjects that accompanied them on the *tabula ante magnum candelabrum*, and that are described as 'wicked lawyers', 'wicked monks', and the punishment of the covetous, have an obvious association with the Seven Deadly Sins. The pronounced 'literary' strain in English art may have originated from, and must have been encouraged by, the very extensive use made of wall-paintings for purposes of homiletic illustration. It has been remarked that from the thirteenth century onward, writers of pulpit manuals were accustomed, in connexion with their themes, to make use of 'vivid little sketches of contemporary men and women and their ways'; [1] and, more and more as their capacity for naturalistic representation increased, the wall-painters followed the writers and preachers in this respect. The employment of amusing or fantastic marginal illustrations in manuscripts has been noted as an English [2] development of the end of the thirteenth century, whatever its origin. It has also been noted that in carving there are at Wells, for instance, capitals, corbels and bosses that surpass in inventiveness and vitality others of equal date at Chartres. [3] One characteristic of our art, a 'delight in the forms of burlesque, connected in some degree with the foulness of evil', is present in Chaucer and Shakespeare, and is often encountered in the fourteenth century. Veritably in all great art extremes meet; and it is partly true to say that the 'virtue of the monkey in the margin, and of the grotesque in general, is that it should remind us of the immeasurable distance between the human and the divine'. [4] However, this effect is incidental rather than otherwise, and, as we have seen, 'babwyns' often have definite meanings. Especially in marginal illustrations to manuscripts they have too readily been accepted as mere follies. It is true that they are difficult for us to understand, however plain they may have seemed to contemporaries. For instance, in the Ormesby Psalter there is a creature with a hand at the end of its tail. [5] It has been thought that the hand is in the position of benediction, and this has been taken as an instance of irreverence. But on close inspection the hand is seen to be reversed, that is, with its back towards the spectator, and thus it is not blessing, but cursing. The association on the page is with a small illumination of Christ before Pilate, below which, as well as the grotesque, is to be seen a female figure. This is intended for Pilate's wife, who was considered in medieval times almost to have prevented the Sacrifice of Cavalry and so the redemption of mankind by her attempt at intervention in the drama of the Passion.

It has been remarked that in *Piers Plowman* the 'personalities' of some of the Deadly Sins alternate. For instance, Sloth changes from priest to layman and back again, and Pride from male to female. [6] The suggestion has been put forward that Langland was clumsy in this respect, because he had not freed himself from the conventions of the homily-book. But it is just as likely, and perhaps more likely, that he was 'translating'

---

[1] Owst, *Literature and Pulpit*, 1933, 87; for the paintings at Bury St. Edmunds, see Tristram, *Eng. Med. Wall Painting*, 1950, catalogue.

[2] Michel, *Histoire de l'art*, tome ii, pp. 349, 351.   [3] Harvey, *The Gothic World*, 1950, 74.

[4] Sir Herbert Read, *Burlington Magazine*, LXIII, 1933, 244–53.

[5] See E. G. Millar, *English Illuminated Manuscripts*, 1928, p. 3, pl. II. For Pilate's wife see *Handlyng Synne*, 1303, 1901, 28, and Queen Mary's Psalter.   [6] Owst, *Literature and Pulpit*, 1933, 88.

into his own medium of words and phrases paintings with which he was familiar, and in which, as at Ingatestone, different aspects of the same Sin appeared side by side on the wall, with inevitable 'transformations'.

THE SEVEN CORPORAL WORKS OF MERCY; AND THE SEVEN DEADLY SINS

Theologians of the early centuries evolved the symbolism that was embodied eventually in Trees of Virtues and of Vices. The seven fruits of the latter, suggested by the seven heads of the Apocalyptic Dragon, were each an 'image' of one of the Seven Deadly Sins, and each therefore framed a Sin within its jaws. This Tree of Evil may be considered in some detail later.

The Tree of Virtues, to quote from the *Ayenbite of Inwyt*,[1] 'is Christ', and the 'boughs' are in one sense His virtues and in another 'all the elect'. The tree is also, in one of its aspects, the Tree of Life, and, further, there is an obvious association with the Tree of Jesse. The 'boughs', too, symbolize the Seven Beatitudes. In fact, every part of the Tree, even the leaves and fruit, incorporates a double or triple symbolism. The fruit, by contrast with that of the Tree of Evil, consists in the Seven Corporal Works of Mercy. Like the Sins, they are constantly mentioned in treatises and sermons, with repeated recommendations to 'give mete to the houngre; give drynke to the thursty; clothe the naked and nedye; vysytte the seke; comforte folke in prysone; reseyve straungers; berye the dede'.[2] The last was added, apparently after the twelfth century, to complete the mystic number, seven, and is drawn from the two first chapters of Tobias; but the others are taken from the concluding verses of the twenty-fifth chapter of St. Matthew. Collections of homilies contain numerous exhortations to charity; the parish priest's duty included instruction not only in the Paternoster, the Commandments, the Creed and the Sacraments, but also in the Corporal Works of Mercy and the Deadly Sins. There are fourteen representations of the Works of Mercy from our period. Among them are three types; the Tree, the Wheel, and a set of seven scenes, the last being sometimes placed around a large central figure, or else treated as a series. At Trotton, in Sussex, there is a combination of treatments. The 'branches' of the Tree of Evil, with their dragon-fruit, spring from the nude body of Satan, and opposite is the modestly-clad figure of the Good Man, surrounded with scrolls that were formerly inscribed with the names of the supernatural and cardinal virtues, and with medallions, each of which frames one of the Works of Mercy. At Edingthorpe in Norfolk there is a much-defaced Tree; and at Cranborne in Dorset, apparently another, though little remains but the trunk. A figure of Christ Blessing is placed at the apex, and Angels are decipherable, but of the Works only one can be seen clearly, that is, Clothing the Naked. At Dalham in Suffolk an Angel is said to have been shown in the midst of scenes representing the Works of Mercy; but the information is confused and little more is now visible than 'Feeding the Hungry', with a beggar or a pilgrim receiving a loaf. A Wheel of the Works, at Arundel in Sussex, has been so much repainted in the past as to be unreliable; another, at Kingston, in Cambridgeshire, is very defaced; and what

[1] *Ayenbite of Inwyt*, 1340, 95.   [2] *Middle English Sermons*, ed. Ross, 1940, S.7, 31–2.

was almost certainly a third, above a Weighing of Souls at Nassington in Northampton-shire, has practically disappeared. In stained glass, the Last Judgment is, or was, seen above the Works at Lammas in Norfolk and Brandeston in Suffolk,[1] but no parallel example survives in wall-painting from our date. The presence of the Judgment emphasizes the preacher's warning that 'oure Lorde God at the day of dome shall . . . aske of us howe that we have spende the vii workes of mercy'. Representations of the Works that survive in fair condition are all of the third type mentioned above.

The earliest in date, as well as the most interesting, are at Potter Heigham in Norfolk. There, some of the main features are derived from poems such as the *Ayenbite of Inwyt* and Deguilville's *Pilgrimage*. In the centre of the group of paintings there is the tall figure of a woman, with a nimbus,[2] richly dressed in the fashion of the day, her mantle being clasped upon the breast by a brooch, her kirtle having 'fitchets', and her surcoat being of the 'sideless' type. She raises her right hand, and in the left holds a very small building. In the doorway of this stands a bearded man holding a staff. Now, in associa-tion with the Works of Mercy, in various treatises, etc., there are to be found a variety of personifications, such as those of Mercy, Charity, *Grace Dieu*, and the Porter, who represents Dread or Fear of God. It seems reasonable to think that we have here either Mercy or Charity, or possibly *Grace Dieu*, carrying the Porter in his small lodge. In the *Ayenbite of Inwyt*, Dame Charity is the Queen of Virtues, and Dread the Door-keeper.[3] Deguilville, on the other hand, says that Mercy performs the Works,[4] and also that she entreats God for withdrawal of His judgment against the children of Adam, while the Porter brings messengers, namely Prayer and Alms, to show the dying Pilgrim the way to the Heavenly City. In *The Abbey of the Holy Ghost*,[5] the Abbess is Charity, the Porter, Dread, and the walls 'almes dedes and werkes of mercy and holy werkes'. Apart from the central figure, the most interesting subjects at Potter Heigham are the following: Visiting the Prisoner, who is in the stocks and seated on a rush mat; Receiving the Stranger, where Mercy or Charity takes his bourdon from a pilgrim as she invites him into her house; and Visiting the Sick, with the sick man in bed, being fed from a large spoon, with a curtain behind him (Plate 64a). There are remains of inscriptions in Middle English, and the scenes, though at some time partly retouched, are well composed, and show a certain dramatic sense. The date would seem to be *c.* 1380.

The paintings at Hoxne in Suffolk are in a poor state; but it may be seen that in 'Clothing the Naked' Mercy gives a garment to a nude man, and in 'Giving Drink to the Thirsty' hands him a cup. Other scenes at Moulton (Plate 29b) and Wickhampton, both in Norfolk, are also now somewhat defaced, especially those at Wickhampton, but pictorial records show that there were formerly various points of similarity between these two series. They are most marked in the renderings of 'Giving Drink to the Thirsty' and 'Clothing the Naked'. At Wickhampton a figure of Christ Blessing

---

[1] Owst, *Preaching in Medieval England*, 1926, 339; Woodforde, *The Norwich School of Glass-Painting in the Fifteenth Century*, 1950, 211–12.

[2] Woodforde, ibid., 194; Blomefield says that the figure of Mercy is that of the Blessed Virgin, but this does not seem to have been intended at Lammas, nor at Potter Heigham.

[3] *Ayenbite of Inwyt*, 1340, 1866, 80, 121.

[4] Lydgate, *Pilgrimage of the Life of Man*, 1899, 156.   [5] Owst, *Literature and Pulpit*, 1933, 80–2.

terminates the set, but at Moulton it comes towards the centre. Both the sets of scenes have architectural settings, in which perspective is rendered, but of course incorrectly. It is noticeable that in almost all representations the Works are performed by a woman, most probably the personification of Mercy. From the medieval point of view, an eighth repetition of her figure, presiding over all the Works, as shown at Potter Heigham, would not have been strange. The nimbus she has there does not necessarily identify the figure as that of the Blessed Virgin, or some Saint, but is most probably the equivalent, though in an opposite sense, of the nimbus of evil that sometimes surrounds the seven heads of the Apocalyptic Dragon. However, although it is most unusual to see the Blessed Virgin clad in the fashionable clothes of the day, this may be an exception. This is suggested by a passage in *Piers Plowman* that reads (in paraphrase): 'Thus, quoth Piers the Plowman, Mercy is a maiden with power over all; she is sib to all sinful men and her son also.' In a window at Combs in Suffolk, a man and woman together perform the Works of Mercy, while an Angel blesses them; [1] but there seems to be no rendering comparable to this in surviving wall-paintings or in records. The long persistence of the various ideas connected in medieval times with the Works of Mercy is illustrated in the Whinney Moor Song, sung at 'wakes' in Yorkshire as late as the early seventeenth century. In this song occurs not only the conception of reward after death for the practice during life of the Works of Mercy, but the idea expressed in Deguilville that Prayer and Alms help the dying Pilgrim on his way to the Heavenly City:

> *Fire and Fleet and Candle-light, and Christ receive thy Sawle*
> *When thou from hence dost pass away, every night and awle . . .*
> *To Whinny-moore thou comest at last, and Christ receive thy sawle.*
> *If ever thou gave either hosen or shoon, every night and awle,*
> *Sit thee downe and put them on, and Christ receive thy sawle . . .*
> *If ever thou gave either milke or drink, every night and awle,*
> *The fire shall never make thee shrink, and Christ receive thy Sawle.*

The names of the Deadly Sins, in Latin, or often enough in Middle English, are found or recorded in various wall-paintings, as at Trotton in Sussex and Potter Heigham in Norfolk respectively. They are: *Superbia*, *Avaritia*, *Luxuria*, *Ira*, *Gula*, *Invidia*, and *Accidia* (or *Socordia*); or, Pryde, Couetize, Lechery, Wrathe, Glotenye, Envie, Slouth, which stand for Pride, Covetousness, Lust, Anger, Gluttony, Envy and Sloth. The spelling in Middle English is of course variable. It is not unlikely that the Sins were included in expensive and elaborate schemes, and presented with much of the extraordinary and minutely imagined symbolism found in Deguilville's *Pilgrimage*. There, for instance, Envy is an old hag who glides in the grass like a serpent, while carrying two others on her back. Both of them are differently armed, one with a knife held behind her and spears in her eyes, the other with a sword. As will be recalled, Chaucer's *Persone's Tale* consists in discussion and denunciation of the Deadly Sins. Further, a passage in the *Romaunt of the Rose* describes paintings of them on the outer face of a

[1] Woodforde, *The Norwich School of Glass-Painting*, 1950, 194–6, pl. XLII. See also Brown, *Lyrics of the Fourteenth Century*, 1924, no. 95, lines 37–108, 'Merci passeth alle thinge'.

garden wall: 'Sorowe was peynted next Envye upon that walle of masonry', and so on. Another line in the same poem—'Alle these things . . . with gold and asure . . . depynted were upon the walle—' serves to indicate that the Deadly Sins indeed found their place, as might be expected, in schemes of the richest type.

There are some twenty wall-paintings of the Deadly Sins from our period. Two of them, at Ingatestone in Essex and Hurstbourne Tarrant in Hampshire, were not Trees, but Wheels of the Sins, and thus were very similar in general outline to Wheels of the Works of Mercy. The two seem but very seldom to have been placed side by side; at Arundel, for example, there is a Tree of the Sins, but the Works are set within a Wheel, with an Angel at the hub. The Tree is obviously the contrasted counterpart of the conception that has been noted already, in the *Ayenbite of Inwyt*,[1] of the Tree of Virtues. Some features of the Tree of Evil, just as those of the Tree of Jesse, seem to have been inspired by Seth's vision of the Tree of Paradise in the Legend of the Cross; for the roots of the last were in Hell, entwined with the body of Cain, and the Tree of Evil usually rises from the gaping jaws of Leviathan. Sometimes it is being sawn across at the base by demons, so that it may fall into 'the throat of the lion of Hell',[2] the 'dragon that devoureth all'. The figure of Satan that often forms the trunk was originally in some instances phallic; and it is curious to note that the phallic demon survived on the stage in Shakespeare's day, so late as 1620.[3] On the branches of the Tree of Evil, framed within the gaping jaws of the dragon-fruit, the various Sins are depicted. Usually the heads of the dragons turn upward, but occasionally, as at Hoxne and Kentford in Suffolk, they are pendent. As well as the fruit, there are leaves, often so conventionalized in treatment as to be unrecognizable, but now and then identifiable as those of the holly or the ivy. The latter is mentioned in connexion with death in a carol of the time of Henry VI,[4] and so the other may have had some such association. Pride, Avarice, Lust and Envy[5] seem to have been the Vices most commonly and vigorously denounced from our pulpits, and so representations of one or two of them may be considered in some detail, with reference also to representations of other of the Deadly Sins.

Pride, the chief of the vices, sin of Lucifer, 'that bright Angel that fell so far', is in wall-painting most often represented as male, but occasionally as female. In either case, the aspect emphasized is that of vanity, vain-glory, or 'ydel-blisse'.[6] Painters seem to have made no attempt to represent spiritual Pride, even by means of symbolism, or, if they did, no example has survived.[7] In a French manuscript of 1276 there is a Tree of Evil with spreading roots that each end in a woman's head, in every case symbolic of one of the Deadly Sins, and at the summit, surrounded by black birds, appears a Queen, with crown and sceptre. This is evidently a representation of Intellectual Pride, so that the birds are opposites of the Seven Doves which in the Jesse Tree sometimes stand for the seven influences of the *Spiritus Domini*.[8] At Ingatestone Pride was seated

---

[1] 1866, 95.   [2] ibid., 173.   [3] Summers, *The History of Witchcraft and Demonology*, 1926, 277.
[4] Brand, *Popular Antiquities*, I, 286–7.   [5] Owst, *Preaching in Medieval England*, 1926, 323, n.2.
[6] Dan Michel, *Ayenbite of Inwyt*, 1340, E.E.T.S., 217.
[7] Unless by the central demoniac figure, from which all the Sins spring, as at Trotton in Sussex.
[8] Mâle, *Art in France of the Thirteenth Century*, London, 1913, 107–8; Watson, *The Early Iconography of the Tree of Jesse*, 1934, 168–9, pls. I–III, XI, XV, XIX, XXIII, XXVI.

'in a chair of dignity, like a Duchess', and had a tiring-woman at her right and at her left a devil. In *Jacob's Well* it is said that 'the devyl hath maryid Pride to wommen; for wommen settyn all here stodye in pride of aray of her hed and of here body, to lokyn in myrrourys,[1] in kemyng here heed' . . . If at Ingatestone Pride once had a mirror, it was defaced before the painting was recorded. As so often throughout the centuries, women much disturbed moralists at our period, and are rebuked, among other things, for self-conscious vanity—'looking aside like costly horses'.[2] The medieval woman had every temptation to indulge in pride of apparel, and Margery Kempe admits to it in amusing terms: 'her bodice with the tippets were dagged. Her cloaks also were dagged,[3] wyth dyvers colours be-tween the daggys that it schuld be the more staryng to mennys sygth, and hir-self the mor ben worshepd'. But her male contemporaries were not much behind her in this; and Myrc recommends that a penitent be asked whether he has been proud of his dress 'as fools are wont to be'.[4] At Brooke in Norfolk and Hoxne in Suffolk Pride is a gallant in gay attire, holding a mirror, at Hoxne in the left hand, the right being occupied by a sceptre. There he is also crowned, and at Brooke he has about his head a fillet ornamented with roses, and holds in one hand a double-edged comb, while his cote-hardie is fantastically striped. The mirror, in the texts, is held before Pride by Flattery,[5] and here there is a glance at the Bestiaries, where the Unicorn, a symbol of Pride, is rendered harmless by seeing itself in reflection. At Cranborne in Dorset the Tree of Evil springs from the bust of a richly-clad woman, presumably representing Pride. There seems to be here some repetition of ideas, and perhaps confusion with those relating to Gluttony, in a crowned male figure at a loaded table, with a devil and a trumpeter just behind him, all seen at the apex of the Tree. However, this painting has at some time in the past been retouched extensively, and the resulting confusion is such that it can no longer be 'read' with any confidence. Deguilville says [6] that Pride makes a great noise in the world, like the bagpipes, and 'his hornys he bloweth al the day'; also, that he chatters like a jay or a magpie. At Bardwell in Suffolk Pride is, or was, accompanied by three trumpeters clad in parti-coloured gipons of red and blue, who blow vigorously at their instruments with heads and bodies well thrown back, and are preceded by a smaller figure with the bagpipes. A trumpeter also appears in a much-defaced painting at Alveley in Shropshire; there the central figure of Pride is recorded as crowned, nude, and female, with a skeleton on her right, emblematic of Death, who aims an arrow at her. At Padbury in Buckinghamshire the skeleton is armed with a spear—'hys dredful spere'.[7] The biblical allusion to the wages of sin is too obvious to call for comment.

Avarice, as depicted in the thirteenth-century scheme of the Painted Chamber, was named *Covoitise*, in Norman French. Loaded with money, he was shown prostrate beneath the feet of *Largesce*, or Bounty, who was engaged in choking him with gold.[8] In a most unusual painting of even earlier date at Chaldon, in Surrey, Avarice [9] is the only one of the Deadly Sins still without doubt recognizable, and this by the money-

[1] Owst, *Literature and Pulpit*, 1933, 96.   [2] *Ayenbite of Inwyt*, 1340, 216.

[3] *Booke of Margery Kempe*, E.E.T.S., I, 1940, 9.   [4] Myrc, *Instructions for Parish Priests*, 1868, 33–46.

[5] Lydgate, *Pilgrimage of the Life of Man*, 1899, 682.   [6] ibid., 389.   [7] ibid., 211.

[8] Tristram, *Eng. Med. Wall Painting*, 1950, 105, pl. 20.   [9] Ibid., 1944, 36–9, pl. 48.

bags tied about his waist. In works of our period, he has them at Crostwight in Norfolk and Hoxne in Suffolk, where he is busy filling a large chest. A similar strong-box is seen at Bardwell, with a flying devil nearby; it is also found at Trotton and Ingatestone. At the latter place there are two attendant demons, and Avarice counts out coin from his chest with claw-like, crooked fingers. These hideous fingers bring to mind the remark in Deguilville that Avarice has the paws of a gryphon and her six hands grip everything fast.[1] In the *Pilgrimage*, she is not weighted down with money-bags, but tied to her riches like an ape to a clog.[2] Her 'hands' are named Ravine, Cut-purse, Usury, False Semblance, Symony, and Treachery (or Cheating). She does no work, but gains money by means of gaming.[3] At Broughton in Buckinghamshire there is a representation of Avarice under the guise of gambling, for two men are shown quarrelling over a gaming-board.[4] Above is another painting, in which Our Lady of Pity holds the Body of Christ and is surrounded by men in elaborate costume, who each hold different portions of the Body, such as the heart, hands, feet and bones, as well as a cross and a wafer. This work as a whole clearly relates to swearing in one of its most sacrilegious forms. In the *Ayenbite of Inwyt*[5] the sin of swearing comes under the general heading of Envy: 'the envious man sinneth by the mouth, for his heart being full of venom it leapeth out by the mouth, in cursing'. Sacrilegious swearing is nevertheless also treated as the fruit of the 'tenth bough' of Avarice, and it is pointed out that 'wicked games', as 'of dice and of table', give occasion for many sins, including 'great blasphemies'. It is therefore reasonable to 'read' both the paintings just mentioned as related to the Sin of Avarice. It may be noted at this point that William of Wykeham[6] forbade the scholars of New College, Oxford, to play chess since this and similar games led to much gambling and quarrelling. 'Queke' or 'quek' has been identified as a game played on a chess-board, which was known by the same name, and, in an inventory of 1376 there is mention of a 'pair of tables on the outside of which was painted a chequer-board that is called a "quek"'. From this it would seem very likely that a duck shown as saying 'quek' in one amusing marginal illustration[7] is not a mere drollery, but may have been inserted at the wish of the owner of the book as a warning against a specific temptation. Much the same might be said of many similar marginal drawings. To return after this digression to the painting at Broughton in Buckinghamshire, it may be noted that this is quite a straightforward illustration of numerous passages in homiletic literature, such as may be found in Robert of Brunne's *Handlyng Synne*[8] (1303) and Myrc's *Festial*.[9] In the former, those in the habit of swearing 'grete othys grysly' are warned by a tale of a dying man, who was said to have seen a vision of the Blessed Virgin with her Son, covered by wounds, in her arms. When asked the meaning of the vision, she replied: 'Thou . . . with thy othys wykked and wylde . . . thus hast drawen my dere chylde-alle hys flessh thou teryst, whan thou falsly by hym swerest.' Wyclif denounces 'comyn swereris by Goddis herte, bonys, nailis, and sidis, and othere

---

[1] Lydgate, *Pilgrimage of the Life of Man*, 460-70.   [2] ibid., 469.   [3] ibid., 492.
[4] *Ayenbite of Inwyt*, 1340, 45.   [5] ibid., 26-7, 28.
[6] Coulton, *Chaucer and his England*, 1937, 274.   [7] Millar, *English Illuminated Manuscripts*, II, 3, pl. 2.
[8] Robert of Brunne, *Handlyng Synne*, 1303, pt. I, 1901, 25-7; 'Gentyl men, for grete gentry, wene that grete othys beyn curteysy'.   [9] Myrc, *Festial*, pt. I, XCVI, 113, 114.

membris'.[1] At Broughton the figure of Christ, and indeed the whole work, have at some time been repainted. It may be noted in passing that the symbolism of the 'twigs' of the Tree of Evil varies in different accounts, and they may be transferred from one 'branch' to another.

The most consistent of the representations is that of Lust, showing invariably the figures of a man and woman closely embraced. Anger, however, takes two forms—that of a combat between two enraged men, or a single figure in the act of committing suicide. Wrestlers engaged in their sport seem at first sight to be harmless enough, and to have little connexion with Anger; though among the most popular of medieval sports, wrestling had however its darker side, and was used to dispatch enemies through foul play. Further, numerous fatal bouts are recorded in assize rolls; [2] and so it became representative of the Deadly Sin of Anger, shown especially in carving, as at Lincoln. At Ingatestone, two youths (not, however, wrestlers) struggle furiously with each other; but at Brooke a man is depicted stabbing himself. With brow contorted, he plunges two knives into his breast, one of them grasped in either hand, and blood streams down his gay garments. Like all the Sins at Brooke, he emerges from the Jaws of Leviathan, each, that is, from a separate representation of these. This series, now lost, is exceptional, since there is neither Tree nor Wheel, and the Sins are framed separately, each within an arched compartment. They are placed below a large painting that seems to have represented the parable of the Prodigal Son, so far as may be judged from descriptions of it that were written c. 1852. If this was so, it was obviously introduced with a view of impressing on the beholder the necessity of penance for sin. The representation of Sloth was most unusual for wall-painting; since a bear was shown walking on its hind legs and dragging behind it, head downward, a youth whose ankles were tied just behind its head. There is here a symbolism that combines both the human and the animal varieties. The bear, in the homilies, is sometimes compared to the Glutton, because, just as the Glutton wastes the fruit of other men's labours, so the bear wastes those of the bee's industry. However, if the painting under consideration was well understood and accurately recorded, the symbolism was in this case transferred quite appropriately, from Gluttony to Sloth.[3] At Crostwight and Hoxne respectively, a woman and a man recline with cheek resting on the palm of the hand,[4] while at Ingatestone and Trotton the emphasis is laid on slothful neglect of religious duties. At the former place, a figure slumbers with a devil brooding over it and there is a church window in the background; at the latter there are beside the couch a fallen book and a rosary. Gluttony in the form of drunkenness is often included both in the homilies and their derivative paintings. At Brooke a drunkard vomits into a cask full of flames. This idea may be traced both in the *Ancren Riwle*, where it is said that the toss-pot [5] should have boiling brass to drink, and in Hampole's *Pricke of Conscience*, where the 'throats of the wicked' are described as being filled with 'molten brass'. At the same time, in wall-paintings, those who cheated in the sale of drink were pilloried; thus, at

[1] *Works*, III, 332. See Chaucer, *Persone's Tale* and *Pardonere's Tale*.
[2] See, for example, Coulton, *Chaucer and His England*, 1937, 275-6.
[3] Owst, *Literature and Pulpit*, 1933, 326, n.2, 445.   [4] See chap. I, p. 9.
[5] *Ancren Riwle*, 216; *Pricke of Conscience*, l. 9433.

Brooke, the Fraudulent Alewife carries in her left hand a vessel of flaming liquid, and in her right the bung of the cask, also flaming. A small winged figure, apparently nude and having a nimbus, is mentioned in a description of the painting. It is difficult to account for this figure, for the drawing made from it is as confused as the verbal description; most probably it is a devil, and the 'nimbus' merely a misreading on the part of the recorder. On the other hand, the nimbus may possibly be that of evil, though if so it would be a unique instance as shown on an ordinary demon.[1] The painting of Gluttony at Ingatestone, in which a man vomits into a bowl, has been mentioned before. Since he holds a rosary in the left hand, and a devil tempts him, the double sin of sensual indulgence on holy days may be intended.[2] Casks of liquor are to be seen beyond this figure, and another urges a third to drink. At Bardwell, a woman fills a jug from a large cask, and near her a man and woman are seated on a bench, engaged in drinking. Cranborne in Dorset and Trotton in Sussex each have a figure tilting a jug to its lips; the one at Cranborne has a protuberant stomach; the other at Trotton stands between a large flagon and a dish. Gluttony's 'bely round, no thyng smal' is mentioned by Deguilville,[3] who also says that when it is overloaded he is sick.

In the homilies and treatises the Deadly Sins are compared to a great variety of creatures;[4] e.g. Envy to a serpent or scorpion; Wrath to the spined hedgehog or the allegedly venomous toad; Avarice to the griffin, to an ape tied to a clog, to a medieval variant of the 'dog in the manger', or to a spider sucking a fly. Devils, too, frequently take the form of various animals in the homilies, and the animals are often the same as those representing the Sins. Much of this very varied symbolism, and in fact probably most of it, would have been familiar to numbers of people through sermons.[5] It is not therefore at all surprising to find Gluttony, for instance, in many strange guises, whether in wall-paintings, in marginal illuminations, or in carvings. Let us name a few of these: —the hound chasing a hare, in illustration of 'a strong [6] craving for meat'; the bittern,[7] or the fabulous miredromble, a bird with two stomachs, as big as a swan; or a fox carrying off a goose.[8] Lest it be imagined that in medieval times Gluttony in its grossest forms was widespread, it should be recalled that under this heading were included 'lusty taste', and the 'cherishing of the body with sweet meat and soft clothing.' [9] It may be as well to point out here that many scenes, in addition to drawings of animals and birds, that are found in the margins of books, and especially on the Beatus pages of psalters, seem to have both an obvious and a symbolic meaning. The parable of Dives and Lazarus,[10] for example, may stand for Gluttony contrasted to Sobriety, and the story

[1] Seen, as stated previously, on the Beast of the Apocalypse; and also probably at Idsworth in Hampshire; see p. 88.

[2] Owst, *Preaching in Medieval England*, 1926, 180.

[3] Lydgate, *Pilgrimage of the Life of Man*, 349.

[4] Owst, *Literature and Pulpit*, 1933, 112, 196.

[5] The bittern is a favourite bird, and the fabulous miredromble.

[6] *Ayenbite of Inwyt*, 1866, 55. [7] Owst, *Literature and Pulpit*, 1933, 439.

[8] Saxl, *A Spiritual Encyclopedia*, etc., *Journ. Warburg and Courtauld Inst.*, 116.

[9] Myrc, *Instructions for Parish Priests*, 1868, 33–46.

[10] *Somme le Roi*, Brit. Mus. Add. MS. 28162, no. 15.

of David and Goliath for Work and Sloth.[1] Goliath, at times, even represents the Devil.[2]

In one of the treatises,[3] the Sins are likened to 'sevene sundry bestis: as Pryde to the lyon; Covetyse to the urchon; Wrathe to the wolfe; Envye to the hound; Slowthe to the asse; Glotonye to the bere; and Lecherye to the swyne'. It will be noted that here Covetousness becomes an 'urchon', or hedgehog, whereas previously we have found the creature representing Wrath. When it stands for Covetousness there is a side-glance at the Bestiaries, for they sometimes say that the hedgehog gathers fallen grapes on its spines by rolling on them. Further, in the quotation given above, Envy is a dog, whereas previously the likeness was to a serpent. Changes such as these are rung endlessly; and so, while we may suspect that any individual drawing or carving of an animal may represent a given vice, we can only identify it positively through a context too often lacking. Animal symbolism was taken to great lengths, with no attempt at consistency. Man himself, since he was regarded as a microcosm of the world,[4] might be called 'hardy [brave] as a lyon, dredfulle [timid] as the hare, bold as the cock, and as a hound covetous; . . . simple as the lambe, and lyke the foxe malicious'.

THE FIVE SENSES

The Five Senses, or 'Five Wittes' are mentioned almost as often in the homilies and treatises as the Deadly Sins, and frequently in connexion with them. In the *Ayenbite of Inwyt* it is pointed out that the Senses should be under the command of Reason,[5] or Conscience. Elsewhere, they are termed the 'five gates of the castle', i.e. the body, through which the devil may enter. The 'sovereign' of the castle is God Himself, who resides in the Reason like 'a lord in the principal place of his township.'[6] In the *Ancren Riwle* the Senses are the heart's wardens; Langland, in the account of Dowell, calls them the five sons of Conscience. Finally, Myrc recommends in detail the questions that should be put to a penitent regarding possible misuse of his Senses,[7]—'the five golden talents that the Lord entrusted to his thrall in order to gain therewith'. There may well have been Wheels of the Senses on church walls, but there are no identifiable examples among the large incised circles found here and there that are almost certainly remains of Wheels of one kind or another.[8] Our only known Wheel of the Senses is in a secular building, namely, Longthorpe Tower near Peterborough (Plate 64*b*), where it is to be seen on the east wall of a room, above the fireplace. At its hub, from which there radiate five spokes, in correspondence with the number of the Senses, there is a crowned figure, undoubtedly that of Reason, or Conscience; about the rim are two rings of

---

[1] ibid., no. 12. [2] *Middle English Sermons*, ed. Ross, 1940, S.18, 105.

[3] Sermon of Dan John Gaytryge, *c.* 1440, ed. Perry, E.E.T.S. (MS. Harl. 211).

[4] Lydgate, *Pilgrimage of the Life of Man*, 679.

[5] *Ayenbite of Inwyt*, 1340, 23; 1866, 153–4, 177, 204.

[6] Owst, *Literature and Pulpit*, 1933, 29–30.

[7] Myrc, *Instructions for Parish Priests*, 1868, 43–6; to judge from a passage in the *Ayenbite of Inwyt*, the Wheel at Longthorpe might be more accurately termed a Wheel of Lust, for there it is said that to 'lechery' of the 'five wits' 'belongeth drunkenness and gluttony, the love of soft bedclothes and ease of body' (46). [8] Tristram, *Eng. Med. Wall Painting*, 1950, 261–2, 286–8.

creatures that symbolize the Senses. The choice made of the larger of them, in the inner ring, serves to show that this Wheel had as its main motif warning against abuse of the Five Wittes, for the monkey and the spider have almost always a bad significance. The outer ring, of smaller creatures, is much defaced, but the presence of an unmistakable squirrel, so amiable an animal in the Bestiaries, suggests that they were chosen by way of antithesis. The squirrel was thought to cross water on a leaf, or a piece of wood, using its bushy tail as a sail; and when the moralists dwelt on its habits, they pointed out that similarly those who cross the troubled waters of this world should 'hold fast to the wood of the cross'. So far as the creatures around the Wheel at Longthorpe Tower survive, they are well drawn, and the head of Reason or Conscience has some nobility. There are several birds elsewhere in the room, filling the lower sections of the wall-space, and it has been supposed that their presence shows an interest in natural history on the part of the owners of the house, quite early in the fourteenth century. They have therefore been claimed as one of the so-called purely 'secular' features of the scheme. However, though they are not all recognizable, it is to be observed that the peacock symbolizing pride or vanity, is in a significant position immediately below the Three Corpses, in the *Trois Vifs et Trois Morts*.[1] The bittern representing Gluttony comes just beneath a painting of December, with a man killing a pig, in a series of Labours of the Months. In the Psalter of Robert de Lisle the seven Offices of the Hours are related not only with the seven scenes of the Passion but also with the Five Senses.

WITCHCRAFT AND 'JANGLING'

The small group of paintings, only seven in number, that we are about to study under the two headings of Witchcraft and 'Jangling', are of great interest from the historical point of view. They are, however, in all cases save one, virtually devoid of aesthetic qualities. The most that can be claimed for them is a certain dexterity in handling, and some power in rendering a stock subject with confidence and clarity in almost purely linear style. Four of them exist or existed at Colton, Little Melton, Seething and Stokesby, all in Norfolk, each depicting two women seated in the centre of a long bench with heads close together, and behind them a large devil, who extends his arms widely to enclose the group. At the sides there are smaller fiends, and at Colton and Seething are scrolls filled with meaningless letters, often repeated throughout the length of each scroll. As we shall see, these scrolls and their inscriptions are of some importance for identification of the subjects. At Little Cornard in Suffolk a fragment remains (or formerly remained) of a similar painting, consisting only in the head of one woman, and part of a demon behind her. There is a thirteenth-century example at Wiston in Suffolk,[2] and another at Brook in Kent, which is however of doubtful identification. The representation at Stokesby, lost but recorded, is the most interesting of all. There, as well as the central group of two women, with a great devil above them, are three or four minor fiends, and a third woman holding a rosary

---

[1] See the section on *The Three Living and the Three Dead*, p. 112 *et seq.*
[2] Tristram, *Eng. Med. Wall Painting*, 1950, 279–80, 351.

between her knees. Further, at the opposite end of the bench from the third woman, are two of the minor fiends, one being armed with a pointed instrument, and before them, on the bench, is something that in Winter's drawing looks like the leg of a small child.

Apart from slight variations in the gestures of the arms, the central group of two women is almost identical at Stokesby, Colton, Little Melton and Seething. It would appear to have been repeated, in any subject it would suit, from a painter's 'pattern book'. Nevertheless it is obvious that the painting at Stokesby was not only the most elaborate, but differed in meaning from the others, and so we may study the other three first. Two of them certainly, and the third most probably, are Moralities painted in reproof of 'jangling', that is, idle talking or chattering, especially in church.[1] The third, at Little Melton, retains only a slight trace of the huge central demon, and if there were once scrolls inscribed with gibberish they are now altogether defaced. As at Colton and Seething, each of the women holds a rosary in the right hand and raises the left to her breast, or her heart. The gesture may mean little or nothing, but on the other hand it may signify that the two women are indulging in 'charms or conjurations'.[2] But at Colton and Seething the scrolls with their strange inscriptions, and, at Seething, a small devil who escapes with a rosary, identify the subject beyond reasonable doubt. It comes from a favourite story of the medieval moralists and was attributed by them to many different sources: by Myrc to 'an holy byschop';[3] by the Knight of La Tour Landry, when admonishing his daughters, to St. Martin of Tours;[4] in Handlyng Synne, to 'a holy man';[5] and elsewhere, to St. Augustine.[6] The tale is a warning to women not 'to be ever jangelyng,[7] as a pye, other a jay'. In Handlyng Synne, prefaced both by the very ancient legend of the Sacrilegious Carollers,[8] who danced in a churchyard and would not cease at the priest's bidding, and the warning that 'jangelyng longeth to sacrylage', it runs as follows: There was a deacon who began to laugh while reading the Gospel at Mass, and, on being reproved explained that he had seen two women chattering near him, and behind them a fiend 'with penne and parchemen yn honde', who 'wrote alle that ever they spake, pryvyly be-hynde here bake'. The devil, when he had filled his scroll, tried with his teeth to draw it out and lengthen it, but it broke suddenly so that he hit his head against the wall behind him, whereat he went away shamefaced. It followed that, up to a point, the women with their tongues had defeated even the devil himself. The small fiend at Seething, who is carrying off the rosary, has of course succeeded in drawing their attention from their prayers. There is a connexion here with those devils who run 'among the pepullys fete hedyr and thedyr'.[9] Sometimes admonitions against jangling are of general application, and are not confined to one class or one sex. In The Lay Folks Mass Book occurs the passage —'Thou shulde gode tent take, that thou at the messe no jangling make.'[10] Elsewhere,

---

[1] Coulton, Chaucer and his England, 1937, 140–1; Owst, Preaching in Medieval England, 1926, 175, n.1, 176–7; Myrc, Festial, 279–80; The Babees' Book, ed. Rickert, 32.

[2] Middle English Sermons, ed. Ross, 1940, S.5, 21.   [3] Myrc, Festial, 279–80.

[4] Book of the Knight of the Tower, 1371, E.E.T.S., 41.

[5] Handlyng Synne, 290.   [6] The Lay Folks Mass Book, 1879, 4, 136–7.

[7] Owst, Literature and Pulpit, 1933, 44.   [8] Handlyng Synne, 238–89.

[9] Myrc, Festial, 277.   [10] The Lay Folks Mass Book, 1879, 4.

labourers are reproved for 'jangling and japing' [1] in church; and in the *Golden Legend* there is a story about what befell monks who stood by a river and 'jangled there of fables and idle words'.[2]

We may now consider the painting once at Stokesby. As at Colton, two women seated on a bench clasp right and left hands, but here neither holds a rosary. The woman on the spectator's right has her right hand on the left shoulder of her companion, while on the other shoulder is a large insect which also appears on the left shoulder of the former woman. At the extreme right of the bench, beside the third woman, who has a rosary hanging between her knees, and has been mentioned before, are the heads of three more insects. Balancing them, at the other end of the very long bench, as has been said, are two small fiends and what is perhaps the leg of a child. The gigantic devil, presiding as usual over the scene, is of exceptionally terrifying aspect, with curved horns and immense bat's wings outspread. To 'read' this painting with absolute assurance is impossible; but it is certain, from the presence of the insects and the action of the minor fiends, that this is a Morality concerned with witchcraft. The rosary held by the third of the women was no doubt intended for some superstitious use. For instance, the Lord's Prayer, written or said backward, was employed in Norfolk as a charm within the first quarter of the present century; [3] and as for the insects, they are probably 'familiars', but it is also possible that a chapter in *The Bulleymung Pit* [4] may have some bearing on their presence in this painting.

There is a second, and perhaps also a third painting, concerned with witchcraft. They are at Melbourne in Derbyshire and Crostwight in Norfolk respectively. For 'jangling' one is claimed for Peakirk in Northamptonshire; but it is much defaced, and the 'action' of what has been thought to be the presiding devil is false by comparison with that seen in all other examples. The so-called 'arms' and 'hands' do not widen to embrace the two central figures, but hang limply down behind their heads; and the 'hands' are in fact no more than two blotches, in shape like gloves without fingers. There is in fact nothing to be deciphered with certainty beyond parts of two figures, the one on the right being female; they face each other, as in representations of Lechery, before semi-defaced remains of a tree, with intertwined branches, probably a Tree of the Deadly Sins. Well within living memory, East Anglia and the West Country have been considered as main strongholds of the belief in witchcraft.[5] The unusual creatures at Stokesby call for some further comment. It has been noted that the domestic 'familiars' of witches are confined to this country, and that they are always small creatures, kept in the house and used to carry out the commands of the witch. They are recorded most frequently in East Suffolk, and the eastern counties, where mice, rats, toads and moles are usual among them. In the Middle Ages, certain creatures, such as frogs and mice, were thought to be 'imperfect', in

---

[1] Owst, *Preaching in Medieval England*, 1926, 172.   [2] *Golden Legend*, IV, 253.

[3] B. J. Armstrong, Vicar of East Dereham, *A Norfolk Diary*, 1850–88, 110, 237; A. R. Wright, *English Folklore*, 1928, 76.

[4] Mathena Blomefield, London, 1946, VI, 56–64; Summers, *The History of Witchcraft and Demonology*, 1926, 101—'domestic animal familiar most frequently met with in Essex, Suffolk, and the eastern counties'. 'Familiars' were animals of many kinds, and even some insects.

[5] Murray, *The God of the Witches*, 83, 151.

that they might be generated from putrefaction.[1] Frogs and toads no doubt gained their ill repute partly from the mention in the Apocalypse of the 'unclean spirits like frogs'.[2] The insect-like creatures at Stokesby, if they are not intended for actual insects of any kind, may be the painter's attempt to represent a 'spirit familiar', described as 'much like a ferret'.[3] As well as beetles' wings, they have curved and pointed 'beaks', as though to indicate that they are suckers of blood. Only the slightest of suggestions can be offered in regard to the two small demons with perhaps a child between them. The pointed instrument held by one of them may be that employed to make the 'witches mark', which was normally placed on the left shoulder. Alternatively, it might be used for murdering a child, for midwives were said to do this for purposes of magic.[4] Myrc lists, with persons to be excommunicated, all that destroy children by means of drinks or witchcraft, whether born or unborn, and all witches and charmers; he says, further, that penitents should be asked if they have had any dealings with evil spirits, or with love philters and so forth.[5] Again, witches were believed capable of producing sterility and abortion.[6] As might be expected, the avoidance of witchcraft and superstition is emphasized in homilies.[7] In *Handlyng Synne*, under the First Commandment,[8] there is this warning to penitents:

'If thou ever through folye dydyst ought do nygromauncy, or to the devyl dedyst sacryfyse . . . or any man gave the mede for to reyse the devyl . . . thou has synned and do a-mys . . . thurgh thys . . . commaundement.' [9]

In the Carew-Pointz Horae (1350–60) there is a miniature showing Theophilus, the most notable medieval example of a devotee of Satan who became penitent,[10] seated in the company of three devils, on a bench precisely like those in the wall-paintings we have been discussing.

The painting at Melbourne in Derbyshire is of the Black Mass. It is now much defaced, but it may be seen from a pictorial record that a gigantic horned devil, with a smaller one on either side, extended its arms to embrace a group of two women kneeling before it and holding between them a circular object that can only be intended for a wafer. The great demon bears a scroll, and on it, c. 1860, there was still to be seen part of an inscription, recorded as IC EST CELIA DEABOL; the word *Celia* is mistakenly read. The phrase may have been '*Ic est cellam Deabol*[*i*]', that is, 'this is the secret place, or storehouse, of the devil'; but the first letter, as given in an engraving in the *Reliquary*, resembles a G rather than a C, and there is in fact no space for the six letters of *cellam*. By a process of elimination the conclusion may be reached that the words were either IC EST GAUDA DEABOLI (or Diaboli)—this is the devil's gaud, or jewel,—or that they parodied words of consecration in the mass.[11] The reference would be to the profaned

[1] Summers, *Malleus Maleficarum*, 1928, 122.　　　[2] Druce, *Archaeological Journal*, 1909, LXVI, 329.
[3] Murray, *The God of the Witches*, 86.
[4] Myrc, *Instructions for Parish Priests*, 71; *Malleus Maleficarum*, v, 2.
[5] Myrc, *Instructions for Parish Priests*, 12, 21–3, 30.　　　[6] Murray, *The God of the Witches*, 137–8.
[7] Owst, *Preaching in Medieval England*, 1926, 243.
[8] *Handlyng Synne*, pt. I, 13.　　　[9] *Middle English Sermons*, ed. Ross, 1940, S.5, 21.
[10] Fitzwilliam Museum, Cambridge, ff. 176b and 177a; *Archaeological Journal*, XCII, 1935, pls. 11, 12.
[11] ? Ic est calix diaboli.

wafer, which, as is well known, was used for purposes of witchcraft. From the head-dress of the two women it may be judged that this painting is the earliest among those mentioned here. There is a reference to abuse of the Host in the *Ayenbite of Inwyt*,[1] and there are others in similar works. During proceedings in 1324 against Dame Alice Kyteler,[2] in Ireland, it was deposed that in her closet a wafer had been found with the name of the fiend stamped upon it. During the fourteenth century, and also later, witchcraft was much in men's minds, and there were various notable prosecutions, such as that, about 1303, of Walter de Langton,[3] Bishop of Lichfield and Coventry. In 1324 as many as twenty-seven defendants stood their trial [4] for an alleged attempt to kill Edward II by the practice of magical arts. Much later, in 1406, Henry IV [5] was concerned about the number of witches and sorcerers then said to be active in the diocese of Norwich. The trial of the Duchess of Gloucester took place in 1441; she was stated to have confessed that she had acted under the influence 'of the wicche of Eye', in Suffolk.

The third painting with a subject that may be related to witchcraft, at Crostwight in Norfolk, has been very badly defaced owing to penetration of water in recent years. Originally, it could be seen that it was somewhat superior to the others in this group. It is placed over a doorway, with a Tree of the Seven Deadly Sins and a St. Christopher at a lower level on either side. The juxtaposition of these subjects seems significant, in view of St. Christopher's role as a protector of Man the Spiritual Pilgrim. At a long, narrow table, or what is more probably intended for a bench like those noted previously in paintings of the kind, stand three richly-dressed couples, with their arms twined about each other. Behind them is the usual immense demon, with its all-embracing arms. It may be suggested, though with diffidence, that we have here a representation of a Sabbat, with its attendant feasting and debauchery.

THE THREE LIVING AND THE THREE DEAD

The Morality of the Three Living and the Three Dead, commonly known by the title of *Les Trois Vifs et Les Trois Morts*, appears first in our wall-painting in the early fourteenth century; but, as with the Works of Mercy and Seven Deadly Sins, representations seem to have become general only about 1350. It is doubtful how far the spread of this rather morbid subject was encouraged by a frame of mind which came about through the calamity of the Black Death. The association is one that appears almost too obvious; yet little doubt can be felt that the terrible experiences of that time must have exerted at least some influence upon those who frequented the churches, were responsible in part for their upkeep, and therefore no doubt had had some voice in the matter of painted decoration for them. However, this Morality of the Three Living and Three Dead has not been fully understood. It is not, primarily, a warning

---

[1] *Ayenbite of Inwyt*, 1340, 1866, 40.
[2] *Proceedings against Dame Alice Kyteler*, Camden Soc., 1843, 46.
[3] Summers, *The History of Witchcraft and Demonology*, 1926, 138.
[4] id., *Malleus Maleficarum*, 1928, xix.   [5] Rymer's *Foedera*, IV, pt. 1, 93.

that all must die, as it has often been interpreted, but one against Pride, the head and fountain of the Deadly Sins; it therefore includes by inference an insistence upon the virtue of Humility, Pride's opposite, or remedy. This becomes obvious if we study certain features of this Morality. Contrasted with the Three Corpses are, not merely ordinary men, but Kings, and though no example survives in England, St. Macarius the Hermit is often associated with the subject. According to his legend, he not only talked familiarly with such corpses as he happened to come across, but, on enquiring from the devil [1] the reason for the latter's failure to overcome him, received the reply that it was so in virtue of his humility, 'and thy meekness by which I may not prevail against thee'.

The close association between the subject of the Trois Vifs and that of the Deadly Sins becomes obvious from a poem such as one on the Sins having the refrain, 'remember man thow art but wormes meat';[2] that these two subjects are not more often found together in wall-painting, as at Bardwell in Suffolk, is probably due to the accidents of time. Among remedies against Pride, the contemplation of dead men's bones was suggested in medieval times;[3] and in this may doubtless be found the origin of the *cadavre*, so often seen from the fifteenth century onward on the lower stage of a magnificent tomb, rich with carving and painting. To impress upon an audience the hollowness of earthly vanities, it was not unknown for a preacher suddenly to reveal a skull previously concealed beneath his cloak.[4]

Representations of the Three Living and Three Dead have more variety than might be expected from the nature of the Morality they illustrate. They developed equally in England and in France, but it has been suggested that the origin of the 'Dit des trois morts et des trois vifs' may have been English.[5] The early representation found in MS. Arundel 83 has been carefully studied; and it has been noted that the gestures of Kings and Corpses alike, as depicted there, coincide with words assigned to them in accompanying verses. Thus, the third of the Kings wrings his hands—'*destreint ses meins*'—and the last of the Corpses, both wealthy and powerful in life, is denuded even of worms. In sermons, connected with the fate of the dead, the numerous references to toads and worms [6] find illustration in wall-paintings; at Bardwell and Kentford in Suffolk, for instance. At Bardwell there are also, apparently, newts, and at Peakirk in Northamptonshire, where is found an unusually good and quite early rendering of the subject, newts, lizards, and a variety of creatures of ghastly aspect are skilfully used to pattern the background. Here, the third of the Kings wrings his hands, and the second, clad in richly-embroidered garments rendered by the painter with considerable skill in his brush-work, bears the sword of sovereignty. It is thus easy to connect the figure with the words assigned to it in the poem . . . '*Trop ay fet de mes voluntez*', and the wish expressed for amendment of life as due '*al dieu rei de misericorde*'. The

---

[1] *Golden Legend*, II, 218.
[2] Lydgate, *Reson and Sensuallyte*, I, 1901, xiv, poem on the Seven Deadly Sins.
[3] Myrc, *Instructions for Parish Priests*, 1868, 51.
[4] Owst, *Preaching in Medieval England*, 1926, 344, 351.
[5] Saxl, *A Spiritual Encyclopedia of the Early Middle Ages, Journ. of the Warburg and Courtauld Institutes*, V, 1942, 98; Freyhan, *Burlington Magazine*, LIV, 320–30.　　[6] Owst, *Literature and Pulpit*, 1933, 487.

Corpses, in wall-painting, are usually stiff and awkard in conception, and seldom show any hint of the imaginative ingenuity in treatment characterizing the miniature referred to above; but the Kings often show considerable power in delineation. To depict skeletons on a large scale, seems understandably to have embarrassed the average painter. At Charlwood, in Surrey, the Kings on horseback formed an unusually spirited group, but this painting is now almost defaced. At Longthorpe Tower the Morality is placed opposite, or almost opposite, the Apostles Matthias and Jude, whose scrolls would originally have borne, as has been noted previously, the words CARNIS RESVRRECTIONEM and ET VITAM ETERNAM. The paintings at Charlwood and Longthorpe are among the earliest of this subject. Wensley in Yorkshire, however, has what is not only an example of similar date, but in some ways the most interesting; for there is upon it, running perpendicularly between the Corpses, a very early inscription, taken in essentials, from the verse usually assigned to the second Corpse. This verse is given in English: 'As we are nove thus sal the be . . .bewar wyt me.' It is in excellently-designed and executed Lombardic capitals, and there is no division between the words. The normal inscription, in paraphrase, above the Kings, runs: 'I am afeard at what I see, methinketh these be devils three'—and over the Corpses 'I was once fair, but as I am so shalt thou be; for God's love be warned by me'. Around the tomb of the Black Prince, part of the inscription, which he himself chose, runs:

TIEL: COME: TU: ES: JE: AUTIEL: FU: TU: SERAS: TIEL: COME: JE: SU[1]: DE: LA: MORT: NE: PENSAY: JE: MIE: TANT: COME: J'AVOY: LA: VIE: EN: TERRE: AVOY: GRAND: RICHESSE: DONT: JE: Y: FYS: GRAND: NOBLESSE

At Wickhampton, in Norfolk, there is a late version of the subject, with gigantic figures, that in their original condition must have been most impressive. In the foreground, in front of the Corpses, a huntsman with hounds in leash chases a hare or rabbit. This is a feature found now and then in representations of the Morality, and not included either by a whim of the painter, nor for the amusement of the beholder, as has usually been thought. Unlikely though it may seem at first sight, the group is intended to convey the warning that the mind should be held by things of the spirit rather than of the flesh, for it is found, in verbal form, for example, in the *Ayenbite of Inwyt*: [2] 'The hare runneth, the greyhound followeth. The holy man runneth as the greyhound. All day his eye is to heaven, and he forgetteth all else, as does the hound with his prey before his eyes.' There has previously been occasion to allude to the hare and the greyhound, in connexion with Gluttony; but, bearing the context in mind, as it is always important to do when 'reading' pictorial symbols, there seems little doubt as to their meaning here.

ST. CHRISTOPHER

St. Christopher, to judge from the large number of extant and recorded representations, was increasingly by far the most popular of the Saints, from the fourteenth

[1] As thou art, so once was I; as I am, so shalt thou be, etc.   [2] 23, 75.

century onward. There are about fifty examples from that century—though a few are of doubtful identification—and from the next, over four hundred. This is the more remarkable because, as painters usually attempted to give at least an impression of the legendary stature of twelve cubits, they covered a considerable area of wall and their work was correspondingly vulnerable. Sometimes no more remains than a single, large bare foot, or traces of water and fish; but the evidence thus afforded is not as slight as it would seem to be, if it is considered in conjunction with that to be derived from the position in which the fragments are found. St. Christopher was normally painted either facing the common entrance of a church, or else above it, so that he might readily be seen in the first case by people passing the open door, in the second, by those leaving the edifice after their devotions. To look at his image, since the act of doing so was regarded as being in the nature of a prayer, was to ask for his help in many difficulties and dangers, and also in temptations, as we shall see later. Perhaps the chief of all physical dangers, in the medieval view, was that of sudden death without benefit of the sacraments, and it was against this calamity in particular that the Saint's aid was probably most often invoked. It may be conjectured with likelihood that the great increase noticeable in fifteenth-century representations may have been connected with the intensified peril of the times, and especially with the dangers incidental to the Wars of the Roses. Inscriptions on the paintings have seldom survived in good condition, but a remarkable early example is to be seen at Wood Eaton, in Oxfordshire, on a work of *c.* 1350 above a doorway, now blocked, in the north wall of the church. It is on a long pendent scroll beside the Saint's figure, and reads KI CEST IMAGE VERRA LE JUR DE MALE MORT NE MURRA—'who sees this image shall not die an ill death this day'.

A considerable rise about the middle of the fourteenth century in St. Christopher's popularity would seem to have been associated with the Great Plague, and to have resulted not only from the reliance on him as a guardian against sudden death, but from the belief, stated in the *Golden Legend* and elsewhere, that by prayer he had gained power to 'put away sickness and sores from them that remember his passion and figure'. Recurrent and sometimes widespread outbreaks of pestilence of course continued long after the Black Death, and the repeated attacks no doubt had the incidental consequence of establishing his cult. No paintings of him have survived here on external walls, like one recorded as having existed in Florence, nearly twenty feet in height, or those of which Molanus speaks, saying:

'Men are wont to paint him . . . where he can easily be seen. Nay, I hear that in many places of Germany he is painted outside the church, about the entrance or on the outer wall.'

Molanus goes on to quote the Latin version of the inscription from Wood Eaton given above, a very common one.

St. Christopher was famous also as a sustainer against fatigue, and at Pakefield, near Lowestoft, a representation once bore the lines:

Christophori Sancti speciem quicunque tuetur
Illa nempe die nullo languore gravetur.

It may be recalled that Chaucer's Yeoman in the *Prologue* to the *Canterbury Tales*, as being no doubt mindful of more than commonly strenuous activities, and also of dangers, had 'a Cristofre on his brest of silver shene'. Likewise the labourer might glance at the Saint's image as he passed by to daily toil. According to the legend, St. Christopher, when carrying the Christ Child across a river in flood, bore upon his shoulders not only the whole world, but also Him who had created it.

The Holy Child is shown first as supported on the Saint's left arm, but in works of the fourteenth century and later on his left shoulder and, as time went on, always higher on the shoulder. In some very late examples, He is placed almost immediately behind the Saint's head. He is clad in a simple tunic, raises the right hand in blessing and holds an Orb of the Universe [1] that is not infrequently divided into sections framing the elements of water, earth and air. The Orb, small in early representations, grows steadily larger as time goes on, and is depicted with increasing elaboration and often surmounted by the Vexillum. Palimpsest paintings of St. Christopher are not infrequent, and have given rise to some strange errors. For instance, one at Sedgeford in Norfolk, apparently showing three children on the Saint's shoulder, was interpreted by Didron [2] as a representation of the Trinity, since he thought that the Holy Child was depicted there with three heads. In fact, three layers of painting had been confused by those who had discovered the work and had attempted to reveal it fully. Little more than a bare outline now remains, and the 'three heads' are no longer distinguishable. There was originally an inscription reading:

> *Wyth al thys world in hand*
> *Thy dry staff withouten let*
> *Shall beren leaves in land*
> *Where thou it set.*

The Saint sometimes carries an eel spear, though this is rare in later work—for instance, at Peakirk in Northamptonshire (*c.* 1340); or, though seldom, the pilgrim's staff or bourdon, with a knob at the top and another below it on the shaft. There is an example of the bourdon at Seething in Norfolk, but the lower knob is defaced, and there was evidently another at Babingley in the same county. In one pictorial record, however, it has been misread as being a spear and in consequence conjecturally provided with an 'appropriate' head—as has happened on occasion also with the herald's baton borne by the Archangel of the Annunciation.[3] From the end of the fourteenth century onward, St. Christopher's staff was generally formed from a branch bursting into leaf at the top. In a German version of his story it miraculously became a living tree when the Saint, crossing the river, received baptism [4] from the Holy Child. According to the *Golden Legend*, this happened after the passage, when the staff had

---

[1] *Golden Legend*, IV, 119; or Orb of Sovereignty: '*Super te totum mundum habuisti.*' The orb used at Coronations was known as the 'mundus'.

[2] Didron, II, 59. Didron had not seen the work, as is evident from the fact that he calls it a statue.

[3] See chap. IV, p. 79.

[4] Rushforth, *Medieval Christian Imagery*, 1936, 223–4. The baptism in the midst of the stream is shown in a window of *c.* 1400 at Birtsmorton in Worcestershire.

been planted on the shore, where it was found on the morrow 'like a palmier bearing flowers, leaves and dates'. Yet another form of the staff, but one not very often seen, is Tau-headed, as at Willingham in Cambridgeshire (c. 1350); in glass slightly later at Mere in Wiltshire; and in another wall-painting at Lambourne in Essex (c. 1400). The Tau, the cruciform letter like a cross without its shortest limb,[1] was regarded as the letter of salvation, and inspired much complicated symbolism. It was associated with the idea of pilgrimage; for example, in Deguilville's *Pilgrimage of the Life of Man* the Pilgrim is told that banners charged with it should hang from the windows of the 'castle', which symbolized his own body.

St. Christopher, as is fairly well known, has for centuries been regarded as the patron Saint of travellers, and was no less the patron of Man as spiritual pilgrim. The medieval conception of spiritual pilgrimage has been well expressed by Mâle, thus:

'—la vie du pèlerin était la vie même du chrétien. Car, qu'est ce que le chrétien? sinon un voyageur qui ne se sent nulle part chez lui, un passant en marche vers une Jérusalem éternelle.'[2]

St. Christopher's head-covering varies. The late-thirteenth-century figure in Westminster Abbey[3] has the cloak drawn over the head, but in miniatures that are roughly contemporary there is sometimes a hat of helmet shape. An example of the latter existed in the early-fourteenth-century wall-painting at Coombes in Sussex, now almost obliterated, and still exists at Edingthorpe in Norfolk. At Willingham in Cambridgeshire (c. 1350), Paston in Norfolk (c. 1380) and Fritton in Suffolk (c. 1400) the Saint wears, or once wore, a soft cap, while at Paston he also has, though this is somewhat exceptional, a cusped nimbus. At both Willingham and Paston he is bearded, the beard in the latter case being elaborately designed and very well drawn; there also, as in some other instances, his cloak is lined with *vair*. In fourteenth-century paintings, his gipon, or doublet, is frequently looped over his belt, to clear the water through which he wades, and beneath it are seen breeches tied at the knee; but in the following century he is swathed in a voluminous cloak, floating free behind him and to the sides, so that little or nothing is seen of his other garments. At Fritton his gipon is, or was, patterned in green and blue, and on the background are traces of a diaper of ermine tails and quatrefoils—the former a type of ornament found with some frequency on backgrounds, at least from the early fifteenth century onwards. One of the most interesting representations to survive from our period is that at Fring in Norfolk, of c. 1330, where the river, with fish in it,[4] is drawn in archaic manner, as though heaped up about the Saint's legs, and there is black underpainting to the flesh tints, which have, however, fallen away almost entirely. The gipon was once green, as may still be deduced from remaining traces, and on the background is a diaper of quatrefoil flowers in red. The whole is framed by borders of scroll-work in green on

[1] Didron, I, 373; Ezekiel, IX, 4.
[2] Mâle, *L'Art religieux du XIIe siècle en France*, Paris, 1922, 245-6; Lydgate, *Pilgrimage of the Life of Man*, 329-30.
[3] Tristram, *Eng. Med. Wall Painting*, 1950, 123-4, pls. 11, 12.
[4] ibid., 1944, pl. 33 (Hardham, Sussex, example of 'heaped' water, in Baptism of Christ).

black, and the work, in its original state, was clearly of the best type. At Brisley in Norfolk a painting of *c.* 1360, also a superior example, is flanked in most unusual fashion, by two small figures, respectively those of St. Andrew, with titular cross, and perhaps St. Bartholomew.

St. Christopher evidently enjoyed very great esteem as one of the group of Saints, known, chiefly abroad, as the Fourteen Holy Helpers, who became most popular, here as elsewhere, about the time of the Black Death.[1] It therefore seems strange at first sight that 'histories' of his life and martyrdom, as distinct from single figures of him, are so rare with us. None, in fact, survive from the fourteenth century, although several most elaborate 'histories' illustrate the legends of less prominent 'Helpers' like St. Catherine and St. Margaret. The explanation is evidently that, despite the rich content of his story, it was eclipsed as a subject for wall-painting by the complex symbolism that gradually came to be associated with representations of him, because he was regarded as protector of Man the Spiritual Pilgrim.[2] Thus, as time went on, his personal story, for some reason never very popular as a theme for illustration, was almost entirely neglected, and paintings of him became, to an ever-increasing extent, allegorical in content. Together with those of his 'companion', St. George, though it is less obvious in the latter case, they in fact were in large part allegories.

St. Christopher, too, in some degree typified the Third Estate, or the Common Man, and St. George, who is often found opposite to or near him on our church walls, represented the Second Estate, and, in particular, Knighthood.[3] As is well known, the obligations of the different Estates frequently provided themes for sermons; and at our period ordinary church wall-paintings, as should never be forgotten, undoubtedly fulfilled the function of sermon illustrations. The obligations of Knighthood were thus defined:—to support the Church; to defend the weak; to uphold the right; and to punish evildoers. How these duties, or some of them, were 'translated' into pictorial symbols, may be seen in renderings of the legend of St. George, which show the symbolic Lamb, the helpless Princess, and the defeated Dragon of Evil.

Towards the end of the fourteenth century and in the fifteenth, representations of St. Christopher, when they developed fully as allegories, gave considerable scope to painters. At the sides of the river forded by the Saint, in its waters, or in the trees and hills about it, are seen various figures, creatures, and so on, some of them familiar, some fantastic, and all, as can hardly be questioned, included for the sake of their symbolism. Even the mill, sometimes on the heights above the river; the fisherman, often on the banks of the stream; the hermit, with lantern and hermitage (though they related primarily to the Saint's legend)[4]—none of these are idle fancies, nor were they introduced by the painter merely in order to fill his allotted space, and to complete his picture, however delightfully they may do so. It is true that in 'reading' his work, it must be borne in mind that there is much confusion in pictorial symbolism of this kind; and, in particular, that the animals and birds represented may have varying and

---

[1] The cult is traceable to Krems in Austria as early as 1284.

[2] *Ayenbite of Inwyt*, 253; Owst, *Literature and Pulpit in Medieval England*, 1933, 103; *Middle English Sermons*, ed. Ross, 1940, S.14, 74.　　　　[3] Owst, *Preaching in Medieval England*, 1926, 264.

[4] As are the Princess and the Dragon to that of St. George.

even conflicting significations. Nevertheless, in the case of paintings of St. Christopher, there is no reason to despair of reaching approximate certainty in interpretation; for in them subsidiary features evidently relate to one of their main motifs—that of the Saint as protector of Man the Spiritual Pilgrim. These features, too, are drawn from the sermons and religious literature of the times. The idea of Christian pilgrimage through the world and its perils was prominently in men's minds during the fourteenth and fifteenth centuries. For example, in the *Ayenbite of Inwyt*, or Remorse of Conscience (1340),[1] it is said that all good men are strangers in the world, because they are out of their country, Paradise, and so think only of completing their journey through life to reach their abiding place, the Heavenly City.[2] The last cry in *Piers Plowman* (1362–1393)[3] rings out—'I will become a pilgrim, and wander world-wide, to seek Piers the Plowman'—or Christ. From a brass of 1407 to a man called Palmer, named like the pilgrim from the Holy Land who was distinguished by carrying a branch of palm strapped to his bourdon,[4] there is recorded this punning inscription:

> *Palmers al our faders were*
> *I a Palmer livyd here*
> *And travylled still, til worne wyth age*
> *I endyd this worlds pylgrymage*
> *On the blyst assension day*
> *In the cherful month of May.*

With all this in mind, we may first consider in detail the chief persons and objects seen in paintings of St. Christopher, and then the animals and birds. The Hermit, according to legend, was encountered by the giant Reprobus (as the Saint, before conversion, was named) in the course of his search for 'the greatest Prince that was in the world' to 'serve and obey'. Though instructed 'diligently' by the Hermit, Christopher would have none of advice tendered to him that he should serve God by fasting and prayer, but said bluntly 'I wot not what it is; I may do no such thing'. He agreed however to the suggestion that his service should take the form of acts of mercy, and that he should use his great strength by helping those who were unable to ford a dangerous torrent. Over it, as we know from the legend, he eventually bore the Holy Child. The Hermit and his chapel would seem to have symbolized in the pictures prayer or contemplation, and his lantern the light of faith, but about this we cannot approach certainty, however probable it may seem. The Fisherman, however, harmless enough in aspect and often dressed in the latest fashion, is without doubt Satan, the 'fisherman of Hell' who takes the fish (man) by the throat.[5] The Mermaid, rocking on the waves with her mirror, represents Worldly Gladness,[6] or else Pride; these are closely allied dangers, the latter being, of course, chief of the Seven Deadly Sins. Near by, the Ship

[1] Owst, *Literature and Pulpit*, 1933, 103; *Middle English Sermons*, ed. Ross, 1940, S.14, 74.

[2] *Ayenbite of Inwyt*, 23: 'All good men in this world are strangers and pilgrims . . . they think only of fulfilling their journeys to come to their heritage, which is the city of paradise.'   [3] C. text.

[4] The palm may be seen strapped to the bourdon in the painting of St. Edward and the Pilgrim at Forthampton Court near Tewkesbury, and was formerly visible at Faversham in Kent.

[5] *Ayenbite of Inwyt*, 23, 1866, 238, 150; Owst, *Literature and Pulpit*, 1933, 395, 396, n.1.

[6] ibid., 61; Lydgate, *Pilgrimage of the Life of Man*, 396, 573, (merman) 574.

at rest on the waters signifies Religion, and is there to help the Pilgrim 'to pass the great sea of the perilous world'. [1] A popular homiletic figure, the Ship is found as far back as the eleventh century. Occasionally it is, however, a type of the Good Man—good 'not because painted with gay colours', not because the prow is silvered or gilt, but as being steady, firm and swift to meet 'the oncoming sea'. The Sea, [2] in the homilies, is always the 'Sea of the World'—the bitter sea of this dangerous world. The Windmill —at first sight most puzzling of all features in the paintings we are studying—if it is intended for 'a mill that turns but does not grind', [3] symbolizes Sloth, another Deadly Sin, and one of the Pilgrim's greatest perils. But even if, as seems very likely, it should most often be interpreted thus, it may, by a characteristically medieval reversal, signify the Heavenly Bread, [4] made of corn brought to the Mill and ground, the grindstones being scorn and derision, and the mill-sails turned by the winds of envy. A closely similar idea has been traced in the carving of a twelfth-century capital at Vézelay in France, where St. Paul turns a hand-mill [5] to grind corn. The Mill was once to be seen also in the landscape background to a wall-painting of St. George at Kersey [6] in Suffolk, and at Belton in the same county it appeared in a rendering of the Three Living and the Three Dead. In the latter, it may have stood for Sloth, and as a reminder of the passage of time. It is to be noted, however, that at Fairford in Gloucestershire it is seen in the east window, of *c.* 1490, in the *Corpus Christi* Chapel. At St. Mary-in-the-Marsh, in Kent, a chalice of the late sixteenth century has on the base a small post-mill, which may or may not be a goldsmith's mark. In wall-paintings of St. Christopher, the Mill is, or was, seen at Baunton in Gloucestershire, and Henstridge and Ditcheat in Somerset, Gawsworth in Cheshire, and Whimple in Devonshire. It is occasionally found in illumination; opposite the magnificent *Beatus* page of the famous Windmill Psalter, *c.* 1270, for instance.

Fish swim in the water around St. Christopher's feet, and are seldom, if ever, omitted; in course of time, different recognizable species appear, and one may suspect an unpleasant significance in the snake-like eel sometimes twined about the Saint's ankles and evidently hindering his passage. But the ordinary fish represented are more likely to be 'the fish that bathes and nourishes itself in running water' [7]—that is, man strengthened by patience in adversity. The Crab, that is occasionally seen, may have served as a warning to bailiffs who sinned [8] in carrying out their duties—or, perhaps more probably, as an admonition [9] to the worldly, for its 'sidewise sidling' did not escape observation. The Owl, 'that of death the bode bringeth', [10] seems an obvious warning, but may signify blindness in matters of faith, and hatred of the light of truth. [11] It is noticeable that paintings of St. Christopher are not infrequently placed close to representations of the Seven Deadly Sins, as at Cranborne in Dorset and Crostwight in Norfolk.

[1] *Ayenbite of Inwyt*, 1340, E.E.T.S., 23, 1866, 112–13; Owst, *Literature and Pulpit*, 1933, 68.
[2] ibid., 68, 69.   [3] Lydgate, *Pilgrimage of the Life of Man*, 375.
[4] ibid., 142.   [5] Mâle, *L'Art religieux du XIIᵉ siècle en France*, 1922, 167.
[6] See Salmon, *The Windmill in English Medieval Art*, B.A.A.J., 3rd ser., VI, 1941, 88–102.
[7] *Ayenbite of Inwyt*, 1866, 167.   [8] Owst, *Literature and Pulpit*, 1933, 326, n.2.
[9] Lydgate, *Minor Poems*, ed. Halliwell, 58–60.   [10] Chaucer, ed. Skeat, Oxford, 1915, 106.
[11] Mâle, *L'Art religieux du XIIᵉ siècle en France*, 1922, 333; also a figure of Envy—*Ayenbite of Inwyt*, 23, 27. The significance of the paintings would appear to have been largely forgotten by the time of Molanus.

THE CHRIST OF THE TRADES

Widely separated areas of England and Wales, in counties as far apart as Buckinghamshire, Berkshire, Gloucestershire, Sussex, Suffolk, Cornwall, Monmouthshire and Pembrokeshire, show an unusual type of wall-painting in which Christ is depicted, not enthroned as in the Doom, but standing, almost always with arms upraised, to display the wounds in the palms of the hands, as was usual in a Doom. The wounds in the feet are visible and also that in the side, since the figure is clad only in a loin-cloth. Around the Body are tools of different kinds. They are sometimes arranged as a 'glory' about the head, as, in a painting which once existed at Stedham in Sussex; almost invariably they also encircle the entire figure, which they sometimes seem intended to pierce at the edges. In considering this last feature, it should however be borne in mind that all surviving English examples of the subject are of a poor type, and so were hastily executed in return for low pay. One natural result of this would be, that having completed the Christ, a craftsman would surround it as quickly as possible with the numerous implements, and in his haste would not be very careful to finish strokes of the brush exactly short of its outline. In England at least there are no known examples of which it can be said with confidence that the intention was to show the tools cutting into the figure; and foreign works, like that at Ormalingen in Switzerland are so heavily repainted that they are not in detail convincing.

It seems evident, however, that the idea emphasized in these paintings is that of labour, and of labour in some relation to Christ. It is clear also that sometimes, as at Stedham where the tools form a 'nimbus' about the head, and at Fingringhoe in Essex, where hands hold them up to Him, they are intended to show that through honest labour they become worthy offerings. By contrast, in certain paintings, and perhaps in almost all, they have no doubt also been introduced to illustrate means by which He may be wounded, as, for example, through Sabbath breaking. Both aspects of the main idea —labour in relation to Christ—may sometimes be combined, as is indicated by an inscription on a scroll held by an Angel above the figure at Fingringhoe, which reads: IN OMNIA OPERE MEMENTO FINIS—in all work remember the end—the true end, that is, of man. A proverb of the fifteenth century offers a slight variant in expression of the same idea—'Thinke on the ende or thee begyn, and thou schalt never be thral to syn.' The latin phrase quoted above is recorded as formerly visible in the windows of a house at Norwich.[1] On account of one or two other inscriptions found abroad, it has been thought that the sole relation of the Christ of the Trades is to Sabbath-breaking; but the phrase we have just been considering in its various forms shows conclusively that this alone is too narrow an interpretation of it.[2] The painting at Fingringhoe, with its inscription, is obviously of some general application.

[1] Woodforde, *The Norwich School of Glass-Painting in the Fifteenth Century*, 1950, 199–200.

[2] Tristram, *Burlington Magazine*, XXXI, 1917, 135; d'Evelyn, *Modern Language Notes*, Baltimore, XXIV, 1919, 247; Saxl, Aller Tugenden und Laster Abbildung, *Festschrift für Julius Schlosser*, 1927, 104; Borenius and Tristram, *English Medieval Painting*, Paris, 1929, 29–35; Ryan, *Art Bulletin*, xl, 1929, 302; James, *Suffolk and Norfolk*, 1933, 74–5; Woodforde, *Downside Review*, LV, 1937, 1–6; Evans, *English Art, 1307–1461*, Oxford, 1949, Appendix A; Woodforde, *The Norwich School of Glass-Painting in the Fifteenth Century*, 1950, 185–96.

As we shall see, when studying the various paintings, their central theme, of Christ surrounded by the tools of the trades, and other objects, is often slightly varied in meaning by emphasis derived through association; this might be expected, since medieval thought was seldom so static as to be confined to only one aspect of a subject. As well as a large variety of tools—including saw, axe, hammer, mallet, wheel, knife, pincers, hatchet, anvil and tongs—objects used purely for idle amusement are depicted. At Amney St. Mary, in Gloucestershire, in our earliest painting of the kind, which is late fourteenth century, there is on the left an archer, and opposite him a man with a 'singing arrow', held in such a way as to suggest that he is about to aim it at the Body of Christ. Such arrows as this, still in use in Tibet,[1] have a blunt, wooden head, perforated in order to hum like a whistling top, when passing through the air. In a marginal illumination of the fourteenth century,[2] a woman, poised gracefully, is about to loose one at a dismayed rabbit. Further, Stow gives an account of a May-time visit to the woods on the part of Henry VIII and his Court, when these arrows were a feature of the day's entertainment. Dice and playing-cards are also seen in the paintings, as at Hessett in Suffolk. It is not necessary, once again, to go further than the sermons for an explanation, for among sins of the labouring classes there are enumerated—shooting at the butts; useless and unnecessary occupations[3] such as chess and dice-playing; 'games' and 'drinkings'; as well as Sabbath-breaking, the last being excused by craftsmen on the plea that others would do whatever they themselves might refuse.

It is not improbable that the scales seen in some of the paintings, as at Littleham in Devon, relate, not to some specific occupation, or, if so, only in part; but are symbolic, and connected with 'fals labour, taking more than thou hast deserved in fals servys, in falsenesse of thi craft', or hardly doing in two days what could be done in one. As the Scales of Justice, they form what may be termed 'pictorial shorthand' for the Weighing of Souls, or Divine Justice. The medieval association of the scales with the idea of Divine Justice is illustrated, for instance, in a poem of the fourteenth century, where it is said that the Christ of the Apocalypse, who 'rod on ye blak horse', had a 'weye in His hand', in token that He was just.[4] Then, too, among the Orders of Angels, Thrones hold the Scales, representing as they do Divine Justice. When found in a Christ of the Trades, as is not infrequently the case, wheels also may have been included for the sake of association with their complex symbolism, as well as for their obvious connexion with the wheelwright's craft. If it be objected that all this complicated symbolism would not have been understood by the craftsman in the fourteenth and fifteenth centuries, the reply is that he was familiar with much comparable symbolism from sermons delivered in his parish church. It is hardly surprising that, as has been noted by one of our best-known historians, the 'mysterious allegorical style' of John Ball's well-known message in the rising of 1381, 'seems to have been the favourite of the lower classes of the day'.[5]

---

[1] *National Geographic Magazine*, vol. XC, no. 2, Aug. 1946, 191.
[2] Millar, *English Illuminated Manuscripts*, II, 1928, pl. 50; Stow, *Survey of London*, 90 (Everyman ed.).
[3] Owst, *Literature and Pulpit*, 1933, 362-3.   [4] *Lyrics of the Fourteenth Century*, ed. Brown, 1924, 258.
[5] Trevelyan, *England in the Age of Wycliffe*, 1912, 204; he notes the popularity at the time of *Piers Plowman*.

The idea of Christ as 'chief of all craftsmen and source of all the arts in the world' is expressed in an invocation opening a letter from an Icelandic painter of the thirteenth century to a monk who was his friend and who had evidently asked him for a certain recipe.[1] In a painting of the Sienese School, St. Catherine of Siena, who is represented in her life as wise and subtle of mind, appears as patroness of the arts,[2] against a background patterned with implements, such as shears, hammer, saw, carpenter's rule and plane, pestle and mortar, combs for carding wool, spindle and distaff, and a pair of compasses. The compasses are frequently seen in the hands of the Almighty in medieval pictures of the Creation, just as they sometimes appear on gravestones of master-masons. The spindle and distaff are borne triumphantly through the Gates of Heaven in a wall-painting placed beside the Christ of the Trades at Amney St. Mary. At Ramersdorf in Germany an Angel leads the Blessed into Heaven, and they carry the tools of their labour. A painting of St. Osyth, patroness of housewives, at Horley in Oxfordshire, has the background covered with implements of housewifery. Mâle has remarked that, in French cathedrals, knowledge and manual labour hold places of equal honour;[3] at Chartres and Bourges, there are shown in windows given by the Guilds, the badges of the trades—including trowel, hammer, wool-carding comb, baker's shovel, and butcher's knife. It seems evident from all this that the tools around the Christ of the Trades have a very wide significance. The suggestion that in all these paintings Christ is shown as wounded by the sins of all manner of people, is too narrow in its scope, as becomes clear beyond reasonable doubt if an attempt is made to relate them to contemporary preaching and to literature. Another suggestion, that the tools are not in fact tools, but Instruments of the Passion, the list of which was very much extended in the fifteenth century, is ingenious but does not survive close examination.

There is abundant evidence to show that medieval moralists and preachers did not regard the poorer craftsman and labourer solely as a sometimes hardworking and meritorious social inferior. Admonition formed a part of the content of the 'Piers Plowman' paintings, as they have with some reason been termed, but, by comparison, the negative part. The mendicant preachers, and in fact most preachers, as well as Langland and other writers, championed and encouraged in their hard lot those of the poor who were honest and hardworking:[4] 'the simple working folk . . . the righteous poor'; 'patientes pauperes'; 'fideles simplices'; 'the trewe pore peple'; 'goddes knyghtes', proved by 'angres, tribulaciouns and woo'. It has been remarked that in the preachers Bozon and Bromyard there is not merely sympathy with the fate of the good labourer, but the belief that of such is the kingdom of Heaven.[5] 'Les pauvres seront élévés au jour de Jugement', said Nicol Bozon the Franciscan, speaking strongly in sympathy with the poor man, defenceless before the spoilers; and near him, on the wall, as he preached may have been visible the wounded hands, raised Heavenward, of the Christ of the Trades. Manual labour, said Bromyard the Dominican, is 'sometimes worthy of a place amongst good works meritory of life eternal'; Langland gives unqualified praise to the

---

[1] Tristram, *Eng. Med. Wall Painting*, 1950, 404–5.   [2] Jameson, *Sacred and Legendary Art*, II, 478.
[3] Mâle, *Religious Art in France of the Thirteenth Century*, 1913, 64–75.
[4] Owst, *Literature and Pulpit*, 1933, 568–9.   [5] ibid., 570.

virtuous labouring poor, and Sloth is the Deadly Sin that he sees as Pride's companion in leading the attack on Conscience. Lydgate has this passage: [1]

> Ploughman, carterys, with othir laborerys
> Dichers, delverys, that great travaylle endure,
> Which berne up alle, and have doon many yerys,
> The staatis alle set here in portrature.

From which it seems reasonable to conclude that they found some place in the paintings on the walls of our churches. Langland has what is in effect a good verbal picture of a Christ of the Trades:

> Ich fel eft-sones a slepe and sodeynliche me mette,
> That peers the plouhman was peynted al blody,
> And cam yn with a croys by-fore ye comune peuple,
> And ryght like in alle lymes to our lord ihesu;
> And thenne calde ich conscience to kenne me ye sothe.
> 'Is this ihesus ye Iouster?' quath ich 'that Iuwes duden to dethe,
> Other is hit peers plouhman? ho peynted hym so rede?'
> Quath conscience, and kneolede tho 'these aren christes armes,
> Hus colours and hus cote-armuer and he that cometh so blody
> Hit is crist with his crois conquerour of crystine'. [2]

It may now be considered whether any significance can be seen or suspected in the apparently deliberate juxtaposition of the Christ of the Trades with other subjects. It is sometimes, as at Amney St. Mary and Stedham, placed opposite a painting of St. George, representations of whom in some degree symbolize the duties of knighthood. In such an arrangement it hardly seems far-fetched to discern intentional 'illustration' of such passages as that in *Piers Plowman*, where Piers and a knight exchange comments on the general theme, that all should work in their different ways for the good of the community. Piers ends thus: [3]

> Yow profre yow so faire,
> That I shal swynke and swete and sowe for us bothe,
> And other laboures do for thi loue al my lyf-tyme,
> In couenaunt that thow kepe holi kirke and myselve
> Fro wastours and fro wykked men that this worlde struyeth.

In the Rebellion of 1381 it seems hardly surprising that the insurgents, led by Wat Tyler, bore with them two banners of St. George. Further, the poor and oppressed must have seen in their condition the fruit of the Deadly Sin of Pride: 'Whan adam delf and eve span . . .whare was than the pride of man that now mars his mede' (meed, reward). It is well known that many of the poorer clergy sympathized with, or even

---

[1] Lydgate, *Minor Poems*, ed. Halliwell, 1831, 211; Bozon, ed. Toulmin Smith and Meyer, Paris, 1889, 11, 12, 13, 19, 38, 39, 143.
[2] *Piers Plowman*, C. text, 1362–1393, ed. Skeat, 1873, 399.
[3] ibid., 311.

led, the rebels in different parts of the country; [1] and it has been remarked that 'we must acknowledge the sermons, however little so intended, as a primary literature of secular revolt, and their authors as the heralds of political strife and future social liberties'.[2] 'Carte and Plowh', as Lydgate says, 'they ber up al, the clergye and the chevalrye.'[3] At Stedham, the Christ of the Trades stands on a cart, probably in allusion to this saying. Further, the painting is linked in design with a *Mater Misericordiae*, who is framed within a niche and extends her protective cloak about a crowd of suppliants. Fingringhoe, where, as we have noted, hands hold up instruments of toil before the Christ, has near it an Image of Pity. At Breage, in Cornwall, there is, or was, a Christ, whose Body is covered with wounds, but whose head is crowned, no doubt in allusion to the crown of 'life eternal', believed to be in some circumstances merited through a life of manual labour.[4] This painting, with one other, are perhaps the only examples in England in which the hands are not raised to display the wounds, as they are in a Doom, for here the left hangs downward and the right is brought forward across the chest. At Broughton in Buckinghamshire there is, or was, a painting of Christ mounted, perhaps as Langland's 'Jesus the Jouster', and nearby is a representation of St. George.

The shortcomings of the labourer were not forgotten in these paintings. At Walsham-le-Willows, in Suffolk, to one side of Christ's feet, is a representation of the Deadly Sin of Wrath, with two youths fighting, and opposite are two meeting, with a mounted man in the background. It may be suggested, though with diffidence, that Wrath's opposite, or remedy, Concord, is shown here. Hessett has a Tree of the Seven Deadly Sins high on the wall, and below it a Christ of the Trades. Among the tools around it, which include a wheel and scythe, are also a jug, a playing-card—the six of diamonds —and a musical pipe; thus the allusion to failings and temptations is unmistakable. None the less, neither here nor elsewhere was the thirty-ninth chapter of Ecclesiasticus forgotten, where it is said of the craftsmen and labourers—'All these put their trust in their hands . . . they will maintain the fabric of the world, and in the handywork of their craft is their prayer.'

[1] Trevelyan, *England in the Age of Wycliffe*, 1912, 195–6, 204, 220, 222, 254–5. See map showing area of rising in 1381. *Lyrics of the Fourteenth Century*, ed. Brown, no. 81. A Song of Mortality.

[2] Owst, *Literature and Pulpit*, 1933, 236.   [3] Lydgate, *Pilgrimage of the Life of Man*, 310–11.

[4] There are one or two doubtful examples of paintings of St. Christopher, perhaps with the same crown. Didron (I, 354–60) mentions numerous instances of tools in great variety as represented on tomb-stones, from very early times, both in Italy and France; but the significance is different to that which is discussed above. For references relating to the Christ of the Trades, other than those given previously, see Owst, *Preaching in Medieval England*, 80, 94, 295, 296; idem, *Literature and Pulpit*, 220, 557, 585–6; *Piers Plowman*, ed. Skeat, pt. IV, 1885 (as Christ), xxi, 148, 308, 347, 432; Wells, *The Vision of Piers Plowman*, xxv, 299. For list of Instruments of the Passion, to compare with tools seen in the paintings, see, for example, *Legends of the Holy Rood*, E.E.T.S., 46, 1871. Those among the *Piers Plowman* paintings that were executed in the poorer churches may well have had for some of the priests and their congregations a double meaning, more safely expressed in painting than otherwise. They are almost all of a comparatively unskilled type.

BIBLIOGRAPHY

The list of books given below refers only to works frequently consulted during preparation of Chapters I–V.

In the Catalogue section a short bibliography is given at the end of each separate account; these bibliographies, had there been sufficient space, might in most cases have been much extended. A fair number of descriptions in the Catalogue are based solely on notes made over a long period by E. W. Tristram and Mrs. M. Bardswell, and exchanged between them; further, a large number of such descriptions, though a reference to some publication or publications may be given, have been much amplified and also corrected by them.

Apocryphal New Testament, ed. Wake & Lardner.

Ayenbite of Inwyt, ed. Morris, E.E.T.S., 1866.

Bernath, *An East Anglian Primitive in Germany, Burlington Magazine*, LII, 1928.

Bishop and Prideaux, *The Builders of the Cathedral Church of St. Peter in Exeter*, 1922.

Black Prince's Register, IV, 1933.

Blackburne, *Decorative Painting*, 1847.

Booke of Margery Kempe, E.E.T.S., I, 1940.

Borenius, *English Primitives*, British Academy, 1924; *St. Thomas Becket in Art*, 1932.

Borenius & Tristram, *English Medieval Painting*, 1927.

Bozon, *Les Contes Moralisés*, ed. Toulmin Smith & Meyer, 1889.

Brand, *Popular Antiquities*, 1813.

Brayley and Britton, *History of the Ancient Palace and Late Houses of Parliaments at Westminster*, 1836.

Brindley, *Notes on the Mural Paintings of St. Christopher in English Churches, Antiquaries Journal*, IV, 1924.

Bunim, *Space in Medieval Painting & the Forerunners of Perspective*, N.Y., 1940.

Butler, *Lives of the Saints.*

Carleton Williams, *Mural Paintings of the Three Living and the Three Dead in England, Journal British Archaeological Association*, VII, 1942.

Cave, *Archaeologia*, vol. 85, 1936, *The Roof Bosses of Lincoln Cathedral*; *Roof Bosses in Medieval Churches*, 1948.

Cennino Cennini, *The Book of the Art of*, trans. Herringham, 1899.

Chaucer, *The Complete Works of*, ed. Skeat, 1915.

Christie, *English Medieval Embroidery*, 1938.

Collins Baker & James, *British Painting*, 1933.

Constable, *Catalogue of Exhibition of British Primitive Paintings*. Royal Academy of Art, 1923.

Conway, *English Medieval Painting, Burlington Magazine*, LIII, 1928: ibid., LV, 1929.

Coulton, *Art and the Reformation*, 1928; *Chaucer & his England*, 1937; *Life in the Middle Ages*, 1928, 4 vols.; *Medieval Panorama*, 1947.

Dart, *Westmonasterium*, 1742, I, II; *History and Antiquities of Canterbury Cathedral*, 1726.

Devon, *Issues of the Exchequer*, 1837.

Didron, *Christian Iconography*, I, II.

Druce, *The Medieval Bestiaries, British Archaeological Association Journal*, XXV, 1919; *Symbolism of the Crocodile in the Middle Ages, Archaeological Journal*, 1909, LXVI.

Dugdale, *Monasticon Anglicanum*, 5 vols.; *History of St. Paul's Cathedral*, 1818.

Early South-English Legendary, ed. Horstmann, E.E.T.S., 1887.

Eastlake, *Materials for a History of Oil Painting*, 1847.

Englefield, *The History of the Painter-Stainers Company of London*, 1923.

Evans, *English Art, 1307–1461*, 1949.

BIBLIOGRAPHY

Freyhan, *The Three Living and the Three Dead, Burlington Magazine*, LIV.

Golden Legend, I–VII, Temple Classics, 1900.

Green, *Painted Lid of a Reliquary Chest*, Hampshire Field Club and Archaeological Society, X, 1926–31.

Handlyng Synne, ed. Furnivall, E.E.T.S., 1901.

Harvey, *Gothic England*, 1947; *The Gothic World*, 1950.

Hastings, *Parliament House*, 1950.

Hudson Turner, *Some Account of Domestic Architecture in England from Edward I to Richard II*, 2 Vols., 1853.

James, *Sculptured Bosses in the Roof of the Bauchun Chapel in Norwich Cathedral*, 1908; *An English Medieval Sketch-book*, No. 1916 in the Pepysian Library, Magdalene College, Cambridge, Walpole Society, XIII, 1924–5; *Blomefield's Norfolk Supplement*, 1929; *Suffolk and Norfolk*, 1930.

Jameson, *Sacred and Legendary Art*, I, II.

Johnson: *English Painting from the Seventh Century to the Present Day*, 1932.

Journal of the Warburg and Courtauld Institutes, V, 1942; VI, 1943.

Jusserand, *English Wayfaring Life in the Middle Ages*, 1891.

Keepe, *Westminster Abbey*, 1682.

Kelly and Schwabe, *A Short History of Costume and Armour*, I, 1066–1485, 1931.

Keyser, *List of Buildings Having Mural Decorations*, 1883.

Lay Folks Mass Book, ed. Simmons, E.E.T.S., 1879.

Lethaby, *Medieval Art*, 1904; *Westminster Abbey and the King's Craftsmen*; *London and Westminster Painters in the Middle Ages*, Walpole Society, I, 1911–12; *Medieval Paintings at Westminster*, Proceedings British Academy, 1927.

Lillie, *The Retable at Thornham Parva, Burlington Magazine*, LXIII, 1933.

Little, *Franciscan History & Legend in English Medieval Art*, 1937.

Lydgate, *Minor Poems of Dan John Lydgate*, ed. Halliwell, E.E.T.S., 1831; *Minor Poems of John Lydgate*, ed. MacCracken, E.E.T.S., 1911; *Pilgrimage of the Life of Man*, from Deguilville, E.E.T.S., 1899, 1901, 1904; *Reson & Sensuallyte*, I, E.E.T.S., 1901.

Mâle, *L'Art religieux du XIIe siècle en France*, 1922; *Religious Art in France of the Thirteenth Century*, trans. Nussey, 1913.

Malleus Maleficarum, trans. Summers, 1928.

Middle English Sermons, ed. Woodburn O. Ross, E.E.T.S., 1940.

Millar, *English Illuminated Manuscripts*, I, II, 1926, 1928.

Mirk, *Festial*, ed. Erbe, E.E.T.S., pt. I, XCVI, 1905; *Instructions for Parish Priests*, E.E.T.S., 1868.

Neale and Brayley, *History and Antiquities of the Abbey Church of St. Peter, Westminster*, 1818, I, 1823, II.

Noppen, *The Westminster Apocalypse and its Source, Burlington Magazine*, LXI, 1932.

Oakeshott, *The Sequence of English Medieval Art*, 1950.

Owst, *Preaching in Medieval England*, 1926; *Literature and Pulpit in Medieval England*, 1933.

Parker and Turner, *Domestic Architecture in England during the Middle Ages*, 1851–9.

Piers Plowman, ed. Skeat, I–IV.

Prior and Gardner, *Medieval Figure-Sculpture in England*, 1912.

Proceedings Against Dame Alice Kyteler, Camden Soc., 1843.

Prymer, or Lay Folks Prayer Book, pt. I, ed. Littlehales, E.E.T.S., 1895.

Read, *English Stained Glass*, 1926; *English Art., Burlington Magazine*, LXIII, 1933.

Religious Lyrics of the Fourteenth Century, ed. Carleton Brown, 1924.

Rickert, *Chaucer's World*, 1950.

Royal Commission on Historical Monuments.

Westminster Abbey, I, 1924.

Rushforth, *Medieval Christian Imagery*, 1936.

Rymer's *Foedera*, I, 1066–1377, 1869.

Salmon, *The Windmill in English Medieval Art, British Archaeological Association Journal*, VI, 1941.

Saunders, O.E., *English Illumination*, II, 1928; *A History of English Art in the Middle Ages*, 1932.

Scharf, *The Westminster Abbey Portrait of King Richard II*, 1867.

Scott, *Gleanings from Westminster Abbey*, 1863.

Seinte Marherete, ed. Mack, E.E.T.S., 1934.

BIBLIOGRAPHY

Shaw, *The Early English School of Portraiture, Burlington Magazine*, LXV, 1934.

Smith, *Antiquities of Westminster*, 1807.

St. John Hope, *On a Painted Table or Reredos of the Fourteenth Century in the Cathedral Church of Norwich*, Norfolk Archaeology, XIII, 1898; *Windsor Castle*, 2 vols., 1913.

Storck, *Aspects of Death in English Art and Poetry, Burlington Magazine*, XXI.

Summers, *History of Witchcraft and Demonology*, 1926.

Swartwout, *The Monastic Craftsman*, 1932.

Thompson, *The Materials of Medieval Painting*, 1936.

Three Kings of Cologne, ed. Horstmann, E.E.T.S., 1886.

Trevelyan, *England in the Age of Wycliff*, 1912.

Tristram, *English Medieval Wall Painting*, I, 1944; II, 1950; *Piers Plowman in English Medieval Wall Painting, Burlington Magazine*, XXXI, 1917; The Wilton Diptych, *The Month*, N.S.I, II, 1949.

Vallance, *English Church Screens*, 1936.

Vices and Virtues, Stowe MS., 240, *c.* 1200, ed. Holthausen, E.E.T.S., 1888.

Victoria and Albert Museum, *Cat. of an Exhibition of English Medieval Art*, 1930.

Wall, *Medieval Wall Paintings*, 1914.

Watson, *The Early Iconography of the Tree of Jesse*, 1934.

West's *Notebook*, Victoria and Albert Museum, 1844, 1860–4.

Whaite, *St. Christopher in English Medieval Wall-Painting*, 1929.

William of Palerne, E.E.T.S., 1867, ed. Skeat.

Woodforde, *The Norwich School of Glass-Painting in the Fifteenth Century*, 1950.

PART TWO

The Catalogue

ABINGDON, Berks ST. HELEN

In the fourteenth century a general reconstruction of the church was undertaken, in the course of which the earlier building was converted into two aisles, the inner of these being used as a Lady Chapel; here the ceiling was decorated with some elaboration (?) c. 1390. About 25 ft. 7 in. in length, it comprises a central horizontal portion flanked by two sloping sections; the former, 4 ft. 4 in. in width, is divided into square and triangular panels by means of moulded ribs, with carved bosses at their intersections and rich tracery between them, the whole having doubtless been coloured originally, though now nothing survives; the latter are composed of panels of an average height of 4 ft. 9 in. and a width of 9 in., arranged in pairs, thirteen on either side. Each pair is divided from the next by a slender buttress terminating in a crocketed finial, and is framed by a crocketed ogee arch with tracery in the spandrels over it, enclosing two narrow arches, their heads cusped and the spandrel between them filled by a quatrefoiled circle. Within these arches figures are depicted, thirty-eight of which survive, some of them in a good state of preservation, and others much perished; but few of them are in their original positions, and the sequence has thus been lost owing to changes made during a restoration in 1872. They originally formed part of a Tree of Jesse, and stand upon the branches of a painted vine trail, which once ran horizontally from end to end of the ceiling, passing over the dividing ribs; and they represent, alternately, Prophets and Kings, the latter having evidently been arranged in chronological order and usually paired with a contemporary Prophet. Their names, some of which survive, were painted in 'black letter', with red capitals, on the coloured and carved wall-plate immediately below them. The Kings are crowned and hold sceptres, the Prophets bear in their hands inscribed scrolls; and the scheme culminates in a Crucifixion, in panel 25, in which the cross is composed of a lily rising from a pot of lilies placed between the kneeling figures of the Arch-angel Gabriel in panel 24 and of the Virgin, in panel 26, which form an Annunciation occupying these two panels. Gold is freely used, and the tints comprise green, blue, scarlet and plum colour, with some brown and yellow, against a ground of vermilion. The vine stem is carried out in dark grey, with the leaves in green.

Lysons, vol. I, 2 (Berks), 225; Blackburne, *Decorative Painting*, 1847, 46–7; Keyser, *Mural Decorations*, 1883; *Victoria County Hist., Berks*, 1924, IV, 443; Preston, *Berks B. & O.A.J.*, 1936, XL, 115–45, reprs.; Borenius, *Burl. M.*, 1936, LXVIII, 268–76, reprs.

ABBOTS LANGLEY (near Watford) Herts
ST. LAURENCE

The Chancel and Nave

In both chancel and nave are traces of fourteenth-century decoration.

The South Chapel

The chapel appears to have been painted in entirety soon after erection. Around the window in the east wall are remains of colour, the coign-stones and voussoirs having been picked out alternately in red and white; on the wall, on either side of the window-head, is a figure of a Saint, on the north St. Thomas of Canterbury, and on the south St. Laurence. The former, facing frontally, is clad in mass vestments, raises his right hand in blessing, and in his left holds the archiepiscopal cross; the latter, vested as a deacon in alb and dalmatic, turns slightly towards the window-arch, bearing upraised in his right hand the Grid, at which he gazes, and in his left the palm of martyrdom. Both figures, executed in ochres on a ground of white, are of approximately life-size; they are somewhat perished as to detail. On the wall below them, traces remain of horizontal borders, indicating that one, or more, tiers of subjects formerly occupied the lower part of the wall-space.

On the south wall, between the two windows in this wall, and also westward from the westernmost of the two, traces exist of subjects framed within rectangular panels bordered by bands of red ochre, but, apart from vestiges of a fret pattern in one of them and fragments of figures in others, very little remains.

Within a large recess near the doorway is a diaper of roses.[1]

Keyser, *A.J.*, 1901, LVIII, 49; *Victoria County Hist., Herts*, 1908, II, 327; *R.C. Historical Monuments R., Herts*, 1910, 28; *The Times*, viii, ii, 1933; Rouse, *St. Albans A. & A.S.T.*, 1933–5, 29–34, repr. Plate 54*a, b*.

ST. ALBANS, Herts
CATHEDRAL CHURCH OF ST. ALBAN

The Choir and Presbytery

In the north-east corner of the feretory, St. William of York, with a shield of the arms of Fitz-william—*Lozengy argent and gules*, beneath the feet, and below it the inscription SCS WILLMUS; upon the head, inclined slightly towards the right shoulder, a blue mitre, banded in gold and jewelled, is set high upon curled and waved yellow hair, and the face is bearded; the hands are covered by white gloves, the right, with a ring on the second finger, being raised in blessing and the left holding a cross-staff; the figure is vested in a red embroidered amice and red chasuble, a blue dalmatic lined with red, and an alb with an apparel of embroidery in red; on the feet are black, somewhat pointed shoes. The painting is exceptionally well preserved. *c.* 1330.

In a similar position on the opposite side of the chapel, a fragmentary figure of another archbishop, against a white background diapered with quatrefoils and crescents in red; vested in a blue jewelled mitre, an orange embroidered amice, and a purple chasuble lined with blue and having an orphrey embroidered with crosses in red; the dalmatic and alb are not distinguishable; from the left arm hangs an embroidered maniple, coloured orange and fringed with blue, and the left hand holds the cross-staff, the cross, painted in red, being unusually large.

Within the niches round the pedestal which once bore the shrine of St. Alban, remains of painting which comprise leopards and fleurs-de-lis on grounds of red and blue diapered with stars and small roundels.

In the retro-choir, a pattern of roses.

A.J., 1850, VII, 86; Keyser, *Mural Decorations*, 1883; Page, *Archaeologia*, 1902, LVIII, 289; *Victoria County Hist. Herts*, 1908, II, 494–5, frontis.; *R.C. Historical Monuments, Herts*, 1910, 185; Wall, *Medieval Wall Paintings*, 1914, 185, fig. 79.

The Nave

Formerly, the western face of the fifth pier from the west bore a painting in outline of the Adoration of the Magi, a subject repeated in its immediate vicinity towards the south; only a few traces of these works now exist.

'Before this painting stood the altar of St. Mary at the Pillar, erected at the cost of William Wynturshulle, almoner of the monastery, *c.* 1380, in the time of Abbot Thomas de la Mare.'

Lloyd, *A.J.*, 1882, XXXIX, 67, quoting de Amundesham, *Annales*, R.S., I, 442; Keyser, *Mural Decorations*, 1883.

The South Aisle

In the spandrels of a late fourteenth-century doorway, known as the abbot's door, two carved shields, that on the east side charged with the arms of Richard II, that on the west side with those of the abbey, both painted in proper heraldic colours.

Victoria County Hist., Herts, 1908, II, 502.

The North Transept

A vine pattern survives on the splay of one of the windows.

Formerly the pier supporting the central arch on the east side retained ornamental painting, described in the *Builder*, 1864, 722, as follows:

'The face of the pier under the arch is divided into lozenges charged with lions passant and fleurs-de-lys alternately, the colours being buff on a red ground. The return of the face has a single row of vertical lozenges with alternately a lion rampant and a foliated ornament. The next face parallel with the soffit is divided into white and yellow masonry like the Norman [i.e. thirteenth-century] painting. The next return has a row of lozenges charged alternately with crosses and fleurs-de-lys . . .'

Builder, 1864, 722, repr.; Keyser, *Mural Decorations*, 1883; Page, *Archaeologia*, 1902, LVIII, 290, repr.

The Lady Chapel

On the splay of a window on the south side, remains of a scroll and vine pattern on a vermilion ground, with traces of inscriptions in black; and formerly in the passage leading to the chapel, a scroll pattern.

Page, *Archaeologia*, 1902, LVIII, 291.

---

[1] Since this description was written, all the survivals, with the exception of the two figures of Saints, have been whitewashed over.

ALPHETON (near Sudbury) Suffolk
ST. PETER AND ST. PAUL

The Nave

Opposite the south door, a St. Christopher, 10 ft. 9 in. in height by 4 ft. 4 in., discovered in 1903; he is bearded, clad in a red cloak, carries a staff (the top obliterated), and bears on his left shoulder the Holy Child, wearing a cloak spotted in red and holding the Orb. Late fourteenth century.

Munro Cautley, *Suffolk Churches and Their Treasures*, 1938, 218.

ALTON (near Uttoxeter) Staffs
ST. PETER

On the north wall of the nave, at the western end, above the arcade, remains of (?) a rendering of *Les Trois Vifs et les Trois Morts*, consisting of the figure of a man, clad in a hip-length gipon, belted low, dagged at the lower edge and fastened down the centre front with buttons, long hose and pointed shoes, standing, with a hawk on his left wrist, beside a large tree, with birds in its branches. The painting is partially covered by later texts, and the head of the figure is missing. After 1380.

Hurst, *North Staffs Field Club Transactions*, 1934–5, LXIX, 80.

ALVELEY (near Kidderminster) Salop
ST. MARY

The South Aisle

On the east wall, but now almost entirely defaced, an Annunciation and a Visitation.

On the south wall, over the piscina, the Fall of Man; and further to the west, the Seven Deadly Sins, the upper part only surviving, in the centre a crowned female figure, nude, representing Pride, with scrolls terminating in demons, issuing from various parts of the body, on the right a skeleton, emblematic of Death, aiming at her an arrow, and above a trumpeter. On the background a diaper of roses. Late fourteenth century.

Keyser, *Mural Decorations*, 1883; id., *A.J.*, 1892, XLIX, 343; *Shropshire A. & N.H.S.*, 1893, 2nd ser., V, xii; Cranage, *Churches of Shropshire*, 1901, I, 264.

AMBERLEY (near Arundel) Sussex
ST. MICHAEL

The Nave

Near the chancel arch, on the south side, traces of four nimbed figures, apparently survivals from a series of representations of Saints, painted upon a red ground and framed within squares formed by vertical bands decorated with scroll-work in red on yellow, and horizontal bands, of which the only section remaining intact is enriched with bent-riband pattern in red on cream. The lower part of the painted area of wall is covered by a later text, through which, for a distance of approximately 8 ft. downwards from the figures just mentioned, remains of early colouring are visible; and at a height of 9 ft., roughly, from the present floor level, fragments are discernible of a fifth nimbed figure, painted, like the others, upon a red ground. The surviving portions of the decorated bands have in the past been mistaken for a large cross, framed within a panel of oblong shape, and the subject misinterpreted in consequence as perhaps an Adoration of the Cross. The figures, apart from the much-defaced fifth figure, which appears to have escaped notice, were identified tentatively as 'Angels', though no traces of wings are visible. *c.* 1300, or possibly even earlier.

On the north wall, traces of a consecration cross paty within a circle, in red; and, formerly, at the eastern end of the wall, scroll ornament.

The South Aisle

On the south wall, two female heads, one of them with a nimbus, both executed in black outline, and retouched with black chalk; and in the north-east corner, above the string-course, a Virgin and Child, with an ecclesiastic kneeling below—the whole subject now almost entirely defaced.

Clarkson, *Sussex Archaeological Collections*, 1865, XVII, 231; Keyser, *Mural Decorations*, 1883; André, *Sussex Archaeological Collections*, 1900, XLIII, 222.

AMNEY or AMPNEY CRUCIS (near Cirencester) Glos
HOLY CROSS

The North Transept

The north and west walls are encircled by a string-course, below which scenes from the Life of Christ were originally painted within contiguous barbed quatrefoils; those on the west were eventually destroyed by re-plastering, but evidence of their former existence is afforded by tracings made at the time of their discovery. On the north wall slight remains of the paintings still survive, but sufficient only to show that the execution was exceptionally delicate. On this wall the string-course is taken up to a rather higher level than on the other, and the space thus left between it and the line of quatrefoils below is filled by a series of coats-of-arms, on which most of the charges are defaced, although vair and part of a lion rampant may be distinguished, the tinctures not being adhered to, but represented by the usual ochres.

Above the string-course, at the northern end of the west wall, are two windows, their splays originally decorated with niches framing figures of Saints, one of which, St. Helena holding the cross, survives, though much defaced, on the northern splay of the southern window; above the niche the wall is diapered with conventionalized roses, or cinquefoils. Narrow chevroned shafts are depicted at the angles of the windows, and the voussoirs are picked out in red and white, the joints being indicated by double lines in black. The space between the two windows, as that between the northern window and the angle formed at the juncture of the west and north walls, is filled by a painted niche, with cusped head and a canopy of elaborate design; each frames the figure of a Saint, that between the windows being defaced apart from the outline of the nimbus and shoulders, but the other, St. James the Great, facing north, with scrip and bourdon, clad in a white tunic and reddish-brown mantle, comparatively well-preserved. The small area of wall-space left free by these paintings, is filled with masonry pattern enriched by cinque-foils, as described fully below.

A window occupies the centre of the north wall; and on either side of it two more niches, similar in type to those already described, frame, that on the west side an Archbishop, that on the east a Bishop, with no distinguishing emblems, at least in their present condition. On the upper part of the window-splays an Annunciation is depicted, the Angel Gabriel being represented on the western and the Virgin on the eastern splay, but both paintings are somewhat defaced. Below, on either side, is a pattern of circles with small quatrefoils filling the interspaces, the circles themselves framing fleurs-de-lis in all cases but one, that in the highest row on the eastern splay, near the window-edge, which frames a dove. The coign-stones at the angles of the windows are picked out in red and umber, and the window-arch encircled by a band of scroll-ornament. It is recorded that similar scroll-work, discovered beneath the wall-plate on the east wall, was destroyed.

The South Transept

On the north wall a fragment of masonry pattern survives, of a type identical with that in the north transept; the joints are indicated by bands of deep yellow outlined in black, and the centre of each block is decorated with a cinquefoil, or conventionalized rose in umber, supported by a curling stem in pale

blue adorned with triple groups of pointed leaves in the same tint.

All the surviving painting is of *c.* 1300; works formerly existing in both chancel and nave may have belonged to the same period, but there is no certain evidence to this effect.

Keyser, *B.A.A.J.*, 1914, N.S., XX, 5–10, repr.; Bird, *Mural Paintings, Glos*, 1927, 12, repr.; Borenius, *St. Thomas Becket in Art*, 1932, 18n.

AMNEY or AMPNEY ST. MARY (near Cirencester) Glos

ST. MARY

The Chancel

Remains of a masonry pattern of unusually elaborate type are to be seen on the walls, and notably on the splays of two windows on the north side, executed in red and enriched with stalked cinquefoils or conventionalized roses.

The Nave

Plain masonry pattern originally covered all the wall surfaces with the exception of the space below the windows, at the angles of which are painted representations of shafts and capitals, while scroll ornament surrounds their arches; in one case, on the soffit, are the head and shoulders of a figure, accompanied by an inscription now indecipherable. On the west wall are large medallions bordered by scroll ornament in red and black; if they once framed subjects, no traces now survive. This decorative scheme, like that in the chancel, appears to be of early fourteenth-century date; over it, in the nave, towards the end of the period, a second scheme, comprising subject-paintings, was applied, the extant remains being as follows: On the south wall, to the east of the doorway, a figure of Christ, the head being of the traditional type, but without nimbus; blood is shown trickling down the forehead, and issuing from the wounds in the hands and feet, the former being displayed palm outward as in the Last Judgement. Occupying a considerable area around the figure are implements of varied types, some of them closely packed around the head where the nimbus would normally be placed. Among the objects represented are a mallet, wheel, hammer, knife, comb, dish, saw, axe, ball of cord and pincers, while a saddle and a horn hung from a ring also appear. To the east are traces of an archer holding his bow, and to the west, above the doorway, of a seated man with a 'singing' arrow. The entire subject was once surrounded by an ornamental border composed of large leaves with serrated edges. Above the outer arch of the doorway is a diaper of cinquefoils, or conventionalized roses, and over the inner arch part of a second subject (which extends westward on the wall), viz. a battlemented and masonried building, with traces of five figures in front of it, some of them bearing distaffs, and all proceeding westward towards a figure of St. Peter, identifiable only by means of a fragment of a nimbus and triple tiara, with remains behind him of flying Angels bearing musical instruments before the Gates of Heaven. Late fourteenth century.

On the north wall, immediately opposite the paintings just described, against a background diapered with stars, the head and other parts of the figure of St. George are visible; he wears a crested helm and holds a long black lance, the trappings of his horse, where they are discernible, being partly black and partly banded in red and white. To the east, above a blocked doorway, are the walls of a town, with a group of people, including the King and Queen, observing the combat with the dragon from the battlements. Late fourteenth century.

The paintings are executed in the normal ochres and black, and are now in a very fragmentary condition.

Keyser, *B.A.A.J.*, 1914, N.S., XX, 84-9, reprs.; Tristram, *Burl. M.*, 1917, XXXI, 135-40, reprs.; Borenius and Tristram, 1927, *Eng. Med. Painting*, 29-35; Bird, *Mural Paintings, Glos*, 1927, 11; Carleton Williams, *B.A.A.J.*, 1942, 3rd ser., VII, 30.

ARUNDEL (near Chichester) Sussex
ST. NICHOLAS

The Nave

Formerly, on the walls in every bay, a consecration cross, six of which still exist, but have been retouched. *c.* 1380.

Over the north doorway, the Seven Deadly Sins and the Seven Corporal Works of Mercy, executed in red outline and dating from *c.* 1390; the former represented by small scenes framed within the mouths of dragons issuing from different parts of a nude figure standing in the centre; the latter, slightly to the east of the Sins, within a Wheel divided by means of the spokes into seven sections, the centre being occupied by an Angel, with upraised hands, framed within a circle, and the surrounding sections by small scenes representative of the Works, four of which survive, two to the right and two to the left in the lower part. They are as follows:

1. To the left, above, Feeding the Hungry—two figures seated at a table covered by a cloth which falls from it in regular folds, and a third standing on the left, apparently serving them.

2. To the left, below, Clothing the Naked—a male figure, wearing a hat with up-turned brim, placing a garment over the head of another, scantily clad, or perhaps nude, on the right of the scene.

3. To the right, above, Visiting the Sick—one, or perhaps two figures beside a bed, where another was once shown half-reclining, but is now almost entirely defaced.

4. To the right, below, Burying the Dead—a group of three figures, the central one holding a book and an aspergillum, but with the head repainted as that of a layman having bushy hair and a soft cap, and the other two, on either side, shown lowering a corpse into an open grave.

All the paintings have been extensively retouched in the past and are now much defaced.

Within the bay to the west of the north door, fragmentary traces of paintings in red, largely concealed by whitewash, but perhaps of the same date as those just described.

The FitzAlan Chapel

Remains of gilding and colour on the fourteenth-century wooden vaulting.

B.A.A.J., 1851, VI, 440; *Ecclesiologist*, 1857, XVIII, 341; Burges, *Archaeologia*, 1860, XXXVIII, 432; Keyser, *Mural Decorations*, 1883; Dewick, *A.J.*, 1908, LXV, 21; Johnston, *Memorials of Old Sussex*, 1909, 245, 273-4, 279; Wall, *Medieval Wall Paintings*, 1914, 200.

ASHAMPSTEAD (near Pangbourne) Berks
ST. CLEMENT

On the tympanum are remains of a Crucifixion, with the Virgin and St. John, painted upon a red ground, within a rectangular panel; but the surviving traces are slight, since the work was practically destroyed when it was uncovered towards the close of the nineteenth century, owing to a confusion which then arose between this layer of painting and another of the thirteenth century. Above, in the angle formed by the roof, a rayed medallion, sun, or sunflower, visible some years ago, may have been of approximately the same date as the Crucifixion, or perhaps slightly later.[1]

Keyser, *A.J.*, 1896, LIII, 177; *Reliquary & Illustrated Archaeologist*, 1896, II, 53; Keyser, *Berks B. & O.A.J.*, 1915, XXI, 36; *Victoria County Hist.*, Berks, 1923, III, 451.

---

[1] 1950: the slight traces described either lost or obscured by dirt.

ASHBY ST. LEDGERS (near Daventry) Northants
ST. LEODEGARIUS

On a section of ancient wall towards the eastern end of the south aisle, which was evidently incorporated in the re-building, is a painting of the scourging of St. Margaret, about 2½ ft. in height, identified as a scene in the Passion of that Saint, rather than in that of St. Catherine, by the fact that the hair is knotted above the head in accordance with the story as related in the *Golden Legend*, that St. Margaret, when tortured, was hung by the hair. In the centre stands the Saint, draped from the waist, with her hands bound before her; on the spectator's left is an executioner in a parti-coloured gipon of red and green, and black hose, with a green band about the hair, wielding a triple-thonged whip, and on the right a few remaining fragments of a complementary figure.

Tristram, *Associated Architectural Societies R. & P.*, 1927, XXXVIII, 352, repr.; id., *Apollo*, 1929, IX, 166, repr.; Long, *Burl. M.*, 1930, LVI, 226, repr.

ASHWELL (near Baldock) Herts
ST. MARY

The Nave
In the spandrel on the north side of the chancel arch, an adoring Angel, and in the corresponding spandrel on the south, traces of another.

The North Aisle
Remains of a diaper of small roses; and on the east wall, formerly, a painted bracket.

Keyser, *Mural Decorations*, 1883; and notes supplied by Mrs. M. Bardswell.

ASTON CLINTON (near Aylesbury) Bucks
ST. MICHAEL AND ALL ANGELS

The Chancel
On the south wall, between two windows, the upper part of a large figure, clad in a robe of pink and white outlined in yellow, and a cloak of deep red, lined with vair.

The Nave and South Aisle
Decorative painting survives on the mouldings and capitals of the nave arcade; on the window-splays, chevron and other patterns; and on a window-moulding in the south aisle, a chevron design.

Rouse, *Records of Bucks*, 1933, XII, 401.

BABINGLEY (near Castle Rising) Norfolk
ST. FELIX

Until *c.* 1883, a St. Christopher, of *c.* 1380, survived above the main doorway; the Saint, bearded and with long hair, was shown supporting the Holy Child on his left arm, and holding in his right hand a spear, instead of the usual staff, a feature so unusual and so dubious in character as to suggest that it was misunderstood when the painting was recorded. The Saint was clad in a gipon, closely buttoned down the front, with the skirt looped up over a belt, and breeches tied at the knee, and about his feet were depicted the normal water and fish; and the Child, in his left hand, supported an Orb of the Universe. On each side of the stream rocks were visible. The church is now a ruin.

B. Mus., *Dawson Turner Collection*, Add. I, 77; Keyser, *Mural Decorations*, 1883.

BARBY (near Daventry) Northants
ST. MARY (formerly St. Lawrence)

During a restoration of the church in 1897–8, 'four distinct layers of designs' were discovered on various parts of the walls, the lowest of them of late fourteenth-century date; they were described as consisting of 'figure subjects illustrating scriptural incidents with spaces filled in with floral patterns'. On the north wall of the north aisle there are some slight remains of a St. Christopher, viz. a foot of gigantic proportions, part of a bare leg, and fish of various sizes; further on the same wall, are remains of scroll-work. On the north side of the east window, in the same aisle there was formerly a figure of an ecclesiastic, beneath a richly decorated canopy.

On the chancel arch, the voussoirs of the soffit are painted alternately in red and white, with some 'marbling' in a deeper red.

Associated Architectural Societies R. & P., 1897–8, XXIV, 547–8; Keyser, *A.J.*, 1901, LVIII, 51.

BARDWELL (near Bury St. Edmunds) Suffolk
ST. PETER AND ST. PAUL

The Nave
On the north wall, a 'history' of St. Catherine, comprising:

1. The Dispute with the Philosophers, the Saint standing to the left, clad in a patterned kirtle, the Philosophers seated on the right, in round caps trimmed with vair, but, apparently, gipons and hose in place of long gowns, and 'piked shoon'; their

gestures indicate that they are emphasizing points under discussion.

2. The Burning of the Philosophers. Maximinus, bearded and with peaked cap surrounded by a crown, in a long blue cloak opening on the left shoulder, and white gipon patterned in red, stands on the right, directing the two executioners, in gipons dagged at the lower edge, who thrust the victims into the fire with staves.

3. The Breaking of the Wheels. In the centre, the Saint, crowned and clad in a white kirtle, patterned in blue and buttoned down the centre front, with hands clasped in prayer, between two wheels, each supported upon a post, and above each an Angel with drawn sword; below, to the left, one of the stricken executioners, or 'paynims', the others being defaced.

4. The Decollation of St. Catherine. Only the head of the Saint, crowned and bowed, her hands clasped in prayer, and the head and right arm of the executioner, bearing a sword, formerly visible. Adjacent to the St. Catherine subjects, on the east, the Three Corpses, from a *Trois Vifs et Trois Morts*, all crowned, the trunk of each being covered with representations of toads and lizards.

On the south wall, a Tree of the Seven deadly Sins, the remains comprising: on the highest of the four branches, to the spectator's right, Pride, represented by three trumpeters in parti-coloured gipons of red and blue, and long hose, blowing vigorously at their instruments, with heads and bodies well thrown back, and preceded by a smaller figure playing the bagpipes; on the second branch, *Luxuria*, identified by an inscribed scroll, with male and female figures embracing near the trunk of the Tree, and on the extreme outer end of the branch a devil, grasping a figure held head downwards; on the lowest branch, *Gula*, part of the inscription surviving—near the tree trunk, a large cask, from which a woman draws ale, in the centre, a man and woman, seated on a bench and drinking, the former clad in parti-coloured gipon and hose of white and yellow the latter in a parti-coloured kirtle of green and white, with a male figure, mainly defaced, on the end of the branch; on the lowest branch, three figures grouped about a large chest, with remains of a flying devil—*Avaritia*.

The painting is much defaced on the opposite side, the slight remains formerly visible near the second and third branches of the Tree suggesting that *Invidia* and *Socordia* may have been represented in these positions. All *c.* 1390–1400; now obliterated.

Keyser (1883) mentions a Martyrdom of St. Edmund as existing or having existed, on this wall,

but the account written soon after the works were discovered in 1853 makes no mention of this subject; and since the entire scheme in the church was white-washed over again shortly after the discovery and recording of the paintings it seems probable that he is in error on this point.

Dunlap, *P. Suffolk Institute & N.H.P.*, 1859, II, 41–50, reprs.; Syer Cuming, *B.A.A.J.*, 1872, XXVIII, 124–5; Keyser, *Mural Decorations*, 1883; James, *Suffolk & Norfolk*, 1930, 70–1; Munro Cautley, *Suffolk Churches and Their Treasures*, 1938, 221.

BARNSTAPLE, Devon   ST. PETER

The Nave

Formerly, on the south side over the tower arch, occupying a space 16 ft. in width by 8 ft. 9 in. in height, *Les Trois Vifs*, executed in black outline, with traces of six other figures; the figure of the King on the extreme left was partly defaced, that in the centre perfect, and the third, holding a hawk on the left wrist, nearly so. The background was sown with barbed quatrefoils. Above the heads of the figures were traces of lettering; below them a fragment of an ornamental border, and part of a donor's figure, holding a scroll with an inscription recorded as THER YS JOHN WARD PAYER, J.B.

Chanter, *Memorials Descriptive and Historical of the Church of St. Peter, Barnstaple*, 25–7, repr.; Keyser, *Mural Decorations*, 1883; Storck, *Burl. M.*, 1912, XXI, 314; Carleton Williams, *B.A.A.J.*, 1942, 3rd ser., VII, 39.

BARTON (near Cambridge) Cambs   ST. PETER

The Nave

In both the north and south walls there are four windows, and a doorway between the second and third of these from the west. Above the string-course, which runs below the windows at a height of 6 ft. 9 in. above the present floor level, there are subject-painting viz:

North wall: Between the first and second windows, reading from west to east, against a background composed of foliated branches in which are birds of various types, the Virgin, crowned, suckling the Child, the whole much defaced; to the west of the adjacent doorway, St. Thomas de Cantelupe (1218(?) –1282) Chancellor (1265) and Bishop of Hereford (1275), depicted standing within a pavilion, and vested in alb, amice, dalmatic charged with wolves' heads, mitre and gloves, the right hand raised in blessing, in the left a crozier, at his feet on the spectator's right, a small figure kneeling in supplication;

above the doorway, St. Michael Weighing Souls, clad in a green tunic and white mantle, standing with wings outspread and holding the balance, with fragmentary remains of grotesque figures in the left pan, which devils armed with hooks attempt to depress, one of them being large in scale and having a tail terminating in a bird's head; opposite St. Michael a figure of the Virgin, crowned, who with her right hand depresses the balance on the opposite side with a rosary, a small figure kneeling in supplication in the pan and another at her feet. To the left of the spectator, immediately above the large demon previously mentioned, a knight, probably St. George, clad in chain mail and a white surcoat charged with a cross in black, and armed with shield, sword and lance, strikes with the lance at a devil perched upon the extreme end of the balance-beam. The background is sown with six-petalled flowers. Later painting somewhat obscures the base of this subject. To the east of it, traces of a large St. Christopher, with the Divine Child seated on his left shoulder, partly covered by and somewhat confused with a later (probably fifteenth-century) rendering of the same subject, in which the Child is shown on the Saint's right shoulder, the combination of these remains creating the impression that he is depicted here carrying two children. The traces of the earlier painting also include part of the Saint's staff, held in his right hand, traces of drapery of somewhat involved design, a fish in the water at the base of the composition, and, to the left, a small figure kneeling in adoration. At the edge of the third window, immediately above the string-course, St. Antony Hermit, in alb, amice, dalmatic and chasuble, bearing a book and a crozier, standing on a pig, and having at his right side a small supplicating figure. Above the arch of the third window, on the western side, a large head of Christ, with a cruciform nimbus, complete in itself and not the surviving part of a large figure; on the eastern side, St. John Baptist, clad only in a black mantle, with an Agnus Dei in his left hand to which he points with his right; below, a small figure of a man kneeling in supplication, and, directly in front of him, a bell. Immediately to the east, within a border ornamented partly by bent-riband pattern and partly by a waved design, a large subject so much defaced as to elude identification; the remains of which comprise a man on horseback, apparently turning to look back at three small figures, some of their drapery alone surviving; between the front hoofs of the

horse, a small dog-like animal and traces of foliage; and various birds, scattered over the background.

South wall :[1] Reading from east to west: between the first and second windows, remains of two tiers of subjects separated by an ornamental border; in the upper tier are (1) two kneeling figures, facing east, sole remains of the first subject, and (2) (?) a Baptism of Christ, of which the lower part only survives. A third subject must originally have filled the remaining wall-space but it has perished entirely. In the lower tier, a Last Supper; in the centre, Christ, with a cruciform nimbus, His right hand raised in blessing, and very slight traces of the figure of St. John, resting upon His breast; to the right of Christ, three Apostles, the figure next to Him turned towards Him, that beyond holding a cup, and the third raising food to his mouth; to His left, a bearded figure, facing towards Him, and two others apparently in conversation, though the second of the two is much defaced; on the table before them, a fish on a plate, and a ewer.

On either side of the doorway, the figures of an Annunciation; on the eastern side, the Angel Gabriel, holding in the right hand a scroll which extends over the arch, and bears remains of the inscription AVE MARIA, to the west the Virgin, standing beneath an arch, a book in her left hand, her right hand raised, and her head turned slightly upwards to the descending Dove. Between the second and third windows, traces of a large subject, of which insufficient survives for identification, but having a background enriched with birds and foliage.

All these works, of *c.* 1350, now exhibit only their main lines and masses, almost all detail having been lost.

Morning Post, 7th Aug. 1929.

BARTON MILLS (near Mildenhall) Suffolk
ST. MARY

Two consecration crosses survive, one just within the chancel on the south side, the other on the north wall, to the west of an ancient blocked doorway.

Munro Cautley, *Suffolk Churches and Their Treasures*, 1938, 223.

BAULKING (near Wantage) Berks ST. NICHOLAS
Nave, north wall
To the west of the doorway in this wall are fragmentary remains of (?) a Nativity series, the heads of

---

[1] 1953. The paintings on the south wall are now much defaced by yellowed varnish, damage due to penetration of water, and white-washing around the edges. Eileen Tristram and Monica Bardswell.

the Ox and Ass from a Nativity scene being discernible, together with various much-defaced figures The work seems to be of the early fourteenth century.

Keyser, *Berks B. & O.A.J.*, 1914, XX, 36; Long, ibid., 1942, XLVI, 28.

BECKLAY (near Oxford) Oxon
THE ASSUMPTION (*now St. Mary*)

The Nave
Over the tower arch at the east end, a Last Judgement, with the dead rising from their graves, the just ascending to Heaven, and the lost cast by demons into the jaws of Leviathan, grouped towards the base of the composition on the south side; immediately above the arch, remains of an indecipherable Latin inscription. Below the inscription, on the north side of the arch, St. Peter bearing the Keys, and on the south side, St. Paul, clad in a scarlet cope lined with vair, holding a book in the left hand and a sword, pointed upwards, in the right.

The South Aisle
On one of the tower piers, the Virgin with the Holy Child at the breast, enthroned beneath a cusped, gabled canopy, against a background diapered with roses within quatrefoils, a kneeling figure, almost entirely defaced, beside her to the spectator's left; above the canopy, beneath a cusped framework of indeterminate form (the work being here much damaged), part of an Angel with the left arm outstretched towards a kneeling figure, apparently clad in a hooded cloak, on the right, upon a ground sown with roses; and above this composition again, masonry pattern enriched with roses, part of an inscription, and a fragment of a representation of the Torments of the Damned.

Jewitt, *A.J.*, 1847, IV, 257–8, repr.; *Builder*, 1864, 725; Keyser, *Mural Decorations*, 1883; Howard, *A.J.*, 1910, LXVII, 174.

BEDALE (near Northallerton) Yorks
ST. GREGORY

The Chancel
On either side of the east window, a heater-shaped shield 24 in. in height by 18 in. in width; on the north side—*Argent, a lion rampant sable, on the shoulder an annulet of the first*, for Stapelton or Stapleton of Bedale; on the south side—*Argent, three bars azure over all a bendlet gules*, for Grey of Rotherfield. *c.* 1320.

The Nave
On the chancel arch, an Angel, traces of the Heavenly City, and of Hell, the remains of a Doom.

York A.J., 1926, XXVIII, 450, repr.

GREAT BEDWYN (near Hungerford) Wilts
ST. MARY

The Nave
On the west respond of the north arcade is cut a late fourteenth-century panel with a traceried head, which frames a representation in low relief of the Virgin and Child, retaining traces of red, blue and gold; covered with plaster in 1851.

The North Transept
Formerly, diaper ornament, and remains of figures of St. John Baptist, St. George, and other Saints; early fourteenth century.

The South Transept
Formerly, a Crucifixion, and ? the history of a female Saint, both of the early fourteenth century; and on the east wall, above the former site of the altar, 'paintings of ten or twelve Saints', whitewashed over, perhaps of the same date.

Within a recess in the south wall, the effigy of Sir Adam de Stokke, bearing remains of colour; early fourteenth century.

Gent. M., 1842, N.S., XVIII, 413; Ward, *Wilts A. & N.H.M.*, 1860, VI, 278–80; Keyser, *Mural Decorations*, 1883; Ponting, *Wilts A. & N.H.M.*, 1896, XXVIII, 144; ibid., 1922, XLI, 130; Carleton Williams, *B.A.A.J.*, 1942, 3rd ser., VII, 32.

BEIGHTON (near Buckenham) Norfolk
ALL SAINTS

One consecration cross, of cross paty type, painted in red, yellow and white, survives.

BELCHAMP WALTER (near Sudbury) Essex
ST. MARY

The Nave
On the north wall, between the blocked doorway and the north-east window, the upper part of a Virgin and Child, with traces of two, or more, censing Angels, originally framed by an ogee-headed canopy supported on slender shafts, as is clear from remaining traces; the Virgin is crowned, has long, fair hair falling upon her shoulders, and is shown suckling the Child, part of whose head, surrounded by a cruciform nimbus, alone remains. The composition must originally have been about 6 ft. in height. Towards the west on the same wall, traces

of paintings divided by a narrow strip of foliated ornament, and arranged in two tiers; they are probably of approximately the same date as the Virgin and Child, but are largely obliterated with colour-wash. c. 1350.

On the south wall, the fragments of what was once a large Wheel of Fortune, approximately 12 ft. in diameter; the head of Fortune, and that of a man, are discernible through the super-imposed colour-wash. Above the south door further fragments of painting are to be seen.

R.C. Historical Monuments R., Essex, 1916, I, 20; Benton, *Essex A.S.*, 1928, N.S., XVIII, 239, repr.; id., ibid., 1930, N.S., XX, 86–9, reprs. (see frontispiece).

BELTON (near Yarmouth) Suffolk ALL SAINTS

The Nave

On the north wall, the lower part of a mid-fourteenth-century St. Christopher, comprising the legs (with black underpainting showing, the super-imposed flesh tints having perished), a portion of the gipon, drawn in simple folds, and of the staff, and the usual water and fish about the feet; the remainder of the work (the original height of the figure having been probably about 12 ft.) is covered by a later rendering of the Three Living and the Three Dead, which has been retouched.

B. Mus., *Dawson Turner Coll.*, Add. II, 1848, 208; *A.J.*, 1864, XXI, 218; *East Anglian N. & Q.*, 1866, II, 326; Keyser, *Mural Decorations*, 1883; *Suffolk I.A. & N.H.P.*, 1888, VI, xvi; Whaite, *St. Christopher*, 1929, 15, pl. 13; James, *Suffolk and Norfolk*, 1933, 111; Munro Cautley, *Suffolk Churches and Their Treasures*, 1938, 227.

BENGEO (near Hertford) Herts ST. LEONARD

The Chancel

On the splay of a window, a mitred bishop holding in his hands some object now unidentifiable, and traces of another figure.

On all the walls, remains of a lozenge pattern in red and white.

The Nave

On the south side of the chancel arch, a pattern of contiguous barbed quatrefoils, much defaced, each formerly framing a subject, now unidentifiable; within one of the quatrefoils is a crowned king, with a group of other figures to the right, and above them, terminating the pattern, a narrow band of colour with a border over it ornamented with half-quatrefoils. When presumably in better condition than they are now, two of the subjects were described as a scene from the history of St. Catherine and an ecclesiastic, ? St. Leonard, preaching. The work was carried out in the usual ochres, but traces of green are also visible. On the north side of the arch are vestiges of a medallion pattern corresponding to that already described.

Keyser, *Mural Decorations*, 1883; *R.C. Historical Monuments R., Herts*, 1910, 50; *Victoria County Hist., Herts*, 1912, III, 427.

BERKELEY CASTLE, Glos THE CHAPEL

The roof, nearly flat, is supported by heavy tie-beams, the spaces between them being divided by purlins and ridge-pieces into panels which are approximately square in shape, and on the flat sides of all these timbers are remains of inscriptions in Norman French, executed in black on a white ground, the initial letters being rubricated, and the spandrels picked out in red; the texts given, so far as they are decipherable, are drawn from the Apocalypse. Similar inscriptions, much decayed, are traceable on the walls of an arched passage extending along the southern side of the building; it has been thought probable that originally there were paintings to illustrate all these inscriptions, which seem to be mentioned in Trevisa's *Higden*, where, in giving reasons for the translation of the Bible, in the form of a dialogue between Thomas, eighth Lord Berkeley, and a clerk (his patron and himself) he says 'Also thou wotest where the Apocalyps is wryten in the walles and roof of a Chappell both in latyn and in frensshe'. The walls of the chapel at Berkeley have been replastered, so that no traces of inscriptions survive except in the passage previously mentioned and, of course, upon the roof beams; and if there were formerly inscriptions in Latin as well as in French, they have vanished.

Trevisa's *Higden*, R.S., XLI, introductory dialogue; Cooke, *Bristol & G.A.S.R. & P.*, I, 1876, 138–46, reprs.; Keyser, *Mural Decorations*, 1883.

BERKHAMPSTEAD (GREAT), Herts
ST. PETER

Paintings survived as late as c. 1855 on the walls of the nave, together with one on a column; they included the following:

1. On the column under a cusped and crocketed arch, the head of a woman, wearing a crespine and barbette.

2. A female figure, holding a child in swaddling clothes, and mounted on a horse or ass, (?) the Flight into Egypt.

3. The Massacre of the Innocents. To the left, the

seated figure of Herod, to the right a figure stabbing an infant held head downward.

4. A female figure, with right hand raised and the left pointing downward.

5. The bust of a figure holding an open book in the left hand.

6. A ? female figure, apparently crowned and with a rayed nimbus, entering a doorway.

7. The bust of a demon, with bat's wings outspread.

8. A church or castle, with a scroll pattern to one side of it.

So far as may be judged from sketches made before the eventual destruction of the works, they were all of a date *c.* 1360, with the possible exception of 4, which may have been later.

B. Mus., *John Carter Collection*, 1878, II, 133; Sketchbook of the Hon. Charlotte Grimston, in the possession of the Revd. E. H. Evans, of Hertford.

BIRMINGHAM, Warwick ST. MARTIN

The Chancel

Formerly, in the north-east angle, and extending over the northern jamb of the adjacent east window, a 'history' of St. Martin, in two tiers, separated by wide bands ornamented with delicately-executed scroll-work in white on red, and finished above and below by similar bands, that above surmounted by painted arches filled with similar decoration. Reading from the north, in the upper tier:

1. ? St. Martin seated, clad in episcopal vestments, one hand, part of the pastoral staff and of the maniple remaining together with fragments of a ground diapered with fleurs-de-lis: at this point there intervened a broad space, extending downward into the lower tier and bordered on either side by scroll-work elaborated with leaves and tendrils, in white on black.

2. St. Martin Dividing his Cloak with the Beggar, a scene so painted as to follow over the angle of the wall on to the window-splay; in the centre, the Saint, bearded and on horseback, dividing the cloak with his sword and turning towards the beggar who follows his horse; the background patterned with a large fret having fleurs-de-lis at the intersections.

3. In the lower tier, ? the Translation of St. Martin, part of a pinnacled shrine, of a figure apparently carrying it, and a *Manus Dei* above it, visible.

4. Beyond the broad space previously mentioned, against a ground diapered with fleurs-de-lis, in the centre a large oak tree, to the right parts of the figure of the Saint, in pontificals, and on the left, above, the hooded head of a man with tongue protruding, and below him a bearded man with hair cut to the level of the ears, clad in a gipon buttoned down the front, long hose and somewhat pointed shoes, holding an axe over his left shoulder and facing a beardless figure, who has a wound in the neck and is apparently about to drop an axe grasped in both his hands. This last subject, like that of St. Martin Dividing his Cloak, was carried over the angle of the window-splay.

On the east wall, and the jambs of the north window, a diaper of white roses on a ground of dull red ochre. All *c.* 1380.

On a window jamb, the position of which is not stated in the account, ? the Charity of St. Nicholas, apparently of the same date as the paintings just described.

Holliday, *Birmingham & Midland A.S.T.*, 1870–1905 (1874), IV, 57–9, reprs.; Keyser, *Mural Decorations*, 1883.

BISHOPSBOURNE (near Canterbury) Kent
ST. MARY

The Nave

Above the arches of the arcade on the north side, the following paintings were discovered in 1935:

1. St. Nicholas with the Three Boys; beside the tub, a kneeling woman.

2. An Angel with outspread wings, and below, four chained figures descending into a pit; since these fragments are at the western end of the arcade, they probably once formed part of a Doom, which would in the main, have been depicted on the adjacent western wall.

3. St. Michael Weighing Souls.

4. The Martyrdom of a Saint, comprising three figures, the central one pierced with arrows, and that on the right an archer with a drawn bow; probably the Martyrdom of St. Edmund the King.

5. An unidentified subject, described on discovery as a tall figure, the neck pierced by swords, bearing a bow, a quiver and another weapon.

6. A plain masonry pattern executed in red.

These works appear to be of early fourteenth-century date.

The Times, ii, ix, 1935.

BISHOP'S CLEEVE (near Cheltenham) Glos
ST. MICHAEL

The North Transept

At the back of an altar recess in the east wall, remains of a Crucifixion, with the Virgin and St.

John in the usual positions, and, originally, two supporting figures; on the south, St. John Baptist bearing a disc charged with the *Agnus Dei*, now entirely defaced; on the north, a king, without a nimbus or any identifying emblem, cut off at the level of the knees by a band of bent-riband pattern crossing the recess horizontally at the level of about 4 ft. from the floor, i.e. just above the former position of the *mensa*. A sceptre is visible, as well as the crown, the short beard is yellow and the hair curled at the tips, the mantle light vermilion in colour, with a pale yellowish-green lining, and the tunic white, delicately shaded with pink. A strong outline in black is used to define the forms, except the head, which is outlined in red. This figure is now the only one surviving in fairly good condition, although, in addition to the crucifixion group itself, a small kneeling donor is distinguishable.

Keyser, *A.J.*, 1901, LVIII, 52; *A.A.S.R. & P.*, 1901–2, XXVI, xvii; Bird, *Mural Paintings, Glos*, 1927, 14.

BLEDLOW (near Princes Risborough) Bucks
HOLY TRINITY

The Nave

On the walls above the arcading, remains of an ornamental treatment; upon the main wall-space a masonry pattern in single red line, and in the spandrels between the arches scroll ornament executed in red, yellow and black. *c.* 1300.

The South Aisle

At the eastern end, a pattern of roses in red, and indecipherable traces of painting.

On the south wall, immediately beneath the wall-plate and above the doorway, the Condemnation of Adam to Labour and Toil; on the spectator's right Adam, a bearded figure clad in a mantle, wielding a spade, to the left, Eve, with long hair, in a tunic and mantle, holding a distaff in one hand and a ball of thread in the other; the lower part of this figure is destroyed. Above the group, a *Manus Dei*, with the index finger pointing towards Adam. *c.* 1300.

Cruikshank, *Records of Bucks*, 1909, IX, 445; *R.C. Historical Monuments R., Bucks*, 1912, I, 54; Skilbeck, *Records of Bucks*, 1927, XII, 144; ibid., XIII, 64–5.

BRADWELL (near Braintree) Essex
HOLY TRINITY

The Chancel

At the eastern end, high upon the wall, to the north side of the (later) east window, formerly traces of an Angel; above, from end to end of the wall, remains of a wavy border, in dark red ornamented

with roundels in white. In the centre of the border, traces of a large nimbus. To the south of the window, a Norman window, partly blocked, the arch edged with masonry blocks in yellow and white alternately, outlined by double lines in black; on the splays, masonry pattern in red single line, and at the right side a small pillar depicted in red and yellow.

On the soffit of the arch of the north-east window, an abbreviated Last Judgement, comprising a figure of Christ in Judgement, flanked by Angels holding Instruments of the Passion; on the western splay of the same window, Christ bearing the Vexillum; and on the opposite splay, a Trinity, the Dove being virtually obliterated.

The Nave

On the walls, fragmentary traces of painting.

On the soffit of the arch of the north-east window in the north wall, a circle surrounded by wavy pattern in red on white and framing a bird, ? a phoenix or pelican; on the eastern side of the circle vine-scroll in red on pink.

On the same wall, near the west end, a small head, probably of the Holy Child; since it faces the south door, perhaps the remains of a St. Christopher.

On the soffit of the arch of the south-east window in the south wall, an *Agnus Dei* on a red ground within a medallion having a light-coloured border of wavy pattern enriched with small roundels, and surrounded by vine-scrolls; on the eastern splay of the same window, against a yellow ground ornamented with groups of three spots in red, an Incredulity of St. Thomas, the figure of Christ surviving but that of the Saint obliterated, apart from a hand; on the opposite splay of the same window, St. James, the Great, with scrip and bourdon, against a ground diapered with groups of spots disposed in threes.

The paintings, which were uncovered in 1908, are executed in the usual ochres, together with black, and a little green. *c.* 1325–50.

Curling, *Essex A.S.*, 1909, X, 36–8; *R.C. Historical Monuments R., Essex*, 1922, III, 13.

BRAINTREE, Essex ST. MICHAEL

In *The Builder*, 1864, XXII, 724, the following description is given of decorative painting then surviving about the vestry door:

'A broad string-course, of various colours, runs along the wall, and rises into an arch over and concentrical with the doorway. The colours in the band are, beginning at the top narrow stripe, of buff and then broader stripes of chrome yellow, bright red, bright blue, a strong line of black, and then a broad stripe of yellow. Over this coloured arch is a crocketed and finialled gable in red outlines. The space between the arch and gable is filled in with a buff foliated scroll, outlined in red on a ground of blue. The wall itself is covered with red masonry pattern in which the stones are of unusual length and the vertical pointing lines double, while the horizontal lines are only single. To the right of this canopy there is a painted pillar, blue, which seems to have formed a part of another ornamental design; perhaps of such a canopy as that which was formed on another part of the wall. This was a painted trefoil arch under a crocketed and finialled gable: the arch of three colours, yellow, red, white, the gable only outlined in red and the spaces between the arch and gable filled in with plain blue.'

Essex A.S., 1869, IV, 138; Keyser, *Mural Decorations*, 1883.

BRILL (near Thame) Bucks ALL SAINTS

On the soffit of the chancel arch, on the north side St. Peter, tonsured, with a red nimbus and robe, holding the Keys and a book, and on the opposite side, St. Paul, with a yellow nimbus and a red robe, bearing the Sword and a book. *c.* 1300.

Keyser, *Records of Bucks*, 1897, VII, 227; *R.C. Historical Monuments R., Bucks*, 1912, I, 64, repr.

BRINSOP (near Hereford) Hereford ST. GEORGE

The Chancel

On the south side, to the east of the south-east window, an Annunciation, and on the eastern splay of the same window, a Visitation; much defaced. Above the Visitation, remains of masonry pattern, and below the Annunciation, a scroll border in red. *c.* 1300.

The Nave

Over the south door, part of a Crucifixion, *c.* 1330–40; and to the east of the south-eastern window, remains of foliage decoration.

Keyser, *Mural Decorations*, 1883; *R.C. Historical Monuments R., Hereford*, 1932, 28.

BRISLEY (near East Dereham) Norfolk
ST. BARTHOLOMEW

The South Aisle

Between two windows in the south wall, St. Christopher, holding the staff in the right hand, and the Holy Child on the left shoulder; the Child and the head and feet of the Saint are much defaced, but

part of the latter's mantle, swathed around the shoulders, and his knee-length gipon, belted at the waist and enriched with a delicate pattern, are clearly seen. To the left, a much smaller figure of a Saint, ? St. Bartholomew, since there are traces of ? a knife, in the right hand; and to the right another small figure, of St. Andrew, carrying the titular cross in the left hand and a book in the right. *c.* 1360.

Keyser, *Mural Decorations*, 1883; Whaite, *St. Christopher*, 1929, 18–19, pl. 5; James, *Suffolk & Norfolk*, 1930, 181.

BRISTOL, Glos
CATHEDRAL CHURCH OF THE HOLY TRINITY

The Eastern Lady Chapel

The altar screen, except for the cresting (1526–37), and the central portion, reconstructed in the nineteenth century, is of *c.* 1320; during the process of cleaning some years ago, superimposed coats of cement-wash and white oil paint were removed, and considerable remains of original colour decoration were discovered; among them carved heads of kings, larger than life-size, painted in natural colours, with red on cheeks and lips, the eye-balls white, the iris blue, delicately gradated and outlined in black, and the pupils black; the hair and beards retaining fragments of gilding in the pitted surface of the stone. The blue background behind the heads was enriched with large flowers in red, outlined in black, with scroll ornament in white issuing from them. Carved shields-of-arms, large in scale, were treated in true heraldic colours, and behind them the ground was green, diapered in gold. Carved ornament about the arches was also decorated in gold and colour. The colour on the shields-of-arms, on the ground behind them, and on the ornament about the arches, was found to be in a fragmentary condition, but all the rest was unusually well preserved.

On the north and south walls, at the western ends, barbed quatrefoils framing traces of subjects, are all now practically defaced.

BROOKE (near Loddon) Norfolk ST. PETER

The Nave

Formerly, on the west wall, a painting 6–7 ft. in height and 7–8 ft. in breadth, the lower edge about 10 ft. from floor level, showing on the left a female figure, in kirtle with a pouch at the waist in front, and on her head what may have been intended for a 'ruffled' veil, but this, probably rather defaced in the original, is not clear in Winter's drawing; she holds in her left hand a vessel of flaming liquid, and in her right the bung of the flaming cask whence she has drawn it, set upon trestles under which are flames. Above, issuing from flames, is a small winged figure, apparently nude, with a nimbus: (evidently misunderstood).

On the south wall, a painting approximately 6–8 ft. square, beginning at a level of about 5 ft. from the floor, the upper part devoted to a scene thus described soon after the discovery of all these paintings in 1849:

'One part represented a building of large dimensions and great beauty, with three gables, giving it the look of a cruciform church, and with windows of an ecclesiastical character. Outside the open door stood a human figure, with arms partly extended, and in a stooping posture; evidently receiving with welcome a tattered, bare-legged, disconsolate-looking individual, who, half-bent towards the ground, seemed to implore help, yet almost to despair of receiving it. On the right hand was a third figure, stalking away with indignation; his back turned on the others in evident displeasure. He was well clad. In the distance, within what appeared to be some kind of inclosure, were swine, running as though to some one engaged in feeding them; but we could discover no remains of the swineherd.'

In the lower part were four arched compartments, drawn in black outline with some use of grey wash, each containing a figure of one of the Seven Deadly Sins standing every one in the Jaws of Leviathan; the order in which they were placed not being clearly indicated in Winter's drawings. One, much defaced, represented *Gula*, of which there survived a man's head, a stream, but it is uncertain whether of fire or, as more usually in this subject, of vomit, issuing from his mouth, as he bends over a cask containing flames; on either side were parts of two more vessels, and below a trace of Leviathan. *Ira* was shown with head bent to the left and brow contorted as if in agony, plunging into his breast two knives; blood runs down the hip-length gipon parti-coloured in red and white, dagged at the edges and having a rich belt at hiplevel, in which he is clad; he has a short beard, and hair curled all over his head; the Jaws of Hell, defaced in the centre, are otherwise clearly seen. The background is plain. *Avaritia*, painted against a ground diapered with roses in red, but barbed in green, holds in either hand a bag of money, with loose strings and small tassels at the corners, while fixedly regarding that in his right; his gipon, hiplength and striped, is buttoned down the entire front and dagged at the edges, and about his hips is a rich belt; he has a short, pointed beard and his hair is curled all over his head. Only the tips of the Jaws are visible, the rest being defaced. A youth, rather more fantastically clad than *Avaritia*, since the stripes on his otherwise similar gipon run downward on the shoulders, but horizontally on one side of the waist and at the hips, represented *Superbia*; his head, with loose, slightly wavy hair, cut to the level of the ears, and bound by a fillet ornamented with roses, is turned slightly to the spectator's left, towards a round mirror held in the right hand, and in the left he holds a double comb. Roses, identical with those in the *Avaritia*, diaper the ground, and the Hell-mouth is almost entire. On the same wall, some distance above the large painting first described, evidently as part of a series once representing the remaining three Sins, was *Socordia*; a bear is shown walking on its hind legs to the left, dragging, by means of a white band held in its fore-paws, a youth whose ankles are tied just behind the animal's head; his figure was partly defaced, but it was discernible that his head was being dragged along the ground, and that he was clad very much as were the others previously described, but with long tight hose, parti-coloured in pink and yellow. The bear has a white belt and is girt with a sword in a green scabbard. All the paintings appear to have been of *c.* 1400.

B. Mus., *Dawson Turner Collection*, Add. 1849, I, 225–30; Beale, *Norfolk Archaeology*, 1852, III, 62–70, reprs.; Keyser, *Mural Decorations*, 1883; James, Blomefield's *Norfolk Supplement*, 1929, 17–25, reprs.; id., *Suffolk & Norfolk*, 1930, 126.

BROUGHTON (near Newport Pagnell) Bucks
ST. LAURENCE

The Nave

From floor level to a height of 6 ft. on both north and south walls vertical stripes of red and white, the latter enriched with roses, which have largely perished; this treatment finished at the top with a chequer pattern, the colours being those of the stripes below counterchanged, and the white squares charged with the Sacred Monogram in red. On the north wall, *Mater Dolorosa*, supporting the Body of Christ (the right arm and right leg mutilated), and surrounded by figures of men in late-fourteenth-century dress, several holding portions of the Body, one the heart, others the hands, feet or bones; also one the Cross, and another a wafer. Below the painting two men are depicted quarrelling over a gaming board. The work has been, at some time extensively retouched. *c.* 1400.

A.J., 1849, VI, 176; *Builder*, 1864, 725; Sheahan, *History and Topography of the County of Buckingham*, 1851, 508; Keyser, *Mural Decorations*, 1883; *R.C. Historical Monuments R.*, *Bucks*, 1913, II, 71; Tristram, *Burl. M.*, 1917, XXXI, 139; *Records of Bucks*, 1920–26, XI, 355–6.
Plate 60b.

BROUGHTON (near Banbury) Oxon
ST. MARY

The Chancel

North wall: Originally two tiers of painting, the higher now much defaced, illustrating the Death of the Virgin.

1. Lower tier reading from the west: The Angel Gabriel giving the Palm to the Virgin. The Angel, with wings extended, genuflects, holding in the left hand a scroll and in the right the palm, which the Virgin, seated, takes with her right hand; to the left of her head, and above it, is another scroll, the lettering on both being indecipherable. Approx. 5 ft. × 3 ft. 6 in.

2. Beyond an intervening window, traces of several figures, one bearing a book; probably Apostles in the Gathering of the Apostles.

3. Between a second and third window (?) the Death-bed of the Virgin.

4. To the east of the third window, the Burial of the Virgin, the tomb, and figures of Apostles and Angels being decipherable; further to the east, the Assumption of the Virgin, who is depicted within an almond-shaped glory supported by Angels, her girdle falling at her left side and grasped by St. Thomas, kneeling below. Immediately above the two paintings just described in the upper tier, the Coronation of the Virgin, part of her figure alone remaining, together with a small tonsured figure, kneeling beside her, to the spectator's left, and bearing a scroll with a repainted inscription reading LEUEDY FOR PI JOYZES FYVE LED ME PE WEY OF CLENE LIVE.

Earth colours are employed, with the use of blue in the first scene.

The Nave

On a column of the arcade, a Crucifixion, of approximately the same date as the works described above.

Keyser, *Mural Decorations*, 1883; Wyatt, *A.J.*, 1888, XLV, 446; Keyser, ibid., 1896, LIII, 178; Howard, *Bristol & G.A.S.R. & P.*, 1930, LII, 39; Long, *Burl. M.*, 1940, No. 76, 162, repr.

BURITON (near Petersfield) Hants ST. MARY

The Chancel

On the eastern jamb of a window towards the western end of the south wall, traces of painting, the best-preserved portion a representation of the Virgin and Child, under a trefoiled canopy with foliated capitals. *c.* 1300.

Victoria County Hist., Hants & I.O.W., 1908, III, 92.

BURLINGHAM ST. EDMUND, or SOUTH BURLINGHAM (near Norwich) Norfolk
ST. EDMUND

The Chancel

On the south wall, a Martyrdom of St. Thomas of Canterbury, *c.* 1400; a somewhat unusual rendering of the scene, as being set in a landscape with trees, through which the knights advance towards the figure of St. Thomas, who kneels partly within a small building (representing the cathedral), supported upon four slender columns, and having a spire and battlements, and a gabled subsidiary portion with a Decorated window. Behind the altar are traces of Grim the cross-bearer, and the Saint's mitre is shown on the ground beside him; two of the attackers strike him on the head with their swords, the second being intended for le Bret, carrying a shield emblazoned with a bend engrailed between two crescents, all within a bordure engrailed. Behind him is Fitzurse, holding an axe in the right hand, his shield charged with a bear rampant, and following him the fourth knight, who draws his sword, and carries a targe. The painting is much defaced, little more than the silhouette of the figures surviving, though here and there some detail is still to be seen.

The Nave

Opposite the south door, fragments of a St. Christopher, showing part of the hips, with gipon looped up over the belt, part of (?) the staff and a tree, and a scroll and rose border, painted over masonry pattern with courses drawn in single line and the divisions between the blocks in double line; this pattern appears to have been elaborated originally with (?) flowers having serrated petals, a few of which survive. (?) *c.* 1350. All now much defaced.

Morant, *Norfolk Archaeology*, 1859, V, 185, repr.; Keyser, *Mural Decorations*, 1883; André, *A.J.*, 1888, XLV, 409; Kent, *B.A.A.J.*, 1926, XXXI, 15, 16, 83, 85; Blomefield, *Norfolk Supplement*, 1929, 341; Whaite, *St. Christopher*, 1929, 26, pl. 18; Borenius, *Archaeologia*, 1929, LXXIX, 52, repr.; id., *St. Thomas Becket* in Art, 85, n. i, 98, 101; James, *Suffolk and Norfolk*, 1930, 142.

BURTON LATIMER (near Kettering) Northants
ST. MARY THE VIRGIN

The Nave

Above the chancel arch traces of colour only survive of work recorded as 'probably two series of paintings', with 'some medallions and figures on the north side'.

In the spandrels of the arches of the arcade, on both sides, covered by post-Reformation work, traces of very early fourteenth-century painting, which, in a spandrel on the southern side, comprise a group of several heads, with a tall figure to the left of, and slightly above, them.

The North Aisle

North wall: scenes from the legend of St. Catherine (of which three remain in fair condition), arranged in a continuous sequence framed above and below by borders composed of scroll-work in red, enriched with trefoils, between a narrow band of yellow patterned with roundels in black at the upper edge, and at the lower by a counter-change wavy pattern in yellow and white, outlined in black, both borders being approximately $11\frac{1}{2}$ in. deep, and the band of subjects about 3 ft. 6 in. The lower of the two ornamental borders is placed at a level of approximately 8 ft. from the present floor; below it there are slight traces of another series of subjects, executed on a plain ivory ground. The ground of the existing series, also of plain ivory, is covered with a masonry pattern executed in thick double line in red. The paintings were not carried out on the original wall-surface, but imposed upon a thin layer of lime-putty laid over it as a preparation for them. That they must have been begun while this layer was freshly laid, is indicated by the fact that setting-out lines, visible in places, are deeply scored into its surface. When the wall was heightened in the fifteenth century, and large windows inserted, many of the subjects were destroyed. They begin at the western end of the aisle, and are as follows:

1. St. Catherine before the Emperor Maximinus. His figure alone remains, bearded and with curled hair, seated facing westwards, cross-legged upon a throne, its long, curved arms terminating in animal heads; his left hand is raised in command and his right rests on his knee. He is clad in a white mantle lined with pink, its folds being depicted in black line, a black cote-hardie with wide bell-mouthed sleeves, enriched by bands of an elaborate diamond pattern

in deep buff on a paler buff ground, purplish-buff hose, and shoes adorned with a diamond design in black.

The next few subjects, which may have included the Dispute with the Philosophers, the Scourging of St. Catherine, etc., are defaced.

2. St. Catherine in Prison. The Emperor, on the eastern side of the composition, facing westwards, is shown as in the first scene, except that he is here wearing white gauntlets. The figure, however, is less well-preserved than in that. St. Catherine, clad in a long cream-coloured kirtle, walks from his presence, followed by a gaoler who grasps a thong attached to her person and over his shoulder carries a short, round-headed staff with a bunch of keys hanging from the head. He is clad in a gipon, with yellow hose.

Immediately to the west of the Saint there are fragments of a second figure, either a gaoler or a figure belonging to another scene. The gap in the sequence which here occurs, was doubtless filled by other scenes from the legend, such as the Visit of the Empress to St. Catherine in Prison, and the Saint again before the Emperor.

3. The Breaking of the Wheel. St. Catherine, disrobed to the waist, with her long yellow hair hanging about her, stands frontally, but facing slightly westwards, her hands raised in prayer; on her left is the broken Wheel, a portion of which on her right is represented as being struck by an Angel wielding a sword. At the Saint's feet are the bodies of some of the 'four thousand paynim', slain by broken parts of the Wheel, which lie among them; and to her left, immediately below the broken Wheel, remains of a falling figure, perhaps of one of the executioners.

4. The Decollation of St. Catherine. Only part survives of the kneeling figure of the Saint.

The work is carried out in ochres, black, and white, solid white being used for parts of the flesh and for certain objects, to make them tell against the ivory ground.

A.A.S.R. & P., 1865, VIII, cxiii; Keyser, *Mural Decorations*, 1883; Bailey, *The Antiquary*, XXXIV, 210-213, repr.; *Victoria County Hist.*, Northants, 1930, III, 184; *The Times*, 22, v, 1933.

Plates 47, 48.

BURY ST. EDMUNDS, Suffolk
ABBEY OF ST. EDMUND

Douai Register, list of benefactors to the Abbey (Register *c.* 1425):

'Johannes Lauenham sacrista (13..) soluit pro

continuacione celaturae cum pictura in naui ecclesie ad similitudinem presbiterii £100; pro pictura furni [1] super feretrum £12 13s. 4d.'

Edmund de Brundish gave two pictures for the altar in the choir.

James, *The Abbey of St. Edmund at Bury, Cambridge Antiquarian Soc. Octavo Publications*, 1895, XXVIII, pp. 130, 133, 135, 182.

For paintings on wall or panel already adorning the church *c.* 1300 or early in the fourteenth century, and records of inscriptions from them, giving some idea of the subjects depicted, see *English Medieval Wall Painting*, vol. II, Catalogue, under Bury St. Edmunds.

BYFLEET (near Weybridge) Surrey ST. MARY

The Nave

Over the north doorway, remains of a seated figure of a king, under a canopy; and to the west of the doorway a consecration cross.

Formerly, on the walls generally traces of a masonry pattern elaborated with flowers.

Keyser, *Mural Decorations*, 1883; *Victoria County Hist.*, 1911, III, 403.

CANTERBURY, Kent

CATHEDRAL CHURCH OF CHRIST

The Choir (c. 1180)

On both north and south sides, on the walls and the lower parts of the columns, vestiges of fourteenth century decoration, viz. traces of large chevrons in green and white, and, on the coping of the wall on the south side, remains of a diaper of stars.

Formerly, on the outer walls of the aisles: on the north, a painting of (?) a pilgrimage to a shrine, with a tower in the background upon a conical hill:—on the south, a figure surrounded by rays, perhaps Christ or a Saint. Both these works are shown in a seventeenth-century painting of the Cathedral by Thomas Johnson, dated 1657, in the possession of A. Caroë, Esq.

A.J., 1896, LIII (2nd ser., III), 260. In an inventory of the goods of Prior Henry of Eastry (d. 1331) painting in the Prior's Great Chamber and other chambers mentioned.

1392–3: Whitewashing of the choir and choir vaulting mentioned in the sacrist's accounts; also the following:

'Carboñ ligna vitrum et colores . . . lxxixs. iiijd.

Et tantum hoc anno propter picturam mensure beate marie virginis. Et tabulam inferiorem ad altare sancti Stephani et ij tabulas parvas superiores ad altare sancti Martini.

'*Lambeth MS. 20, f. 210 b. Kalendar of Obits* (Works carried out in the time of Prior Chillenden, 1390–1411). Majus vero altare cum duobus altaribus sanctorum Dunstani et Elphegi opere argenteo aureo ac ligno subtiliter inciso decenter ornavit . . . Et tercium ex parte australi sancti Johannis evvangeliste laudabili pictura et opere ligneo strenue decoravit.'

From the *Inventories of Canterbury Cathedral*, in list of new works of Chillenden's time:

'Item novum altare cum tabula argentea et deaurata cum apparatu altarium sanctorum Elphegi et Dunstani . . . Item iiij altaria unde ij ex parte chori et duo ex altera de novo depicta. . . . Item j magnus pannus cum toto apparatu ad cooperiendum summum altare et altaria sanctorum Elphegi et Dunstani depictus cum historia [apparently to cover the three altars during Lent].'

The Screens of Prior Henry of Eastry (erected 1304–5). At the western end (concealed by stalls of comparatively recent date), gold rosettes on a green ground, and a border of lions and fleurs-de-lis on a ground of red and blue; the decoration extends on to the piers, where these adjoin the screen; two compartments of solid masonry on the eastern side are painted in imitation of stone tracery. On the south side of the choir, near the altar steps, carved and painted decoration comprising: elaborate diaper work composed of hexagons, each framing a sexfoil flower, surrounded by six trefoils with points between the cusps, the flowers and trefoils being coloured light red and surrounded with a wavy line in blue; above and below this decoration a band of dark green bordered in blue and charged with quatrefoils in white; below this again an arcade with trefoils between the arches, the trefoils and the panels framed by the arcading being painted dark red and dark green in alternation; the general colour scheme being green, red, gold and white. Further to the west, on a portion of the cornice of the screen, which survives partially built into and obscured by the canopy of Archbishop Stratford's tomb, remains of rich colour decoration in gold, blue, red, white, green, black and stone colour, comprising: on the upper part, stone colour on the flat surfaces, black in alternation with red on the round mouldings, and red within a border of pierced trefoils; and, on the lower part, a leaf pattern in gold on blue decorating

---

[1] Perhaps a canopy, or the **wooden cover** of the shrine.

the wide hollow moulding, with, on the flat surface, a border of roundels in red on white, and, on the narrow hollow moulding, green.

Dart, *History and Antiquities of Canterbury Cathedral*, 1726, pp. 13, 15, 17; Scott, *A.J.*, 1875, XXXII, 87, repr.; Scott Robertson, *A. Cant.*, 1876, X, 72; Keyser, *A.J.*, 1878, XXXV, 276; Keyser, *Mural Decorations*, 1883; Wickham Legg and St. John Hope, *Inventories of Christ Church, Canterbury*, 1902, pp. 101, 105, 107, 108, 111, 114; Caroë, *Archaeologia*, 1911, LXII, 356; Woodruff, *A. Cant.*, 1936, XLVIII, pp. 47–8.

The Tomb of the Black Prince (c. 1376)

On the tester above the tomb are remains of a painting of the Trinity, which upon close scrutiny afford ample evidence, not only of the general lines of the composition in its original state, but also of the details of the design. The Trinity is framed by an aureole of diamond shape, broken into by a large arc on either side towards the top, and another two similarly disposed near the base, the whole elaborately cusped in gold. God the Father is enthroned on a rainbow, executed in gold partially covered with transparent colour, and between His feet, as also at the foot of the Cross which He supports, and which formerly bore the figure of the Crucified, now partly defaced, is the Orb of the Universe, patterned in zones representing water, clouds and sky. The head, surrounded by a cruciform nimbus, is defaced but immediately below it are slight traces of the Dove; the hands are raised, the right in the act of blessing. The tunic is green, diapered with fleurs-de-lis and rosettes in gold, and the mantle pink, enriched by a pattern composed of suns in splendour, each charged with the sacred monogram I.H.S., in alternation with a motif of four-petalled flowers with sprigs between them; the gold border to the mantle is decorated with a delicately executed pattern in colour, and its lining is red. The background of the painting generally, of a deep greenish blue, is sown with small gilt roses in relief, outside the aureole, and stars within it. In each of the four spandrels formed by the lines of the aureole as they impinge upon the edges of the panel, one of the Symbols of the Evangelists is depicted, and identified by an inscribed scroll. The edges of the tester are adorned with rosettes and diamond patterns in gilt relief on a black ground elaborated with a foliated pattern in white; the carving is gilt, the members of the mouldings picked out in colour, and the battlements of the parapet painted with quatrefoils in black.

The effigy of the Black Prince, made, according to the provision in his will, of 'laton overgilt', and described in early records as gilded, was thought to have lost its gilding until, in 1935, this was again revealed upon the removal of an obscuring coat of darkened varnish.

Blore, *Monumental Remains*, 1826, p. 10; West's *Note-book*, Victoria and Albert Museum, 1844, p. 10, 1860–4, pp. 67, 69; Carter, *Collections*, B. Mus., vol. II, 246; Stothard, *Monumental Effigies of Great Britain*, 1876, pp. 122, 123; Keyser, *A.J.*, 1878, XXXV, 276; Keyser, *Mural Decorations*, 1883; Scott Robertson, *A. Cant.*, 1897, XXII, 34; Conway, *Burl. M.*, 1929, LV, 212, repr.; *Friends of Canterbury Cathedral*, 3rd Annual Report, 1930, pp. 42–50, repr.; Tristram, *Apollo*, 1935, XXII, p. 26, repr.; Harvey, *Gothic England*, 1947, pp. 62, 65–6, repr.
Plates 13, 14, 15a, b.

St. Andrew's Chapel

This chapel which is on the north side of the ambulatory, opposite St. Anselm's Chapel on the south, dates from c. 1100.

Survivals of fourteenth-century decoration in the Chapel comprise:

On the north and west walls, painted hangings with wide vertical stripes in red and white, charged with rosettes, the colours counter-changed. c. 1304.

In a recess in the north wall, masonry pattern, the courses shown in single and the joints in double lines, elaborated with crescents surmounted by small roundels, grouped in threes, stars, and saltires bottony.

Architectural Association Sketch Book, 3rd ser., 1906, X, pl. 2.

The Chapel of Our Lady Undercroft

This Chapel occupies two bays of the Norman crypt, and is enclosed, at the eastern end, by a reredos, and on the north and south by screen-work in stone, all of the fourteenth century.

Remains of decoration are as follows:

The reredos; on the vaulting above the central niche, discs of cement or composition, perhaps the remains of 'prints', but more probably bedding for jewels, whether real or imitation; on the screen-work, red and green colouring, on the shafts, 'barber's poling' in black and white, and on the carving, gold; on mouldings, 'prints'.

The vaulting of the Chapel: now black in colour, but, as appears from remaining fragments, originally a deep blue, with the black as an underpainting, the whole diapered with suns and stars, their sharp-faceted rays formed in a hard, shiny composition in relief, their centres, now very fragmentary, convex, with 'mirrors' laid over them, made of talc backed by silver leaf. Each 'sun' is represented by a disc 8 in. in diameter, with 24 rays emanating from the convex centre, each 'star' is similar, but smaller, with only six rays. In the centre of the vaulting, four suns, conjoined so as to form a quartefoil.

At the eastern end of the screen on the southern side, a figure of a cleric, about 18 in. in height, now much defaced.

On the Norman piers, bands in red and black, and on their capitals, re-cut in the fourteenth century, traces of red and azure.

Formerly, on the south-east pier of the sacrarium, a shield of the Black Prince, possibly of fourteenth-century date.

A. Cant., 1880, XIII, 522, 535–6; Keyser, *Mural Decorations*, 1883.

The Jesus Chapel

In this Chapel, at the eastern end of the crypt, the remains of late-fourteenth-century decoration comprise a simple masonry pattern, elaborated with horizontal bands of zigzag ornament, and a diaper of crowned Ms and Js in black.

Keyser, *A.J.*, 1878, XXXV, 282.

The Chapter House

At the back of the Prior's seat (*c.* 1304) are confused vestiges of painting of different dates, but all of the first half of the fourteenth century, comprising remains of (?) a Coronation of the Virgin. In the central section of the canopy a portion of the original decoration (of *c.* 1304) remains in fair condition, although the greater part is repainted; it consists of delicate ornament painted in translucent colour, mainly in reds and greens, upon a ground of gold leaf, and covered with clear, greenish glass, the whole executed in imitation of enamel and resembling the ornamentation (of *c.* 1269) on the Westminster Panel. In the side sections of the canopy similar ornament, composed of trefoils framing leaf and other patterns, has at some time been entirely repainted.

Keyser, *A.J.*, 1878, XXXV, 276; id., *Mural Decorations*, 1883.

CANTERBURY, Kent ST. DOMINIC

The Refectory

On the south wall, to the left of the pulpitum, remains of a shield of arms, about 18 in. in height, bearing—*on a field ermine a cross invected gules*; below, traces of a subject comprising a figure with a nimbus. On various parts of the same wall, masonry pattern in single red line; and elsewhere, coign-stones and voussoirs painted in red and yellow ochre and white. *c.* 1300.

CASTLE HEDINGHAM (near Halstead) Essex
ST. NICHOLAS

A fragment of plaster, painted with the head of a Bishop or a King, against a background diapered with stars, is preserved in a glass case at the western end of the church. Early fourteenth century.

R.C. Historical Monuments R., Essex, 1916, I, 51.

CASTLEACRE PRIORY (near Swaffham) Norfolk

The Prior's Chapel

At the eastern end of the chapel, on the soffit of a Norman arch, on the south side, fragments of figures, originally crowned (one having a green mantle outlined in black), on a vermilion ground; above them, a star, like the crowns, in gold; ? an Adoration of the Magi. On the north side, remains of a subject framed within a medallion or an almond-shaped glory; in the centre a nimbus, and on the left a genuflecting figure, with another behind it. Below the string-course, at the springing of the arch, and crossing the east wall, traces of a fret pattern elaborated with a geometrical motif, extending to the floor and also to the adjacent parts of the north and south walls; perhaps a wall-hanging about the altar. On the splays of the eastern window, one on each, two bishops or abbots, holding croziers, and a border of lions leopardy; to the north of the window, part of a painted niche with cusping in black, and to the south, similar remains. On two carved corbels, re-used in Perpendicular times to support the roof timbers, that to the north bears *France ancient and England, quarterly, with a label of five points*, that to the south, for William de Warenne, *checky or and azure*; both are carved, painted and gilt, the chequers in the second having been adorned with 'prints' (generally taken to be carving).

Keyser, *Mural Decorations*, 1883; St. John Hope, *Norfolk Archaeology*, 1895, XII, 146–7.

CASTOR (near Peterborough) Northants
ST. KYNEBURGA

North Aisle

North wall, western end: Scenes from the legend of St. Catherine, in three tiers, as follows:

Highest tier, much damaged; under a canopy, to the extreme left a building and to the right a group of figures—? the Saint Imprisoned and the Saint before the Emperor.

Middle tier: the Burning of the Philosophers; a seated bearded figure (? the Emperor), directing the casting of a bearded man clad in a long robe and borne upon another's shoulders into a pit, in which are about ten male figures, apparently dead. The scene is covered with a canopy. To the left, under a smaller canopy, the Saint encouraging the martyrs.

Lowest tier: St. Catherine on the Wheel. Under a canopy, the Saint, draped from the waist, is bound between two toothed wheels, turned by a pair of executioners, while, above, an Angel is about to break them with blows from two swords. On the left a seated male figure, probably the Emperor. To the extreme left, under a narrower canopy, St. Catherine, draped as above, is shown with bound hands and wrist grasped by a hand. The remainder of the subject has perished.

The backgrounds to all the scenes are powdered with fleurs-de-lis.

Keyser, *Mural Decorations*, 1883; *Victoria County Hist., Northants*, 1906, II, 481.

CATHERINGTON (near N. Havant) Hants
ST. CATHERINE

The Hyde Chapel

The east wall is pierced by a round window above and two lancets, one on each side, below, between them being a painting of the Trinity (much defaced and now almost indecipherable), within an almond-shaped glory framed by a rectangular patterned border. On either side is a censing Angel, and to left and right, above the lancets, two more Angels, that on the left almost entirely destroyed, that on the right playing a harp. The background everywhere, including that within the aureole surrounding the Trinity, is patterned with cinquefoils. Narrow borders composed of scroll-work follow the contours of the lancets, and two very wide borders of a similar type and of unusually free and beautiful design fill the splay of the circular window above.

The Nave

On the wall above the north arcade, St. Michael Weighing Souls with wings outspread and a sword held perpendicularly in the right hand. He is clad in an alb diapered with small crosses, and having deep apparels at neck and hem, the former patterned with spots in groups of three; at the waist is a broad girdle supporting, by means of a loop, the beam of the Scales. In the pan on the spectator's right are traces of a devil, and another devil clings to the beam above; in the second pan a Soul is seen, and behind it stands the Virgin, crowned as Queen of Heaven, resting her rosary upon the beam on this side.

All the work described is of *c.* 1350, but the St. Michael has unfortunately been largely repainted.

P. Society of Antiquaries, 2nd ser., 1885, X, 55; Keyser, *A.J.*, 1896, LIII, 170–1; id., *Memorials of Old Hants*, 1906, 148, 150; *Victoria County Hist., Hants & I.O.W.*, 1908, III, 101.

CERNE ABBAS (near Dorchester) Dorset
ST. MARY

The Chancel

On the north wall, at the eastern end, and continued on to the eastern splay of a window in the same wall, a History of St. John Baptist, in three tiers divided by bands of plain colour, the subjects in the highest now being indecipherable. In the second tier, on the window-splay, the Baptism of Christ, who stands in the centre with hands folded in prayer, St. John and a smaller figure, bearing the garments of Christ, being on the left, and an Angel, also holding garments, on the right; in the third tier on the splay, traces of two figures, beneath an arch, turning towards each other, that on the left with the left hand raised, that on the right with the right hand raised and the left lowered—(?) remaining parts of a rendering of Herod's Feast. On the window-splay, in the second tier, St. John Baptist before Herod; the Saint, nimbed, long-haired, bearded, and clad in the usual loose, knee-length garment, stands on the left of the composition, his left hand raised and a book in his right; his head is turned towards Herod, seated on the right, crowned, bearded, and clad in a red mantle lined with ermine, behind him being Herodias, in a red kirtle and grey mantle, a crespine upon her head. These two figures are on the whole somewhat defaced, but Herod's head is exceptionally well-preserved. In the third tier, before the entrance to a building, presumably the prison, an executioner brandishes in his right hand a sword, and in his left holds the severed head of the Saint over a platter borne by two serving-women, or perhaps Salome and an attendant. *c.* 1360. The paintings are partially retouched.

Also on the north wall, a consecration cross in incised line, executed by means of compasses, and composed of a sexfoil pattern framed by a circle, the latter originally, as appears from traces, painted red.

Long, *Dorset A.S.*, 1928, L, 105; id., *Burl. M.*, 1930, LVI, 231.

CHALFONT ST. GILES (near Amersham) Bucks
ST. GILES

The South Aisle

On the east wall, on either side of an open archway, subjects arranged in two tiers, separated both vertically and horizontally by borders of wavy design in yellow and white, and terminated immediately below the wall-plate by a running scroll. In the upper tier to the north of the arch, St. Anne teaching the Virgin, a subject in a fragmentary condition, and in the lower tier, no survivals; above, on the south side, in a similarly poor state of preservation, ? the Virgin, veiled and crowned, with traces of several figures before her, the subject unidentifiable; and, below, another scene almost entirely defaced, in which a small figure, perhaps that of an Angel, is decipherable in the upper left-hand corner.

On the south wall, adjacent to the subjects just described, and framed like them, as are all the paintings on this wall, the Virgin saving the Jewish Boy from the Baker's Oven, and the Legend of the Youth betrothed to the Virgin. In the former, which is represented in two 'moments' she is shown, on the left, standing by the slight figure of the child at the oven's mouth, and on the right grasping his hand to save him, and also sheltering him (for his figure is twice represented) within her cloak; in the latter, she stands behind the Youth, who kneels with his back to her, at the foot of an altar upon which is a statue of the Virgin and Child. On the other side of two perished subjects, and further to the west, beyond a window, are the Temptation and the Expulsion from Eden. In the former, the Tree of Knowledge is placed in the centre of the scene, a human-headed serpent entwined about its trunk, and to the left stands Eve, handing the apple to Adam, on the right, who takes it in his left hand, raising the other to his mouth as though in doubt; immediately behind him, the Avenging Angel, clad in tunic and mantle, with upraised wings and sword held horizontally above the head, expels them from the Garden. Only the figure of Eve survives in good condition, that of Adam being much defaced. A second window intervenes at this point, and above it is a scroll pattern with large vine-leaves and tendrils. Next in sequence is a well-preserved Crucifixion, with the Virgin and St. John. Christ hangs on the Cross, bent in a double curve, and the sway of the attendant figures, especially that of St. John, is very pronounced; the background is powdered with small crosses having spots in the angles of the shafts. Beneath the Crucifixion, the remains of a Resurrection, comprising the upper part of the figure of Christ, with cruciform nimbus, bearing the vexillum, and to the right, probably one of the Holy Women, against a ground diapered with stars. To the west of the Crucifixion in the upper tier of paintings, Herod's Feast, with Salome represented on the left, bearing the head of the

Baptist in a charger, and yet again in front of the table, on the right, dancing, her body bent in a curve so that her head touches the ground; dishes and covered cups are shown upon the board, and two figures are decipherable seated at its far side, one with hands raised as if in horror; the background is diapered with stars. Below this scene, the Decollation of the Baptist, who stands bent forward in the doorway of a building, presumably intended as that of the prison, towards an executioner, in particoloured gipon and peaked hood, who raises a sword; behind this figure is that of Salome, holding a dish in readiness to receive the head when severed; the background has a diaper resembling that seen in the Crucifixion. A doorway here intervenes in the series, with slight vestiges of painting above it; to the west are the remains of a Jesse Tree, which must originally have occupied a space about 12 ft. in length by 9 ft. in height. The identifiable remains comprise David playing a harp, in the centre, with slight traces of a Virgin and Child above, and branches of vine, bearing bunches of grapes and tendrils, and framing the remains of nine Prophets holding scrolls, some of the figures being much clearer than others.

The work, which may be dated *c.* 1330, is executed mainly in red and black line against an ivory-tinted ground, portions, however, being filled in with solid colour. (1954: obscured by dirt.)

Keyser, *Mural Decorations*, 1883; Phipps, *Records of Bucks*, 1886, VI, 86, 87, repr.; R.C. *Historical Monuments R., Bucks*, 1912, I, 81; Tristram, *Apollo*, 1929, IX, 276–80; Rouse, *Records of Bucks*, 1927–33, XII, 108–18; James, ibid., 288.

CHALGRAVE (near Dunstable) Beds
ALL SAINTS

The Nave

The general scheme (c. 1310). Below the wall-plate on both sides of the nave, and extending from end to end of the building above the arcade, a scroll border in red between two narrow bands in black, the scroll composed of a stem executed in double line and decorated by ternate leaves with serrated edges; lower down, at the apices of the arches, another ornamental border, of the same extent as that just described, consisting of a fret pattern in red between two narrow black bands; the wall-space between these two borders being left plain. In the spandrels of the arches, shields of arms (approx. 2 ft. 6 in. × 1 ft. 11 in.), outlined in black and suspended by 'guiges', also in black, from loops represented as attached to the ornamental border above; on each side of the shields, sprays of foliated ornament springing from central bosses and painted in red. On the columns, remains of colour; on the carving of the arcading generally, colour decoration; on sculptured corbels, the lips and cheeks painted red, the iris of the eyes black, the hair in yellow or brown, and the head-dresses, mitres, etc., in a variety of colours; at the bases of the columns, about 4½ ft. from the present floor level, a black band 3½ in. in depth, and below this, in some instances, remains of colour decoration in red; remains of similar decoration on the lower part of the tower arch at the western end of the church.

Charges on the shields.

South wall, reading from the east:

1. *Argent, a cross gules.*[1]

2. *Argent, a fesse gules, a chevron of the same in base, a label of five points of the same.*

3. *Quarterly argent and gules, a bendlet gules,* Loryng.

4. *Argent, two chevrons gules, five roundels three and two of the same.*

5. Doubtful; probably once *Argent, a fesse sable between three crescents sable.*

6. Destroyed.

North wall, reading from the west:

1. Destroyed.

2. *Argent, two chevrons gules.*

3. *Quarterly argent and gules, a bendlet gules,* Loryng.

4. *Gules, three crescents argent.*

5. *Ermine, a chief dancetty gules.*

6. *Gules, a fesse between two chevrons argent.*

The South Aisle

On the west wall, as part of a scheme which extended also to the south wall, and to the west and south walls in the north aisle, three Apostles (one being St. Paul bearing the Sword), depicted as of slightly less than life-size, each within a painted niche having a trefoil-headed arch surmounted by a crocketed gable, and supported upon shafts terminating in chevroned pinnacles; the whole much defaced. On the south wall only a single niche survives. With one exception, ? St. Peter, who wears a chasuble, all the figures in both aisles are clad in cloaks and long tunics.

Between two windows on the east of the doorway in the south wall, a niche like those already described, but rather larger in scale, framing the figure of an Archbishop in Mass vestments, much defaced. On the splays of the windows, masonry pattern in double line, enriched with roses, and, on one of the splays,

a fragment of a crowned figure framed by a canopied niche.

On the north wall, above the arcade, and also in part on the south wall, a series of shields disposed like those in the nave, except that the sprays of foliated ornament on either side of the shields are omitted. The charges are as follows:

South wall, reading from the east:

1. Destroyed.

2. Partly defaced; *Argent, a fesse sable,* ? part of a bordure with martlets in red.

3. *Argent, a fesse gules between two chevrons of the same.*

At this point a large window now breaks the series.

Above the doorway:

4. *Argent, a chevron gules,* with traces of other charges, viz. on the chevron ? 3 scallop shells, and on the dexter chief ? a mullet sable.

North wall, reading from the west:

1. *Argent, a saltire engrailed gules.*

2. *Gules, a fesse indented of three points or.*

3. *Gules, a lion rampant argent within a bordure engrailed of the same* (? or).

4, 5, & 6. Destroyed.

The North Aisle

On the west wall, four of the series of Apostles within niches remain, one of them being St. James the Great, with palmer's hat, with two on the adjacent north wall.

On the north wall, traces of an Angel with outspread wings, and of three other figures.

On the east wall, an Annunciation, approximately 2 ft. × 3 ft. in size; the Virgin, wearing a white veil, a mantle of dark red, and a tunic of a lighter red, is depicted to the south of the composition. She raises her right hand and holds a book in her left; the figure is outlined in black, and the shoes are black. The Angel Gabriel (the upper part defaced), clad in a red mantle and a white tunic, raises one hand in salutation and in the other holds a scroll inscribed AVE MARIA. On the border below the painting, delicate scrollwork in white on red.

Near the blocked north door, within a niche decorated profusely with crocketed pinnacles and ornamental buttresses, a large figure bearing a staff; to the east of it, a second similar figure; elsewhere on the same wall, remains of another richly decorated niche; and south of the east window, traces of a fourth (c. 1380).

[1] The metals are generally impossible to identify with certainty, owing to the use of a cream tint, indifferently for the one or the other.

On the south wall, above the arcade, a series of shields, disposed like those in a similar position in the south aisle. The charges are as follows:

Reading from the east:

1. Destroyed.

2. *Argent, a fesse sable between six martlets gules* (some of the martlets much defaced).

3. *Argent, a fesse gules between two chevrons of the same.*

4. *Argent, a chevron sable between three billets of the same.*

5. *Argent, a bend sable between six martlets of the same.*

6. Destroyed.

On two tombs of the Loryng family, respectively on the north and south sides of the nave, the effigy in each case wears a surcoat charged with the Loryng arms—*Quarterly argent and gules, a bendlet gules*; on the shields at the sides of the monuments are traces of colour; and on the eastern end of the tomb to the south, remains of a small figure, painted in bright colours, including vermilion.

Over the north door, fragments of a St. Christopher, of *c.* 1400.

Keyser, *Mural Decorations*, 1883; *Victoria County Hist., Beds.*, 1912, III, 348; Rouse, *A.J.*, 1936, XCII, 81–97, reprs.

Plates 59a, b, c, 61b.

CHALGROVE (near Oxford) Oxon
THE ASSUMPTION OF THE VIRGIN

The Chancel

Above a level of about 7 ft. from the floor, subjects are arranged in three tiers, not separated as usually by horizontal bands of ornament, or by any architectural features, whether horizontally or vertically disposed. They are as follows:

North wall: The Life of Christ, in fifteen scenes, from the Nativity to the Ascension, prefaced by a Tree of Jesse.

Lowest tier, reading from the west:

1. The Tree of Jesse, springing from the first, but extending into the second tier; it is divided into two branches, which intertwine to form two almond-shapes, one above the other, with curved branches springing from them laterally, and supporting prophets holding scrolls. Within the lower of the almond-shapes, King David is depicted playing a harp; and within the upper, the Virgin and Child.

2. On the splays of an intervening window, the Annunciation; the Angel Gabriel, a tall, standing figure, with right hand raised in salutation, within a painted niche on the western splay, faces the Virgin,

framed by a similar niche on the eastern splay, having her right hand raised and a book in her left.

3. The Nativity, immediately to the east of the window; a couch extending from the eastern angle of the composition, and for the greater part of the distance across it, with the Virgin reclining, her head supported by a cushion patterned with a fret, and at her feet the seated figure of St. Joseph; behind the couch, traces of (?) two other figures, and of the Holy Child.

4. The Adoration of the Magi; on the western side, the Virgin and Child, with a kneeling King before them, and traces of two others standing behind him; somewhat defaced.

At this point the series is continued in the second tier.

5. Immediately to the east of the window, the Massacre of the Innocents. On the western side of the composition, Herod, enthroned, and holding a sword in the right hand, leans forward to direct the massacre; before him, a soldier holds one of the children transfixed by a spear, and beyond him a woman struggles for her child with another of the attackers; and just beyond her traces of more figures.

6. The Presentation in the Temple. The Virgin, attended by a bearded man and a woman with a circular hat and barbette, holds the Child over the altar towards the extended arms of St. Simeon.

7. The series, from this point, is continued at the western side of the westernmost window, in the highest tier, above the Tree of Jesse, with the Betrayal. Christ, receiving the kiss of Judas, stands in the centre of a group of figures (much defaced); to the spectator's left St. Peter cuts off the ear of Malchus.

8. To the east of the same window, in the same tier, the Trial before Pilate; the head of Christ, together with that of Pilate and those of two guards, being visible, but the remainder of the subject destroyed.

9. In the same tier, adjacent to the scene just described, the Mocking of Christ. The head and bound hands of Christ, and the heads of two figures with their tongues protruding survive.

10. The series continues in the uppermost tier, to the west of the easternmost window, with the Flagellation, the figure of Christ being visible, with fragments of those of the executioners.

11. In the same tier, immediately adjacent to the window, the Carrying of the Cross. Christ is preceded by a man clad in a parti-coloured tunic, and bearing a basket, and followed by another similar figure.

12. In the same tier, beyond some foliated ornament at the apex, to the east of the window arch, slight traces of a Crucifixion.

13. In the central tier, immediately below the Crucifixion, the Descent from the Cross. On the left, St. Joseph of Arimathaea receives the Body into his arms, and, behind him, the Virgin tenderly clasps the extended right arm; to the right stand St. John, and Nicodemus, who extracts the nails from the feet of Christ.

14. In the lowest tier, immediately beneath the Deposition, the Entombment, with the Body lying in the tomb, surrounded by the Virgin, St. John, and Nicodemus, the last-named shown in the act of anointing, with an attendant behind him bearing a pot of spices.

On the splays of the intervening window, St. Helena, holding the Cross, and another female Saint, perhaps St. Mary Magdalen. *East wall:* to the north of the east window, the conclusion of the Life of Christ:

1. The Harrowing of Hell, in the lowest tier, adjacent to the window-splay. Christ, holding the vexillum in His right hand, with His left leads Adam and Eve, followed by other Souls, from the gaping jaws of Leviathan.

2. Immediately above the subject just described, the Resurrection. Christ, bearing the vexillum, His right hand raised in blessing, and with an Angel on either side of Him, emerges from the tomb, and within the arches supporting it traces are to be seen of the sleeping Roman guards.

3. The Ascension. A group of the Apostles, with the Virgin in their midst, and St. Peter, holding the Keys, just behind her, gaze upward towards Christ, whose figure disappears in clouds above them.

On the northern splay of the east window, St. Peter, with the Keys, in his left hand, the right being covered by his mantle; on the opposite splay, St. Paul with the Sword, which he holds in an upright position in his right hand, pointing to it with his left.

On the south of the window, concluding scenes from the Life of the Virgin, which will be described in connexion with that series. *South wall:* reading from the west, the Last Judgement. Christ is shown in the highest tier, enthroned upon a rainbow and displaying His wounds, with the Virgin kneeling in intercession on His right, and in the second and third tiers Souls are depicted rising from their graves; among them are bishops and monks, and all have hanging upon them grave-clothes, which in some cases are patterned with crosses.

Above the window which here intervenes there is foliated ornament; on its western splay, St. Bartholomew, with the knife by which he was flayed, and on the opposite splay, St. Lawrence with the gridiron. Beyond the window there begins a series of the Death of the Virgin, as follows:

1. Adjacent to the second and easternmost window in this wall, in the lowest tier, a subject destroyed by the insertion of a monument with the exception of a single surviving figure immediately adjacent to the western splay.

2. To the west of the monument, part of a second scene, with the Virgin praying to be preserved from the sight of the Evil One at the moment of her death.

3. Still farther to the west, the Angel giving her the palm, and announcing that the hour approaches for her re-union with her Divine Son. Behind her to the east, and forming a division between this scene and the previous one, hanging drapery is represented, presumably intended for the 'clothes of immortality', the 'vestments' brought for her, with the palm, by the heavenly Messenger.

4. On the western side of the central tier, a subject combining the Gathering of the Apostles and the Assembling of the Neighbours, with the Virgin standing centrally, and addressing St. John, who stands before her while the remaining Apostles kneel behind him, their hands held to their heads in grief. The Neighbours, represented by a complementary group of six women, three kneeling and three standing, join their hands in prayer; two have their heads uncovered, and their hair loose, one has it braided, another wears a wimple and veil, and two have bands about their heads, together with barbettes and crespines.

5. To the east of the scene just described, Christ Receiving the Soul. He stands in the centre of the composition, His hand raised in blessing, and above and to the right, two Angels bear the Soul heavenward in a cloth; behind Him to the east is a group of four Angels with upraised wings, their hands clasped in prayer, and part of the drapery of the death-bed, patterned in stripes, most of which has been defaced by the insertion of the monument previously mentioned. On the western side of the subject is a group of Apostles, one, doubtless intended for St. John, touching the head of the Virgin, the greater part of whose figure is destroyed.

6. Extending over the entire length of the uppermost tier, between the two windows and the foliated ornament at their apices, the Funeral Procession and the Miracle of the Jews. Immediately to the east of

the window the Apostles are shown carrying the bier, which has a cross at each end and is covered with a pall richly patterned with stripes ornamented in various ways; three Apostles are at the head, and another three at the feet. At the side of the bier, and clinging to it, is the 'prince of priests', the leader of the Jews in the attack on the procession, whose hands were withered, and below the bier two of those who were blinded. The remainder of the subject is somewhat defaced, but it can be seen that two more episodes in the legend are represented, viz., St. Peter sprinkling with an aspergillum the penitent 'prince of priests', who kneels before him, and the penitent himself advancing with the heavenly palm towards his blinded followers, that those who declared their belief in Christ might be miraculously cured.

On the splays of a window which here intervenes, on the western side, St. John the Evangelist bearing a palm, and on the eastern side, St. John Baptist with the *Agnus Dei*.

7. To the east of the window, in the highest tier, the Burial of the Virgin, a much-defaced scene, in which the tomb, the figure of St. John, fragments of another figure, and the head of the Virgin, may be discerned.

8. The Apostles at Table, with St. Thomas who, having been absent at the time doubted the Assumption of the Virgin, showing them her girdle, fallen from Heaven. St. John and St. Peter turn toward him, the former touching the girdle. Two of the other Apostles hold, respectively, a jug and a cup, and a third raises food to his mouth.

East wall: to the south of the east window, concluding scenes from the series of the Death of the Virgin, as follows:

1. In the lowest tier, St. Thomas, standing beside the tomb, receives her girdle.

2. The Assumption. In the centre stands the Virgin, her hands joined in prayer, supported by an Angel on either side.

3. The Coronation of the Virgin. Christ and the Virgin are seated side by side, and she raises her hands in prayer and bends her head to receive the crown.

The paintings, of *c.* 1350, were discovered in 1858. They are set out in incised line and executed on a ground of deep cream, against which the hands and faces of the figures, painted in a lighter tone, stand out in some degree. Earth colours, black and white are used, the colours being mixed with white, but seldom with one another, so as to form intermediate tints. Window arches and all plain spaces are diapered with sexfoil flowers.

Buckler, *Gent. M.*, 1860, N.S., VIII, pp. 274, 367, 547–56, repr.; Keyser, *Mural Decorations*, 1883; *Oxon. A. & H.S.P.*, 1886, N.S., V, 38; Wall, *Medieval Wall Paintings*, 1914, pp. 135–44, reprs.; Borenius & Tristram, *Eng. Med. Painting*, 1927, 21–2, repr.; Tristram, *Archaeologia*, 1927, LXXVI, 200–2, repr. Plates 30–8, 39*a, b,* 40*a, b.*

CHARLTON-ON-OTMOOR (near Oxford) Oxon

ST. MARY

The Chancel

South wall: a consecration cross of cross paty type, in red, within a double circle in grey; and another similar cross on the back of the central seat of the sedilia.

The Nave

The north arcade: on the soffits of the arches, crescents, stars, and scroll patterns elaborated with trefoils, and on the piers, chevrons in red.

The South Aisle

On the splays of a window at the eastern end, a scroll pattern in red on white.

Gent. M., 1860, VIII, 274; Keyser, *Mural Decorations*, 1883; Bruton, *Oxon A. & H.S.P.*, 1884, N.S., IV, 290.

CHARLWOOD (near Reigate) Surrey

ST. NICHOLAS

The South Aisle

Paintings survive on two areas of the south wall, respectively to the east and west of a two-light Early Decorated window. To the east, a 'History' of St. Margaret, arranged in three tiers, separated by narrow borders, as follows:

Highest tier, reading from the east; St. Margaret seated spinning, approached by the messenger from the Prefect Olybrius, clad in a hooded cloak and bearing a banner, charged with a cross upon a fretted field; he is followed by the Prefect himself mounted on horseback, but apparently engaged in hunting, since a dog coursing a hare is shown in the foreground, and behind him an attendant winding a horn and bearing a bow, or perhaps a hunting-staff. In the background is a conventionalized tree.

Central tier, reading from the east:

1. The Saint is scourged.

2. She is thrown into prison, with a gaoler in the act of thrusting her through a doorway surmounted by a cusped arch.

3. She is swallowed by the fiend in the form of a dragon (the head of the monster alone being clearly

visible), represented beneath a cusped arch, wherein appears a *Manus Dei* together with a few stars.

Lowest tier, reading from the east:

1. A defaced subject.

2. The Saint is beheaded, Olybrius being enthroned to the left, the executioner, with upraised sword, before him, with traces of the Saint's figure; above her a bird, flying heavenward, and a powdering of stars.

To the west of the window, previously mentioned, in the higher of two tiers, a subject from the 'history' of St. Nicholas, namely, the Resuscitation of the Three Boys, and in the lower the morality of *Les Trois Vifs et Les Trois Morts*; the three Kings, a spirited group of riders, all crowned, approaching the Three Corpses; immediately adjacent to the latter, the lower part of a Martyrdom of St. Edmund the King, the whole of which extends on to the higher part of the wall, a composition executed late in the century and on a large scale, whereas the works previously mentioned may be dated *c.* 1350. The two tiers of painting are separated by a band of chevron ornament, and the lower bordered below by another similar band. All the works described are now much damaged, as the result of an application of varnish.

Burges, *A.J.*, 1859, XVI, 89; *Gent. M.*, 1859, VI, 55; Way, *A.J.*, 1864, XXI, 209–17, repr.; Keyser, *Mural Decorations*, 1883; André, *Surrey Archaeological Collections*, 1893, XI, 13–18; *County Churches, Surrey*, 1910, 47; Johnston, *Memorials of Old Surrey*, 1911, 183–6, reprs.; *Vict. County Hist., Surrey*, 1911, III, 188; Wall, *Medieval Wall Paintings*, 1914, 204, repr.; Johnston, *Surrey Archaeological Collections*, 1927, XXXVII, 64–70, reprs.; *B.A.A.J.*, 1935, N.S., XL, 170; Carleton Williams, *B.A.A.J.*, 1942, 3rd ser., VII, 33–4, 39.

CHEDGRAVE (near Reedham) Norfolk
ALL SAINTS

Thomas Martin, *MS. Church Collections*, 1738, I, 211, illustrates a painting and comments:

'This painted but much defaced upon a wooden tabernacle yet standing in the steple, which steple I believe was once the north transept of the church, because there are several paintings on the wall and niches and a small old window northward, and IHS frequently, with angels painted about the sides.'

Features to be noted in the illustration are:—a man kneeling, an inscription reading DEPICTU[M] FUIT HOC TABERNAC[ULUM] . . . REGIS RECARDI SECŪDI VII: a large figure, bearing an emblem, the left hand raised; in the lower corner on the left, a fox and goose; and at the base on the right a figure with an inscribed scroll.

Norwich Free Library.

CHESHAM (near Berkhampstead) Bucks
ST. MARY

On the north-west pier of the tower (its south-west aspect) a bishop in mass vestments, holding a pastoral staff and with the right hand raised in blessing; also a consecration cross; and near by, on the respond of the north arcade, paintings of a hammer, pincers and horse-shoe.

In the north aisle, on the north wall, formerly one of St. Michael Weighing Souls.

Chapple, *Records of Bucks*, 1870, IV, 27–8; Keyser, *Mural Decorations*, 1883; *R.C. Historical Monuments R., Bucks*, 1912, I, 94.

CHESTER CASTLE, Cheshire

The vaulted chapel of St. Mary de Castro in Caesar's tower was formerly decorated with fourteenth-century wall-paintings; traces of scroll ornament in red, with leaf terminals, survived on the vaulting in 1937.

Simpson, *B.A.A.J.*, N.S., XXXII, 1926, 31; and notes by Mrs. M. Bardswell.

CHESTERTON, Cambs ST. ANDREW

In the Fitzwilliam Museum at Cambridge there is preserved a stone taken from Chesterton church, but from what position is unknown; upon it is painted the figure of a girl with long, curling hair, clad in a purple tunic and a bright blue mantle lined with pink. She has a nimbus, stands in a graceful pose, and holds in one hand a small pick or hammer and in the other a filled basket. Above her head is a cusped arch, and the background to the figure, which is of the natural colour of the stone, is covered by a small diaper pattern executed in black. The drawing, in black line, is very delicate in character. The work is very well preserved, and the colour of some beauty.

Within the splays of the east window, on the north side of the north aisle, formerly, an unidentified subject, ? The Works of Mercy.

Naylor, *Cambridge A.C.*, 1876, IV, 3–5, repr.; Keyser, *Mural Decorations*, 1883; Foster, *Cambridge A.C.*, 1908–9, XIII, 185–211.

CHEVELEY (near Newmarket) Cambs
ST. MARY

North transept: a masonry pattern executed in red

and black upon the walls, and on the splays of a small window, reopened *c.* 1853, a diaper of fleurs-de-lis in the same colours.

Fairlie, *Illustrations of Cheveley Church*, 1851, pl. VII; Bennet, *Suffolk I.A. & N.H.P.*, 1853, I, 237, 244; Keyser, *Mural Decorations*, 1883; Evelyn-White, *Churches of Cambridgeshire*, 1911, 47.

CHRISTCHURCH PRIORY, Hants

The Choir

The magnificent stone reredos, representing a Tree of Jesse, retains traces of its original colouring.

It is recorded that in 1848 remaining portions of the rood screen showed traces of colour.

Above the imitation stone vaulting of the nave a fine wooden roof exists, complete with its original painted decoration, comprising large flowers and leaves, and grotesque heads; the various members are picked out in colour, with red predominating.

A.J., 1848, V, 73, 142, 144; Sutton, *A.A.S.R. & P.*, 1868, IX, 254; Keyser, *Mural Decorations*, 1883.

CLIFTON CAMPVILLE (near Tamworth) Staffs

ST. ANDREW

The South Aisle

At the back of a tomb recess in the south wall, traces of a Coronation of the Virgin, of mid-fourteenth-century date, with supporting figures of a knight and his lady, all executed in red ochre, with a sparing use of black and light red, the treatment being linear; Christ has a cruciform nimbus, is clad in a tunic and mantle, holds an orb surmounted by a cross in the left hand, raises the right in benediction, and is seated on a throne of simple design, while the Virgin, enthroned beside Him, her hands raised in adoration, wears a crown. The background is pink in colour, diapered with crescents and stars in black. The knight, clad in chain mail, executed in black, and a light-coloured surcoat, has ailettes apparently once bearing charges, but, if so, these are no longer decipherable; his lady, veiled and having a crespine, is clad in a kirtle and a mantle coloured in pale pink. With the remains of this painting two shields, evidently executed at a slightly later date, towards the close of the century, are confused. Originally they both had charges, but only the charge on the one on the left is now decipherable—*Argent, a fret sable,* i.e. the arms of Vernon. Formerly under the arch over the recess—*On a fret sable a canton gules,* with the inscription 'Here lyeth the founder of the church';

on the wall at the back of the recess, another inscription 'This is the tomb of the founder of the church', and within an arch opposite, 'Here lyeth the founder's wife'. These three inscriptions apparently belong to, or were repainted at a later date.

The North Chapel

At the back of an altar recess in the east wall and on the wall above it, remains of painting, including traces of figures, approximately of the same date as those previously described.

The South Chapel

On the north wall in the spandrels of the arcade, formerly, remains of large medallions bordered by concentric bands of colour; recorded in a sketch in the possession of a former Rector, the Rev. R. Reed.

Cossins, *Birmingham & Midlands Inst.*, 1902, XXVII, 3–7.
Plate 57.

COLTON (near Kimberley) Norfolk

ST. ANDREW

The Nave

In a painting discovered in 1938, high on the west wall above the gallery, two women are represented seated upon a long bench, leaning towards each other with their heads close together, clasping hands, each holding a rosary in her free hand, the one on the spectator's left in her left, the other in her right. Both are veiled, and wear kirtles buttoned down the centre front, that of the woman on the right being red, the other, originally, green. Above them a devil is depicted, with one foot on the head of one, the other on the head of the other, with the tail hanging between them; its arms are akimbo and resting upon its knees. Two others, standing upon the ends of the bench, one on either side, appear to be pressing the women's heads together, as though encouraging them in undesirable conversation. Three scrolls in the upper part of the composition, two proceeding from the central devil, the third from that on the right, bear inscriptions, apparently meaningless arrangements of very similar letters, frequently repeated.

The painting is approximately 2 ft. 9 in. in width by 3 ft. 3 in. in height.

On the north wall, between the second and third windows from the west, a consecration cross incised in the plaster and framed by three bands of colour, two of them narrow, but of different widths, the outermost broader, and about $1\frac{1}{2}$ in. wide, originally painted green.

COLTON (near Rugeley) Staffs ST. MARY

The South Chancel Aisle and South Aisle

Extensive remains of painting, discovered *c.* 1851, and soon afterwards obliterated, comprised:

A diaper of cinquefoils in red on the usual lime-washed ground; parts of an ornamental border; a Temptation and Expulsion from Eden on the south wall of the south aisle, together with the lower part of a General Resurrection; and various figures of Bishops and Saints, one perhaps a St. Christopher, on the west wall of the south aisle and on the splays of the west window.

The Chancel

On the south wall, St. Nicholas and the Three Boys; and a Visitation.

Street, *The Ecclesiologist*, 1851, N.S., IX, 373–5; Keyser, *Mural Decorations*, 1883.

COOMBES (near Steyning) Sussex
DEDICATION UNKNOWN

The Chancel

On the north, south and east walls, masonry pattern in double red line enriched with cinquefoils in red, or, alternatively, in black, one in the centre of each block.

On the south side of the east window, a nimbed figure holding a scroll with traces of an inscription; the remains consist chiefly of underpainting in black, and red outline.

On the south wall, a Bishop in mass vestments holding a pastoral staff, and standing, within a niche, on a low platform decorated with small lancet windows; the whole much defaced.

On the north wall, opposite the figure just described, and also depicted within a niche, St. Christopher, with a nimbus, a hat with brim and slightly pointed crown, and hair cut to the level of the ears, holding a staff in his right hand and the Holy Child, whose head is faintly visible, on his left arm; he is clad in a gipon reaching just below knee level. The entire painting is much defaced.[1]

Johnston, *Sussex Archaeological Collections*, 1898, XLIII, 232.

CORBY (near Grantham) Lincs
ST. JOHN THE EVANGELIST

The North Aisle

On the north wall, to the east of the north door, St. Anne teaching the Virgin, a subject approximately 8 ft. × 4 ft. in size, executed on a cream ground. St. Anne, with a green and yellow nimbus and a veil, is clad in a light-coloured cloak falling in intricate folds on her right side and fastened at the neck with an ouch of diamond shape patterned in green, and a cream kirtle with folds drawn in grey, held at the hips by a long girdle patterned in green and black. She passes her left arm about the slight figure of the Virgin, who looks down towards the original position of the book, now defaced, to which her mother points; her long, wavy hair, bound by a fillet, is drawn in red outline, as are her and St. Anne's features, and she is clad in a brown kirtle and 'sideless' gown of green, having fitchets. The group is supported upon a long, shallow step or pedestal, ornamented with quatrefoils in black outline. *c.* 1325.

To the east of the subject just described, between two windows and opposite the south door, remains of a St. Christopher, of the usual gigantic proportions, now measuring approximately 9 ft. × 5 ft., and originally, as seems probable, nearly 11 ft. in height. The figure is much damaged, the head and that of the Holy Child being entirely destroyed; but it may be seen that the gipon reaching to the knees, was painted in red ochre on cream, with a black outline, a border in double black line elaborated with small roundels in black being placed at the neck, while the cloak, draped in heavy folds, is pink in colour and lined with green. The right hand grasps the staff, painted green, and the left supports the Child, who, once raising the right hand in blessing, holds in the left an Orb of the Universe, the lower part patterned with wavy lines in green and yellow, outlined in black, to represent water, the upper part, almost totally destroyed, having apparently been coloured yellow. The slight figure is clad in a cream tunic with folds executed in grey, the whole being patterned with large spots in green, outlined in black and surrounded by a circle of small spots in vermilion within a black outline; at the hem, neck and wrist is a narrow border in green and vermilion, composed of small spots within black outlines. Colour survives on the window mouldings, and on a small image-niche in the wall; and on the splays of the windows are traces of a masonry pattern in double line, enriched with roses. *c.* 1350.

The South Aisle

On the south side of the east window, a scroll pattern elaborated with vine-leaves and tendrils, executed in black on a pinkish ground, with a narrow border composed of red, pink and white lines and an outer, wider one patterned with a diamond fret in

[1] The whole almost entirely defaced and virtually unidentifiable since the above description was written.

deep red and pink, each diamond enclosing a quatre-foil. *c.* 1325. On the north of the same window, indecipherable remains of a figure framed within a canopied niche, of approximately the same date.

In the south-east corner of the aisle, and continued on to the east wall traces of a Tree of Jesse, with the fragment of the figure of a kneeling donor and of an inscription reading ORATE P̃ ANI . . ., the first letter rubricated; though the work is much defaced, it may be seen that the background was originally red, and the foliage green, the stems, outlined in red ochre, having been painted in yellow and green.

Rouse, *Lincs. A. & A.S.R.*, 1938, II, pt. 1, 7–12; id., *A.J.*, 1945, C, 150–76, reprs.

GREAT CORNARD (near Sudbury) Suffolk
ST. ANDREW

On the wall near the Lady Chapel, remains of a female figure with a devil behind her.

NORTH COVE (near Beccles) Suffolk
ST. BOTOLPH

The Chancel

In three tiers on the north, and one on the south wall, a Passion series, and between two windows on the south, a Doom, the entire space on both walls not occupied by subject-paintings being filled with a vine-scroll pattern having numerous bunches of grapes; the whole repainted at some time in an unusually incompetent manner. North wall, reading from the east:

In the highest tier, only the feet of a number of figures, and, to the east of the easternmost window, the Resurrection.

In the central tier, the Entry into Jerusalem, and the Harrowing of Hell.

In the lowest tier, reading from west to east, the Flagellation, the Nailing to the Cross, with executioners in parti-coloured garments, and the Descent from the Cross. Formerly, the Last Supper and the Crucifixion.

South wall, reading from the east:

The Ascension, and the Last Judgement, the latter comprising all the normal features, including Angels with Instruments of the Passion, others blowing the Last Trump, and St. Michael separating the Blessed and the Lost, with a General Resurrection below. *c.* 1300.

Keyser, *Mural Decorations*, 1883; Bryant, *County Churches, Suffolk*, 1912, 220; Munro Cautley, *Suffolk Churches and Their Treasures*, 1928, 244; James, *Suffolk and Norfolk*, 1933, 110.

COVENTRY CATHEDRAL ST. MICHAEL

As the result of bombing and consequent vibration during the recent war, a painting of the Blessed Virgin and Child, and above it a head of Christ, the latter with a cruciform nimbus, were revealed on the north wall of the nave; the head, however, was soon afterwards destroyed. The Blessed Virgin bore the Child on her left arm and in the right hand held flowers resembling in shape the wild tulip. *c.* 1330.

Catholic Herald, 1941, x, iv.

COWLEY (near Oxford) Oxon ST. JAMES

Towards the end of the last century paintings then discovered in the church were destroyed; tracings of some of the subjects, made before this took place, are preserved in the Bodleian Library, and suffice to show that they were of high quality and mainly of late fourteenth-century date. They are as follows:

1. St. Anne teaching the Virgin. On the right, the tall, standing figure of the Saint, wearing a crespine and head-band, holds an open book before the slight figure of the Virgin, who, veiled and clad in a tunic and mantle, with black shoes, extends both hands towards it. The background is diapered with roundels, and the scene is framed within a scroll-work border. *c.* 1350.

2. The head of the Virgin; well drawn, it is of life-size, and above it are traces of a small Angel holding a crown.

3. A crowned Saint, bearing a book, with the figure of a donor.

4. Two censing Angels.

5. A Trinity, of normal type, formerly over the east window.

6. Christ as Creator; a large figure, facing left, the right hand raised in benediction and in the left an Orb of the Universe; the head is crowned and the beard forked. Formerly on the east wall of the chancel, to the south side.

The majority of the surviving subjects appear to have been in the chancel. Besides the Trinity and the Christ, mentioned above, a Virgin and Child (to which the head of the Virgin, previously described, may have belonged), and a Presentation in the Temple, are stated to have existed on the north side of the east wall; on the north wall, a 'row of Saints'; and on the south wall a Descent from the Cross. On the containing arch of the east window masonry pattern was visible. In the nave, apart from an unidentified subject, said to have existed in the south spandrel of the chancel arch, in which were two figures 'one presenting a church to the other', only masonry pattern, on the north and south walls, and about the arch a diaper of cinquefoils, are recorded.

Keyser, *Mural Decorations*, 1883; *Oxon A. & H.S.P.* 1888, N.S., V, 7.

CRANBORNE, Dorset
ST. MARY AND ST. BARTHOLOMEW

The Nave

In the spandrels between the arches of the south nave arcade, on its south side, reading from east to west:

1. Fragments of three skeletons—no doubt remains of a *Trois Vifs et Trois Morts*.

2. Opposite the north door, St. Christopher, 13 ft. in height, in a fragmentary state, the head, the right hand holding the staff, and the left supporting the Holy Child, the legs, with breeches tied at the knee, and some fish about the ankles, being decipherable.

3. The Seven Deadly Sins. A Tree with holly leaves, springing from the bust of a woman clad in veil, wimple, and mantle with a narrow border, holding her left arm upraised; at the apex of the Tree a crowned (?) male figure seated at a table laid with a variety of vessels, who turns towards a devil, with a trumpeter just behind him, perched upon a branch to the left; on either side of the trunk, three branches with nude figures at the ends, representing the Sins; that placed centrally on the left has the right arm grasped by a devil, but like all the others except one opposite, is unidentifiable. The exception, a figure with a jug upraised to the mouth, and a protuberant stomach, evidently represents Gluttony under the form of Drunkenness, though Gluttony appears also to be represented by the feasting figure at the apex of the Tree. The work has been almost entirely repainted in outline, and having been partially misunderstood by the restorer is suspect in many of its features—notably the curious fan-shaped objects attached to the highest figure on the left, below the devil and the trumpeter.

4. The Seven Corporal Works of Mercy. Apparently also a Tree, although the trunk is almost, and the branches are entirely, defaced; at the apex, Christ Blessing, with a censing Angel on either side; at the base, a kneeling female figure, facing east, with hands upraised in prayer, and two more Angels; on both sides, against a ground diapered with cinquefoils, small figures, originally representative of the Works, but now unidentifiable as such, apart from one on the right, a woman casting a cloak about a smaller figure, doubtless Clothing the Naked.

Dorset A.S., 1902, XXIII, xxxv–vi; Fletcher, ibid., 1924, XLV, xxxii; Long, ibid., 1928, L, 106; Whaite, *St. Christopher*, 1929, 21, pl. 8(a).

CRANFORD (near Hounslow) Middlesex
ST. DUNSTAN

The Chancel

On the east wall, a masonry pattern, the horizontal lines being single and the vertical double, enriched with a voided sexfoil in the centre of each block, all in red. *c.* 1300.

Upon later plaster on the same wall a stencilled diaper of crowned Ms in black; and above the east window, rays and traces of the lower part of a subject; all *c.* 1400, or perhaps of slightly later date.

CROSTWIGHT (near North Walsham) Norfolk
ALL SAINTS

The Nave

Paintings were discovered on the north wall *c.* 1847, and in 1938 a further exploration was made. Reading from the west, the subjects are as follows:

1. A Tree of the Seven Deadly Sins, its base to the left of the north door, its top rising above it; at the apex a figure of (?) *Superbia*, much defaced, as is also the highest of the three Sins depicted on the left side, the survivals being *Luxuria*, with two figures in an embrace, and *Socordia*, a woman resting her head on her hand, identified by an inscribed scroll; on the right side the Sin depicted in the highest position is *Gula*, holding a cup, with *Avaritia*, laden with money-bags, below, and immediately below again a bearded male figure with the right hand raised and the left on the hip, perhaps *Ira*, in which case the remaining Sin, that at the top on the left side, and now indecipherable, would have been *Invidia*. As well as the usual dragon-heads, with their mouths framing the Sins, the tree bears ivy-shaped leaves; on the left, within the Jaws of Leviathan at its root, is a large devil, and on the right slight traces of three (?) seated figures. The painting measures 9 ft. 3 in. × 4 ft. Below it is a consecration cross, of cross paty type, incised in the plaster and painted red.

2. Immediately adjacent, over the north door, is a subject in which three richly-dressed couples are represented as seated at a long, narrow table, supported on four legs, the entire group depicted within the arms of a gigantic demon, as follows:

i. Left. A man, hooded, wearing an elaborately dagged gorget and cote-hardie with tippets, passes his left arm about a woman (probably, but the kirtle is not discernible since the lower part is destroyed, and the upper is indistinct), who twines her right arm about the man's waist and leans her head against his.

ii. Middle. A man and a woman stand, with heads close together, embracing each other; on the left, the woman clad in a travelling hood with a gorget and a cote-hardie, embroidered with small shields, and tippets to her sleeves; the man bearded and bare-headed, with hair curled at the level of the chin, clad in a low-necked cote-hardie.

iii. Right. The figures of the third pair, also locked in an embrace, are so defaced that of their attire only the dagged gorget of the woman, and the single remaining shield upon her robe are clearly visible.

3. Immediately to the east of the doorway is a St. Christopher of the usual gigantic proportions, now mainly a silhouette against a ground of dark red, with little detail surviving; the knee-length gipon is yellow, and a short yellow cloak is draped about the shoulders. In the right hand is a staff, and the left supports the Holy Child, clad in a long red tunic; water is visible about the Saint's legs, but no fish are discernible. To the east, fragments of other subjects are seen where they show around the edges of a memorial tablet; they comprise the bare legs of another figure on the same gigantic scale as the St. Christopher, part of a red cloak, and of the white drapery of another figure. Below the memorial, near the left foot of the St. Christopher, is a consecration cross having foliated terminals, within a circle incised in the plaster.

4. Between two windows in the same wall, further to the east, are three tiers of paintings, divided both vertically and horizontally by narrow bands of scroll-work, the subjects thus framed being depicted against grounds alternately red and yellow, as follows:

A Passion series, opening in the second tier with the Entry into Jerusalem; on the left a group of Apostles, Christ and the Ass in a fragmentary state, and to the right a man throwing a garment before it, with indications of several smaller figures above. Immediately to the right, slight traces of a Last Supper, the head of Christ and those of some of the Apostles surviving, and the Washing of Feet, with Christ, in a red tunic, bending towards St. Peter, seated, with other Apostles behind him. The series continues on the western splay of the window on the spectator's right with the Agony in the Garden, Christ in a kneeling position, accompanied by three Disciples. At this point the series is continued in the highest tier with (reading from the west) Christ

Before Pilate, a better-preserved subject than the others, in which it may be seen that the work was technically once somewhat elaborate, the flesh tints having been painted solidly upon a dark ground, and white shaded with grey used upon certain of the garments represented, while the background was enriched with a pattern of quatrefoils; on the left stands Christ, bound and held by a man in a white gipon and short red cote-hardie with a dagged border. Pilate, seated to the right on a yellow throne, is almost indistinguishable. There follows a much-defaced subject (?) the Scourging; and a Crowning with Thorns is at this point placed between the highest tier of paintings and the second—a small scene in which the figure of Christ, and those of the two tormentors engaged in placing the crown upon His head, are of half-length. The next subject, the Carrying of the Cross, is much damaged; to the east of it is the Crucifixion, in which the two thieves, Longinus thrusting the spear into the side of Christ, Stephaton holding the sponge upon a reed, the Virgin in a fainting attitude, and St. Mary Magdalen at the foot of the cross, are all decipherable. At the edge of the window on the spectator's right part of an Entombment remains, and the tomb, the body of Christ laid within it, and some attendant figures may be made out. The series is concluded in the lowest tier by the only subject remaining there, the Ascension, with a group of Apostles gazing upward; but the feet of Christ, as usually shown in this scene, dis-appearing into clouds, are defaced. Below, to the west, is a third consecration cross, of elaborate design, with foliated terminals and trefoils about the centre, executed in red on white within a circular border. To the extreme left of the highest tier, adjacent to the Christ Before Pilate, is a female Saint, wearing a wimple and coronet or head-band, and carrying an object, the nature of which is not clear; and immediately below, in the second tier, a figure, yellow-haired, raising the right arm—part of a painting now almost indecipherable.

On the south side of the east wall are fragments of a fourth consecration cross, similar in design to that just described, painted over a subject of rather earlier date, from which there remains within the cross a small head. Further to the south is a fragment of a scroll-work border in red, and above and to the north of the chancel arch, which retains traces of colour, another similar fragment.

P. Society of Antiquaries, 1849, I, 269; B. Mus., Dawson Turner Collection, N.S., II, 109–22, 125, 126; Keyser, Mural Decorations, 1883; André, A.J., 1888, XLV, 416; Blomefield's Norfolk Supplement, 1929, 312.

CROUGHTON (near Brackley) Northants

ALL SAINTS

The South Aisle: south wall, in three tiers, separated by borders of bent-riband pattern, the Life and Death of the Virgin and the Holy Infancy. *c.* 1310.

Highest tier, reading from east to west:

1. The Rejection of St. Joachim's Offering. On the left, the High Priest, mitred and wearing an amice and chasuble, the bearded head, bust and extended hands only visible; he turns slightly to the right to face St. Joachim, who, bearded, and clad in a red tunic and light-coloured mantle, raises his right hand.

2. Beyond an intervening window, a fragment only of a subject, ? the Appearance of the Angel to St. Anne; the lower part of a figure facing left, clad in a red mantle and tunic of faded black, similar to those of St. Anne in the next scene, alone survives.

3. The Meeting of St. Joachim and St. Anne at the Golden Gate. Beneath the trefoiled round-headed arch of the Gate, with battlements above it, St. Joachim and St. Anne embrace, she caressing his face with her left hand, he passing his arms about her; he, on the left, is clad in a yellow mantle, light-coloured tunic, and black shoes, and has a hat of bee-hive shape hanging on his back; she wears a red mantle lined with cream and a tunic of a pale bluish colour, and on her head a head-dress comprising a barbette, and a fillet with its upper edge shaped as if battlemented.

4. The Birth of the Virgin. The centre of the scene is defaced; to the left there remains the arm of a woman clad in red, and ? the corner of a pillow, or part of a vessel; on the right, beyond the blank space, a woman in a red tunic, wearing a white head-dress and facing left, with traces of a child's figure before her, and below, ? part of a striped coverlet; probably St. Anne, half-reclining on a couch and holding her infant. To the right is a cradle with balustered sides, foliated terminals to the head and foot posts, and bedclothes fastened down by three cream-coloured bands attached to the side rails.

5. The Presentation of the Virgin. On the left St. Anne, clad as in the previous scene, and standing before a wide-open door, consoles St. Joachim, who, wearing a red mantle and light-coloured tunic, holds ? the empty purse which had contained his offering and turns away from the slight figure of the Virgin (mainly defaced, except for the head) who mounts the fifteen steps of the Temple behind him towards the High Priest (largely defaced), standing on the highest step before an altar draped in red.

6. The Departure of the Virgin from Home. On the left, St. Anne, in red mantle and light-coloured tunic, with a fillet about her head and a barbette, is seated holding an open book before the Virgin, a slight figure with a head kerchief, red robe, and white under-tunic with long sleeves, whose left hand is grasped by St. Joachim as he prepares to lead her away for the Espousals; with his left hand he points towards the right, but turns his head back towards St. Anne. He wears a red cap, a cloak of the same colour with a dark lining, fastened by a yellow brooch, and a light-coloured tunic; near him on the right are two sheep, and a tree. This part of the painting, together with the figure of St. Joachim, is somewhat defaced.

7. The Espousals of the Virgin and St. Joseph. On the left are seven figures, three of them perhaps young men, and, if so, probably suitors, and four women, three of them veiled, and one with a fillet and barbette. All look towards an open doorway, before which the High Priest, standing frontally, vested in a chasuble and alb, performs the ceremony; St. Joseph is on his right, with a bare-headed stripling in a cream-coloured robe behind him, and the Virgin (an almost defaced figure) is on his left. A flight of four steps, leading to an altar draped in red on the extreme right with some slight traces of a figure before it, may form part of the same scene, or perhaps of another, such as the Appearance of the Angel to Zacharias.

Central tier, reading from east to west:

The space beneath the Rejection of St. Joachim's Offering, in the higher tier, is now blank, but must originally have been occupied by an Annunciation.

8. Beyond the intervening window, the Visitation. Of this only the lower part of the embracing figures survives.

9. The Nativity. Extending across the greater part of the scene, is the couch, with a red coverlet from beneath which appears white drapery, and at its foot St. Joseph is seated in a chair, leaning with both hands on his staff. Behind the couch is the manger, with the Holy Child, and to the right the head of the Ox; the upper part of the Virgin's figure is defaced.

10. The Appearance of the Angel to the Shepherds. On the left is the Angel, in a red mantle and tunic of deep cream colour, with the right wing lowered and the left raised behind the head, pointing with the right hand towards the shepherds, and holding a scroll, now blank, in the left; to the west traces only remain of a shepherd's figure, viz. a hand holding a staff, and the pendant end of a bag-pipe, and at the feet, a small barking dog.

11. The Magi before Herod, above the arch of a door. On the left are fragments of two of the Magi,

the foremost figure being the most complete; he is crowned, and raises his left hand towards Herod, who, crowned and bearded, is seated to the right, holding a sword, point upward, in the left hand.

12. The Adoration of the Magi. This scene beginning above the level of the door extends to the right. One white and one reddish brown horse (perhaps two), both saddled, are led westward by a bearded attendant in a yellow and black tunic, the colours counter-changed, and a black hood, ornamented by a zigzag line running round the edge of the gorget. Holding a spear upright in the left hand and grasping the reins in the right, he has his head turned back towards the horses. Immediately to the right, just beyond the arch of the door, are the Magi. The first is facing westward, a covered cup held in the right hand and the left extended towards the second who, with a covered vessel clasped in both hands, stands frontally and looks back. The third with a goblet held upraised in the right hand, kneels immediately before the Virgin, enthroned, crowned and veiled, supporting erect upon her knee the slight figure of the Holy Child, who extends the left hand as if to receive the goblet and gives His blessing with the right.

13. The Massacre of the Innocents, beyond an intervening window. On the left a soldier in mail armour, with a yellow surcoat over it, brandishes above his head a sword held in the right hand, while he tramples on the bodies of two children and grasps with the left the wrist of a bigger child, standing on its mother's knee, who, seated on the ground, embraces and attempts to protect it. On the earth beside her are the heads of two children, and behind her a second soldier, in a red surcoat and a broad helmet, grips the ankle of another victim, which he holds head downward.

14. The Flight into Egypt. The Virgin, clad in a black mantle drawn up over her head, and holding the Child, swathed in black, in the crook of her left arm, is seated on a yellow donkey which is led westward by St. Joseph, who, clad in a red tunic, but without any head-covering, looks back towards her, and over his right shoulder carries a staff with a white cloak hanging upon it. To his belt are fastened a purse and a sheathed knife.

Lowest tier, reading from east to west:

15. The Presentation in the Temple, of which little remains but the heads, viz. on the extreme left, St. Joseph's, nimbed, and covered with a cap, next to him, the maid's or midwife's, with fillet and barbette, one hand holding a candle, then the Virgin's, with a red nimbus encircled by a white line within its edge, and a white veil, and, finally, the Holy

Child's, with a cruciform nimbus, the cross black on yellow.

16. Beyond an intervening window, the Death of the Virgin series opens with the Appearance of the Angel with the Palm; but of this only a fragment remains, showing a part of the Virgin's red nimbus, again edged with a white line, and of her white veil and red mantle.

17. The Virgin giving the Palm to St. John. She stands, nimbed, and clad as before, raising the left hand and extending the right with the palm towards St. John, who receives it in his left. He has yellow hair, is nimbed, and wears a light-coloured mantle over a red tunic.

18. The Gathering of the Apostles. A much-defaced subject, of which there survives part of the Virgin's figure, the heads of five of the Apostles, and the lower parts of their draperies.

19. The Death of the Virgin. Almost entirely defaced, fragments of two nimbed heads, and of the drapery of the couch, alone remaining.

20. The Funeral of the Virgin, and the Miracle of the Jews. Of this scene, part of the red pall, ornamented with a lozenge pattern enriched with four-petalled flowers, to which two Jews are clinging, survives.

21. Beyond the doorway, The Burial of the Virgin; fragments of nimbed figures are decipherable, together with a small part of the tomb; one, in a red tunic and a light-coloured cloak fastened with a morse, holds a book in the left hand and extends the right.

22. The Assumption. Within a yellow mandorla, supported by two Angels on either side (those on the right almost defaced), the Virgin stands frontally with hands joined in prayer.

Beyond an intervening window is a blank space, probably once occupied by the Coronation of the Virgin.

The North Aisle: north wall, in two tiers, separated by a border of bent-riband pattern, and finished above and below by borders ornamented with scroll-work, a Passion series.

Higher tier, reading from the west:

1. The Entry into Jerusalem. The upper part of the scene is defaced, as is also a portion on the extreme left. In the centre Christ clad in a white robe, rides on an ass towards the gate of the city, on the right. He is followed by a group of Apostles, their figures, except in one instance, where a hand holding a book and part of the mantle and tunic survive, obliterated except for the feet. On the ground beneath the hoofs of the ass are trefoil leaves, and immediately in front

of it a man in a short tunic holds a red, long-sleeved garment in its path; behind him stands another figure, in a tunic of three-quarter length, holding a staff. The heads of both are obliterated.

2. The Last Supper. A table covered with a white cloth, falling in folds at regular intervals, stretches the entire length of the composition; upon it are vessels and knives of different types, including a flagon, with a covered cup beside it, and another covered vessel (? a salt) on three legs, and below it are visible the drapery and bare feet of those seated. At the far side, in the centre, Christ caresses with his left hand the head of St. John on His right, as it lies upon His breast; His right arm passes over the Saint's neck as He hands the sop to Judas, kneeling on the near side of the table. Immediately beyond St. John is St. Peter, looking towards Christ, and raising both hands; still further to the spectator's left are four more Apostles, one holding a small object partly resting on the board, another raising food to his mouth, a third, at the far end, who is beardless, with left hand raised, the fourth mainly defaced. To the right of the centre are traces of five more, all except one who is beardless, facing east, with left hand raised, much defaced.

Above an intervening door is a space now vacant, perhaps originally filled by the Agony in the Garden.

3. The Betrayal. The lower part is entirely defaced; in the centre, Christ receives the kiss of Judas, who, in giving it, passes the right arm about His neck; to the left are the heads of two Apostles, to the right a soldier putting out his tongue and brandishing a sword held in his left hand, and beyond him traces of two more, bearing spears.

4. The Trial before the High Priests. Christ, clad in a long, light-coloured tunic, and without a mantle, stands between two guards, one with a close cap or hood, its peak turned upwards from the forehead. The High Priests, on the right, wear, respectively, a 'Jewish' cap, and a cap or hood with a long peak rising up behind. All the figures are much defaced.

5. An almost entirely obliterated scene, probably the Mocking; among the indistinct traces, a man in a light-coloured hood and a red tunic, the arms upraised.

6. The Flagellation. Christ, clad in a loin-cloth, His arms about the pillar, is in the centre, His head inclined to the left, where survives part of the figure of an executioner, wearing a tall, winged cap. The pillar supports a miniature building, surrounded by battlements, and having a gabled roof; to the right is a second executioner, in a close cap and short, parti-coloured tunic, grasping a scourge, which he holds above his head, leaping to add more force to the blow he is about to inflict.

7. The Carrying of the Cross. To the left is a gaoler or executioner in a red and white tunic (the colours counter-changed) who holds up an indecipherable object in his right hand, and jumps in the act of pushing forward, with his left, Christ, who carries the Cross upon His right shoulder and turns His head to look back at him. The Cross is tau-shaped, and its long shaft extends into the adjacent Crucifixion scene, passing across a group composed of:—an executioner in a peaked hood or cap, just behind Christ, the Virgin, swooning, with her head drooping to the left and her body supported by an unknown Saint, with nimbus and veiled head, and Longinus, who pierces the side of Christ upon the Cross, and points to his eyes; in this manner the group in question is made to play a part both in the scene of the Carrying of the Cross, and in the next.

8. The Crucifixion. Christ hangs upon the Cross, His feet fastened to it by a single nail, and His head inclined to the left towards Longinus who is clothed in a long red tunic, showing a white garment beneath it, and the Virgin, who is swooning; to the immediate right of the Cross is the lower part of a man's figure, clad in a light-coloured tunic, and beyond, St. John, somewhat defaced. Except for a few traces, the remainder of the composition, on this side, is obliterated.

9. The Deposition. On the left, the Virgin watches the lowering of the Body from the tau-shaped Cross into the arms of Joseph of Arimathaea, and on the right, St. John clasps the extended left arm; in front of and rather below him, Nicodemus draws the nails from the feet.

10. The Entombment. To the left, the Virgin supports the Body, and to the right Joseph of Arimathaea, with St. John behind him, anoints the left arm from a large, white bottle; the tomb, of a bluish-grey colour, is supported upon three cusped arches, the lower part of the Virgin's white drapery appearing through that on the left, and through the other two, the red tunic and cloak of St. Joseph and St. John respectively.

11. The Harrowing of Hell. On the left side are the gaping jaws of Leviathan with traces of figures inside them, and above, of two small demons, both long-eared, one tailed, and the other winged. To the right Adam and Eve follow Christ, who holds a tall cross (not the vexillum). The entire scene is much damaged.

12. The Resurrection. Still more defaced, the left

portion only surviving, in a fragmentary state, and including only a part of the figure of the risen Christ, emerging from the tomb, on the left side of which is a small kneeling Angel, with upraised wings.

The remainder of the series, which probably filled the spaces on either side of the intervening doorway, has been destroyed. Near a window, beyond the door, is a pot of lilies, much defaced, which may have formed part of the Lady Chapel scheme at the end of the same wall. The first subject in this scheme is that of St. Anne teaching the Virgin. St. Anne, clad in a light-coloured mantle, fastened by a brooch, and a red tunic, and with a fillet and barbette on her head, holds an open book before the Virgin, a slight figure standing by her side. The lower part of the work is defaced. To the left is the Angel of the Annunciation, in light mantle and red tunic, pointing with the right hand and holding a blank scroll in the left, with the right wing lowered and the left extended, above a pot of lilies in the direction of the Virgin, towards whom the Dove descends. She has fair, flowing hair, a red nimbus encircled by a white line, and raises her left hand. The lower part of the figure is defaced.

Keyser, *B.A.A.J.*, 1921, XXVII, 135; Tristram and James, *Archaeologia*, 1927, LXXVI, 179; Borenius and Tristram, *English Medieval Painting*, 1927, 20, repr.; Noppen, *Burl. M.*, 1930, LVII, 77–8; Saunders, *English Art in the Middle Ages*, 1932, pp. 169–70, repr.; Long, *Oxon. A.S.*, 1932–6, 19–20. Plate 21.

DALHAM (near Newmarket) Suffolk ST. MARY

The Nave

Between the western and the central arch of the north pier arcade, a Tree of the Seven Deadly Sins, the branches ending in dragons' heads with traces of figures within the jaws, and of devils; there are remains of inscriptions in black letter.

Between the central and the eastern arch, the Corporal Works of Mercy, one, on the spectator's right, Feeding the Hungry, with a figure giving a loaf to a beggar or pilgrim in a hood having a gorget and surmounted by a hat, still clearly decipherable; formerly, a figure, described as an Angel, depicted on a large scale, in the centre, pointing to the representations. *c.* 1400; in the main, now much defaced.

On the central space of the north aisle wall, traces of horses, now almost indistinguishable, apart from some hooves.

Keyser, *Mural Decorations*, 1883; Bryant, *County Churches, Suffolk*, 1912, I, 167; Munro Cautley, *Suffolk Churches and Their Treasures*, 1928, 249.

ST. DAVID'S, Pembroke CATHEDRAL OF ST. DAVID

Considerable remains of painting on Bishop Gower's rood screen (1328–47) comprise:—in a tomb recess on the north side of the entrance, on the west wall, a Crucifixion with the Virgin and St. John, on the eastern wall, the Reception of a Soul into Heaven, and on the vaulting over the recess, symbols of the Evangelists, grotesques, and foliage, the latter including rose and holly. On the eastern face of the western entrance arch, an owl and two magpies.

Jones and Freeman, *The History and Antiquities of St. David's*, 1856, 127–8; Keyser, *Mural Decorations*, 1883.

DODFORD (near Daventry) Northants ST. MARY

North Aisle

North wall, within the arch covering the tomb of Hawise Keynes, who died after 1329, and of Wensiliana de Keynes, her great-grand-daughter, who died in 1376, a painting of the Soul taken to Heaven by Angels; and a *Manus Dei* appearing from clouds above, near the apex of the arch to the spectator's right. Below is a row of five shields, the three in the middle defaced, that to the extreme left—*Barry argent and gules*, that to the extreme right—*Ermine, a cross gules*.

Traces of colour remain on the two effigies.

Baker, *History & Antiquities of Northants*, 1822–30, I, 360; Bloxam, *A.J.*, 1878, XXXV, 258, repr.; Keyser, *Mural Decorations*, 1883; Wall, *Medieval Wall Paintings*, 1914, 24, repr.

DORCHESTER (near Oxford) Oxon
ST. PETER AND ST. PAUL

The South Aisle

East wall, western face, within a large but shallow recess placed high above the altar, a Cross in red, measuring approximately 10 ft. × 6 ft., upon a white ground retaining slight traces of a diaper in yellow; around the arch of the recess remains of bands in black and red; and on the wall to the south, of a patterned hanging in red, much defaced.

Immediately above the altar, a Crucifixion with St. Mary and St. John, entirely repainted, but evidently on the general lines of the original; Christ hangs upon the Cross with body bent in a double curve, the feet fastened by a single nail, and to the left is the Sun, represented after the manner of an estoile, and to the right the crescent Moon. The red background is patterned by a diamond fret, each diamond enclosing a constellation of spots, and borders of wavy pattern frame the subject both above and below. On either side a painted hanging, stencilled with large flowers in red on white, evidently in detail a conjectural restoration. All the works described would appear to be, or to have been, of the early fourteenth century.

On the eastern face of the same wall, a pattern of small connected roundels, in red on cream, framing delicately-executed ornament, now much defaced; perhaps of the early fourteenth century.

The Ecclesiologist, 1846, V, 24; Keyser, *Mural Decorations*, 1883.

DORNEY (near Eton) Bucks ST. JAMES

The Chancel

On the north wall, an Annunciation. The Angel Gabriel, with a nimbus, clad in a white tunic, and a mantle of pink and red, lined with black, holding a scroll in the left hand and raising the right in salutation, is on the western side of the composition, framed within a niche surmounted by a painted arch with a finial at the apex. The Virgin, veiled, and clad in a black tunic and a white mantle, the latter fastened at the neck by a brooch, bears a book in the left hand, and raises the right in acknowledgement of the Angel's message; the upper part of the head and the entire arch over the niche formerly framing the figure, are missing. The work is executed in line, in the normal ochres and black. *c*. 1300.

The Nave

On the north side of the tower arch, formerly, traces of a nimbed figure framed within a small niche.

On the west wall, traces of a subject, and remains of colour here and there in other positions.

R.C. Historical Monuments R., Bucks, 1912, I, 127–8; Rouse, *Records of Bucks*, 1933, XII, 399–400.

DUCKLINGTON (near Witney) Oxon
ST. BARTHOLOMEW

The South Aisle

On the southern splay of the east window, a Trinity, framed within a crocketed and cusped arch and executed in ochres and black, of *c*. 1325; the figure of God the Father, with a cruciform nimbus, is enthroned, with the feet resting on a footstool and the hands raised, and clad in a light-coloured tunic and a black mantle. A representation of Christ on the Cross survives in the usual position, but all traces of the Dove have vanished. To the left are remains of a kneeling figure.

Other paintings discovered in the same aisle some thirty years or more ago were obliterated, tracings

being preserved by the Revd. Christopher Tristram. From them it may be seen that a subject on the south wall was a Betrayal, since the name MALCVS was inscribed beside one of the figures. Some fragmentary lettering still remains on the same wall, together with the head of a crossed staff and a rosette.

N. Oxon Archaeological Society, 1891, XXVIII, 11; Keyser, *A.J.*, 1895, LIII, 181.
Plate 58.

DURHAM
THE CATHEDRAL CHURCH OF THE BLESSED VIRGIN MARY

On the south side of the choir is the monument of Bishop Hatfield, who died in 1381; the entire structure was once richly gilded and coloured and still retains much of its colour; on the walls at both the eastern and western ends are in each case two Angels, those at the eastern end bearing shields, now blank, those at the other end too damaged for it to be possible to ascertain whether they, also, were depicted holding shields.

Keyser, *Mural Decorations*, 1883; *Victoria County Hist., Durham*, 1928, III, 107.

DURLEY (near Bishop's Waltham) Hants
HOLY CROSS

Paintings were discovered and again obliterated before 1888; a figure holding a scroll and 'figures of Saints' are mentioned in the accounts, but there can be no certainty regarding the date of any of these; the only work now visible, a representation of a ship, showing the bow and forecastle, the mast with fighting top and yard, and the figure of a man in the rigging, appears to be of the fourteenth century.

Keyser, *A.J.*, 1896, LIII, 171; id., *Memorials of Old Hants*, 1906, 151; Sansbury, *The Mariner's Mirror*, 1945, XXXI, 107–8, repr.

DYMCHURCH, Kent ST. PETER AND ST. PAUL

The Nave

South wall, eastern end: within a recess, masonry pattern in black on white, the horizontal courses indicated in single line, the vertical divisions between the blocks, which are ornamented with quatrefoils and scrolls, in double line.

Description supplied by Mrs. Bardswell.

EATON (near Norwich) Norfolk ST. ANDREW

Two consecration crosses survive from a scheme of painting discovered in 1860, which seems to have been largely of fifteenth-century date, but included, on the south wall of the nave, a Martyrdom of St. Thomas of Canterbury, of *c.* 1400; to the spectator's left, a small building, within which is an altar and behind it Grim the cross-bearer, in front St. Thomas, kneeling (the figure mainly defaced), his mitre at his side; the four knights approach from the right, the first and third drawing their swords. Both have plumes on their helmets, the fourth knight a crest to his.

Norfolk Archaeology, 1864, VI, 161–9, repr.; Keyser, *Mural Decorations*, 1883; *Norfolk Archaeology*, 1923, XXI, lvi; James, *Suffolk & Norfolk*, 1930, 133.

EDINGTHORPE (near North Walsham) Norfolk
ALL SAINTS

The Nave

North wall: St. Christopher, framed within a border of deep red, against a background diapered with small plants, the upper part of the composition, with a few traces of the lower part, alone surviving. The Saint, facing east, clad in a yellow gipon, a mantle the colour of which has perished, so that it now appears white, and a helmet-shaped hat, bears the Holy Child on his left shoulder, and holds in his left hand a staff bursting into foliage at the top. The Child, with a cruciform nimbus, is clad in a yellow tunic and holds the Orb of the Universe. At the base of the composition are traces of water, in which fish are swimming.

Between the second and third windows from the west, remains of a Tree representing the Seven Corporal Works of Mercy, the right-hand half alone surviving; three branches spring laterally from the tree, with leaves growing from them, and originally divided the composition into eight sections, of which four remain, reading from the base on the right, as follows:

1. A woman's figure, and some small heads, are decipherable.

2. A small figure, the hand on the breast, and a larger figure on the right, with extended hand.

3. Two figures clasping hands, that on the left in a full white mantle, the other in red—clearly the Fourth Work, Welcoming the Homeless.

4. Two small kneeling figures with raised hands face eastward, towards a large *Manus Dei*, or perhaps the right hand of a figure of Christ, which may have been depicted originally above the adjacent window. The colours used are green, yellow, red and black.

Above the doorway to the rood loft is a niche with carved tracery around the head and an elaborately carved corbel below; the ground within it is painted red, and on the wall about the niche is a deep border of rosettes in dark red between red lines, the spandrels at the base being filled with painted tracery on a black ground; below the border and just above the door are traces of an inscription, ORATE PRO . . ., in black letters, the capital being rubricated.

All the paintings are of *c.* 1400, but have been retouched at some time subsequent to 1937.

Keyser, *Mural Decorations*, 1883; B. Mus., *Dawson Turner Collection*, Add. II, 257.

EDSTASTON (near Wem) Salop ST. MARY

The Chancel

On the splays of a window, masonry pattern executed in double lines; between two of the windows, traces of painting; below a window in the south wall, a diaper formed of constellations of six spots, and at the back of the sedilia a consecration cross.

The Nave

About the south doorway, traces of paintings in two tiers, with many figures, executed on a large scale, the upper tier cut in half by the fifteenth-century roof, *c.* 1400; at the eastern end of the south wall, a consecration cross; elsewhere in the nave, an arcade of four round-headed arches framing figures, fragments of a diaper of spots like that already noted in the chancel, and traces of theme-paintings carried out on a large scale, together with remains of riband pattern and of an inscribed scroll.

The work, executed in the usual ochres and black, appears to have been of various dates in the fourteenth century, is in a much defaced condition, and not of good quality.

B.A.A.J., 1846, Glos. vol., 308; Keyser, *Mural Decorations*, 1883; Cranage, *Churches of Shropshire*, 1912, II, 684.

ELSING (near Dereham) Norfolk ST. MARY

The Nave

South wall: formerly a 'history' of St. John Baptist, including:

1. The Dance of Salome, represented with her body bent in a bow, her hair touching the ground.

2. St. John preaching before Herod and Herodias; the latter in 'the costume of the period', St. John in a blue mantle.

3. St. John being led from Prison; Herodias, a guard, and the Saint decipherable, together with a representation of the prison gate, with a portcullis.

4. The Beheading of St. John; a soldier seizing the Saint, to force him on to the block, the executioner raising a weapon of scimitar shape.

Discovered in 1860, the paintings were later plastered over, a brief and rather confused description having previously been made.

Norfolk Archaeology, 1861, VI, 201, and 2nd Annual Rep., II; *East Anglian N. & Q.*, 1864, I, 100–1; Keyser, *Mural Decorations*, 1883; James, *Suffolk & Norfolk*, 1930, 182.

ELY, Cambs
CATHEDRAL CHURCH OF THE HOLY TRINITY

The Choir

Beneath the eastern window, a series of figures of kings, of almost life-size, depicted within niches; within the central niche, three figures, and in the two outer niches, one figure only, that on the northern side being the best preserved. It is drawn in black outline against a background of light blue; the hair is short and curled, but there does not appear to be a nimbus, and there is no indication of identity. The ground above the head of the niche is painted red.

On the north wall, formerly, paintings of Wulstan, Osmund, Alwin, Elfgar, Ednod and Athelstan, bishops of Ely, and of Duke Brithnoth.

In the south choir aisle, on the vaulting, a masonry pattern executed in double line, in red ochre; and at the intersections of the vaulting a deep band elaborated with cusping terminated by a maple leaf, in the same colour. On the soffit of the arch opening into the nave, a similar masonry pattern enriched with a diapering of small sprigs, also in the same colour.

The Octagon

The original decoration, of *c.* 1335, still clearly visible *c.* 1850, was unfortunately repainted at a later date.

The Lady Chapel

The exterior: remains of colour decoration, and at the backs of the niches in the western wall, diaper patterns composed of lozenges and circles and carried out in deep red.

The interior: remains of colour decoration on carving, mouldings and architectural features generally; in the vaulting, a diaper of roses in red; on the ridge ribs, alternate blocks of between 12 in. and 15 in. in length, painted in red and green, and, for about 6 in. from the intersection of the ribs, remains of gold and colour; on the bosses, remains of gold and colour; at the backs of the stalls, vermilion and bright green in alternation; on the carving of the canopies, vestiges of gold, vermilion, green and bright blue.

The Prior's House

In the Great Hall, within an arch over the fireplace, figures of two bishops were discovered *c.* 1882; some remains of this work were still visible in 1930.

Sacrist Rolls of Ely, ed. F. R. Chapman, 1907 (2 vols.).

'Mention of a "Painted Chamber" in a document of 1541, in a house identified by Chapman as one still in the possession of the Canon of the "second stall", and described as a building of fourteenth-century date (vol. I, appendix B, p. 140).

'*Vol. II. Roll III.* 1322–23. In iij lagenis et dimid. olei pro ymaginibus super columpnas depingendis. 3s. 6d. (p. 34.)

'*Roll IV*, Alan de Walsingham Sacrist, 1323–24. In vadiis Johannis Pictoris cum auro et argento et card. et pro aliis rebus emptis pro pictura, ymaginis magni cum stipendio unius garcionis auxiliantis. £4. 4. 11½ (p. 44).

'*Roll VI.* 1334–35. Nova pictura. In xxiiij libris rubei plumbi empt. pro volta novi Campanilis depingend. una cum xx libris . . . plumbi . . . prec. libr. ij d. Item in xviij libris rubei plumbi empt. pro eodem 3s. 9d. Item in xx libris de Verny empt. pro eodem prec. lib. iijd. 5s. Item in iij libris de gold coleir empt. ad idem 2s. 2d.

Summa xxvijs. vij d. (p. 73.)

'*Roll VII*, 1336–37. Nova Pictura. Account for materials bought, including vermilion, verdigris, white lead, oil, silver leaf and gold leaf, and for wages, as follows:

Item solut. Nich. Pictori pro volta nova dealband. in parte per iij septimanas ad tasc. 3s. 6.

Item cuidam pictori pro eodem per iij septimanas ad mensam domini 1s. 9d.

In solut. Magister Will. Shank pro dict volt. depingend. cum le chapitral et bocio deasurand. ex pingend. cum le chapitral et bocis deaurand ex convencione in grosso. £10. 0. 0.

Summa xiiij li xixs. ijd. (p. 83).

'*Roll VIII.* 1339–40. Item in j roba empt. pro Waltero Pictore 7s. Item j garniamento empt. pro Waltero Trulboke garciaone pictoris, 4s. 4d. (p. 97.) In stipend. Walteri pictoris per xlij septimanas (et non plus) quia stetit cum Dna. de Clare per x septs. capientis per sepm. viijd preter mensam et robam £1. 8s. (p. 99). Marginal note. Custus noue Picture. In xxxj lagenis di. olei empt. de quodam homine de Wycham pro colore temperando prec. lagen. viijd. £1. 1s. In mccc de silverfoile empt. per vices de Radulpho le goldbetere et de aliis apud London ut patet per parcellas prec. cent. vjd, 6s. 9d. There follows a list of materials bought, including:—dccc de Goldfyn £1.12.0; mcc de goldparti £1.16.0; 1 libra de orpiment 6d. iiij buss. de strowes empt. pro cole inde facient, 1s. 6d.; vj lib. vermiloun at 10d. lb. (p. 98).

'*Roll IX*. 1341–42. Dat Waltero garcioni pictoris. 4s. (p. 118). In stipend. Walteri Pictoris de die Lune prox. post fest. Sci. Andree usque in diem dominicam in festo Sci. Mich. per xliij septs. capientis per septm. viijd. preter mens. et rob. £1.8.8. (p. 119).

'*Roll X*. 1345–46. In stipend. Walteri pictoris per ann. . . . per sept. js. iiijd. preter robam suam sine mensa, £3.9.4. (p. 137).

'*Roll XIII*. 1354–55. Marginal note. Pictur, et stannum emp. In xxiii lb. stanni empt. prec. lib. iijd £1.0.9; 1 quart. Synopre 5s.; vi lb. dimid de Azure empt. prec. lib. iiijs. iiijd. £1.8.2. Solut. Johanni Peyntori pro ymaginibus pingendis apud Tydbr. Stunteneye et Ely. 7s. (p. 169).'

Gough, *Funeral Monuments*, 1786, I, pt. 1, clvi; Stevenson, *Supplement to 2nd ed. of Jas. Bentham's History & Antiquities of Ely Cathedral*, 1817, 23, and not es, 144; Keyser, *Mural Decorations*, 1883; *A Notebook of Drawings*, Anon, Victoria & Albert Museum, 93, E.5; *Cambs & H.A.S.T.*, 1930, IV, 250.

ENBORNE (near Newbury) Berks ST. MICHAEL

At the eastern end of the north wall is an Annunciation, executed in ochres, the treatment being linear. The arrangement is that normal for this subject at this period; in the centre of the composition is the pot of lilies, to the spectator's left the Angel Gabriel with the right hand raised and in the left a scroll, to the right the Virgin, the head slightly inclined to the left and the hands upraised.

Ditchfield, *The Reliquary*, 1892, N.S. VI, 146, repr.; *Victoria County Hist.*, *Berks*, 1924, IV, 173; Long, *Berks.*, *B. & O.A.J.*, 1942, XLVI, 29, repr.

EXETER, Devon
CATHEDRAL CHURCH OF ST. PETER
The Choir

During cleaning carried out *c.* 1930 extensive remains of gold and colour were found on the corbels and bosses, the carved foliage having been gilt against a ground of deep red in the hollows of the carving.

The bishop's throne, work upon which, with the reredos, sedilia and pulpitum, was begun in 1316–17, was originally painted and gilt. The sedilia retain, on the backs of the seats, parts of a painted hanging ornamented with horizontal stripes enriched with roundels and delicate scroll and leaf patterns; and on the carved heads of a king and queen, and a bishop, visible above the level of the painted drapery, colour

survives. On either side of them are traces of a painted lion. It is recorded that the richly-carved reredos, subsequently almost totally destroyed, was coloured and gilt and also the pulpitum. The Fabric Rolls show that a certain Nicholas, painter and 'imager', John and Benedict Lena, painters, and two others named Boteller and Berested, were employed between 1320 and 1325, with another whose initial 'R' alone is given. Their wages ranged from 1s. 3d. to 2s. the week, as compared with 1s. 1d. to 2s. 2d. for carpenters and woodcarvers, 2s. 9d. a week for the chief stone-carver down to 2s. for his assistants, (stone-carvers or stone-masons), and 3s. a week for the master glazier; but none of the painters seem to be termed 'magister', and their work probably went no further than the application of colour, gilding and patterning upon stone and woodwork. The Rolls also provide evidence that the colouring of 49 bosses in the presbytery was paid for at Midsummer, 1302; of those in the choir aisle in the summer of 1309; of those in the Chapels of St. Paul and St. John, and in the high vault of the choir respectively at Christmas, 1311 and 1317.

Bishop Stapledon's tomb, on the north of the high altar, has on the under-side of the canopy a painting of Christ in Judgement, of which hardly more than the silhouette survives.

The Nave

The corbels and bosses, when cleaned *c.* 1930, were found to have retained a large proportion of their original gold and colour; and very extensive remains of colour were discovered on the Minstrels' Gallery. Two complementary bosses at the crossing retained their colour in an almost perfect state, although the gilding was naturally broken. On that representing the legend of the Tumbler, the ground is vermilion, the foliage gilt, with some green on the stems; the hood and gipon of the Tumbler blue, patterned with groups of small roundels in yellow and red; the musician's gipon white, sown with golden leaf-forms outlined in black; and his shoes black; and the head of each figure is painted in natural colours, with bright red on the lips and cheeks and the eyebrows outlined in black. On the second boss, carved with the Virgin and Child, the ground is also red; the wings of the censing Angels green and their tunics white; the crown and mantle of the Virgin gilt and her tunic white; and the tunic of the Holy Child gilt, likewise outlined in green.

The Transepts

The wooden bosses under the transept towers were painted in 1320 (*Fabric Rolls*).

The West Front

The Rolls show that the great west door was completed in 1332, and, after a gap of six years (1334–40), for which the accounts are lost, there occurs an entry referring to gold and colours for 'painting the image of Blessed Peter' and, a few weeks later, for 'painting of the bishop in the gable'; which latter entry, considered in connexion with a small painted head of a carving found loose some time ago in a protected position high up on the front, and now preserved in the Chapter House, indicates that the entire façade was originally painted and gilt, since it is highly improbable that the upper part would have been finished in this way and the lower, and far richer portion, left bare of colour.

Exeter Diocesan Architect. Soc., 1849, III, pt. II, 94–6; ibid., 1861, IV, 45, and VI, 53; Keyser, *Mural Decorations*, 1883; Bishop and Prideaux, *The Building of Exeter Cathedral*, 1922, 70–1; *Friends of Exeter Cathedral*, 1st Annual Rept., 1930; notes from the Fabric Rolls, supplied by Bishop, March 1931; Bishop, *Notes on Exeter Cathedral*, 1935, 11, 13, 14, 15, 17. Plate 28.

EYNSHAM (near Oxford) Oxon ST. LEONARD

The Chancel

North wall, reading from the east:—around a window arch, chevron pattern in red, cinquefoils, and also masonry blocks, all in red; and on the splays, masonry pattern executed in single yellow line and elaborated with cinquefoils in red.

On the adjacent wall immediately to the east, five tiers of decoration; beginning with the lowest tier they are as follows:

1. A large fret pattern in broad yellow line enriched with fleurs-de-lis in red.

2. Part of a series from the legend of St. Catherine; (1) The Breaking of the Wheel, with faint traces of the Saint in the centre of the scene, of fragments of the Wheel to the left and of a number of heads; (2) the Decollation of St. Catherine, much defaced, though parts of figures of executioners, and of the head and the hands raised in prayer of the Saint, together with a Flying Angel above and to the right Maxentius enthroned, are barely decipherable. There is some use of black underpainting.

3. ?A prison scene, perhaps the Imprisonment of St. Catherine; and another, almost entirely destroyed.

4. Only slight fragments remain.

5. Masonry pattern, identical with that on the window-splays, described above.

East wall, on the north side: a niche, with slight remains of vermilion at the head, and on the small pillars at the sides, 'barber's poling' in red, black and white. At the back of the niche, remains of scroll-work, interspersed with small cinquefoils in red, or, alternatively, in white, the whole on a vermilion ground. South wall. Continuing on to the east wall, a large fret pattern, as described above, with fleurs-de-lis; on this wall it may be seen that the fret is voided at the joints. On the piscina, traces of colour. The window in this wall is decorated like that in the north wall, but the decoration is on the whole more defaced, the chevrons and masonry blocks being lost. Traces of half-diamonds in sequence, however, survive here on a narrow moulding, although lost from a similar position on the window opposite. All *c.* 1350.

The Nave

On the north-east piers, colour is recorded as having existed, but is now gone.

Long, *Oxoniensia*, 1937, II, 204.

FAIRSTEAD (near Witham) Essex ST. MARY

The Nave

On the south wall, between the two windows, reading from east to west:

1. St. Christopher, clad in a black mantle lined with red and holding a yellow staff; much defaced.

2. The Annunciation to the Shepherds. Two figures of Shepherds survive, the foremost hooded, shading his eyes with his right hand and raising his left in wonder, the other, immediately behind him, also gazing upward.

3. Just beyond the westernmost of the two windows, the faint silhouette of a standing female figure, clad in a mantle, beneath which the right foot is visible.

Immediately below the paintings, traces of a scroll-border enriched with trefoils, executed in red.

At a height of approximately 4½ ft. from the present floor level, and at 19 in. from the adjacent west wall, a grotesque head in a peaked cap.

A.J., 1908, LXV, 24; *R.C. Historical Monuments R., Essex*, 1921, II, 66, 67; Tristram and Benton, *Essex A.S.*, 1939, XXII, 216–18, reprs.

FAVERSHAM, Kent ST. MARY OF CHARITY

North Transept

In the eastern arcade, the southernmost column, which is octagonal, is completely painted; the decoration begins at a height of 4 ft. 7 in. from floor level, and extends for 6 ft. 4 in. upwards as far as the capital, itself painted in plain colours. The decoration is divided into three tiers by horizontal bands of dark green edged with roundels in white; the two lowest tiers are filled with Holy Infancy subjects, the highest with Passion scenes. Each subject fills two, three, and sometimes four facets of the pier; and they are so arranged that the Virgin and Child, in the Adoration of the Magi is immediately below the Christ on the Cross in the Crucifixion scene, and both face the spectator as he looks eastward. Apparently with the object of achieving this arrangement, the Nativity is placed, not as it normally is in a Holy Infancy series, after the Visitation, but in the middle tier, before the Appearance of the Angel to the Shepherds. The backgrounds to the subjects in the lowest and highest tiers are of green diapered with rosettes composed of a red roundel with six or seven white roundels or annulets disposed about it; whereas the backgrounds in the middle tier are red, patterned with crescents and stars in white, now rather indistinct.

Lowest Tier:

S.W. and S. facets. The Annunciation: the Angel Gabriel, clad in a dark green mantle and a white tunic, and having white wings tinted with pink, holds a scroll with slight vestiges of an inscription; the Virgin, veiled, and clad in a white tunic and pink mantle, raises her right hand in salutation and rests the left on a prie-dieu. The painting is somewhat perished.

S.E. and E. facets. The Visitation; St. Elizabeth, with barbette, and pillbox hat, clad in a white tunic and red mantle, embraces the Virgin, who is veiled, and wears a white tunic and a mantle of dark green.

N.E., N., N.W. and W. facets. The Adoration of the Magi. The last in the advancing group of three Kings is clad in a white tunic and red cloak with arm-slits, and raises his right hand in salutation while in the left he holds a gift; the second, also bearing a gift, has a pink tunic and a dark green mantle edged with white annulets and a narrow line in white, and holds a sceptre in his left hand, the shaft being white and the fleur-de-lis at the top red; the third King, who like the other two, is crowned, stands immediately before the Virgin and Child; this figure is somewhat defaced, but it can be seen that the tunic is white, with the folds drawn in pink line, and the mantle dark green. The Virgin is seated facing frontally with her left arm about the Child, who, clad in a white tunic and dark green mantle, raises the right hand in blessing. She is crowned, but has no nimbus, whereas the Child has a nimbus of the usual cruciform type.

This painting is somewhat defaced in parts, particularly towards the base.

Central Tier:

W. and S.W. facets. The Nativity. The Virgin, in a white tunic and a mantle of pale green, is depicted half reclining on a couch, with her head resting upon a cushion, suckling the Child, who is wrapped in swaddling clothes ornamented with bindings in red. About His head is a cruciform nimbus. All that remains of the figure of St. Joseph, on the S.W. facet of the pier, is a part of his dark green mantle and of the chair in which he is seated. Above are the heads of the Ox and Ass, painted respectively on the S.W. and S. facets of the pier.

S., S.E. and E. facets. The Appearance of the Angel to the Shepherds. The Angel, nimbed, and clad in a white tunic and green mantle, points with the right hand towards the Shepherds, as though emphasizing his message. The foremost Shepherd, his wide-brimmed hat slung on his back, kneels, resting on a staff held in his left hand, and his small white dog in front of him barks at the Angel. The second shepherd, whose hat, similar to that borne by the other, is strapped under his chin, shades his eyes with his right hand and gazes at the Angel. The lower part of the painting is mutilated; if there was formerly a third Shepherd, the figure, which must have been small in scale, to judge from the space available for it, has been destroyed.

N.E., N. and N.W. facets. The Presentation in the Temple. St. Joseph, wearing a white tunic, a dark green mantle, and a black hat with a broad brim, holds a basket containing doves, of which traces of three, or perhaps four, may be discerned. The Virgin, in a white tunic and mantle of pale green, presents the Child to the High Priest, who is bearded, wears a white tunic and dark green mantle, and extends his hands over an altar towards them.

Highest Tier:

N.W., W. and S.W. facets. The Crucifixion. The Virgin, veiled and clad in a white tunic and red mantle, stands on the right of the Cross, which is depicted on the central of the three facets; the figure of Christ has a yellow loin-cloth, and the head is painted with particular delicacy; St. John, to the left of the Cross (the spectator's right), has a white tunic and red mantle, and carries a book.

S., S.E., E. and N.E. facets. The Angel and the Holy Women at the Tomb. The Angel, a somewhat defaced figure, has a white nimbus; the tomb, which extends across three facets of the pier, is 'marbled' to represent purbeck, and has grave-clothes hanging from it. The foremost of the Holy Women, veiled and clad in a white tunic and red mantle, holds a pot of ointment or spices in the left hand and extends the right towards the Angel; beyond her, the second, veiled and wearing a white tunic and dark green mantle, also carries a pot, and turns back towards the third, in pill-box hat, barbette, crespine, white tunic and red mantle, who raises the right hand towards the other as though attracting her attention.

N. facet. A tree occupies this facet, perhaps being intended to complete the scene at the Tomb, or simply to serve as a division between it and the painting of the Crucifixion.

The colour scheme in general consists mainly in an alternation of various tints of red and green, with some black, white and ochre; thus, where the ground of the paintings is red, the tunics on the figures are usually painted in white, the folds being outlined in pale yellow or green, and the mantles light or dark green, whereas, where the ground is green, the tunics may be pale pink, or white outlined in yellow or red, the mantles light or dark red. The draperies are defined by black or dark red outline, emphasized by a narrow inner line in white; and there is some gradation in the painting of the folds. The heads are painted with a greater use of gradation than are the draperies; upon the cheeks is a circular patch of red, merged at the edges into the flesh colour; the lips are painted red, and the hair is delicately drawn. Originally the paintings were finished with minute care for detail, as may still be seen in some parts where they have escaped much wear. *c.* 1300.

The Chapel of St. Thomas of Canterbury

Paintings, well-preserved when discovered in this chapel in the north aisle in 1851, now much perished, are hidden by an organ; however, they were carefully drawn and described soon after discovery by Thomas Willement.

The south wall of the chapel, pierced by an archway which opens into the chancel, was formerly covered with a masonry pattern executed in double red line and enriched with roses, and finished beneath the wall-plate by a border of vine-scroll in white on red. Superimposed upon the masonry pattern, just below the apex of the arch on either side, were two large figures, 7 ft. in height—on the north side St. Edward the Confessor, on the south St. John the Evangelist in the guise of a pilgrim. St. Edward, crowned and holding a sceptre in the left hand, was bearded, had hair falling below the ears and curling at the ends, wore a light-coloured tunic and red mantle lined with vair, and was shod

in black; he stood on a pedestal, extending his right hand, with the Ring of the legend. St. John, bending forward with his right hand outstretched to receive it, was on rough ground, his weight resting on the bourdon or pilgrim's staff held in his left with a palm attached to it by thongs; his hair and beard were long, he was clad in sheep-skin, and had at his side a scrip, hung by thongs passing over his shoulders, and on his back, slung by a cord across his chest, a pilgrim's hat.

Below and to the east of the St. Edward was a painted tabernacle of very elaborate design, within which, against a background ornamented with intricate scroll-work and cinquefoils, the donor of the painting was depicted. His dress was that of a layman, and comprised a white coif, and a red mantle lined with vair and having a deep collar-cape. His hands were raised in supplication, and between them was a long scroll, inscribed, according to Willement, with the words: ✠ FERRE: POLI: SERTVM: FAC: REX: EDMVNDE: ROBERTVM: DOD: FAVERSHAMIE: QVEM: REGE: THOMA: PIE. The paintings were evidently exceptionally skilled, and of high quality. *c.* 1340.

A Martyrdom of St. Thomas of Canterbury, perhaps of the same date, was discovered on the north wall of the chapel in 1874, but appears to have perished without further record.

Gent. M., 1859, VII, 244; Keyser, *Mural Decorations,* 1883; Willement, *A. Cant.,* 1858, I, 150–3; ibid., 1874, IX, lxi; *P. Society of Antiquaries,* 1861, 2nd ser., I, 40.

FELSTEAD (near Dunmow) Essex   HOLY CROSS

In 1876 the entire length of the wall over the north arcade was found to have been painted, the painting in the spandrel between the two westernmost arches being the best-preserved, since it had been covered by a gallery, at that time in course of demolition. It dated from the fourteenth century, and represented a Tree of the Seven Deadly Sins, of which the lower part only remained. Within two circles composed of branches having leaves somewhat like those of the vine, *Avaritia* was to be seen, represented by the figure of a miser counting his money at a four-legged table, with a demon standing on either side of him, and a coffer to his left; below, two other demons were shown sawing through the trunk of the Tree with a cross-cut saw, at the point where it rose from the gaping jaws of Leviathan. At the top of what remained of the general composition, part of a third circle, with fragments of a figure, were discernible. The colours used were the normal ochres and black.

Benton, *Essex A.S.,* 1926, N.S., XVII, 30–2, repr.

FINGRINGHOE (near Colchester) Essex
ST. OWEN, or ST. ANDREW

In the spandrel over the central pier of the north nave arcade, a Coronation of the Virgin, somewhat defaced, particularly on the right side, where the figure of Christ is missing; on the left one censing Angel survives. Traces remain of masonry and other patterns in red. Early fourteenth century.

On the south-west respond of the nave arcade, a consecration cross.

R.C. Historical Monuments R., 1922, III, 101; Benton, *B.A.A.J.*, 1937, 3rd ser., II, 172 et sqq.

FLAMSTEAD (near St. Albans) Herts
ST. LEONARD

The Nave

Over the chancel arch, a Doom, confused with remains of another of later date. The figure of Christ is visible, seated on a rainbow, on His left an Angel, with a cross on the brow, and upraised wings, holding the Spear, on His right another with the Scourge. Above the second Angel, the walls of the Heavenly Jerusalem. Low on the wall, to the spectator's left, fragment of the Mouth of Hell. Traces remain of figures of censing Angels, but whether these belonged to the earlier or to the later painting, is uncertain.

The North Aisle; the Beauchamp Chantry

On the north and east walls, a Passion series, arranged in two tiers, as follows:

On the north wall, in the upper tier, reading from west to east:

1. The Last Supper. The table is visible, but only the hands of the seated figures, with the lower parts of their robes, and their feet, and part of the representation of Judas, placed in front of the board, survive.

2. ?Christ Before Pilate. The figure of Christ remains, and also that of a Roman soldier, with other figures.

On the east wall, in the upper tier, reading from north to south:

3. The Mocking of Christ. The figure of Christ, being blindfolded, and another figure, are decipherable.

The series continues on the north wall, in the lower tier, reading from west to east:

4. The Crucifixion. The figure of Christ, the head retouched, and that of St. John survive, together with a flying Angel on the right of the cross, and the hand and spear of Longinus.

5. The Entombment. Christ lies in the tomb, behind which are two figures, one of them shown in the act of anointing the Body, while a third stands at the feet.

The series is concluded on the east wall, in the lower tier, with

6. A Resurrection, only the right arm of Christ, with the pierced hand raised in blessing, and an Angel in adoration on the spectator's left, remaining.

The paintings are executed in the normal ochres.

Conquest Clare, *St. Albans Quarterly*, 1929.

FORTHAMPTON (near Tewkesbury) Glos.
FORTHAMPTON COURT

Forthampton Court, now a private residence, was originally the grange of the Abbots of Tewkesbury; and here, for an indeterminate period, at least a century, has been preserved a painting in oil, or an emulsion of oil, executed on two panels of wood joined vertically a little to the left of the centre, the whole measuring 2 ft. 6 in. in length by 2 ft. 4 in. in width, the subject depicted being taken from the Legend of St. Edward the Confessor and the Pilgrim.

On the spectator's left stands the King, extending his right hand, with the Ring held between the first and second fingers, towards St. John the Evangelist, habited as a pilgrim, who takes it in his upraised right hand. St. Edward is clad in a pink gipon, its straight-cuffed sleeve being visible on the forearm, a long pink super-tunic shaded in red, reaching almost to the ankles and having three-quarter-length sleeves, and a green cloak collared with vair and fastened on the right shoulder, from which it falls in straight folds, by means of three round buttons, but thrown back over the left upper arm. On his head is a golden crown ornamented with leaves somewhat resembling those of the strawberry, and his loosely-waved yellow hair falls from beneath it to the level of the jaw; he has a slight moustache and a short forked beard. His hose are green in colour, and his long, pointed shoes, patterned with a fret in black upon cream, are cut high at the heel and fastened by a strap around the ankle. St. John, whose hair and beard resemble those of the King, though they are curled rather than waved, is bare-headed and bare-footed; his dark green tunic, which has three-quarter-length sleeves, clears the ankles by some inches, and his cloak, which is of a lighter green lined with pink shaded in red, opens in front and falls in elaborate and beautifully-designed folds on either side. About his shoulders the brown gorget of his hood is visible, and a pilgrim's hat, dark green in colour like the

173

tunic, but turned up with pink, is slung at his back; in his left hand he bears the bourdon, with a palm attached to it by thongs. Neither the Evangelist nor the King has a nimbus, and both stand on ground represented as a series of small brown hillocks. The background was originally of vermilion, but is largely obliterated by a coating of Indian red, applied at some time to disguise blemishes where the paint had perished, and carelessly carried over the left hand of the Confessor, which was found intact beneath it; apart from the ground colour, the painting is in exceptionally perfect condition. The state of the wood panels, which had become worm-eaten at the back, made it necessary that they should be to some extent strengthened.

The work, extremely skilled and of high quality, dates from c. 1360.

Tristram, *Burl. M.*, 1943, LXXXIII, 160–5, repr. Plate 25.

FRING (near Docking) Norfolk ALL SAINTS

The Nave

North wall, opposite the south door, framed by borders of scroll-work in green on black, a St. Christopher, the head and shoulders and the figure of the Holy Child missing. The Saint, clad in a knee-length cote-hardie (originally green) looped up and held by the belt, showing the lower part of the gipon, and loose breeches tied at the knees, leans on the staff held in his right hand; about his feet are traces of water, drawn as though heaped up, and swimming fish. The underpainting to the flesh tints and other light colours, which have almost disappeared, is black. On the background is a diaper of quatrefoil flowers in red. The remains of the painting occupy a space 7 ft. in width by about 10 ft. in height. c. 1330.

On the east wall, to the south of the chancel arch, beside a carved image niche with considerable traces of colour decoration, remains of an Annunciation, framed by a representation of a niche, part of the canopy still being visible. The entire work is much defaced, but traces of the nimbed head of the Angel and of portions of a wing, the scroll between the two figures, and fragments of the upper part of that of the Virgin, veiled and clad in a red mantle and green tunic, with the right hand raised, survive against a ground of a warm grey.

Around the chancel arch, scroll-work in black enriched with four-petalled flowers in blue.

On the south wall, in the angle between the east wall and an adjacent Decorated window, within a painted niche, a female Saint clad in a red tunic and holding a palm branch in the left hand, against a blue ground; and on both splays of the window just mentioned, slight remains of similar figures within niches, that on the western splay, of which a bare foot and part of a staff survive, having probably been an Apostle. All these works, of c. 1330, were originally of good quality, as may be judged from the range of colours employed and from the excellence of the drawing, where it survives.

Keyser, *Mural Decorations*, 1883; Brindley, *Antiquaries Journal*, 1924, IV, 228; Whaite, *St. Christopher*, 1929, 19, pl. 6; James, *Suffolk & Norfolk*, 1930, 204.

FRITTON (near Lowestoft) Suffolk ST. EDMUND

The Nave

On the north wall, a St. Christopher of late-fourteenth-century date, framed within a scroll-work border; the Saint, bearded and with long hair, clad in a gipon patterned in green on blue, a mantle, and soft cap with upturned brim, holds the staff in his right hand and turns his head towards the Holy Child on his left shoulder; the background has a diaper pattern composed of ermine spots and quatrefoils. Apart from the green and blue on the gipon, the colours are the usual ochres. c. 1400.

In many parts of the church, including the chancel arch, scroll pattern similar to that bordering St. Christopher.

On the south side of the nave, in the splay of a window, St. Thomas of Canterbury.

Keyser, *Mural Decorations*, 1883; Bryant, *County Churches, Suffolk*, 1912, II, 159; Whaite, *St. Christopher*, 1929, 22, pl. 10; James, *Suffolk & Norfolk*, 1930, 111; Munro Cautley, *Suffolk Churches and Their Treasures*, 1938, 262.

GLASTONBURY, Somerset
ABBEY CHURCH OF ST. PETER AND ST. PAUL

In John of Glastonbury's *Historia de rebus Glastoniensibus* (ed. T. Hume, 1726, I, 263), the following passage occurs in relation to Abbot Adam de Sodbury:

'*Navem ecclesiae pro maxima parte voltavit. Splendidisque ornavit picturis.*'

GLOUCESTER CATHEDRAL CHURCH OF ST. PETER

Historia et Cartularium Monasterii Sancti Petri Gloucestriae, ed. W. H. Hart, 1863, I (Rolls Series).

'p. 44. Tempore istius abbatis [John Thoky 1306–29] Edwardus rex secundus post conquestum, filius regis Edwardi primi, veniens in Gloucestriam, abbas et conventus eum honorifice suscepit, qui sedens ad mensam in aula abbatis, et ibidem videns depictas figuras regum praedecessorum suorum jocose sciscitabatur ab abbate utrum haberet eum depictum inter ipsos an non . . . '

'p. 46. Similiter dum prior [John Wigmore 1329–37] ejusdem monasterii extiterat cameram abbatis juxta gardinium infirmariae construxit. Similiter et tabulam ad altare prioris cum imaginibus politis et deauratis sumptibus suis adornavit. Et aliam tabulam quae nunc est in capella abbatis de eodem opere composuit, qui in diversis artibus multum delectabatur, ut ipse saepissime opereretur, et multos diversos operarios in diversis artibus praeexcelleret tam in opere mechanico quam in textura.'

GLOUCESTER ST. MARY-LE-CRYPT

The Chancel

In both north and south walls large arched recesses, within which are remains of subjects, in a perished condition.

On the canopy to the Sedilia, two Angels, bearing scrolls, and on the back a small consecration cross; the latter has a small cross incised in the centre, is framed by an incised circle, and executed in black, green and white, the two first-named colours predominating; all the work is much defaced. Late fourteenth century.

When the Sedilia were first discovered, during a restoration of the church *c.* 1845, each had a painting on the back, that on the westernmost much defaced, but thought to have represented 'the consecration of a bell', that on the middle identified improbably as 'the lifting up of the brazen serpent in the wilderness', and that on the easternmost, evidently the best-preserved, as the presentation, by 'an Earl with a numerous retinue', of a chalice to an Abbot, attended by 'a band of monks'. Above the Easter Sepulchre was a painting of the Holy Women, and at its back a Resurrection, with Christ emerging from the tomb, and the sleeping guards. An Adoration of the Magi and (?) the Prophecy of Simeon are also recorded as having existed in the chancel, within the large arched recesses mentioned above. All the work is stated to have been of exceptionally high quality.

Gent. M., 1845, XXIII, N.S., 189; Keyser, *Mural Decorations*, 1883; *Bristol & Glos. Arch. Soc.*, 1903, XXVI, 302; *A.J.*, 1908, LXV, 34; Bird, *Mural Paintings, Glos*, 1927, 20.

GORLESTON (near Yarmouth) Norfolk
ST. ANDREW

The Nave

On the easternmost pier of the south nave arcade, traces of figures, thought on their discovery in 1880 to be St. Anne and the Virgin, and below them, St. Catherine or St. Etheldreda.

On the north wall, formerly, *Les Trois Vifs et Les Trois Morts*; three life-size figures of Kings confronted by three skeletons, against a background of floriated scroll-work; the two foremost of the Kings bearded men in flowing red cloaks, red stockings, shoes enriched with a diaper pattern, and gauntlets, the third a youth, crowned and with flowing yellow hair, in an embroidered yellow cloak, red gipon, flesh-coloured hose, and gauntlets; the entire composition framed by an ornamental border; *c.* 1380.

North Chancel Chapel

Formerly, on the splays of the two north windows, Angels against backgrounds diapered with the foliage and fruit of the vine.

Within a fourteenth-century Easter Sepulchre recess, formerly the Holy Trinity; against a diapered background, God the Father supporting the cross with the figure of Christ the Son, the Holy Ghost descending in the form of a Dove, and on either side a censing Angel, the whole richly executed in gold and colour; below 'figures on a large scale', unidentified. On each side of the canopied arch, a shield, one of the Trinity, the other with Emblems of the Passion.

Bately, *B.A.A.J.*, 1880, XXXVI, 437–9; Keyser, *Mural Decorations*, 1883; *Burl. M.*, 1912, XXI, 317; James, *Suffolk & Norfolk*, 1930, 112–13; Munro Cautley, *Suffolk Churches and Their Treasures*, 1938, 265; Carleton Williams, *B.A.A.J.*, 1942, 3rd ser., VII, 39.

GRIMSTON (near King's Lynn) Norfolk
ST. BOTOLPH

On the east wall of the south transept, a Crucifixion within an architectural setting, painted under a low crocketed arch against a red ground; there survive—the upper part of the Cross (with label visible, and on it traces of lettering); a cruciform nimbus, obviously that of the figure of Christ; and to the left part of another nimbus, coloured in blue —probably from its position, that of the Blessed Virgin—with indications of the figure of Longinus with the Spear. To the extreme left, slight traces of a painted niche and of the blue-green ground within it. The whole is large in scale, and though now almost lost, it is evident that this was originally a work of fine quality.

In the nave, on the south wall, a consecration cross in red on white, within a black border.

HADDISCOE (near Reedham) Norfolk
ST. MARY

The Nave

South wall, between the first and second windows from the west, a consecration cross of cross paty type, in red, within a circle. A painting of *Les Trois Vifs et Les Trois Morts*, on the same wall, and between the two easternmost windows, another, of a figure on horseback, both probably of fourteenth-century date.

North wall, opposite the south door, part of a St. Christopher, viz. the head, the right hand holding the staff, and the Holy Child, borne on the left shoulder, holding in the left hand an Orb of the Universe, on which are traces of clouds and trees. *c.* 1400.

Keyser, *Mural Decorations*, 1883; Blomefield's *Norfolk Supplement*, 1929, 302; Whaite, *St. Christopher*, 1929, 24, pl. 13.

HALES (near Loddon) Norfolk ST. MARGARET

The Chancel
Around the east window, foliated scroll ornament: early fourteenth century.

The Nave

On the eastern splay of the easternmost window in the south wall, a band of foliated ornament in red on a white ground, outlined by inch-wide bands in black; below, a much-defaced figure, facing west, about 3½ ft. in height, of St. James the Great, habited as a pilgrim, with scrip and bourdon, red tunic, pilgrim's hat slung at his back, and feet bare, holding in the left hand a scroll with an inscription, now illegible. Probably of early fourteenth-century date.

Between the south door and the westernmost window, a St. Christopher of the usual gigantic proportions, mainly defaced, part of the Saint's head, with yellowish-red hair and curled beard, red cote-hardie with hanging sleeves, a bare leg, and traces of fish being visible, together with the figure of the Holy Child, in white tunic with dark belt and collar, cruciform nimbus in red and white, raising the right hand in blessing and holding in the left an indecipherable object. The flesh tints are superimposed on a dark underpainting. Probably of *c.* 1400.

The paintings were discovered when the walls of the church were in course of being cleaned down in November 1950. From notes supplied by Mrs. M. Bardswell.

HALESOWEN (near Birmingham) Worcs
CHAPEL OF ST. KENELM

The following works, since destroyed, are recorded through tracings preserved in the Victoria and Albert Museum (E. 701-9-1921, dates 1839 and 1845).

The Legend of St. Kenelm, King of Mercia

1. St. Kenelm's sister Quendred plots to murder him, and bribes Askeberd, 'chief ruler about the King', to effect her purpose. On the left of the scene Quendred, with one hand raised and index finger pointing upward, extends the other hand to Askeberd, who grasps it. He has a sword slung from the right shoulder, is clad in a knee-length gipon, parti-coloured in red and white, and wears pointed shoes. Her cote-hardie has tippets and is belted low on the hips.

2. St. Kenelm's Dream of the Tree that Reached Heaven, combined in one scene with the Story of the Widow's White Cow. On the right the young King is seen seated in the branches of the Tree, clad in a parti-coloured gipon. Below, a yoked cow (painted to contrast with the white of the background) is driven 'into the wood of Clent' in the 'valley of Cowbage', by a man in knee-length gipon and hood with traces of a liripipe. At the foot of the Tree the Widow, in white hood and red kirtle, raises her left hand to her breast and extends the other towards the animal. The background is patterned with groups of five spots in red.

3. The Body of St. Kenelm is Raised from the Grave. Two figures (recorded as Angels) in albs apparelled in red, bear the headless corpse. The background is patterned as in the last scene.

4. Quendred's Eyes Fall from her Head. She is seated to the right of the scene, crowned and holding a sceptre, on a throne with a red cushion. With one hand she takes the Psalter onto the pages of which her eyes fell. It is held before her by a kneeling man, to whom she points with her other hand, the left. Under her crown is a 'ruffled' veil, and she is gloved and wears a cote-hardie with tippets. The man, perhaps Askeberd, is bearded and clad in a short gipon barely reaching to the knee. Behind him is a group of seven men, the foremost bearded and wearing a gipon dagged at the lower edge and belted about the hips. The background is treated as in the previous scene.

5. ? From the same series:—the figure of a man in red knee-length gipon, belted low, and yellow shoulder-cape, with ? a staff in his hand, and to his

right traces of another male figure. After 1380. (*Golden Legend*, IV, 60-6.)

Scenes from the Legends of St. Martin of Tours and St. Nicholas of Myra. They are framed under low crocketed and pinnacled canopies. St. Martin Restores to Life a Man 'that was Hanged'. On the right is a figure on a gibbet, and to the left the Saint, vested as a Bishop, gloved, and with maniple, bears a crozier in his right hand and lays his left on the shoulder of the dead man (*Golden Legend*, VI, 145). St. Nicholas Defeats the Devil in the Shape of 'the Evil and Foul Diana'. From a sailing ship the Saint empties into the sea a phial from which issue ? flames, and flames rise from the waves below. The phial is handed to him by a youth with hair curled at the level of the ears, who has a belt set low at the hips with a purse pendent from it. To the left of the ship's sail is depicted what is in fact an earlier scene from the story. A youth, apparently intended for the same lad, receives a phial from a veiled woman with an ugly profile—'Diana', or the Devil, for in the legend the latter was disguised as a woman. (*Golden Legend*, II, 113-14.)

The series just described was earlier in date than that related to St. Kenelm, to judge from details of costume and architecture as shown in the tracings. *c.* 1350.

Keyser, *Mural Decorations*, 1883 (the legends of St. Martin and St. Nicholas either unidentified by Keyser or omitted by him); *Victoria County Hist.*, 1913, III, 147.

LOWER HALSTOW (near Sittingbourne) Kent
ST. MARGARET

The Nave

South arcade, easternmost arch: on the soffit, two sailors in a storm-driven boat, one with his hand raised as though invoking the aid of St. Andrew, painted above upon a St. Andrew's cross. On the pier beneath, a palmer, or pilgrim Saint, wearing a pilgrim's hat; an indecipherable subject; and a shield charged with bars. On the southern face of the arch, a figure of approximately life-size, the silhouette only remaining, seated on a throne under a trefoil-headed and canopied arch.

Second arch from the east: above, a Queen, and below, consecration crosses.

North arcade, easternmost arch: figures of Saints, placed one above the other.

Second arch from the east: a woman and child, in fourteenth-century costume, before a Saint, drawn on a larger scale than the other figures. On the northern face of the arch, a bishop bearing a chalice.

On the west wall, a Coronation of the Virgin, with the figures of Christ and the Virgin seated on a bench in place of the customary throne.

On the soffit of the chancel arch, a leaf pattern, large in scale.

On the wall opposite the entrance, towards the west, remains, comprising heads, of two tiers of subjects, separated by a border of wavy design.

South aisle, south wall: fragments of a narrow dado-band.

All the work, executed in the usual ochres, is much perished, with the exception of the subject first described.

Aymer Vallance, *A. Cant.*, 1918, XXXIII, 164, 165, repr.; Keyser, *B.A.A.J.*, 1918, XXIV, 17, footnote; Borenius, *St. Thomas Becket in Art*, 18, footnote 2. (Halston for Halstow.)

EAST HANNINGFIELD (near Chelmsford) Essex
ALL SAINTS

The Nave

At the west end of the south wall, paintings executed *c.* 1300, or early in the fourteenth century, and now in poor condition as the result of exposure to the weather during many years. There were originally two tiers of subjects, separated by a scroll and trefoil border:

1. *The upper tier:* The Condemnation of Adam to Labour and Toil; Adam and Eve facing eastward, appear to be receiving implements of labour from the (?) hands of an Angel; the last-named figure now entirely defaced.

2. Eve seated, spinning with a distaff, while Adam digs; they are clothed in tunics, as in the first scene, and between them is a conventionalized tree.

3. St. Catherine, framed within a niche which extends into the lower tier of paintings, veiled and crowned, and bearing the Wheel in her right hand; formerly she held a book in her left, but this, together with the lower part of the painting, has perished.

4. The Sacrifice of Cain and Abel; on the left a figure, presumably that of Abel, with the sacrifice of a lamb before him, the smoke ascending to Heaven, on the right the sacrifice of Cain, represented by sheaves of corn, the smoke from them descending into the Jaws of Leviathan. The figure of Cain is missing. On the ground is a diaper of circular groups of spots.

5. Cain Slaying Abel, only parts of the figure of Cain decipherable.

In the lower tier, only fragments of heads survive, the subjects being unidentifiable.

The colours are a dark red ochre, a deep yellow

ochre, and solid white. Part of the painting was re-moved, in 1933, to the Victoria and Albert Museum.

Some years ago, on the north wall, immediately opposite the works described above, an Entry into Jerusalem still existed, but this has now perished entirely. (Notes, E. W. Tristram, 1931.)

A.J., 1896, N.S., LIII, 163; *R.C. Historical Monuments R., Essex*, 1923, IV, 36, repr.; Benton, *Essex A.S.*, 1928, N.S., 105–18; id., ibid., 1933, XX, 297.

HARBLEDOWN (near Canterbury) Kent
ST. NICHOLAS

The Chancel

On the splays of the east window, an Annuncia-tion, *c.* 1350, the Angel Gabriel on the northern and the Virgin on the southern splay. Both figures are framed by painted niches with cusped and crocketed canopies, executed in black and yellow ochre; the background within the niches is red, that above them and on the soffit of the window-arch black. The Angel Gabriel, with one wing raised and the other drooping, has a white nimbus and yellow hair, is clad in a white tunic, bordered at the neck, and a black mantle, and extends his hands towards the Virgin, who holds a black book in the left hand and raises the right in acknowledgement of his salutation. She has a yellow nimbus and yellow hair, a white tunic and a black mantle; and her face and hands, like those of the Angel, are black, the underpainting for flesh colour, which has perished. Before her is a tall black pot filled with lilies, painted black and out-lined in white.

On the north side of the window, traces of a diaper composed of the letter M, crowned, apparently in alternation with rosettes. *c.* 1400.

The Nave

South aisle, east wall; remains of a diaper com-posed of the Sacred Monogram, I.H.S., crowned, in alternation with the letter M, crowned. *c.* 1400.

Keyser, *Mural Decorations*, 1883; Newman, *P. Society of Antiquaries*, 1904, XX, 46.

HARDWICK (near Harleston) Norfolk
ST. MARGARET

The Nave

North wall, opposite the south door, St. Christo-pher, against a ground diapered with ermine, clad in a red gipon patterned with delicate scroll-work in white, and a voluminous red cloak lined with green, bordered at the neck with yellow and fastened by a brooch; he holds the staff, with traces of branches at the top, in the right hand and on the left arm sup-

ports the Holy Child, who has a cusped nimbus in yellow and green, raises the right hand in blessing and holds in the left an Orb of the Universe sur-mounted by a cross. On each side is a conventional-ized tree, with birds in the foliage, including an owl; and on the left the figure of an angler, in soft cap with rolled brim, shoulder-cape, short hip-length gipon, belted low, and long hose. The painting, all the features of which were clearly decipherable when it was recorded by Dawson Turner, is now much defaced, only the general mass of the chief figures, with traces of the trees, the owl, and the ermine diaper, now being visible. *c.* 1390.

B. Mus., *Dawson Turner Collection*, Add. 23055, vol. III, 156–7; Keyser, *Mural Decorations*, 1883; Blomefield's *Norfolk Supplement*, 1929, 305, repr.; Whaite, *St. Christopher*, 1929, 18, pl. 4.

HAYLES (or HAILES) Glos

The Chancel

The splays of the east window are painted in ver-tical stripes of red, yellow and black, a treatment terminated above and below by a horizontal border of ornament, that above being placed at the springing of the window-arch, with scroll-work in red line filling the soffit. The arch has voussoirs defined in outline, with every third block painted in solid yellow; the border of ornament at the springing, already mentioned, is continued from the splays on to the adjacent wall-surfaces on either side, and in the spandrels above it, also on either side, is a censing Angel, kneeling on uneven ground, clad in a black tunic and white mantle, and having the wing feathers painted in rows of white, black and pink. Framing these figures, and following the contour of the roof, is a scroll border elaborated with leaves having ser-rated edges, tendrils, and small cinquefoils, between a narrow upper border of wavy pattern and a lower, equally narrow, composed of chevrons in black, white and red.

On the north wall, reading from the west, the remains of the scheme are as follows:

Above the level of the wall-plate is a painted frieze about 4 ft. in depth, now broken at intervals by struts supporting the roof joists, but originally continuous, since the struts were plastered over and the frieze thus carried across them; an arcade was represented, the six narrow eastern bays framing single figures of Apostles, but the six wider western bays, which have more elaborately cusped heads than the eastern, and are supported on shafts ter-minating in chevroned pinnacles, framing subject-paintings. Little of these is decipherable, and no more can be said than that a bier or tomb, attended by Angels, is seen in a central position, with the figure of a bishop to the east of it, and traces of groups of figures in the bays to the extreme west and east respectively. It is evident that the backgrounds, in some cases at least, were diapered with a fret pattern, each diamond framing a quatrefoil flower. Below the frieze, the wall-space between the north-west angle of the wall and the first of the two windows is filled with a large chequer pattern charged with two heraldic devices in alternation, namely—*Argent, an eagle displayed sable*, and—*Gules, a castle argent*. The arch of the adjacent window is outlined with a lozenge pattern, and the spandrels above it filled with grotesque beasts, that on the west being goat-headed but having the body, apparently, of a wyvern, that on the east, united to the head of an elephant, a cater-pillar-like body with scalloped edges to the wings. The wall-space between this window and the second is filled by barbed quatrefoils, on a black ground, in closely serrated ranks, twelve deep and four wide, with small pink cinquefoils in the interspaces: each quatrefoil originally framed a shield of arms, placed centrally on the cream field provided by the plaster of the wall; but the colours used are simply black, white and red ochre, so that, at least in the majority of cases, the true heraldic tinctures must necessarily have been disregarded. Many of the charges have perished entirely; among the clearest of those still decipherable are: *A bordure semy of martlets; Gules a bar argent between three mullets of the same:—Argent an eagle displayed gules; Argent three piles gules, a canton of the same;—Gules a chevron argent;—Argent three lions rampant gules;—Sable three chevrons argent;—Gules a bar argent;—Argent a chevron gules;* and—*Barry of argent and gules.* The arch of the second window is bordered in the same manner as that of the first, but the grotesques in the spandrels above are virtually indecipherable.

Between the two windows in the south wall is a large diamond pattern, filled with two coats of arms in alternation, viz. *Argent a lion gules within a bordure sable bezanty*, and *Argent an eagle displayed sable*; but every third row of diamonds, in place of the charges described, has *paly argent and gules*. Over a niche in the splay of the south doorway an owl is painted; and within the head of the niche is a small linear pattern, reminiscent of vaulting ribs, the bosses at the intersections being represented by small quatre-foils; above another niche is a fragment of a Pietà. The frieze above the wall-plate is now almost en-tirely defaced; but it may be seen that Apostles were represented in the six westernmost bays.

On the eastern face of the west wall a fragment remains of a large lion executed in black, but no other traces of painting survive in this position.

The Nave

Over and around the chancel arch, a powdering of roses and five-petalled flowers, in red ochre and white respectively, on a ground of dark red.

James, *Abbeys*, 1926, 121; Bird, *Mural Paintings, Glos.*, 1927, 20, repr.; Borenius and Tristram, *Eng. Med. Painting*, 22, pl. 55.

HEACHAM (near Hunstanton) Norfolk
ST. MARY

The Nave

On the southern face of the south-west pier at the crossing, St. John Baptist, holding in the left hand, veiled by the mantle, a disc charged with an *Agnus Dei*, to which he points with the right hand. His head is defaced; his figure is drawn in red outline, against a background composed of a fret pattern in black and red, the black nearly obliterated. The paint-ing was evidently once framed by a representation of a canopied niche (its upper part now destroyed), from the sides of which spring delicately-executed floral forms, somewhat resembling cornflowers, supported on slender stalks. Below, part survives of the canopy of a similar niche. *c.* 1340.

Around the chancel arch, good scroll-work in red, and remains of red colouring. ? *c.* 1300.

Plate 55b

HEADINGTON, Oxon ST. ANDREW

About the year 1864 well-preserved painting was discovered in the nave and south aisle, but was later obliterated, having first been recorded in detail. The survivals were as follows:

The Nave

The arches of the arcade between the nave and south aisle were coloured red on the exterior and yellow on the interior chamfers, and on the soffits was a scroll pattern resembling that employed else-where in the church; above the hood-moulding was a masonry pattern in double red lines; over the chancel arch a pointed 'arch' composed of foliated scroll-work and a representation of a Majesty; while at the eastern end painted hangings, as described below, were continued from the scheme in the south aisle, and above them the wall-space was filled by four horizontal stripes in red, each patterned with a row of stars, the plain space between them having stars in red.

The South Aisle: south wall

Below the level of the window-bottoms there was a painted hanging, bordered at the upper edge by a horizontal band ornamented with scroll-work bearing roses and trefoil leaves and framed by two narrow bands charged at regular intervals with small roundels, and at the lower edge by another narrow band, also charged with roundels and finished with a fringe, the space between these two borders being filled with vertical stripes of different colours. The upper part of the wall, above the hangings, where it was not occupied by subject-paintings, was treated with a masonry pattern, its stones being painted yellow and the broad joints between them pink with a central line in white. Reading from the east, the subjects depicted were:

In the south-east angle, above the painted hanging, in two tiers: below, an Angel with right hand raised and a scroll in the left; above St. Anne teaching the Virgin, who, clad in a long tunic and veiled, kneels before a prie-dieu on which lies an open book, with St. Anne behind her, clad in a dark mantle and light tunic and with a head circlet and barbette, her right hand upraised above her daughter's head. The series was interrupted at this point by two adjacent windows, with masonry pattern around them: in the first, on the eastern splay, painting in three tiers, in the highest a bust of St. Peter with the Keys; in the central tier, a Nativity, the Holy Child, with a cruciform nimbus, being placed centrally, the Ox and Ass behind Him, and the Virgin and St. Joseph respectively to the left and right; and in the lowest tier, the Flight into Egypt, the Virgin, holding the Child, being seated on the Ass, which is followed by a figure, apparently of a youth and led by St. Joseph, who holds his staff over his right shoulder with a cloak slung from it. On the western splay, also three tiers of painting; in the highest a bust of St. Paul, holding the Sword upright by its point, and painted, like the St. Peter on the opposite splay, against a light ground powdered with roses; in the central tier, Herod commanding the Massacre of the Innocents, seated cross-legged to the right of the composition, crowned and holding a sword, and before him two soldiers, the foremost bearing a spear, the second a hatchet; in the lowest tier, a man in a short tunic, leading a horse and preceded by a larger figure, probably part of a (?) Journey of the Magi, on the immediately adjacent eastern splay of the second window. In this second window, on the eastern splay, again three tiers of painting, in the highest of the three, against a ground powdered with roses, the bust of a Queen; in the central tier, the Massacre of the Inno-

cents, with Herod seated cross-legged on the left of the scene, a sword held upright in his right hand, and his left extended in a gesture of command towards a soldier who transfixes a child upon a spear, and has behind him two smaller figures and at his feet a second child; in the lowest tier, probably the Magi on their Journey, only two figures on horseback being visible, one crowned, preceded by a man in a short tunic, holding a sickle. On the western splay, in the highest of the three tiers, a bust of a Bishop, against a ground diapered with roses; in the central tier, the Entry Into Jerusalem, with Christ upon the Ass to the left, to the right Zacchaeus in the tree, and below him a man spreading a garment before the hoofs of the animal; in the lowest tier, probably an Annunciation to the Shepherds, misunderstood in many of its details as represented in the engraving from it, in which the crooks of the Shepherds seem to have been rendered as spears and swords, and one of the sheep, in file in the foreground, apparently provided with a nimbus, while a tall standing figure, presumably the Angel, is mis-drawn, with what seems to be a cap upon the head.

All the tiers of subjects in both windows are separated by narrow bands of a dark colour, patterned with roundels; in the easternmost window, the spaces beneath the lowest tier are patterned with scattered roses, while in those in the westernmost window they are filled by scroll-work enriched with the same flower.

Immediately adjacent to the westernmost window was a large St. Christopher, filling the entire wall-space above the painted hanging. Clad in a tunic clearing the ankles, about which water is represented, a mantle, and soft cap, he holds a crooked stick in his right hand, and supports with his left, covered by his mantle, the Holy Child, who has a cruciform nimbus and raises His right hand in blessing. Immediately to the west of this painting was a door, the wall-space above it decorated with roses, and the arch ornamented by painted cusping terminating in trefoils. The entire scheme appears to have dated from 1310 to 1325.

Builder, 1864, 733, 741, repr.; Parker, *Oxon A. & H.S.P.*, N.S., 1860–64, I, 302, repr.; *Gent. M.*, pt. I, 1865, 323–4; Keyser, *Mural Decorations*, 1883.

HEREFORD

CATHEDRAL CHURCH OF ST. MARY AND ST. ETHEL-BERT

Formerly, on a Norman arch at the end of the south aisle of the nave, leading to the south transept:

checker and chevron patterns and heraldic shields, among them ? FitzAlan, Pembridge, Sudeley, Harley and England; on the capitals, large ? half-roses; on the shafts, half-diamonds, chevrons, fleur-de-lis, large diamonds in two colours, smaller diamonds framing sexfoils or roses, and roundels enclosing ? animals or grotesques; on the abacus of one or other of the capitals, 'wavy' ornament, or, alternatively, bold intertwined scroll-work. On the wall beside the arch, a diaper of small shields, each one charged with ermine; scroll-work; and a bent-riband pattern.

Havergal, *Fasti Herefordenses and other Antiquarian Memorials of Hereford*, 1869, 155, pl. XV.

The Tomb of Joanna de Bohun, Countess of Hereford: in the Lady Chapel, north wall, eastern end. 1327.

R. Gough, *Sepulchral Monuments*, 1786, I, pt. ii, 194. 'On the wall within the arch [over the tomb] is painted the Virgin Mary sitting crowned with a nimbus. A lady habited in a mantle and wimple, kneeling on an embroidered cushion, offers a church, formed *en croix*, with a central spire, and behind her kneel eleven or twelve religious chanting a *gorge deployée* after the foremost, who holds up a book with musical notes, and *Salve Sca parens*. Fleurs-de-lis are painted about within and without the arch, and on the spandrels *a bend cottised, the lioncels rampant*, Bohun, effaced, and *Ermine a bend fusily gules* [Plugenet].'

During cleaning undertaken in 1946, which included the removal of later colouring, considerable remains of original colour were found, including light and dark green, vermilion, light blue, and black on the arch mouldings; on the effigy, natural colour on the face, on the 'sideless gown' vermilion, diapered in gold, on the kirtle dark green, and on the shoes, black; the veil and wimple, white; the cushion under the head, dark green patterned in grey; and on the canopy over the head, small windows painted in black, but much defaced. Above the arch and at the sides, yellow or gold fleurs-de-lis and rosettes in green, all on a red ground. Only traces survive of the subject-painting described by Gough, since it was repainted at a later date; cleaning in 1946 revealed some fragments of the original work.

Also in the Lady Chapel, within an arched recess in the south wall, the tomb of ? Chancellor Gilbert de Swinfield; at the back of the recess, traces of colour, the remains of a painting illustrated by Carter (Gough, *Sepulchral Monuments*, 1796, II, part ii, plate LXXVI) wherein a Dean of the Cathedral was shown, with hands raised, kneeling before St. Anne, in fillet, barbette and crespine, traditionally represented as instructing the Virgin, who, with an open book before her, received a rose

from her mother. The mouldings of the arch, when cleaned in 1948, were found to have been painted red and green in alternation, and the carvings of boars upon them had each upon the back a small coat blazoned with the arms of the Deanery—*Or, five chevrons azure* (which shows some variation from the present blazoning). In the spaces between the animals, remains of delicate foliation in white.

Gough, *Sepulchral Monuments*, 1796, II, pt. ii, 196.

HOLCOT (near Brixworth) Northants
ST. MARY AND ALL SAINTS

The North Aisle

At the eastern end of the north wall, a Martyrdom of St. Thomas of Canterbury, the Saint depicted in choir habit, and not, as usually, in Mass vestments. Grim the cross-bearer attempts to avert the blows of the knights from the kneeling Archbishop,

On the north wall, in the higher of two tiers of subjects, St. Catherine before the Emperor Maximinus, and in the lower tier, six Apostles, one probably St. John, bearing the Cup, and another St. Bartholomew, with the Knife; the tiers divided by a band of scroll-work in red, and finished below the wall-plate by another in faded black.

On the window-splays, single figures of Saints, one being St. Andrew; and on the soffits of the window arches, a scroll pattern in red.

Around the blocked north doorway, a border in red, faded black, and buff.

The South Aisle

At the western end, the Ascension, the Descent of the Holy Ghost, and a doubtful subject; adjacent, ? the Incredulity of St. Thomas; and near the south door, the Resurrection.

HONINGTON (near Thetford) Suffolk
ALL SAINTS

The Nave

On the wall above the south door, a 'history' of St. Nicholas, and a Martyrdom of St. Thomas of Canterbury; much defaced.

Bryant, *County Churches, Suffolk*, 1912, I, 28; James, *Suffolk & Norfolk*, 1930, 71; Munro Cautley, *Suffolk Churches and Their Treasures*, 1938, 276.

HORLEY (near Banbury) Oxon   ST. ETHELDREDA

The Nave

North aisle, reading from the west:

1. Between the second and third windows, remains of a subject, comprising traces of a figure, and of an ornamental treatment consisting of a diaper of

black fleurs-de-lis in alternation with quatrefoils in pink, evidently the remains of a painted hanging, since hooks are depicted at the upper edge; the figure subject, when discovered in 1853, seems to have been in a good state of preservation, being then described as a St. Michael Weighing Souls.

2. Between the third window and the east wall, a much-defaced subject, including two figures, that on the left side having bare feet and a blue tunic and red mantle, that on the right a red tunic; ? an Annunciation.

3. On a column of the north arcade, St. Osyth, veiled and clad in a tunic, red mantle lined with white, and black shoes; her yellow nimbus is rayed, and she holds a rosary and bears a green book. On the black background are various objects, among them a purse, four keys, a cauldron, a tub, and a brush or bell. *c.* 1400.

The Tower

Fragments of a treatment comprising: on the eastern splay of the north window, a shield about 2 ft. in height, with guiges, charged with—*Gules on a fesse sable a crescent argent, in chief two mullets sable:* above the shield delicate ornament in white on a ground of black, and below it an indecipherable inscription. High upon the walls, in the north-west, north-east, and south-west angles, medallions 2 ft. 6 ins. in diameter, bordered in red and having black backgrounds, one in each angle. If another formerly existed in the south-east angle it has been destroyed. Such subjects as may have been framed by the existing medallions have vanished without trace, excepting that in the north-west angle, of which fragments survive comprising a scroll with traces of an inscription, the letter W being decipherable, and remains of wing feathers; ? the Symbol of the Evangelist Matthew.

A.J., 1853, XIII, 416; Keyser, *Mural Decorations*, 1883.

HORNTON (near Banbury) Oxon
ST. JOHN BAPTIST

The South Aisle

It is recorded that the 'walls, roof and screen were painted in brilliant party colours and gilt', and that on the walls there was a Virgin and Child, with St. Joseph, and a kneeling figure of a bishop.

Beesley, *History of Banbury*, 1848, I, 125-6; Keyser, *Mural Decorations*, 1883.

HORSHAM, Sussex ST. MARY

The North Aisle

Formerly, on the south wall above the arcade, and

originally filling one of the spandrels between the arches, a painting of Christ, with cruciform nimbus, facing frontally, between a tonsured figure, on His right, and another, bearded, on His left, (?) St. Peter and St. Paul; the whole superimposed upon a masonry pattern in single line elaborated with stalked quatrefoils and finished above with a band consisting of blocks of masonry depicted in alternating colours. Elsewhere upon the same wall, the exact position not being specified in the account, a tonsured head superimposed upon a masonry pattern having the horizontal joints executed in single line and the vertical joints in double line, with small chevrons between the lines, each block being enriched with a stalked cinquefoil.

Part of a Passion series is recorded as having existed on the north wall; the surviving subjects, reading from the west, were Christ being Mocked, Christ carrying the Cross, and the Crucifixion, in the last-named only traces of an unidentifiable figure and of the penitent thief remaining; the backgrounds were diapered with spots in groups of three, and above the scenes ran a border like that over the Christ with (?) St. Peter and St. Paul, described above, and below a chevron border.

Keyser, *Mural Decorations*, 1883; André, *Sussex Archaeological Collections*, 1892, XXXVIII, 6, repr.; id., ibid, 1900, XLIII, 236.

HOUGHTON CONQUEST (near Ampthill) Beds
ALL SAINTS

Over the chancel arch, a Doom: in the centre, within an almond-shaped Glory, Christ enthroned upon a rainbow, displaying His wounds, the Orb of the Universe beneath His feet; to the right, an Angel holding the cross and spear, to the left another with the pincers and nails; below, shields bearing Emblems of the Passion.

A.A.S.R. & P., 1870, X, xcvi; Keyser, *A.J.*, 1881, XXXVIII, 85; Keyser, *Mural Decorations*, 1883; *Victoria County Hist.*, *Bedfordshire*, 1912, III, 295.

HOXNE (near Eye) Suffolk
ST. PETER AND ST. PAUL

The Nave

On the north wall, above the arcade, separated by the clerestory windows, reading from the west:

1. St. Christopher, traditionally represented as of gigantic stature, bearing the Holy Child on his right shoulder. The painting is in a somewhat defaced condition, the river-bank, with the hermit and hermitage, being barely decipherable. To the south, two

standing figures with scrolls, one having a nimbus, the other clad in a green robe.

2. The Seven Deadly Sins. In the centre, a tree, bearing as its fruit seven dragons, one at the apex and three on either side; in the mouth of the highest a figure of *Pride*, represented as a richly clad gallant, in a cote-hardie with bell-mouthed sleeves, and a belt at the waist, crowned, and holding a sceptre in the right hand and in the left a mirror; in the mouths of the others *Avarice* and *Sloth* may be recognized, the former represented as a bearded man grasping a money-bag and taking coins from a box, and the latter as a man with eyes closed, lying in a lazy attitude. Both have high hats and cote-hardies with pointed long sleeves and bugle cuffs. *Envy*, *Lust*, *Anger* and *Gluttony* are much perished. At the base of the tree, two devils sawing through the trunk. Hell Mouth, into which it might be expected to fall, and which was doubtless represented originally at the base of the composition, is utterly defaced. On the south wall, immediately opposite this painting, a large incised circle is all that remains of what was perhaps originally a representation of the Seven Ages of Man.

3. The Seven Corporal Works of Mercy. In 'Clothing the Naked', Mercy, represented as a female figure, veiled and clad in a kirtle, gives a garment to a nude man; in 'Giving Drink to the Thirsty', she hands another figure what was probably a cup, now indecipherable; 'Visiting the Imprisoned' is defaced, apart from traces of a building; in 'Feeding the Hungry' she gives a bearded man, clad in a long belted gown and holding a staff, a slice of bread, and in 'Harbouring the Homeless' a seated male figure in large hat and high-necked, closely buttoned cote-hardie, receives from her a bag of money; in the final scene (since 'Burying the Dead' is destroyed), that of 'Visiting the Sick', Mercy feeds a figure lying upon a couch. Scrolls, with inscriptions, now indecipherable, accompany most of the figures, and a border ornamented with quatrefoils, now largely perished, frames the series of subjects. All *c.* 1390–1400.

4. The Last Judgement, arranged within a semicircle formed by the arch of a rainbow; at the top a figure of Christ in Judgement, the Orb of the Universe at His feet, on either side Angels bearing Instruments of the Passion, and the Apostles as Assessors; below, the separation of the Blessed and the Damned, and St. Michael Weighing Souls, with a General Resurrection beneath. Much defaced.

White, black and green are used, as well as the usual ochres.

Other subjects, among them a Crucifixion, are recorded as having existed on the south wall in 1835, but there appears to be no information regarding their probable date.

Gent. M., 1835, N.S., III, 420; Page, *History of Suffolk*, 1844, 402; Keyser, *Mural Decorations*, 1883; Tristram, *Apollo*, 1927, V, 33–4, reprs.; *Burl. M.*, 1930, LVI, 231; James, *Suffolk and Norfolk*, 1930, 80–1; Munro Cautley, *Suffolk Churches and Their Treasures*, 1938, 276.

HURSTBOURNE TARRANT (near Andover) Hants
ST. PETER

The North Aisle

On the eastern splay of the first window from the east in the north wall, a diaper of fleurs-de-lis.

Between the same window and that next to it on the west, *Les Trois Vifs et Les Trois Morts*, executed on a large scale: on the eastern side of the composition the skeletons, separated from each other in each instance by a tree, and on the western side the kings, likewise separated by trees; reading from the east, the first is shown richly dressed and bearded, raising his left hand, the next as young and beardless—the third is much defaced. The painting is terminated at the upper edge by a scroll border and at the lower by a patterned band.

Between the second and third windows in the same wall, a Wheel of the Seven Deadly Sins: the rim is decorated with a scroll pattern, and representations of *Luxuria* and *Socordia* are decipherable. Both this painting and that previously described were discovered *c.* 1896, and are now much damaged.

Keyser, *A.J.*, 1896, LIII, 171–2; id., *Memorials of Old Hants*, 1906, 147; *Victoria County Hist.*, *Hants & I.O.W.*, 1911, IV, 323; Storck, *Burl. M.*, 1912, XXI, 317; Carleton Williams, *B.A.A.J.*, 1942, 3rd ser., VII, 34, 39.

ICKWORTH (near Bury St. Edmunds) Suffolk
ST. MARY

The Chancel

On the southern side of the east window, within a painted niche surmounted by a cusped and crocketed arch, an Angel, in a three-quarter-length tunic and a mantle draped to fall in intricate folds from the left shoulder, holding a scroll, now blank, in the left hand and raising the right; the figure has a nimbus, and the wings are half-extended, the right wing being partially covered by scroll-work. Extensively retouched.

Suffolk I.A. & N.H.P., 1912, XIV, 57; Wall, *Medieval Wall Paintings*, 1914, 189, repr.; James, *Suffolk & Norfolk*, 1930, 33, repr.; Munro Cautley, *Suffolk Churches and Their Treasures*, 1938, 278.

IDSWORTH (near Havant) Hants   ST. HUBERT

The Chancel

Wall-paintings were first discovered in 1864, and a further search was undertaken *c.* 1900; there were indications that all the walls had been painted, but indecipherable remains were cleaned down and the wall-surface whitewashed, while the better-preserved parts of the work were retained.

On the northern splay of the east window, within a painted niche having a cusped and crocketed canopy supported on slender shafts, St. Peter, with short hair and beard, wearing a conical tiara, orphreyed alb, dalmatic, chasuble and pallium, and holding the Keys in the right hand, the left being defaced; bordering the splay, a design of stalked trefoils and free brush strokes. On the chamfer of the window arch, a pattern of chevrons with small roundels between them. At the apex of the soffit, a large estoile, and just below it, on the north side, an Angel, having a nimbus and vested in an alb, with an incense boat in the left hand, the right being destroyed; on the opposite side, remains of a similar Angel.

On the southern splay of the same window, St. Paul, with a nimbus, within a niche similar to that framing St. Peter; he is bearded, but bald on the top of the head, with long hair from the level of the eyebrows, and clad in a tunic and mantle, the latter veiling his left hand, in which he carries a book, while in his right, held by the blade, is the Sword. The pattern of trefoils and brush strokes, together with that of chevrons and roundels, and the figure of a censing Angel, are repeated in the same positions as on the northern side of the window. In both these paintings ochres and black are used; but the latter has faded to greyish-beige. *c.* 1330.

From slight traces appearing from beneath later painting, it may be seen that the wall to the north of the window was originally coloured pink and enriched with a masonry pattern of square blocks, each having in the centre a quatrefoil.

The north wall, divided into three tiers, has well-preserved paintings in the two higher of these, which are separated by a band of bent-riband pattern in red and white on a yellow ground. Reading from the west, there appear to be two subjects in the higher tier, as follows:

1. A hunting scene. At the extreme west of the composition two horsemen, mounted respectively on a white and on a yellow steed, ride eastward, the former clad in a ? cloak reaching to slightly below the knee; the upper part of the painting is here defaced, so that these figures are partly missing. Immediately before the horses' hooves, two hounds and a small dog leap in the direction of a huntsman, who, with another behind him grasping a whip, and three more hounds at his feet, stands beneath an oak tree having large leaves and acorns. He has short, curled hair showing beneath his wide-brimmed red hat, a white tunic, a red super-tunic, a yellow cloak, pink hose and red shoes; at his back is slung a sheaf of arrows, while in his right hand he holds a bow and in his left the horn he is winding. From the hounds about him a sixth breaks away as it leaps in front of a group of three figures, towards a weird, shaggy-coated animal emerging from between the low-growing branches of a second oak-tree, here framing the scene. The central figure in the group bends towards the animal and grasps its right fore-limb, which, unlike the others, ends in a human hand in place of a paw; and as he looks down upon the creature he raises his left hand slightly above its bearded, human head, surrounded by a yellow nimbus, with traces of a red outline. He has hair curled in a roll at the level of the jaw, is clad in a white tunic, reaching to the calf of the leg, a pink super-tunic diapered with roundels in red and having a loose, patterned collar and wide, three-quarter-length sleeves, and in white hose and shoes, and carries a sword at his side. Behind him to the left stands a huntsman in a yellow super-tunic and red hood, holding a horn, and to the right a man in a white super-tunic and yellow hood, pointing downward at the strange beast, with the left hand and extending the other slightly upward over it. His head, like those of all the others in the scene, is bent towards it. Uneven ground, with small plants springing from it, is represented at the base of the composition, but it terminates at the base of the second oak tree, so that the animal's hind legs, unsupported and extending into the next scene, rest upon the border of bent-riband pattern already mentioned.

2. The Arrest of St. John Baptist. The Saint, long-haired, bearded, and with a nimbus, clad in the usual loose, knee-length garment, stands facing eastward, his legs apart, the hind feet of the strange animal in the previous scene appearing between them. His left shoulder is grasped by a man in a yellow tunic who points towards him with the left hand, while his wrist is gripped by another, in a

white tunic and yellow headgear, and having an ugly, mocking countenance, who drags him away.

In the second tier, as it now exists, there are also two scenes, continuing the 'history' of St. John Baptist as follows:

1. The Imprisonment of St. John Baptist. Masonry is shown on the prison building, which has a door with ornate hinges, under a cusped and crocketed canopy, and windows in the eastern side. Through the doorway, and partly concealed by the half-open door, the Saint, clad in a shaggy skin, is being thrust by a warder holding a club, or perhaps an axe, in his right hand; his head is drawn as a hideous caricature and covered by a turban-like winged head-dress.

2. The Feast of Herod, in three 'moments'. In the first, the Presentation of the Head, Herodias and Salome are seated with two companions at a table spread with a white cloth hanging from it in regular festoons and bearing plates and vessels of different types. Salome, on the extreme left, wears a coronet over a crespine and short white veil, and, resting the left hand on the table and raising the right, turns towards Herodias, a slightly larger figure, with a coronet, voluminous veil, and mantle lined with vair, who, with the man and woman at her other side, gazes at the charger containing the head, held by a server standing at the end of the board. He is clad in a full-length, light-coloured super-tunic with elbow-length sleeves, showing the long, close-fitting sleeves of the red tunic, and has feathers in his hair. The second episode, as represented on the wall, is the first in the story itself—the Dance of Salome, who is shown executing a sword dance in the centre of the composition, in front of the table; her body, clad in a red kirtle, is bent backward in a curve with the head almost touching the ground, and in each hand she holds a long sword, while a dagger is suspended in mid-air above her upturned face. Immediately behind her, as part of the third 'moment', the Showing of the Head to Herod, a second server is represented, turning to the east and offering the charger to Herod, who, crowned, bearded, with hair curled in a roll at the level of the ears, and clad in a yellow mantle fastened with a brooch over a loose-sleeved red super-tunic and white tunic, raises his right hand as though in concern. To his right, between him and the server, a youth seated beside him points downward with his right hand across the table at Salome's contorted figure; on his left a bearded man raises his right hand as if in astonishment, and beyond him are traces of another figure. The table at which they are seated is draped and set after the same fashion as the other already described.

The painting is set out on a ground of thin lime putty; and yellow and red ochre, and lime white, but not black, are used. *c.* 1330.

A.J., 1864, XXI, 184; Keyser, *Mural Decorations,* 1883; id., *Memorials of Old Hants,* 1906, 147; *Victoria County Hist., Hants & I.O.W.,* 1908, III, 108–9; Johnston, *Surrey Archaeological Collections,* 1911, XXIV, 76, repr.; Wormald, *Ant. J.,* 1945, XXV, 43–5, repr. Plates 42–6.

IMBER (near Warminster) Wilts ST. GILES

The Nave

On the arches of the arcade, masonry blocks picked out alternately in red and in 'marbling', executed in imitation of Purbeck; and in the spandrels, masonry pattern in red enriched with flowers; on one of the round pillars, chevron decoration in red. *c.* 1300.

The North Aisle

At the western end, masonry pattern in red, elaborated with scroll-work; and near the roof a border, placed diagonally, of scroll ornament in red, between narrow borders. *c.* 1300.

Keyser, *A.J.,* 1901, LVIII, 58.

INGATESTONE (near Chelmsford) Essex
ST. MARY AND ST. EDMUND

A Wheel of the Seven Deadly Sins was discovered in an unspecified position in the church during alterations carried out *c.* 1866, and afterwards covered with whitewash; but in the interval a drawing of it had been made by W. Strutt, and descriptions had appeared in more than one publication. The Wheel, 7 ft. 2 in. in diameter, was divided into seven compartments by means of the spokes, which issued from a 'hub' framing a representation of Hell; around the 'rim' ran an inscription, only a few words of which remained legible. The Sins are represented as follows:

1. *Superbia,* in the central section at the top—a richly-dressed woman in a close-sleeved red kirtle, fastened with a long row of buttons down the front and covered with a 'sideless' surcoat. On her right a tiring-woman standing; and on her left traces of a devil.

2. *Invidia,* below, to the spectator's left—a group of four men, one clad in a short gipon buttoned down the front and finished with dagging, another bearing a small round targe and a sword, with a devil in the rear, standing before two justices, the foremost wearing gloves and a coif, seated behind a barrier.

3. *Gula,* below again, on the same side—at the

narrow end, three casks lying side by side; in the middle, a woman urging another to drink from a shallow bowl; at the broad end next to the rim, a male figure, with a rosary in the left hand, vomiting into a basin; behind him a devil.

4. *Avaritia*, at the base, a seated male figure, coifed and caped, counting money with claw-like fingers; behind him a strong-box and two devils.

5. *Accidia*, at the base on the right side—a figure asleep in bed; in the background traces of a devil and a church window.

6. *Luxuria*, above—a male and a female figure embracing.

7. *Ira*, above, next to *Superbia*—two young men, clad in long hose and brief gipons, engaged in a fight. *c.* 1390.

A St. Christopher, of fourteenth-century date, is recorded to have existed in the church; it seems to have been on the north wall of the nave near the west door.

Gent. M., 1866, pt. 2, 348; *Reliquary*, 1869–70, X, 219–24, repr.; Piggot, *Essex A.S.*, 1869, IV, 140, repr.; Keyser, *Mural Decorations*, 1883; André, *A.J.*, 1888, XLV, 416; Wall, *Medieval Wall Paintings*, 1914, 198, repr.

INGHAM (near Stalham) Norfolk HOLY TRINITY

The Chancel

On the north side stands the tomb of Sir Oliver de Ingham (d. 1344); the effigy has traces of blue on the helmet, and it is evident that the mail was originally executed in raised gesso and gold, of which there are considerable remains; behind the 'weepers' there were once delicately-executed scroll patterns in blue, as may be seen from an example still in fairly good condition behind the second figure from the western end; on the fragments of the canopy are traces of colour and some minutely worked 'marbling'. Formerly, on the wall at the back of the tomb recess, there was a scene with trees, animals, a forester blowing his horn, clad in a short green gipon and a hood, and another drawing his bow, dressed in a gipon buttoned down the front and hooded; ? the Legend of St. Hubert, or that of St. Eustace.

The Nave

Under the easternmost arch of the arcade stands the tomb of Sir Roger de Bois and his wife, upon which there are considerable remains of painted decoration, as follows: on Sir Roger's helmet and also on his surcoat, delicately-executed patterning in gesso, and 'prints', and on the former, traces of red and of blue; on the head-dress of his wife, vestiges of gold and blue, on the pillow under the head a deli-

cate pattern in raised gesso, on the mantle a narrow border in raised gesso, on the gown parts of an elaborate diamond design, on the unbroken portion of the girdle, some colour, and on the folds of the dress about the feet and on the shoes, remains of blue and of red.

B. Mus., *Dawson Turner Collection*, vol. X, 12–15; Stothard, *Monumental Effigies of Great Britain*, 1817, 55, reprs.; *Norfolk Archaeology*, 1879, VIII, 216–18; Keyser, *Mural Decorations*, 1883; Keyser, *Archaeologia*, 1899, LVI, 196.

INGLESHAM (near Swindon) Wilts

ST. JOHN BAPTIST

The Chancel

On the east wall, on either side of the altar, as also at the east end of both north and south walls, a pattern of stars in yellow on a red ground, with a pattern of stripes below; the string-course at the base of the east window painted red; at the back of a recess in the wall, a rosette pattern in bright red on a grey ground; in the piscina recess in the south wall, red colouring. Upon fragments of the original reredos, considerable remains of colour decoration, executed *c.* 1330, as follows: in recessed panels, paintings of four Saints, the heads of the two upper figures missing, the heads and shoulders of the two lower ones being the only parts of these to survive; they are delicately drawn, and the nimbi are wrought in gold, while the drapery is painted in bright colours and outlined in black, and the red background is diapered with small quatrefoils; to one side is a small censing Angel with outspread wings, the feathers being rendered in varied tints. It is obvious that the reredos must have been of fine quality, since the workmanship upon it was of the best.

On the east wall, and also on the north, consecration crosses within circles elaborated with small roundels.

Ponting, *Wilts A. & N.H.M.*, 1927, XLIII, 167; Knowles, *Bristol & G.A.S.R. & P.*, 1931, LIII, 205; Tristram, *Wilts A. & N.H.M.*, 1936, XLVII, 527. Plates 56*b*, *c*, 60*a*, 61*a*.

INWORTH (near Kelvedon) Essex ALL SAINTS

The Nave

A border of scroll ornament in red extends from north to south on the wall above the chancel arch; and another of wavy pattern in red and white, elaborated with small red roundels on the white, follows the contour of the arch. On the western face of the south respond is a 'history' of St. Nicholas, in two tiers, separated by a scroll-work border, and finished at the top by another, similar but somewhat wider. The work in the upper tier is much defaced, and the scenes difficult to decipher in both tiers.

Upper tier:
1. Several figures, mitred and in mass vestments;
2. A Bishop, facing frontally;
3. A figure in red tunic and black mantle, facing south.
4. A larger scene than the first three, with a figure on the north side.

Lower tier:
1. A Bishop in mitre and black chasuble with hands raised, facing a building, and three female figures; ? St. Nicholas and the daughters of the poor nobleman.
2. ? the Saint on the northern side of the scene, facing a ship with striped sails.
3. A small subject, now indecipherable.

The backgrounds throughout are diapered with a pattern of three small roundels.

On the north side of the arch, masonry pattern with vertical joints in double and horizontal in single line, each block enriched by a centrally-placed sexfoil flower. All *c.* 1300.

Keyser, *Mural Decorations*, 1883; *R.C. Historical Monuments R., Essex*, 1922, III, 139.

JERSEY ST. BRELADE'S: THE FISHERMEN'S CHAPEL

The chapel stands in the churchyard of St. Brelade's church. The vaulting, decorated at the apex with scroll foliage, in 1859 bore extensive remains of subjects arranged in three tiers, though some were much defaced, which were as follows:

In the northern compartment, a Passion series, with Christ before Herod, showing Herod enthroned, a scroll above him being inscribed HERODES ROY, and Christ between two guards, and the Binding of Christ, both in the highest tier; and in the second tier the Flagellation and the Carrying of the Cross; the lowest tier obliterated. In the southern compartment, a Nativity series, in which part of a figure and an Annunciation survived; the latter still exists, but has been extensively retouched.

At the western end of the chapel, St. Michael Weighing Souls. All the subjects painted in red outline on a ground diapered with constellations composed of five small circles. *c.* 1400.

Burges, *A.J.*, 1859, XVI, 89; *Builder*, 1864, XXII, 733; Keyser, *Mural Decorations*, 1883.

KEMPLEY, Glos ST. MARY

The Nave
Traces of a fourteenth-century scheme of painting, comprising: On the splay of a window in the north wall, an Archbishop. On the splay of a Norman window in the same wall, a St. Michael Weighing Souls, with the Virgin interceding.

On the south wall, St. Antony, formerly with the pig, which is now entirely defaced.

Masonry pattern elaborated with roses; and a consecration cross.

All the work is in very poor condition.

Keyser, *A.J.*, 1872, XXXIV, 270-5.

KENTFORD (near Newmarket) Suffolk
ST. MARY

The Nave
North wall, reading from the west, between the first and second windows:
1. *Les Trois Vifs et les Trois Morts;* the three kings, elegant figures, apparently clad in cloaks thrown back over the left shoulder, and gipons, on the right, meet the corpses with expressions of horror; the latter have each a toad in the body. The painting is over 11 ft. in length. *c.* 1360-80.
2. St. Christopher, of the usual gigantic height (about 12 ft.), facing the southern entrance to the nave, but much defaced.
3. Between the second and third windows, the Seven Deadly Sins; the Tree of Evil, with its dragon fruit, is decipherable, but only one of the Sins is clearly to be seen—Sloth, represented by a figure lying on a couch.

South wall, reading from the east: to the west of the doorway in this wall, the Seven Virtues, or perhaps, the Seven Sacraments; in the centre a church, with Angels issuing from it, each holding either a Virtue or a Sacrament, now difficult to decipher, since all are somewhat defaced and the inscriptions on the identifying scrolls have perished. Around the doorway, traces of large figures of Saints, and nearby, the Seven Corporal Acts of Mercy, all scarcely discernible. *c.* 1390-1400.

The fragmentary condition of the paintings is partly attributable to the fact that they have been obliterated with limewash, and again uncovered, on two occasions.

Tristram, *Apollo*, 1927, V, 34-5; Long, *Burl. M.*, 1930, LVI, 231; Munro Cautley, *Suffolk Churches and Their Treasures*, 1938, 281; Carleton Williams, *B.A.A.J.*, 1942, 3rd ser., VII, 35, 39.

LITTLE KIMBLE (near Wendover) Bucks

ALL SAINTS

The entire church was evidently painted about the beginning of the fourteenth century, but the chancel walls retain only traces of colour, the survivals being on all four walls of the nave, which are divided into three zones—the lowest, now blank, about 6 ft. in depth, the middle about 7 ft. and the highest, separated from the other by a zigzag border, only 2 ft.

The north wall is pierced by three windows, one of them, that between the door and the west end of the building, being small, and the other two, between the door and the east end, larger. Reading from the west, there is in the upper part of the wall-space a 'History' of St. Margaret; of the first scene, the head of the Saint and her black tunic alone survive; of the second, her head only, bent forward; of the third, her figure, kneeling before a torturer, represented with hideous features; of the fourth, her entire figure, stripped to the waist, and with arms upraised and hair tied to a horizontal bar, standing between two executioners wielding staves; and of the fifth, her figure, kneeling with hands clasped in prayer, the head dragged forward by the hair as the executioner strikes with his sword. In the middle tier are slight traces of a large figure, vestiges of colour on the splays of the small window mentioned before, and between this window and the door part of another tall figure, that of St. James the Great, who, bearded and with long hair, has a pilgrim's staff and hat; the lower part of this painting is defaced. Farther to the east, between the doorway and the next window, the upper part of a St. Christopher survives; the Saint, facing east, wears a red tunic, white mantle and low hat, has a staff in the left hand, and bears on the right shoulder the Holy Child, with a cruciform nimbus, clad in a short tunic, with hand raised in blessing; to the right is a scroll, but no inscription remains upon it. Above the painting just described, to the west of the adjacent window, is the head of a bearded man, facing west and holding, or pointing to, a triptych; in its middle panel is a Virgin and Child, with tracery above, and in the right, a small representation of the Holy Trinity, but that on the left is defaced.

On the splays of the window are four figures, two on each side, represented within painted niches: of those on the western side, one is defaced, apart from the head and some drapery, the other being a bishop in mass vestments, with hand raised in blessing. A similar figure is to be seen on the opposite splay, its companion having disappeared, except for the fingers of one hand, holding a book.

Between this window and the third in the wall there is a St. George some 6 ft. in height; he is in chain mail, over which is a white surcoat charged with a red cross enriched by a delicate running scroll. At his waist is a sword, in his left hand a shield, charged with a similar cross, as are also his ailettes, and his right hand grasps a lance; beside the hand is a shield charged with the lions passant gardant of England. Beneath his feet uneven ground is represented; and the painting is finished with a border upon which the name G[E]OR[G]IVS is inscribed in Lombardic capitals. To the right are traces of a consecration cross, and the figure of a woman, in veil, wimple and long red tunic, holding in her right hand a ball from which hangs in festoon a long thread, its end in her other hand.

On the western splay of the easternmost of the two windows are two figures, the first, on the left, with head defaced, clad in a black habit, holding a book in one hand and raising the other; the second that of a woman in veil, wimple, and long yellow tunic, who also holds a book and faces the first. The eastern splay has remains of a St. Francis preaching to the Birds; his figure is partly defaced, but it may be seen that he was depicted clad in a brown habit with a knotted girdle at the waist, raising a hand as though to emphasize his discourse to the birds of various species perched in the branches of a conventionalized tree, an owl being prominent among them. To the east of the window, in the angle by the east wall, is a St. Lawrence, in alb, amice, and black dalmatic adorned with wide bands in white; he faces west, holding a grid in one hand and raising the other.

On the east wall, to the south of the chancel arch, is a painted niche framing, against a black ground, a much-defaced figure; and above, on the right, a shield, the charge being indecipherable.

The south wall, by comparison with the north, has but few remains. Above the doorway is a Burial of St. Catherine by Angels on Mount Sinai, in a somewhat fragmentary state; to the right of the doorway a tall figure in a tunic and a voluminous mantle drawn over his head, holding a book between his hands, the left being veiled by a fold of the mantle; and, also near the door, another tall figure, almost entirely defaced.

On the west wall, on both sides of the window in this wall, are remains too fragmentary for identification; and it can only be said that on the north side two figures may be made out, apparently of veiled women, falling headlong, with two male heads lying near them, together with some lines in red.

Keyser, *Mural Decorations*, 1883; *The Antiquary*, 1900, XXXVI, 379–81; *Victoria County Hist.*, Bucks, 1910, II, 306; *R.C. Historical Monuments R.*, Bucks, 1912, I, 166; Tristram, *Records of Bucks*, 1932, XII, 313; *Franciscan History and Legend in English Medieval Art*, ed. Little, 1937, 8, repr.; Carleton Williams, *B.A.A.J.*, 1942, 3rd ser., VII, 24, 33.

KIMPTON (near Wheathampstead) Herts
ST. PETER AND ST. PAUL

The Nave

Above the chancel arch, within medallions, the Seven Corporal Works of Mercy, discovered *c.* 1860, now much defaced. Giving Drink to the Thirsty, with the benefactor, in a hooded cloak, to the spectator's left, and a pilgrim to the right, painted against a diapered background, and Giving Bread to the Hungry, with a similarly clad benefactor, again to the left, a basket of bread on a low stool behind him, but the remainder of the scene defaced, are illustrated in the *Church Builder*.

Above the main arcade on the north, facing the principal entrance, formerly, traces of a subject executed on a large scale, ? a St. Christopher.

The Church Builder, 1865, XVI, 167, repr.; *Gent. M.*, 1861, pt. 1, 662; Keyser, *Mural Decorations*, 1883; *R.C. Historical Monuments R.*, Herts, 1910, 132.

KINGSTON (near Cambridge) Cambs
ALL SAINTS AND ST. ANDREW

North Aisle

West wall: a Wheel of the Seven Corporal Acts of Mercy; between the spokes of the Wheel scenes representative of the various Acts, that placed highest on the wall, 'The Burying of the Dead', alone being identifiable. At the sides of the Wheel two Angels are represented in the act of revolving it. Below, traces of what was probably a Tree of the Seven Deadly Sins, including a small head of a devil with a figure held in its jaws, the whole framed by two interlaced bands of colour enriched with a small pattern in white.

North wall, reading from west to east: a tall figure, apparently of a Saint holding a book; a figure almost entirely obliterated; St. George and the Dragon, represented against a background of red, the Saint mounted on a richly-caparisoned white charger, the dragon beneath its hooves, and behind it traces of a figure; between the second and third windows in this wall, St. Christopher bearing the Divine Child, in a perished condition; above some of the paintings, representations of rods, as though for painted hangings, which have not survived. *c.* 1400.

South Aisle

On the soffit of a window arch, a chevron pattern, the points of the chevrons terminating in trefoils, executed in red and white; in the hollow moulding of a capital, a fret pattern in red; and remains of large consecration crosses.

A.J., 1924, IV, xxxii, fig. 2; Brindley, *Cambridge A.C.*, 1931, XXXI, 146–8; Carleton Williams, *B.A.A.J.*, 1942, 3rd ser., VII, 33.

KINGSTON LISLE (near Wantage) Berks
ST. JOHN BAPTIST

The Chancel

On the splays of the east window, life-size figures of St. Peter and St. Paul, bearing their respective emblems, the Keys and the Sword, the former also carrying a church or (?) ship; the background diapered with red roses. On the east wall, to the north and south of the window, traces of subjects now indecipherable.

At the eastern end of the north wall, including the splay of a window in it, scenes from a 'history' of St. John Baptist, in two tiers, one scene remaining in each:

1. In the higher tier, Herod's Feast, with the king seated at a table spread with dishes, Herodias on his right and on his left a partly defaced figure; in front of the table, Salome dancing, her body depicted, in the manner normal at the period, bent in a curve.

2. In two 'moments'; the Decollation of the Baptist; on the left the executioner with sword uplifted, at his feet the headless body of the Saint; and on the eastern splay of the adjacent window, Herodias, crowned, receiving the head. At the apex of the window, a head of Christ, with a cruciform nimbus. The paintings are executed in black line, apart from Herod's hair and the food upon the table, in the banqueting scene, which are in red.

The Reliquary, 1892, N.S., VI, 147; Keyser, *A.J.*, 1901, LVIII, 55; Long, *Berks, B. & O.A.J.*, 1942, XLVI, 31.

KYRE MAGNA, KYRE WYARD, or GREAT KYRE (near Tenbury) Worcs
ST. MARY

In a chapel built in 1330, on the splays of the south-west window, remains of painting; on the eastern splay only a fragment survives, but on the western, against a diapered background, consisting of diamond-shapes enclosing quatrefoils, there survives the figure of a Saint, standing with head slightly bent to the spectator's left, and holding in her left hand a book.

Chatwin, *Birmingham & Midland A.S.T.*, 1913, XXXIX, 59, repr.; *Victoria County Hist., Worc.*, IV, 284.

LAKENHEATH (near Mildenhall) Suffolk
ST. MARY

The Nave

On the flat face of a massive pier immediately opposite the south door, a painted hanging in grey and black, terminated about 5 ft. from the present floor level by a fringe. The pattern upon it is geometrical in character, being based upon intersecting circles, and executed in grey, outlined in black, upon cream, the interspaces being filled with stalked trefoils in black, placed saltire-wise. From the upper edge springs scroll-work, on either side of the base of a 'tree' composed entirely of scroll-work in black, of which the 'branches' spread to fill the spandrel immediately above the column, between the third and fourth arches of the arcade reading from the east; the highest 'branch' on the western side has a dove perched upon it. *c.* 1300. On the soffits and members of the first three arches of the arcade from the east are to be seen bold scroll-work, a wavy pattern in outline elaborated with roundels, or alternatively roundels set at intervals, and a band following the contour of the arch, all in black, but much faded. Above and to the left of the last arch to the east, fragments of scroll-work.

Superimposed upon the paintings on the pier, described above, and partially obscuring them, are the following subjects, executed *c.* 1350:

On the eastern side of the pier a figure, rather under life-size, of St. Edmund, King and Martyr, crowned, the nimbus pink outlined in black, the hair, curled at the level of the ears, yellow outlined in red, the features outlined in red; the tunic white outlined in red, and the mantle black; the left hand raised to touch the cord at the neck of the mantle and the Arrows held in the right. At the centre of the pier, parts of a figure of Christ, comprising traces of the head, with a cruciform nimbus, the tunic, and one hand; and on the western side, and extending on to the western face, remains of a hanging executed in broad red outline and elaborated with roses.

In the spandrel above the pier, and partially obscuring the 'tree' of scroll-work, a Passion series, arranged in three tiers and executed in red and yellow, as follows:

Highest tier:

1. The Harrowing of Hell, the Vexillum being visible, together with parts of two or three figures.

2. The Angel at the Tomb, seated with wings spread and arms outstretched, facing east, with a head (? that of one of the Holy Women) on the western side, and on the eastern, scroll-work.

Middle tier:

1. (?) The Agony in the Garden, part of a figure of Christ, with the cruciform nimbus, alone being visible.

2. The Carrying of the Cross, in which Christ, led by a man with a rope, looks back over His shoulder towards a small figure following Him.

Lowest tier:

1. The Crucifixion, parts of the cross, of the head of Christ and of His left arm, and the nimbed head of St. John, surviving.

On the eastern facet of the pier, painted in black, a life-size figure with hands raised in adoration, much defaced.

On the capital, remains of red; and, following the contour of the arch on the eastern side, remains of boldly-executed scroll-work in red.

On the third pier from the east, three life-size figures with hands raised in adoration, executed in red and black; much defaced.

In the spandrels between the first and second arches of the arcade, reading from the east, in each two Angels with outspread wings, seated on thrones masonried in the upper part, and furnished with a cushion patterned with a fret design; the figures executed in black outline, their cloaks being pink and their tunics white. Below the easternmost pair, in the narrowest part of the spandrel, a smaller Angel, nimbed like the others, with hands raised in adoration, and in a similar position to the west, traces of another. *c.* 1350.

On the Norman chancel arch, traces of colour, and high on the wall to its southern side, a life-size female head, nimbed, and executed in black outline; probably *c.* 1350.

The North Aisle

On the west wall, masonry pattern in red, the courses in single line, the vertical joints in double line.

At the eastern end, between two windows, parts of ? a Christ in Majesty or Judgement, fragments of the head, ? nimbed, and of the feet, being visible; the scale is very large. In the north-east angle, a fragment of an altar hanging ornamented with a large fret design.

Keyser, *A.J.*, 1896, LIII, 161; James, *Suffolk & Norfolk*, 1930, 64; Munro Cautley, *Suffolk Churches and Their Treasures*, 1938, 286.

THE CATALOGUE

LAMBOURNE (near Theydon Bois) Essex
ST. MARY AND ALL SAINTS

The Nave

On the south wall, the upper part of a St. Christopher, discovered in 1951; the head, painted with considerable skill, is exceptionally well preserved, but like that of the Holy Child, cut off at the top by a modern cornice. The Saint turns towards the Child, who is borne on his left shoulder, and holds perpendicularly at his right side a tau-headed staff with a knob on the shaft. His cloak is bright blue, draped around the body and lined with vermilion, and his gipon pale purple with a green band at the neck; his nimbus is red towards the centre, where it is patterned in black, and its border dark green. The Child, with hair curled and golden in colour, wears a pale purple tunic and a dark green cope, draped over the knees, fastened with a morse, and lined with ermine; His right hand is raised in blessing and in His left He holds an Orb, painted a bright red and surmounted by a small, light green cross with trefoil terminals. The background is light red, with traces of a darker red ground appearing in places. Both figures are outlined in black, the flesh tints being solidly painted over a dark underpainting. *c.* 1400.

Of another and earlier painting of St. Christopher (? *c.* 1350) in the same situation as that described above, part only of the beard is visible, seen through colour on the neck of the later figure. There are indications of a late fifteenth-century renovation, namely, remains of a small flower-spray, stencilled on the background in light green, and fragments of dark green.

From notes supplied by Mrs. M. Bardswell.

LEGERWOOD (near Earlston) Berwick

The Chancel

The walls retain traces of ornamentation in red, composed of wheels, each 8 in. in diameter and having 8 spokes springing from a hub; the best-preserved part of this decoration is to be seen at the back of a small recess, 15 in. in width and 11 in. in depth, in the north wall, where it is bordered by scroll-work framed by a narrow band.

R.C. Historical Monuments R., Scotland, 1915, VI, 124, repr.

SOUTH LEIGH (near Oxford) Oxon ST. JAMES

The North Aisle

At the west end, the Mouth of Hell, from which springs the Tree of Evil, traces of it alone remaining; seven dragons' heads, on serpent-like necks and bodies, spring from and cling to the trunk and branches, three being on either side and one at the top of the tree; within the wide-open jaws were originally representations of the Deadly Sins. These are almost entirely defaced, but when clearer than they are now were described as 'figures of fat men, with their names written in old English characters, Envie, Slothe, etc.' Executed in the usual ochres, the work is the only one in the church that escaped repainting in the nineteenth century.

Moultrie, *Oxon A. & H.S.P.*, 1872, N.S., III, 27–9; Keyser, *Mural Decorations*, 1883.

LENHAM (near Maidstone) Kent ST. MARY

The Chancel

On the splay of a window in the south wall, painted against masonry pattern executed in double line and elaborated with roses, a Bishop in pontificals, the right hand raised in blessing.

The Nave

On the south wall, St. Michael Weighing Souls; clad in a yellow mantle and red tunic, and with a red nimbus, he stands with wings outstretched behind him, on a small hillock with traces of trefoil plants upon it, facing west with the scales held in his right hand and the left raised towards the Virgin, who, veiled and crowned, and standing on a similar hillock, throws a rosary upon the balance-beam and raises her right hand as though interceding for the Soul in the scale before her. The other scale, upraised, is grasped by two devils who attempt to weigh it down. A third devil was formerly visible, being described as seated on the upper part of the beam, grasping an unidentified object in the right hand and in the left a horn which he was winding; but all this, together with part of an inscription in Old English, has now disappeared. The figure of the Virgin is partly obscured by a mural tablet. The painting, executed in the usual ochres and black, and framed by a deep band of yellow outlined in red, is skilful in execution and large in scale, the figures being almost life-size. *c.* 1350.

On the effigy of a priest, built into the north wall of the chancel, remains of green, yellow and red colouring.

Gent. M., 1844, XXII, 410, 450; *Antiquarian and Architectural Year Book*, 1844, 173; *A.J.*, 1845, II, 270, 274; ibid., 1846, II, 73; Waller, *Gent. M.*, 1851, XXXVI, N.S., 24; Keyser, *Mural Decorations*, 1883; Wall, *Medieval Wall Paintings*, 1914, 191, repr.

THE CATALOGUE

LICHFIELD THE BISHOP'S PALACE

Formerly, in the hall, built by Walter de Langton, Bishop of Lichfield, 1295–1321, 'excellently well painted, but now much decayed, the coronation, marriage, wars, and funeral of Edward I, and some writing which there is also yet remaining, which expresseth the meaning of the history, where is especially mentioned the behaviour of Sir Roger Pewlesdon and others, against the Welshmen; and also of Almaric de Bailgiol, Burnell, Valence, Earl of Pembroke, of Lord Badlesmere and other barons against the Scots, where the said earls and lords are very lively portrayed, with their banners of arms bravely before them, but it is a great pity that the same is not restored by the Lord Bishop before it be quite decayed.'

Archaeologia, 1786, III, 188; Erdeswick, *Survey of Staffordshire*, 1844, 101; Blackburne, *Decorative Painting*, 1847, 4.

LILBOURNE (near Rugby) Northants
ALL SAINTS

Over the chancel arch, on the south side, part of a Doom, in which the dead rising from their graves remain in the lower part of the work, and in the upper part, several nimbed figures. *c.* 1390–1400. Decoration in red on the arch includes a bent-riband pattern, of *c.* 1300.

From notes made by Mrs. M. Bardswell.

LIMPENHOE (near Loddon) Norfolk
ST. BOTOLPH

The Nave

Paintings discovered on the north wall in 1852, appear to have been of late fourteenth-century date; copies were made by C. J. W. Winter before they were whitewashed over four years later, and subsequently destroyed when the old church was demolished. A History of St. Margaret, at first erroneously described as a History of St. Catherine, was represented in eight scenes. Between the north door and an adjacent window, reading from west to east, the subjects were as follows:

1. St. Margaret, holding a distaff, is seated spinning; the Prefect Olybrius, in a cloak with a dagged collar, approaches on horseback, holding a ring in his right hand.
2. The Saint before the Prefect, who is seated to the right of the scene, on a raised platform; a guard behind her appears to be grasping her arm, and behind

him another, clad in a knee-length gipon, holds a scourge; there are traces of two other figures.
3. The Saint thrown into the Cauldron; two executioners cast her head first into the vessel, from which two birds fly towards her; behind the executioner on the left is a man in a knee-length gipon and a hood with the peak pointing forward over his face, holding a rod in the right hand, and directing the proceedings.
4. The Saint burnt with brands; executioners stand on either side of her, wielding, or about to wield, the brands; both are clad in gipons and the one on the left has his hair standing in upright tufts upon his head; in the background is a gibbet.
5. The Saint held by the hair and scourged; a torturer, clad in a hip-length gipon with dagging at the lower edge and with a richly ornamented belt, placed low, a hood with a gorget dagged at the edge and long liripipe pendent behind, and pointed shoes patterned with a fret, grasps her hair with his left hand and raises the scourge in the other; above her head a large bird with outspread wings.
6. ? A missing subject.

Here the series was continued to the east of the window, between it and the adjacent rood screen, as follows:
7. The Beheading of the Saint to the east of the scene, before a small tower with battlements and an open doorway, dividing this subject from the next, part of the kneeling figure of the Saint, her hands raised in prayer, and before her the executioner, grasping a sword in the right hand and holding her severed head up by the hair in the left; above it a bird flies upward. Behind the executioner a group of figures support the bodies of two men struck by lightning.
8. The Burial of the Saint; she is laid in the tomb, a group of three figures standing at the head, and at the feet a priest with an open book and two more figures behind him.

All the scenes are framed above and below by two borders, both of scroll ornament, one enriched with trefoils, and the other with roses; including these, the paintings occupied an area of approximately 4 ft. 6 in. × 25 ft. *c.* 1390.

Partially concealed by the St. Margaret scenes was a painting of *Les Trois Vifs et Les Trois Morts*, probably of *c.* 1340. The church was entirely demolished in 1881.

B. Mus., *Dawson Turner Collection*, 1852, Add. IV, 81; Husenbeth, *Norfolk Archaeology*, 1859, V, 221–5, repr.; *A.J.*, 1864, XXX, 219; Keyser, *Mural Decorations*, 1883.

LOLWORTH (near Cambridge) Cambs
ALL SAINTS

The Nave

On the partly walled-up nave arcade, traces of painting; in red ochre on the shafts, in red ochre and pale grey on the mouldings of the capitals; together with a fret pattern alternating with a diaper of lozenges and quatrefoils, all in red.

At the extreme western end of the north wall, at a height of 8 ft. from floor level, and measuring approximately 27 in. × 19 in., a painting of the Incredulity of St. Thomas, in which Christ, clad in a yellow tunic, holds against the wound in His side the hand of St. Thomas, who is kneeling, clad in a long red cloak and yellow tunic. The work dates from the end of the fourteenth century.

Benton, *Cambridge A.C.*, 1906-8, XII, 148-51, repr.

LONDON PALACE OF THE ARCHBISHOP OF YORK

The Palace appears to have been occupied by Edward I *c.* 1304-5, since 'the King's great chamber in the Archbishop of York's house', and also the 'chamber of the Lady Mary, daughter of the King', are mentioned in the Accounts Various of the Exchequer, King's Remembrancer, E.101/468/10, E.101/468/11, and E.101/547/18, which relate to painting carried out there at the time. No subjects are specified, but it is evident, from the mention of large sums of money as being expended, and also from the fact that some of the foremost painters in the employment of the King were engaged, that considerable schemes of decoration were undertaken. Among the names of painters are to be found those of Walter of Durham, Thomas of Durham (? of Westminster, his son, as he is named in the Accounts for Westminster Palace), and Alan de Beomond, Beaumond or Beumond, a highly paid painter, all of whom worked also in Westminster Palace.

Other names given are: Walter Marchaund (whitewasher), Philip of Barnby, Philip of Hales, Isaac of Ireland, William Wickeware, Milon of Ailewyk, Richard of Madely, Abraham of Northampton, John of Hastings, Richard Blithe, Ralph of Conford, Richard of Reyndon, Roger of Worcester, Thomas of Wilton, William of Ros (three painters who worked also at Westminster), Thomas of Stockwell, Ralph of London, and William of Birleye.

LONDON ST. PAUL'S CATHEDRAL (*Old St. Paul's;* destroyed in the Great Fire of 1666)

Extracts from records, etc., relating to painting executed in Old St. Paul's during the fourteenth century.

John of Gaunt's Register, 1379-83, Camden Soc., 3rd Ser., 1937, LVI, pp. 76-7, par. 231.

'Johan, etc., a nostre tresame clerc sire William de Bughbrigg, nostre receivour general, saluz. Come noz chers et bien amez Richard Burgate et Robert Davy, peinteurs et citzeins de Londres, eient empris de peinter saffissantement touz les aysshelers et touz les ymages deinz ycelles environ la tombe de nostre tresamee compaigne dame Blanche, qi Dieux assoille, assise en lesglise de Seint Poule de Londres, et de parfornir et parfaire bien et loialment le dite peinture a la feste de la Nativitee de Seint Johan le Baptistre prochein avenir apres la date de cestes; et prendront les ditz Richard et Robert pur le dite depeinturee vynt et sys livres, cestassavoir tresze livres au comencement de meisme le depeinture et tresze livres a la feste de seint Johan desusdit sicome es endentures parentre nous et eux faitz est pleinement contenuz, vous mandons que, maintenant vieues cestes, des issues de vostre receite facez paier as ditz Richard et Robert tresze livres desterlinges en partie de paiement de les vynt et sys livres avantdites, receivant devers vous lettres dacquitances desouz les sealx des ditz Richard et Robert tesmoignantz le paiement quel vous leur ensi ferrez. Par quels lettres et par cestes nous volôns que vous en eiez due allouance en vostre aconte. Donnee, etc., a la Sauvoye le tierz jour de Marz lan, etc., tierz. (3 March, 1380, the Savoy).'

References to paintings, or painted sculpture, it is uncertain which, occur in: Dugdale, *History of St. Paul's Cathedral*, 1716, p. 16 (1309), pp. 32-3 (1325), and p. 17 (1398); and in Sharpe, *A Calendar of Wills in the Court of Husting*, 1889, I, 416 (1336).

LONDON THE TOWER OF LONDON: the Byward Tower, main gatehouse of the outer ward

In a large room on the first floor of the south tower extensive remains of wall-painting were discovered in 1953-4. A heavy beam running the length of the room is decorated with popinjays, fleurs-de-lis and lions-leopardy in gold, a few of them with gilding still brilliant and virtually intact. The birds, collared in vermilion, have beaks and claws of the same colour, and the lions are armed and langued in vermilion. The south wall is covered by a large pattern in which similar popinjays are placed diamond-wise on a ground of green. Between them are fleurs-de-lis, originally gilt and outlined in vermilion, and lions-leopardy, also once in gold, outlined in black and armed and langued in vermilion. Only slight traces of gold remain, except on parts of the beam just mentioned, but yellow ochre underpainting to the metal is everywhere visible. The work is highly skilled, and the date apparently *c.* 1380.

Superimposed on the pattern just described are figure-subjects of *c.* 1400. Reading from the left, they are as follows:

1. St. John Baptist. The Saint is clad in a cloak with folds painted in a greyish-purple tint, and in an undergarment of skin, the hair upon it being skilfully drawn in yellow and brown. The head is well rendered, with long hair and beard in reddish-yellow, while the eyes are a dark brown. The nimbus, originally gilt, has a narrow border in red and is outlined in black. In the left hand is a book, bound in red and with clasps that were once gilt, and upon it there lies the *Agnus Dei,* to which the Saint points with the right hand. From the same hand hangs a white scroll with an inscription still largely intact, in black letter with the first E rubricated; it reads ECCE AGN[US DEI]. The Lamb is painted in white and bears the Vexillum, charged with a cross in vermilion.

2. The Blessed Virgin has her hands clasped in the traditional attitude of grief, as in a Crucifixion. The head, well drawn and modelled, is in a good state of preservation, the flesh tints being predominantly a deep rose. The eyes are a vivid blue, and the nimbus, originally gilt, is edged in vermilion and outlined in black. The cloak is a bright blue, shaded in a deeper tint of slightly greenish blue, while the lining is in dull red, with high lights in yellowish pink. The pink tunic is shaded in lake.

At this point the painting is broken through the insertion of a later fireplace. On the other side of this are:

3. St. John the Evangelist. Only the head and shoulders of the figure survive, with part of the upraised right hand. The features are well drawn and modelled, and the hair, curled closely over the head, is reddish-gold in tint. The pink cloak is shaded in red, and the tunic is blue.

4. St. Michael Weighing Souls. The head is treated like those previously described, and there are traces of a diadem upon the brow. The curled hair is painted in reddish-brown and yellow, and the eyes are grey. The outspread wings are shaded from white, or very pale pink, in the highest range of feathers, through a deeper pink and a brilliant vermilion to crimson. The cloak is grey and the tunic yellow lightly shaded in dull red. One of the feet is visible; it is bare, and well drawn and modelled. Traces of gold remain on the balance-beam. In the pan to the spectator's right is part of a small devil in a dark, rich green, with touches of

vermilion on the features; it is however somewhat confused with remains of one of the lions-leopardy on the green background.

The work, highly accomplished throughout, is executed in oil or an emulsion of oil. There is slight 'crackling' on the surfaces in some parts, in particular in the darker colours.

R.C. Historical Monuments R., East London, V, 1930, 77 (re lions-leopardy, etc., on beam); *The Times,* xii, xii, 1953.
Plates 8*b,* 9*a, b,* 10.

LONDON WESTMINSTER ABBEY

The Abbot's Hall

The hall was built in the second half of the fourteenth century. The ceiling rests on stone corbels of late fourteenth-century date, carved with Angels holding either scrolls or painted shields-of-arms; the shields comprise Edward the Confessor; Litlington, (*Argent ?*) *quartering* (*azure ?*) *fretty or ? over all a bend sable ? with three fleurs-de-lis or ? thereon;* the same, but with *a border charged with six mitres or;* the Abbey of Westminster. The Litlington arms are repeated.

R.C. Historical Monuments R., Westminster, 1924, I, 87.

Chapel of Our Lady of the Pew

This small chapel, measuring only 9 ft. × 6 ft. is formed in the thickness of the abutment between the chapels of St. John Baptist, and Abbot Islip, and seems to have been built towards the end of the fourteenth century; but the inner archway, opening into the Baptist's Chapel, is of later date. The mouldings of the head of the outer doorway are painted in vermilion, with bands of 'marbling' and of white. Two corbel heads in the inner bay are painted, and there are traces of painting on the vaulting; on that of the outer bay are stars of six points. The walls have remains of colour decoration, comprising those of a brocade pattern with white fleurs-de-lis on the blue centres, and a hart with a crown about the neck (much defaced). In the north wall is a niche, its mouldings richly decorated in colour, and patterned with 'barber's poling' in black and vermilion, and small roundels in groups of seven, in white on a ground of black; at the back the outline of a figure survives, with radiations painted around the head. On the north-east side of the chapel, a stone shield of St. George, painted in white and vermilion.

Neale and Brayley, *Westminster Abbey,* 1823, II, 187–8; *R.C. Historical Monuments R., Westminster,* 1924, I, 34, 73, 74, pl. 143.

The Tomb of Aymer de Valence, Earl of Pembroke

The monument has considerable remains of its

original colour decoration and gilding, which was originally as profuse as that adorning the near-by, rather earlier tombs of Edmund Crouchback, Earl of Lancaster, and his wife Aveline de Forz, though it is perhaps executed with slightly less delicacy, and there are no 'prints'. The 'weepers' were originally highly coloured in red, green, blue and white, against backgrounds alternately green and red, diapered with flowers in gold; and between the crocketed gables of the niches within which they stand are quatrefoiled circles each framing a shield with painted arms. The effigy has a surcoat with the Valence arms, and upon the cushions under the head are small shields of Valence. 'Marbling' is much in evidence on the architectural features, being executed by means of white brush-strokes on varied grounds of red, green and black. In the gable of the canopy, on either side of the monument, is a trefoil with a diapered background in relief, painted red with the flowers gilded, framing a horseman in armour, the colour on the figure being fairly well-preserved. The head is damaged, but it is evident that the eyes were painted in full; the mantling, streaming out on either side, is white, barred with red and edged with black. The armour is gilt in parts, and the chain-mail is painted in black with small, curved brush-strokes. The bardings of the horse bear the arms of Valence (except that the martlets are omitted), the lining being painted red; where the harness is seen it is in red or gold. The horse was originally white, but this has largely vanished. The roof of the canopy, on both sides of the monument, is red, and covered with a large masonry pattern having blocks 7 in. × 12 in., with courses and joints executed in white lines ¼ in. in breadth. The effigy is thought to be of *c.* 1310, but the structure generally is dated *c.* 1324.

Dart, *Westmonasterium*, 1742, II, 11, repr.; Neale and Brayley, *Westminster Abbey*, 1823, II, 275, pl. XLIII; Scott, *Gleanings from Westminster Abbey*, 1863, 159–61, 164; Keyser, *Mural Decorations*, 1883; Lethaby, *Burl. M.*, 1918, XXXIII, 170–2; *R.C. Historical Monuments R.*, *Westminster*, 1924, I, 24, pls. 33, 34.

The Coronation Chair, 1300–1

The Coronation Chair, made by Master Walter, King's Painter to Edward I, with the object of housing the Stone of Scone and serving as a 'memorial in perpetuity' of the King, is preserved in the Chapel of St. Edward. Made of oak, it has a high back rising in the centre in an acute gable with carved crockets; immediately below the latter, on the obverse, which is otherwise without ornament in relief, there is between narrow mouldings a flat division, about 3 in. in breadth, retaining traces of the fixing of what were probably 'glass enamels' similar to others of which fragments still survived on the reverse *c.* 1823, when they were thus described:

'Within the spandrels connected with the upper tier of arches at the back, were formerly, according to Mr. Carter, enamelled ornaments representing foliage; but the ornaments thus alluded to were not enamelled; they consisted of small sprigs depicted on a metallic ground, either gilt, or silvered, and covered with plain or coloured glass; as may yet be seen in three or four places.'

These remnants of imitation enamels have since disappeared. In contrast to the reverse, the obverse was evidently left entirely plain, below the flat division mentioned above, with the object of providing space for a subject-painting, of a king enthroned, with his feet resting upon a lion; but only parts of the throne, of the lion in question, of a foot in a somewhat pointed shoe, and of the drapery and diapered background, survive. On the inner face of the right arm of the chair there remains a considerable portion of a diaper pattern executed with extreme delicacy by means of gilding and 'pouncing' upon a ground of gesso, and comprising foliage and grotesques; and on the corresponding face of the other arm an exquisite design, similarly executed, of oak leaves and birds, unfortunately much perished. On the outer side of the same arm, that is, the left, the first of four panels, reading from the spectator's left, is in good condition, and shows a pattern of oak leaves; the second, much defaced in the centre, a pattern apparently of ivy, interspersed with trefoils and ? groups of small berries; the third, also much damaged in the centre, shows unidentifiable leaves with trefoils in the interspaces; and the fourth, the best-preserved of the series, vine leaves, with small clusters of grapes, and trefoils. The technique is similar to that described in connexion with the decoration on the inner faces of the arms; in each case the foliage springs from two broad curving stems, which disappear into the leaves at the apex of the panel. There are indications of a somewhat earlier scheme on the arms than that now visible. Fragments of gilt gesso-work exist all over the Chair.

In the year 1887 it was disfigured by a coating of 'dark brown oak stain', but, after protests had been made, this was removed. It had been the original intention to make it of metal.

Extracts from Records relating to the Coronation Chair,
   1299–1300

'Compotus Adae aurifabri Regis de jocalibus emptis ad opus Regis; et de aurifabria diversa facta per eundem anno XXVII° et anno XVIII° usque

XXVII diem Marcii. Eidem pro diversis custibus per ipsum factis circa quandam cathedram de cupro quam Rex prius fieri preceperat anno XXV⁰ post reditum suum de Scocia, pro petra super quam Reges Scociae solebant coronari inventa apud Scone anno XXIIII^to superponenda juxta altare ante feretrum Sancti Edwardi in Ecclesia Abbathiae Westmonasterii: et nunc eadem petra in quadam cathedra de ligno facta per Magistrum Walterum pictorem Regis loco dictae Cathedrae quae prius ordinata fuit de cupro est assessa: videlicet pro una Cathedra de ligno facta ad exemplar alterius cathedrae fundendae de cupro-c.sol. . . . Et pro duobus leopardis parvis de ligno faciendis depingendis et deaurandis, et liberatis Magistro Waltero pictori ad assidendis super cathedram de ligno factam per dictum Magistrum Walterum . . .

'*Wardrobe Account, XXIX Edward I*

'Magistro Waltero Pictori, pro custibus et expensis per ipsum factis circa unum gradum faciendum ad pedem novae cathedrae in qua petra Scociae reponitur juxta altare ante feretrum Sancti Edwardi in Ecclesia Abbatiae Westmonaster' juxta ordinationem Regis, mense Martii, et in stipendiis carpentariorum et pictorum eundem gradum depingencium, et pro auro et coloribus diversis emptis pro eadem depingenda; una cum factura unius cassi pro dicta cathedra cooperianda, sicut patet per particulas inde in garderoba liberatas, l lib. xix sol. vii den.

'1307. *In a Westminster Abbey Inventory.* Mittebatur per preceptum Regis usque Abbathiam de Westmonasterio ad assedendum ibidem juxta feretrum Sancti Edwardi, in quadam cathedra lignea deaurata quam Rex fieri precepit *ut Reges Angliae et Scociae infra sederent die Coronationis eorundem* (crossed out in the document) ad perpetuam rei memoriam.'

Keepe, *Westminster Abbey,* 1682, 143; Dart, *Westmonasterium,* 1742, II, Bk. 3, 12; Carter, *Ancient Architecture of England,* II, 62, pl. VI; Neale and Brayley, *Westminster Abbey,* 1823, II, 134–5; Hunter, *A.J.,* 1856, XIII, 252–3; Scott, *Gleanings from Westminster Abbey,* 1863, 121–5, reprs.; *P. Society of Antiquaries,* 1887, XI, 2nd ser., 427–8; Lethaby, *Westminster Abbey & the King's Craftsmen,* 1906, 18, 265–7; id., *Burl. M.,* 1918, XXXIII, 169–70; *R.C. Historical Monuments R.,* 1924, I, 9, 28; Noppen, *Westminster Abbey & its Ancient Art,* 1926, 61–3; Lethaby, *P. British Academy,* 1927, 19–20; Borenius and Tristram, *Eng. Med. Painting,* 1927, 19, reprs.

The Portrait of Richard II

The King is represented seated frontally upon a cushioned wooden throne having delicate pinnacles at the angles of the back, which is finished with cusping and a moulding having a hollow section decorated with roses; there is a solid base forming a step. He is crowned, and holds an orb in the right hand, surmounted by a cross with a shaft of some length, and in the left a sceptre terminating in an ornament composed of three tiers of foliation; the crown, enriched with jewels between mascles, all rendered by means of fine 'pouncing', is further decorated with five ornaments resembling that on the sceptre, though not identical with it. The head, delicate-featured and somewhat mournful in expression, with a small, double-pointed beard, is framed by the thick, brown hair, slightly waved and cut to the level of the jaw; about the neck is a richly ornamented collar, fastened in the centre by a morse decorated with a mascle framing a rose. The tippet is of ermine, the mantle red, draped in intricate and well-designed folds over the knees and falling to the feet, which are encased in somewhat pointed shoes, its lining of ermine being visible here and there. The blue tunic is powdered with crowned R's and conventionalized roses, the sleeves having full cuffs falling almost to the knuckles. The background, now of plain gold, was originally patterned with 'prints', each motif framing a small rose surrounded by delicate sprigs of foliage of indeterminate character, the interspaces between the motifs forming crosses clechy; the sole portion of these 'prints' now surviving may be seen towards the upper corner of the painting, to the spectator's left. The 'prints' were removed when the work was treated by George Richmond, R.A., and Henry Merrit, in 1866, who, finding traces of a yet earlier background beneath them, came to the conclusion that they were not contemporaneous with the original work as then recovered; extracts from the account of their activities given by Scharf, are quoted below. A previous renovation, which seems to have comprised heavy re-painting (removed in 1866), had been carried out by a Captain Broome, a print-seller, in 1732; some ten years earlier, it is recorded, the painting had had the lower part damaged by the backs of those using the stall on the north side of the choir in the Abbey, where it had been situated at least since 1631. In [1] 1775 it was placed in the Jerusalem Chamber, and in 1823 cleaned by Charles Muss; it is now hung at the western end of the nave. Its measurements are 7 ft. × 3 ft. 7 in.; the panel is of oak and formed of six planks joined vertically.

[1] Weever, loc. cit., 473.

Scharf, *The Westminster Portrait of Richard II, Fine Arts Quarterly Review*, 1867, 27–63, reprs.

'September 25th, 1866. Mr. Richmond worked cleaning tippet, and removing thick layer of lead. Pure tempera painting found underneath with brown varnish. Cleaned face, which came out as now seen, saving an injury on right temple, particle of the nose, and a spot below the mouth . . . The eyes had been slightly rubbed, and required trifling repairs . . .

'September 29th. Mr. R. occupied in endeavouring to remove morsels of stucco-diaper background, found evidence of an older background under chair ornaments, where the gold is still seen, and around the hair. The older background was apparently reddish, gilt in oil, and covered with undefined sprigs and scrolls, as now seen in the openings of the chairback. Mr. R. found the clumsy diaper-stucco laid on so as to cover and mar the contours in many parts of the chair, and outer tresses of the hair . . .

'October 2nd. Mr. Chance [a practical gilder] slowly uncovered the raised gold, which hid the true crown, sceptre, and globe . . . he uncovered a shadow falling from the right thumb upon the globe, and found also that the little finger of the left hand came outside the sceptre, and was not, as the prints represent, hidden by it.

'October 4th. Mr. C. found gold under pinnacle of crown, further supporting the impression of a plain gilt background prior to stucco.

'October 5th. Mr. R. superintended the removal of the outer raised sceptre, when the top ornament came out in fine drawing and shading.

'October 12th. Found the blue tunic thickly painted over, and upon this ground the letter R, with crown and sprig with the circular ornament, was coarsely stencilled. On removing these ornaments nothing remained save the false blue covering, and on removing that, the letter R, crown, and circular ornament came to light as now seen. . . .

'Two crowns had been successively laid, one over the other, upon the true one. . . . The second crown had been thickly laid on with composition at the time when the diaper pattern was added, and took the general form seen in Vertue's 1718 engraving. The third operation was a re-gilding and re-painting of the ornaments and jewels with a heavy black outline, and probably the work of Captain Broome in 1732. . . . On removing some of the stucco of the crown, and also external portions of the sceptre, it was found that the original work had extended beneath the stucco ornaments of the diaper, and consequently, in order to recover them, parts of the diaper had to be removed. This led to further investigations

and, ultimately, it was ascertained that, in all parts of the background, the original surface of the panel had been lowered excepting just within a quarter of an inch round the edge of the figure itself. Nevertheless, the clumsy workman, in adding the stucco ornament, carried it beyond the well-defined limits, and covered over many parts of the gracefully flowing hair, and the elegant foliage of the sceptre-head. . . . This lowering of the surface of the entire ground might be the natural result of a desire to efface some deeply punctured ornaments already existing, and, indeed, without this course there would have been no very effective means of obliterating them. . . . Instead of a large, coarse, heavy-toned figure, with very deep, solid shadows, strongly-marked eyebrows, and a confident expression (almost amounting to a stare) in the dark-brown sparkling eyes, we now have a delicate, pale picture, in carefully modelled forms, with a placid and somewhat sad expression of countenance; grey eyes, partially lost under heavy lids; pale yellow eyebrows, and golden-brown hair. These latter points fully agree with the King's profile in the small tempera Diptych at Wilton, belonging to the Earl of Pembroke. The long, thin nose accords with the bronze effigy of the King in Westminster Abbey; whilst the mouth, hitherto smiling and ruddy, has become delicate, but weak and drooping in a curve. . . .'

Extract from records, probably referring to the portrait of Richard II.

'*Issues of the Exchequer*, ed. Devon, 1837, 262; Michaelmas, 1395. To Master Peter, sacrist of the Church of the Blessed Peter, Westminster. In money paid him by the hands of John Haxey, as well for painting the covering of the tomb of Anne, late Queen of England . . . and for painting an image to correspond with another of the King [better translated as counterfeit of the King—*contrefacte*] placed opposite, in the choir of the aforesaid church.'

Weever, *Funeral Monuments*, 1631, 473; Vertue, 1718, *Vetusta Monumenta*, I, repr.; Dart, *Westmonasterium*, 1742, I, 62, repr.; Carter, 1780, I, 55, 90, repr.; Walpole, *Anecdotes of Painting* (first published 1786), 1871, 21, n.; Scharf, *Athenæum*, IX, XVII, 1866, 645; id., *Fine Arts Quarterly Review*, 1867, 27–63, reprs.; Stanley, *Hist. Memorials of Westminster*, 1868, 147; Lethaby, *Westminster Abbey and the King's Craftsmen*, 1906, 24, 278–9, 283, n.; Cockerell, *Burl. M.*, 1906–7, X, 126, repr.; Michel, *Histoire de l'Art*, 1907, III, 314, reprs.; Cust, *Burlington Fine Arts Club, Catalogue of Early English Portraiture*, 1922; Constable, *Catalogue British Primitives Exhibition*, R.A., 1923, no. 30; Conway, *Burl. M.*, 1923, XLIII, 225; R.C. *Historical Monuments R., Westminster*, 1924, I, 25, repr.; Borenius and Tristram, *Eng. Med. Painting*, 1927, 26, repr.; *Catalogue French Exhibition, R.A.*, 1932, no. 30, repr.

The Sedilia

The Sedilia are in the first bay of the arcade to the south of the high altar; they are of four bays, constructed in oak, with a canopy of four cinquefoiled and sub-cusped arches surmounted by crocketed gables, each with a trefoiled and sub-cusped circle in the tympanum and with truncated pinnacles, rising from pendants, between them; the entire structure was originally richly painted and decorated, with raised gesso ornamentation, glass 'enamels', composed of transparent glass of various colours—mainly red and blue—superimposed on silver foil, the crowned or mitred heads with which the pendants are carved having been coloured to the life, and the crowns and mitres painted as if set with jewels. The ribs of the vaulting were treated with gold and azure, and the divisions of the web filled with scroll-work in white on a red ground. Much of the decoration survives, in particular on the carved heads and the vaulting. The close boarded back, divided by pairs of slender shafts supporting the vaulting, originally had paintings in all four bays; those that survive, reading from the east, on the north side, are as follows:

1. The figure of a King, of rather more than life-size, facing west, clad in a red tunic and green mantle, lined with vair and edged with a delicately-executed border in gold, which also adorns the neck of the tunic; the mantle is swathed about the body and draped in voluminous and intricate folds from the right arm. The head, inclined slightly to the spectator's right, bears a narrow crown ornamented with strawberry leaves, and the loosely-waved hair is swept back from the face and curled upward somewhat below the level of the ears; the ends of the slight moustache are curled like the moderately short beard. The eyes are raised, the eye-brows are rather long, and the thin nose sharply defined. The hands are covered by cream-coloured gauntlets, enriched with some embroidery, the left being raised with the index finger pointed upward; in the right is a sceptre terminated by a head resembling a small, spired building. The feet, encased in purple stockings and dark blue-green shoes patterned in black, rest on grassy ground having upon it daisies and other small flowers. The background is red; and delicately-painted cusping follows the line of the arched frame-work at the top. The panel is 2 ft. 7 in. in width, and 8 ft. 11 in. in height to the extreme point.

2. Mainly defaced; the painted cusping around the arched frame-work at the head survives, and at the

base are remains showing that a bishop or abbot was depicted, in mass vestments, holding a crosier, and standing on grassy ground.

3. The figure of a king, of rather more than life-size, facing east, clad in a red tunic and dark purple mantle lined with vair; the tunic is girt with a narrow embroidered belt, one end falling to the knees; the mantle, enriched with a narrow border in gold, and swathed about the neck, where part of the vair lining is visible, is caught upon the right shoulder with a brooch and falls over the arms into voluminous folds on either side. The head, held upright but half-turned to the east, has a crown decorated with jewels and strawberry leaves, and the hair is curled upward at the level of the ears. The nose is rather aquiline in type, the mouth firm, or even hard, and the heavy and prominent chin is beardless apart from some stubble. On the hands are cream-coloured gauntlets, their backs embroidered in the centre with a diamond motif, and embroidery also appears on the cuffs and around the base of the little finger. In the right hand is a sceptre, the shaft white, and the head ornamented by three tiers of oak leaves, each tier narrowing towards the top of the cluster; the index finger of the slightly raised left hand appears to be pointing to the sceptre in the other. The base of the painting is defaced for several inches upward. On the background is a close powdering of small lions passant gardant—i.e. lions-leopardy.

4. This panel is now entirely blank.

The south side of the Sedilia, facing the ambulatory, has four boarded panels with trefoiled and sub-cusped heads, surmounted by gables pierced by circles enclosing quatrefoils, the spandrels being filled with painted ornament. The decoration in its general type resembles that of the northern side. Between the panels are buttressed standards. Reading from the west, the paintings upon the panels are, or have been, as follows:

1. No trace of a figure survives, but it may be inferred with strong probability that St. John the Evangelist was here represented as the Pilgrim, since in the adjacent panel to the east the Confessor is shown extending the ring, held between the first and second fingers of his right hand, towards the west.

2. St. Edward the Confessor, crowned and nimbed, with hair curled at the level of the ears, slight moustache, and long beard, clad in a green tunic and voluminous mantle lined with vair and originally red, bearing a sceptre in his left hand; both hands being covered by gloves having embroidery upon the cuffs and at the base of the thumbs. The

background is green. The painting is somewhat damaged.

3. The Angel Gabriel. The upper part is entirely defaced, apart from a few wing feathers; in the lower half of the panel there survive folds of the green mantle and purple tunic, the bare feet, standing on grassy ground, and part of a hand holding a long, pendent scroll, inscribed with the Angelic Salutation. The background is vermilion in colour.

4. The Virgin. In the upper half of the panel, only four fingers, those of the right hand raised in acknowledgment of the Angel's message, now exist; in the lower half are folds of the pink mantle, lined with vair, the blue tunic, and black shoes, against a ground of green.

In the north wall of the ambulatory, immediately below the northern side of the panels, just described, forming the back of the Sedilia, is a recess enclosing a monument erected in 1308 to King Sebert of Essex; the soffit and ends of the recess bear traces of painting, including a crowned female head, a Catherine wheel, and vine foliage, against a white ground.

Vetusta Monumenta, 1780, II, 10–14; Dart, *Westmonasterium*, 1742, I, 6, repr.; Neale and Brayley, *Westminster Abbey*, 1823, II, 278–81; Scott, *Gleanings from Westminster Abbey*, 1863, 115–20, 165; Keyser, *Mural Decorations*, 1883; Lethaby, *Burl. M.*, 1905, VII, 269; id., *Westminster Abbey and the King's Craftsmen*, 1906, 19, 271–4; id., *Burl. M.*, 1918, XXXIII, 8, repr.; *R.C. Historical Monuments R.*, 1924, I, 25–7, reprs.; Lethaby, *P. British Academy*, 1927, XIII, 23–6; Borenius and Tristram, *Eng. Med. Painting*, 1927, 18, repr.; Noppen, *Burl. M.*, 1929, LIV, 207; id., *Apollo*, 1933, XVIII, 353, repr.

Plate 7a, b.

The Tomb of Richard II and Anne of Bohemia

The Tester. The plain oak tester has the soffit divided into five panels by means of moulded ribs, which are ornamented at intervals with painted roses; the grounds of all the panels are enriched with 'prints', mainly oblong in shape, but in parts applied with considerable irregularity, so that they might be the more easily fitted to the outlines of the subject-paintings in four of the five sections. The pattern upon the 'prints' is composed of small contiguous quatrefoils, each enclosing a tiny quatrefoil flower, the latter perhaps intended, like those painted on the ribs, for roses; the whole is gilt, and survives in remarkably good condition. The subjects, beginning with the panel at the head of the tomb, are as follows:

1. Two Angels, supporting between them a shield, now defaced, but originally, as is virtually certain, bearing the King's arms, to correspond with those of the Queen—France and England impaling the Eagle of the Empire quartering the crowned lion of Bohemia—similarly disposed between Angelic supporters in the fourth panel. The Angel on the dexter side stands with a slight sway, bending inward towards the shield, with wings folded; that on the sinister side is in an upright posture, with the right wing partly raised and extended over the shield, the left being barely visible at the edge of the panel. The first apparently holds the shield with the left, the other with the right hand. The corresponding pair of Angels in the fourth panel are similarly drawn, except that both bend slightly towards the centre, extending both hands to support the shield, and in each case both wings are clearly visible, disposed in the same manner as before, the Angel on the sinister side having the second wing folded. The ground beneath their feet, which is well-preserved, is green, diapered with swiftly-executed tufts of grass and the leaves of small plants, in a darker green. Only the silhouettes of the figures are now visible.

2. God the Father. The figure, of which the silhouette alone survives, is seated, facing frontally, with the right hand raised in blessing, upon an oblong throne, its seat represented in rough perspective. In contrast to the figure, the seat is well-preserved, as is also the nimbus about the head, which is ornamented with delicate beading and scroll-work in raised *gesso*.

3. The Coronation of the Virgin. The group is traditionally arranged, but only the silhouettes of the two figures remain; the nimbi are richly wrought after the same fashion as that about the head of God the Father, and the crowns are also executed in raised *gesso*. The throne closely resembles that in the previous panel, and, like it, is well-preserved.

4. Two Angels bearing a shield, as described above.

5. This panel bears only 'prints'.

Gough, in his *Sepulchral Monuments*, 1786, gives a general description of the tester, and says that in the panel numbered 2 above, was 'a figure sitting in a nimbus, the face fine and well-preserved'.

In *Beauties of England and Wales*, 1815 (and Neale and Brayley, *Westminster Abbey*, 1823), the same panel is described as framing 'the Almighty, habited as a venerable old man, in a close garment, his hand in the act of blessing'; a description made when the painting was still evidently at least in part in fair condition, and which indicates that the subject was God the Father. Of the Coronation of the Virgin, it is stated in the former account, that the outlines then remained, but the colours were 'fast disappearing'; that the 'countenances' were 'still very beautiful', and the background richly gilt and 'embossed with multitudes of small quatrefoils and other ornaments'.

Dart, *Westmonasterium*, 1742, II, 44; Gough, *Sepulchral Monuments*, 1786, I, pt. ii, 136; *Beauties of England & Wales*, 1815, X, pt. IV, 32; Neale and Brayley, *Westminster Abbey*, 1823, II, 110; Eastlake, *Materials for a Hist. of Oilpainting*, 1847, 177; Scott, *Gleanings from Westminster Abbey*, 1863, 175–6; Lethaby, *Westminster Abbey & the King's Craftsmen*, 1906, 14, 279, 280–1, repr.; *R.C. Historical Monuments R., Westminster*, 1924, I, 31; Borenius and Tristram, *Eng. Med. Painting*, 1927, 26.

The Tomb of Philippa of Hainault, 1367

It is recorded that the tabernacle-work was formerly enriched in some degree with colour and gilding, the foliage being gilt and the coats-of-arms emblazoned; gold patterns ornamented the dresses of figures, whose eyes were blue, and lips red; and the iron-work formerly about the monument was painted red soon after erection in 1377, ten years after the completion of the tomb itself. On the tester, traces of colour.

Scott, *Gleanings from Westminster Abbey*, 1863, 169–71; Keyser, *Mural Decorations*, 1883; Lethaby, *Westminster Abbey and the King's Craftsmen*, 1906, 251–2.

THE NAVE

The North Aisle

The fifth to the tenth bays, of late fourteenth- and fifteenth-century work, retain little colour decoration on the carving; but in the sixth bay label-stops composed of a small figure of a Saint and a man's head, are painted.

In the spandrels of the wall-arcade are painted shields, two in each bay, with identifying inscriptions; reading from the east, and commencing with the fifth bay, they are as follows:

1. Defaced.
2. *Quarterly gules and or a molet argent in the quarter* for [Hugh] de Vere, Earl of Oxford.
3. *Checky or and azure a border of England and a quarter ermine* dimidiating a defaced coat for John de Dre[ux, Earl of Richmond].
4. *Or a maunch gules* for Henry de Hastings.
5. *Gules a lion argent* for Roger de Mowbrai.
6. Defaced [*Or a chevron gules*] for [Robert] de Stafford.
7–8. Two shields of the arms of Warin de Vernon and William de Malpas have disappeared.
9. Defaced [*Gules three water-bougets argent*] for [Robert] de Roos.
10. Defaced [*Or a fesse between two chevrons gules* for Robert Fitzwalter].
11. *Gules* [*an orle argent* for John Balliol].
12. *Bendy gules and argent* [for Gilbert Talbot].

The South Aisle

The sixth to the eleventh bays are of late fourteenth- and fifteenth-century work. The western processional doorway in the eighth bay is of the late fourteenth century, the middle main spandrels of the four-centred arch over it having spaces left for painted shields, and painting surviving on the labels, carved with a lion and a male human head. In the spandrels of the wall-arcade are, or formerly were, painted shields, two in each bay, some having inscriptions; reading from the east, and commencing with the sixth bay, they are as follows:

1. *Vairy or and gules*, for William, Earl of Ferrers and Derby.
2. *Azure six lions or*, for William Longespee, Earl of Salisbury (both these shields are repainted). The shields in the seventh, eighth and ninth bays are entirely defaced, but it is recorded that as late as 1723 there were to be seen the arms of William de Valence, Earl of Pembroke, Roger de Mortimer, William de Percy, Roger de Clifford, Roger de Somery and John de Verdon. In the tenth bay are: *Argent a fesse gules between three popinjays vert* for [Robert de Thwenge], and *Quarterly fessewise indented argent and gules* for [Fulc Fitz Warren] (both shields repainted); and in the eleventh [*Azure*] *a lion argent* for Roger de Montalt, and *Azure two bars argent* for Roger de Venables.

Dart, *Westmonasterium*, 1742, I, 60: Keyser, *Mural Decorations*, 1883; *R.C. Historical Monuments R.*, 1924, I, 54, 55, 56, 58.

The South Ambulatory

Under a late fourteenth-century moulded and painted arch, a monument to the Princess Catherine, daughter of Henry III, and other children and grandchildren, originally in the Chapel of St. Edward, but moved in 1395 to the South Ambulatory to make room for the tomb of Richard II. On the wall, which is painted red, at the back of the recess, are slight traces of the four kneeling figures shown in the engraving in the *Westmonasterium* of John Dart who remarks: 'over this tomb is something which seems to have been a piece of church-perspective, but scratch'd, and almost entirely defaced'. It seems probable that the four figures shown by the engraver were depicted kneeling in an interior, or within arcading, but, if so, he has failed to represent it.

'*Issues of the Exchequer*, ed. Fed. Devon, 1837, 262. To Master Peter, sacrist of the Church of the Blessed Peter, Westminster . . . for the removal of a tomb near the tomb of the said queen [Anne of Bohemia]; also for painting the same tomb so removed . . .'

Dart, *Westmonasterium*, 1742, I, 104, and II, pl. 8; Neale and Brayley, *Westminster Abbey*, 1823, II, 153; *R.C. Historical Monuments R.*, 1924, I, 34.

Oaken Testers

Two testers, both of oak, and both bearing traces of painting, are preserved one in the Triforium and the other in the Dorter sub-vault. The former, of *c.* 1400, has remains of a large Trinity, but is much defaced; the latter, of about the same date, now has nothing on the soffit beyond traces of colour.

R.C. Historical Monuments R., 1924, I, 45, 82.

The Muniment Room

On the northern face of a plastered partition is a large painting of the White Hart of Richard II, somewhat defaced; and on the boarding of the plastered tympanum of the partition, as also on the western side of a cupboard against it, a pattern of stars in white; late fourteenth century.

A piece of fascia-board, preserved in the room, is patterned with ornamental foliage, and bears three shields-of-arms, as follows: *Gules, a Toulouse cross or; —Argent, a saltire gules and a label of five points azure;* and—*Barry or and sable a border gules;* early fourteenth century.

Dart, *Westmonasterium*, 1742, I, 64; Stanley, *Historical Memorials of Westminster Abbey*, 1868, 146; Keyser, *Mural Decorations*, 1883; Lethaby, *P. British Academy*, 1927, XIII, 30; *R.C. Historical Monuments R., Westminster*, 1924, I, 45, 51, 82.

The Chapter House

The Chapter House, an octagonal building surrounded within except for the bay on the western side where the entrance is placed, by a wall arcade comprising five trefoil-headed arches to each bay, was completed as a structure by the year 1253.

The Majesty

Within five arches of the arcade, on the east side of the building, are remains of a Majesty, thus described when better preserved than it is now, by Sir Charles Eastlake, *Materials for a History of Oil Painting*, 1847, 178–9:

'In the centre niche or compartment there is . . . a figure of Christ (with a gilt nimbus containing the cross) holding up his pierced hands. A scarlet robe, embroidered with gold borders, is fastened on the centre of the breast by an embossed and gilt fibula . . .: the robe, parting again, shows the wound in the side. Two angels sustain a deep blue diapered drapery behind the figure. The instruments of the Passion are held by other angels now partly obliterated; the reed and sponge, the spear, and the nails are still visible. The face of the principal figure is destroyed, perhaps by violence. The four other compartments are filled with angels: in the right and left niches, a single central figure is prominent, standing about a head lower than the Christ; behind and below, smaller nimbi and some heads indicate the rest. The principal angels are covered with wings having eyes like those in the peacock's tail; the lower extremities of all the figures are destroyed. Among the angels, some with fiery vermilion faces represent the seraphim, in the manner of the early Italian painters. The principal angel in the niche next the centre to the right holds up two gilt crowns. On the wings of the upper angels, and round the heads of those below, is inscribed a sort of tabular view of the Christian virtues, according to the dogmas of the time. "Confessio" ramifies downwards into "simplicitas, humilitas, fidelitas"; "Satisfactio" into "oronis devocio", "eleemosina", and perhaps "jejunium", or an equivalent word now illegible. Under "Mundicia carnis" are ranged the virtues of temperance; under "Puritas mentis", those relating to the command of the will. In the centre above, the half word ". . . lateria" (latreia?) is visible. The corresponding angel in the niche to the left holds up an embossed crown with the left hand, and what appears to be a rosary with the right. Inscriptions on this figure have either never existed or they have perished. In the second niche to the right the figures are almost entirely obliterated; in that to the left some portions of heads remain. The general subject of this representation, therefore, is Christ surrounded by the Christian virtues: but many particulars correspond with descriptions in the beginning of the book of the Revelation, and, as the history of St. John the Evangelist is represented on other portions of the walls, they may be so interpreted.

'With respect to the date of this work, Mr. Devon is of opinion that the writing in the inscriptions belongs to the time of Edward III. This agrees with the opinion expressed by Smith (*Antiquities of Westminster*, p. 226). He formed his conclusion from the perfect coincidence of the style and execution with the then existing remains in St. Stephen's Chapel, with which he was certainly well acquainted. The figures are by no common painter; some of the heads and hands, with all their defects, may bear a comparison with the works of the Italians of the corresponding period. The same may be said of the colouring of the flesh; the heads of the principal figures are painted with a good surface and body . . .; pure lake, used in certain parts of the centre subject, is well preserved, as is the gilding of the nimbi. The stone wall is covered with a coating of *gesso*, but there is no cloth underneath the preparation. The inscriptions, unlike those on the other representations in the building, are painted on the figures, not stuck on.' Plate 8a.

Waller, *Trans. London & Middlesex Arch. Soc.*, IV, 377 et sqq.; Lethaby, *Westminster Abbey and the King's Craftsmen*, 1906, 47; *R.C. Historical Monuments R., Westminster*, I, 1924, 79–81, reprs.; Borenius and Tristram, *Eng. Med. Painting*, 1927, 28.

The Apocalypse

A series of paintings, the gift of John of Northampton, a monk at Westminster from *c.* 1372 to 1404, representing subjects taken in part from the legendary history of St. John the Evangelist, but mainly from the Apocalypse, fill the arches of the arcade in the bays on the north-west and north, the two western arches in the north-east bay, and the corresponding arches on the south.

There are indications that the central cusp of each arch originally framed the demi-figure of an Angel, contemporary with the Johannine series, holding a musical instrument; but, if so, many have perished. The arches number 24 in all, 12 on either side. Originally they framed three tiers of paintings divided from one another by narrow borders patterned with roses and in one instance with small dogs, into six panels, approximately 19 in. square, in each arch. The lowest tier of the three (perhaps once filled with scroll-work in green, executed on a vermilion ground and enriched with white roses, as appears from traces in the first bay) contains a Bestiary of somewhat later date and hence outside our scope; the two higher the Johannine series, to which we here confine our attention. In the two higher tiers there were originally 96 panels, four above and four below in each arch, which have below them strips of paper or parchment glued to the wall with inscriptions in black letter upon them giving the biblical text from the Vulgate appropriate to the scene represented above. On the north side thirteen of these scenes survive in excellent condition; but the fourteenth and fifteenth are partly, and the sixteenth entirely defaced. On the south side the paintings are on the whole in a poorer condition than those opposite; but there are remains sufficient for the identification of most of the forty-eight, eighteen of them being fairly well preserved, whereas the last six are almost entirely defaced.

The series begins on the north side within the westernmost arch. Reading from west to east the subjects are as follows:

1. St. John before Domitian. Domitian, bearded, wearing a conical tiara upon his head and holding a sceptre with a floriated head in his left hand, is enthroned to the spectator's left, clad in a mantle having an ermine tippet; behind him stands a figure apparently intended to represent an evil counsellor, since he leans slightly forward and seems to be speaking into the Emperor's ear. St. John, as throughout, nimbed, bearded, and with long hair, is clad in a light green mantle and red tunic; about him is a group of figures, one of them, a man in a pink hip-length gipon and long hose, dragging him forward, and another, similarly clad, but in dark green, on the right, leaping from the ground in a frenzy of vituperation.

2. The Intended Martyrdom. To the left Domitian is represented as before, except that he holds a drawn sword point upward in the left hand, instead of a sceptre; before him St. John stands naked within the cauldron of boiling oil, his hands clasped in prayer, surrounded by a group of torturers, one of them stirring the fire, represented in red and gold, with a two-pronged fork, another working a pair of bellows.

3. The Banishment to Patmos. To the right the Saint, accompanied by an oarsman, is seated in a small boat which is being pushed off by another figure from the shore, where stand two men clad in ankle-length *houppelandes*, both fur-lined and one having the wide sleeves trimmed with dagging.

4. The Arrival at Patmos; in two 'moments'. To the left the boat approaches the shore with the Saint seated in the centre, between two men, one of them with an oar; to the right he stands with a foot resting on the blade of the oar as he lands, his right hand raised to his head and the left, veiled by his mantle, holding a book. This concludes the introductory scenes from the Legend of St. John, and the scenes from the Apocalypse follow, beginning in the adjacent bay of the arcade.

5. St. John with the Angel. St. John seated on a rocky island crowned with trees, the sea at his feet, rests his head on his right hand, as though asleep, and holds a book in his left, while the white-clad Angel with the right hand touches his left shoulder, and with the other points towards the next scene. (*Apoc.*, I, 1–3.)

6. The Seven Churches of Asia. On the left St. John, seated, is writing in an open book, the rest of the scene being filled by seven small churches (each with an Angel in the doorway), arranged in two rows, four churches in the higher, and, originally four in the lower, but one is defaced. (*Apoc.*, I, 4–12.)

7. The Vision of Christ amid the Seven Candlesticks. Christ, with the Seven Stars in His right hand

and a book in His left, the 'sharp two edged sword' issuing from His mouth, is enthroned before an altar upon which stand the Candlesticks, four to the left and three to the right; His face (*et facies ejus sicut sol lucet in virtute sua*), hands and feet are executed in gold, His hair and beard are white, and His robe white, girt with a golden girdle. Below, to the left, with the Angel behind him, is St. John, fallen 'at His feet as dead'. (*Apoc.*, I, 12–16.)

8. The Majesty and the Twenty-four Elders. In the centre, within an oblong panel, is an almond-shaped glory framing, on a dark green ground, Christ enthroned upon a rainbow, His right hand raised in blessing and in His left, veiled by His purple-grey mantle, the Book with Seven Seals, beneath His feet an Orb of the Universe; about Him are the Seven Lamps, and beasts' heads in gold appear below the throne ('*et de throno procedebant fulgura, et voces, et tonitrua*'). Within the spandrels formed by the glory are seen the Four Beasts. On either side of the central oblong panel are four others roughly square in shape, each framing, against a ground of vermilion, figures of six Elders, clad in white, crowned with gold, and playing various musical instruments, including a harp and a portable organ. (*Apoc.*, IV, 1–9.)

9. St. John Consoled by the Elder. St. John, weeping '*quia nemo dignus inventus est aperire librum, nec videre eum*', stands in a central position, with the Angel behind him, facing the Elder, who consoles him; a second Elder stands on the extreme right within the doorway of a small building (? the Gate of the Heavenly Jerusalem). (*Apoc.*, V., 1–5.)

10. The Elders Cast Down Their Crowns. The general disposition of this scene is identical with that of the eighth, but it presents a departure from the strictly chronological arrangement evident so far, since the text illustrated comes from Apoc., IV, 10–11. Within the almond-shaped glory Christ is seated on a throne striped red and yellow, His nimbus, as before painted in red and crossed in gold, and His robe dark red; in His right hand, veiled by His mantle, He holds the Book Sealed with Seven Seals, in His left an orb, and beneath His feet is an Orb of the Universe, divided into the usual three sections. Within the spandrels formed by the glory, in place of the Four Beasts, scroll-work is represented in red on a ground of green. Within the four square compartments, arranged two on either side, the Elders, painted against a vermilion ground, cast down their crowns and musical instruments.

11. The Lamb with Seven Horns and Seven Eyes. The general arrangement of the scene is the same as that of Nos. 8 and 10, but the figure of Christ is replaced by the Lamb, bearing the vexillum and standing upon an altar covered in white and supported upon a pedestal. Within the spandrels formed by the central glory the Four Beasts are depicted; and the Elders in the compartments at the sides play their instruments. (*Apoc.*, V, 6.)

12. The Lamb takes the Book. The general arrangement resembles that of Nos. 8, 10 and 11; but within the central glory the Lamb takes the Book from Christ, who, clad in a dark red mantle, and light green tunic, is seated facing west with His feet on an Orb of the Universe; within the spandrels formed by the glory are the Four Beasts. In the two upper compartments at the sides worshipping Angels descend (*et audivi vocem angelorum multorum in circuitu throni*) and in the two lower compartments the Elders fall down and worship, *habentes singuli citharas, et phialas aureas plenas odoramentorum, quae sunt orationes sanctorum.* (*Apoc.*, V, 7–14.)

13. The First Seal. St. John stands on the left, with the Man (or Angel) speaking into his ear, as he supports a book in his right hand, veiled by his pale green mantle, and points with his left towards the First Horseman, who, mounted on the White Horse, with trappings of red and gold, and bearing a drawn bow, rides eastward '*vincens ut vinceret!*' He is crowned with gold, clad in a short white gipon belted with gold, long hose, and a tippet of ermine. (*Apoc.*, VI, 1–2.)

14. The Second Seal. The lower part of the painting is defaced; in the upper part, on the left, are the head and shoulders of St. John, with the Lion, and on the right those of the Rider on the Red Horse, who, bearing a drawn sword over his left shoulder, glances backward. He wears no crown, but about his neck is a tippet of ermine. (*Apoc.*, VI, 4.)

15. The Third Seal. On the left of the scene stands St. John with the Ox at his right ear; in his left hand, veiled by his mantle, he bears a book, and with his right he points towards the Rider on the Black Horse who, turning back, holds the scales towards him; the lower part of the Rider's figure and the greater part of the horse are defaced. In the background are two conventionalized trees. (*Apoc.*, VI, 5.)

16. The Fourth Seal. No trace of the painting survives, and the thirty-two episodes which undoubtedly once filled the remaining eight arches on the north side have entirely disappeared.

On the south side, reading from east to west, the subjects painted on grounds either of red or of white, are as follows:

1. The War of the Beast upon the Saints. The

Beast, with seven heads and ten horns, and the markings of a leopard, its tail curved over its back, has a shield hung about its neck and in its right paw a spear with which it wounds one of a group of the Saints, lying prostrate to the right. (*Apoc.*, XIII, 7.)

2. The Second Beast. St. John stands on the left, the Beast on the right, with three men worshipping it and behind them the second Beast, enforcing their adoration of the first. (*Apoc.*, XIII, 11–12.)

3. The Second Beast and the Image of the First. In the centre of the scene the Second Beast raises the sword with which he has slain those who lie prostrate on the left, because they refused to worship the Image of the First Beast; with his left hand he touches the heads of others on the right who adore it. St. John stands on the left. (*Apoc.*, XIII, 15.)

4. The Mark of the Beast. The Second Beast, enthroned on the left, has two men kneeling before him and others approaching from the right with hands outstretched; '*et faciet omnes . . . habere characterem in dextera manu sua, aut in frontibus suis*'. (*Apoc.*, XIII, 16.)

5. The Lamb on Mount Sion. The right half of the scene is defaced; on the slope to the left, are three conventionalized trees and below them figures kneeling in adoration and gazing towards the area in which the mountain top must originally have been represented. St. John is seated to the left, bearing a book. (*Apoc.*, XIV, 1.)

6. Entirely defaced.

7. Mainly defaced; the figure of St. John may be distinguished on the left, and towards the centre those of a man with a long grey beard, and, on each side of him, a veiled woman. On the right are slight traces of the Lamb.

8. Almost entirely defaced; on the left, remains of the figure of St. John, and towards the centre a nimbus and slight traces of a head.

9. Entirely defaced.

10. The Third Angel. Entirely defaced; of the text, the words *angelus secutus* survive. (*Apoc.*, XIV, 9.)

11. Entirely defaced.

12. Almost entirely defaced; above, towards the centre, a crown of gold and a nimbus, and a star or sun, and slightly lower, to the right, another nimbus; on the extreme right, traces of a figure; but all are barely decipherable.

13. Almost entirely defaced; only slight traces remain of an architectural setting above, and of green colour below.

14. The Seven Angels with the Seven Plagues. Only traces of the figure of St. John survive; but of the almost indecipherable text M. R. James identified

the phrase *quoniam in illis consummata*. (*Apoc.*, XV, 1.)

15. Entirely defaced.

16. The Appearance of the Seven Angels from the Temple. St. John stands on the left and on the right the Angels are seen coming out. The painting is much damaged. (*Apoc.*, XV, 6.)

17. The First Vial. The painting is almost entirely defaced, but a large golden vial may be distinguished. (*Apoc.*, XVI, 2.)

18. The Second Vial. Entirely defaced, but fragments of the inscription remain sufficient to identify the subject. (*Apoc.*, XVI, 3.)

19. The Third Vial. The Angel, in the centre, pours out his vial '*super flumina, et super aquarum*'; St. John is on the left. (*Apoc.*, XVI, 4.)

20. The Angel of the Altar. The Angel stands on the right behind the altar, holding a scroll which extends above it; St. John, with a book in his left hand, and another Angel before him, is seated to the left. (*Apoc.*, XVI, 7.)

21. The Fourth Vial. Almost entirely defaced, but some prostrate figures are discernible on the right; fragments of the text identify the scene. (*Apoc.*, XVI, 8–9.)

22. The Fifth Vial. The painting is mainly effaced, apart from traces of an Angel on the left; but sufficient remains of the text to identify the scene. (*Apoc.*, XVI, 10.)

23. The Sixth Vial. The Angel, in flight, pours out his vial upon the Euphrates; St. John is seated on the right. (*Apoc.*, XVI, 12.)

24. The Unclean Spirits like Frogs. St. John, on the left, bearing a staff in his right hand, and holding the left to his head, watches as the Frogs issue from the mouths of the Dragon, the Beast, and the False Prophet. (*Apoc.*, XVI, 13.)

25. The Seventh Vial. On the left, the Angel pours out the vial over buildings collapsing upon their inhabitants in the great earthquake; and the '*grando magna . . . de coelo*' falls. On the right, above, a small Angel. (*Apoc.*, XVI, 17, 18, 21.)

26. The Angel Speaking to St. John. On the left the Angel takes St. John by the left hand; on the right the head and shoulders of the Great Whore are barely distinguishable. (*Apoc.*, XVII, 1.)

27. The Scarlet Woman. St. John stands on the left, with his left hand raised and the Angel at his right ear; the Woman, clad in a dark red mantle and purplish tunic, rides upon a red dragon, bearing the cup of abominations in one hand and in the other a ring. (*Apoc.*, XVII, 3–4.)

28. The right half of the scene is defaced; on the

left are the Angel and St. John. The woman *'ebriam de Sanguine sanctorum'* was probably represented. (*Apoc.*, XVII, 6.)

29. Babylon is Fallen. St. John is seated to the left, gazing upon the devastated city; above, on the right the Angel *'habentem potestatem magnam'* descends, *'in fortitudine dicens'*. (*Apoc.*, XVIII, 1–2.)

30. *Exite de illa, populus meus.* St. John is seated to the left, with a T-headed staff in his hands, beside a building from which emerge a number of people, led forth from above by an Angel—the *'aliam vocem de coelo'*. To the right *'negotiatores terrae'* bewail the fall of Babylon, one of them holding a scroll. (*Apoc.*, XVIII, 4–11.)

31. The Mighty Angel with the 'stone, as it were a great millstone'. The left side of the painting is defaced; on the right the white-clad Angel throws the stone into the sea. (*Apoc.*, XVIII, 21.)

32. God is Praised in Heaven. On the left St. John is seated, resting his right hand upon a book lying on his knees, and shading his face with the left from the glory of Heaven. In the upper part of the scene are remains of the lower half of an almond-shaped glory, within which God was no doubt represented enthroned, and from its left side Angels appear blowing trumpets, while just below is one bearing a scroll. To the extreme right, on the ground beneath, a group of Elders kneel in adoration, and in the centre, between them and St. John, the Great Whore lies burning. (*Apoc.*, XIX, 1–6.)

33. The Marriage of the Lamb. On the right the Lamb, standing on an altar, gives a ring to the kneeling Bride; above an Angel bears the fine linen which *'justificationes sunt sanctorum'*. Behind the Bride are attendants, and to the extreme left St. John. (*Apoc.*, XIX, 7–8.)

34. St. John is Rebuked by the Angel. To the left St. John falls at the Angel's feet to worship him, to the right he is raised up with the words *'vide ne feceris'*, while the Angel points upward to the lower part of an almond-shaped glory, within which must once have been visible a figure of God—*'conservus tuus sum . . . Deum adorae'*. (*Apoc.*, XIX, 10.)

35. The Celestial Host. The King of Kings and Lord of Lords, the *'sharp two edged sword'* issuing from His mouth, mounted on a white horse, leads the Host as the Heavens open before St. John, who is seated on the left, holding a T-headed staff. (*Apoc.*, XIX, 11–16.)

36. The Angel Standing in the Sun. Of the Angel's figure nothing survives, but the circular halo formed by the sun is discernible; black or red birds of hideous type fly down to feast on the flesh of kings and cap-tains, while St. John, on the left, looks on. (*Apoc.*, XIX, 17–18.)

37. The War with the Beast and the Kings of the Earth. The painting is much defaced, but the Celestial Host may be distinguished on the left, and the Beast, with a shield and falchion, on the right. (*Apoc.*, XIX, 19–21.)

The rest of the paintings are unidentifiable, except that in the case of the forty-first fragments of text, read by M. R. James as *civitatem dilectam* (*Apoc.*, XX, 8) and *in stagnum ignis et sulphuris* (XX, 9) remain to show that the subject was the attack on the Beloved City and the subsequent casting of Satan into the lake of fire and brimstone; and if so, it is apparent that the subsequent scenes represented the Judgement; in the forty-third are traces of an almond-shaped glory, which probably framed a figure of Christ. (*Apoc.*, XX, 8–10 and 11–15.)

The work is delicate in execution, and some of the more precious pigments, together with gold and, probably, silver (now blackened) were used; the colours comprise blue, vermilion, lake, green and brown.

Eastlake, *Materials for a History of Oil Painting*, 1847, 178–81; Keyser, *Mural Decorations*, 1883; *R.C. Historical Monuments R.*, Westminster, I, 1924, 79–81; id., V, 1930, 114; Borenius and Tristram, *Eng. Med. Painting*, 1927, 28; Noppen, *Burl. M.*, LXI, 1932, 146–59.

Extracts from records relating to painting executed in the Abbey during the fourteenth century.

'Ricardus Merston prior [d. 1376] fieri fecit crucifixum cum pertinentiis in claustro juxta sedem Magistri Noviciorum pro xx marcis . . . Frater Robertus Herford fieri fecit picturam Natalis Domini in claustro juxta hostium hostillarii versus cameram Prioris pro xx marcis. Frater Johannes Northampton fieri fecit picturam de judicio in fronte domus Capitularis pro xj marcis. Item fieri fecit picturam Apocalipsis pro iiij. li. xs. in Capitulo nondum completo. Et similiter Kalendare (xxx.s.) in claustro, cum aliis picturis (xx.s.) ibidem ad hostium ecclesie pro vij. li . . . Willielmus de Reliquiis fieri fecit ymaginem Beate Marie Magdalene ad pedes tumbe Cardinalis [Cardinal Langham, d. 1376] pro x.s. (Et Lodowicus de Britailx de novo fecit eandem ymaginem depingi tempore Regis E. iiij.). . . . Jacobus Palmer clericus domini Regis E. iij fieri fecit clausuram et totum apparatum Altaris Sancti Andree cum pictura ejusdem ubi et ipse postea sepultus est . . . Frater Johannes London' postea reclusus, et frater J. Northampton fieri fecerunt picturam superioris tabule Altaris Sancti Johannis Baptiste pro . . . Frater

Johannes Sutton fieri fecit picturam dedicationis ecclesie Westm' cum censuris scriptis ad Altare Sancti Pauli. Et similiter picturam ad tabulam Regis Sancti Seberti pro . . .'

Stanley, *Historical Memorials of Westminster Abbey*, 1868, 608–9.

LONDON WESTMINSTER PALACE: THE PAINTED CHAMBER

In *Proceedings Society of Antiquaries*, 1881, 2nd ser., VII, 524, the following description is given of fragments of stonework from the Chamber, which apparently came from some fitting of fourteenth-century date:

'These small fragments are portions of tracery with very good mouldings of about the year 1330. The whole has been covered with painting and enriched with gilding. The gilding is laid upon a thick coat of *gesso*, which is modelled on the surface so as to break up the light, and so obtain a richer effect from the metal. One large convex moulding has a row of roundels of gold rather elaborately worked.'

J. G. Rokewode, *Vetusta Monumenta*, 1845, VI, 11–12, quotes entries from the accounts of Nicholas de Tickhull, 1307, then in private possession, showing that Master Thomas of Westminster, with a number of assistants, was at work in the Chamber, '*circa diversos defectus in Camera depicta existentes, tam in cumblea, quam in muris, et fenestris, reparandis et emendandis*'; and also refers to another roll of expenses, covering a period from the first to the thirteenth year of the reign of Edward II, in which Master Thomas is mentioned as engaged for 264 days '*circa depicturas in Camera depicta et ejusdem depictura historias reparandas et emendandas*', at a wage of 6*d*. daily. The following painters are mentioned as working with him: Gilbert of Coueham, William of Weston (? Westm'), Edmund of Marham, William Wyt, John of Norfolk ('*servienti*'), William of Sudbury, Simon of Bradstrete, William of Blida, Simon of Bordeaux, John of Bristol, William of Clousebrug, and John of Yarmouth; the highest paid among them, with wages equal to those of the Master, being Gilbert of Coueham, Simon of Bradstrete, William of Sudbury (who was receiving, in fact, 7*d*. instead of the Master's 6*d*.), Simon of Bordeaux, and William of Blida. A Hugh the Painter is mentioned as working for a fortnight as the '*socio*' of Peter the Paviour, '*circa Cameram Marculphi, Cameram depictam et alias Cameras et Capellas pavandas*'. Rokewode remarks that in 1307 the paintings seem to have been 'thoroughly repaired' and the gilding and inscrip-

tions renewed, no doubt as part of the renovations usual in the Palace on the accession or marriage of a king.

Materials named comprise: parchment strips for making size, white lead, red lead, orpiment, ochre, vermilion, *coloris Indei* (probably Indian red), brown, '*pakthred ad inde faciendas lineas*', red varnish, and white varnish. The mending of brushes, '*reparacione brushorum*', and their making, are also mentioned.

B. Mus. Add. MSS. 30263 contains accounts in parts almost identical with those quoted by Rokewode; the painting of the King's Ship, chambers, Painted Chamber, etc., is mentioned, and the names of the painters are the same, with the addition of those of William of Westminster, at 5*d*. a day, Richard of Glosby and William of Berle. William Wyt or Wyl was employed grinding and tempering colours at 3*d*. a day, while John of Norfolk, '*servienti*' in Rokewode's quotations at 1*d*. a day, ground and tempered colours at 2*d*. a day, and is once mentioned as also '*colando muros*'—? sizing (cole = size) walls.

The Great Hall, The Little Hall, The Marculph Chamber and various unspecified Chapels and Chambers.

It is evident, from entries in the accounts mentioned above, and from British Mus. Add. MSS. 30263, that Master Thomas and his assistants, whilst at work on repairs to the scheme in the Painted Chamber, were also engaged in the execution of paintings in the Great and Little Halls, and of paintings, or of paintings and repairs alike, in the Marculph Chamber and an indefinite number of other chambers and chapels—*et circa alias cameras capellas et alias domos depyngend' et depictur' emendand'*. They were also, in 1307, painting the ship in which Edward II was to go to France for his marriage—*circa navem depingendam in qua Dominus Rex transfretavit in Francia ad nuptias suas.*

St. Stephen's Chapel

With the exception of the crypt, St. Stephen's Chapel was destroyed by fire in 1834. The building of the upper chapel proceeded from 1331, and a rich scheme of painting was begun there in 1350, and substantially completed by the following year.

Descriptions of the Painted Decoration of St. Stephen's Chapel. John Topham, *Some Account of the Collegiate Chapel of St. Stephen, Westminster*, 1795, pp. 8–22.

'8. It is necessary to observe, that the whole of the architecture, and its enrichments, on the inside, are in gilding and colours, appearing extremely fresh; and what is remarkable and singular, the columns are decorated with a sort of patera, and several of the mouldings are filled with ornaments so very minute, that those on the spandrels and grand entablature, could hardly be perceived by the eye from the pavement of the chapel; but the artist designed that the whole of the work should have the same attention paid it, and that one universal blaze of magnificence and splendour should shine around, making this chapel the *ne plus ultra* of the art, worthy of the saint whose name it bears, and of its founder, Edward III, the great patron of ancient architecture.

'9. In the arch [of the windows] is introduced the flower de lis; which, however, is not sculptured, but formed by gilding.

'12. . . . the rich stall work and other decorations, such as the paterae and roses put on in stucco, the numerous paintings with which the walls are decorated, the profusion of gilding and minute tracery and diaper . . .

'13. The paterae which adorn the shafts of the columns, outer mouldings of the arches of the windows, and flanks of the niche on the pier, are of stucco formed in moulds and cemented to the stone.

'13–14. Plate XVI. The paintings given in outline in this Plate, formed the decoration of the east end of St. Stephen's Chapel, on the north side of the high altar. They are in two tiers, or series, totally unconnected with each other. The lower division, which is two feet and an inch in height, exhibits a row of arches, seven in number, but which are divided into three compartments, each having its separate perspective of groins and windows, resembling in some degree small oratories or chapels. In each arch is a figure in armour, kneeling, representing the king, Edward the Third, with his five sons, introduced as it were to the altar by Saint George, the Patron Saint of England. Under each figure has been its name in French, but of these only Saint George and the king are legible. There can be little doubt that these were intended for portraits of the royal family; and it is very much to be regretted, that, by some unaccountable accident, the faces of the four younger princes should have been completely obliterated, while every other part of the picture is nearly perfect. The face of the king may certainly be called handsome; he probably was about forty-four years of age when this portrait was painted. The Prince of Wales, the immortal Black Prince, was about 25 or 26 years old, and represented as a beardless youth, with a likeness to his father. His helmet has a coronet on its brim, which sufficiently distinguishes him. The three last letters of his name are partly visible under his feet. A part of his legs, and the whole lower part of the next figure, probably Lionel, Duke of Clarence, is

cut off by a square place for a small table or shelf 18 in. long and 10 inches high. This seems to have been placed after the original finishing of the work, as it interferes irregularly with the design. The next in order is probably John of Gaunt, Duke of Lancaster. He bears on his coat armour a label of three points . . . Under his feet the letters Jo are visible, a part, probably, of his name. Edmund of Langley, Duke of York, comes next, and the traces of his name appear under his feet. The small figure on a pedestal must have been designed to represent Thomas of Woodstock, Duke of Gloucester, and it is curious that he should be thus brought up to a level with his brothers. As he was not born till 1355, this circumstance places the finishing of this part of the paintings in this or the next year at the earliest. There does not appear to have been any name under this portrait.

'These portraits (with the exception of the little boy), were they standing, would be about 18 inches high, nearly a quarter the size of the life. Though finished with great care, and ornamented with elaborate profusion, they are ill and stiffly designed. The awkward position of their heads may, however, be in a good degree copied from nature, as the cumbrous and inflexible armour in which they are clad, allowed but little motion to the head, and certainly admitted of no grace in the attitude of the body.

'The perspective of the ornaments over the arches, particularly of the small row of battlements which terminate the design, is very inaccurate. Each arch is supposed to be viewed from a near point directly in its centre, and, in consequence, the flanks of the battlements next the centre on each hand are seen; but they are all equally seen, which is false from any assumed point of sight. The perspective of the interior building behind the figures is likewise very defective, but the architecture is very nearly the same in style as that of the chapel itself. The patterns of the glazing of the windows are elegant: it is however observable, that none of them have any tracery or mullions.

'The subject of the upper picture I cannot but suppose, represents the offering of the three kings or wise men of the East; and in this particular alone, I am sorry to be compelled to differ from the very ingenious Artist, whose minute and very curious account of these paintings will be hereafter given in his own words . . .

'The figure of the standing king is just two feet high . . . The throne on which the Virgin is seated, in its form and ornaments very much resembles the venerable Coronation chair still preserved in West-minster Abbey.

'14–15. [Detailed description of the paintings on the east wall of the chapel, as given by Smirke.] "In describing the colouring of these paintings, I begin with the upper subject on the right side of the altar . . . [The Adoration of the Magi.]

' "The background of the figures is diaper work embossed and gilt. The king's crown, embossed and gilt; his hair, reddish brown; cape of his mantle, white ermine. The mantle itself is deep olive green glazed upon silver, the lining of it white and grey fur en vair. His under coat has a crimson pattern on a gilt ground. The ornament of the waist-belt con-sists of blue squares with a gilt rim. A thin lamen of talc covers each blue square. The pantaloons are scarlet, and shoes black, ornamentally pierced, show-ing the scarlet underneath. The sceptre and shrine in his hands are gilt, but not embossed.

' "In the group of three attendants standing behind the king, I begin with the one furthest from him. His cap is pink, faced with white and grey fur en vair; his mantle, crimson, lined with white and grey fur en vair; his coat and sleeve dark green, his right leg black, and shoe white, the left leg light blue, and shoe black. Scabbard of his sword, black. The hilt I sus-pect has been silver; but its colour is now doubtful. The sword belt, black, with a gilt pattern. Middle figure. Feather, white; scroll, gilt; cap, scarlet; beard, dark; left side of his cape, pink; right side, light blue; belt across his shoulders, black and silver. The flowered pattern of his coat and sleeves is light blue on a ground of silver. His left leg scarlet, and shoe, black; his right leg, pink; with shoe also black; his sword belt, gilt. Of his sword hilt I entertain the same opinion as that of figure 1. The scabbard, black. Figure nearest the King. Cap, green; cape, grey; coat, scarlet; legs, pink; and shoes, black. Cap of the groom, crimson; jacket, olive green, with stripes of yellow; pouch, black; legs, naked; and shoes, black; horse, grey; bridle, gilt. Pattern of the tiled floor, alternate lozenges of brown red with white pattern, and white with brown patterns. For the purpose of making the floor appear to recede, it is glazed with transparent brown, which increases in strength as the floor approaches the diaper work. The mantle of the kneeling queen [king], scarlet, sprinkled with gilt fleurs de lys [a leaf pattern]; its lining white and grey fur en vair. Her [his] loose sleeve has a light blue pattern on a silver ground; border of the sleeve em-bossed and gilt, its lining crimson; her [his] right sleeve is white with stripes of light brown; shoes, black; crown, [on the floor, before the figure] em-bossed and gilt. Mantle of her [his] attendant, [in fact, the third of the Magi] light blue; sleeve, crim-son; shrine, flat gilt. Floor consists of triangular tiles, alternately olive green with white pattern, and white with brown pattern. Mantle of the Virgin seated in the chair is pink (seemingly produced by a mixture of red lake and white); the folds are rounded with red lake; the ornaments of its border, gilt; its lining, dark green, glazed on gold; the wavy lines of the pattern have been made while the glazing colour was soft, by pressing a hard point through it to the gold underneath. Her under mantle is light blue; her shoes, black; the swathing of the infant is purple grey; the cloth he sits on is orange, with a pattern of gold and green flowers; cushion, gilt; chair, silvered; the forms upon it made with black lines, and the shadows opake grey. Joseph's mantle, brownish yellow. The squares of the tiled floor are alternately brownish red with a white pattern, and white with a brown pattern. This portion of flooring, as also that under the Queen [i.e. kneeling king] is glazed in the same manner as the King's. The bars separating each have a quatrefoil pattern expressed with white lines on a black ground.

' "In describing the lower subject, I begin on the right with St. George. His helmet is silvered; its rim embossed and gilt; the mail defending the neck and other parts, is embossed and gilt; his surcoat and cross upon it are also embossed and gilt, but the cross is glazed with red lake on the gold; scabbard of his sword, black; that of the dagger, gilt; its handle, silvered; the plate armour is flat gilt, and the form of its parts given by black lines. His spurs are em-bossed and gilt. The crown of the king who kneels under the adjoining arch is embossed and gilt; the helmet, silvered; its rim, gilt. Mail, the same as on St. George. His surcoat is quartered with the arms of England and France; lions embossed and gilt on a red field, made by glazing red lake on gold; fleurs de lys embossed and gilt on a light blue field; the scabbard of his sword, black; that of his dagger, mottled black and gold; handles of both, gilt; sword-belt black with gilt quatrefoils. Without attempting to describe the various colouring of the architectural work of the arches, I must, to prevent confusion, be content to say generally, that the battlements are grey; the piers of the range of windows, blue; those of the pinnacles, pink; but the windows of these last are expressed by a dark brown glazed over gold, whereas the others are black. The walls of the apartment within the arches are dark brown; groin work of the roof, crimson; the windows are silvered, and the form of the panes and their ornament are given by black lines; the pillars, crockets, and mouldings, are every-where flat gilt, their forms expressed by black lines and shadows, by glazing of red lake.

'"Pattern of the tiled floor, white lozenges con-taining red ones, upon a light-blue ground. This flooring is not glazed as in the upper subject. Ground of the inscription at bottom, light opake purple, the letters white. It is unnecessary to detail thus accurately all the remaining arches, or the dress of the king's sons under them, as it would mostly be repetition; I shall therefore confine myself to the mention of those particulars in which they differ. Except the helmet of the first son, the rim of which has an em-bossed and gilt ornament on its upper edge, that and all the others resemble St. George's, already des-cribed. Their surcoats, mail, and plate armour, are like the king's. The first and third sons have an embossed and gilt heraldic label on their breasts. The floor pattern to the first and second sons, is white hexagons containing a blue flower, on a scarlet ground. The floor to the third and fourth sons, a blue square containing a white lozenge inclosing a red flower, alternating with a white square, blue lozenge and white flower. Floor to the youngest son, blue and white chequer; the intervals between the com-partments of arches are white."

'15–16. Plate XVII. This Plate contains the paint-ings on the south side of the high Altar, which are, like those in the former Plate, divided into two dis-tinct tiers, and have, moreover, a small recess to the right hand of the Plate, of which the decorations are entirely independent of the other parts.

'The lower division consists of four arches, similar in their general form to those on the north side of the altar, but differing essentially in their details. In each of them is a female figure kneeling, and apparently looking towards the altar, in an attitude of prayer. These figures are nearly two inches higher than the male figures on the other side.

'There can be no doubt that these are designed for portraits of the Queen Philippa and three of her daughters: their figures are as stiff and meagre as those of the king and his sons, and the heavy platted tresses which load their heads, are nearly as adverse to grace as the mailed gorgets of the princes . . .

'The architecture introduced in the back ground of this picture differs much from that behind the por-traits of the princes. All the windows have mullions, and very elegant tracery in their heads. The small columns too from which the groins spring have wreathed shafts and capitals of a more elegant design.

'The upper subject is evidently the Presentation of our Saviour in the Temple . . . The heighth of these figures is exactly the same as those in the picture of the Epiphany, namely, two feet.

'The small pictures of the Adoration of the Shep-herds, and the Angel appearing to them, which decorate the recess, seem to be the work of a different painter, and perhaps of the same artist who painted the History of Tobias, given in the subsequent Plates. The figures are much less meagre, and the attitudes less stiff and awkward. The sitting boy playing on the double flute to his dancing dog, in the right-hand compartment of the Angel appearing to the Shep-herds, has a great air of truth and nature.

'The attempts at perspective in the picture of the Nativity, are unusually bad; the figures, quite on the fore-ground, are rather less than those about the Infant Saviour, though much nearer to the eye. The general size of the figures is about ten inches.

'Below the subject of the Angel and the Shepherds, is an whole length female figure standing, with her hands joined in prayer. This has been considered as intended for the youngest daughter of the king. This may be so, though she is much smaller than the other portraits of the princesses, and standing.

'The colouring of the whole of this Plate is given, as in the former, in the words of Mr. Smirke.

'"Left side of the Altar. I shall begin at the left with the upper subject. The stone upon which the first figure was painted, has been lost since I made the outline from it. The table cloth between the first and second figures is white with gilt lines. Beneath it may be observed some unconnected patches of ornament introduced to fill up injuries which the original had received. The preparation for them is a dark grey composition, the surface of which is not level with the original painting, and the black and red chequers with gilt tracery upon it are of much inferior execution. This grey composition, I remem-ber to have been very hard when first discovered, but the damp situation it is removed to has destroyed its tenacity. The upper mantle of figure 2, is light blue, lined with white fur; its border, gilt; the stripe, gilt. The upper mantle of figure 3, is purple; hanging-belt, yellow; trefoils upon it, brown; the under mantle is pink; the stripes upon it, yellow; the different borders, gilt; shoes, black.

'"The upper mantle of the Virgin, purplish pink; its folds are rounded with red lake; the border, gilt; its lining is dark green. Her under mantle and sleeve, light blue; its borders, gilt; her hair is light brown, and shoes, black. Joseph's upper mantle, dark olive green; his under vest and sleeve, brownish orange; the work, embossed and gilt. The original floor has been chipped out with some care, and what at first sight seem to be fragments of it, are remains of inferior work upon the grey composition already noticed, which is not level with the other parts.

' "I proceed now to the subject underneath, beginning on the left with the kneeling queen. Her crown is embossed and gilt; her hair, light brown, with small gold ornaments in it; the under vest and sleeves, light blue. A pattern upon it of gilt stars and spots covers the arms and part of the body, and is terminated by a gilt border. The stomacher is of white and brown fur en vair; the stripe of ornament down the middle of the body is gilt; her outer hanging sleeves or flaps are blue, of the same hue as the under one. Fur appears where they are attached to the shoulders, and fur, like that of the stomacher, lines them as low as the gilt pattern of the under vest, terminating with a similar gilt border. The dress of the Queen's first daughter resembles her's in colour and shape; there is only a slight difference in the borders, and pattern on her body. The second daughter's dress is also light blue; it varies a little from the other two figures, and so does her crown . . . The buttresses and external parts of the building containing the above figures, are painted in imitation of grey granite. The mouldings, pinnacles, crockets, and semiquatrefoils are gilt, upon which the forms and shadows are expressed with black lines and red lake. The internal part of each arch exhibits an aperture filled with diaper work embossed and gilt; a silvered window with grey mullions, and a gilt column supporting a groined roof, whose ridges are gilt and intervals crimson; the piers are dark brown; the intervals on each side of the compartments of arches are orange.

' "The subject of the Adoration of the Shepherds is painted on a recess contiguous to the left side of the altar, the sides of which are laid open in the outline, to show what is represented on them. The back ground is diaper work embossed and gilt. The ox, brown; ass, grey; manger, light brown. The Virgin's hair is light brown; her dress, light blue; the pillow and sheet, white; coverlet, scarlet, with a gilt pattern; nimbus round the infant's head, flat gilt, with flat black tracery; its swathing, white. Joseph's cap, black; the facing, pink; his vest and sleeves, pink rounded with red lake; outer mantle, blue; chair, light brown. Shepherd, No. 1. His hair, black; hood, light brown; coat, light green; legs, bare. Shepherd, No. 2. His hair white; cap and coat, grey. Shepherd, No. 3. Hair and beard, black; coat and hood, light brown. Shepherd, No. 4. Cap and coat, purplish pink. The sheep are white. The rocky ground, opake green, shadowed with green of a darker hue. The sides of the recess are finished in a very slovenly

manner . . . The carved leaf in the corner on the right hand is gilt; the diaper work beneath it embossed and gilt; the nimbus of the angel is gilt, his hair, light brown; mantle, pink, and wings light blue; the scroll in his hand is flat gilt. The parts underneath have been lost since I made the outline from them. If I remember rightly, the dress of the female figure was light blue."

'16–17. Plate XVIII. This print represents three of the figures of angels which were probably continued round the whole Chapel, and also the architectural decorations of the lower part of the Chapel, on a larger scale than Plate XV. These figures are about four feet high, and in the same stiff style with the rest of the painting, though there is some grace in the attitudes of the heads and hands.

'Their dress is remarkable. The high embroidered standing collar of their tunics, and the embroidery encircling the upper arms, and repeated at the wrists, though only half round the sleeve, and the embroidery round the waist, have a sort of general resemblance to the sacerdotal dresses, though not exactly similar to any of them . . . The details of colouring both of the figures and architectural heraldic ornaments are given in Mr. Smirke's words.

' "In describing the angels painted on the wall of the south side contiguous to the altar-end of the Chapel, I shall begin with that on the right of the engraved outline, calling it the first. His nimbus is a flat gilt circle, whose outer edge has a diaper border embossed and gilt. The face is carefully painted; the red and grey tints are intermingled with some propriety, and it has tolerable roundness. The colours do not seem to have derived any assistance from glazing, nor does the handling of the pencil exhibit any facility. Though the features are not much out of proportion, they are far from being correct general imitations. These remarks are applicable to the painting of flesh in all the other subjects. His coat is dark blue; the pattern on it consists of two birds whose beaks and legs are scarlet, and a leaf gilt; alternating with a white heart which contains a leaf gilt, and glazed with red lake; the collar, cuffs, and bands round his upper arm and waist, are diaper work embossed and gilt; the linen appearing at the opening of the collar is white. The suspended mantle is scarlet, whose folds are rounded with red lake. All the pattern upon it is gilt, except the heart-shaped foliage, which is opake green. The border of it is embossed and gilt, and its lining is white and brown fur en vair; the wings consist of peacock feathers expressed with black lines and red lake glazing on gold; the centre of the eyes of the feathers is blue enclosed by a circle of green made by glazing green over gold.

' "The head, hair, and nimbus of the second angel resemble the first, but the eyes are blue; his coat, scarlet; most of the pattern on it is gilt; a leaf edged with a white line alternates with a dragon; a white spot in the middle of a black one occurs in the centre of the leaf and wing of the dragon; collar, cuffs and bands, as in the first angel; the suspended mantle is dark blue; the eagle of the pattern with its surrounding rays are gilt; each wing has a stripe of green between two stripes of crimson; the tail also is glazed with red lake. The central part of the intervening foliage is gilt, and the larger branches are either light blue or scarlet, according to the range in which they stand. Its border and lining are the same as those of the first angel. The third angel's nimbus, coronet, hair, coat, collar, cuffs and band are like the first; the suspended mantle is scarlet; the pattern on it, birds and surrounding quadrangular ornament, gilt, alternating with quatrefoil-shaped foliage, opake green, whose central parts are gilt. These three angels have a black back ground sprinkled with embossed and gilt stars; the earth upon which they stand is interspersed with leaves and daisies. The attendant monk, in the compartment on the left, has a white surplice over a coat with tight sleeves and buttons of light blue; his shoes are black, the ground he stands on, grey; the candlestick he holds, gilt; the candle in it yellow; the back ground, scarlet.

' "I will now endeavour to describe the colouring of the architectural parts which are represented in the same outline.

' "The escutcheons of the frieze are painted on a ground of an apple-green hue (in which I find no trace of iron or copper). The grotesque figures and foliage are flesh colour, rounded with red lake. Beginning at the left, the *first* shield quarters lions embossed and gilt on a red field (by red, I wish to be understood a glazing of red lake over gold), with chequers of dark blue and gold. *Second* shield. An engrailed cross embossed and gilt on a black field. *Third* shield. A chevron red, on a diapered and gilt field. *Fourth* shield. Lozenge, red, on a diapered and gilt field. *Fifth* shield. Lions embossed and gilt, on a red field; the rim diapered and gilt. *Sixth* shield. Quarters a manche red on a diapered and gilt field with four bars, scarlet (that is, vermilion) on a dark blue field, which colour has been laid on a ground previously silvered. *Seventh* shield. Three embossed and gilt stars on a blue field, and six crosses embossed and black (seemingly) on a flat gilt field. *Eighth* shield. Quarters, a field diapered and gilt, with a fretty

embossed and gilt on a red field; the bend black. *Tenth* shield. A cross, embossed and gilt on a red field, flourished with black foliage. *Eleventh* shield. Three roundlets, red on a diapered gilt field; two of the roundlets have a black stripe. *Twelfth* shield. A lion, embossed and dark blue on a flat gilt field. The spandrils of the trefoil arches have white window-tracery on a black ground. . . .

' "It appears from a note of the late Mr. Brand . . . that on the mantle, held by another of the angels, were elephants and castles . . .

' "The great beauty and variety of design, both in the tunics of the angels and the mantles they hold, and the extreme richness and elegance of the embroidery with which the draperies of all the figures are bordered, and otherwise decorated, shews that the art of embroidery had attained to a very high perfection at that early period. . . ."

'17–18. Plate XIX. In this and all the following Plates, are exhibited specimens of the paintings which decorated the walls of the Chapel, under the opening of the windows. There were eight subjects in each set, in two tiers, four in each tier, and probably each set formed a separate series illustrative of some scriptural or sacred history. These, which are from the book of Job, filled the first division of the north side of the Chapel nearest to the altar. Those relative to the story of Tobias, were in the opposite southern compartment. Of those in the compartments further westward, no trace or fragment now remains, but that there were paintings in them is known.

'The outlines were all made with great care from the originals by Mr. Smirke, and the details of colouring are given from notes made by him, and marked on the Plates themselves. The paintings are very carefully and minutely finished; so much so, indeed, that at the distance of ten feet from the ground, which is the elevation of the bottom of the lowest range of pictures, much of the detail must have been lost. The general size of the figures is about a foot in height. The Plates are of the size of the original paintings.

'The painting now to be described, represents the destruction of the children of Job, by the fall of the house in which they were feasting. The fore-ground of the picture is an arcade of three rather elegant arches, supported by light pillars; and a panelled ceiling comes up to the top of the picture. The flanks of this arcade are seen in perspective; they are richly adorned with niches and statues . . .

'Six figures in good preservation, and a seventh nearly effaced, are sitting at a table covered with a white cloth. Every one of them appears to have been wounded by the fall of the roof of the hall, the timbers of which appear disjointed, and in confusion behind them; the Demon who directs the Storm, is pushing the beams, and impelling them on the victims of his rage . . .

'The first figure to the left, which seems a female, with her hand to her head, on which a beam has fallen, is dressed in purplish pink, with an elegant ornamented border round the bosom and shoulders. Of the second, the head only is visible. It seems male, with light brown hair. The third seems also a man, dressed in purple grey with a rich collar, and light brown hair. The fourth is a female, who is dying or dead, and is the best figure of the whole group: her dress is light blue, with a very rich collar and bracelets, or embroidered cuffs to the sleeves of her robe, which fits tight to the arms and descends to the wrists. The fifth is a young man looking upwards with terror; his coat is close to his body and arms, and buttoned down before; it comes high up his neck, and over his shoulders there is an ornament which seems rather a rich collar or chain, than an embroidery on the dress itself. The colour of his coat is purple pink; his legs appear under the table, clad in green; his shoes are black. The sixth is a female in light blue, . . . her collar is in shape similar to the others, but less rich. The last is a man nearly effaced, but who seems dying. His dress is pink, his hose the same, with black shoes; the borders and ornaments of all the dresses are gilt.

'The cups and spoons on the table are silver. The figure of Satan is brown, with eyes and lips of red lead; the falling timbers, light brown; the back ground, black; the pillars of the portico in front are orange, with violet capitals; the ceiling and the right flank, dark grey; the left flank and floor, light grey; the diaper border, embossed and gilt.

'It may be observed that the perspective of this porch is much better than is usually seen in the works of this period, and evinces a degree of acquaintance with the principles of that art far beyond its first elements . . .

'18. Plate XX. Fac-similes of Inscriptions, found under the different compartments of scriptural histories, painted on the inside walls of St. Stephen's Chapel.

'No. 1. was underneath a picture not preserved, representing the piety of Tobias in burying the dead bodies of his countrymen

que reperit corpora co . . . pit humo
ter mens.m levat . . . b tempore noctis
em ducit sepius ipse diem
. fessus thobias   regressus.

'No. 2. The painting above this inscription represented the muting of the swallows into Tobias's eyes as he lay sleeping in the open air. A fragment of it remained.

Dormit et ex nido quem fecit hirundo jacentis
. . . . -lapsa fluunt
. . . . ab ejus ocellis
vigilat et ceca frons sine luce fuit.

'No. 3; the painting above which is preserved, and represents Zophar the Naamathite in the act of speaking to Job.

Sophar Anaamatites: parat in solamina lites.
Non consolatur: sed fallax insidiatur.
Multa volens fari: nequit unquam justificari.
Nolens audire: non quibit plurima scire.
Est nota stulticie: meliorem velle docere.
Est nota nequicie: majorem velle juvare.

'No. 4. The painting above this has also been preserved, exhibiting Job's comforters in the act of altercation; the inscription is nearly entire.

Hos tres predictos: Helui culpas quasi victos
Quem Deus ostendit: justum tumide reprehendit
Nititur et verbis: illum maculare superbis.
Set pius et rectus gerit insuperabile pectus.
Arguo majores: junior et juvenis seniores
Quod nimis injusto: tacere simul cum justo.

'No. 5. was on the south wall, under a compartment representing Tobit's marriage feast. The picture remains.

Laudat uterque parens magnificatque Deum
Exhilarat Raguel conjunctio facta duorum
Et vaccas pingues enecat ille duas
. . . nis et eis quos . . .

'No. 6. was under another compartment, representing in the history of Tobit—the Angel's discovery of himself before his departure to Heaven. The picture is in part preserved.

Argentum recipit pater quod ante Gabelos
A socio Tobi . . . quod nomen inhereat illi
Accipe quod queris. Azarias vocor ortus
. . . Dominum rediit Tobisque remansit.

'No. 7. This fragment has been under another compartment of the history of Job, exhibiting the latter end of that Patriarch as much greater than his beginning. The picture is lost.

. . perillata: justi virtute probata.
ma sublata: redduntur ei duplicata
salute data: tibi pace simul reparata
. prius ablata: tibi reddo multiplicata.

'No. 8. This is beneath the representation of the destruction of the house in which Job's sons and daughters were feasting, by a whirlwind excited by the devil.

> *Conveniunt venti: domus impulsu vehementi*
> *concidit in natos: convivendo sociatos.*

'No. 9. is beneath the compartment representing the messenger delivering the sad tidings to Job of the above catastrophe. The picture in part preserved.

> *Cum gemitu tristi: quidam sic nunciat isti.*
> *Igne coruscante: pueros gregesque devorante.*
> *Instat merenti: narrare dolenda dolenti.*
> *Natis orbatus: rebus dispoliatus.*
> *Sum satis afflictus: per cuncta sit hic benedictus.*

'No. 10. under a compartment in which Job has been represented as giving religious instruction to his seven sons and three daughters. A fragment of the picture exists.

> *. . . septem natos: et tres natas generavit*
> *illi servite: qui dat spiracula vite*
> *ille nos plasmavit, animavit, sensificavit.*

'No. 11. underneath another compartment of the history of Job; in which one of the daughters of that Patriarch is represented as in the act of asking her father's permission to go to their brother's feast, to which they had been invited. The picture partly preserved.

> . . . .
> *cum natis natas: concessit adire paratas*
> *ad fratrum mensas: . . . ire rogatas*
> *Felices ite: felicius inde redite.*

'18–19. Plate XXI. The upper subject in this Plate represents Job addressing his sons, and apparently giving them paternal admonition. The merit of this picture is but small; the head of the Patriarch is the best part of it; he is dressed in a light blue mantle, lined with miniver, and a broad cape of the same fur over his shoulders. The mantle is edged with gold; under it appears a pink dress; his shoes are black. The standing figure nearest to him, whose chin only is remaining, is dressed in a tight doublet of light orange brown; over his shoulders is a broad cape of light blue, with a broad border of gold; a black sword-belt, with a golden buckle is girt very low on his hips; his stockings are light blue; his shoes black. Of the next figure little remains. He has a purple doublet, and a broad pink cape, with a black sword-belt, and hose of light olive green. The third son is quite a boy. His hair, light brown; his doublet and hose are pink, but of different shades; his belt black,

with a golden buckle; his shoes, black. Of a fourth figure one leg only is visible: the stocking is grey. Two very slender columns with orange-coloured shafts and grey base, appear in front of the figures. Beneath this figure was an inscription, of which the remains are given in Plate XX, No. 10. Three lines only are legible, which Mr. Brand has restored as follows:

> 'Qui septem natos: et tres natas generavit.
> Illi servite: qui dat spiracula vite
> Ille nos plasmavit: animavit: sensificavit.

'The words *qui* in the first line, and *vite* in the second, are quite lost, but happily supplied by Mr. Brand, who thinks he sees a trace of the name of Job and of his country, Hus, in the mutilated remains of the first line.

'The lower subject on this Plate is from the history of Tobit in the Apocryphal book which bears his name. Tobit is just awakened from his sleep by the pain given by the muting of the sparrows, which is represented as falling directly on his eyes. His hands are lifted to them with a very natural action. His wife, with an air of much anxiety, is coming to his assistance. What remains of her countenance is good, and the drapery on her shoulder and body is thrown with great elegance. By a repetition very common in ancient pictures, where two points of time are frequently represented in the same piece, Tobit, blind and disconsolate, is sitting on the other side of a square pillar; his head is extremely fine, and full of expression; the mouth and beard particularly well drawn. He is clad in a light blue mantle, which is drawn over his head, so as to form a hood. Its border is gilt, and on his shoulder is a large text T. He has an under garment of purple grey. His dress is the same in the recumbent figure; his wife has her head and shoulders wrapt in a white veil with a gold border; her gown sleeve is light blue; her mantle, light purple grey; the pilasters are green.

'Under this picture was the following inscription, which is given in Plate XX, No. 2.

> 'Dormit et ex nido quem fecit hirundo jacentis
> Illius in vultum stercora lapsa fluunt
> . . . . . . radius fulgoris ab ejus ocellis
> Vigilat et ceca frons sine luce fuit.

'It is curious that this and all the other inscriptions remaining relative to the history of Tobit, should be in verse not rhymed, while Job's history is in Leonine rhyme . . .

'It is to be observed, that the inscription speaks of swallows having muted into the eyes of Tobit. The

English bible calls the birds sparrows. The Latin Vulgate however, which the author of the inscription certainly followed, calls them Hirundines.

'19. Plate XXII. The nuptial feast of the young Tobias, on his return home, is here depicted. The old Tobit, known by the T on his cloak, is apparently in the act of blessing the young married couple, of whom only a part of the figure of Sara remains. The gilt coronet or chaplet round her hair, and the modest downcast of her eyes, sufficiently mark her. Next to Tobit, on his left hand, sits a female, probably his wife; next to her another old man, and a woman of advanced age . . . A very small part of three figures sitting with their backs to the spectator, remains. . . .

'The first figure on the left of the picture, whom I suppose to be the bride, Sara, has light brown hair, and a coronet of golden quaterfoils on her head; a small fragment of a white kerchief . . . appears on her neck; her dress is pink.

'Tobit has a light blue conical cap trimmed up with white, and edged with gold; . . . his mantle is scanty, and of light blue, as is his under garment; it is bordered with gold, and has the distinctive T. The female next to him wears a light grey purple hood lined with light brown, and edged with gold; it covers her head, and falls in large folds over her shoulders; a white muffler comes close under her chin.

'The male figure next her has a flat cap of dark grey purple edged with gold; his mantle is light blue, with gold border, and clasped on his breast; his under garment like his cap. The female next to him has a white hood, edged with gold, and a muffler which covers her chin and great part of her cheeks. Her dress is pink. Of the three figures sitting with their backs to the spectator, two are in purple pink. The female head has a white hood. The very small fragment of the third, is dressed in light blue; the bench is brown ochre; the table-cloth white, with an edge and a waving thread above it, of gold; silver vessels are on the table. The room is hung with a rich arras of olive green and roses, alternately white with scarlet spot, and scarlet with white spot. The cord or moulding which marks the angles of the room and ceiling, is white wreathed with scarlet.

'Under this picture is the inscription given in fac-simile, Plate XX, No. 5.

'Mr. Brand reads it thus,

'*Laudat uterque parens magnificatque Deum*
Exhilarat Raguel conjunctis facta duorum
Et vaccas pingues enecat ille duas.
Vicinis et eis quos necat. . . .

The whole word vicinis was legible when Mr. Brand copied the inscription, though now lost.

'19–20. Plate XXIII. This picture, which seems the last in the series of subjects taken from the history of Tobit, represents the parting of the angel Raphael, from the family of Tobias, and, like one of the former ones, has a double point of time in one piece. On the left, Tobit, marked by the T on his garment, with his purse in his hand, and his son, the young Tobit, standing by him, appears to be offering to Raphael a liberal reward for his services . . .

'The Angel, still in his travelling attire, but distinguished by the nimbus round his head, seems courteously attending to their generous offer. Three heads looking out of several windows, shew that this part of the story passed in public.

'In the right hand of the picture, the Angel having, as the text says, "taken them both apart", is in the act of disclosing to them his celestial character. Tobit, and probably his son, kneeling, bend forward in reverence, while the just opening wings of Raphael point out that he is saying, "I go up to him that sent me." Though the figures of Tobias and the Angel in the first half of the picture are far from dignified, yet the attitude and action of both are extremely natural. Tobias has an air of great affection and kindness towards his companion, and the Angel's look is modest and grateful.

'Of the figure of old Tobit too little remains to form any exact judgment of its merit. The heads looking out of the windows are but poor; the right hand group is so much defaced that nothing can be said of it.

'The standing figure of the old Tobit is dressed in a light blue mantle, with a gold border; his under garment is white; his cap, light blue, turned up with white; his shoes black. The purse is gold, with ver-milion tassels; his beard is grey. Tobias wears a coat of purple pink, reaching to the mid-leg . . . His hose are orange; his shoes black. The Angel has a dress similar in form to that of Tobias. Its colour is a grey pink, with light blue hose; the nimbus round his head is gilt. The kneeling figure, probably Tobit, has a mantle of light blue; the wings and nimbus of the Angel are gilt, and his drapery was (from a small fragment yet remaining) probably white. Of the old heads looking out of the windows, the first has a light blue cap; the other a yellow cap, faced with crimson; both have grey beards, touched with great care. The building in the back ground is in very awkward perspective, and rather an odd style of architecture. It is painted in light grey, shadowed with purplish brown; the little arches above the door have their apertures black; the parts of arches seen over the head of Tobit are yellow; the shaded part within them to the left, purple brown; the window casement is silvered, and its sill scarlet.

'The diaper near the ascending Angel, embossed and gilt as usual.

'The inscription under this picture is given in facsimile, Plate XX, No. 6.

'Mr. Brand reads it as follows:

> 'Argentum recipit pater quod ante Gabelo
> A socio Tobius quod nomen inhereat illi
> Accipe quod queris, Azarias vocor ortus.
> . . . Dominum rediit Tobisque remansit.

'I doubt the first words in the second line. I here remark that Mr. Brand, by an odd mistake, uniformly calls the father Tobias, and the son Tobit. A bare inspection of the book shews that the father was Tobit and the son Tobias; the Vulgate however, calls both father and son by the same name, viz. Tobias.

'20. Plate XXIV. This picture seems to represent the three daughters of Job obtaining permission to visit their brothers. It appears to possess more merit than any of the paintings now under consideration. The head of Job has a very dignified character, and his attitude is, with the exception of his right foot, graceful. His drapery is disposed and folded with much elegance, and the whole figure has a striking resemblance to ancient statues of the sitting Jupiter . . . The standing figure of the first daughter has the slender form, characteristic of the art in its early times, but she is gracefully disposed, and what remains of her head is very handsome. The other three figures are so mutilated as to leave little room for observation: the folds, however, of the drapery held up by the last daughter are extremely good.

'The scene appears to be laid in a magnificent room adorned with columns of a very singular design; having a slender shaft wreathed round with a very projecting angular band, very much resembling a deep-cut screw.

'The dress of Job is a light blue mantle, lined with white fur and bordered with gold; his doublet pink (painted with vermilion and white); his shoes, black. His wife, who sits by him, has her head covered with an ample white veil. Her robe is a grey purple.

'The first of the three daughters has a robe of pink; her sleeves, which descend to the wrists, are light blue.

'The second was dressed in grey.

'The third has an upper garment of purple, lined

with white, and bordered with gold, which appears to have been tight to the body, but very ample below the waist. It has no sleeves, but wide openings for the arms, with a rich golden embroidery round them, and the neck. The under garment has sleeves of light blue, and as the upper robe is lifted up by the right hand, it appears that this blue dress reached to the feet.

'The wreathed columns are orange, shaded with red lake; a sort of plain pilasters appear behind them, painted in dark olive green; the ground to the whole is a diaper embossed and gilt. Under this picture was an inscription, of which the remains are given in facsimile, Plate XX. No. 11. Three lines only are legible, and Mr. Brand reads them:

> 'Cum natis natas: concessit adire paratas.
> Ad fratrum mensas: . . . ire rogatas
> Felices ite: felicius inde redite.

.   .   .   .   .

'21. Plate XXV. Job and his wife are here represented sitting in a sort of open porch, and receiving two of the messengers who reported to him the destruction of his property and his family. The heads of both are destroyed, but the attitudes are not ill conceived. The draperies are well folded, but the hands have the long and pointed form, characteristic of that period of the art. The messengers are kneeling on one knee; their attitudes and faces are not destitute of expression, but their figures are meagre and ill drawn. The wife of Job wears on her head a white veil; her upper robe or mantle is purple pink, edged with gold; her under garment is light olive green. Job wears an ample mantle of light blue, lined with white fur, and edged with gold; his doublet is of a purplish grey. The first messenger has a tight dress of olive green, with a loose black sword belt. The other is clad in light olive brown, with olive green hose, and black belt and shoes.

'The architecture introduced into this picture is more similar to that in use at the period than in most of the others; but the perspective is very bad. The pillars of the porch in front have their bases and capitals pale orange; the shafts seem designed to imitate veined wood. The arches in front, purple pink; within, green grey. The smaller porch to the left, has pillars with shafts like the others: the bases are orange, the capitals vermilion; the outer part of the arches is green grey; the interior groins, red lake; the upper part of the edifice seen in perspective is light brown; the ground of the picture, as usual, diaper, embossed and gilt. Under it was an inscription given in facsimile, Plate XX. No. 9. Mr. Brand reads it as follows:

> 'Cum gemitu tristi: quantum sic nuntiat isti
> Igne coruscante: pueros gregesque devorante,
> Instat merenti: narrare dolenda dolenti:
> Natis orbatus: rebus dispoliatus
> Sum satis afflictus: per cuncta sit hic benedictus.

'In the fourth line I should insert et before rebus, which completes the metre, and of which there is an indication in the Plate. Mr. Brand thinks the last line is Job's answer to his wife. I rather think the two last lines are spoken by the afflicted Patriarch.

'21. Plate XXVI. Job is here represented in affliction, sitting on the ground naked, and covered with blotches, accompanied by his three false friends, one of whom is nearly effaced, and Elihu, who is rebuking them. The grouping and attitudes of these figures are not bad; the attitude of Job particularly, is easy and expressive. His head has considerable merit, but the body is almost destitute of drawing. The heads of the other figures are but indifferent, and ill set on. The hands have the stiff and pointed form peculiar to the early age of painting. The draperies are well folded; that of Elihu may be called elegant. The whole appearance of this youth, both in countenance, hair and dress, is so feminine, that did not the inscription under the picture decide him to be Elihu, he might have been taken for the wife of Job. The colour of his mantle is pale crimson, lined with white; his under garment, light blue; his cap is yellow, with crimson flowers turned up with white; his hair is light brown. The person to whom he is speaking wears a purple grey mantle lined with white, and a vest of pale crimson; his cap is pale crimson.

'The figure reclining on his hand has a light blue cap and mantle, with a light crimson vest. The third figure seems to have been clad in light blue, with a pink and white mantle; the edges of all the draperies are gilt. The building in the back ground is painted in a greenish grey; the two reticulated pinnacles are scarlet.

'The diaper in the fond is embossed and gilt.

'Under this picture are the following lines, of which a fac-simile is given in Plate XX, No. 4.

> 'Hos tres predictos: Helui culpas quasi victos
> Quem Deus ostendit: justum tumidi reprehendit.
> Nititur et verbis: illum maculare superbis
> Set pius et rectus: gerit insuperabile pectus
> Arguo majores: junior et juvenis seniores
> Quod nimis injusto: lacere simul cum justo.

'This is Mr. Brand's reading: but in the fifth line I read for junior, minor; and I am not satisfied with the reading of the sixth line, though I cannot amend it.

'Mr. Brand justly observes, that in the first line Helui is in the vocative, and culpas is the second person singular of the present tense, of the verb culpo. . . .

'21–22. Plate XXVII. Job is here represented naked and afflicted, sitting on the ground and conferring with his seeming friend Zophar, the Naamathite. This picture has considerable merit: the action of Job is just, and his countenance has a character of mild and patient sorrow; the naked is, as usual, very ill drawn, and the hands in particular.

'Zophar, both in attitude and expression of head, has the air of pride, and self-sufficience. His cap is light blue, faced with white; his beard, white. He is wrapped in an ample mantle of pink, lined throughout with ermine, and edged with gold; the folds of this robe are very well disposed; his doublet and hose are light blue, his shoes black.

'The ground appears rough and broken, and is painted of a light grey.

'In the back ground is a castellated mansion. The round turrets and walls are painted in a grey purple, the pillars supporting the three small arches are light brown; the openings of the small arches and of the windows are black. It may be a matter of some surprise, that the painters of these pictures, who in the costume of their figures, seem to have copied the dresses of the period in which they lived, should in their buildings have, in this and most other places, totally departed, not only from the architecture then in use, but from any thing that ever was practised in this country. This may lead to a suspicion that Master Hugh of St. Albans, and the other artists employed, had studied in foreign parts, or at least had borrowed their designs from the painters of the Continent, and from Germany in particular; as the style of buildings in their very early pictures much resemble these.

'The ground of this and all the other pictures is diaper embossed and gilt.

'Under this picture is the following inscription, which is given in fac-simile, Plate XX, No. 3.

> 'Sophar Anaamatites: parat in solamina lites.
> Non consolatur: sed fallax insidiatur.
> Multa volens fari: nequit unquam justificari
> Nolens audire: non quivit plurima scire.
> Est nota stulticie: meliorem velle docere
> Est nota nequicie: majorem velle juvare.

'Such is the late Mr. Brand's reading, though I doubt the word volens in the third line; and juvare in the last, is scarcely sense, and (what in these verses is rather worse) scarcely rhyme. It seems as if the painter, who probably was not learned, had made a mistake, and put *juvare* for *monere*. There certainly seems no wickedness in assisting a superior, though there may be presumption, and of course vice, in reproving or admonishing him.

'22. Plate XXVIII. The two figures of armed knights, with the names of Mercure and Eustace under them, are here given from drawings made by George Naylor, Esq., York Herald, and by him presented to the Society.

'These figures were painted on the piers between the windows, and it is probable that every pier was so adorned, although these alone have been drawn previous to their destruction in the general wreck of the interior of the Chapel . . .

'It appears that he [St. Mercurius] was a soldier in the army of Decius, of Scythian race, an Armenian by birth, and by an angel, gifted with a lance of supernatural power. With this he slew the king of a barbarian nation who had invaded the Roman territory, and was by Decius placed at the head of his army; but on his refusal of sacrifice, was with many and most cruel torments put to death by Decius.

'The story of Eustace is to be found in the Golden Legend . . . His wife and family accompanied him in his conversion, and shared in the honours of martyrdom with him, they being enclosed in a brazen bull, and so burned to death. A part of the paintings under the window in the Chapel represented this circumstance in the Legend of St. Eustace, but the barbarous haste of the destroyers prevented any memorial of this picture being preserved, except a very small one in the print of Cotton Garden, by Mr. Smith, in the Antiquities of Westminster.

'In the figures of the knightly saints here given, it may be remarked that Mercure has merely a cross on his shield, surcoat, and pennon, while Eustace has the hart's head on each of them. In the plate the crucifix is scarcely made out between the horns. In Mr. Smith's plate of these figures it is more distinct; and it may be added that he gives beards to the knights, while Mr. Naylor left them with smooth chins. . . .

'It will be observed, that the Plates from the Paintings do not follow the order of the subjects represented, and that the stories of Tobias and Job are mingled in them. The cause of this irregularity is, that it was at first the intention of the Council only to publish the outlines of those of the pictures which seemed the most interesting, but that on considering the great curiosity of the whole of them as works of art, of a period of which no other remains whatever

exist in this country, and which tend to prove that English painters were at that brilliant epoch both numerous and far from unskilled in their art, it was thought proper to give to the world the whole of what was saved from the wreck of that splendid edifice which during four centuries they had adorned, and from the walls of which in the year 1800 they were swept away with a haste so barbarous, as scarcely to allow a moment to artists to endeavour to preserve them by copies; without even the plea of necessity for their destruction, as the space gained by the utter defacement of the interior of the Chapel might have been obtained with the utmost ease, and at an expense much inferior, by other means.'

J. T. Smith, *Antiquities of Westminster*, 1807.

'144. In the year 1800, the number of members of the House of Commons being increased from 558 to 658, in consequence of the Act of Parliament for uniting the two kingdoms of Great Britain and Ireland, the building itself was thought too small for their reception. The original side walls, between the piers, were three feet thick, and it was, therefore, found that by erecting on the same foundation, but so as to range with the external extremity of the old, other walls, of less dimensions, as being only one foot thick, the building might be considerably enlarged internally, and sufficient room might be obtained: and this plan was accordingly determined on. On removing the wainscoting, as a preparatory step to taking down these walls, a discovery was made . . . that the stone walls had been originally painted with a variety of subjects, and that many of them were still in such a perfect state as to admit of their being copied and engraven.

147–8. To describe the building more particularly, it must be said that it is of an oblong shape, and measures about 90 ft. in length by about 30 ft. in width, internal measure, having externally at each corner, an octagonal tower. It consists of five windows on each side, about 12 ft. 6 in. wide, and between each a pier of about 5 ft. 6 in. in width, formed on the outside into a flying buttress, nearly 3 ft. 6 in. thick, and extending in the whole about 10 ft. from the wall of the building. It contained likewise two stories; the height of the upper story, now the House of Commons, from the floor to the top of the battlement of the cornice, just under the springing of the roof, was about 42 ft.; and the height of the under chapel, before the ground was raised, was about 20 ft., making together 62 ft.

'151–52. As to the interior part of the Chapel, it is

to be observed that with the exception of the space for the altar, which was a plain stone projection, all round the Chapel, against the wall, were two seats, of Purbeck marble, one above the other; each about a foot high and of the same width. These were discontinued only where openings for doors, or entrances from other apartments, were necessary, and on the uppermost of these seats rested the base of those columns by which the piers were formed. . . . The flat surface of the pier between the two clusters of columns in front, was sub-divided into two, by one column of like size and pattern with the large one of the three at the angles: and in each of these sub-divisions, at about 14 ft. from the floor, was the figure of a knight in armour, painted on the wall, with his arms, or symbol, emblazoned in proper colours on his shield and banner; and the name of the person under it. Above the tops of the windows ran an entablature, consisting of an architrave, on which were carved in stone grotesque faces or masks, foliage and shields of arms; over that was an open frieze, surmounted with battlements; and all these parts were as exquisitely gilt and coloured as those nearer the eye. Under each of the side windows, at the height of about 12 ft. from the floor, was a frieze projecting about a foot, so as to range with the face of the pier. This frieze was surmounted with battlements similar to those at the top of the building, and had under it an architrave formed by a receding hollow, and upon this cavetto or hollow were painted in their proper colours the arms of the royal family and several of the nobility and others. . . .

'153–4. Of this frieze the open parts had been filled with stained glass, containing flowers, and diapered ornaments of various colours; and it is supposed, that when this Chapel was lighted up, lights were placed behind these parts. The whole entablature, consisting of the architrave, frieze and battlements, which served as a cornice, was formerly supported by eight insulated columns, which had, however, when the paintings were discovered, been broken away, but originally stood on the upper seat. Behind these eight columns the wall, which was also the side wall of the Chapel, was divided into four compartments by three clusters of columns, consisting of three each; and on each of these divisions was painted on the wall a figure of an Angel about 5 ft. high [according to Topham, 4 ft.] with wings composed of peacock's feathers, holding an extended piece of drapery before him, on which were represented, in some instances, the device of two doves, in others that of a spread eagle, in others elephants and castles, in others griffins or dragons, and in others pelicans. . . .

Above this lower frieze, and on the flat surface of the wall of the building, between that frieze and the bottom of the window, were painted, in eight compartments, historical subjects from the Scriptures, and the legends of the Saints, with verses over them; but these paintings and inscriptions were, in many cases, so much mutilated that they could not be copied. Of some of these the subjects are known; that at the west corner, in the upper range under the first window from the altar, on the south side, representing the martyrdom of St. Eustace, by enclosing him in a brazen bull, and roasting him with fire underneath, is to be seen in the print of Cotton Garden, Westminster, lying among the fragments; near which lies also another fragment, containing an inscription which had been over a similar painting; parts of two other such inscriptions, comprising the end of the lines in one, and the beginning of those of the other, were found painted on one and the same stone, and are here inserted as a specimen:

. . . *merito beneficia Christi*	*Hii fide ferven* . . .
. . . *it sic dispersos simul vn it*	*Aras polluta* . . .
. . . *quos credentes sibi crevit*	*Hinc ruit* . . .
. . . *et hinc vide quae vada poscunt*	*Quos inbet a* . . .

Another of these paintings, on the north side, in a similar situation, and directly opposite to the marriage of Canaan before mentioned, was a representation of the Destruction of Job's Children . . .

'156. [Smith remarks that parts "which never were there at all" are represented in the plates published by Topham; that the outlines of some of the figures, particularly that of the King holding a casket, in the Adoration of the Magi, are not "correct"; that his right hand was not there when the wainscot was removed, and the dove, surmounting the sceptre, is omitted, which was then in existence but subsequently defaced.] In the . . . view of the several paintings under the window next the altar, in the south side, a stone arched doorway is seen. Its jambs were painted on the sides with the arms of England and France, alternately, in square compartments; and two elbows, one on each side of it, projected forward into the Chapel, which formed the termination of the Purbeck marble seats . . . Adjoining to this doorway, towards the west, was a flat surface of wall of 10 in., on which was painted a Stand, and on the top of this Stand were represented a bason and spoon gilt. On another flat surface, adjoining the former, but more towards the west, was painted a whole-length figure of a youth, with a thuribulum, or incense pot; and on the pier, at the south-east corner of the Chapel, another youth, with a taper. . . .

'160. On the sloping side of the north-east pier farthest from the altar, occurred another painting like that on the south-east pier; of the same size, and at the same height from the ground; the subject of which was a youth holding a wax taper . . . Of this very beautiful and magnificent building it is not too much to say, that no edifice, existing at the time of its erection in any part of the world, can, in any degree, be compared with it . . .

'163. To give a general and brief summary of the statues and pictures of St. Stephen's Chapel, it may be sufficient to say there were:

46 painted figures of Angels, 5 ft. high.

20 youths, about 3 ft. high, painted on the same level with the Angels.

32 knights, painted also, exclusive of those at the west end.

20 youths, similar to those by the Angels, painted on the same level as the knights.

12 statues of stone, at least 6 ft. high, on brackets on the piers round the Chapel.

80 paintings on the walls under the windows, 8 under each window, many of which contained 10 or 12 figures.

16 subjects painted at the east end . . . besides 2, of a bishop and an old man in blue . . .

'164. Above the statues on brackets, were paintings; so there were also on all the flat faces of the piers; and the whole west end was also painted; without reckoning the coats-of-arms, with the grotesque supporters between each shield—the paintings and decorations about the east window—the painted and gilt parts of the architecture all over the building—and the wood-work and carving of the ceiling, which was, probably, painted and gilt in the same manner.'

At the Society of Antiquaries drawings and tracings, many of the former in colour, by John Carter, made in 1791 and 1792, are preserved; together with various drawings and tracings by R. Smirke and others. Reconstructions by E. W. Tristram are to be seen in the Houses of Parliament.

Topham, *Some Account of the Collegiate Chapel of St. Stephen, Westminster*, 1795, pp. 8–22; Smith, *Antiquities of Westminster*, 1807, 144, 147–8, 151, 153, 155–64, 174–223; Michel, 1907, *Histoire de l'Art*, III, 312, 313, repr.; Borenius and Tristram, *Eng. Med. Painting*, 1927, 22–4; Bunim, *Space in Medieval Painting and the Forerunners of Perspective*, New York, 1940, pp. 162–9; Harvey, *Gothic England*, 1947, 60–1, 66, 69; Hastings, *Parliament House*, London, 1950, 58, 59, 110, 113.
Plates 1–5, 6a, b.

LONGTHORPE TOWER (near Peterborough)
Northants

In the tower, probably an addition of *c.* 1300 to an earlier edifice still in part surviving, of a farmhouse at Longthorpe, originally a defensible Manor House, there are three stages, the second of which, with a contemporary fireplace and a vaulted ceiling of four bays, has extensive remains of an early fourteenth-century scheme of decoration, as follows:

The North Wall. Centrally placed, above a window recess of some width and depth, a Nativity (the middle defaced) with the Virgin, reclined against the draped head of a couch and suckling the swaddled Holy Child, on the spectator's left, and St. Joseph, seated in a chair at the foot, on the right; in the space between these two figures traces survive of the Ox and the Ass. Above the Nativity, arranged in an arc roughly following the contour of the vaulting, the Seven Ages of Man, which commence on the left near the springing of the arch over the recess with *Infans*, a child in a cradle, and continue upward with *Puer*, a boy playing with a whip and ball, and *Adolescens*, almost defaced, to *Pubertas*, in the centre, just over the Nativity, shown as a young man with hawk on wrist and belt, dagger, jess and lure at his waist; and then, following the curve of the arch, proceed downward with *Adultus*, much defaced, *Senectus*, who holds a bag of money, and, finally, *Decrepitus*, hooded, bearded, and walking with crutches. On the vault above, David, enthroned and playing a harp, and opposite him another enthroned figure, unidentified, with a psaltery; and between and slightly above them, at the apex of the vaulting, remains of a barbed quatrefoil which once framed the Sign of St. John, but one claw of the Eagle and a scroll inscribed JOHANNES are all that are now visible. Below, on either side of the window recess, two tiers of painting, in the higher of these, on both sides, being two Apostles, and in the lower, also on both sides, two large birds painted against a background of scroll-work. On each splay of the recess, a similar figure of an Apostle, and on the soffit of the arch parts of four shields of arms.

The South Wall. Divided horizontally into two sections at the level of the springing of the vault by a band of some depth, painted in red and ornamented with a wyvern, birds and flowers, above which is a second band, in this case, of lettering, now much defaced, but evidently related to the subjects over it, namely, two kings, enthroned and with arms outstretched towards each other, perhaps in disputation (the one on the western side much defaced) flanked each with a shield, that on the left charged with the arms of England, the other indecipherable apart from a bordure. On the lower part of the wall-space, a heraldic diaper of diamond design, with the Thorpe arms repeated—a fess between six fleurs-de-lis; and over the two doorways which break the space on the western side, the Bonnacon, and part of the figure of a man drawing a bow. In the vaulting above, on either side, two musicians, and in the centre part of the Ox of St. Luke.

The East Wall. Also divided, just above the springing of the vault, into an upper and a lower area; the subject above mainly defaced, in the centre being part of a standing figure, originally tall, and on the right a youth with hair curled at the level of the ears and hood thrown back, in a gipon covered by a calf-length cote-hardie having elbow-length sleeves ending in a flap, who raises the right hand and holds in the left a pair of gloves; at his heels is a small dog. Immediately below the painting just described, over the fireplace, a Wheel of Lust or the Five Senses, with a crowned figure in tunic and mantle at its centre, from which radiate five spokes; at their ends, about the rim of the Wheel symbolizing the Senses, are the Monkey for Taste, the Vulture for Smell, the Spider for Touch, the Boar for Hearing, and the Cock for Sight. Arranged in an outer circle about these creatures, smaller ones, mainly defaced, a squirrel, near the upper part of the Wheel, to the left, and two small long-tailed animals, on the right, being decipherable. On the vaulting above two musicians, the one on the right holding a portative organ; but the remainder of the painting in this position is defaced. Within the door recess, two Apostles, on the north side, and below them, within a subsidiary recess, a bearded figure, not nimbed, holding a scroll in the left hand and pointing to it with the right, as though teaching a group of three youths who stand before him; the letters surviving on the scroll are E, N or M, T, U and perhaps V. On the space over the door the painting is much defaced, but the upper part of the figure of a king survives from a *Trois Vifs et Trois Morts* which continues over the south side of the door recess with the third king, in red cloak and diapered tunic, who raises the left hand with index finger pointing towards the three Corpses, the first two draped in their shrouds, with hands crossed on their breasts; the third nude, with right hand raised to the breast and the left arm pendant. In the lower tier of painting, below the Corpses, a peacock, somewhat defaced.

The West Wall. A wall differing structurally from the others, in that it is mainly occupied by a wide, pointed recess of some depth, within which, on the right, is a small lancet window. Around the arch of the recess, the Labours of the Months, the first, January, at the springing on the left side, represented by a man seated on a stool, warming himself before a fire and holding a bowl; then February, too fragmentary for description, apart from the fact that the figure was evidently a standing one; March, a man digging; April, with another fragmentary standing figure; and, after a considerable space now without survivals, near the springing of the arch on the right side; December, a man killing a pig, mainly defaced. Below these subjects, on the wall at either side of the recess, on the left delicate scroll-work, with a bird, and on the right, a large bittern, with a curlew below it. On the southern splay of the recess, a shield, with a pig-like animal over it; on the southern splay of the lancet window, St. Paul with the Sword; and on the northern splay of the recess, which extends from the northern splay of the same window, St. Peter with the Keys, and St. Andrew, with titular cross. Within a small recess below the latter Saint, a female figure with veil and wimple seated in a chair, behind which are traces of one standing, the former holding a scroll (with the surviving letters of an inscription vs asovdra . . . del . . .) in the left hand and pointing with the right towards a child. On the wall-space within the main recess, divided, as elsewhere, at the level of the springing of the arch (in this case by a border with a plover or hoopoe, a pigeon and an owl painted upon it, among floral forms) are two scenes. That above the border shows, on the left, a barefoot figure, perhaps nimbed, clad in a hooded cloak and a tunic, with a staff resting between the arms, which are raised before him with hands placed palm to palm; behind him is a 'tree' composed of scroll-work, with five or six birds in the branches, and at the base two rabbits, that on the left apparently about to enter its burrow, the other, on the right, facing the opposite way towards the standing figure and raised on the hind legs. In the sky above, within the apex of the arch, traces of painting, now indecipherable, and opposite the standing figure a seated figure, shod and clad in hood and tunic, who, with hammer held in the right hand, is making something, perhaps a receptacle, from fenland withies. Behind him is a second figure, standing and holding in the right hand an indecipherable pendant object; like the other, he is shod, and clad in a long tunic and hood. On the lower part of the wall, two seated male figures of approximately life-size, of which only the setting-out lines survive, with a tree between them; that on the left, who is bearded and wears a wide, soft cap, cloak and tunic, holds the right hand up—raised toward the left hand of the other, clad in mantle and tunic, as though in discussion with him. The decorated border, mentioned above, as dividing the upper part of the wall-space from the lower, extends around this subject at the sides, but is here much defaced. On the vaulting, traces of two musicians, one of them with bag-pipes, and of one of the Signs of the Evangelists, too defaced for identification. On the chamfers of the vaulting ribs, in all four bays, traces of red and of white.

The series of Apostles, each of them, with the exception of St. Paul, carrying a scroll inscribed with one of the Articles of the Apostles' Creed, begins on the south splay of the lancet window within the recess in the west wall with St. Paul and continues with St. Peter, opposite him, the inscription (defaced) on whose scroll would have read CREDO IN DEUM PATREM OMNIPOTEN-TEM CREATOREM CAELI ET TERRAE; St. Andrew, formerly with the inscription ET IN JESVM CHRISTVM FILIVM EJVS VNICVM; DOMINVM NOSTRVM; then, on the north wall, left side, St. James the Great, with scrip and bour-don, and a scroll inscribed QVI CONCEPTVS EST DE [1] *SPIRITV SANCTO*, NATVS EX MARIA VIRGINE; (?) St. John, with the inscrip-tion PASSVS SVB PONTIO *PILATO*, CRVCI-FIXVS, MORTVVS ET SEPVLTVS; on the west splay of the window in the same wall, St. Philip, with the inscription *DESCENDIT* AD INFEROS, TERTIA DIE RESVRREXIT A MORTVIS, etc.; on the opposite splay, St. Bartholomew, with the inscription CREDO IN *SPIRITVM SANCTVM* (perhaps originally preceded by INDE VENTVRVS EST, etc.); on the north wall, right side, (?) St. Matthew, young and beardless, with curls around his forehead, with the inscription SANCTAM ECCLESI*AM CATHOLICAM, SANCTORVM COMMVNIONEM*; St. Simon, with the inscrip-tion REMISSIONEM PECCATORVM; and with-in the door recess in the east wall, opposite the *Trois Morts*, two more Apostles, presumably St. Matthias and St. Jude, with scrolls originally bearing the inscriptions CARNIS RESVRRECTIONEM and ET VITAM ETERNAM. All the Apostles are depicted as bearded, with the exception of that appar-ently intended for St. Matthew, or perhaps St. John, on the north wall immediately adjacent to the eastern splay of the window recess.

Rouse, *Country Life*, IV, iv, 1947, 604–8, reprs.; id., *Illustrated London News*, v, xi, 1949, reprs.
Plates 41*a*, *b*, 64*b*.

LUDDESDOWN COURT (near Rochester) Kent

In the Great Hall of this ancient house, dating from *c.* 1100, is a painting of a ship, thought to be of a date *c.* 1320.

Peake, *Luddesdown, the Story of a Kentish Manor*, 1920.

LUTTERWORTH (near Rugby) Leics

The South Aisle

On the south wall, a group of the Kings, from a rendering of *Les Trois Vifs et les Trois Morts*, was discovered *c.* 1867; it presented the features usual in a painting of this subject of *c.* mid-fourteenth-century date, but though described at the time in some detail, was misunderstood and identified as 'portraits of two kings and a queen'. The colours included bright red and green. At a later time it was extensively retouched.

Formerly, scroll patterns and chevron patterns were visible on the pillars and arches of the church.

A.A.S.R. & P., 1867–8, IX, 253; *Leics A. & A.S.T.*, 1874, III, 361; ibid, 1882, V, 293; Keyser, *Mural Decorations*, 1883; *B.A.A.J.*, 1900, VII, 210; *Leics A. & A.S.T.*, 1926–7, XXXVIII, xlvi; Carleton Williams, *B.A.A.J.*, 1942, 3rd ser., VII, 35, 39.

MALMESBURY, Wilts
ABBEY CHURCH OF ST. MARY AND ST. ALDHELM

The Nave

On a pier in the north arcade, and also on the corresponding pier in the south arcade, stencilled patterns which appear to have been experiments or first trials, comprising: (1) a circle framing a cross fleury in pink, the whole within a square repeated; a fret pattern in pale blue having in the centres con-ventional leafage in red; a semicircle framing a trefoil leaf, in pale blue and purple.

On the bosses in the vaulting, which are exception-ally fine examples of West of England sculpture, considerable traces of the original colour decoration, the colours which remain brilliant, comprising ver-milion, lake, red lead, yellow ochre, azure and a copper green; the colour treatment of each boss being as varied one from the other as the carving, the grounds sometimes blue and sometimes a bright red, the ornaments and leaves either gilt or else picked out in red, green and yellow; heads painted in a lifelike manner in naturalistic tints, the eyes painted in and the features forced by the use of dark line; drapery, in the comparatively few cases where figures are carved, brightly coloured and enriched with delicately-executed patterns; the dominant colour, a

---

[1] Letters in italics survive, wholly or in part.

bright scarlet vermilion, used to define the contours of the bosses against the contiguous parts of the vaulting ribs, which also retain traces of colour of a comparatively subdued type, consisting primarily of yellow ochre, in the hollow mouldings; capitals at the sides of the windows treated in the same way as the bosses in the vaulting.

MARTIN (near Fordingbridge) Hants
ALL SAINTS

In the south transept are two windows of the mid-fourteenth-century, the splays of the eastern one bearing remains of painting; viz. on the northern side, part of an inscription evidently embodying the Angelic Salutation, since the remaining letters read .ACIA PLENA, and on the opposite side a small figure kneeling in supplication and holding a scroll inscribed O BEATA MAR . . . M(ISERERE MEI).

Victoria County Hist., Hants & I.O.W., 1911, IV, 593.

MARTLEY - WITH - HILLHAMPTON (near Worcester), Worcs
ST. PETER

The Chancel

On the east wall, on either side of the east window, a painted curtain, having framed within its loops small animals, a fox, a dragon, a winged monster, a rabbit, a wolf and a hart; above the curtain, a border of lozenge design, partly in green; and around the entire east window, chevron ornament in black and white.

On the south wall, above a doorway, an Annunciation, with small kneeling figures below.

On the eastern splay of the south-east window, remains of a figure; and around the window-head and the western splay, the quartered arms of Mortimer, le Despenser, Clare and Cornwall. All *c.* 1340.

The Nave

On the north wall, remains of a large painting, ? St. Martin of Tours, with a small subject, unidentified, above its eastern end; and a fragmentary Adoration of the Magi. *c.* 1300.

Victoria County Hist., Worcs, 1924, IV, 295.

MELBOURNE (near Derby) Derbyshire
ST. MICHAEL

On the western face of the north-western pier of the tower, a large figure of a horned Devil with outspread wings, holding a scroll with an inscription now illegible but recorded as IC EST CELIA DEABOL . . .; kneeling in front of him, and holding between them

a round object, two women in fourteenth-century costume, each with a smaller devil on her back, that on the left head downwards and apparently with a trumpet-like object in its mouth; immediately below the round object just referred to, a very small demon.

On the opposite pier, formerly, traces of a Passion series, including remains of a Crucifixion and a Flagellation which, to judge from accounts made before its total destruction, was probably of the same date as the work just described.

Deans, *The Reliquary*, 1860, I, 31–3, repr.; id., *B.A.A.J.*, 1860, XVI, 286–7, repr.; Keyser, *Mural Decorations*, 1883.

LITTLE MELTON (near Great Melton), Norfolk
ST. MARY AND ALL SAINTS

The Chancel

Extending over the wall on both sides of the east window, an Annunciation; to the north the Angel Gabriel, clad in a black cloak and a yellow tunic, the wings executed in black, white and red, a scroll held in the left hand and the right extended with the index finger pointing; to the south, the Virgin, with long yellow hair, in a white cloak over a black tunic; above her and to the right, traces of the Dove, and below a pot of flowers.

The Nave

Over the door at the western end of the north wall and facing the south door, a St. Christopher, the lower part only surviving; it is evident that the staff was originally held in the right hand, and it may be seen that the cote-hardie is pink and the breeches are tied below the knee.

Near an arch of the arcade, a painting of two women, each veiled and clad in a kirtle fastened down the front by large buttons, seated side by side on a bench, their heads together and their attitudes suggestive of intimate conversation. Each holds a rosary in her right hand and extends it towards the other figure, and each raises her left arm to her breast. On either side are traces of devils, the horns, tail and hoofs of the one who stands on the end of the bench to the spectator's right being clearly visible. Traces of painting immediately above the group may be remains of a large devil with arms extended to embrace it, as at Crostwight and Seething in the same county.

In the Lady Chapel, on the north side of the nave, the east wall and the adjacent part of the north wall retain traces of a wall-hanging in red with a border approximately 6 in. in width executed in pink, bordered by half-inch bands of grey, and patterned with scroll-work in dark red elaborated with large sexfoil flowers in grey.

From notes supplied by Mrs. M. Bardswell.

MEONSTOKE (near Bishop's Waltham) Hants
ST. ANDREW

In the chancel, between two windows, at a height of 8 ft. from the present floor level, a large consecration cross within a cusped border, the cusps terminating in trefoils.

Cox and Jowitt, *Little Guides, Hants*, 1949, 114.

MILTON REGIS (near Sittingbourne), Kent
HOLY TRINITY

In a chapel to the north of the chancel, on the east wall, immediately above the site of the original altar, below the base of the east window, is a Crucifixion, with the Virgin and St. John on either side of the cross, and, also on either side, traces of two other figures, now too indistinct for identification.

To the south of the east window is a tall figure of a bearded man, clad in a mantle and wearing long shoes: he raises his right hand, and around his head is a scroll with an indecipherable inscription. At his feet is a bird and a small male figure.

Traces of painting exist in other parts of the chapel.

Beneath the floor fragments of plaster have been found, bearing fragments of painting, very delicately executed in gold and bright colours. All *c.* 1390.

Nave, south aisle. On the south wall is a large St. Christopher, mutilated in part by a later monument. The head is of a fine type, and the orb borne by the Holy Child is unusually large, with a wavy line upon it executed in blue and representing water; otherwise the painting presents no features which distinguish it from renderings of the subject normal for its date, *c.* 1390. To the right are remains of an inscribed scroll, to the left buildings; but the latter probably once formed part of another subject, since destroyed.

On the jamb of the chancel arch is a scroll with bunches of grapes upon it, executed in red: *c.* 1400.

There are many slight traces of painting throughout the church.

Salmon, *A.J.*, 1936, XLI, 107.

LITTLE MISSENDEN (near Great Missenden) Bucks
ST. JOHN THE BAPTIST

The Nave

Above the chancel arch, traces of a Last Judge-

ment, of *c.* 1400; in the centre, fragments of a figure of Christ, and of an Angel on His right; to the north, of two figures, one having a nimbus bordered with a pattern composed of half-circles; and to the south, of small figures in the Jaws of Hell.

The North Chapel

At the back of an arched tomb recess at the western end of the north wall, a Christ in Judgement, seated on a wide throne, its front pierced with narrow round-headed windows in black on a white ground; the nimbus is scarlet, with a white cross, and the mantle red, so arranged as to show the wound in the side, and fastened at the neck with a red morse. The hands are raised to display the wounds. On either side is an Angel, in alb and orange-pink mantle, genuflecting and swinging a censer, and with wings outspread. The general background to the composition is greenish-blue, and a horizontal band terminates it at the base, with traces of colour below. The arch mouldings are picked out in red and yellow ochre.

Tristram, *Records of Bucks*, 1932, XII, 313–14; Rouse, ibid, 318; Skilbeck, *Ant. J.*, 1932, 3rd ser., XII, 305–6.

MOULTON (near Acle) Norfolk ST. MARY
The Nave

South wall, just below the wall-plate, a band of painting about 5–6 ft. in depth, comprising several scenes representative of the Corporal Works of Mercy, with a figure of Christ towards the centre; each scene framed within a bay of a painted arcade having canopies drawn in perspective and supported by slender shafts. The backgrounds are of black and red alternately, except for the two westernmost, which are both red. Reading from the east, the subjects are as follows:

1. Cut into by the insertion of a window, and the eastern side destroyed. Receiving the Stranger or Feeding the Hungry—on the right a female figure in white kirtle with folds drawn in red outline, extending the right arm; in the centre of the composition, and above her head, a wide scroll with traces of an inscription, and on the black ground remains of stars in white.

2. Feeding the Hungry or Giving Drink to the Thirsty—on the left, a pilgrim with a long beard, clad in a calf-length garment, apparently of sheepskin, who has the scrip at the waist and bourdon in the left hand. He extends the right hand to receive a bowl held out to him by a veiled woman clad in a white cote-hardie patterned with stars in black and with folds drawn in red, its sleeves having long

tippets; the kirtle is black, and the cuffs of the sleeves extend to the knuckles. From the left hand hangs an inscribed scroll, and another stretches across the top of the scene.

3. Clothing the Naked—on the left, a man with short, forked beard, bare-footed and nude to the waist, where his breeches are supported by a waist-string; with the bourdon resting against the right arm, he extends both arms to receive a voluminous white garment, lined with red and spotted in black, from a woman in widow's head-dress with barbe, the latter grey spotted in black, and a red kirtle spotted in black. On the black background are stars in white.

At this point a window breaks the sequence, and two, or perhaps even three scenes, are destroyed. Extending from the western side of the window and over the south door, five scenes survive, though much defaced:

1. Two figures facing each other, that on the right apparently holding a book; the background black.

2. A figure of Christ, with a nimbus, blessing, surrounded by a wide scroll with traces of an inscription; the background red.

3. Defaced, apart from remains of a scroll, of the black background, and of the canopy.

4. Burying the Dead—two figures are decipherable, standing beside a bier, that on the left partially framed by an inscribed scroll, the inscription virtually destroyed; parts of a floor covered with a diamond pattern and of the red background survive.

5. Defaced, except for part of the canopy, and fragments of a figure, floor with diamond pattern, and red background.

All these paintings are of c. 1400.

North wall, between the first and second windows from the west, St. Christopher, about 12 ft. in height, against a ground of red, with traces of inscribed scrolls and a wide border in white enriched with scroll-work in red. The Saint leans upon the staff held in the right hand, and supports the Holy Child upon the extended left arm and hand; he is clad in a white cote-hardie, breeches tied at the knee, and a voluminous red mantle having a narrow border of roundels in red outline. Beside the right foot, one fish survives, and there are traces of others; the painting as a whole is much damaged. Near the lower left-hand corner, a large incised circle, perhaps all that is left of a consecration cross. Probably late fourteenth century.

James, *Suffolk and Norfolk*, 1930, 142.
Plate 29b.

MUSÉE DE CLUNY, PARIS ALTAR PANEL

Probably the reredos for a Lady altar; the frame is decorated, on its wide, flat moulding, with golden lions *passant gardant* on a red ground (the lions-leopardy of England) and between them roses in gold framed by diamond-shapes, outlined in white on a green ground. On a second and narrower flat moulding are half-circles in green and red; and the innermost, small round moulding is gilt. Reading from left to right, the subjects depicted, each surrounded by cusping represented in green and gold, are as follows:

1. The Nativity. On the left, with a striped curtain hanging behind her head from a rod, the Virgin reclines on a couch, its red drapery ornamented with star-shapes in green and vermilion; she suckles the Holy Child, and in her left hand holds a gaily-coloured bird, its beak and right wing touching the Child's outstretched left hand. Her gold nimbus is cusped and outlined in black, like the cruciform nimbus of the Child, whose hair, like hers where visible, curls around the forehead; her rose-coloured mantle, drawn over her head, is lined with vair and clasped at the neck by a brooch composed of a diamond-shaped 'print' showing addorsed doves. Below the couch the Ox and Ass are represented in natural colours beside a manger with small lancets in the sides; and at the Virgin's feet St. Joseph, with long white hair and beard, rests his head on his right hand, his right elbow and left hand being supported by a T-headed staff. His round hat is brown and its rolled-back brim vermilion; his mantle a purplish brown, lined with orange-red. On the background are squares in deep blue, each charged with a golden fleur-de-lis, in alternation with 'prints', originally gilt, but now brown, ornamented by a fleur-de-lis within a quatrefoil, the spandrels formed by the latter being filled with minute quatrefoil flowers.

2. The Dormition of the Virgin. She lies with her head upon a pillow patterned in gold, red and black, under a coverlet of red lined with green; her nimbus resembles that in the previous scene, but her hair, reddish-golden in colour, is uncovered and waved around her face. Christ, with a cruciform nimbus, stands behind the bed, His right hand outstretched in blessing and His left supporting the Soul, partially wrapped in the folds of His mantle, which is purplish in colour and lined with red, while His tunic is green. The Apostles, six of them shown in front of the bed, and six grouped at its foot, are clad in tunics and mantles, and their golden nimbi are outlined and cusped in black; St. Peter, towards the left at the base of the scene, is recognizable by his tonsure, and the

figure next to him on the right, with hair curled around the forehead and hands clasped in grief, is probably that of St. John. On either side of Christian Angel appears from clouds, with hands clasped in prayer; each is nimbed in gold, the one on the left having a red mantle and green wing-feathers, the other red feathers and a green mantle. The background is covered with 'prints', patterned by addorsed doves framed by diamond shapes set within squares, small trefoils filling the angles.

3. The Adoration of the Magi. The Virgin is seated at the left of the composition, on a throne painted in white, black and gold, with small lancets in the base; she is crowned, the crown being gilt, decorated with strawberry leaves, outlined in black and 'jewelled' in colour, and her hair is golden-red; her mantle, of a purplish-red, is lined with vair. She supports the Holy Child with her left hand, and in her right holds a golden apple, which He touches with His right hand, resting His left on coins in the golden bowl extended towards Him by the foremost of the Magi. His nimbus is cruciform, His hair curled closely around the forehead, and His tunic purplish-brown in colour. The first King, whose hair and beard are long and white, kneels, his crown on the ground before him, holding the lid of the bowl just mentioned in his left hand; his tunic is red and his mantle blue-green. The second, clad in a mantle of yellowish-green, lined with vair, and a red tunic, stands behind the first, the upper half only of his figure being visible; he raises his right hand in a pointing gesture, as though indicating the Star, which, however, is not shown, its place being taken by a fleur-de-lis on the background; and in his left he bears a covered cup of gold. Behind him the third King, in purplish-brown mantle, lined with vair, and purplish-red tunic, approaches with right hand raised palm outward, and in his left holds a cup like that borne by his predecessor; both are crowned, the crowns being decorated with strawberry leaves, gilt, and 'jewelled' in colours. The background is like that in the Nativity scene.

4. St. Anne Teaching the Virgin. On the right of the composition, St. Anne, a tall figure in white veil and wimple, dark green mantle lined with vair, and tunic of olive green, bends forward, touching with her left hand the slight, standing figure of the Virgin, over whose right shoulder she points to the inscription (from Psalm XLIV, 10, Vulgate, *Audi filia et vide, et inclina aurem tuam*, etc.,) on the open pages of a book laid on a reading desk, the latter being painted in grey, gold and green. The Virgin bends her head and lays her hands upon the volume, with the index finger of the left pointing to the left page; her long, red-gold hair is bound by a fillet decorated with small roses; and her sleeveless surcoat is purplish red and her kirtle green. The background is ornamented with squares painted red and charged each with a golden lion-leopardy, in alternation with others filled with 'prints', identical with those on the 'dormition' scene.

Clemen, *Repertorium fur Kunstwissenschaft*, 1911, XXXIV, 62 et sqq.; Storck, *Monatshefte fur Kunst-wissenschaft*, 1911, IV, 125, n. 3; Borenius and Tristram, *Eng. Med. Painting*, 1927, 19-20, repr.; Evans, *English Art, 1307–1461*, 1949, 48, repr.

NASSINGTON (near Oundle) Northants
ST. MARY AND ALL SAINTS

The Nave

On the north wall, in the spandrel between the second and third arches of the arcade from the west, St. Martin dividing his cloak with the beggar; the Saint, depicted on horseback, in the centre of the spandrel, rides eastward, but turns back, holding his fur-lined cloak extended towards the beggar, who grasps it with his left hand and holds a staff in his right. The head of each figure is missing and the entire subject much defaced. *c.* 1400.

The North Aisle

On the western splay of the third window from the west, a Saint with nimbus in red, veiled in white and clad in a white tunic and red cloak, the latter swathed about the figure and falling in folds on either side.

Between the fourth and fifth windows from the west, paintings in two tiers, as follows:

The higher tier. Remains of a Wheel? of the Works of Mercy, a figure in red kirtle or tunic with tippets pendent on either side, standing behind the hub. The rim of the Wheel is clearly seen to the right; and there are apparently two arms holding it, those of a figure now entirely defaced. Traces of painting in black on the opposite side and slightly below the centre of the subject appear to have belonged to superimposed work, now almost entirely destroyed.

The lower tier. St. Michael Weighing Souls: to the west of the scene, the Archangel, with a red nimbus, in red cloak lined with white and draped in voluminous folds, stands with a pronounced sway, holding the balance beam, weighed down by the rosary of the Virgin, who faces him, her right hand raised with index finger pointing upward to the Wheel. She is clad in a dark red mantle and tunic of light red, but the upper part of her figure is mainly defaced. Low in the centre of the scene, between the main figures, is a small, kneeling donor, bearded and with hair cut to the level of the ears; he is clad in a yellow cloak and a white tunic, and his hands, raised towards the Virgin, are clasped in prayer. On the western side of St. Michael are traces of a small devil, painted in red, and ? fragments of others.

On the western splay of the fifth window from the west, a Saint, with yellow nimbus, but otherwise depicted like the figure on the splay of the first window mentioned above; and on the opposite splay, the lower part only of another figure.

On each splay of the next window, a figure similar to those previously described; so far as can be ascertained, all the figures seem to have been those of female Saints, but no attributes have survived from which they may be identified.

On the north side of the east window, a figure under a pointed canopy, in red cloak and white tunic, standing with a pronounced sway. All *c*. 1350.

Victoria County Hist., *Northants*, 1906, II, 590.

NEWINGTON (near Sittingbourne), Kent
ST. MARY
North Aisle
Flanking the site of an altar which formerly stood at the eastern end of the aisle are painted hangings ornamented with large chevrons in red and white. The upper part of the wall is occupied by a representation of the Last Judgement, divided into two zones by a band of clouds. In the centre of the upper zone Christ is enthroned, displaying His wounds, with the Virgin and St. John kneeling on either side in intercession, and two Angels, vested in albs ornamented with bands placed horizontally, bearing the Emblems of the Passion, the Spear, Cross, Nails and Scourge. To the extreme right St. Peter, at the Gate of Heaven, receives the Souls of the Blessed, who rise with outstretched hands from the clouds below. In the lower zone are two Angels, one blowing the Last Trump, with Souls of the Blessed to the left, and to the right a small demon, a Lost Soul, and some traces of the Jaws of Hell.

The western wall seems to have been covered originally with a large scroll pattern with leafage resembling that of the ash, which spreads also over the north wall, extending to a height of about seven feet from the floor. On the jambs of a door in the north wall is a similar pattern, but here ivy leaves are depicted. At the extreme western end, above the scroll-pattern, are remains of a Nativity, the head and part of the figure of the Virgin surviving, and also St. Joseph, with one hand resting on his staff

and the other pressed against his forehead. Above the door is a bare foot, and some lines representing water. Between the second and third windows from the west, on the upper part of the wall, are clouds and a large star; and another large star in a corresponding space further to the east.

On the splays of the three windows in this wall are figures of Saints, painted on a large scale. Reading from the west, they are as follows:

1. St. Andrew, bearded, holding a small saltire, and clad in a tunic ornamented with a fret pattern.
2. An indistinguishable figure on the opposite splay.
3. Slight traces only.
4. St. John the Evangelist, a youthful figure, bearing a book and a palm branch; this painting is well preserved, and the folds of the drapery are rendered skilfully.
5. St. Paul, bearded, bald-headed but with long hair from the level of the ears, carrying a sword.
6. St. Peter, much defaced.

Below the window and also at the sides, are traces of a third variety of scroll pattern.

At the extreme eastern end of the wall fragments survive of a figure of St. Margaret, with the dragon below: it can be seen that her tunic is covered with a fret pattern.

On one of the piers of the arcade separating the aisle from the nave there are vestiges of bands of pink and yellow, about 18 in. in depth; and on a pier in the south arcade, of chevrons in red and white.

Keyser, *A.J.*, 1881, XXXVIII, 85, 87; Keyser, *Mural Decorations*, 1883; Grayling, *County Churches*, 1913, 54; Wall, *Medieval Wall Paintings*, 1914, 211 and fig. 68.

SOUTH NEWINGTON (near Deddington) Oxon
ST. PETER AD VINCULA, or ST. MARY AND ST. PETER
The Nave
A scheme of painting, executed *c*. 1330–40, embraces the wall above the chancel arch, the eastern end of the north wall of the nave, and the eastern end of the wall above the arcade in the north aisle. Partially uncovered in 1897, and somewhat unskilfully repaired in parts, it was completely freed of whitewash and carefully treated in 1931.

Above the chancel arch are remains of a Doom, including traces of a Christ in Judgement supported by Angels, a General Resurrection with Souls rising from their graves, St. Michael Weighing Souls, and the Torments of the Damned, all occupying the customary places in the composition; to the north side of the arch is the lower part of a St. John Baptist, and, below this, a painted niche with traces of what may have been a Virgin and Child; and on the upper part of the wall, adjacent to the arch, are remains of two unidentifiable figures, and of two shields, one charged with three cups or chalices, the other apparently with a chevron. All these works are much damaged by the hacking of the surface carried out at some later time preparatory to the application of another layer of plaster.

The North Aisle

On the southern splay of the window in the east wall, is a figure of St. Margaret, in a good state of preservation. The Saint is tall, and stands gracefully upon a painted corbel composed of two large green leaves, with a heater-shaped shield between them, charged with—*Gules, three lions passant argent*, for Gifford. She is crowned, wears a green mantle edged with vermilion, and holds a book in her left hand and in her right a spear with which she impales the Dragon, supine beneath her feet.

At the eastern end of the north wall is a Virgin and Child, framed within a painted niche and supported by a corbel and shield arranged like those seen in the St. Margaret subject, and set against a background of pale pink enriched by delicately executed foliated scroll-work in red, the main stem being painted in double lines. Masonry joints are depicted on the supporting shafts of the niche, together with single-light windows in alternation with quatrefoils, all executed in black upon a white ground; the capitals are foliated, and surmounted by pinnacles, and the arch decorated with crockets, outlined in black, and with cusping in red and white. Above the niche are remains of a background of dark red, together with the lower parts of two shields with similar charges to that seen below the St. Margaret. The Virgin, crowned, with long golden hair and a nimbus of dark red, stands in a swaying pose, facing westward bearing the Divine Child on her right arm, and in her left hand a green rod terminating in a fleur-de-lis, and further ornamented with another on the shaft just above the point where it is held in the hand. She is clad in a pink tunic having the folds delineated in red, and edged around the neck by a line of spots in white, and a mantle of light green, drawn across the body and falling in elaborately-designed folds on either side, the folds being shaded in a darker green and defined by means of black line. The Child, whose nimbus is painted dark red and charged with a cross in yellow, is clad in a tunic of a yellowish-pink colour; He holds a red apple in the right hand and with the left touches the neck of His mother in a gesture as of tender affection. To the

west of the niche kneel two supplicating donors, one being placed on the wall above the other; the higher of the two is a man with hair curled at the neck and a short beard, clad in a long tunic of red adorned with vertical stripes in green, having a hood of the same colour decorated with the same design, but with a lining of green, and black shoes. About his waist is a black belt patterned with white stars, to which is secured a black purse with its lock prominently displayed, and a dagger thrust through the attaching thongs. The lower figure is that of a woman, wearing a veil and wimple, a red kirtle, and a mantle of an intense dark green, edged with red. The background to both figures is dark red, enriched with a scroll pattern in a lighter tint of the same colour. Below the paintings is a horizontal border ornamented by a bent-riband pattern having constellations of white spots in the triangular interspaces, and below this again vertical stripes in red and white, which are the remains of decoration originally covering the remaining wall-space to floor level.

Further to the west in the same wall is a window, on the eastern splay of which two subjects survive, namely an Annunciation, and St. James the Great. The former is placed at the higher level. In it the Angel Gabriel is seen on the spectator's left, clad in a pale pink tunic with folds drawn in red, and a mantle of very rich, dark green, edged with red and outlined in black. The wing feathers are painted in red, yellow and green, the nimbus is red, the curling yellow hair is bound with a fillet ornamented by red roses set at intervals, and the features are delicate in type, a round red spot appearing at the centre of the cheek. In the left hand is a scroll, originally inscribed with the Angelic Salutation, some letters now being defaced, and the right is raised in an expressive gesture, towards the Virgin, who stands with head bent, her right hand raised in assent and in her left a book. She is clad in a cream-coloured tunic, the folds drawn in red, a dark green under-tunic, visible only on the upper part of the figure, and a red mantle edged with white and outlined in black, draped in voluminous folds. The top of the head and of the nimbus are defaced. Between the two figures is a pot with narrow ornamental bands about its centre and foot, from which springs a plant bearing flowers of tulip shape, the whole supported upon a shield charged with—*Ermine, a chief dancetty gules*, for Mortayne. The background is painted a light red and enriched with foliated scroll-work in a darker red, and at the base the composition is terminated by a wavy border in green and white. The Annunciation has been deliberately defaced at some time.

In the second subject, St. James the Great is shown on the left of the composition, standing, unshod, on green, uneven ground, carrying a large scallop shell in his left hand and in his right a pilgrim's staff. He has a red nimbus, long hair, a beard, and a black pilgrim's hat patterned with a band of white rings about the crown; his tunic is white, and his mantle red, edged with white and lined with green. At his feet a donor kneels in supplication, with a shield above him similar to that seen in the Annunciation above. His beard is short, his hair curled at the neck, and he is clad in a white gipon and vermilion cote-hardie striped in white, each stripe having upon it a narrow line in red. The cote-hardie has sleeves with pendent flaps, and there is a hood, which falls at the back of the neck. The background is like that in the Annunciation.

On the opposite splay of the window some traces of colour alone remain to suggest that there was formerly painting in this position also. Beyond, and for some distance to the west, the wall is bare of traces, but approximately half-way towards its juncture with the west wall two Martyrdoms are to be seen, to the east the Murder of St. Thomas of Canterbury, to the west the Beheading of Blessed Thomas of Lancaster. The upper part of the former subject is defaced, but it is otherwise in reasonably good preservation. St. Thomas is depicted to the spectator's right, facing eastward as he kneels before an altar, clad in mass vestments, which in parts are elaborately patterned, his hands raised in prayer and his mitre falling to the floor. The altar, draped with hangings richly decorated in bright colours, has a chalice upon it, and behind it is seen a part of the figure of the monk Grim, with a book in the left hand and the right arm outstretched. The four knights approach from the left, all wearing chain-mail, hauberks, sword-belts, decorated knee-cops and elbow-cops (or demi-brassarts and demi-vambraces), greaves or shin-guards, and sollerets, strapped over the feet. The only one with head and shoulders still partially visible, on the extreme left of the composition, has a mail-coif, a conical helm, and, around his neck, guiges from which a shield hangs at his back. He is in the act of drawing his sword; another, immediately to the east, holds his drawn, while the next in order cleaves the Saint's skull, and the fourth, the upper part of whose figure is entirely defaced, seems to have been in the act of striking the first blow which, according to the accounts, was warded off by Grim; his surcoat is charged with Gules, a bear statant proper, so that he would appear to have been intended for Reginald Fitzurse, said to have been the first of the attacking group. The head of St. Thomas, noble in character, is finely drawn, with hair of moderate length curled at the neck, short beard and moustache; blood runs in streams down his forehead, and is spattered on his neck, hands and vestments. The latter are as follows: an alb, having orphreys ornamented with quatrefoils on a green ground within a pattern of squares executed in white line; a red chasuble edged by a border composed of black and white lines, and white spots; an amice embroidered in green, with a fret pattern in white; a stole patterned with rectangles in yellow enriched with a fret pattern in black, in alternation with scroll and quatrefoil designs in blue and white; and red shoes with white straps. The mitre is red, banded at the centre and edged with white spots; and Grim has a green under-tunic and white habit. The altar drapery has a large fret pattern, the diamonds being framed by narrow bands of pink, with a white line running down the centre, and edged with black line, a small quatrefoil foliated pattern ornamenting the crossings. The diamonds themselves bear:—in the highest row, a delicate foliated pattern in white on green; in the next below, in alternation, a foliated pattern in black on yellow, or in white on red; then, fylfots, in white on green; and foliated patterns in white on green within cusped borders in white; the fifth and sixth rows being largely defaced. The superfrontal is ornamented with squares of green, yellow and red in sequence, charged respectively with fylfots in white, black, and white. The knight immediately following Fitzurse has a blue surcoat charged with a chevron in white; the next in order, one lined with green and charged (?) with a chevron gules; and the fourth, azure, several dogs' heads erased proper. The finely-drawn head of St. Thomas is painted in flesh colour, gradated, with pink on the cheeks, the features being drawn in dark red line and its general outlines in black. The drapery everywhere is either painted in a flat tone, or in one slightly shaded, the folds being boldly drawn in black line. The background is a deep red.

In the Martyrdom of Blessed Thomas of Lancaster there are two figures only, the executioner and his victim. The former is shown in a vigorously active pose, with one leg raised from the ground, about to strike, and wielding a sword of which the hilt and cross-bar only survive; the raised hand grasping it is gauntleted, the shoes are black, the hose pink, the cote-hardie red, belted at the waist and with elbow-length sleeves ending in a tongue-shaped flap. The head and left arm are missing. Blessed Thomas kneels with his back turned to the executioner; and upon his neck, below the short curled hair, are two deep, blood-bespattered gashes. The head,[1] in which use is made of a green underpainting, is, like that of St. Thomas, fine in type, with beard of moderate length; the long cloak is red, ornamented with vertical stripes in grey edged with a white line, and the shoes are elaborately patterned with a complicated fret. The arms have been destroyed. Below this painting and that of St. Thomas runs a border of bent-riband pattern in red and green, its interstices ornamented with cusping. All the paintings are carried out in oil or an emulsion of oil upon a plaster surface.

Keyser, *A.J.*, 1901, LVIII, 54; Whitehead, *Oxon A.S.*, 1907, LIII, 14–15, repr.; Borenius, *Archaeologia*, 1931, LXXXI, 30, repr.; id., *Folklore*, June 1932, 180; id., *St. Thomas Becket in Art*, 1932, 98, repr.; Tristram, *Burl. M.*, 1933, LXII, 114–29.
Plates 16*a*, *b*, 17, 18*a*, *b*, 19*a*, *b*, 20.

NEWTON (near Sudbury) Suffolk ALL SAINTS
The Nave
Formerly, on the north wall, about 6 ft. from floor level, a horizontal scroll border, and above it remains of large figures and of a Visitation, *c.* 1330; and on the south wall, traces of colour appearing from beneath lime-wash.

NORTHMOOR (near Oxford) Oxon ST. DENIS
The North Transept
In the north wall, two tomb recesses, each with an effigy at the base, that on the east of a knight bearing a shield charged with the arms of Delamore, that on the west of his wife; both retain slight, almost indistinguishable, traces of colour. Above each recess, a painting of the Soul Borne Heavenward by Angels, and about it remains of seven shields of arms, set out in incised line, one of them, at the eastern side of the easternmost recess, charged with a stag's head cabossed. To the west of this recess, part of a delicately-executed scroll border in dark red; and within it a Coronation of the Virgin, with kneeling figures at the sides, all almost defaced. Within the westernmost recess, on either side of a Virgin and Child, ? members of the Delamore family kneeling in prayer, the foremost of the best-preserved group, a woman, having hair, veil and wimple disposed after the fashion seen in the effigy below. Immediately adjacent to this recess, on the west wall, where it forms an angle with the north wall, a painting of Christ in Majesty, blessing, and bearing in the left hand a large Orb of the Universe, surmounted by the Vexillum

and with three divisions marked upon it; on either side is a censing Angel. All the paintings, with the exception of the upper part of the Majesty, are much damaged.

Keyser, *A.J.*, 1896, LIII, 181; Brabant, *Little Guides, Oxon*, 1933, 211.

NORWICH, Norfolk
CATHEDRAL CHURCH OF THE HOLY TRINITY
The Nave
On the soffit of the arch of the west door, mainly concealed by the later doorway built beneath, between bands of wavy ornament, a vine-scroll with fruit and tendrils, in ochres and green on a light ground. After 1350.

The South Aisle
Figures of Saints, of early fourteenth-century date, were discovered in the south aisle in 1862, within the arcading of the south wall; they included St. Wolstan, as a Bishop, receiving his crosier from St. Edward the Confessor, with the inscription SCS WVLSTANVS; a figure, apparently female, clad in a red garment and kneeling before ? a prie-dieu, under a vaulted roof supported by clustered columns; and a Bishop.

The Presbytery Aisle
Outside the Bauchun Chapel, on the vaulting, masonry pattern in black; bands about 6 in. in width in black, edged with narrow borders of indented pattern in black and white, on the arrises; and at the crown of the vaulting a square panel with corners terminating in small trefoils, framing a medallion surrounded by an indented border like that of the bands just described, and enclosing an *Agnus Dei* in black on a yellow ground; the spandrels formed by the circle and its enclosing square are filled with foliated ornament and trefoils. Contemporary with the scheme in the Bauchun Chapel.

The Bauchun Chapel
There are in this chapel remains of a scheme of painting executed, in all probability, soon after it was built, and carried out entirely in black, except for some yellow, sparingly used. Around a later window in the south wall is a scroll pattern enriched with five-petalled flowers and buds; and below the level of the window bottom masonry pattern of diamond form, executed in yellow line about an inch in width, with small squares in black at the intersections, each diamond having a quatrefoil in black in the centre. On the north wall, over the arch leading into the

---

[1] (1954.) The head is partially defaced, through ? the effects of damp.

aisle, fragments survive of a subject framed within a large quatrefoil, and, below this, of a masonry pattern in black line, enriched with flowers like those on the south wall. Remains of a large subject, comprising four Saints depicted under canopies, these and the heads of the figures alone surviving, are visible on the east wall. An inscription formerly existed, as follows: IN HONOREM BEATE MARIE VIRGINIS ET OMNIVM SANCTORVM WILLMVS BAVCHVN CAPELLAM HANC ORDINAVIT ET EX PROPRIIS SVMPTIBVS CONSTRVXIT.

The Ante-Reliquary Chapel

The chapel is in the form of a bridge spanning the northern ambulatory of the presbytery; the vaulting is quadripartite and square in plan, with a span of about 14 ft. The fourteenth-century scheme of painting, of *c.* 1325, includes the vaulting and the western transverse arch.

The Vaulting: at the crown is a small medallion framed by a narrow border of red, within which is depicted a figure of Christ, clad in a blue mantle, and seated on a branch of vine which, springing from the edge of the medallion, fills the background; the leaves are in white, outlined in black, against warm grey. A second medallion, about 5 ft. in diameter, surrounds the first and smaller one; it is divided into four sections by bands of red which follow the intersections of the vaulting, and each of these four sections is filled, on a ground of deep ivory colour, with interlacing vine-scrolls springing from the inner medallion, and executed in bluish-green outlined in black, every section being finished by a band of Lombardic lettering in black, giving the names of the twelve Saints depicted below, three in each division of the vaulting, against a ground of pale ivory colour enriched with beautifully-designed vine-scrolls in bluish-green. The figures in the four bays are as follows: The eastern bay: in the centre, the Virgin, crowned, in a white tunic and a blue mantle, draped about her in intricate and graceful folds, holding in the right hand an apple, towards which the Holy Child, supported on her left arm, extends His left hand, while caressing her face with the other. To the north St. Margaret, in a white tunic and mantle of emerald green, holds in her right hand a palm branch, and in her left a crossed spear, which she thrusts into the mouth of the dragon beneath her feet: above her head S: MARG . . . On the south St. Catherine in tunic and mantle of identical colours with those of St. Margaret, raises her left hand, and in her right, covered by her mantle, bears the Wheel.

The western bay: in the centre, St. Peter, vested in an alb, a green dalmatic and chasuble of the same colour, pallium, maniple and conical tiara, holding the Keys in his right hand, covered by a fold of his chasuble, and in his left a crossed staff. On the north, St. Andrew, bearded and clad in a white tunic and a green mantle lined with pink, holding the cross of his martyrdom, small in scale and painted green; and on the south, St. Paul, in a tunic of reddish brown and a green mantle, bald, but with hair from above the level of the ears, and bearded, holding the Sword in his right hand. The inscription above is indecipherable.

The southern bay: the painting is here much defaced, little surviving of the three figures beyond their mitred heads, and the tops of their crosiers, except for the right hand, raised in blessing, and the left hand, holding the crozier, of St. Richard of Chichester, on the western side, together with a foot and the lower part of his alb and chasuble. The inscription above the heads is decipherable, and reads S: MARTINVS: S:NICHS: S: RICS: CICES . . .

The northern bay: in the centre, an Archbishop, perhaps St. Thomas of Canterbury, on the west, a king, ? St. Edmund, on the east, a Deacon, probably St. Laurence or St. Stephen; the painting is much defaced and the inscription indecipherable.

The soffit of the western transverse arch: the Twelve Apostles, in pairs, between narrow chevroned borders, in black, white, pink and green, under elaborate architectural canopies, in white outlined in black, the roofs, however, being blue, supported on slender green shafts. The Apostles, barefooted, stand on grassy ground against backgrounds of pale ivory, holding, alternately, a book or a scroll; they are clad in tunics and mantles of varied colours, comprising blue, pink, purple and green.

Husenbeth, *Norfolk Archaeology*, 1864, VI, 272–6, repr.; *East Anglian N. & Q.*, 1864, I, 287–8; Keyser, *Mural Decorations*, 1883; *Victoria County Hist.*, *Norfolk*, 1906, II, 533–5, repr.; James and Bensley, *Sculptured Bosses in the Roof of the Bauchun Chapel of Our Lady of Pity*, 1908, 1–7, reprs.; Borenius and Tristram, *Eng. Med. Painting*, 1927, 16, repr.; James, *Suffolk and Norfolk*, 1930, 118; Tristram, *Friends of Norwich Cathedral, Annual Report*, 1934, 13–15, repr. Plates 11*a*, 12*a*, *b*, 29*a*.

The Cloisters

In 1937–8, during the cleaning of the vaulting and roof bosses in the cloisters, remains of colour decoration and gilding were found upon the carving.

Cranage and Tristram, *Norwich Cathedral Cloisters*, 1938, 1.

An Introduction to the Rolls of Norwich Cathedral Priory, 1930, Saunders. For notes concerning the re-decoration of the edifice after the fire of 1272, and onwards into the fourteenth century, see pp. 107, 109; for repairs of walls and 'decoration of images' in the early years of that century, p. 106; for the painting of panels, benches and tombs, and the use of gold and silver leaf, vermilion, verdigris, saffron, white lead, varnish, and stones, p. 107; for the painting of a cross in the Refectory, and for whitewashing of the Refectory, p. 143.

The Shrine of St. William

111. Roll of 1325. In C and 40 leaves of gold bought for the shrine of St. William, 6s. 8d. In CCC and ½ silver, 11d. In 12 lb. white lead, vermilion and orfainment, 2s. 2d. In oil for painting 10d. In stipend and victuals of Simon the Painter and groom for 9 weeks, 25s. 6d.

NORWICH, Norfolk ST. SAVIOUR

The Chancel

Formerly, on the east wall, two consecration crosses with these inscriptions: ET PORTA COELI; ET AVLA VOCABITVR DEI.

L'Estrange, *Norfolk Archaeology*, 1872, VII, 352; Keyser, *Mural Decorations*, 1883; Cox, *Churches of Norfolk*, 1911, 189.

NOTGROVE (near Cheltenham) Glos
ST. BARTHOLOMEW

The Chancel

On the windowless east wall, an elaborate scheme of painting was discovered *c.* 1872; immediately above the level of the altar a series of Passion subjects, executed in red line, and seven in number, stretched from end to end of the wall, the central one being a Crucifixion and that on the extreme left a St. Mary Magdalen washing the Feet of Christ, but the others were indecipherable. It is recorded that the scenes were divided by bands composed of a broad line in vermilion between two narrower bands in dark red, that the hair of the figures was yellow, and some of the nimbi dark in colour. Above these paintings were three niches, with cusped ogee heads, surmounted by large finials, all cut off flush with the wall-surface, that on the left retaining traces of colour on the remaining mouldings; within it, on the wall at the back, was painted a *Manus Dei* issuing from clouds, above the former site of carved figures of ? the Angel Gabriel, to the left, and ? the Virgin, to the right, the background being diapered with flowers. The corresponding niche on the right framed a 'brightly gilt star' and a hand pointing to it, against a dark green ground enriched with 'an elegant flowing pattern' in white, the surviving fragments of a Nativity or Epiphany (the carved figures missing), but probably of the former. The central niche had once held a third sculptured group, apparently of the Coronation of the Virgin, on a projecting base. On the upper part of the wall, between the finials at the heads of the niches, were painted trefoil-headed arches, two on either side of the central finial, and one to the north and south of the remaining two finials, and within them were figures of six Saints, drawn in strong red outline and having dark nimbi and yellow hair; between the heads of the arches painted quatrefoils were placed, and just above them, immediately below the wall-plate were battlements 'painted in rough perspective'.

The south wall was covered with a masonry pattern in single line enriched with flowers; and on the upper part of a splay of the easternmost window, was a male figure. Foliated scroll-work was visible between this window and the angle of the wall.

On the north wall a masonry pattern reproduced exactly that on the south wall, and a blocked niche, similar to those in the east wall, when opened up, was found to have had the surface at the back coloured red and patterned with two different designs, one executed in red, the other in black; there was also evidence to show that the mouldings of the niche itself had been coloured. The statue originally standing in this niche had been made use of as part of the blocking. Late fourteenth century.

The Nave

On the face of the inner order of the arcade, fragments of scroll-work, masonry pattern on the soffits, and on the label a spot design, probably contemporary with the painted decoration in the chancel but perhaps earlier.

The Church Builder, 1872, 151; *Glos. N. & Q.*, 1879–81, I, 367–9; Keyser, *Mural Decorations*, 1883; Bird, *Mural Paintings, Glos.*, 1927, 24, repr.

OAKSEY (near Cirencester), Wilts ALL SAINTS

Traces of a fourteenth-century painted scheme of purely ornamental character survive, as follows: near the chancel arch, high upon the wall, indecipherable traces; in the north aisle, on the north wall, scroll pattern; in the south aisle, on the west wall and on the window-splays, masonry pattern elaborated with scroll-work and cinquefoil flowers, the latter in black, and on the south wall a rich vine-scroll; all *c.* 1300.

Goddard, *Wilts A. & N.H.M.*, 1935–7, XLVII, 632–6.

OAKWOOD (near Dorking) Surrey
ST. JOHN BAPTIST

The Nave

Formerly, on the splays and jambs of all the windows, scroll patterns and other ornamental designs, some of them of fourteenth-century date.

On the north wall, two large figures (both destroyed); and towards the eastern end of the south wall, a Visitation.

A.J., 1883, XL, 239; Keyser, *Mural Decorations*, 1883; André, *Surrey Archaeological Collections*, 1900, XV, 14; Johnston, *Memorials of Old Surrey*, 1911, 169 n.

OCKHAM (near Guildford) Surrey ALL SAINTS

The Nave

Over and around the chancel arch a scroll pattern on a ground of dark red, the stem being yellow, the leaves dark green, and the daisy-like flowers white, with blue centres. North of the arch, an image bracket, retaining traces of blue, green and red.

South of the doorway, a line of trefoil arches, depicted as resting on shafts with rudimentary capitals, the shafts being disproportionately short and without bases, executed in red. *c.* 1300.

Keyser, *Mural Decorations*, 1883; Bloxham, *Surrey Archaeological Collections*, 1937, XLV, 16, 17, 40-1, repr.

ORLETON (near Ludlow) Hereford ST. GEORGE

On the west wall, an Annunciation to the Shepherds, and a decorative pattern.

Keyser, *Mural Decorations*, 1883.

OXFORD CHRIST CHURCH CATHEDRAL

The South Choir Aisle

Early in the fourteenth century changes were made at the eastern end of the south choir aisle, a large window being inserted and the adjacent division of the Norman vaulting divided into four sections by ribs carved with leaves and ball-flower. In each of the divisions an Angel with upraised wings was depicted, mainly in red outline; the two westernmost are shown dancing, and below one of them, that on the north side, a musician is playing a stringed instrument. The figures in the eastern divisions are larger than the others, and stand motionless with arms upraised; their mantles are drawn in red outline, but their tunics are painted in solid black. Both, in contrast with those previously described, which are well-preserved, are somewhat defaced, and below each

are remains of a medallion framed by concentric bands of black, white and red, enclosing shields, the charges defaced, upon a ground of black. The hair, in all cases, is yellow, as is also the instrument borne by the musician.

On one of the choir piers in the same aisle traces exist of a figure in a swaying pose similar to that of the dancing Angels; but only the general mass is now discernible. It probably once formed part of the same scheme of decoration, executed *c.* 1325.[1]

The Lady Chapel

Fragments of colour remain as indications that all three bays of the chapel were painted, probably as part of a scheme undertaken when the tomb of Lady Montacute was erected after her death in 1353; but in the central bay alone there are considerable remains. Here the intersections of the vaulting are defined by parallel bands of yellow, red and black, and the ribs and arch mouldings in red, black and pale blue, and both capitals and shafts have remains of colour. In the vaulting itself, against a ground of light blue, censing Angels are depicted, placed as if radiating from the centre, each swinging a censer, with one wing outstretched and the other lowered, there being eight figures in all, now much defaced. It may be seen, however, that all stand upon clouds, have golden hair and a circlet of gold about the head, a rayed nimbus, and wings of a deep orange colour, some ranges of the feathers being painted in pale blue, and wear albs shaded in pale blue and orphreyed with embroidery in gold and red.

The Tomb of Elizabeth Lady Montacute

Both the carving and colour decoration of this tomb are well-preserved. The effigy is clad in a kirtle, ornamented by a square pattern with small circles at the angles, the squares framing much smaller squares enclosing quatrefoil flowers and having foliation at the angles, the whole executed mainly in green; a 'sideless' gown, having a broad white edging and diapered with leopards' masks in gold interspersed between foliage and flowers in green on a ground of bright red; a mantle clasped at the neck with a brooch of gold and patterned in relief with fleurs-de-lis which were originally gilt; and black shoes. The dog at the feet is painted brown. On the head and hands traces of flesh-colour remain; and the former rests on two cushions, supported by two Angels in white albs, one cushion being ornamented with foliated pattern in red and the other painted brown and decorated in white. At the sides of the tomb are carved figures of Lady Montacute's ten children,

---

[1] These figures are now almost concealed by dirt (1954); see Preface.

against backgrounds alternately red and green, all being realistically painted in bright colours with patterned borders to the drapery. Set in the tracery between the panelling of the sides, which is all richly coloured and gilt, are coats of arms, minutely patterned in certain parts, of which one bears—*Argent three lozenges in fesse gules*, for Montacute, and another *Azure four bendlets argent*, for Montfort. In the panels at the head and foot of the tomb are carvings of the Virgin and Child, of Symbols of the Evangelists, and of a Saint, all coloured and gilt. The colours used on the structure generally cover a wide range, and include vermilion, red lead, lake, a bright green, a deep blue, purple, black and white. There is evidence to show that 'prints' in the form of gold rosettes diapered the backgrounds in places, but few of them have survived.

The Sutton Tomb (1316)

This tomb retains some traces of painting, from which it may be seen that the vestments were once bordered with elaborate patterns, and also treated with ornaments in relief ('prints').

Hollis, *Monumental Effigies*, 1840, pt. 2, pl. 5, pt. 3, pls. 5 & 6; Bloxom, *Gent. M.*, 1850, N.S., pt. 2, 260–2; id., *A.J.*, 1852, IX, 153; Keyser, *Mural Decorations*, 1883; James and Tristram, *Walpole Soc. Annual Publication*, 1928, XVI, 1–8, reprs. Plates 26, 27*a*, *b*, 52*a*.

PADBURY (near Buckingham) Bucks
THE NATIVITY OF THE VIRGIN

The North Aisle

Traces of colour are visible on the eastern arch of the north arcade and all along the north wall, and at the eastern end, above an arched recess, are remains of subjects which, reading from the east, are as follows:

In two tiers, a 'history' of St. Catherine, two scenes surviving; (1) in the upper tier, the Breaking of the Wheels, in which the Saint, with golden hair, and stripped to the waist, stands between the Wheels, the Emperor being enthroned at the side, holding the sword; the figures of Angels have perished, but the diapering of leaves upon the yellow background is discernible; (2) an unidentifiable scene, painted upon a ground of pale pink, in which the Saint extends her hands towards two figures, one of a man clad in a gipon, the other, perhaps a woman, kneeling; in the background is a female figure. Both paintings are framed by a scroll border.

The Seven Deadly Sins; in the centre of a Wheel 6 ft. in diameter, Pride, crowned and richly clad, surrounded by scrolls terminating in dragon heads

which frame each a representation of a Sin and an attendant demon; except for *Luxuria*, and, probably, *Avaritia* and *Ira*, the two latter represented respectively by a figure with a sack across the shoulders and a soldier, they are unidentifiable. Outside the circle, a large, gaunt figure of Death, having claws upon the knees and elsewhere, thrusting a spear into the figure of Pride.

Below and to the west of the Sins, a consecration cross of cross paty type, not framed, as normally, within a circle.

On either side of the north doorway, traces of red and black, and within an adjacent niche, a pattern of fleurs-de-lis and an inscription in black.

All the works mentioned appear to be of the mid fourteenth century.

Keyser, *Mural Decorations*, 1883 (the Deadly Sins erroneously described as a Wheel of Fortune); Keyser, *A.J.*, 1892, XLIX, 340–1; id., *Records of Bucks*, 1897, VII, 215, 228; *R.C. Historical Monuments R., Bucks*, 1913, II, 233.

PASTON (near North Walsham) Norfolk
ST. MARGARET

The Nave

On the north wall, between the first and second windows from the west, opposite the south doorway, St. Christopher, about twelve feet in height, carrying on his left hand the Holy Child, who raises the right hand in blessing and holds an Orb of the Universe in the left. The Saint's head, surrounded by a nimbus with a cusped edging, and covered with a close cap, is turned towards the Child, and his beard and hair are elaborately drawn and well designed; his cloak is lined with vair, and his breeches are tied at the knees; about his ankles are traces of water and fish. *c.* 1380.

Between the second and third windows from the west in the same wall, *Les Trois Vifs et Les Trois Morts*; to the spectator's left, three standing corpses, with part of an indecipherable inscription in black letters above and to the right of them; and beyond, two Kings (the first of the three being defaced), and an attendant. The foremost of the two kings wears a hip-length black cote-hardie buttoned down the centre and adorned with stripes and roundels; his right hand is stretched towards the Corpses, and his head turned away from them, and on his left hand he carries what appears to be a hawk. The second King's gesture is similar; his cote-hardie is light in colour, with ornament over the breast and shoulders, and traces of tippets; his hair, like that of the first, is curled at the level of the chin, and he has a forked beard. The attendant, who appears to be holding to his lips a bugle, slung from his neck, is clad in a short gipon, parti-coloured, red on one side, striped in red and white on the other, and dagged at the lower edge. *c.* 1370.

Below *Les Trois Vifs*, slight traces of a subject, comprising a fragment of ? a large figure, and a small nude Soul; perhaps originally a St. Michael Weighing Souls.

Above the chancel arch, what alone remains of a painting is a representation of a pair of feet.

A.J., 1923, LXXX, 353–4; Bardswell, *Norfolk Archaeology*, 1923–5, XXII, 190–3, lxxi, repr.; Whaite, *St. Christopher*, 1929, 20, repr.; James, *Suffolk and Norfolk*, 1930, 155–6; Carleton Williams, *B.A.A.J.*, 1942, 3rd ser., VII, 36, 40, repr.
Plates 62, 63*a*, *b*.

PEAKIRK (near Peterborough) Northants
ST. PEGA

The Chancel

In the north-west angle, traces of masonry pattern executed in single line in red, and much defaced; perhaps of thirteenth-century date, but more probably part of extensive painting undertaken in the following century; it is not of the heavily-executed twelfth-century type. (See *Eng. Med. Wall Painting*, 1944, I, 74.)

The Nave

In the spandrel between the first and second arches of the north arcade, facing the south door, and framed by a border of patterned diamonds in black, white and red, St. Christopher, painted against a light background enriched by vigorously-executed scroll-work in red; the figure of the Holy Child, supported on his left shoulder, and the head of the Saint, are defaced, but the eel-spear, held in the Saint's right hand is, exceptionally, decipherable almost throughout the entire length, although at some time part of the shaft, covered by an oblong template, has been continued by means of retouching over the metal. At the top of the spear, a pommel, and just above the Saint's hand a second pommel, as commonly seen in representations of the bourdon; the blade is visible in the point of the spandrel between the arches. St. Christopher is clad in a mantle lined with vair and what was once apparently a gipon reaching just below the knees; water is depicted as though piled up around the legs, but any fish once existing are defaced. Low on the west side of the painting is a small figure of a donor, with hands raised in prayer,

and on the opposite side traces of another figure. *c.* 1340.

Filling the remainder of the wall from end to end, a Passion series, framed above and below by bent-riband pattern executed in red and white on a band of black, each scene being divided from that next to it, where such division survives, by a small column painted in yellow. Reading from the west, the subjects are as follows:

Higher tier

1. The Last Supper; the figures defaced, apart from the arm of one in the centre ? that of Christ, extended towards a dish; numerous other vessels are visible, including two small flagons with handles, and also some loaves of bread.

2. The Washing of Feet, with Christ kneeling on the left, the rest of the scene being mainly defaced, and cut into by a later window.

3. Almost entirely defaced; ? the Betrayal.

4. Defaced; there follow two, or perhaps three, defaced subjects.

5 or 6. Mainly defaced; ? the Mocking of Christ.

Lower tier

1. Mainly defaced; ? the Scourging.

2. Christ led to Crucifixion; on the left, an executioner thrusting Him forward, as He turns to gaze upon His tormentor, on the right another, also in knee-length red gipon, who points eastward and apparently holds the end of a rope in the right hand.

3. The Crucifixion; Christ hangs on the Cross, His body bent in a double curve; to the left, the kneeling Longinus, with red hair and beard, pointing to his eyes with the left hand and with the right wielding the spear, and on the other side of the Cross the bearer of the Sponge, holding a bag in the left hand.

4. The Deposition. The Body of Christ falls into the arms of a much-defaced figure on the left; to the right, in parti-coloured gipon and 'Jew's hat' turned back with vair, Nicodemus, bearded and with hair cut to the level of the jaw, crouches at the foot of the Cross and draws the nails from the feet.

5. The Entombment: much defaced—to the left, two figures, one of them probably that of the Virgin; the lower half of the subject is occupied by the arches beneath the tomb, painted in black.

6. The Resurrection. In the centre, traces of the figure of Christ, and of the Vexillum; to the right, an Angel, kneeling on the tomb, with arms extended towards Him; and below, as in the previous scene, the arches supporting the tomb, painted in red, black and white, traces of the sleeping Roman soldiers

being visible on the black ground within them. On the chancel arch, indications of a cube border, and on the soffit, of chevron decoration. c. 1360.

On a column in the south-west angle, traces of painting, as also at the east end of the north chancel chapel.

The North Aisle

Reading from the west, the surviving paintings are as follows:

1. Traces of a bearded head, executed on a fairly large scale, and confused with remains of fifteenth-century decorative work.

2. Over the north door, a fragment of ? a Tree of the Seven Deadly Sins; on the left, part of the head of ? a male figure, with right hand extended towards a woman opposite him, who is veiled and clad in a black kirtle with fitchets, into one of which she thrusts her left hand; in the background, the intertwined branches of a tree; ? *Luxuria* (since there are no traces of a devil behind the figures, where, instead, the branches of a tree are seen, this subject cannot be that of scandalbearing, as suggested in notes dated April 1951, and available in the church. Shapeless blurs, apparently accidental and meaningless, have been misread as the 'hands' of a devil). c. 1340.

3. The Three Living and Three Dead; framed by a border of bent-riband pattern, executed in red and black on a white ground diapered with groups of seven small roundels in red. The first King, on the west, young, beardless, and with hair curled slightly above chin level, clasps his hands at his breast in anguish, and holds a sceptre in the crook of his left arm; he wears a shoulder-cape over a knee-length cote-hardie turned back with white, and having tippets in dark red. His belt, set low on the hips, is white, and from it there hang a seal and a purse ornamented by a diamond pattern in black and white, a floral ornament in red appearing on the central diamond; his hose are black. The second King holds a sword in his left hand, and places his right on the shoulder of the first, as though in reassurance; his hair is cut like his companion's, but he is bearded. He wears a light-coloured cloak, caught at the neck by a brooch, and decorated with scroll-work in black, over a cote-hardie reaching below the knees and elaborated with scroll-work painted in red, with black stems; his red hose show a diamond pattern in white. The figure of the last King is partially defaced, the arms missing; his red mantle is lined with yellow, and his cote-hardie, grey in colour, reaches below the knees; on it, at chest level, are two narrow bands of embroidery in red and black, and there is a third

near the hem. Beyond this figure a plaster repair has destroyed the first of the Three Dead; the second has a shroud hanging from the head and floating free, and places its left hand on the right shoulder of the third, represented as a nude and decaying corpse. On the white background are lizards, insects, and creatures resembling tadpoles and newts, all these being executed in red, or, alternatively, yellow. c. 1340.

4. At the east end of the aisle, beyond a window, a subject almost entirely defaced, apart from a head in the upper corner on the left side; the framework, of bent-riband pattern, is well-preserved.

The South Aisle

At the east end, remains of a large scene, with traces of two figures, that on the left raising ? a sword or baton. The border, in a good state of preservation, is of wavy pattern in red and white, ornamented by roundels of the same colours counterchanged, the four angles being filled with leaf ornament.

Artis, *A.J.*, 1845, I, 158; Keyser, *Mural Decorations*, 1883.

SOUTH PICKENHAM (near Swaffham) Norfolk
ALL SAINTS

The Nave

Around the blocked archway at the western end, which formerly opened into the tower, scroll-work enriched with trefoils.

On the south wall, to the east of the south doorway, and almost opposite the north door, a St. Christopher, only the lower part being clearly decipherable; drawn in red outline, the figure has bare legs (the feet missing), a short green gipon, and a red cote-hardie shaded in white, which is looped up on each side, the ends being thrust through a white girdle. The staff seems to have been held perpendicularly in the left hand, and the Holy Child to have been supported on the right arm or shoulder. The heads of two fishes are decipherable in the water about the ankles. The painting, which is framed on either side by a narrow band in red, would originally have been about 10 ft. in height by 4 ft. in width.

From notes supplied by Mrs. M. Bardswell.

PICKWORTH (near Grantham) Lincs
ST. ANDREW

The Nave

Above the chancel arch, a Doom, the upper part mutilated, but the remainder well-preserved; the feet of Christ are visible, together with the Orb of the Universe upon which they rest (divided into three sections, containing the three elements of air, earth and water) and on the right, as normally, kneels the Virgin, but on the left, exceptionally, not St. John the Evangelist, but the Baptist, whose bare legs, with a portion of his garment of skin, are visible. Beyond, on either side, an Angel, the feet and the hem of the apparelled alb being decipherable, and beyond again, also on either side, the bare feet of Apostles acting as Assessors.

At the eastern end of the north clerestory wall, an Ascension, the feet of Christ being seen above, and below, on the spectator's left, the Virgin and St. Peter, who holds the Keys, in front of a group of Apostles, their robes in some cases decorated with scroll-work; on the right is a similar group, but much defaced.

Filling the entire wall-space between two clerestory windows to the west, *Les Trois Vifs et Les Trois Morts*, painted upon the normal cream-coloured ground stencilled with double sexfoils in red, these being evidently part of a later renovation. The entire subject is much damaged; on the eastern side are traces of the Kings, the heads defaced, clad in hip-length gipons, belted low, gauntlet gloves, long hose and somewhat pointed shoes, patterned with a fret in black; on the western side, the Corpses, facing frontally, in a rigid posture, the first with arms hanging at its sides, the second pointing with the right hand towards the Kings and with the left arm hanging, the third with right arm pendent and the left across the body. Kings and Corpses alike stand on small patterned hillocks, and are separated each from the other by stiffly-designed trees. Below the painting, a border of triangles, alternately black and cream, ornamented with roundels, the colours counter-changed.

In the spandrels between the arches of the arcade below the Three Living, on a ground diapered with double sexfoils, as before, traces of an unidentifiable subject; and in the adjacent spandrel to the west, against a similar ground, further enriched with small fleurs-de-lis that are painted, and not stencilled, a Weighing of Souls, also much damaged; to the spectator's left, remains of a St. Michael, and the balance-beam with two pans pendent from it, a small soul being visible in that on the right, which falls within the point of the spandrel and before the figure of the Virgin.

Beyond the next clerestory window to the west, a St. Christopher, against a plain background; the figure is much defaced, and the head cut into by a later roof-bracket, but it may be seen that the staff is held in the right hand and the Holy Child sup-ported on the left shoulder. All the paintings appear to be of the late fourteenth century.

Rouse, *B.A.A.J.*, 1950, 3rd ser., XIII, 24–33, reprs.; id., *Lincs A. & A.S.R.*, 1951, N.S., IV, 57–9.

PLUSCARDINE PRIORY CHAPEL (near Elgin)
Moray

Formerly, on the north of the chancel arch, an Angel, with a pattern of stars and clouds, which appears to have been of fourteenth-century date; and elsewhere; a figure of Christ, one of the Virgin, and others of St. John and other Evangelists and Apostles, perhaps of the same period. Consecration crosses survive.

Keyser, *Mural Decorations*, 1883; *The Catholic Herald*, vii, ix, 1943.

POTTER HEIGHAM (near Yarmouth) Norfolk
ST. NICHOLAS

The North Aisle

At the eastern end, indecipherable remains, consisting mainly of plain red, and superimposed upon them a border about 6 in. in width, executed in white and patterned with scroll-work in grey; lower on the wall, fragments of a masonry pattern in double line.

On the eastern splay of the easternmost window, indecipherable remains of painting in red.

On an area of wall further to the west and approximately 6 ft. in width by 12 ft. in height, painting in three tiers, reading from the west as follows:

Highest tier

1. (?) The Appearance of the Angel to Joachim. An Angel emerges from clouds before a kneeling figure in the head-dress of a priest of high rank; the subject is partially destroyed by the insertion of a window.

2. (?) The Meeting of Joachim and Anna at the Golden Gate. A figure facing east (largely destroyed by a roof truss), clasping with the right hand the left hand of a woman, veiled and clad in a red kirtle and white mantle, who, apparently standing before a gateway, lays her right hand upon her breast.

3. (?) The Departure from Home of the Virgin. On the left, a female figure, facing east, veiled and clad in a red kirtle having a white girdle, her left hand raised and her right extended to clasp that of another, with a nimbus, and long hair falling on her shoulders, who stands in a doorway holding her cloak about her with the left hand.

4. (?) The Presentation in the Temple, partially destroyed by the insertion of a window. In the upper

part, a bearded man with the head-dress of a priest of high rank, resembling a conical tiara, accompanied by two others having soft caps, and immediately below and slightly to the right, a veiled female head and a smaller but similar head, below and to the left.

Second tier

1. A king, crowned and enthroned, facing east, with traces of a figure advancing towards him from that direction.

2. In the centre, a tub having two or more small figures within it, their hands upraised in prayer, and beside it, to the right, traces of a nimbed figure with a hand upraised over them; presumably St. Nicholas and the Three Boys.

3. Indecipherable.

Third tier

1. Head of a King, facing west, the left arm bent with the hand raised towards the chest, and beside him to the east traces of a figure with arm extended towards him.

2. On the western side, indecipherable traces; in the centre, low on the wall, a small head; on the east, remains of a female figure, standing and facing west, clad in a white kirtle and black shoes, and behind her, still further to the east, parts of a male figure in parti-coloured gipon and long hose of red and white, facing towards her; beyond him again, another, having one white stocking and one striped in white and red, advancing eastward; both the male figures have maces pendent from the waist-belt. (?) A Massacre of the Innocents.

The borders to all these subjects are enriched with a wavy pattern in black and white. In the centre of the wall, beneath the lowest tier of paintings, remains of a consecration cross.

At the western end of the aisle, between the westernmost window and the north door, St. Anthony Abbot, a figure approximately 7 ft. in height, nimbed, a crozier in the right hand with the pendent infula, and in the left an indecipherable object, with a tau cross immediately below it.

To the east of the north door, remains of a St. Christopher, as usual of gigantic dimensions; traces of several fish remain, and also of (?) a ship, confused with relics of a later painting of the same subject.

All the work, with the exception of parts of the (?) Joachim and Anna series, is much defaced.

The South Aisle

Between the first two windows at the eastern end of the south wall, the Corporal Works of Mercy: in the centre a female figure of approximately life-size, nimbed and veiled, clad in a pink mantle with folds drawn in red, which is clasped upon the breast by a brooch of diamond shape, and a 'sideless' surcoat over a red kirtle with fitchets. She faces east, raises the right hand and in the left bears a small building, with a bearded figure in its doorway, grasping a staff in the right hand. She is surrounded by scenes representing the Works, as follows:

1. Above, on the eastern side, Feeding the Hungry: an inscription in which the word Hunger is decipherable, extends across the top of the scene; to the left, cut into by an adjacent window of later date, a man with a forked beard receives in his left hand a loaf, and in his right (?) a bowl, from a woman, clad in a 'sideless' surcoat over a red kirtle .The background is white, diapered with groups of four spots in red.

2. Immediately below this a subject now indecipherable, only a veiled female head surviving.

3. Immediately below again, another indecipherable subject, comprising a hand extended eastward, and part of a figure clad in a red garment, against a white background diapered with groups of four spots.

4. In the centre, below the life-size female figure described above, Visiting the Prisoner; a man with a long, forked beard and shaggy hair is seated on a rush mat (of this only faint traces exist) with wrists shackled and feet in the stocks; the background is white, diapered with single spots arranged diamond-wise.

5. On a level with this scene to the west of the large central figure, Receiving the Stranger: on the left stands a man with forked beard, garbed in pilgrim's habit with hat and bourdon, clasping the latter with the left hand and extending the right towards a veiled woman standing in a doorway to receive him, who grasps his right wrist with the left hand and with the right takes the bourdon from him. Across the top of the scene and around the doorway is an inscribed scroll, and the background is white, diapered with groups of four spots in red.

6. Immediately above this scene, Visiting the Sick: a bearded man, nude, reclines on a couch under a coverlet striped in white and yellow, the right hand resting upon it and the left on the breast; above the head and to the side hangs a white bed-curtain. A veiled female figure on the right, clad in a 'sideless' surcoat and red kirtle, feeds him with a spoon from a bowl held in the left hand. Above runs an inscription, originally of three lines, with the capitals rubricated; the background is white, diapered with red spots set diamond-wise.

7. Immediately above again, Burying the Dead. On the left, part remains of the figure of a priest in

mass vestments who receives in the right hand a coin proffered by a kneeling woman, veiled and clad in a pink kirtle and 'sideless' surcoat, who extends the left hand towards the foot of (?) a bier. Above the scene, which is broken into on the western side by a window, runs an inscription of three lines; the background is white patterned with red spots in groups of four. *c.* 1380.

Borders 3 in. in width, in pale grey ornamented with large white roundels set at intervals, surround all the subjects, which are well executed and well drawn. They have, unfortunately, at some time been disfigured by pencilling, and to some extent retouched.

Dawson Turner, *Norfolk Archaeology*, 1849, II, 358–9, note; Keyser, *Mural Decorations*, 1883; James, *Suffolk and Norfolk*, 1930, 146; Long, *Burl. M.*, 1940, LXXVI, 156.

Plate 64a.

PRESTON (near Brighton) Sussex ST. PETER

The Nave

A series of paintings formerly existing was almost entirely destroyed by fire in 1906; discovered in 1828, they had remained in a fairly good state of preservation, although, unfortunately, retouched to a considerable extent *c.* 1878. Photographs taken before their destruction are preserved in the Victoria and Albert Museum.

The Nave

The paintings on the north wall, between two lancet windows near the eastern end, were arranged in three tiers, the highest, and also the lowest—the latter finished with a scroll-work border enriched with trefoils—being narrow, but the middle one almost twice the depth of the others, i.e. approximately 5 ft. The highest tier was entirely occupied by a Last Supper, in which the table, laid with vessels (two of them containing fish), and covered with a cloth represented as hanging in festoons, had behind it the figures of Christ and the Apostles, their heads destroyed, and before it Judas. The subject depicted in the middle tier showed many unusual features: in the centre stood an altar, with a covering, patterned by a fret, and a draped antependium, and towards its centre a chalice of gigantic size, holding the recumbent figure of the Holy Child, with a cruciform nimbus, wrapped in swaddling clothes. Immediately above was a star, and on either side the Ox and the Ass, with the manger behind them. At the side of the altar, to the spectator's left, a hooded figure, in tunic and cloak,

raised the right hand with palm extended as though in adoration, and held in the left a T-headed staff; partially obscured by this figure, between it and the altar, was, apparently, a high stool bearing a cushion, or perhaps a vessel, and behind it a second figure, in tunic, cloak and soft cap, with arms extended over the *mensa* towards the chalice, the folded hands just touching its lip. On the opposite side of the altar, a female Saint, nimbed, and clad in a long tunic and cloak, also extended her arms over the *mensa*, the left, however, being slightly lowered and the right touching the nimbus of the Holy Child; behind her a hooded figure in a long tunic stood with arms outstretched in a gesture almost identical with hers, except that in the left hand was held a short pendent scroll. Behind both these figures appeared a slanting bar. The subject was terminated above and below by a border of wavy design, beneath which, in the lowest tier, against a background of scroll ornament, were demi-figures of the Magi, holding their gifts.

Other paintings were arranged in two tiers around the chancel arch. In the upper tier, on the northern side, reading from north to south, were:

1. The Incredulity of St. Thomas: Christ, on the right of the scene, with the vexillum in the left hand, and the mantle drawn back to show the wound in the side, guided towards it with His right hand the right hand of the kneeling St. Thomas, who raised his left in adoration. In the background were traces of scroll ornament.

2. The *Noli Me Tangere*: this was represented in much the same way as the preceding subject; except that the kneeling Magdalen raised her hands clasped in prayer, while Christ extended His right towards her, the two figures being separated by a conventionalized tree.

3. St. Catherine, facing the *Noli Me Tangere*, veiled and crowned, but not nimbed, clad in a tunic and mantle, the latter covering her right hand, in which she held the Wheel.

In the lower tier, on the same side, at and just above the level of the springing of the chancel arch, a Martyrdom of St. Thomas of Canterbury; to the right of the scene, immediately adjacent to the arch, the monk Grim, represented with a nimbus (doubtless an error of the restorer), extending the right arm, with the hand wounded and bleeding, across an altar bearing a chalice, in defence of the Saint, who, half-turning backward to face the approaching knights, knelt on the highest of the seven altar-steps. The foremost of the knights, who all bore heater-shaped shields, was shown striking him on the head with a sword, the second, immediately behind, also striking, but extending at the same time the left hand with index finger pointed to the chalice, above which was a *Manus Dei*; the third advancing, his weapon brandished, and the fourth turning slightly backward, with sword half-drawn. Beneath the scene was a band of fret patterning, with scroll-work below it.

In the upper tier, to the south of the arch, the subjects were as follows:

1. Within a canopied and crocketed niche, St. Margaret, facing south, nimbed, veiled and clad in a tunic and mantle, standing upon the dragon, and with raised right hand thrusting into its mouth a spear.

2. A mitred Bishop, unidentified, facing towards St. Margaret, his right hand raised in blessing and in his left a crozier, painted against a background of scroll-work elaborated with trefoils; between this figure and the preceding one, a consecration cross of somewhat elaborate design.

3. Within a niche, St. Thomas the Apostle, nimbed, bearded, bare-footed and clad in tunic and mantle, in his right hand a lance and in his left a book, facing the Bishop; the remainder of the wall-space occupied by scroll-work enriched with leaves and trefoils. Above this tier, a border of fretwork, badly restored.

In the lowest tier on this side, a St. Michael Weighing Souls, with the Virgin interceding; her figure, misunderstood by the restorer, repainted as an Angel, with upraised wings.

So far as can be judged from the photographs taken after the paintings had been retouched, they seem to have been of the early fourteenth century.

Archaeologia, 1831, XXIII, 311, reprs.; *Builder*, 1864, 725; Keyser, *Mural Decorations*, 1883; *Sussex Archaeological Collections*, 1900, XLIII, 241, repr.; Williams, *The Antiquary*, 1904, XL, 340–5; Johnston, *Memorials of Old Sussex*, 1909, 266; Perry, *Burl. M.*, 1912, XXII, 215, repr.; Borenius, *St. Thomas Becket in Art*, 1932, 98.

PURTON (near Cricklade) Wilts

The South-eastern Chapel

South wall: to the west of the large window in this wall, filling a space approximately 4 ft. 6 in. × 6 ft. 8 in., the Death of the Virgin. In the lower part of the composition, the body of the Virgin lies on a bier, behind which stands Christ receiving her Soul; to the spectator's right are remains of figures of five Apostles, their nimbi alternatively white or dark red, and to the left vestiges of two more. The entire composition is much defaced, with the exception of the Virgin's figure, which is in a fair state of preservation, in particular the head. To the east of the same window are indecipherable traces of painting. All the work is of the late fourteenth century.

The South-east Transept

Above the arch leading to the south-eastern chapel, fragmentary remains of a Crucifixion; in the centre, traces of Christ on the cross, and above, to the right of the centre, of a small Angel; below, in the spandrel above the arch, on the spectator's right, traces of another figure, apparently that of another and much larger Angel. About two feet to the south of the work just described, on the same wall, confused traces, possibly of a large painted niche formerly framing the figure of a Saint. Late fourteenth century.

Ponting, *Wilts Archaeological Society*, 1887, XXIII, 237 (erroneous interpretation of subject in S.E. Chapel, corrected above from notes taken during cleaning in 1947).

QUATT (near Bridgenorth) Salop ST. ANDREW

The Nave

When the rebuilding was about to take place in 1763, paintings were discovered, apparently to the north and south of the chancel arch. On the north side were the Corporal Works of Mercy, with a half-figure of Christ above them, represented with a cruciform nimbus, the right hand raised in blessing and in the left an orb surmounted by a cross; immediately below were four Angels with wings outspread; and below again, the Works reading from the spectator's left, as follows: 1. ? Visiting the Imprisoned; 2. Clothing the Naked. 3. Feeding the Hungry. 4. Giving Drink to the Thirsty. Below again, in a very fragmentary state, ? Burying the Dead. On the south side, the upper part of a Tree of the Seven Deadly Sins, comprising a central figure with lines radiating from the mouth, and a devil on the left, two figures, apparently nude, with an attendant devil, ? *Luxuria*, and traces of more devils and other figures.

These works are known only through some drawings made before their destruction, by a certain Richard Colley, and formerly preserved at Dudmaston, the manor-house of Quatt; so far as may be judged from such rudimentary sketches, they would appear to have been of a date *c.* 1400.

'On vellum nailed to a board' (? part of a wooden tympanum) 'the Resurrection'; also found in 1763, this painting may have formed part of the scheme described above, the whole tympanum having perhaps been painted with a Doom, since a 'Day of Judgement' is mentioned in one account.

Hulbert, *Hist. & Description of the County of Salop*, 1837, 338; Bagshawe, *Gazetteer of Shropshire*, 1851, 655; Keyser, *Mural Decorations*, 1883. Photographs of the sketches by Colley were kindly supplied by Mr. W. Watkins-Pitchford.

RAINHAM (near Chatham) Kent ST. MARGARET
The Nave

Between the first and second windows from the east in the south wall, an Annunciation, *c.* 1340. The figure of the Angel Gabriel, on the left, is much defaced; it is considerably shorter than that of the Virgin, and may originally have been represented as genuflecting; one hand is raised, holding a scroll. The Virgin, also holding a scroll, and a clasped book, stands in a slightly swaying pose, clad in a white tunic and a red mantle, the folds of the latter being intricate in design. Both figures are nimbed, and between them a pot of flowers is represented in black outline.

Between the second window and a doorway, a Last Judgement, with a General Resurrection below, all much defaced; the figure of St. Peter, in conical tiara, beneath an architectural canopy, is alone clearly distinguishable.

Further to the west, beyond a doorway, traces of a St. Christopher, confused with remains of a later painting of the same subject.

Elsewhere, two consecration crosses.

Long, *Burl. M.*, 1930, LVI, 232.

RAMSEY (near Huntingdon) Hunts
ST. THOMAS OF CANTERBURY

The Nave

Over the easternmost arch of the north arcade, a painting of a cloaked and bearded man with hand raised to his forehead, and on the right the wing of an Angel, against a ground diapered with rosettes— probably part of an Annunciation to the Shepherds. *c.* 1300.

R.C. Historical Monuments R., Hunts, 1926, 207.

RISBY (near Bury St. Edmunds) Suffolk
ST. GILES

The Nave

West wall, next to the tower, a painting of a bishop, and to the east of it another of a *Noli Me Tangere*. *c.* 1380.

On either side of the chancel arch, a canopied niche with cusped and crocketed head, retaining traces of original colour decoration.

Suffolk I.A. & N.H.P., 1903, XI, 60–1; James, *Suffolk & Norfolk*, 1930, 33; Munro Cautley, *Suffolk Churches and Their Treasures*, 1938, 307.

ROCHESTER, Kent
CATHEDRAL CHURCH OF ST. ANDREW

The Choir

The wall-surface above the stalls to the height of the string-course is painted with a heraldic pattern, originally continued also over the screen at the western end of the choir. It consists of a series of contiguous quatrefoils bordered in pink, white and green, framing golden lions passant gardant on a vermilion field, the octagonal interspaces being filled with golden lilies on a blue field. This pattern is terminated immediately above the stalls by a border of interlaced riband pattern in red and blue, inset with sexfoil flowers in yellow upon roundels of red and blue counterchanged, and tracery in black and white, the whole outlined strongly in black. Beneath the string-course is another and deeper band of ornament, in which similar riband pattern in red, green and blue alternates with shields in white on green, many of these having apparently been left blank originally, but in 1876, when the decoration was discovered, filled with the arms of the Bishops of Rochester. The greater part of all this decoration was heavily restored at the date just mentioned, but a portion of about a foot in depth immediately above the stalls was retouched comparatively lightly, and a coat of arms, charged with a cross fleury, near the thirteenth-century Wheel of Fortune on the north wall, and in the higher of the two ornamental borders just described, was left, and still remains, intact. Part of the decoration, comprising the lions passant gardant, may also be seen in its unspoilt state upon a piece of boarding removed from the screen mentioned above and preserved in the south choir transept. The work is executed in oil, and vermilion, pink, green, blue, white, gold and black are used; it is of an early date in the fourteenth century, not long after 1330.

It is recorded that in 1840 colour and gilding remained upon the sedilia, and upon the arms of the church of Rochester, Christ Church, Canterbury, and Bishop Thomas Brinton (1373–89) decorating them; also that below the arms there were formerly figures of three bishops, with the inscription:

*O altitudo divitiarum: sapiencie et scientie
Dei quam incomprehensibilia sunt
Judicia ejus et investigabiles vie ejus.*

Gent. M., 1840, pt. 2, 137–8; Spence, *A Walk Through Rochester Cathedral*, 1840, 15; Phippen, *Descriptive Sketches of Rochester*, 1862, 113; Scott Robertson, *A. Cant.*, 1876, X, 70–4, repr.; Keyser, *Mural Decorations*, 1883; St. John Hope, *A. Cant.*, 1898, XXIII, 304, 310.

The North Choir Transept (Site of the Shrine of St. William of Perth)

On the piers are slight remains, little more than silhouettes, of a series of subject-paintings; and traces are to be found here and there showing that the shafts were originally painted black (some of them, to judge from slight traces, having perhaps been patterned in vermilion), the hollow mouldings of the ribs red, the round mouldings with 'marbling', and the fillet yellow, while the bosses were picked out in bright colours and the vaulting decorated with a masonry pattern executed in black line upon the usual ground of cream. This general scheme of decoration seems to have been carried out *c.* 1360.

At the back of a recess in the north wall, said to have housed the tomb in which St. William of Perth was first interred, is scroll-work composed of maple and vine leaves, with tendrils, further elaborated by what may be described as a diaper comprising pink long-tailed parakeets, or 'popinjays', so placed in relation to one another that any four among them form the sides of what is approximately a diamond shape. The whole pattern, executed in oil colour, is painted upon a ground of vermilion, and appears to be of *c.* 1330; it is to be seen also surrounding the arch over the recess at the angle of a pier approximately opposite, as also, in a very fragmentary state, in many other parts of the transept.

In the south-eastern corner is the effigy of Bishop John of Sheppey (1353–60). In 1825 this was discovered walled up, and was eventually repainted, but the later painting has been removed of late years as far as possible to expose the ancient work, of *c.* 1361. The Bishop is vested in an alb with elaborate apparels executed in gesso and colours, a pinkish dalmatic enriched with a floral pattern in black, and edged with gold, and a chasuble, originally vermilion, but now a lake colour, powdered with a pattern in gold. The amice, mitre, gloves and ring are 'jewelled' with gesso and gilding. The treatment of the maniple is particularly rich; upon it there are sunken diamond shapes, 1 in. in width and $1\frac{1}{2}$ in. in length, gilt and ornamented with a minutely executed pattern in black, and covered with glass about $\frac{1}{16}$ in. in thickness. The face, with widely-opened dark eyes, is painted in gradated flesh tints, and beneath the head are two patterned cushions. The effigy, in every part, even to the dogs at the feet, with their red collars and golden bells, is embellished with colour, gilding, or gesso-work. In the Cathedral Museum portions are preserved of a stone canopy said to have covered the tomb; but it is uncertain whether they may not in fact have formed part of an altar-piece. They comprise parts of figures of the Virgin and Child, of a representation of the Coronation of the Virgin, and of Angels holding censers, scrolls, and musical instruments, and are all highly coloured and gilt, blue and green predominating, with some use of natural colour, e.g. upon a fragment carved with grapes.

West's *Notebook*, 1844, p. 4; *Gent. M.*, 1825, pt. i, 76; *Archaeologia*, 1834, XXV, 122–3, pls. VII and VIII; *Gent. M.*, 1840, XCV, pt. 2, 226; St. John Hope, *A. Cant.*, 1898, XXIII, 314, 318.

The South Nave Transept, or Lady Chapel

Built *c.* 1322 and enlarged in the late Perpendicular period.

The decoration at the eastern end of this chapel seems to have been carried out *c.* 1350; of the general colour treatment vestiges alone remain, viz. traces of light red on marble shafts in the north-western corner; but about the lofty arch over the former site of the Lady altar there are survivals of subject-paintings, now in a much defaced condition, being decipherable largely by means of the remaining setting-out lines, stain from the medium used, which penetrated the plaster, and fragments of paint still adhering to the surface. There are three tiers of paintings, the middle and the lowest tiers being separated by a band of green ornamented with quatrefoils. The subjects are framed within painted niches of very elaborate design, the vaulting, piers, capitals and masonry all being drawn in great detail, by means of incised line as previously mentioned, and the canopies and supporting piers richly ornamented. The colour used on the architectural features is cream, or light buff, outlined in red. The figures stand upon painted consoles composed of foliage resembling maple and ivy; their drapery is cream in colour, shaded in bright green, the linings to mantles, etc., being tinted generally with pink or light red. The subjects are as follows:

Highest tier: above the apex of the arch (the soffit of which is painted green and ornamented with red lions rampant within medallions), at either side, a censing Angel, kneeling, is painted on a larger scale than the rest of the figures on the wall, against a background semy of lions; on the north side, immediately behind the Angel on that side, an elaborately designed empty niche, and beyond that again a standing figure of the Angel Gabriel, holding a scroll in the left hand and extending the right towards the Virgin, who is represented in a corresponding position on the opposite side of the arch, bearing a book in the left hand and raising the right in salutation. Further to the north from St. Gabriel two female Saints are depicted, but they are not identifiable, and on the south side of the arch there are some remaining indications that the scheme here was similar to that on the north, but part of one female Saint alone survives.

Central tier: filling the spandrel at the side of the arch, on the north side, St. Margaret, spearing the dragon beneath her feet, and, immediately beside the arch, a kneeling donor, extending the arms in supplication, probably a male figure,[1] but much defaced; on the south side of the arch another donor, a woman clad in a kirtle, with a veil, and, apparently a wimple, her hands raised and joined in prayer, kneeling before a prie-dieu on which lies an open book. Beyond her to the south are traces of a St. Catherine, fragments of the Wheel alone being decipherable.

Lowest tier: On the north side, the head of a female Saint may be deciphered, on the south side, nothing more than traces of colour.

The arch mouldings terminate, on the north in the carved head of a king, on the south in that of a queen, and a shaft springing from the apex of the arch is supported by that of a monk, all of them retaining traces of colour.

St. John Hope, *A. Cant.,* 1898, XXIII, 297.

The Nave

On the northern side of the first pier from the west in the south arcade, a St. Christopher, so defaced that little remains but the silhouette and a few fragments of colour. *c.* 1340.

Formerly, on the capital, carved with oak leaves and acorns, of the second pier westward from the crossing on the south side, colour and gilding; and on the bases of some of the vaulting shafts, marbling.

St. John Hope, *A. Cant.,* 1898, XXIII, 253, 271, 286; Whaite, *St. Christopher,* 1929, 17, pl. 3.

The Crypt

On the vaulting of the bay beneath the altar of St. John Baptist in the upper church, painted over a simple masonry pattern of thirteenth-century date, are decorative patterns of the fourteenth century, viz. roses in black and white on a cream ground; a scroll-pattern with black and white oak leaves; and various others, much defaced. One bay is treated with especial elaboration, as is also an adjacent arch;

here the quadripartite vaulting has in each division two large medallions and one smaller one (framing remains of subjects which will be described below), the borders being either of wavy or zig-zag ornamentation, sometimes elaborated with small roundels in black and red. In the spandrels immediately above the capitals are shields of arms, the ground between these and the medallions, as also between the medallions themselves, being covered with a scroll and maple-leaf pattern in cream, outlined in black, upon a ground of red ochre.

The subjects within the medallions, so far as they survive, are as follows: in five of the large medallions (3 ft. in diameter), the 'history' of a Saint, represented as having a patterned nimbus and as clad in a tunic and mantle, who is shown (1) taking the hand of a kneeling man, bearded and with curled hair, and pointing with the right hand to an open door, as though inviting him to rise and pass through it; (2) (?) before a couch or a bier, on which lies either a veiled woman or a corpse in grave-clothes, with a woman at the head who raises both hands as if in wonder; (3) standing, apparently in a group of figures, one of them an Angel, whose wing breaks into the enclosing framework of the medallion; an almost entirely defaced subject; (4) standing to the extreme left of the composition, but whether on shore or upon the water is not distinguishable, blessing two persons, the foremost seemingly bearded, who are seated in a small boat surrounded by waves in which fish are shown swimming. In another medallion, immediately adjacent to that just described, the boat is again depicted, with one man only in it, approaching a shore where lies a draped figure, apparently female, but much defaced, accompanied by a child, or perhaps a small nude figure, raising its arm as if in appeal, and partially enveloped in the drapery of the other draped figure; in this scene no representation of the Saint is decipherable. One subject only survives, even in part, of those formerly filling the smaller medallions (2 ft. in diameter) i.e. a scene in which a monk, clad in a dalmatic, or perhaps a tunic with wide sleeves, kneels before an altar above which the Saint appears, extending a hand towards him.

The broad soffit of the arch on the western side of the bay is divided into twelve square cusped panels, the interstices of the cusping being painted red; the subjects which they formerly framed are almost entirely defaced, and it is only possible to distinguish that episodes in the 'history' of a Saint are depicted,

---

[1] From St. John Hope's account, identifiable as a male figure in 1898.

the majority of them as scenes taking place in the open air, since trees are discernible in all of them except three; that in one scene, three women veiled in black are represented; and that in a second, the best-preserved of the series, a figure stands before a couch or bier upon which another is lying, while Angels with upraised wings are placed at the head and feet.

The charges on the shields which, as previously mentioned, ornament the spandrels of the vaulting immediately above the capitals, are as follows: at the north-west angle, (1) Quarterly 1 and 4, *Or, a lion rampant double-tailed gules* (the field apparently fretty sable); 2 and 3, *sable, a lion rampant double-tailed* (?), *argent*; (2)—*Argent, an eagle displayed sable*, the ground enriched with a fret or; at the south-west angle (3) a much-defaced shield, (?) a lion rampant (?) gules, upon a field the colour of which cannot be determined, within a bordure (?) argent, and (4) now completely defaced, but formerly—*Argent, a cross gules*, again upon a diapered field. At the south-east angle, (5) and (6) are defaced. At the north-east angle, (7)—*Argent, three chevronels gules*, the field patterned with scroll-work in red.

All the work described is of early-fourteenth-century date, and it is evident that, in its original condition, it was of high quality.

Keyser, *Mural Decorations*, 1883; St. John Hope, *A. Cant.*, 1898, XXIII, 327–8.

ROTHERFIELD (near Tunbridge Wells) Sussex
ST. DENYS

The Nave

On the east wall, around the chancel arch, remains of a Doom, painted *c.* 1300 or soon after; only fragments survive, apart from an exceptionally well-preserved St. Michael Weighing Souls, on the north side of the arch. St. Michael stands with one wing raised and the other folded, bearing the scales in the left hand and with the other pointing to the pan on his right, which is the lower of the two; near it being traces of a devil. The Archangel's head is slightly bent, his hair yellow, and his nimbus bordered with cusping; the folds of the tunic and cloak are executed in red line, with some use of modelling, and the wings in red, yellow and black. Immediately below this painting are remains of two subjects, of the same date, separated by a narrow band of plain red, and apparently once framed by a continuation of a scroll border, a part of which is visible beneath the St. Michael. Owing to extensive repairs to the plaster, fragments only of the subjects now exist, viz. in one,

part of a small figure clad in a tunic, and in the other, two figures on the left, one with head and feet defaced, apparently vested in a dalmatic enriched with horizontal bands of ornament, and the other, immediately behind the first, standing frontally and perhaps holding an object in a cloth; ? possibly remains of a 'history' of the Martyrdom of St. Lawrence, recorded as once having existed 'near the pulpit'.

Formerly, on the nave piers, decoration comprising diamond, wavy and chevron patterns, with some remains of scroll-work and chevron patterns on the capitals; and on the wall adjacent to one of the piers, bold scroll-work.

The Nevill Chapel

On the northern splay of the east window, the Archangel Gabriel genuflecting, with one hand raised in salutation, clad in an alb and a mantle falling in complicated folds; above the head is a scroll, now blank. The figure survives mainly as a silhouette against the ground of dark red, diapered with small flowers in white, and the companion figure, no doubt that of the Virgin, has disappeared from the opposite splay.

Keyser, *Mural Decorations*, 1883; id., *Sussex Archaeological Collections*, 1896, XL, 218–21; id., *A.J.*, 1896, LIII, 168, 169; Johnston, *Memorials of Old Sussex*, 1909, 271; Wall, *Medieval Wall Paintings*, 1914, 85, repr.
Plate 50a.

ROWNER (near Gosport) Hants ST. MARY

In what was originally the north chapel, remains of painting were found in 1874, but were subsequently destroyed; they included what was thought to be perhaps an Ascension, upon a splay of the east window, an Adoration of the Magi, on the north wall, diaper patterns, and over what is now the chancel arch, traces of inscriptions. *c.* 1350.

Keyser, *Mural Decorations*, 1883; id., *Memorials of Old Hants*, 1906, 148; *Victoria County Hist., Hants & I.O.W.*, 1908, III, 219.

SALISBURY, Wilts THE SUB-CHANTRY HOUSE

Formerly, on the north and west walls, a pattern composed of diamonds and squares, the former white, charged each with a bird in blue, the latter red, charged each with a lion-leopardy in white, larger intervening squares in white being left blank.

On the south wall a masonry pattern in single red line, elaborated with cinquefoil white-centred flowers in red borne upon stalks in black, the latter springing from the angles of the blocks either out of, or else in alternation with, groups of four small leaves in blue.

Harding, *Wilts A. & N.H.M.*, 1896, XXIX, 95–7, repr.; Wordsworth, ibid., 1917, 433.

SANDERSTEAD (near Croydon) Surrey
ALL SAINTS

The Chancel

To the north of the east window, St. Edmund, King and Martyr, crowned and nimbed, clad in tunic and mantle, and somewhat pointed shoes, with the right hand raised, the index finger pointing to the Arrows held in the left, standing on a low platform decorated with small lancet windows; to the south, St. Edmund of Canterbury, in mitre and mass vestments, identified by means of fragments of an inscription above the head; the first figure is moderately well-preserved, but the second much defaced. Plate 55a.

SARRATT (near Rickmansworth) Herts
HOLY CROSS

The South Aisle

On the east wall, two tiers of paintings, separated by a scroll-work border enriched with roses; in the higher of the two, Holy Infancy scenes, in the lower a Passion series. Reading from north to south in each tier, the subjects are as follows:

The Higher Tier. 1. The Annunciation. Part only remains of the figure of the Angel Gabriel, who is shown entirely feathered,[1] with bare feet, the right hand raised and in the left a scroll. The Virgin, with head slightly bent and both arms upraised, is a tall, graceful figure. 2. The Appearance of the Angel to the Shepherds. The Angel, whose head, wings and feet alone are decipherable, is on the left of the scene, with the first Shepherd, a much-defaced figure, standing before him and leaning on a staff. Of the second Shepherd the strongly-characterized head, and part of the shoulders, survive, the former in good condition; as far as can be made out, he was depicted holding on its back a ram, which is clearly seen. In the foreground sheep are grazing, and to the right the third Shepherd, the head again strongly characterized, wearing a hood and a gipon buttoned down the centre front, is playing the pipes. 3. The Nativity. Very little of this scene remains; a tall figure at the head of what must originally have been the couch, and the head and upraised right hand of St. Joseph are alone decipherable.

The Lower Tier. 1. ? The Last Supper, two heads, apparently of Apostles, are visible. 2. The Resurrection. Almost entirely perished, apart from the *Vexillum*. 3. The Ascension. Above, the feet of Christ, and below the Apostles, with upraised heads and hands, the lower parts of their figures destroyed.

The paintings, executed in the usual ochres, are in the main of *c.* 1370; but there are traces of a renovation of *c.* 1400 or later, notably on the scroll-work border. (1954, the paintings obscured by dirt.)

Cussans, *History of Herts*, 1879–81, III, pt. 2, 114; Keyser, *Mural Decorations*, 1883; R.C. *Historical Monuments R., Herts*, 1910, 201.

SEDGEFORD (near Hunstanton) Norfolk
ST. MARY

The Nave

In the spandrels between the arches of the arcades, bold foliated scroll-work in red line with central stem and trefoil terminals, the latter painted in solid red with surrounding outline in red; also masonry pattern in red, with single line between the courses and double between the blocks, elaborated with roses; and around the arches wavy pattern. All apparently *c.* 1300, and partially obscured by lime-wash.

The South Aisle

Between the first and second windows from the west, and almost facing the north door, the upper part of a St. Christopher, of the usual gigantic proportions, holding a T-headed staff in the right hand and supporting with the left the Holy Child, who bears a large Orb in the left hand and raises the right towards His bearer's head. The Saint is clad in a voluminous cloak, and a gipon with skirt caught up to the waist by a belt; it was formerly to be seen that he also wore breeches tied at the knee, but the lower part of the work is now obliterated by a monument. When first discovered, *c.* 1840, there were remains of at least two later repaintings, including two more versions of the Holy Child; the Saint wore a soft cap, and his mantle was lined with vair, but it is impossible to decide whether these features belonged to the earlier paintings of the subject, or the later. Only the outline drawing now survives. *c.* 1360.

Tower Arch, south pier

Masonry pattern with large blocks outlined in black, there being double lines between the blocks and single between the courses.

---

[1] A very early example of this treatment.

B. Mus., *Dawson Turner Coll.*, vol. XX, 149, 150–1; *Gent. M.*, 1843, N.S., XIX, 381, repr.; Waller, *Surrey Archaeological Collections*, 1874, VI, 296; Keyser, *Mural Decorations*, 1883; Brindley, Blomefield's *Norfolk Supplement*, 1929, 304–6; Whaite, *St. Christopher*, 1929, 20, pl. 8.

SEETHING (near Bungay) Norfolk
ST. MARGARET

The Nave

North wall, west end, to the east of a window, which cuts into the only one of the three Skeletons now surviving, *Les Trois Vifs et les Trois Morts*; the three Kings, clad in long hose, hip-length gipons, belted low, and pointed shoes, are ranged somewhat stiffly in a row beyond a tree to the east of the skeleton. Below the feet of the two easternmost figures a rabbit escapes westward. Traces of a figure, perhaps that of an attendant, are to be seen to the extreme east of the scene, confused with parts of an ornamental border of considerably later date.

On the same wall, further east, St. Christopher, clad in a voluminous cloak, a knee-length gipon, evidently caught up to the waist by a belt, though this is concealed by the mantle, and breeches tied at the knee; he grasps a staff in the right hand and in the left bears the slight figure of the Holy Child, who holds an orb in the left hand and raises the right towards the Saint's head.

North wall, at east end, high on the wall, the head of a Saint with rough hair and long beard; the right hand also survives, in a pointing attitude, as though indicating some object formerly held in the left, now defaced. ? St. John the Baptist.

South wall, west end, remains of a consecration cross, only part of the enclosing circle, incised in the plaster, surviving. At the east end of the wall, between two windows, a painting of two women seated on a long bench with a large devil behind them, resting its hands on their heads; the woman on the spectator's left holds a rosary in her pendent right hand and below her a small devil is apparently running away with a second rosary. A second small devil is behind one of the women, and to the left of the group is part of an inscription consisting of apparently meaningless arrangements of similar letters, frequently repeated. The entire work is much defaced.

The *Trois Vifs* and the St. Christopher, first discovered in 1861, were subsequently obliterated; revealed again in 1925, they were once more obliterated, but again uncovered, the first in 1937, the second in 1949.

Norwich Mercury, xxv, vi, 1870; Keyser, *Mural Decorations*, 1883; Bardswell, *Norfolk Archaeology*, 1926, XXII, 338–40, repr.; James, *Suffolk & Norfolk*, 1933, 126; Carleton Williams, *B.A.A.J.*, 1942, 3rd ser., VII, 37, 40.

SELLING (near Faversham) Kent ST. MARY
The South Chancel Chapel

On the eastern splay of the easternmost of two windows in the south wall, a masonry pattern in double line, executed in red and elaborated with curling stems terminating in small leaves originally painted green, and sexfoil flowers in red, one in the centre of each block; on the southern splay of the southernmost of two lancet windows in the east wall, the same pattern.

On the splays of the two windows just mentioned, figure paintings, as follows:

On the northern splay of that on the north side, remains of a crocketed canopy framing the nimbed head of St. Paul, mainly bald, but with hair from just above the ears, bearded, and with wrinkled brow; the rest of the work is defaced. On the opposite splay, a well-preserved figure of St. Peter; standing frontally, with head turned to the right, and vested in a conical tiara, amice, orphreyed alb, dalmatic, chasuble and maniple, he holds in the left hand a cross, and gives a blessing with the right. The nimbus, if there was one, is defaced. Below are two large crossed Keys, in white on a field of red, with (?) a sword between them.

On the northern splay of the window on the south side, St. Bartholomew, nimbed, bearded, and with long hair, facing left and holding in the right hand a large knife; he is clad in a tunic and loose mantle. On the opposite splay, painted over the masonry pattern previously described, St. John the Evangelist, facing to the right; he is nimbed, with loosely waving hair and a slight down on the chin. Clad in a tunic and mantle, he rests the left hand on his breast and holds in the right a scroll, which falls vertically to touch the head of the large Eagle upon which he stands.

All four paintings are executed in ochres and black, in outline.

Grayling, *Churches of Kent*, 1913, II, 96; Cox, ed. Johnston, *Little Guides* (Kent), 1935, 268.
Plates 51*a*, *b*, 52*b*, 53*a*, *b*, 61*c*.

SHEERING (near Harlow) Essex ST. MARY

Below the south-west window in the nave, a consecration cross with foliated terminals, within a circle approximately 14 in. in diameter executed in red outlined with black. *c.* 1400.

R.C. Historical Monuments R., Essex, 1921, II, 210.

LITTLE SHELFORD (near Cambridge) Cambs
ALL SAINTS
The Chancel

The traceried panels of the stalls, of *c.* 1370, are enriched with the de Freville arms, the powdering of ermine spots and crescents having been recoloured.

The Nave

On the splays of an early window, scroll pattern. Remains of colour on the arch leading from the nave to the de Freville chantry.

The Tomb of Sir John de Freville, temp. Edward II.

On the wall at the back of the table tomb, an inscription in Norman French.

Keyser, *Mural Decorations,* 1883; Evelyn-White, *County Churches, Cambridgeshire,* 1911, 153-4.

SHORNCOTE (near Cirencester) Glos   ALL SAINTS
The Chancel

The Norman light in the north wall is decorated with radial lines having fan-like terminals, *c.* 1300; and on the adjacent wall, as also on the eastern side of the chancel arch, is a masonry pattern in double line, enriched with large multi-petalled flowers, and terminated at the top of the wall by a band of delicately-executed scroll-work between two narrow bands of wavy pattern.

Bird, *Mural Paintings, Glos.,* 1927, 27, repr.; id., *Old Glos. Churches,* 1928, 161.

SHORTHAMPTON (near Charlbury) Oxon
ALL SAINTS
The Nave

North wall: adjoining a Norman window, traces of a figure, thought to be that of a priest vested in an alb and stole, but without either cope or chasuble; the ends of the stole painted in a bright red and as if fringed, and decorated with a small curly-stemmed trefoil leaf, in place of the normal cross. Early fourteenth century.[1]

Johnston, *A.J.,* 1905, LXII, 163.

SHUDY CAMPS (near Cambridge) Cambs
ST. MARY

In 1895 the walls were partially cleared of white-wash, and the following survivals were found: on the

south wall, scroll-work, part of a large subject, apparently not identifiable, and an Angel; above, and at the sides of the chancel arch, a Doom, with Christ in Judgement, in the centre, attendant Angels on either side, on the right the Virgin in an attitude of supplication, and on the left, another nimbed figure, probably St. John the Evangelist; behind the Virgin the heavenly mansions, with Angels above them, and before them an indistinct figure of St. Peter with the Keys; round the arch, a procession of Souls, those on the northern side advancing towards the Heavenly Jerusalem, those on the southern encircled by a chain and dragged to Hell by demons; the entire subject terminated below by a wavy border. In 1930, of all the work mentioned above, the Doom alone survived, and that in a fragmentary state, most of the incidents having become indecipherable; but enough remained to make it clear that this subject at least was of late fourteenth-century date.

Keyser, *A.J.,* 1896, LIII, 184.

SIDBURY (near Sidmouth) Devon   ST. GILES
The Chancel

Traces of painting on all the walls except the west, which make it evident that a band of bent-riband pattern, arranged diamond-wise with cusping in the spandrels, between a border, enriched with a wavy line above and a plain, narrow border below, originally encircled the walls about 10 ft. from the present floor level, having beneath it a masonry pattern with joints in single line, executed in grey (or black faded) and 5 ft. below this a second ornamental band, consisting of a wavy pattern in grey and white. The masonry pattern continued over the splays of the window in the north wall, which had at its angle a shaft with a foliated capital, in grey outlined in black, the voussoirs of the arch having been picked out in grey, white and yellow, the last 'marbled'. There are indications that the window in the south wall had been similarly treated.

The North Transept

Remains of a general painted treatment of the entire transept; and above an arch of the arcade remains of figures, the drapery executed in yellow and white and outlined in red, one of them, the lower part alone surviving near the apex of the arch, being an ecclesiastic, vested in an alb and a yellow dalmatic (a deacon, perhaps St. Stephen, St. Lawrence, or St. Leonard), standing on a floor of square tiles adorned with roundels; behind him, at a slightly

[1] 1953. Only the ends of the stole, with trefoil leaf, still visible, the remainder having been obliterated with limewash.

lower level and to the spectator's right, a layman in red gipon, white cote-hardie and slightly pointed shoes, facing towards the cleric, his right hand upraised with the index finger pointing. On the outer member of the arch, voussoirs picked out in light red, yellow and white, those in yellow being 'marbled' in red, and the wide masonry-joints outlined in red. On the arch of the east window, masonry pattern similar to that just described. On another arch, delicate scroll-work in white upon a ground of black, as also on the south arcade.

SILCHESTER (near Basingstoke) Hants
ST. MARY

The Chancel

Within the splays of lancet windows, masonry pattern enriched with cinquefoil flowers, and on the soffits, chevrons; probably *c.* 1300 or earlier, but largely repainted.

The Nave

At the back of a monumental recess in the south wall, within which lies the effigy of a lady, of the earlier part of the fourteenth century, formerly a painting of the Soul Borne Heavenward by Angels. Wright, *Archaeological Album*, 1845, 154; *B.A.A.J.* 1860, XVI, 95; Keyser, *Mural Decorations*, 1883; id., *Memorials of Old Hants*, 1906, 142; Ditchfield, *Berks, B. & O.A.J.*, 1929, XXXIII, 108, repr.

SLAPTON (near Towcester) Northants
ST. BOTOLPH

The Nave

Remains of painted schemes dating from *c.* 1350 or just after the early part of the following century, the former being as follows:

On the first pier of the arcade from the east, a slight trace of a trefoil pattern in red.

On the north wall, in the spandrel between the first and second arches from the east, St. Michael Weighing Souls, with the Virgin interceding; she is clad in a white tunic and a black mantle, holds a book in her left hand and rests her rosary on the right-hand pan of the scales, in which is a small supplicating Soul; St. Michael, with outspread wings, stands on the left, holding the scales.

The South Aisle

In the north-east angle, parts of a hanging, painted in red and covered with scroll ornament in grey.

At the east end of the south wall, a miracle of St. Eloy, partly obscured by later painting; on the left the Saint, in full Mass vestments and bearing a crozier, stands before an anvil, holding in his left hand the leg of the restive horse, which, according to the legend, he detached for the purpose of shoeing it, afterwards replacing it on the animal's body; on the right an attendant figure, clad in a gipon buttoned down the front and belted at the waist, holds some unidentifiable instrument, presumably one used in the blacksmith's craft.

Between the window and the door in the south wall, partly covered with later painting, remains of *Les Trois Vifs et les Trois Morts*; two skeletons are visible, together with slight traces of the Kings, and on the ground there are flowers, with fragments of an inscription below.

On the north wall, in the spandrel between the first and second arches from the west, a portion of a painted arcade, in one bay of which a woman, veiled and clad in a long red kirtle, is seated with a book upon her knees; beside her are traces of another figure: St. Anne teaching the Virgin.

On the same wall, in the spandrel between the second and third arches from the west, an Annunciation; the Angel Gabriel, clad in a tunic and mantle, stands on the left, with outspread wings, holding a scroll with indecipherable traces of an inscription; on the right is the Virgin, wearing a long mantle, with her hands raised in the manner of an Orante; between them a pot of lilies.

On the soffit of the westernmost arch, an enthroned figure in red, much defaced.

Ochres and black and white are used, and *veneda* appears beneath the flesh tints. Where detail survives it is delicate in execution. Use has been made of incised line in setting out the work.

A.A.S.R. & P., 1874, XII, lxxxv; Waller, *A.J.*, 1877, XXXIV, 233–41; Keyser, *Mural Decorations*, 1883; Leach, *A.A.S.R. & P.*, 1907, XXIX, 121–8; Carleton Williams, *B.A.A.J.*, 1942, 3rd ser., VII, 23.

SMARDEN (near Headcorn) Kent   ST. MICHAEL

The Chancel

An unusual scheme of painting of *c.* 1300, which, judging from what is still extant, formerly consisted of a series of twelve large medallions each framing the Emblems of the Passion, within a circular border ornamented by one of the twelve articles of the Creed, in Lombardic capitals; to the left of the east window is a medallion with the inscription CREDO IN DEUM, PATREM OMNIPOTENTEM, CREATOREM COELI ET TERRAE, and on the opposite side another, with a defaced inscription. On the north wall, between the windows, is a fourth medallion with remains of an inscription as follows: ET VITAM . . . AMEN, and on the south yet another, the inscription reading QUI CONCEPTUS EST DE SPIRITU SCTO.

The Nave

To the north of the chancel arch, remains of an altar-painting, a Pietà; in the centre, the Virgin, supporting the Body of Christ, flanked by four, or perhaps five, nimbed figures, against a ground diapered with flowers.

Haslewood, *A. Cant.*, 1882, XIV, 20–30, repr.; Keyser, *Mural Decorations*, 1883.

SNODLAND (near Rochester) Kent ALL SAINTS

On a pier on the south side of the nave, a Crucifixion of *c.* 1300, largely repainted.

SOBERTON (near Bishop's Waltham) Hants
ST. PETER

The South Transept

In the centre of the eastern wall, a statue-niche, between two single-light windows, the mouldings of the tracery at the top and the sculptured heads which form part of the pedestal at the base being picked out in black, yellow, red and green; on the wall-surface, masonry pattern elaborated with roses; immediately below the wall-plate and at the level of the window-bottoms, a band of foliated scroll ornament; traces of strips of colour edging the architectural features. On the window-splays, figures of Saints, against a masonry pattern enriched with roses, drawn in black line, and but little shaded, namely, St. Anne teaching the Virgin, St. Cathérine trampling on the Emperor Maximinus and bearing the Wheel, St. Margaret Spearing the Dragon, and another Saint, unidentified, Within an aumbry, decoration comprising roses. *c.* 1300.

Victoria County Hist., 1908, III, 266.

WEST SOMERTON (near Yarmouth) Norfolk
ST. MARY

The Nave

On the north wall a Passion series, painted against grounds of deep red, the figures being 3–4 ft. in height. Reading from the west, the subjects are as follows:

1. The Entry into Jerusalem: Christ, clad in a green cloak, blessing with the right hand and holding an Orb in the left, rides eastward upon the ass; traces of painting further to the east, two or three upraised hands only being decipherable, are probably part of the same subject.

2. Beyond the intervening north door, ? The Mocking; in the centre, apparently, a seated figure with bowed head and hands crossed, but much defaced.

3. The Scourging: Christ stands in the centre, clad in a green loin-cloth diapered with white spots, His arms bound behind Him and His head bent to the left; there are two almost indecipherable figures of executioners, one on either side, the one on the right having his right arm raised behind his head. The figures are drawn in red outline, surrounded by a broader, white line.

4. Between the first and second windows from the west, beyond a considerable area of wall from which all traces have perished, the Resurrection: Christ steps from the tomb, its slanting lid being barely visible, with His right hand raised in blessing and the vexillum in His left; a green mantle is thrown about Him and over His left shoulder, and his hair and beard are of a golden-yellow tint. There are fragmentary traces of other figures. Pink flesh-tints appear throughout this series of paintings.

On the south wall, between the second and third windows from the east, a Doom, painted upon a ground of dark red diapered with roses; when it was discovered in 1867, parts of a figure of Christ were visible in the centre, but the wall-space has here been largely replastered during the intervening years, and there now remain only the Orb of the Universe upon which His feet rested and the silhouette of the rainbow upon which He was enthroned. On the spectator's left are remains of a kneeling figure of the Virgin, in a green mantle, and on his right parts of a figure of St. John, in a grey mantle, and slightly below them, one on either side, two Angels blowing the Last Trump, each having upon the head, a diadem with a small central cross and hair painted in yellow and outlined in red, an alb outlined in yellow, and wings executed in grey and white. Immediately below are the heads and upraised hands of Souls rising from their graves, among them, on the extreme left, the head of a woman with long hair, towards the centre, parts of a mitred head, and on the right a head covered by a hood and having a moustache and forked beard. The chief figures in this painting are about life-size: they are surrounded by a wide outline in white.

Between the third window from the east and the blocked south doorway, opposite the north door, remains of a St. Christopher, of the usual gigantic stature, the parts still visible being the right hand with the staff and the left supporting the Holy Child, who is clad in a yellow tunic with folds defined in red and shaded in buff. All the work is of late-fourteenth-century date.

l'Estrange, *Norfolk Archaeology*, 1872, VII, 256–9, repr.; ibid., 1879, VIII, 336; Keyser, *Mural Decorations*, 1883; André, *A.J.*, 1888, XLV, 414; Blomefield's *Norfolk Supplement*, 1929, 314; James, *Suffolk and Norfolk*, 1930, 146.

SPORLE (near Swaffham) Norfolk   ST. MARY

The South Aisle

On the south wall, occupying a space about 11 ft. 5 in. in length by 7 ft. 8 in. in height, 25 scenes from the history of St. Catherine of Alexandria, each separated from those adjacent by narrow bands of red, and the whole framed within a border of bent-riband pattern in umber and white on a ground of black. The episodes depicted are as follows:

1. Saint Catherine Upbraiding the Emperor Maximinus before the Gates of the Temple. The Saint, hearing that preparations were being made to force all the people of the city of Alexandria, even those who were Christian, to sacrifice to idols, approached the Emperor and upbraided him outside the Temple; to the left of the scene, the Emperor and Empress stand at the door of a building with towers, the Saint facing them, and extending her right hand as though in remonstrance; behind her two spectators.

2. The Emperor Sacrificing to Idols. In the centre, an altar, with a devil above it and figures kneeling on either side; to the extreme right, a guard with a spear, another figure, and the Saint, raising a hand in protest.

3. The Saint Disputing with the Emperor. Maximinus is seated cross-legged on the left, a drawn sword in his right hand, his left being raised as though in emphasis; the Saint, facing him, raises her right hand; behind her stands an attendant, clad in shoulder-cape, a red knee-length cote-hardie with the lower edge dagged, and shoes with long points.

4. The Dispute with the Philosophers. The Emperor is seated on the left, with three Philosophers, clad in long robes, in one case enriched with bands of ermine, immediately before him; behind them is the Saint, with both hands raised as if emphasizing the points of her argument, and to the extreme right another of the disputants.

5. The Burning of the Philosophers. On the left the Emperor enthroned, wearing a triple crown, a drawn sword in his right hand; in the centre, a group of Philosophers in the furnace, with an executioner behind them throwing one of their number into the flames; to the right, the Saint, encouraging the martyrs.

6. The Emperor Tempts the Saint. To the left, Maximinus, enthroned, tries to win over the Saint by promising that, if she will renounce Christ, she shall rank next to the Empress, and shall be 'adored of all the people as a goddess'. Beside him a tall courtier stands, joining in the endeavour to overcome her resistance by fair promises; an attendant or gaoler, in knee-length cote-hardie and long hose, stands behind her.

7. The Saint Condemned to Imprisonment. The composition resembles that of the previous scene, except that she is being led away by two gaolers or attendants.

8. The Saint in Prison. Her head is seen framed in a window, before which stands Porphyry, the 'prince of knights', clad in a knee-length cote-hardie, dagged at the lower edge.

9. The Conversion of Porphyry and Two Hundred Knights. To the left, the towers of the prison, and, apparently, the head of the Saint; towards the centre, immediately below a half-figure of Christ which appears in the sky, the kneeling Porphyry, with a group of knights behind him, together with some other figures, one of them apparently wearing a mitre or tiara.

10. The Saint Before the Emperor. Maximinus enthroned to the left of the scene, as throughout; before him the Saint, stripped to the waist and bearing marks of scourging, and beyond her a gaoler and an executioner, the latter flourishing a three-thonged knotted whip.

11. The Saint Condemned by the Emperor to be broken on the Wheel. Maximinus seated as before, with the Saint and a gaoler facing him.

12. The Breaking of the Wheel, a subject occupying the space of two. To the left, Maximinus, enthroned, struck by a fragment of the Wheel, the blood streaming from his face; in the centre the Saint, with fragments of the Wheel or Wheels, and parts of stricken figures, some lying supine where they have been struck down; to the extreme right, the kneeling Empress, crowned, like the Emperor, with a triple crown; and in the sky above, to left and right of St. Catherine, a half-figure of an Angel with drawn sword.

13. The Condemnation of the Empress. Maximinus enthroned, a huge scimitar grasped in his right hand and before him the Empress, with triple crown and clad in a long kirtle, being grasped and led away to execution by two gaolers, dressed in short cote-hardies, belted low; they have maces slung from their belts and wear extravagant head-dresses.

14. The Decollation of the Empress. She kneels on the right, her back turned to the executioner, who

prepares to strike; he is clad in a cote-hardie, elaborately dagged at the lower edge, a short, patterned cloak, and an elaborate, turban-like head-dress.

15. Porphyry Buries the Body of the Empress by Moonlight. The 'prince of knights' stands in an open grave, wielding a shovel, above him the line of a hill and the sky over it, with the moon and some stars; in the foreground the headless corpse of the Empress; on either side, a conventionalized tree.

16. The Emperor Condemns the Two Hundred Converted Soldiers of his Guard. A double scene; to the left Maximinus, as before grasping a large scimitar, a courtier standing beside him whose head is rendered as a hideous caricature; before him, traces of the condemned soldiers.

17. ? The Emperor Condemns Porphyry. A somewhat defaced subject, with Maximinus on the left and an elaborately gowned courtier standing beside him, facing two figures of which traces only remain.

18. The Massacre of the Soldiers of the Guard. A double scene; four executioners, two of them brandishing scimitars above their heads, fall upon a group of soldiers, all in armour and pointed bascinets, striking them to the ground; to the right, a hillside covered with grass and flowers, and a conventionalized tree.

19. The Saint Before the Emperor. The general arrangement resembles that of the other condemnation scenes.

20. The Saint between Executioners or Gaolers. She stands in the centre, facing frontally, clad, as in the previous scene, in a long robe; on each side is an executioner or gaoler, his head a hideous caricature as in 16, in cote-hardie, long stockings, their colours counterchanged, and bizarre head-dress, the one on the right holding a large implement.

21. In the centre of the scene ? a small nude Soul, surrounded by devils.

22. ? The Saint Condemned to be Beheaded. The left of the scene is defaced; to the right St. Catherine is led away by a gaoler in parti-coloured cote-hardie and hose.

23. The Decollation of St. Catherine. The Saint kneels in the centre of the scene, gazing heavenward, where Angels appear in the sky; behind her the executioner raises a scimitar.

24. The Burial of St. Catherine on Mount Sinai. In the upper part of the scene, a sarcophagus having the Saint's body within it, attended by two Angels with outspread wings; below, against a background of flowers and grass, two more Angels, censing.

25. Pilgrims at the Tomb of St. Catherine. In the upper part of the scene, the sarcophagus, and on the left a single tree; in the foreground, against a bank of grass and flowers, three pilgrims kneeling in prayer, one tonsured and another, on the extreme left, with scrip and bourdon.

The paintings were discovered c. 1855, when they seem, on the whole, to have been in good condition. At that time various details such as jewels, chaplets of flowers, curling hair, forked beards, and 'piked shoon', were visible, but most of them have now disappeared. The description given above was taken from Winter's drawing, preserved in the Norwich Castle Museum, and checked by comparison with the remains of the original paintings, which are now in the main much defaced. The colours found in them are a copper green, red and yellow ochre, and black. Their date would appear to be c. 1390–1400.

P. *Society of Antiquaries*, 1867, 2nd ser., III, 386–90; Winter, *Norfolk Archaeology*, 1872, VII, 303–8, repr.; Keyser, *Mural Decorations*, 1883; James, *Suffolk & Norfolk*, 1930, 190.

STANFORD RIVERS (near Chipping Ongar) Essex
ST. MARY or ST. MARGARET

The Nave

On the splays of the easternmost window in the south wall, traces of two figures, each framed within a painted niche having a gabled and crocketed canopy with a trefoil arch and flanking pinnacles; immediately above the niches, traces of shields of arms, largely defaced. Early fourteenth century.

R.C. *Historical Monuments R., Essex*, 1921, II, 221.

STANION (near Kettering) Northants ST. PETER
The Chancel

On the north side of the east window, the lower part of a figure, perhaps clad in a chasuble, painted in white line on a buff ground, and a deer in red; on the south side painting too indistinct for identification; early fourteenth century.

STANLEY ST. LEONARD (near Stroud) Glos
ST. LEONARD

The Chancel

On the east wall, to the north of the window, a kneeling Angel, bearing a sceptre, painted in yellow and outlined in red, and clad in a red mantle, lined with green; a companion figure probably once existing on the opposite side of the window may have been that of the Virgin, the two together forming an

Annunciation. The whole is painted over a masonry pattern executed in double red line and enriched with red flowers stalked in blue, upon a ground of white. On the window-splays and arches, freely-drawn scroll-work in red and blue; and on the eastern splay of the north-east window a standing figure, like the Angel previously mentioned, of life-size, holding in the left hand the model of a church, to which he points with the right; on the opposite splay, another figure, bearing a scroll, much defaced. On the south side, near the chancel arch, a knight in armour with hands folded in prayer. All these paintings, to some extent defaced when discovered c. 1880, are now barely decipherable, where they are not entirely destroyed.

The Nave

Remains of a scheme, apparently more or less of the same date as that described above, were discovered on the south wall about the same time, and destroyed when the plaster was stripped from the walls; they were described as 'beautiful pictures', with colours 'vivid and fresh', and it may be inferred from this that their condition was good. The subjects mentioned, some of which seem to have been misunderstood, include 'a hart at cooling streams', the 'miraculous draught of fishes', and, on a deep window-splay, 'a bishop confirming'.

Middleton, *Bristol & G.A.S.R. & P.*, 1880–1, V, 129–31, repr.; Keyser, *Mural Decorations*, 1883; Swynnerton, *Archaeologia*, 1921, LXXI, 219, repr.

STANTON (near Evesham) Glos   ST. MICHAEL

The North Transept

On the north wall, to the west of a window, traces of a large subject, confused with remains of an eighteenth-century text; perhaps a Presentation in the Temple, since traces of what may be an altar are seen between two figures, that on the right, possibly the Virgin, clad in tunic and mantle, apparently holding the Child, of Whose figure only an arm survives, towards another much-defaced figure with extended arms. To the east of the same window, an almost indecipherable figure, and another, a woman clad in a tunic and wearing a girdle. On the east wall, below the string-course, traces of red.

The South Transept

Around the window in the east wall, masonry pattern, with courses and joints in yellow ochre, and in the centre of each block a cinquefoil or conventionalized rose in red ochre.

All the work is of the early fourteenth century.

STANTON HARCOURT (near Witney) Oxon
ST. MICHAEL

The Nave

Considerable remains of a scheme of painting, apparently of c. 1350, were discovered in 1846 and soon afterwards destroyed. There were two tiers of subject-paintings, elaborated with long inscribed scrolls, the first letter of each inscription being rubricated; but of the higher of the two tiers only the feet of some of the figures survived.

South wall, reading from the east: 1. The Last Supper, traditionally arranged, with Judas in front of the long table, covered by a cloth festooned in a formal manner; 2. The Washing of Feet, Christ kneeling before one of the Disciples.

North wall, reading from the west: 1. The Descent from the Cross, much defaced, part of the cross being visible, as also portions of the figure of Christ, and a fairly intact figure of a man in a short tunic, standing upon a ladder and engaged in freeing His left arm; below this subject, remains of an Entombment. 2. To the east of the two subjects just described, between the two north windows, a Descent into Hell, with Christ bearing the vexillum and trampling upon a devil who clutches a triple hook; within the Jaws of Hell the Souls, and upon the point of the upper Jaw a small devil winding a horn.

Below the paintings the walls were decorated with a pattern which, from the description, would appear to have been of later date.

In the church is an effigy, of c. 1392, representing Maud, daughter of John, Lord Grey of Rotherfield, which retains traces of painting and gilding, as does also the canopy over the monument of Isabel, daughter of Richard de Camville, which also served as an Easter Sepulchre. c. 1300.

Dyke, *A.J.*, 1846, II, 365–8, reprs.; *Builder*, 1864, 725; Keyser, *Mural Decorations*, 1883.

STANTON LONG (near Cambridge) Cambs
ST. MICHAEL

North aisle, north wall, eastern end: a masonry pattern with the horizontal joints executed in single, and the vertical in double line, simple scroll-work being placed immediately above.

Description supplied by Mrs. M. Bardswell, 1934.

STARSTON (near Harleston) Norfolk
ST. MARGARET

The Nave

In 1872, in the process of pulling down part of the

north wall for the purpose of constructing an organ chamber, an arched recess, which had at some time been bricked up, was discovered; it was 4 ft. in width, the same in height, and about 1 ft. in depth, the base being about 2 ft. from the ground, and on the wall at the back of it was found a painting, but this was, unfortunately, destroyed in the course of an attempt to remove it together with the plaster from the wall. It is recorded that at the time of the discovery 'the colours were exceeding bright and perfect' and that 'the painting of parts . . . was very beautiful', especially the shield [in fact, a small panel] with the crucifixion. . . . It was a perfect miniature and would bear looking into with a magnifying glass'. The subject was erroneously identified as a Death of the Virgin; it was actually, as may be seen from a drawing by C. J. Winter, a fourteenth-century funeral scene, painted in the usual earth colours against a green background. A bier, covered with a pall ornamented by a diamond pattern elaborated with quatrefoils in alternate diamonds, and with white drapery at one end (where, presumably, the head of the deceased was shown, but this part of the painting was much defaced) and supported upon an elaborately carved base, stretched across most of the lower part of the composition; behind it, on the western side, were ? part of an altar, a small panel painting of the Crucifixion, with a small shield above it, over which the officiating priest (with an acolyte behind him), vested in alb and pink chasuble, stretched out his arms, apparently towards a scroll, held in the left hand of a bearded and tonsured attendant figure (perhaps a server), and bearing the inscription PRECOR TE MARIA. Behind this figure was another, also bearded, but not tonsured, and evidently a layman, standing frontally with hands clasped against his breast as though in distress, and clad in a grey tunic, perhaps a faded black. Immediately beyond the officiating priest, in the centre of the scene, were two female figures; that on the west, clad in a long red 'sideless gown' and pink kirtle, and having on her head a circlet with a fretted edge, a crespine and a barbette, clasped her hands as if in sorrow and gazed with solicitude at her companion, who in a grey cloak and darker grey kirtle, with a white veil over her head, held a prayer-book in her left hand and rested her head upon her right, as though overcome by grief. Immediately above, in the apex of the arch, the Soul, represented as a small nude figure, was shown being carried to Heaven in a cloth by two Angels emerging from clouds on either side. To the east of the mourner last described, a male figure of youthful appearance, clad in a long

pink tunic, extended his arms towards her as though in an attempt at consolation; he was accompanied by ten others, similarly clad, and, like him, with hair cut straight across the forehead and curled at the level of the ears at the sides, except in the case of one figure, who perhaps had the head covered. The work was of very early fourteenth-century date.

Phipson, *Norfolk Archaeology*, 1872, VII, 300–2, repr. (from a drawing by Winter); Keyser, *Mural Decorations*, 1883; *Victoria County Hist.*, *Norfolk*, 1906, II, 532; James, *Suffolk & Norfolk*, 1930, 127. Plate 56a.

STAVELEY (near Chesterfield) Derby
ST. JOHN BAPTIST

A richly carved recess, now built into the outer wall of the north aisle, but once in the north wall of the nave, formerly framed in its upper half a figure of Christ supported by two Angels, variously described as a Resurrection, or a Baptism, but probably the former.

Cox, *Churches of Derbyshire*, 1875, I, 350–1; Keyser, *Mural Decorations*, 1883.

STEVENTON, Hants ST. NICHOLAS

On the south side of the chancel arch, masonry pattern in double line, elaborated with cinquefoils in black, and some marbling in red; traces of painting in red within a large niche; on both responds of the arch, scale-work elaborated with trefoils, and masonry blocks in yellow and white alternately.

Little Guides, Hants, 1949, 163.

STIFFORD (near Grays) Essex ST. MARY

On the east respond of the south arcade is a corbel, patterned in black, red and gold, the carved head forming the terminal being painted with the same colours, and the hair and crown gilt; on the wall, about the corbel, are remains of a diaper of rosettes in red on a ground of black. c. 1300.

Formerly, on the east wall of the chantry chapel, the Angel appearing to Zacharias; and on the north wall of the nave, St. Dunstan and the Devil. Both these paintings were executed in black and red. c. 1300.

Palin, *Stifford and its Neighbourhood*, 1871, 53, 60; Keyser, *Mural Decorations*, 1883; R.C. *Historical Monuments R., Essex*, 1923, IV, 153.

STOKESBY (near Yarmouth) Norfolk
ST. ANDREW

The Nave

Formerly, to the west of the north door, a painting in which two women, veiled and clad in kirtles buttoned down the front for some distance, are depicted seated in the centre of a long bench, their heads close together, their right and left hands clasped, and on the left shoulder of the one and the right shoulder of the other a beetle-like creature of some size. The woman on the spectator's right has her right hand on the left shoulder of her companion, whose kirtle is yellow, while hers is grey. Immediately behind them, a large Devil, horned and with bat's wings outspread; to the left of the group, parts of a devil, apparently in front of the bench, and behind it another, horned, and holding in the right claw a pointed instrument; ? part of child's figure; to the right of the group, a veiled woman, clad like the two others, seated on the end of the bench, a rosary held in her hands and hanging between her knees, and to the extreme right, the heads of three medium-sized creatures, unidentifiable, but apparently beaked.

A drawing by Winter, made in 1858, is preserved in Norwich Castle Museum; the painting is erroneously described in *Norfolk Archaeology*, 1859, V, 291–2, as the Seven Deadly Sins.

STOKE DRY (near Uppingham) Leics and Rutland
ST. ANDREW

The Chancel

On the east wall, to the north side, a Martyrdom of St. Andrew, with a small female figure, probably that of a donor, below, and also, still further to the north, traces, perhaps of figures, covered by whitewash; on the south side, an ecclesiastic, with an altar behind him, standing under a round-headed arch with remains of masonry pattern above it; below this figure, another round-headed, but somewhat shallow arch, framing a group of figures whose gestures are animated. Around the east window, a foliated scroll pattern in red and black between two narrow bands of wavy pattern, the higher in black on white, enriched with roundels in red, the lower in red on white.

The South Chantry Chapel

On the south wall, opposite a small door, St. Christopher, bearing the Holy Child on his right arm and a staff in his left hand; he wears a hat with upturned brim (much defaced) and is clad in a red three-quarter-length gipon and light-coloured cloak, while about his feet large scaly fish are swimming.

To the east of the St. Christopher, on the same wall, the Martyrdom of St. Edmund the King, depicted as crowned, tied to a tree, and pierced with many arrows, on either side being an archer with a drawn bow. On the western splay of a window, ? the Martyrdom of a female Saint (probably St. Catherine or St. Margaret), who stands stripped to the waist between two male figures clad in short gipons, and long shoes, the one on the left apparently holding some instrument; on the eastern splay, the head, crowned and veiled, and the shoulders, of a female figure, the remainder being defaced.

On the north wall, to the west of the doorway, a man in short pink gipon and long black hose, who stands in ? the doorway of a building, either welcoming an ecclesiastic in a black habit, or receiving something from him, while to the right are two more figures also apparently of ecclesiastics, one in a white habit and the other in one of black and white.

Keyser, *Mural Decorations*, 1883; *Little Guides, Leics & Rutland*, 1924, 210; Whaite, *St. Christopher*, 1929, 21, repr.

NORTH STOKE (near Wallingford) Oxon

The Nave

Both the north and the south walls are pierced by three windows, and encircled at the level of the window-bottoms by a string-course, below which the walls are devoid of painting, though above it there are considerable remains of a fourteenth-century scheme. *c.* 1300.

North wall, reading from the west: 1. Between the first and second windows, a large rendering of the Three Living and the Three Dead, the former, as usual, being shown richly clad, the latter as emaciated corpses; at either side is a tree. 2. Between the second and third windows, two tiers of subjects, separated by a horizontal band of scroll-and-maple-leaf ornament in yellow; in the upper tier, St. Stephen before the 'prince of the priests', who is seated cross-legged upon a throne and holds a sword, while the Saint stands facing him, vested in a black dalmatic and holding a book; and the Stoning of St. Stephen, with Stephen kneeling in prayer, three executioners, one with a basket of stones, and an Angel receiving the soul of the martyr. In the lower tier, St. Catherine tied to the spokes of a wheel, is tortured (much defaced), and in a second scene appears to be undergoing further torment, since two executioners are shown wielding rods, and there are remains of other figures, one perhaps being that of the Saint. The executioners, if such they are intended to be, are hooded and clad in parti-coloured gipons, black hose, and light-coloured shoes, and their heads are rendered with much realism of expression, amounting almost to caricature. At the extreme eastern end of the wall, remains of a figure, perhaps that of a king.

South wall, reading from the east: Between the first and second windows, three tiers of subjects between the string-course and the wall-plate, separated by running borders of green scroll-work between bands of pink and white, the former enriched with leaves of an unusually naturalistic type. In the lowest tier, which occupies the same amount of space as do the two above it together, is a traditionally-arranged Last Supper; and in the central tier, other subjects belonging to the Passion sequence, viz. —the Betrayal, with Christ facing Judas and surrounded by guards: Christ kneeling before Pilate, seated on a throne and holding a drawn sword; and the Flagellation; in the highest tier the Resurrection is the best-preserved scene, the others, the Deposition and the Carrying of the Cross, being identifiable, but much perished. Over the door are two defaced figures, one an Angel, ? perhaps parts of an Annunciation.

On the east wall the paintings, with one exception, a Martyrdom of St. Thomas of Canterbury, low on the north side of the chancel arch, are ill-preserved. Above and around the arch is a Last Judgement, there being on the north side three souls rising from their graves, one of them, a woman, being received by a bishop in mass vestments, probably meant for St. Peter, attended by a deacon—either St. Stephen or St. Lawrence. On the south side another deacon is seen, receiving a Vested Bishop; and low down on the wall is a small Crucifixion, with the attendant figures of the Virgin and St. John. Of the Martyrdom of St. Thomas the figures of the four knights remain; they are clad in chain mail and surcoats, the first, with a bend sinister upon his shield, being shown in the act of striking down the martyr (whose figure is defaced) with his sword, the second in the act of drawing his, the third with sword already drawn, and the fourth pointing in the direction of the Saint. There is a pronounced tendency towards caricature in the rendering of the heads. The range of colours is exceptional, including as it does black, yellow, vermilion, pink, a dark brownish-red, a dark, warm green, and an emerald green.

The splays of all the windows have lost their painted treatment, with the exception of the eastern splay of the central window in the south wall, where survives part of a St. John Baptist, including the head of the Saint and the disc he bears, charged with an *Agnus Dei*; and the corresponding splay of the westernmost window, upon which is discernible the figure of a demon.

The paintings were first discovered in 1884.

Keyser, *A.J.*, 1896, LIII, 178; id., *B.A.A.J.*, 1918, N.S., XXIV, 15–18, repr.; Borenius, *St. Thomas Becket in Art*, 1932, 99; Carleton Williams, *B.A.A.J.*, 1942, 3rd ser., VII, 40.

STOW BARDOLPH (near Downham Market) Norfolk
HOLY TRINITY
The Chancel

This was rebuilt in 1850; on the east wall, to the south of the altar, a consecration cross was formerly visible, and around the chancel arch cusping terminating in trefoils.

The Nave

Over the south door, a Martyrdom of St. Edmund, partly covered by a later St. Christopher. St. Edmund crowned, bound, and pierced by numerous arrows, and on either side an archer drawing his bow.

Dashwood, *Norfolk Archaeology*, 1852, III, 134, 136, repr.; B. Mus., *Dawson Turner Collection*, Add. Vol. VIII, 173–4; Keyser, *Mural Decorations*, 1883.

SUTTON BINGHAM (near Yeovil) Somerset
ALL SAINTS

A scheme of painting, apparently of the late thirteenth or of the early fourteenth century, formerly covered the walls of both nave and chancel; discovered in 1868, the decoration in the chancel was mutilated and rendered all but valueless as an example of its period through repainting carried out, according to one record, 'by an amateur artist, with a free pencil'. It comprised: masonry pattern, enriched with flowers; a Coronation of the Virgin; and figures of various Saints. Survivals in the nave, which were uncovered at a later date and escaped repainting, include a consecration cross, part of a Crucifixion, and a Death of the Virgin, the last-named being traditionally arranged, and painted in ochres and black, against a background sown with cinquefoils.

Keyser, *Mural Decorations*, 1883; Batten, *Historical and Topographical Collections Relating to South Somerset*, 1894, 35–6; Long, *Dorset A.S.*, 1928, L, 101.

SWANSCOMBE (near Northfleet) Kent
ST. PETER AND ST. PAUL

Within two recessed niches on either side of the chancel arch figures were discovered in 1875, and described as perhaps St. Peter and St. Paul; further, floral and leaf patterns, and scroll-work, are recorded as having existed in the church.

Sparvel-Bayly, *History of Swanscombe*, 1875, pp. 39–40; Ross, *P. Society of Antiquaries*, VI, 2nd ser., 233; Keyser, *Mural Decorations*, 1883.

SWINSTEAD (near Bourn), Lincs   ST. MARY

On the first pier of the early-thirteenth-century north arcade, reading from the east, seven heater-shaped shields of arms, the two facing north into the aisle and south into the nave respectively measuring 16 in. × 18 in. and the remaining five approximately 10 in. × 11 in.; the charges comprise—*Gules a daunce (or a fess dancetty) or (? argent)*; on the large shield on the south, *Or (? argent) a lion rampant gules; Or (? argent) a cross gules; Barry of twelve or (? argent) and gules; Argent a fess between two chevrons gules*; on the large shield on the north, *Or (? argent) a maunche gules*; and *Argent (? or) two bars gules. c.* 1300.

Rouse, *Lincs A. & A.S.R.*, 1940, II, N.S., pt. 1, 1–6, repr.

TARRANT CRAWFORD (near Blandford) Dorset
ST. MARY

The Nave

South wall, reading from the east:

The Annunciation. Beneath an architectural canopy of Decorated type, the Angel Gabriel, bearing a sceptre and scroll, faces the Virgin, a pot of lilies between them. Scroll-work above the canopy.

Beyond a window which here intervenes, two tiers of painting, framed above and below, by ornamental borders (that beneath the wallplate confused with remains of a scroll-work border) and separated by a band in white outlined in red and ornamented with small roundels.

First tier, extending to the end of this wall: Thirteen subjects from the history of St. Margaret of Antioch, each approximately 3 ft. × 2½ ft. and separated from the next by a narrow band in black outlined in white and black. They are as follows:

1. The Saint, seated with a kneeling figure before her, perhaps the messenger from the Provost Olybrius.
2. The Approach of the Provost, with an attendant.
3. The Saint before the Provost.
4. The Imprisonment of the Saint.
5. The Saint refuses to worship idols.
6. The Saint Scourged.
7. The Saint again defies the Provost.
8. An indecipherable subject.
9. The Saint hung up by the hair and tormented.
10. The Saint tortured in a vessel of boiling water.
11. The Saint burnt in a fire and tormented with brands.
12. The Saint swallowed by the devil in the form of a dragon, but emerging unharmed, raising her left hand towards an Angel in the sky above, and extending her right towards a figure on the left of the composition, perhaps the gaoler.
13. The Saint vanquishes devils.

The series was probably concluded on the adjacent west wall, where only fragments of colour survive.

Second tier: Les Trois Vifs et les Trois Morts, represented in two 'moments' so as to fill the entire tier, with the feet and lower part of the legs of the figures painted over the ornamental border below; on the eastern side, vestiges of a group of Three Kings, presumably once shown as observing the Corpses, and rather to the west, but filling the greater part of the tier, their approach to the latter and receipt of the warning. The first King is shown as a young man, the third carries a hawk on his left wrist.

Beyond the blocked south doorway, a Crucifixion, painted over an earlier subject; in the former, Christ on the Cross and figures of the Virgin and St. John are discernible, in the latter two small heads. Above these paintings, between them and the band separating the two tiers, traces of colour.

North wall, reading from the west:

1. Between the north door and the north-west angle of the wall, remains of an indecipherable subject.
2. To the east of the door: traces of St. Michael Weighing Souls, of which parts of the wings and the balance-beam remain; of a St. Christopher, bearing the Divine Child on his left shoulder; and of a female Saint, perhaps St. Catherine, as complementary to St. Margaret, since parts of what appear to be the spokes of the Wheel survive.
3. Between a window and the north-east angle of the wall, remains of a figure, with pendent drapery before it.

All the paintings appear to be of the fourteenth century, the better-preserved among them, i.e. the Annunciation, the St. Margaret series, and *Les Trois Vifs*, being of a date towards 1350; they are executed in ochres (in the St. Margaret series, against grounds of white and red in alternation), and show signs of good workmanship, but their condition is very fragmentary.

Almack, *Dorset A.C.P.*, 1918, XXXIX, 109; Long, *Dorset A.S.*, 1928, L, 107; Rouse, *St. Mary's Church, Tarrant Crawford* (pamphlet pub. 1948).

TETTENHALL (near Wolverhampton) Staffs
ST. MICHAEL AND ALL ANGELS

Extensive remains of painting were discovered in the church in 1841, including coats-of-arms, and 'various devices', but almost all the work was destroyed, apart from three skeletons, no doubt the remains of a representation of *Les Trois Vifs et les Trois Morts*, in the Wrothesley chapel.

Gent. M., 1842, N.S., XVIII, pt. 1, 199; Way, *A.J.*, 1864, XXI, 219; Keyser, *Mural Decorations*, 1883; Storck, *Burl. M.*, 1912, XXI, 318; Carleton Williams, *B.A.A.J.*, 1942, 3rd ser., VII, 40.

TEWKESBURY, Glos
ABBEY CHURCH OF THE BLESSED VIRGIN
The Choir

The roof was formerly painted and gilt, but has been repainted.

The Presbytery

The second chantry from the west, on the northern side, the Founder's Chapel, to Robert Fitz-Hamon, was erected in 1397, and on the east wall are fragmentary paintings, now indecipherable, said to have represented scenes in the life of St. Thomas of Canterbury.

The third and easternmost chantry, that of Hugh Le Despenser (d. 1349) and his wife, retains traces of rich colouring on the canopy.

The single chantry on the south side, known as the Trinity Chapel, is that of Edward Le Despenser, who died in 1375; on the east wall is a painting of the Trinity, traditionally represented, with the Dove, and censing Angels on either side, together with the figures of Le Despenser and his wife; below was originally a series of scenes framed in an architectural setting in perspective, of which the Coronation of the Virgin alone survives, though a Resurrection is recorded as having been visible *c.* 1849. At that date, the donor figures were thus described:

'The figures of the lord and lady are somewhat defaced. The outline is all red, the shading blue; the collar, his girdle and buttons, are yellow, the flowers of his coat gold . . . the lady has a close under-dress of cloth of gold, the pattern of which (nearly worn off) appears in the opening of her upper-dress under her arm.' [She wears a 'sideless' surcoat.]

On the damaged Sedilia are traces of the original colour and gilding; the canopies and backs were originally decorated with a diaper of fleurs-de-lis and flowers.

The Nave

On the roof, traces of the original colouring.

Lyson, *Antiquities of Gloucestershire*, 1803, pts. lvi and lxxix; Dyde, *History of Tewkesbury*, 1803, 50; Blackburne, *Decorative Painting*, 1847, 39, 61; *Gent. M.*, 1849, N.S., XXXII, 122, 471–2, repr.; Keyser, *Mural Decorations*, 1883; Biver and Howard, *A.J.*, 1909, LXVI, 13–14; James, *Abbeys*, 1926, 48–9; Bird, *Mural Paintings, Glos.*, 1927, 30, repr.

THORNHAM PARVA (near Eye) Suffolk
ST. MARY
The Nave

On the north wall, remains of figure subjects arranged in two tiers, about 4 ft. 6 in. in depth, divided by a narrow border of scroll ornament enriched with trefoils, the lower tier being terminated at approximately 5 ft. from the present floor level by a similar but wider border, about 8 in. deep. In the lower tier, remains of a 'history' of St. Edmund the King, comprising a representation in red outline of the translation of his body to Bury, in which two monks are portrayed lifting it from the grave; two others were formerly visible, bearing it away, within a portable shrine covered with a red pall, but this part of the painting is now defaced, and all the other scenes, even when first uncovered, were too damaged to be decipherable. In the upper tier, to the west, a small quatrefoil in red, and to the east (?) part of a 'tree' composed of scroll-work, also in red. Around the head of the north door, a wavy pattern in red and white, and immediately above the door a large wheel about 4 ft. in diameter, painted in red outline filled in with yellow, apparently placed before a fence or gate; above it an ornamental border of scroll-work enriched with trefoils which extends the length of the wall below the wallplate, above the upper tier of paintings. On the lower part of the wall, below the second tier and just to the east of the north door, a consecration cross in red within a double border of the same colour, and another to the east of the only window in this wall. On the eastern part of the wall masonry pattern elaborated with quatrefoils.

On the south wall, in the lower part of the space, masonry pattern like that just described, and above it, to the east of the south door, remains of two tiers of painting and of scroll-work borders resembling those of the north wall. In the upper tier, a fragmentary subject, only part of a figure, clad in a red tunic and white mantle, with arms outstretched towards another, mainly defaced, being decipherable; and in the lower tier, adjacent to a small round-headed window ornamented with wavy pattern in red and white, a crowned female figure, holding a book and having upon her knee a child, also crowned and behind her a figure clad in a red tunic and white mantle, but much defaced. A third consecration cross is to be seen on this wall, near the south door. On the west wall only traces of scroll-work survive.

Johnston, *A.J.*, 1904, LXI, 340; Harris, *Suffolk I.A. & N.H.P.*, 1925–7, XIX, 292–311; Long, *The Guardian*, vii, v, 1937.

The Thornham Parva Retable

The Retable, which had been preserved at Thornham Hall since its purchase by an ancestor in 1778, from a family named Fox, which had made use of it in an attic chapel at Rookery Farm, Stradbroke, was presented to the Church by Lord Henniker in 1927.

It is 12 ft. 6 in. wide, consisting of nine panels made up of narrow vertical boards, $36\frac{3}{4}$ in. high by approximately 5 in. wide, the central panel being 25 in. wide, and the other eight $13\frac{1}{2}$ in. on an average. They are framed as the three sections of a triptych, and each is set within a cusped arch, the spandrels between the arches, painted vermilion, being ornamented with carvings of foliage and flowers, coloured mainly in natural tints, the rose (gilded), heartsease, and oak leaves, with acorns, being recognizable; the majority are in good condition, but the central leaf of the heartsease pattern between the arches framing the St. Catherine and the St. John Baptist is damaged, thus weakening the design. The framework is entirely painted, the shafts supporting the arches in red and green, the colours counterchanged, the red being enriched with cinquefoils in gold and the green with golden fleurs-de-lis, and the backgrounds were originally gilded; the latter are ornamented with 'prints', each design being enclosed within a square, and varied in each panel, as to the motifs employed. In alternate panels, every square is filled with 'prints', or else every other square, in place of a 'print', is painted green and (formerly) adorned with a central fleur-de-lis in gold, many of which survive. The central panel contains a Crucifixion, and the eight flanking panels figures of Saints, all delicately executed in oil colour, or, more probably, in an emulsion of white of egg and oil, upon a white priming. Reading from the spectator's left, the subjects are as follows:

1. St. Dominic, standing on a grassy hillock, clad in the habit of his Order, facing towards the centre of the Retable, and holding a long preaching cross in the left hand and a book in the right. The face is slightly scratched; the nimbus, the book, and the head of the cross were regilt during a nineteenth-century restoration of the work, and patterns in green added to the two former; and the habit was repainted to a considerable extent, especially in the lower part, where about a third is nineteenth-century repainting. The background is completely covered with 'prints', the design being an eagle displayed within a quatrefoil, the corners of the containing squares being filled with minute fleurs-de-lis; it was, as were all the other panels, painted over with a stone colour during the restoration previously mentioned, but this overpainting has been removed.

2. St. Catherine, crowned, with her brown hair covered by a transparent veil, standing in a slightly swaying pose and facing towards St. Dominic; she wears a tunic of dark green and a red mantle lined with vair, drawn up to cover her right hand, from which it hangs in graceful folds, and in which she holds the Wheel, pointing to it with her left. The face is slightly scratched, and some retouching is visible. The crown and Wheel are regilt and the left hand partially repainted. On the lower part of the drapery, as in the case of the St. Dominic, about a third of the work is restoration. The background is of 'prints' in alternation with squares painted in green and once patterned in gold, the design of the former being a fleur-de-lis within a quatrefoil, the corners of the containing squares filled with small trefoils.

3. St. John Baptist, facing away from St. Catherine towards the Crucifixion in the centre; he stands, with legs bare to the knees and feet wide apart, upon a grassy hillock, holding a red disc charged with an *Agnus Dei* in his left hand and raising his right, with the fingers spread. He has long hair, curled slightly about the brow, and a long beard, and is clad in a chasuble-shaped garment of brown, patterned with tufts of white hair and edged with similar tufts, and lined with green. The background is entirely covered with 'prints', the design being an *Agnus Dei* within a circle enriched by cusping, a trefoil leaf filling the angles of the containing squares. Some retouching is discernible on the head, mantle and legs.

4. St. Peter, tonsured, turning towards St. John Baptist, his right hand raised palm outward, and in his left the Keys; his tunic is red, shaded with pinkish yellow and his mantle, drawn up over the breast in heavy folds and hanging from the right shoulder, is a reddish purple, lined with green; the tunic clears his bare feet, which rest on a grassy mound. The background is of 'prints' in alternation with green squares once patterned in gold, and the design of the former comprises addorsed birds within a diamond shape, small trefoil leaves filling the angles of the enclosing squares. The face is somewhat scratched, one eye being defaced, and the nimbus and Keys regilt, but

the drapery is less retouched than in the panels previously described.

5. The Crucifixion, with the Virgin, on the spectator's left and St. John the Evangelist to the right; her tunic is red, her mantle green, lined with vair and draped to fall in intricate folds on the left, and her brown hair is covered with a transparent veil. She bends her head towards the cross and clasps her hands in grief. St. John has a tunic of deep green, and a red mantle shaded in yellowish pink; he also turns towards the cross, leaning his head on his right hand and holding a book in his left. His hair is curled about the brow, and his bare feet are visible, resting on grassy ground. The figure of Christ hangs upon the cross bent in a double curve, the left foot fastened over the right by a single nail; the loin-cloth, of a dark yellowish green lined with pink, falls in folds on either side. The cross is painted in brown, and the superscription in black, the first letter being rubricated. The background is entirely covered with 'prints', the design being composed of a quatrefoil flower framed within a barbed quatrefoil. The nimbi of all three figures, and the book held by St. John, have been regilt and repatterned. Some retouching is discernible, especially on the figure of Christ, and more particularly on the loin-cloth.

6. St. Paul. Like St. Peter, he turns outward from the Crucifixion group, but points in its direction with upraised right hand; with his left he leans upon the Sword, his bare feet resting upon a grassy mound. The 'sway' in this figure is more pronounced than in any of the series, even in that of the Virgin. The head, which is exceptionally well-preserved, with no sign of retouching, like that of St. Peter is represented according to the traditional 'portraiture' of these two Apostles; the tunic is red, the mantle a bronze-green lined with yellow. Both hands are slightly retouched, and the hilt and cross-bar of the Sword, as also the nimbus, regilt and the outlines repainted. The mantle draped in voluminous folds from the right arm, has been retouched to some degree. The background, like that of the St. Peter, is of 'prints' in alternation with green squares once patterned in gold, the design of the former comprising lions rampant, facing to the sinister side.

7. St. Edmund, King and Martyr. Facing towards St. Paul, he is shown standing with a slight sway on grassy ground, holding the Arrow in his left hand and pointing to it with his right; both hands are covered by white gauntlets. The mantle is green, lined with vair, the tunic red, with yellowish highlights. The figure, as a whole, is perhaps the best-preserved in the series, with only slight retouching

on the head and tunic and on the ground, though the crown and Arrow-head have been regilt and their outlines repainted. The head, like the majority of the male heads in the series, is long-nosed and long-jawed, and somewhat austere in type, the hair in this instance, however, being curled in a full roll at the level of the jaw. The background, like that of the Saint Catherine, is patterned with 'prints' comprising fleurs-de-lis, within quatrefoils, trefoil leaves filling the angles; but on this panel they cover the entire space.

8. St. Margaret. Facing away from St. Edmund, she stands in a slightly swaying pose upon the Dragon which is painted in brown and red; her crossed staff, grasped in her left hand, is thrust into the mouth as it turns its head upwards towards her, while it raises its tail, which is knotted in the centre. Her head, exceptionally well-preserved, is crowned and covered by a transparent veil falling to her shoulders; in her right hand she holds a book, ornamented with 'prints' of the eagle displayed within a quatrefoil, as seen on the background of St. Dominic; her tunic is green, and her mantle, swathed across the body and draped in intricate folds from her right arm, is lined with vair and held at the throat by a morse, formed of a 'print', enriched with an *Agnus Dei*. The cross and crown have been regilt, and the outlines repainted; and the right hand and the tunic are alike considerably retouched.

9. St. Peter Martyr. This figure, facing towards St. Margaret, resembles that of St. Dominic, except that a short weapon is shown lodged in the wound of the scalp, from which the blood drips, and an open wound is depicted upon the breast, the blood flowing from it over the white portion of the habit. In his left hand he bears a long preaching cross, and in his right a book, the cover enriched with 'prints'. The head is well-preserved, but the habit and the grassy ground beneath the feet have been much repainted. The background is entirely covered with 'prints', the design being identical with that seen in the St. Dominic.

The nineteenth-century repainting, mentioned throughout the description given above, was carried out, in the main, carefully and, except for the over-painting of the background, now removed, with careful attention to the original work, which it did not obscure, being employed only where the medieval paint had perished; hence, when the Retable was cleaned some years ago, it was allowed to remain.

Suffolk I.A. & N.H.P., 1927, XIX, 364; Lillie, ibid., 1933, XXI, 153-65, repr.; id., *Burl. M.*, 1933, LXIII,

99–100, reprs.; Munro Cautley, *Suffolk Churches and Their Treasures*, 1938, 326.

THORNTON ABBEY (near New Holland) Lincs

This was a house of Augustinian Canons, founded in 1139.

Extracts from records relating to painting carried out in the Abbey church during the fourteenth century.

'1313. 8s. paid for painting an image of the Virgin on a column; and 10s. 4d. for two cartloads of soil from Leeds "pro tegula ecclesie coloranda".

'1315. Nicholaus Lynwoodi magister fabrice emit viii c. folia auri et vi c. folia argenti xii libras plumbi rubei x libras plumbi albi pro celatura chori iii li. xvid. Item 1s. 11d. pictori chori pro xlvi septimanis.

'1328. Item in stipendio pictoris pro choro, coloribus et aliis necessariis circa depingendum xli precium pictor', xli. xiis, iid.

'1336. Item solutum pro una tabula depingenda ad altare Sancti Augustini. liiis. iid.

'1341. Solutum magistro Johanni Bernetby pictori pro tabula et tabernaculo magni altaris depingend' xv li.'

A.J., 1846, II, 364; Major, ibid., 1946, CIII, 174–8.

TROSTON (near Bury St. Edmunds) Suffolk
ST. MARY

The Nave

North wall, reading from west to east:
1. St. George and the Dragon, c. 1400; much defaced. A smaller version of the same subject thought to be of thirteenth-century date, appears further east on the wall, and has been mentioned in *English Medieval Wall Painting*, vol. II, Catalogue, under Troston.
2. St. Christopher, the top of the head and the greater part of the Holy Child, defaced, but otherwise in fair condition; traces about the upper part of the head, tentatively described in one account as those of a crown, are almost certainly remains of a representation of a soft cap, or other headgear.
3. A Martyrdom of St. Edmund the King.

Over the chancel arch is the central part of a Doom.

Keyser, *Mural Decorations*, 1883; Brindley, *Ant. J.*, 1924, IV, 234, repr.; James, *Suffolk and Norfolk*, 1930, 71; Carleton Williams, *B.A.A.J.*, 1949, 3rd ser., XII, 23–4, 35.

TROTTON (near Midhurst), Sussex
ST. GEORGE

The Nave

Covering the whole of the west wall, paintings comprising a simplified Last Judgement, having below them on the south side, the Seven Deadly Sins, and on the north, the Seven Corporal Works of Mercy. High upon the wall, in a central position, Christ in Judgement, seated upon a rainbow and displaying the wounds, the earth beneath His feet, and a canopy of clouds above His head, immediately beneath Him Moses with the Tables of the Law; at His right hand a scroll inscribed ITE MALEDICTI, and an Angel (much defaced) bringing into His presence a small nude Soul; at His left a second Angel (likewise almost entirely defaced), escorting another Soul, the scroll in this case bearing the words VENITE BENEDICTI. Below the condemned Soul a nude figure (when first discovered, phallic), about 9 ft. in height, with arms extended to the sides, and dragons issuing from various parts of the body, their gaping jaws in each case framing a group illustrative of one of the Deadly Sins, as follows; above the head, *Superbia*, the inscription barely decipherable, with two figures apparently male and female, extravagantly dressed, and facing each other; proceeding from the mouth, to the spectator's left, *Gula*, represented by a man drinking thirstily from an upraised jug, and having a large flagon to one side of him and a dish to the other; at the main figure's left hand, on the same side, *Avaritia*, showing a man seated before an open chest, and apparently repelling a small devil holding a three-pronged fork; immediately below again near the left foot, *Accidia*, represented by a man cloaked and lying on a couch which stands on a floor or carpet patterned with a fret, his head resting on his hand, and his fallen prayer-book and rosary lying neglected at his side; at the right hand of the chief figure on its other side *Ira*, with a man clad in parti-coloured clothing stabbing himself in the breast; proceeding from the loins on the same side, *Luxuria*, partially defaced; and finally, by the left leg, *Invidia*, so much damaged as to be virtually indecipherable.

Below the central figure, remains of the gaping Jaws of Leviathan within which are traces of a long-horned devil, holding a three-pronged fork.[1]

Below the Blessed Soul, a figure comparable in size to the large nude figure, but of a modestly-clad man, bearded and with long hair, in an ankle-length gown with a hood, turned back from the head and lying upon the gorget, and narrow sleeves;

[1] The Deadly Sins now almost entirely defaced (1954) and also some of the Works of Mercy.

surrounding him scrolls no doubt originally bearing the names of the Supernatural and Cardinal Virtues, *Fides*, *Spes* and *Caritas* being still decipherable, and on either side large medallions, seven in all, three being placed on each side and one above the head of the large central figure, framing the Seven Works of Mercy, as follows: immediately above the head, *Clothing the Naked*, a woman placing a garment over the head of a man who is otherwise almost unclothed; below this scene, on the south side of the chief figure, *Feeding the Hungry*, a woman standing at the door of a house who has just given a bowl to a man accompanied by a second woman, and still holds in her hand a flagon; below again on the same side, *Harbouring the Stranger*, a man in parti-coloured garments receiving at the door of his house a traveller or pilgrim, a chamber containing ? a bed, or table laid with a cloth, being visible on the spectator's right. The complementary subjects on the opposite side are *Visiting the Sick*, a woman who, having just passed through the door of a house, tends an invalid; *Visiting the Imprisoned*—a group of men, in high-collared and long-sleeved houppelandes, approaching a stronghold having a window, from which peers the prisoner; and, finally *Burying the Dead*—a woman standing at the foot of a grave while a priest attended by ? acolytes, sprinkles holy water upon the corpse. *c.* 1380.[1]

Above the west door, a consecration cross within a circle;[2] and two others, respectively to the north and south of the doorway. Formerly, approximately at dado level, a row of heraldic shields, two being still clearly visible on the north side.

On the north wall, traces of a large subject, now indecipherable, said to have included large figures, dogs, and horses; and opposite, on the south wall, remains of a figure.

Johnston, *A.J.*, 1904, LXI, 340; id., *Memorials of Old Sussex*, 1909, 274–8; id., *B.A.A.J.*, 1931, XXXVII, 75. A large photograph, taken *c.* 1910, is in the possession of Mrs. E. W. Tristram.

TURVEY (near Bedford), Beds ALL SAINTS

South Aisle

Within a monumental recess, a Crucifixion, with the Virgin and St. John, executed upon a ground of dark green enriched with a diaper of flowers; Christ hangs upon the cross, the body bent in a double curve, and about the head is a cruciform nimbus, in red on a white ground; the Virgin is clad in a white

cloak and veil, and stands with her hands clasped in grief; St. John raises his right hand to his head, and in his left holds a book.

Harvey, *History of Willey Hundred*, p. 206; Keyser, *Mural Decorations*, 1883; *Victoria County Hist.*, 1912, III, 115; Long, *Burl. M.*, 1936, LVIII, 96.

UPCHURCH (near Chatham) Kent ST. MARY

The South Chancel Chapel, east wall; discovered beneath the east window, in 1875, fragments of paintings: one of two knights in combat, another of two priests.

Archaeologia Cantiana, 1877, XI, 42–3; Keyser, *Mural Decorations*, 1883.

WALTHAM ST. LAWRENCE (near Twyford) Berks

ST. LAWRENCE

On the first pillar from the east on the north side of the nave, a Virgin and Child, much defaced; below, a well-preserved scroll pattern in red and yellow ochres. On the corresponding pillar on the south side, traces (?) of a figure.

Victoria County Hist., Berks., 1923, III, 182–3; Long, *Berks. B. & O.A.J.*, 1942, XLVI, 77.

WARBLINGTON (near Havant), Hants
ST. THOMAS OF CANTERBURY

In the course of repairs made to the structure in 1852 subjects framed 'by the stem of a tree or vine', and painted against a background diapered with stars, were discovered on the south wall; they appear to have been of fourteenth-century date, so far as may be judged from a description written before the work was plastered over. The account, however, is confused and the identification of the scenes evidently conjectural and inaccurate. A coat-of-arms painted upon the wall behind the pulpit was considered to be of the fourteenth century.

Longcroft, *A Topographical Account of the Hundred of Bosmere*, 1856, 115; Keyser, *Mural Decorations*, 1883.

WAREHAM, Dorset ST. MARTIN

The Chancel

At the eastern end of the north wall, a vertical band of red with the sacred monogram IHC, crowned; probably part of a painted hanging around the high altar. *c.* 1400.

---

[1] 1953. Most of the detail in these paintings, and in particular in those representing the Deadly Sins, is no longer visible.   [2] Now almost defaced.

The Nave

On the east wall, near the chancel arch, a powdering of stars.

WELLS, Somerset

CATHEDRAL CHURCH OF ST. ANDREW

The Tomb of Bishop William de Marchia (1308); extensive remains of gold and colour, especially of red and green, and of a small diaper in black, were revealed during cleaning in 1948.

The Tomb of John de Drokensforde, Bishop of Bath and Wells (1329): on the vestments and the cushion supporting the head of the effigy, delicate patterning, with gilding and colour; and on the base, 24 small shields of arms, the majority still retaining their colour, on alternating grounds of red and green, enriched with foliated scroll-work in white.

The Chapter House: on the arcade, remains of decoration, best preserved in one bay on the east; on the wall within the arcading, a pattern of large and small medallions in black, white and gold, dark red and pink; on the mouldings of arches and canopies, traces of vermilion and bright green; in the spaces between the canopies, heraldic devices, a saltire and a cross fleury still being decipherable; on the human heads at the springing of the arches, natural colours; on the finials, marbling in red, and on the shafts, spiral brush-strokes in red; and on the cavetto mouldings, marbling executed by means of wavy brush-strokes around 'eyes' in red and green on a ground of greyish-white.

Keyser, *Mural Decorations*, 1883.

WELLS, Somerset

HALL OF THE COLLEGE OF THE VICARS CHORAL

A representation of the Vicars, kneeling before their benefactor, Bishop Ralph of Shrewsbury, who incorporated them into a College in 1346. Both they and the Bishop hold inscribed scrolls. The painting was much altered in Elizabethan times.

Pugin, *Gothic Architecture*, 1840, III, 9; *B.A.A.J.*, 1857, XIII, 36 et sqq.; Evans, *English Art*, 1949, 1307-1461, 187-8.

WENDENS AMBO (near Audley End) Essex

ST. MARY

The Chancel

On the south wall, remains of three tiers of paintings of *c.* 1330, separated by a border, 6 in. in width, composed of bent-riband pattern in red and white, with cusping in red line filling the interstices. In the highest tier, subjects from the History of St. Margaret; reading from the east, these are as follows:

1. The Instruction of St. Margaret. Her nurse, shown as a tall figure veiled and clad in a kirtle and mantle and seated on a bench with a cushion on the seat ornamented with a fret pattern, raises her left hand, with the index finger pointed as if emphasizing her words, towards a child who is no doubt intended for the Saint (much defaced) holding a book; below, on the left part remains of a similar childish figure, kneeling and holding an open book and two others are seen on the right, the foremost looking intently at a volume she holds, the other gazing over her shoulder. A narrow border 1 in. in width, painted in red, divides this scene from the next, as is the case with all the scenes in the series.

2. St. Margaret approached by the Prefect Olybrius. The Saint is seated on a hillock to the left of the composition, clad in a tunic and mantle, and holding a distaff, and about her feet are sheep, two of them butting each other. In the foreground a dog chases a hare. Slightly to the west, the Prefect's servant, clad in a dark gipon and light hose, with a small object at his waist which may be intended for a purse, extends his right hand, grasping a large ring, towards her, and holds in the left a spear. The Prefect, crowned and mounted on a white horse, follows him, with a companion, also on horseback; they are attended by a bearded figure, clad in a shoulder-cape and gipon and holding a short staff over the left shoulder, while raising the right hand as though in expostulation.

3. The Imprisonment of the Saint. Part of the building, battlemented and with the courses of masonry defined, may be seen, together with the upper part of the Saint's figure, being thrust through a doorway by a figure in a dark gipon (mainly defaced). A little above the latter, towards the left, is a female head, with a coif.

4. The Saint before the Prefect. Only the enthroned and crowned figure of the Prefect survives, and even this in a defaced condition.

In the central tier, at the east end, are traces of what must once have been a subject elaborately treated; and above the piscina remains of heads and hands, and of a wing.

On the north and east walls only traces of colour exist, apart from a consecration cross on the latter, reputed to survive though covered by (?) a reredos.

Tristram and Benton, *Essex A.S.*, 1936, N.S., XXII, 20-7, repr.

Plates 49, 50*b*.

LITTLE WENHAM (near Ipswich) Suffolk
ALL SAINTS

The Chancel

Within painted arcading on either side of the east window, to the north, the Virgin and Child, and to the south St. Margaret, St. Catherine, and St. Mary Magdalen; early fourteenth century.

The Nave

On the north wall, under a trefoil-headed canopy, St. Christopher; in a defaced condition.

Keyser, *Mural Decorations*, 1883; *Suffolk I.A. & N.H.P.*, 1886, V, 184; Bryant, *County Churches, Suffolk*, 1912, II, 200; James, *Suffolk & Norfolk*, 1930, 52; Munro Cautley, *Suffolk Churches and Their Treasures*, 1938, 207, 335.

WENSLEY (near Leyburn) Yorks

Les Trois Vifs et les Trois Morts, the lower half, apart from the figure of the third king, which is entirely destroyed, surviving; what are apparently intended for worms hang from the Corpses, and beside each Corpse is a somewhat defaced inscription, in boldly-designed and well-executed Lombardic capitals as follows:

Beside the central Corpse—

[AS] WE A[RE] NOVE (As we are now).

Beside the second Corpse—

[THUS] SAL THE BE (shalt thou be).

Beside the third Corpse—

[B]EWAR WYT ME (be warned by me).

The inscriptions run perpendicularly between the figures of the Three Dead, and there is in fact no actual division between the words. Below is a narrow border, mainly defaced, and below again traces of a wide scroll border. *c.* 1330.

Elsewhere in the church, part of an unidentified subject; to the left, a bearded man in knee-length parti-coloured gipon, a sheaf of arrows slung at his waist, holding ? a faggot over his right shoulder and in his left hand grasping the reins of a horse, its head only remaining. Below the reins, the coifed head of a man in ? a gipon and cote-hardie, holding a claw hammer in his right hand, and perhaps originally depicted as kneeling and about to shoe the animal. ? St. Eloi in craftsman's habit.

Country Life, 1927, LXII, 934. (No reference to *Les Trois Vifs*; and the other subject described as Jacob and Esau.)

WESTHIDE (near Hereford) Hereford
ST. BARTHOLOMEW

The South Aisle

On the soffit of the east window, remains of foliated scroll-work and to the north of the same window, traces of an inscribed scroll and of ? a figure subject.

R.C. Historical Monuments R., Hereford, 1932, 206.

WESTON (near Beccles) Suffolk ST PETER

The Nave

On the south wall, between two windows, at a height of 10 ft. from the present floor level, and covering an area of approximately 4 ft. 6 in. in length by 2 ft. 4 in. in height, an Entry into Jerusalem, probably of *c.* 1300, in a fragmentary state, parts of the ass, and of three figures clad in tunics and holding in their left hands what were originally palms, surviving; the background is pink in colour, the hair and features drawn in red, and the drapery, where it is still distinguishable, in yellow.

From notes supplied by Miss Janet Becker; Munro Cautley, *Suffolk Churches and Their Treasures*, 1938, 339.

WESTON BEGGARD (near Hereford) Hereford
ST. JOHN BAPTIST

On either side of the chancel are two early-fourteenth-century tomb recesses, one of the two being referred to by Gough as follows:

'In the chancel of Weston Bagard Church is a monument, without inscription, but three chevronels on a shield, and under the arch is or was painted the Virgin and Child; on each side kneels an Angel with a censer, and from the point of the arch descends a glory.'

Gough, *Sepulchral Monuments*, 1796, I, pt. 2, 195; Blackburne, *Decorative Painting*, 1847, 60; Keyser, *Mural Decorations*, 1883.

WESTON LONGVILLE (near Dereham) Norfolk
ALL SAINTS

The North Aisle

On the north wall, occupying a space between two windows, and approximately 15 ft. 9 in. × 9 ft., a Jesse Tree. An interlacing vine stem, having occasional large leaves, tendrils, and small bunches of grapes, or flowers of the vine, springs from the base at the centre of the composition, where would originally have been the figure of Jesse, now destroyed. It forms three central compartments, almost medallion-shaped, one above the other, and its branches, extending laterally from the main stem form four more, rather narrower compartments, on either side, that is to say 35 in all, some of them however, at the sides being much defaced, and those at the base obliterated, except for some of the heads; within them are represented Prophets and Kings, some in conversation, but the majority gazing, and many pointing, towards the three central compartments, where the highest frames a Virgin and Child, the middle a King, enthroned, his head partially obscured by another (apparently by the same hand and a correction made by the painter) and the lowest King David, playing a harp. The Prophets are clad in long cote-hardies and mantles, and wear shoes and contemporary headgear, one having a long liripipe and tippets on his sleeves; and all bear scrolls, formerly, as appears from fragments of lettering upon them, inscribed, probably with their names. The Kings seem all to be seated cross-legged. The mantles on the figures are in some cases lined with ermine, in others patterned with sprigs. One of the Kings has the end of his rather long beard plaited, and his hair also plaited and hanging down behind him.

The subject is set out on smooth plaster by means of incised line, and the colours, besides the usual ochres, comprise black and green, the latter, as appears in places, having once been bright and fair in tint. Of a date later than 1350. Discovered in 1916, the painting was not fully revealed until 1937.

Plates 22, 23a, b, 24.

OLD WESTON (near Kimbolton) Hunts
ST. SWITHIN

The South Aisle

On the northern splay of the east window, St. Margaret, crowned, long-haired, holding a book and trampling on the dragon, under a trefoiled canopy with a ridged roof and a spire; below, masonry pattern in double line. On the opposite splay, St. Catherine, holding the Wheel and Sword, under a trefoiled canopy; below, masonry pattern like that under the companion painting.

On the south wall, ? the enthronement of a bishop by two others, the figure of a woman behind the throne, and traces of another figure on the left; above, remains of a border, with lettering. Further to the west, two subjects, one above the other, separated by a band of scroll-work; the higher of the two, part of a Wheel of Fortune, with figures between the spokes; and the lower, an unidentified scene, with a building on the left, a figure, perhaps seated, facing right, and another on the right, with hands raised in supplication.

R.C. Historical Monuments R., Hunts, 1926, 290, reprs.

WHADDON (near Stony Stratford) Bucks
ST. MARY

The Chancel

On the north wall (but now concealed) part of a Martyrdom of St. Thomas of Canterbury, framed by a border of wavy design enriched with small roundels; to the spectator's left, traces of the feet and lower parts of the vestments of a kneeling figure of the Saint, and to the right the four knights, the foremost, presumably Tracy, with sword raised, the second, identified as Fitzurse, by the charge upon his shield, just behind him, the third with sword held high above his head, and the fourth, Hugh de Morville, with his hand on the hilt of his sheathed sword; all helmeted, and clad in mail and the usual surcoats. Above this painting (formerly) traces of another, the upper part destroyed, and below it of yet another, representing *Les Trois Vifs et Les Trois Morts*, but of this only the three skeletons, a green tree, and an indecipherable inscription remained. Formerly, in the splays of a window in the south wall, St. Edmund, King and Martyr, crowned and clad in a tunic and mantle, holding a sceptre in the right hand and two arrows in the left, and an Archbishop, unidentified, but probably intended for St. Edmund of Canterbury, clad in mass vestments, his right hand raised in blessing and in his left the archiepiscopal cross; and on either side of the east window, the Symbols of the Four Evangelists. The paintings were discovered in 1851.

Sheahan, *History and Topography of the County of Buckingham*, 1851, 770; Pigott, *A.J.*, 1866, XXIII, 78; Lowndes, *Records of Bucks*, 1870, III, 270–3, reprs.; Keyser, *Mural Decorations*, 1883; id., *A.J.*, 1892, XLIX, 333; Storck, *Burl. M.*, 1912, XXI, 318; Borenius, *Archaeologia*, 1931, 30, 81; id., *St. Thomas Becket in Art*, 1932, 99; id., *Folk Lore*, June 1932, 181; Carleton Williams, *B.A.A.J.*, 1942, 3rd ser., VII, 40.

WICKHAMPTON (near Yarmouth) Norfolk
ST. ANDREW

The Nave

On the north wall, to the west, now much defaced, and with little detail surviving, *Les Trois Vifs et les Trois Morts*; the figures of more than life-size, divided into two groups, one of the Kings and the other of the Corpses, by a central tree, and flanked by a tree on either side; above every figure a scroll with an indecipherable inscription. The Corpses, on the western side of the wall, are of normal type; that nearest the Kings raises its left arm towards them. The first of the group of Kings, reading from the west, bearded and with long hair, is clad in a short cote-hardie, with remains of a diaper pattern upon it and tippets on the sleeves, and long hose; he turns towards the second, whose left hand he grasps with his right. The second, who raises his right hand as though emphasizing a remark, is similarly clad, except that his cote-hardie is plain; he is bearded and has hair cut to the level of the jaw. The third is a beardless youthful figure, in shoulder cape and short cote-hardie enriched by a diamond pattern and dagged at the lower edge. He extends his right arm to touch the shoulder of his nearest companion, and looks back towards him; his left hand is encased in a hawking glove, and on it he carries a hawk with jesses, while in the same hand grasping a second glove. His crown, like those of his fellows, is almost entirely defaced. In the foreground, in front of the Corpses, is a huntsman with hounds in leash, straining after a hare or rabbit which escapes westward; the figure, which is much smaller in scale than the others described, is bearded, and wears a cap and parti-coloured gipon and long hose, the colours counterchanged; much black mixed with white to form a bluish grey, having been used, as also in depicting the Kings. Immediately below the Kings are traces of ? battlements over the arch of the north door, but this is all far from clear in C. J. Winter's drawing made *c.* 1850; and below the Corpses a consecration cross of simple cross paty type, in red. The paintings were uncovered in 1851. *c.* 1380.

On the same wall, to the east of the north door, St. Christopher, as usual of gigantic proportions, holding a staff in the left hand and bearing the Holy Child, who has a cusped nimbus and a robe patterned with a diaper, on the right shoulder; the Saint, facing slightly east, holds up his mantle with the left hand, and wears a bluish-grey cloak lined with white, and a green gipon with a lozenge pattern upon it. Near the top of the staff are slight remains of a green leaf, and in the water about the feet are traces of fish, including a crab and a conger eel. To the right and left of the painting, a scroll-work border, in red on white, is visible; and just below it, to the west, is a consecration cross. A small shield charged with a cross, recorded as having existed near this, is now completely lost; and the entire work has become much defaced, many of its features being decipherable only with the aid of descriptions made before this occurred. *c.* 1380.

The same wall, between the first and second windows from the west, arranged in two tiers, each about 4 ft. 6 in. in depth, the Seven Corporal Works of Mercy, and a figure of Christ Blessing, forming eight subjects framed within a painted arcade having canopies drawn in rough perspective and supported on slender shafts. The scenes, almost all of them now much defaced, which are rendered intelligible chiefly through comparison with a drawing by Winter preserved near them, are as follows:

1. Feeding the Hungry—on the left a pilgrim clad in a calf-length garment, and a black hood with a gorget, who carries the bourdon, is received by a veiled woman with her right hand extended towards him; scrolls, their inscriptions defaced, surround the heads of both figures.

2. Giving Drink to the Thirsty—a bearded pilgrim with a bourdon accepts a cup from a woman; scrolls appear, as in the first scene.

3. Clothing the Naked—a man, nude to the waist, has a garment placed over his head by a woman clad in a spotted kirtle; between them is a scroll, the inscription defaced.

4. Receiving the Stranger—a man in knee-length cote-hardie, walking with the aid of two sticks, is received by a woman; a scroll, the inscription defaced, extends above the scene and between the figures.

5. Visiting the Prisoner—a man with a forked beard, clad in a cote-hardie, apparently particoloured in black and white, buttoned down the front and with sleeves having bell-cuffs reaching to the knuckles, is seated in the stocks; a scroll extends over his head, one letter of the inscription surviving, and also over the top of the scene; a woman standing on the right, clad in a black kirtle and hooded cloak, bends over him, clasping his left hand with her right. This scene is the only one now in passable condition.

6. Visiting the Sick—a man lying in a bed with a spotted coverlet is visited by a woman wearing a spotted kirtle, the pattern now almost vanished. There are scrolls over both figures, that above the woman being painted red, with lettering, now indecipherable, in white.

7. Burying the Dead—the corpse lies in a tomb stretching across the front of the scene; at its foot is a grave-digger, holding a spade, in hip-length spotted gipon and a hood with gorget and long liripipe, at its head an acolyte in an alb, bearing a book, and in the centre of the scene, a priest with an aspergillum.

8. Christ Blessing, clad in a robe patterned with squares; the figure is surrounded by scrolls, the inscriptions vanished. All *c.* 1400.

Gent. M., 1851, pt. 2, 414; B. Mus., *Dawson Turner Collection*, Add. IX, 1853, 184–92; Manning, *Norfolk Archaeologia*, 1872, VII, 2; Keyser, *Mural Decorations*,

1883; Storck, *Burl. M.*, 1912, XXI, 250, repr.; James, Blomefield's *Norfolk Supplement*, 1929, 125–30, repr.; id., *Suffolk and Norfolk*, 1930, 143; Carleton Williams, *B.A.A.J.*, 1942, VII, 36, 40.

WIDFORD (near Ware) Herts   ST. JOHN BAPTIST
The Chancel

On the east wall, on either side of the window, a figure of a Saint; that on the north, in poor condition, delineated against a ground of red, with ? an open door behind it; that on the south, painted upon a ground of the same colour, diapered, however, in white and surrounded by a white border engrailed, much better preserved than the other, represents a bishop vested in an alb, dalmatic and amice, and a buff-coloured chasuble, lined with white and falling in intricate folds at the sides. In his left hand is a crozier and on his head a mitre, but there are no attributes by which he may be identified. *c.* 1340.

On the north wall are remains of what was probably once a large rendering of the Last Judgement; Christ, nimbed, is seated on a rainbow, clad in a grey mantle lined with white, the arms raised, as normally in this subject, to display the wounds, and, what is exceptional in wall painting of this date, the 'Sharp two-edged sword' of the Apocalypse issuing from His mouth. To the spectator's left are traces of an Angel bearing one of the Emblems of the Passion, the Cross. Little more than the silhouette of the original work survives, and the background, the head of Christ, and the rainbow have all been retouched at some time. *c.* 1300.

Neal and Webb, *Durandus*, 1843, 57; Cussans, *History of Herts*, 1870, I, pt. 1, 57, repr.; Keyser, *Mural Decorations*, 1883; Gerish, *East Herts A.S.T.*, 1903, II, 124, 125–6, repr.; *R.C. Historical Monuments R., Herts*, 1910, 241.

WIDFORD (near Witney) Oxon   ST. OSWALD
The Chancel

On the north wall, two tiers of painting, separated by a band of bent-riband pattern; in the higher, part of a Martyrdom of St. Lawrence, and ? remains of a Martyrdom of St. Edmund the King; in the lower, occupying a space 9 ft. in length by 6 ft. in height, *Les Trois Vifs et Les Trois Morts*; the three Kings, one in a hood and cote-hardie, having elbow-length sleeves terminating in a tongue-shaped flap, holding a hawk and having a dog at his feet, another in a red mantle enriched with ermine, at the western end of the wall, the Corpses on the eastern side; between the figures are conventionalized trees. On either side of the east window is an image-bracket, originally painted blue, the background being ornamented with a diaper. Little remains on the south wall, where the subjects depicted are unidentifiable. *c.* 1340.

Bristol & G.A.S.R. & P., 1911, XXXIV, 28; ibid., 1925, XLVII, 42; Carleton Williams, *B.A.A.J.*, 1942, VII, 33, 40.

GREAT WILBRAHAM (near Cambridge) Cambs
ST. NICHOLAS

On the four arches at the intersection of the transepts, traces of red, and on the soffits of those of the nave and south transept a checker pattern in red and white; on the capitals of the columns, and on their upper part, a deep blue, forming in part a ground for a running scroll design in red. On the chancel arch, a scroll design in various colours. On the splays of a lancet window at the north-east end of the nave, a powdering of sexfoils in black and on either side of the window a masonry pattern, also in black with double vertical and single horizontal joints, each block charged in the middle with a cinquefoil voided in the centre, and in the angles with small leaves. Early fourteenth century.

Benton, *The Antiquary*, 1910, XLVI, 67–8, repr.

WILLINGHAM (near Long Stanton) Cambs
ST. MARY AND ALL SAINTS
The Nave

At intervals on the north and south walls, a rich diaper of roses and other flowers on a red ground, interspersed with shields; the latter charged with:

1. The Five Wounds and the Crown of Thorns.
2. Again the Five Wounds, represented by the wounded Hands, Feet and Heart.
3. A 'Tau-shaped cross' (? the Pillar of the Flagellation) and two scourges.
4. *Party per pale on the dexter side* (?) *a bear, on the sinister a lion rampant gules.*
5. *Gules, three crowns or,* for Ely, the crown in base having a sceptre in it; the charges on other surviving shields of arms are indecipherable.

St. Christopher, 8 ft. in height, in a voluminous cloak, calf-length gipon, breeches tied at the knee and a soft cap, supporting the Holy Child on his left arm and holding a T-headed staff in his right hand; about his feet water in which fish are swimming; mid fourteenth century.

A consecration cross paty in red on white.

In the Brunes chapel at the eastern end of the south aisle, a consecration cross; on the northern side of the chancel arch another.

North aisle, east end; a parclose screen, the panels painted in red and the carved mouldings in red and green, the former ornamented with a series of 'popinjays' set lozenge-wise in groups of four round a central star framed by small roundels.

Keyser, *Mural Decorations*; 1883, id., *A.J.*, 1896, LIII, 185, 188–90; James, *Cambridge A.C.*, 1894–6, IX, 98; Bligh Bond, ibid., 1908, XIII, 74; Whaite, *St. Christopher*, 1929, 21, pl. 23.

WILTON (near Brandon) Norfolk   ST. JAMES

The Nave

North Wall, a large area covered with a fourteenth-century masonry pattern in red and grey, the blocks being enriched with stalked roses in red; the masonry pattern is executed by means of double line between the blocks and single line between the courses. A border of scroll-work in red runs along the top of the wall.

From notes supplied by Mrs. M. Bardswell, 1933.

WIMBORNE, Dorset   MINSTER OF ST CUTHBERGA

The South Choir Aisle

Formerly, at the side of the east window, parts of two tiers of paintings (separated by a band of scroll ornament) representing the Death of the Virgin; in the lower tier, four nimbed figures, in tunics and mantles, in attitudes of mourning, presumably from an Assembling of the Apostles, and in the higher tier five similar figures bearing a bier, and beside it the head and outstretched arm of the Mocking Jew, all that remained of a Funeral Procession of the Virgin.

The North Transept

Within an altar recess, remains of a Crucifixion, with the Virgin and St. John, the lower part of the figure of Christ, the upper and lower part of that of the Virgin in a vermilion tunic, and most of that of St. John, being visible, in part confused with two other versions of the same subject, one of rather earlier and the other of rather later date, but too fragmentary to be dated with precision; below, a border ornamented with a square diaper pattern and finished with a narrow band of bent-riband pattern, each square of the diaper enclosing a different ornamental motif, among them being eight-and-ten petalled flowers, circles within outer circles composed of spots, and various diamond designs.

Taylor, *A.J.*, 1856, XIII, 103, 104; Mayo, *History of Wimborne Minster*, 1860, 45, 133; Hutchins, *History of Dorset*, 3rd ed., 1868, III, 203, repr.; Keyser, *Mural Decorations*, 1883; Fletcher, *Somerset & Dorset N. & Q.*,

1893, III, 249–50, repr.; Keyser, *A.J.*, 1896, LIII, 174; Long, *Dorset A.S.*, 1928, L, 108.

WINCHELSEA, Sussex   ST. THOMAS THE APOSTLE

Within a tomb recess in the north aisle, a kneeling Angel bearing in a cloth a Soul, the companion Angel, which doubtless originally bore the opposite end of the cloth, having perished.

WINCHESTER, Hants
CATHEDRAL CHURCH OF ST. SWITHIN

The South Transept

The Central Bay on the East: on the east wall, immediately below the base of a window inserted during the first quarter of the fourteenth century, a painted arcade of seven bays extending over the entire width of the wall, 2 ft. 3 in. in height by 13 ft. 9 in. in length, with its base line 3 ft. 9 in. from the present floor level, framing a series of subjects apparently relating to the Order of St. Benedict, painted against grounds of a bright greenish-blue. The shafts supporting the arcade are inset with small traceried windows, and terminate in richly foliated pinnacles framed within cusped and crocketed arches. The arches of the arcade itself are intricately cusped, and ornamented with crockets of elaborate design; the whole is drawn in black line upon a ground of white, with certain features picked out in yellow—perhaps originally an underpainting for gold, which has disappeared. Though much defaced, the three subjects to the extreme left of the spectator are the best-preserved, the others being fragmentary to the point of illegibility; the series reading from left to right is as follows:

1. On the right of the scene, a tall, standing figure of Christ, clad in a long green tunic and yellow mantle, with the right hand raised, though not in blessing, and before Him two men, the foremost bearded, with right hand raised and the left grasping what may be a piece of drapery.

2. To the extreme right, as before, Christ, raising the right hand and bearing a book in the left; before Him a group of three persons, the foremost a woman, veiled, possibly a nun, the other two youths in long tunics.

3. To the extreme right, as before, Christ, the lower part of whose figure is destroyed, with cruciform nimbus (apparently once gilt) clearly visible (as in the second scene, but not in the first) raising, as in the two previous scenes, the left hand; kneeling in front of Him, a tonsured monk with a nimbus, clad in a black habit, raising the left hand in a gesture

as of acceptance, and holding a book in the right; behind him another kneeling monk, whose feet are bare.

4. Traces of a figure of Christ and of other figures.

5. (To the right of the centre.) Slight remains of a figure of Christ, giving a book to a group of almost-defaced figures.

6. Traces, apparently of figures in monastic habits.

7. One foot alone surviving.

The paintings have evidently been treated at some time in the past with a preparation which has darkened the plaster surface and thus obscured them; a very small portion of one figure upon the removal of adhering lime-wash when they were examined a few years ago showed colour that was clear and bright. *c.* 1325–50.

The adjacent bay to the north has in it traces of painting in a similar position to those just described, but they are too fragmentary to be understood.

(1952. The whole series almost obliterated.)

WINDSOR CASTLE, Berks

St. George's Chapel

'*Records relating to paintings executed for the Chapel in the fourteenth century. c.* 1353–4 . Devon, *Issues of the Exchequer*, 1837, 160. To John, a Canon of St. Catherine's, the King's picture painter, in money delivered to him for painting a picture which the same John was commanded to paint by the Lord the King, with images for the chapel in Windsor Castle. £13 6s. 8d.

'1365. To John, a Canon of St. Catherine's, painter to the Lord the King, in money paid to him for making a table whereon the said John was directed by the Lord the King to paint images for the chapel within Windsor Castle. £13 6s. 8d. (As above, 184–5.)

'W. H. St. John Hope, *Windsor Castle*, 1913 (extracts from Pipe Rolls). 194. £4 for painting a table in the King's Chapel (table = reredos, bought in 1362–3).'

The Round Tower; and elsewhere in the Castle

St. John Hope, *Windsor Castle*, 1913.

'148. 100s to Richard Assheby for painting the woodwork in the canons' chambers according to his own devising with varnish and ochre. (Also 165, where it is stated that "some of this colouring was found in the upper story of one of the houses a few years ago, but defaced by an over-zealous painter before arrangements could be made for its preservation".)

'156. Purchase of 66 lbs. of white lead for the painting of the vault of the treasury house, 22s., 12 gallons of painters' oil 24s., etc.

'157. Payment of wages of three painters who carried out work in the treasury house; Gilbert Pokerich 8s. 4d. for 10 days, at 10d.; Thomas Rothewell, 5s. for 7½ days at 8d. Clays Colkyrte 3s. 9d. for 7½ days at 4d. (Also 163, where the entries are given in Latin.)'

The above entries date from 1353 to 1354.

'159. The making of an iron lectern, the painting of a lectern, of two seats, and a sepulchre in the King's Chapel, mentioned.

'178. Account of William of Wykeham, surveyor of the King's works; Richard of Taynton, John the Painter, and Ralph of Dodlesfold, clerks of the King's works, under Wykeham. (1356–61.)

'179. Richard of Ashby paid for pargetting and whitewashing the hall of the King's and Queen's lodgings in the High Tower, and painting the chapel of the Castle and other lodgings with oker, oil and varnish, etc. (1356–7.)

'179. Payment to William Hirlond . . . and to Richard of Ashby for pargetting (*parietacione*) and whitewashing the hall of the King's and Queen's lodging etc., as above.

'189. To John Peintour of Iver for painting the windows of the King's Chamber 6s. 8d. (Also 208; 1363–5.)

'194. A Painted Chamber mentioned among the King's chambers. (Also 195.)

'196. Three clay pots bought for the painters, 3d. (1364–6.)

'197. To divers '*pacches*' for making cole [size] for the painters, 10d.

'List of colours purchased for a certain tower called La Rose, the total expenditure being £13 15. 6; William Burdon received £6. 3. 6. for working upon the painting of the tower for 123½ days at 12d. a day, and was assisted by five painters who worked for 77 days at 8d. daily, nine others who worked for 107 days at 6d. daily, five more who worked for 75½ days at 5d. daily, and two others who worked for 41 days at 4d. daily. (1365–6.)

'200. To Silvester Hereford and his mates for mending and 'okering' the High Tower, 13s. 4d. (1367–78.)

'201. To William Burdon for painting a table in the great chapel of the Canons and a reredos for the upper chapel, £40.

'210. William Burdon "*Pictoris*" mentioned.'

Hudson Turner, *Domestic Architecture in England*, 1853, II, 27, states that in William Burdon's accounts for 1365–6, mentioned above, 67 lb. of white lead,

12 lb. of verdigris, 18 lb. of red lead, and 8 lb. of vermilion, 1 lb. of brown and 7 lb. of blue, altogether about a cwt. of colour, are mentioned; also 22 gallons of oil, 1,400 leaves of gold, 6 lb. of fine varnish and 3 lb. of inferior varnish.

WINTERBOURNE (near Bristol) Glos

ST. MICHAEL

The Tower

A scheme of painting carried out after alterations in the Decorated period;—the corbels supporting the first floor painted with seeded roses; below, remains of wall-paintings, including the figure of a knight in armour, bearing a flag, now indistinct, but said to have been charged originally with the arms of Bradeston, a family holding the manor of Winterbourne in the time of Edward III, viz., *Argent on a canton gules a rose or barbed proper*; on the splays of the south window, on either side, traces of a figure under a crocketed canopy with heraldic shields above; on the walls, soffits of arches, etc., scrollwork, lozenge ornament, rosettes, and bent-riband pattern, executed in the usual ochres.

Bristol & G.A.S.R. & P., 1926, XLVIII, 37; W. H. Bird, *Mural Paintings, Glos*, 1927, 33.

WOOD EATON (near Islip) Oxon

In the tower and nave are remains of an ornamental scheme, executed *c.* 1350. The walls are covered with masonry pattern executed in double red line, and coign stones and voussoirs are picked out alternately in red and white; the north and south doorways in the nave are bordered with a scroll pattern in double red line, enriched with leaves in black; between the two windows in the south wall are traces of a consecration cross of simple design; and on the chancel arch traces of colour, and to its southern side remains of a fret pattern in red.

Above the blocked doorway in the north wall is a St. Christopher, the head of the Saint and the upper part of the figure of the Holy Child being defaced by new plaster, although otherwise the work is moderately well preserved. The Saint is clad in a green gipon, an ivory-coloured mantle, lined with red, and breeches tied at the knee; in his right hand he holds a staff and bears the Child on his left, from whose figure depends a long scroll with an inscription in Lombardic capitals, reading KI CEST IMAGE VERRA LE IUR DE MALE MORT NE MURRA. About the Saint's feet is the traditional water, with fish swimming in it, among them a small squid, an eel, and a flat-fish.

c. 1350. A rough outline of a head was painted on the new plaster in 1932, to indicate its former position.

Long, *Oxon A.S.*, 1932, LXXVII, 19; Tristram, *Burl. M.*, 1933, LXII, 129.

WOOTON WAWEN (near Henley-in-Arden) Warwick

ST. PETER

The Lady Chapel

On the east wall, a Coronation of the Virgin, and a much-damaged figure of an unidentified saint.

On the south wall, at the western end, within quatrefoils arranged in two rows and framed by narrow interlacing borders in red on white, subjects identified as scenes from the lives of Saint John Baptist, St. Anne [1] and St. Catherine, described as being:

1. The Baptism of Christ, 'St. John preaching and in the Wilderness' (bearing an *Agnus Dei*).

2. The Rejection of Joachim's Offering, the Meeting of Joachim and Anna at the Golden Gate, the Birth of the Virgin; and

3. St. Catherine before the Emperor Maximinus, and her Decollation.

Parts of a Passion series, viz. the Holy Women at the Sepulchre, the Harrowing of Hell, and the Ascension are also recorded, together with an Annunciation and the Seven Deadly Sins; but the accounts are confused, and the paintings since their discovery in 1918 have deteriorated so much as to be difficult to decipher.

Turpin, *Burl. M.*, 1919, XXXV, 249; *Victoria County Hist.*, 1947, IV, 204.

WORCESTER CATHEDRAL CHURCH OF ST. MARY

The North Transept

Around an arch opening from the transept to the north choir aisle, roses or cinquefoils, and bent-riband pattern, in red, yellow and black. *c.* 1300.

The Crypt

At the eastern end (formerly), 'an arcade of four principal five-foiled arches of equal height, with two smaller lateral arches. In the three spandrels above this arcade are as many shields, the central one being England, three lions passant, and the others Beauchamp and Clare. Beneath each of the four principal arches is the figure of a bishop in full vestments, in benediction, with a nimbus. One of the figures is tolerably perfect, but the other three are much

---

[1] In reality part of a Life of the Virgin.

defaced; all were evidently drawn by an accomplished hand . . . This wall painting is on the northern side of an Early English bay which now terminates towards the east the (otherwise) Norman crypt beneath the chapel to the south of the southern choir aisle.'

West's Note Book, 1844, 25, V.& A. Mus.; Boutell, *The Builder*, 1857, 606–7; Keyser, *Mural Decorations*, 1883.

WORCESTER THE GUESTEN HALL

The Guesten Hall was built *c.* 1320, near the Cathedral. Formerly, at the upper end of the hall, near the site of the dais, Christ in Majesty, within an almond-shaped glory framed by a square, the spandrels thus formed being filled with the Symbols of the Evangelists; and on either side subjects (those on the left of the Majesty indecipherable, apart from an Annunciation and one other, somewhat vaguely described as 'the Virgin and our Lord', and of those on the right an Adoration of the Magi alone remaining), 'divided by architectural canopies and tracery into two divisions, in one of which the Magi are represented making their offerings to Our Lord, who, in the arms of the Blessed Virgin in the stable, and with St. Joseph seated by His side, appears in the other compartment'.

Below the subjects, and 'covering the whole of the north wall to the height of about 12 ft.', was a diaper of star-shapes formed by super-imposed squares, these and the interspaces alike having each in the middle, a small shield, the charges, however, being without exception 'almost entirely effaced'.

B.A.A.J., 1849, IV, 95; *A.A.S.R. & P.*, 1854, 146–8, repr.

WYMONDHAM, Norfolk ST. MARY
The Nave

On the south side, within three arches of the triforium, formerly *Les Trois Vifs et Les Trois Morts*; also a figure on horseback wearing a triple crown, and beneath him a wood in which were to be seen wild beasts, with hares and hounds, and a floral pattern, perhaps intended to represent a rose window.

Woodward, *Archaeologia*, 1836, XXVI, 290, note; Keyser, *Mural Decorations*, 1883; Carleton Williams, *B.A.A.J.*, 1942, 3rd ser., VII, 40.

GREAT YARMOUTH, Norfolk ST. NICHOLAS

'Over the high altar, a loft . . . called the rood loft, which supported a large crucifix behind which was a vestry . . . which said rood loft was erected by Roger de Haddesco, Prior of St. Olave's, in 1370, and ornamented with curious decorations and devices . . . The remains discovered on the south side of the apse consist—to begin with the easternmost—of a piscina and five sedilia. The first being the Prior's seat, has an hexagonal back panelled, the upper panels being charged with the arms of the See, the Deanery and the Priory . . . The backs of the sedilia have been tinted alternately pink and green and the colours appear to have been extremely rich . . . and the spaces in the wall over each seat between the pinnacles alternately green and pink.'

The Ecclesiologist, 1842, I, 202; Morant, *Norfolk Archaeologia*, 1872, VII, 220–1; Keyser, *Mural Decorations*, 1883.

YATELEY (near Farnborough) Hants ST. PETER

In 1870 remains of paintings were discovered on the north wall, and subsequently obliterated; among them was a figure of a crowned king, holding a sceptre, the upper part alone surviving, against a ground diapered with fleurs-de-lis; above the head, and slightly to the left, a large bird. An exploration of the wall-surface undertaken in 1949 showed that no traces exist under the modern plaster.

P. Society of Antiquaries, 2nd ser., 1867–70, IV, 449; Keyser, *Mural Decorations*, 1883; id., *Memorials of Old Hants*, 1906, 147; *Victoria County Hist., Hants*, 1911, IV, 25.

YAXLEY (near Peterborough) Hunts ST. PETER
The North Chapel

On the south wall, above the arcade, in the four easternmost spandrels reading from the east, post-Resurrection scenes, as follows:

1. The Risen Christ.
2. *The Noli Me Tangere*, with Christ on the right, holding the vexillum and clad in a pink cloak, and on the left the kneeling Magdalen, in a black cloak.
3. (?) The Meeting at Emmaus, with three male figures, standing, one in a white cloak, having the hood thrown back, and carrying a staff, the second in a red cloak lined with black, the feet bare, the third with a hat on his head, a staff in his right hand, and a dull red cloak; the background powdered with red cinquefoils.
4. The Incredulity of St. Thomas, traditionally represented, against a background powdered with cinquefoils in red.

Sweeting, *Parish Churches Around Peterborough*, 1868, 190; Keyser, *Mural Decorations*, 1883; *R.C. Historical Monuments R., Hunts*, 1926, 307.

YORK CATHEDRAL CHURCH OF ST. PETER

The Chapter House

In the year 1736, in *Eboracum*, F. Drake described the painted decoration of the Chapter House, as then surviving, in the following terms: 'At your entrance into the house, the first thing you observe are the canon's seats, placed round the dome, which are all arched over; every arch being supported by small marble pillars which are set at due distance round and separate the stalls. Over these arches, which are built like canopies, runs a gallery about the house, but so exquisitely carved, and has been so richly gilt and painted as to be above description . . . The whole roof has been richly painted with the effigies of Kings, Bishops, etc., and large silver knots of carved wood at the uniting of the timbers; all of which are now much defaced and sullied by time.' He also mentions the 'picture of an archbishop between those of a king and queen over the entrance'.

From his account, from a number of later drawings and engravings, and from painted panels removed from the vaulted roof of wood when it was rebuilt, and which are still preserved, it is possible to form a picture of the painting of the edifice, and in particular of the roof, as it was originally. At the crown of the vault were sixteen compartments, each tapering to a point at the apex, $4\frac{1}{2}$ ft. in width at the base, and $13\frac{1}{2}$ ft. in height, framed by painted borders 7 in. in width, and of very varied design, though all were composed of foliated ornament; within these borders the ground, of a cream colour, was diapered with medallions of different sizes, and also with trefoils filled by geometrical patterns, and with large birds, painted in black with beaks and legs in red. At the base, these compartments met others, of the same width at the point of juncture, but tapering towards the clusters of shafts between the large windows surrounding the edifice, and of a height of 23 ft.; with the remaining compartments of the vaulting, immediately above the windows, there were 48 sections in all, 32 of them being filled by large figures, about 12 ft. in height, framed within plain narrow bands of colour, and the rest by decorative devices similar to those already described. Among the figures were kings, bishops, the Church and the Synagogue, and grotesque creatures. Portions of three of the large figures survive, the most perfectly preserved being that of the Synagogue; she is graceful and long-haired, and inclines slightly to the spectator's right, where the golden crown falls from her head; in her right hand is the broken lance, with its floating pennon, in her left the Tablets of the Law, painted red and bordered in gold. Her tunic is

green, and her eyes bound by a semi-transparent veil, through which they show faintly; the entire painting, executed in oil colour, is outlined strongly in black, and the colours of face, hands and tunic are delicately shaded. From Drake's engraving, it may be seen that the Church, placed next to the Synagogue, was depicted as a crowned figure bearing a chalice. The other two surviving figures are somewhat mutilated; they are those of St. Edmund the King, and of an archbishop unidentified. The Saint, young and beardless, with hair curled at the tips, clad in a golden mantle and a tunic of rose-pink, holds a sceptre in the left hand, and in the right three arrows; the archbishop, bearded, is mitred and vested in a green chasuble having a golden morse, and bears an archiepiscopal cross.

The wall above the richly decorated doorway is filled with tracery resembling that of the windows, and was originally decorated with two tiers of figures; the higher of these was much damaged, when the work was recorded, but in the lower were five figures, the central one that of an archbishop, bearing the cross in the left hand and raising the right in blessing, represented against a background enriched with foliated ornament of a delicate type. On either side of him were kings (not a king and a queen, as stated by Drake); both held foliated sceptres, and were clad in long tunics and mantles lined with vair, and the background in both cases was diapered with cinquefoils; the figure to the spectator's left held the right hand palm outwards. The two outermost figures on either side were probably bishops, although it is not clear from the records whether that on the right held a crozier or an archiepiscopal cross; the background to this figure was enriched with a diaper of geometrical character, but the background to the other with foliated scroll-work. All the figures so far as can be ascertained from existing drawings of them, stood upon lions, or perhaps, in one case, upon a hound.

The Vestibule

In the vestibule, or passage, leading from the north transept to the Chapter House, although the wall-space is mainly occupied by windows, so as to leave little space for subject paintings, there are considerable remains of colour decoration upon the architectural features; it is evident that the mouldings were once richly coloured, largely in red, and the hollow mouldings painted with the same colour, diversified with a white or cream chequer pattern outlined in black and set in small sections at intervals. Upon the vaulting is a plain masonry pattern, and the ribs are outlined by a red band enriched with a row of contiguous lozenges in white. Wherever there is any wall-space free of carving, it has been filled with coats-of-arms in alternation with rosettes. On the wall over the entrance from the transept blind tracery in the form of a window is edged with a band of red charged with contiguous roundels in white. In an engraving in Britton's *York* figures are shown on the vaulting, and in a second engraving in the same scroll-work and grotesques appear within quatrefoils and spandrels. The carving of the capitals retains traces of gilding, and its hollows show remains of red.

'*The Fabric Rolls of York Minster*, Surtees Society, 1859, No. 35, pp. 3–4. At the Eastern end of the Presbytery, about the site of a Lady Altar, "many traces of painting" were still to be seen in 1859.

'Idem vero Archiepiscopus ut verus amator virginis, capellam ejusdem Dei genetricis et Virginis Mariae mirabili arte sculptum, atque notabili pictura peregit.

'pp. 7–8. Et in c de vitro emptis de Edmundo Pictore, 26s. 8d. (1371.)

'p. 11. Pictura celurae supra magnum altare. Et in pictura celurae supra magnum altare cum stellis per Ricardum Kyng, ex. convencione, 47s. 3d. (1371.)

'p. 13, footnote. Et de 3s. 9d. de xv stellis de plumbo venditis ecclesiae Scti. Sampsonis. Et de 2s. de veteribus ymaginibus venditis uni pictori.

'p. 278. St. Blaze. j tabula depicta. (1360.)

'p. 289. St. John of Beverley. Una parva tabula depicta pro pace. St. John Baptist (1364).

'p. 290. Unus pannus depictus extensus desuper altare (1360).'

Drake, *Eboracum*, 1736, II, 476–8; Halfpenny, *Gothic Ornaments in York Cathedral*, 1795, 460, pl. 95; Britton, *York*, 1836, 157, pls. xxvi and xxvii; B. Mus., *John Carter Collections*, V, 100; Browne, *History of the Metropolitan Church of St. Peter, York*, 1847, I, 99, 102; Keyser, *Mural Decorations*, 1883.

ABBREVIATIONS USED IN THE
BIBLIOGRAPHY OF THE CATALOGUE

A.A.S.R. & P.	Associated Architectural Societies Reports & Papers.
A. Cam.	Archaeologia Cambrensis.
A. Cant.	Archaeologia Cantiana.
A.J.	Archaeological Journal.
Ant. J.	Antiquaries Journal.
B.A.A.J.	Journal of the British Archaeological Association.
Berks B. & O.A.J.	Berkshire, Buckinghamshire & Oxfordshire Archaeological Journal.
Bird, Mural Paintings, Glos.	W. H. Bird, The Ancient Mural Paintings in the Churches of Gloucestershire, 1927.
Bristol & G.A.S.R. & P.	Bristol & Gloucestershire Archaeological Societies Reports & Papers.
Birmingham & Midlands A.S.T.	Birmingham & Midlands Archaeological Society Transactions.
Burl. M.	Burlington Magazine.
Cambridge A.C.	Cambridge Antiquarian Communications, being Papers presented at the Meetings of the Cambridge Antiquarian Society.
Cambridge & H.A.S.T.	Transactions of the Cambridge & Huntingdonshire Archaeological Society.
Chester A. & A.H.S.J.	Journal of the Architectural, Archaeological & Historic Society for the County, City & Neighbourhood of Chester.
Derby A. & N.H.S.J.	Journal of the Derbyshire Archaeological & Natural History Society.
Dorset A.C.P.	Proceedings of the Dorset Natural History & Antiquarian Field Club.
Dorset A.S.	Proceedings of the Dorset Natural History & Archaeological Society.
East Anglian N. & Q.	East Anglian Notes & Queries.
East Herts A.S.T.	East Herts Archaeological Society Transactions.
Essex A.S.	Transactions of the Essex Archaeological Society.
Exeter D.A.S.	Exeter Diocesan Architectural Societies Transactions.
Gent. M.	The Gentleman's Magazine.
Glos. N. & Q.	Gloucestershire Notes & Queries.
Hants F.C.P.	Papers & Proceedings of the Hampshire Field Club & Archaeological Society.
Keyser, Mural Decorations, 1883.	C. E. Keyser, A List of Buildings in Great Britain & Ireland Having Mural & Other Painted Decorations, 1883.
Lincs A. & A.S.R.	Lincolnshire Architectural & Archaeological Society Reports.
Newbury D.F.C.T.	Transactions of the Newbury District Field Club.
Oxon A.S.	Oxfordshire Archaeological Society Reports.
Oxon A. & H.S.P.	Oxfordshire Archaeological & Historical Society Proceedings.
P. British Academy.	Proceedings of the British Academy.
P. Society of Antiquaries	Proceedings of the Society of Antiquaries.
R.C. Historical Monuments R.	Royal Commission on Historical Monuments Reports.
Rutland A. & N.H.S.	Annual Report & Transactions of the Rutland Archaeological & Natural History Society.
St. Albans A. & A.S.T.	St. Albans Architectural & Archaeological Society's Transactions.

ABBREVIATIONS

St. Paul's E.S.T.	St. Paul's Ecclesiological Society's Transactions.
Shropshire A. & N.H.S.	Transactions of the Shropshire Archaeological & Natural History Society.
Somerset & Dorset N. & Q.	Somerset & Dorset Notes & Queries.
Somerset A.S.	Proceedings of the Somersetshire Archaeological & Natural History Society.
Suffolk I.A. & N.H.P.	Proceedings of the Suffolk Institute of Archaeology & Natural History.
Victoria County Hist.	Victoria County History.
Whaite, St. Christopher.	H. C. Whaite. St. Christopher in English Medieval Wallpaintings, 1929.
Wilts A. & N.H.M.	Wiltshire Archaeological & Natural History Magazine.
Woolhope C.	Transactions of the Woolhope Naturalist's Field Club.
York A.J.	Archaeological Journal, Yorkshire.

APPENDICES

A. LIST OF SUBJECT-PAINTINGS OF LESSER INTEREST, WHETHER EXTANT OR RECORDED

ADORATION OF THE MAGI
Canterbury, Kent (St. Alphege): Keyser, *A.J.*, 1896, LIII, 166.

ANGELS
Landbeach (near Cambridge) Cambs: Walker, *Cambridge A.C.*, 1879, IV, 258–9, repr.; Keyser, *Mural Decorations*, 1883.

ANNUNCIATION
? Carlby (near Stamford) Lincs: Rouse, *Lincs A. & A.S.R.*, 1937, I, pt. 2, 127–132, repr.

BISHOP (unidentified)
Adderbury (near Banbury) Oxon: *Gent. M.*, 1834, I, N.S., 163; Keyser, *Mural Decorations*, 1883.

CHRIST IN MAJESTY
Eggington (near Leighton Buzzard) Beds: Keyser, *Mural Decorations*, 1883; (with censing Angels).
Oving (near Aylesbury) Bucks: Keyser, *Records of Bucks*, 1897, VII, 215; *R.C. Historical Monuments R., Bucks*, 1913, II, 230.

CHRIST, CRUCIFIXION OF
Hatfield Peverel (near Witham) Essex: *R.C. Historical Monuments R., Essex*, 1921, II, 124.

CHRIST, RESURRECTION OF
? Rothwell (near Kettering) Northants; Sharp, *A.J.*, 1879, XXXVI, 58; Keyser, *Mural Decorations*, 1883.

LAST JUDGEMENT
Madley (near Hereford) Herefordshire: Keyser, *Mural Decorations*, 1883; *R.C. Historical Monuments R., Hereford*, 1931, 196.
Wiggenhall St. Mary Magdalen (near King's Lynn), Norfolk: Keyser, *Norfolk Archaeology*, 1907, XVI, 308

CONSECRATION CROSSES
Barningham Winter (near Holt) Norfolk: Keyser, *Mural Decorations*, 1883.
Heckfield (near Odiham) Hants: *Victoria County Hist., Hants & I. of W.*, 1911, IV, 48.
Hughley (near Much Wenlock) Salop: Cranage, *Churches of Shropshire*, 1901, I, 197.
West Mersea (near Colchester) Essex: *R.C. Historical Monuments R., Essex*, 1922, III, 231.

North Scarle (near Lincoln) Lincs: *A.A.S.R. & P.*, 1897, XXIV, lxx.
Stansfield (near Clare) Suffolk: Bryant, *County Churches, Suffolk*, 1912, I, 46; Munro Cautley, *Suffolk Churches & Their Treasures*, 1938, 317.
Uggeshall (near Halesworth) Suffolk: Keyser, *Mural Decorations*, 1883.

HERALDRY
Anstey (near Buntingford) Herts: Keyser, *Mural Decorations*, 1883.
Ingham (near Stalham) Norfolk: Ingham Old Hall: Bolingbroke, *Norfolk Archaeology*, 1907, XVI, 201.
Narborough (near Swaffham) Norfolk: British Mus., *Dawson Turner Collections*, 1845, XIII, 5.

KINGS (unidentified)
Great Livermere (near Bury St. Edmunds) Suffolk: James, *Suffolk & Norfolk*, 1930, 72.
Lydd (Romney Marsh) Kent: Scott Robertson, *A. Cant.*, 1880, XIII, 435; Keyser, *Mural Decorations*, 1883.

KNIGHTS, FIGURES OF
Barrow-upon-Trent (near Chellaston) Derbyshire: *The Antiquary*, 1892, XXVI, 3, repr.
Braybrooke (near Market Harborough) Northants: Hakewill, *Northants N. & Q.*, 1894, V, 16.

SAINTS (identified)
St. Anthony: Braybrooke (near Market Harborough) Northants: Hakewill, *Northants N. & Q.*, 1894, V, 16: ? North Rauceby (near Sleaford) Lincs: Trollope, *A.J.*, 1854, XI, 68; id., *P. Society of Antiquaries*, 1856, III, 54; Keyser, *Mural Decorations*, 1883.
St. Catherine and St. Andrew: Marholme (near Peterborough) Northants: Sweeting, *Parish Churches in and Around Peterborough*, 1868, 7; Keyser, *Mural Decorations*, 1883.
St. Christopher: Shotteswell (near Banbury) Warwick: *The Builder*, 1876, 669; Keyser, *Mural Decorations*, 1883: Whaite, *St. Christopher*, 1929, 43.
St. Edmund, King and Martyr: Stow Bedon (near

Swaffham) Norfolk: *Watling Collection*, Christ Church Museum, Ipswich, vol. C, p. 107 (church destroyed by enemy action, 1941).

St. George: Boxgrove (near Chichester) Sussex: Popham, *Round and About Boxgrove Priory*, 1935, 7; Silk Willoughby (near Sleaford) Lincs; *A.A.S.R. & P.*, 1908, XXIX, lxxi; *A.J.*, 1909, LXVI, 372.

St. Helen, St. Anne and St. Laurence: Harting (near Petersfield) Sussex: *A.J.*, 1862, XIX, 91; Keyser, *Mural Decorations*, 1883; Johnston, *Sussex Archaeological Collections*, 1900, XLIII, 235.

St. Thomas of Canterbury: (Martyrdom) Easton (near Norwich) Norfolk; *A.J.*, 1861, XVIII, 269; Keyser, *Mural Decorations*, 1883; Borenius, *St. Thomas Becket in Art*, 98.

THE TEMPTATION AND FALL

Elford (near Tamworth) Staffs: Keyser, *Mural Decorations*, 1883.

THE SEVEN DEADLY SINS

? Great Hampden (near Wendover) Bucks: *R.C. Historical Monuments R., Bucks*, 1912, I, 162; *Little Guides, Bucks*, 1935, 130.

THE THREE LIVING AND THE THREE DEAD

Edworth (near Biggleswade) Beds: Keyser, *Mural Decorations*, 1883; *Victoria County Hist., Beds*, 1908, II, 225–6; Guernsey (Ste. Marie du Chastel), Keyser, *Mural Decorations*, 1883; *A.J.*, 1885, XLII, 264; Storck, *Burl. M.*, 1912, XXI, 317: ? Great Livermere (near Bury St. Edmunds) Suffolk: James, *Suffolk & Norfolk*, 1930, 72.

B. LIST OF PLACES WITH REMAINS OF STRICTLY DECORATIVE PAINTING OF LESSER INTEREST, EITHER EXTANT OR RECORDED

ALBURY (near Guildford) Surrey
Johnston, *Surrey Archaeological Collections*, 1921, XXXXIV, 52–89.

ALFORD (near Boston) Lincs
A.A.S.R. & P., 1869, X, xii; Keyser, *Mural Decorations*, 1883.

AVEBURY (near Marlborough) Wilts
Bryan King, *The Antiquary*, 1881, III, 45; Keyser, *Mural Decorations*, 1883.

BEACHAMPTON (near Stony Stratford) Bucks
Keyser, *Mural Decorations*, 1883.

CANEWDON (near Rochford) Essex
R.C. Historical Monuments R., Essex, 1923, IV, 22.

COLCHESTER, Essex (Priory of St. Botolph)
R.C. Historical Monuments R., Essex, 1922, III, 50.

CRANTOCK RURAL (near St. Agnes) Cornwall
Journal of the Royal Institute of Cornwall, 1901–2, XV, 142.

EDGCOTT (near Buckingham) Bucks
R.C. Historical Monuments R., Bucks, 1913, II, 106.

FEN DITTON (near Cambridge) Cambs
Keyser, *Mural Decorations*, 1883.

FOXTON (near Cambridge) Cambs
Keyser, *Mural Decorations*, 1883.

HAMBLE (near Netley) Hants
Little Guides, 1945, 89.

HAREFIELD (near Uxbridge) Middlesex
Hugo, *London & Middlesex Archaeological Society*, III, 1, 23, repr.

HARLINGTON (near Woburn) Beds
Keyser, *Mural Decorations*, 1883

HARTLEY WINTNEY (near Hook) Hants
Little Guides, 1949, 92.

HATFIELD BROAD OAK, or HATFIELD REGIS (near Bishop's Stortford) Essex
Galpin, *Essex A.S.*, 1898, N.S. VI, 329, 334.

HISTON (near Cambridge) Cambs
The Ecclesiologist, 1846, V, 270; Hill, *Churches of Cambridgeshire*, 1880, 21; Keyser, *Mural Decorations*, 1883.

GREAT HORKESLEY (near Colchester) Essex
Laver, *Essex A.C.*, 1930, N.S., XIX, 340.

HORLEY (near Reigate) Surrey
Keyser, *Mural Decorations*, 1883; Johnston, *Memorials of Old Surrey*, 1911, 204, repr.; *Victoria County Hist., Surrey*, 1910, III, 206.

HORNINGSEY (near Cambridge) Cambs
Cambridge A.C., xxxviii, 40; Keyser, *Mural Decorations*, 1883.

HUNSTANTON, Norfolk (St. Mary)
A.A.S.R. & P., 1868, IX, 253; Keyser, *Mural Decorations*, 1883.

LANDBEACH (near Cambridge) Cambs
Walker, *Cambridge A.C.*, 1879, IV, 258–9, repr.; Keyser, *Mural Decorations*, 1883.

LANGFORD (near Biggleswade) Beds
Victoria County Hist., Beds, 1908, II, 236.

LINDRIDGE (near Tenbury) Worcs
Victoria County Hist., Worcs, 1913, III, 447.

MELBOURNE (near Royston) Cambs
Keyser, *Mural Decorations*, 1883; Lloyd, *Cambridge A.C.*, 1927, XXIX, 50–8.

OCLE PYCHARD (near Hereford) Herefordshire
R.C. Historical Monuments R., 1932, II, 150.

RADWINTER (near Saffron Walden) Essex
R.C. Historical Monuments R., 1916, I, 215.

SALISBURY, Wilts (Leadenhall)
Wordsworth, *Wilts A. & N.H.M.*, 1917, XXIX, 439–40

SHERE (near Guildford) Surrey
Victoria County Hist., Surrey, 1911, III, 119; Johnston, *Memorials of Old Surrey*, 1911, 212, repr.

SOLIHULL (near Birmingham) Warwick
Victoria County Hist., Warwick, 1945, III, 225.

STEBBING (near Braintree) Essex
R.C. Historical Monuments R., Essex, 1916, I, 282.

LITTLE STUKELEY (near Huntingdon) Hunts
R.C. Historical Monuments R., 1926, 268.

SWAFFHAM PRIOR (near Newmarket) Cambs
Keyser, *Mural Decorations*, 1883.

THURNE (near Acle) Norfolk
Cox, *County Churches*, 1911, I, 108.

WELLINGTON (near Hereford) Herefordshire
R.C. *Historical Monuments R., Hereford*, 1932, 202.

GREAT WENHAM (near Ipswich) Suffolk
The Builder, 1864, XXII, 724; Keyser, *Mural Decorations*, 1883; Harris, *Suffolk I.A. & N.H.P.*, 1927, XIX, 311.

WORTH (near Three Bridges) Sussex
Johnston, *Sussex Archaeological Collections*, 1900, XLIII, 247.

WRITTLE (near Chelmsford) Essex
R.C. *Historical Monuments R., Essex*, 1921, II, 275.

C. TABULATION OF ITEMS IN ACCOUNTS FOR THE DECORATION OF ST. STEPHEN'S CHAPEL, WESTMINSTER PALACE

	one shilling	tenpence	ninepence
20–27 June		John Elham & Gilbert Pokerig, priming walls at east end, and working on 'tablements', six days.	
4 July.	Master Hugh of St. Albans & John Cotton, drawing for four days and a half.	John Elham & Gilbert Pokerig. five days.	
11 July.	Master Hugh, working on 'ordination' & drawing, two days; Cotton working for six days.	The same, six days.	
18 July.	Master Hugh & Cotton, four days.	The same, five days.	
25 July.	Master Hugh working 'on the ordination of several images', for four days; Cotton painting, for five days.	The same, five days.	
1 August.	Master Hugh & Cotton, both painting, the former for three days, the latter for five.	Elham & Pokerig, six days.	
8 August.	Master Hugh, working on the 'ordination of images to be painted', three days. Cotton, painting & drawing, five days.	„ „ „ „	
15 August.	Master Hugh, two days; Cotton, five days.	The same, five days.	
22 August.	Cotton, five days.	„ „ „ „	
29 August.	Master Hugh, three days.	„ „ „ „	
5 September.	Master Hugh, three days.	Pokerig, six days.	
12 September.	Cotton, five days.	Elham & Pokerig, with Wm. Walsingham, five days.	
19 September.	Master Hugh and Cotton, five days.	Elham & Pokerig, six days.	From 19 September, for five days: Wm. singham, Ric. Norwich, Wm. May John Exeter, Thomas Ruddok, G Prince, John Davy, John de Camb Lowen Tassyn, Janyn Godmered, Blithe, eleven painters.
26 September.	Master Hugh & Cotton, four days.	The same, five days.	From 26 September, for five days, 'e painters', presumably as above.
3 October.	Master Hugh & Cotton, 'painting & drawing several drawings of images', six days.	Elham, Pokerig & John Porkele, six days.	From 3 October, for six days, nine pai R. Norwich, Wm. Walsingham, Maynard, John Exeter, Thos. Ru Gilb. Prince, Henry Bleche, John bridge, Lowen Tassyn; & for a day & a John Davy.
10 October.	Master Hugh & Cotton, both drawing for four days.	Elham & Pokerig, drawing, five days.	From 10 October, for five days, ten pai including John Davy & Richard Nor
17 October.	Master Hugh, painting for two & a half days.	Elham, Pokerig & Porkele, again painting, four & a half days.	From 17 October, for six days, eight pai including Wm. Walsingham.
24 October.		Elham & Pokerig, again drawing, five days.	From 24 October, Wm. Walsingham & Exeter for five days.
30 October.	Master Hugh, drawing for three days.	Elham & Pokerig, again painting for five days.	From 30 October, J. Exeter, Wm. Walsing Thos. Ruddok & Wm. Maynard, four

eightpence	sevenpence	sixpence	fivepence	fourpence halfpenny
		Ed. Paynel & Roger Norwich, 5 days. Ed. Paynel, Roger Norwich & Benjamin Nightingale, painting the 'tablement', 6 days.	Ed. Burton & John Leveryngton, 5 days. Ed. Burton & John Leveryngton, 5 days.	Ric. Lincoln, 5 days, grinding colours. The same, grinding & tempering colours for 5 days.
		Paynel, Nightingale & Norwich, on the 'tablement', 5 days.	Burton, Leveryngton & Ralph Tatersete, 5 days.	Lincoln, as above.
		Paynel, Nightingale & Norwich, as above, 6 days.	Burton, Leveryngton & Tatersete, 6 days.	Lincoln, as above, 6 days.
		Paynel, Norwich, Nightingale & Tatersete, 5 days.	Burton & Leveryngton, 5 days.	Lincoln, as above, 5 days.
		Norwich, & 'three others', 5 days.	Burton & Leveryngton, 5 days.	Lincoln, as above.
		Norwich, & Tatersete, 5 days, Paynel, 6 days.	Burton & Leveryngton, 4 days, on the 'table-ment'.	Lincoln, as above.
		Norwich, Tatersete & Paynel, 6 days.	Leveryngton, 5 days.	Lincoln, as above.
		Tatersete, Norwich & Paynel, 5 days.	Leveryngton, 6 days.	Lincoln, as above.
		As above.	As above, 5 days.	„ „ „
Richard Croydon, four days.		Norwich & Paynel, 5 days.	As above.	„ „ „
Richard Croydon, five days.	Wm. Estwick, 5 days.	Tatersete, Norwich & Paynel, 5 days.	As above.	Lincoln & Thomas Davy, grinding & tempering colours.
	Wm. Estwick, 6 days.	As above.	Leveryngton, 6 days.	Lincoln, Reg. Wal-singham & Thos. Davy, as above.
Richard Croydon, six days.	Wm. Estwick & Thos. Jordan, 5 days.	'6 painters', for 5 days.	Leveryngton & Thos. Prittlewell, 5 days.	As above, 5 days.
Richard Croydon & John Palmere, for six days.	Wm. Estwick & Thos. Jordan, 6 days.	As above.	Leveryngton, 6 days.	Lincoln and 4 others, as above.
Croydon & J. Pal-mere, for six days.	Estwick, Jordan & Thos. Burnham, 5 days.	Tatersete, Norwich, Adam Burgate, Paynel, Peter Stoke-well, Wm. Larke, 6 days.	Leveryngton, 2 days.	Lincoln, Thos. Davy, Reg. Walsingham, Thos. Prittlewell, Thos. Cambridge, 6 days.
...ic. Croydon, J. Pal-mere, Ric. Forde & Thomas Burnham, for five days.	Estwick & Jordan, 5 days.	Tatersete & '5 others' gilding, 6 days.	Leveryngton, gilding.	Lincoln & '4 others', 5 days.
...ic. Croydon '& three others', for five days.	Estwick & Jordan, 5 days.	Norwich & '6 others' gilding, 5 days.	As above.	As above.
...ic. Croydon, Ric. Forde, & J. Palmere, for five days.	As above.	Tatersete, Burgate, Paynel, Stokewell, gilding, 5 days.	As above.	As above.
...ic. Croydon, Ric. Forde, & Wm. [sic] Palmere, four days.	As above, 4 days.	Tatersete, Norwich, Burgate, Paynel, Stokewell, 5 days.	R. Lincoln, 4 days.	As above, 4 days.

one shilling	tenpence	ninepence
7 *November*. Master Hugh drawing for three days.	Elham & Pokerig, five days.	Wm. Walsingham & 'three others', for days.
14 *November*. Master Hugh painting for two days.	Pokerig, six days.	As above.
21 *November*. Master Hugh painting for three days.	Pokerig, five days.	The same, for five days.
28 *November*. Master Hugh painting for two days.	,, ,, ,,	,, ,, ,, ,, ,,
1351 *30 January.*	Elham & Pokerig, five days.	
27 *February*. Master Hugh, two days.		
19 *March*	Elham, Pokerig & Wm. Walsingham, 'painting tabernacles & images', six days.	
26 *March.*	Elham, Pokerig & Wm. Walsingham, six days.	
26 *March.*	As above.	Thos. Ruddok, for six days.
2 *April.*	Elham & 'two others', six days.	
12 *April.*	Walsingham & Elham, two days & a half.	
16 *April.*	Walsingham, Elham & Pokerig, six days.	Thomas Ruddok, John Davy, John Oxfor John Athelard, 'painting and drawing', six days.
30 *April*. Master Hugh 'ordering the drawings for the painters', one day.	Pokerig & Walsingham, five days.	
7 *May*. Master Hugh, 'working on the disposition of the painting', three days.	Walsingham & Pokerig, 'painting Angels for the tabernacles', six days.	Davy, Oxford, Wm. Somervill, Athe Prince, Ric. Norwich & Wm. Mayn 'painting Angels & tabernacles', six day
13 *May*. Master Hugh, 'disposer of the works of the painters', painting for two days.		
21 *May.*		Roger Norwich '& four others', laying on gold in the tabernacles', six days.
28 *May.*	Walsingham 'working on the painting of the Angels'.	Richard Norwich, 'working on the paintin the Angels'.
4 *June.*	Walsingham, Elham & Pokerich, painting Angels for tabernacles, 6 days.	Thomas Ruddok '& six others', pain Angels, five day.
2 *July*. Master Hugh, 'drawing images', for three days.		
24 *July.*	Wm. Walsingham & Pokerig, five days.	John Exeter, Wm. Maynard, & John D four days.

eightpence	sevenpence	sixpence	fivepence	fourpence halfpenny
Croydon & J. Palmere, for six days.		Tatersete & '4 others', painting & gilding, 5 days.	Leveryngton, 5 days.	Lincoln & 3 others, 5 days.
above.		Tatersete, Norwich, Paynel & Stockwell, 6 days.	Leveryngton, gilding 'lysur' ? border of windows, 6 days.	As above, 6 days.
same, for five days.		As above, 5 days.	Leveryngton, 5 days.	As above, 5 days.
„ „ „ „		Norwich, Paynel, Stockwell, as above.	The same, gilding, 5 days.	
Palmere, for six days.		Roger Norwich & 'three others', 6 days; & Wm. Larke, 2 days.	Leveryngton & 'two others', 6 days.	
above.		John Lark & 'five others', 6 days.		
above.		Norwich & Paynel, 'painting tabernacles & walls', 2 days & a half.	Wm. Heston, Thos. Shank, & Leveryngton, gilding & 'placing the preynts on the marble columns', 2 days & a half.	
Palmere, six days.				
		Norwich & 'seven others', gilding, 5 days. Norwich 'and four others', laying on the gold 'in the tabernacles', six days.	Peter de Cambridge & Leveryngton, gilding, 5 days. Leveryngton & 'three others' gilding 'the tabernacles' & priming walls, 6 days.	
		Paynel & 'three others' 'laying gold & pryntes', 6 days. Paynel & '5 others' 'making pryntes' & placing them, 5 days.	Heston, Shank & Peter de Cambridge, doing the same, 5 days (at fivepence halfpenny a day'.	

one shilling	tenpence	ninepence
1354. Painters working at wages of one shilling daily, apart from John Barneby, at two shillings daily.		
27 July. John Barneby, six days; John Barneby, jun., & Wm. Maynard, the same.	Pokerig, six days.	Wm. Lincoln, six days.
3 August. John Barneby, six days; 'two painters' (probably Barneby jun., & Maynard) the same.	Pokerig, six days.	Wm. Lincoln, six days.
10 August. John Barneby, five days; 'two painters', the same.	Pokerig, five days.	Wm. Lincoln, five days.
17 August. John Barneby, six days; 'two painters', the same.	Pokerig, six days.	Wm. Lincoln, six days.
24 August. As above.	As above.	„ „ „ „
30 August. John Barneby, six days.	As above.	„ „ „ „
14 September. Maynard, six days.	As above.	„ „ „ „

1356–7. Master Hugh, sixteen working days & two holidays and a half, 12 September–4 October.		
Wm. Maynard, seventy-five working days and seven holidays and a half, 10 July to 6 November; forty-five working days and five holidays and a half (at elevenpence a day) 6 November to 29 January; sixty-four working days and five holidays and a half (again at one shilling daily) 29 January to 4 June.★	Pokerig, thirty-two working days and two holidays and a half, 5 June to 17 July.	
★ Maynard's hours and pay seem to have been cut slightly during the darker and shorter days of the year.		

Observations.

Master Hugh of St. Albans was working for only 18½ days, in September to 4 October, 1356.

William Maynard began before him, in July 1356, and worked throughout, until 4 June 1357.

Pokerig worked only for roughly a month, in June to July 1357: and William Heston the same, at about the same period. Only the apprentices worked for periods as long as seven months, apart from William Maynard. Sinople, verdigris and vermilion, with white lead, were used, but not in quantity. Gold leaf was used extensively.

Master Edmund Canon, stone-cutter, was at work in the Chapel on stalls from 5 June 1356 to 4 June 1357. His activities would appear to have been connected with those of some of the painters mentioned above, since they took place at the same time (Smith's *Westminster*, 200).

eightpence	sevenpence	sixpence	fivepence	fourpence halfpenny
			'2 painters', 6 days.	
				'two painters', 6 days.
				As above.
				" "
				" "
				" "

servations. A quantity of gold leaf, but only white lead & sinople, no other colours; probably only decorative work.

'm. Lincoln, for 84 working days & five holidays & a half, 29 January–4 June. Wm. Somervill, for 64 working days & 5 holidays & a half, the same dates as above.		Wm. Heston, for 31 working days & two holidays & a half, 27 June–8 August.		John York & Wm. Cambridge, for 62 working days & six holidays & a half, 23 October–29 January. York for 64 days & 5 holidays & a half, 29 January–4 June. Cambridge for 83 days & 5 holidays & a half, 29 January–4 June.

D. LIST OF PAINTERS
WORKING BETWEEN 1300–1400 IN LONDON
AND ELSEWHERE

ABRAHAM DE NORTHAMPTON
Accs. Var. Exchequer, E. 101, 468–10, m. 5.

ADAM BURGATE
Smith, *Antiquities of Westminster*, 1807, 210–17.

ALAN DE BEAUMOND
Accs. Var. Exchequer, E. 101, 547–8, m. 5; Tristram, *Eng. Med. Wall. Painting*, 1950, 457.

ALAN THE PAINTER
Accs. Var. Exchequer, E. 101, 547–8, m. 5 (? the same as above).

ALAN *parvo*
Accs. Var. Exchequer, E. 101, 468–10, m. 8.

ALEXANDER THE IMAGER
Cal. Letter Books, ed. Sharpe (1312–14), 156, 160, 179, 289; Tristram, *Eng. Med. Wall Painting*, 1950, 457.

ALEXANDER LE PEYNTOUR [1]
Close Rolls (1313–18) 23 et sqq., 1313, 1315, 1316, 1317; (1318–23), 30 et sqq., 159, 276; (1327–30), 10, 171, 324, 501, 513; (1330–3) 110, 264, 506; (1333–7) 161, 236.
Patent Rolls (1307–13), 27, 137, 315, 587; (1317–21) 240; (1327–30) 33, 306; (1330–4), 334. Englefield, *Hist. of the Painter-Stainers' Co. of London*, 1923, 19; Tristram, *Eng. Med. Wall Painting*, 1950, 457.

BENEDICT NIGHTEGALE, or NIGHTINGALE
Rymer's *Foedera*, I (1066–1377), 366; Patent Rolls (1348–50), 481.

BENJAMIN NIGHTEGALE
Smith, *Antiquities of Westminster*, 1807, 210–17.

CLAYS COLKYRTE
St. John Hope, *Windsor Castle*, 1913, 157.

EDMUND DE MARHAM
B. Mus. Add. MSS. 30, 263, fo. 4; fo. 14d; Rokewode, *Vetusta Monumenta*, 1845, VI, 11–12.

EDWARD BURTON
Smith, *Antiquities of Westminster*, 1807, 210–17.

EDWARD PAYNEL
As above.

GEOFFREY LE PURTREOUR
Englefield, *Hist. of the Painter-Stainers' Co. of London*, 1923, 28.

GILBERT DE COUEHAM
B. Mus. Add. MSS. 30, 263, fo. 2d, fo. 4, fo. 9, fo. 14d; Rokewode, *Vetusta Monumenta*, 1845, VI, 11–12.

GILBERT PRINCE. [2]
For references in the following: *Close Rolls; Patent Rolls; Wardrobe Accounts;* London Corporation Records, *MS. Calendar of Husting Rolls; John of Gaunt's Register*, 1372–6; F. Devon, *Issues of the Exchequer*, 1837; J. T. Smith, *Antiquities of Westminster*, 1807; T. F. Tout, *Chapters in Medieval Administrative History*, IV, 1928; and R. R. Sharpe, *Wills*, II, see—W. A. Shaw, *The Early English School of Portraiture*, Burlington Magazine, LXV, 171–5, and John Harvey, ibid., LXXXIX, 303–5. See also W. A. D. Englefield, *Hist. of the Painter-Stainers' Co. of London*, 1923 46.

GILBERT POKERIG, or POKERITCH
St. John Hope, *Windsor Castle*, 1913, 157; Smith, *Antiquities of Westminster*, 1807, 210–17.

GREY FRIAR, A
MacEwen, *History of the Church in Scotland*, I, 294–5. [3]

HENRY BLECHE
Smith, *Antiquities of Westminster*, 1807, 210–17.

HENRY BLITHE
Smith, *Antiquities of Westminster*, 1807, 210–17.

HENRY DE DENECOUMBE [4]
Cal. of Letter Books, 1899–1903, ed. Sharpe, 234;

---

[1] The name, Painter or Payntour, is quite often found in documents, but in default of definite evidence of occupation has never been included above.
[2] King's Painter, Governor of the Painters' Guild, and Common Councillor.
[3] King's Painter (Scotland).   [4] Governor of the Painters' Guild, 1328.

Englefield, *Hist. of the Painter-Stainers' Co. of London*, 1923, 28, 29, 46.

HUGH LE PEINTOUR
B. Mus. Add. MSS. 30, 263, fo. 16; Rokewode, *Vetusta Monumenta*, 1845, VI, 11–12.

HUGH OF ST. ALBANS
For references to the following: *Close Rolls; Patent Rolls; Black Prince's Register*, IV; W. Page, *The St. Albans School of Painting, Archaeologia*, LVIII, 1902; *Husting Rolls;* J. T. Smith, *Antiquities of Westminster*, 1807; and R. R. Sharpe, *Wills*, II, see—John Harvey, *Some London Painters of the Fourteenth & Fifteenth Centuries, Burlington Magazine*, LXXXIX, 303–5.

ISAAC DE IRLAUNDE
Accs. Various Exchequer, E. 101, 468–10, m. 5.

JACK OF ST. ALBANS
Lethaby, *Westminster Abbey & the King's Craftsmen*, 1906, 275; Coulton, *Medieval Panorama*, Cambridge, 1947, 561.

JANYN GODMERED
Smith, *Antiquities of Westminster*, 1807, 210–17.

JOHN ALBOUN
Close Rolls, VI (1396–9), 118, 204.

JOHN ATHELARD
Rymer's *Foedera*, I (1066–1377), 1350, 366; Patent Rolls, 348–50, 481; Smith, *Antiquities of Westminster*, 1807, 210–17.

JOHN BARNEBY (? or BERNETBY)
? *Archaeological Journal*, 1846, II, 364; ? ibid., 1946, CIII, 174–8; Smith, *Antiquities of Westminster*, 1807, 210–17.

JOHN BARNEBY, junior
Smith, *Antiquities of Westminster*, 1807, 210–17.

JOHN DE BETOYNE
Close Rolls (1374–7), 516.

JOHN OF BRISTOL
Rokewode, *Vetusta Monumenta*, 1845, VI, 11–12.

JOHN, A CANON OF ST. CATHERINE'S BY THE TOWER [1]
Devon, *Issues of the Exchequer*, 1837, 160, 184–5.

JOHN, ? OF CANTERBURY
Documents in Canterbury Cathedral Library; notes supplied by the late Mr. Blore.

JOHN DE CAMBRIDGE
Smith, *Antiquities of Westminster*, 1807, 210–17.

JOHN COTEREL
Englefield, *Hist. of the Painter-Stainers' Co. of London*, 1923, 28–9.

JOHN COTTON
Accs. Various Exchequer, E. 101–471, 6, 25–8; Smith, *Antiquities of Westminster*, 1807, 210–17.

JOHN DAVY
Smith, *Antiquities of Westminster*, 1807, 210–17.

JOHN ELHAM
Accs. Various Exchequer, E. 101–471, 6, 25–8; Smith, *Antiquities of Westminster*, 1807, 210–17.

JOHN OF HASTINGS
Accs. Various Exchequer, E. 101–468, 10, m. 7.

JOHN HAWKYS
Husting Roll 96 (100); Harvey, *Burlington Magazine*, LXXXIX, 305.

JOHN KEYLE (1434) [2]
Englefield, *Hist. of the Painter-Stainers' Co. of London*, 1923, 46.

JOHN KYNGE
Englefield, *Hist. of the Painter-Stainers' Co. of London*, 1923, 23.

JOHN LARKE
Smith, *Antiquities of Westminster*, 1807, 210–17.

JOHN LEVERYNGTON
Smith, *Antiquities of Westminster*, 1807, 210–17.

JOHN MUSARD
Cal. of Letter Books, ed. Sharpe, 1899–1903 (1314–1337), 7.

JOHN DE NORFOLK
B. Mus. Add. MSS. 30, 268, fo. 2d, fo. 4, fo. 9, fo. 14d; Rokewode, *Vetusta Monumenta*, 1845, VI, 11–12: ? the same, Englefield. *Hist. of the Painter-Stainers' Co. of London*, 1923, 35.[3]

JOHN OXFORD
Smith, *Antiquities of Westminster*, 1807, 210–17.

JOHN PALMERE
Smith, *Antiquities of Westminster*, 1807, 210–17.

JOHN PEINTOUR OF IVER
St. John Hope, *Windsor Castle*, 1913, 189, 205.

JOHN LE PEYNTOUR OF WYGETON
Close Rolls (1333–7), 54; *Cal. Inquisitions Miscellaneous* (1348–77), 329.

JOHN PHIPPE OF LONDON
Close Rolls, IV (1389–92), 100.

JOHN DE POLILEY
Cal. Inquisitions Miscellaneous (1348–77), 85, 166.

JOHN PORKELE
Smith, *Antiquities of Westminster*, 1807, 210–17.

JOHN STOKWELL or STOCKWELL
Cal. of Wills in the Court of Husting, ed. Sharpe, I (1336–7), 417.

JOHN OF YARMOUTH (Jernemuta)
B. Mus. Add. MSS. 30, 263, fo. 4; Rokewode, *Vetusta Monumenta*, 1845, VI, 11–12.

JOHN YORK
Smith, *Antiquities of Westminster*, 1807, 210–17.

[1] King's Painter.   [2] Governor of the Painters' Guild in 1433.   [3] Governor in 1415.

LOWEN TASSYN
  Smith, *Antiquities of Westminster*, 1807, 210–17.
MILON DE AILEWYK
  Accs. Various Exchequer, E. 101, 468–10, m. 5.
PETER DE CAMBRIDGE
  Smith, *Antiquities of Westminster*, 1807, 210–17.
PETER, Sacrist of Westminster (termed 'Master')
  Devon, *Issues of the Exchequer*, 1837, 262.
PHILIP OF BARNEBY
  Accs. Various Exchequer, E. 101, 468–10, m. 5.
PHILIP DE HALES
  As above.
RALPH DE CONFORD
  Accs. Various Exchequer, E. 101, 547–8, m. 4.
RALPH DE LONDON
  Accs. Various Exchequer, E. 101, 547–8, m. 5.
RALPH TATERSETE
  Smith, *Antiquities of Westminster*, 1807, 210–217.
REGINALD WALSINGHAM
  Ibid.
RICHARD ASSHEBY
  St. John Hope, *Windsor Castle*, 1913, 148, 179.
RICHARD BLITHE
  Accs. Various Exchequer, E. 101–468, 10, m. 7.
RICHARD BURGATE
  John of Gaunt's Register, Camden Soc., LVI, 76–77.
RICHARD CROYDON
  Smith, *Antiquities of Westminster*, 1807, 210–17.
RICHARD DAVY (of County Glos.)
  Englefield, *Hist. of the Painter-Stainers' Co. of London*, 1923, 35.
RICHARD FORDE
  Smith, *Antiquities of Westminster*, 1807, 210–17.
RICHARD OF GLOSBY
  B. Mus. Add. MSS. 30263, fo. 2d.
RICHARD KYNG
  York Fabric Rolls, Surtees Soc., 1859 (1371).
RICHARD LINCOLN
  Smith, *Antiquities of Westminster*, 1807, 210–17.
RICHARD OF MADELY
  Accs. Various Exchequer, E. 101–468, 10, m. 5.
RICHARD NORWICH
  Smith, *Antiquities of Westminster*, 1807, 210–17.
RICHARD DE REYNDON
  Accs. Various Exchequer, E. 101–457, 18.
RICHARD DE STOCKWELL [1]
  Cal. of Letter Books, 1899–1903, ed. Sharpe, 234; *Cal. of Wills in the Court of Husting*, ed. Sharpe, I (1336–7), 417, 542; Englefield, *Hist. of the Painter-Stainers' Co. of London*, 1923, 29, 46.

ROBERT DE CLACTONE
  Cal. of Letter Books, 1899–1903, ed. Sharpe, (1331–1332), 267.
ROBERT DE CONFORDE
  Accs. Various Exchequer, E. 101–547, 18, m. 5.
ROBERT DAVY [2]
  Close Rolls (1385–9) 346; (1389–92), 158; *John of Gaunt's Register*, Camden Soc., LVI, 76–7; *Cal. of Letter Books*, 1899–1903, ed. Sharpe, 234; Englefield, *Hist. of the Painter-Stainers' Co. of London*, 1923, 46.
ROBERT THE PAINTER
  (1325–6) Swartwout, *The Monastic Craftsman*, 1932, 158.
ROBERT LE PEYNTUR OF CERTESEYE
  Close Rolls (1313–18), 474
ROBERT SQUYRY (1434) [3]
  Englefield, *Hist. of the Painter-Stainers' Co. of London*, 1923, 46.
ROBERT DE TRUNCH
  (1380) Swartwout, *The Monastic Craftsman*, 1932, 45.
ROGER MERRY
  Englefield, *Hist. of the Painter-Stainers' Co. of London*, 1923, 23.
ROGER NORWICH
  Smith, *Antiquities of Westminster*, 1807, 210–17.
ROGER THE PAINTER
  (1320) Swartwout, *The Monastic Craftsman*, 1932, 169; ? the same (1320), *Bicester, Sacrist's & Bursar's Rolls*.
SAMSON AUMONEY OF LONDON
  Close Rolls (1396–9), 49.
SIMON DE BORDEAUX
  B. Mus. Add. MSS. 30, 263, fo. 9; Rokewode, *Vetusta Monumenta*, VI, 1845, 11–12.
SIMON DE BRADSTRATE
  B. Mus. Add. MSS. 30, 263, fo. 9; Rokewode, *Vetusta Monumenta*, VI, 1845, 11–12.
SIMON DE COUDREY
  Black Prince's Register, IV (1359), 327–8.
SIMON THE PAINTER
  Saunders, *An Introduction to Rolls of Norwich Cathedral Priory*, 1930, 107–43.
STEPHEN DOGET
  Black Prince's Register, I (1347), 47.
SYLVESTER HEREFORD
  St. John Hope, *Windsor Castle*, 1913, 200.
THOMAS DE BOURNHAM, or BURNHAM
  Smith, *Antiquities of Westminster*, 1807, 210–217.

---

[1] Governor in 1328.   [2] Governor of the Painter's Guild.   [3] Governor.

APPENDIX D

THOMAS ? OF CANTERBURY
Documents in Canterbury Cathedral Library; notes supplied by the late Mr. Blore.

THOMAS DAVY
Smith, *Antiquities of Westminster*, 1807, 210–17.

THOMAS GLOUCESTER
Close Rolls (1396–9), 118.

THOMAS JORDAN
Smith, *Antiquities of Westminster*, 1807, 210–17.

THOMAS KENT [1]
Harvey, *Burlington Magazine*, LXXXIX, 303–5.

THOMAS LITLYNGTON, alias PRINCE
Patent Rolls (1396–9), 573; (1399–1401), 106, 180, 205. Accs. Various Exchequer, E. 101–402, 13, m. 7; 403, 5, m. 5. Close Rolls (1389–92), 158.
Harvey, *Burlington Magazine*, LXXXIX, 303–5.

THOMAS PRITTLEWELL
Smith, *Antiquities of Westminster*, 1807, 210–17.

THOMAS RICHER [2] (1415)
Englefield, *Hist. of the Painter-Stainers' Co. of London*, 1923, 46.

THOMAS ROTHEWELL
St. John Hope, *Windsor Castle*, 157.

THOMAS RUDDOK
Smith, *Antiquities of Westminster*, 1807, 210–17.

THOMAS SHANK
Smith, *Antiquities of Westminster*, 1807, 210–17.

THOMAS STOCKWELL
Accs. Various Exchequer, E. 101–547, 18, m. 5.

THOMAS OF WESTMINSTER (or OF DURHAM) [3]
Accs. Various Exchequer, E. 101–547, 18, m. 5; B. Mus. Add. MSS. 30, 263, fo. 2d.; fo. 4; fo. 5d; fo. 7; fo. 9; fo. 14d: Page, *Archaeologia*, lviii, 1902, 275; Tristram, *Eng. Med. Wall Painting*, 1950, 84, 88, 100, 115, 355, 396–7, 414, 423, 429, 436, 451–2.

THOMAS OF WILTON
Accs. Various Exchequer, E. 101–547, 18, m. 4.

THOMAS WRYGHT [3]
Harvey, *Burlington Magazine*, LXXXIX, 303–5.

WALTER OF DURHAM [4]
Accs. Various Exchequer, E. 101–547, 18, m. 4, m. 5; Tristram, *Eng. Med. Wall Painting*, 1950, 70, 84–6, 88–9, 96, 98, 100, 102, 113–15, 122, 125, 140, 153, 157, 205, 210, 231, 355, 366, 414, 420, 423, 425, 428, 429, 431, 436, 444–5, 446, 450–3, 454, 456, 458.

WALTER ? OF ELY
Tristram, *Eng. Med. Wall Painting*, 1950, 15.

WALTER THE PAINTER
(1339–40) Swartwout, *The Monastic Craftsman*, 1932, 158–61.

WALTER DE STOCKWELL
Cal. of Wills in the Court of Husting, ed. Sharpe, I, 1350, 640.
Englefield, *Hist. of the Painter-Stainers' Co. of London*, 1923, 23.

WILLIAM DE BIRLEYE
Accs. Various Exchequer, 547, 18, m. 5; B. Mus. Add. MSS. 30, 263, fo. 9.

WILLIAM OF BLIDA (or BLYTHE)
Rokewode, *Vetusta Monumenta*, 1845, VI, 11–12.

WILLIAM BURDON
St. John Hope, *Windsor Castle*, 1913, 197, 210, 291.

WILLIAM CAMBRIDGE
Smith, *Antiquities of Westminster*, 1807, 210–17.

WILLIAM DUTON
Husting Roll, 96, 100; Harvey, *Burlington Magazine*, LXXXIX, 305.

WILLIAM ESTWICK
Smith, *Antiquities of Westminster*, 1807, 210–17.

WILLIAM DE GLOUSBRUG' (or CLOUSEBRUG')
B. Mus. Add. MSS. 30, 263, fo. 4; Rokewode, *Vetusta Monumenta*, 1845, VI, 11–12.

WILLIAM HESTON
Smith, *Antiquities of Westminster*, 1807, 210–17.

WILLIAM HIRLOND
St. John Hope, *Windsor Castle*, 1913, 179.

WILLIAM LARKE [5]
Patent Rolls, 1392, 170, 172; Close Rolls (1389–1392) 546; (1396–9), 503; Englefield, *Hist. of the Painter-Stainers' Co. of London*, 1923, 46.

WILLIAM LINCOLN
Smith, *Antiquities of Westminster*, 1807, 210–17.

WILLIAM MAYNARD
Ibid.

WILLIAM THE PAINTER
Accs. Various Exchequer, E. 101–468, 10, m. 7, m. 8.

WILLIAM DE PORKELE. [6]
Cal. of Letter Books, ed. Sharpe, 1899–1903, 234; Englefield, *Hist. of the Painter-Stainers' Co. of London*, 1923; 29, 46.

WILLIAM DE ROS
Accs. Various Exchequer, E. 101–547, 18, m. 4.

WILLIAM SHANK
(1336–7) Swartwout, *The Monastic Craftsman*, 1932, 158–61.

---

[1] King's Painter. [2] Governor of the Painters' Guild. [3] Governor of the Painters' Guild.

[4] King's Painter. [5] Governor. [6] Governor.

APPENDIX D

WILLIAM SOMERVILL
Smith, *Antiquities of Westminster*, 1807, 210–17.

WILLIAM DE STOCKWELL
Englefield, *Hist. of the Painter-Stainers' Co. of London*, 1923, 26; *Husting Roll*, 74 (75).

WILLIAM DE SUDBURY
Rokewode, *Vetusta Monumenta*, VI, 1845, 11–12.

WILLIAM OF WALSINGHAM
Patent Rolls (1361–4), 345; Smith, *Antiquities of Westminster*, 1807, 210–17.

WILLIAM OF WESTMINSTER (or DURHAM ?)
B. Mus. Add. MSS. 30, 263, fo. 2d. fo. 9, fo. 14d; ? Rokewode, *Vetusta Monumenta*, VI, 1845, 11–12; Tristram, *Eng. Med. Wall Painting*, 1950, 458.

WILLIAM WICKWARE
Accs. Various Exchequer, E. 101–468, 10, m. 5.

WILLIAM WYT
B. Mus. Add. MSS. 30, 263, fo. 2d, fo. 9; Rokewode, *Vetusta Monumenta*, VI, 1845, 11–12.

E. LIST OF PLACES WHICH HAVE OR ONCE HAD FOURTEENTH-CENTURY WALL-PAINTINGS, ARRANGED UNDER COUNTIES

★ Destroyed.   † Of lesser interest.

ENGLAND

BEDS. Chalgrave; Edworth ★; Eggington ★; Harlington; Houghton Conquest; Langford †; Turvey.

BERKS. Abingdon; Ashampstead; Baulking; Enborne; Kingston Isle; Waltham St. Lawrence; Windsor (Castle).★

BUCKS. Aston Clinton; Beachampton ★; Bledlow; Brill; Broughton; Chalfont St. Giles; Chesham; Dorney; Edgcott †; Great Hampden; Little Kimble; Little Missenden; Oving; Padbury; Whaddon.

CAMBS. Barton; Cheveley; Chesterton; Ely (Cathedral); Fen-Ditton ★; Foxton ★; Horningsey ★; Kingston; Landbeach ★; Lolworth; Melbourne †; Little Shelford; Shudy Camps; Stanton Long; Swaffham Prior ★; Willingham.

CHESHIRE. Chester Castle.★

CORNWALL. Crantock Rural.★

DERBY. Barrow-upon-Trent; Melbourne; Staveley.★

DEVON. Barnstaple ★; Exeter (Cathedral); Sidbury.

DORSET. Cerne Abbas; Cranbourne; Tarrant Crawford; Wareham †; Wimborne (Minster).

DURHAM. Durham (Cathedral).

ESSEX. Belchamp Walter; Bradwell; Braintree ★; Canewdon †; Castle Hedingham; Colchester (Priory of St. Botolph †); Fairstead; Felstead; Fingringhoe; East Hanningfield; Hatfield Broadoak or Hatfield Regis ★; Hatfield Peverel; Great Horkesley †; Ingatestone ★; Inworth; Lambourne; West Mersea; Radwinter †; Sheering; Stanford Rivers; Stebbing †; Stifford ★; Wendens Ambo; Writtle.†

GLOS. Amney or Ampney Crucis; Amney or Ampney St. Mary; Berkeley (Castle); Bishop's Cleeve; Bristol (Cathedral); Gloucester (St. Mary-le-Crypt); Hayles or Hailes; Kempley; Notgrove ★; Shorncote; Stanley St. Leonard; Stanton; Stoke Orchard; Tewkesbury (Abbey); Warblington ★; Winterbourne.

GUERNSEY. Ste. Marie du Chastel.

HANTS. Ashley; Buriton; Catherington; Christchurch (Priory); Durley; Heckfield; Hurstbourne Tarrant; Idsworth; Martin; Rowner ★; Silchester; Soberton; Winchester (Cathedral); Yately.★

HEREFORD. Brinsop; Hereford (Cathedral); Madley; Meon Stoke; Ocle Pychard †; Orleton; Stretton Grandison; Wellington †; Westhide; Weston Beggard.★

HERTS. Abbots Langley; St. Albans (Abbey); Anstey ★; Ashwell; Bengeo; Flamstead; Kimpton; Sarrat; Throcking; Widford.

HUNTS. Ramsey; Little Stukeley †; Old Weston; Yaxley.

JERSEY. St. Brelade's.

KENT. Bishopsbourne; Canterbury (St. Alphege) ★; Canterbury (Cathedral); Canterbury (St. Dominic); Dymchurch †; Faversham; Lower Halstow; Harbledown; Lenham; Luddesdown Court; Lydd; Milton Regis; Newington; Rainham; Rochester (Cathedral); Selling; Smarden; Snodland; Swanscombe ★; Tonge; Upchurch.

LEICS. Lutterworth; Stoke Dry.

LINCS. Alford ★; Carlby; Corby; Pickworth; North Rauceby ★; North Scarle ★; Silk Willoughby ★; Swinstead; Thornton (Abbey).★

LONDON. Palace of the Archbishop of York ★; Westminster Abbey; Westminster Palace ★; Old St. Paul's ★; Tower of London.

MIDDLESEX. Cranford; Harefield.★

NORFOLK. Babingley ★; Barningham Winter; Beighton; Brooke ★; Burlingham St. Edmund, or South Burlingham; Castle Acre (Priory); Chedgrave ★; Colton; Crostwight; Easton; Eaton; Edingthorpe; Elsing ★; Fring; Gorleston; Haddiscoe; Hardwick; Heacham; Hunstanton ★ :Ingham (church); Ingham (Old Hall); Limpenhoe ★; Little Melton; Moulton; Narborough; Norwich (Cathedral); Norwich (St. Saviour); Paston; South Pickenham;

Potter Heigham; Sedgeford; Seething; West Somerton; Sporle; Starston *; Stokesby *; Stow Bardolph; Weston Longville; Wickhampton; Wiggenhall St. Mary Magdalen; Wilton †; Wymondham *; Great Yarmouth (St. Nicholas).

NORTHANTS. Ashby St. Ledgers; Barby; Braybrooke *; Burton Latimer; Castor; Croughton; Dodford; Holcot; Lilbourne; Longthorpe (Tower); Marholme; Nassington; Peakirk; Rothwell; Slapton; Stanion.

OXON. Adderbury *; Becklay; Broughton; Chalgrove; Charlton-on-Otmoor; Cowley *; Dorchester; Ducklington; Headington *; Horley; Hornton *; South Leigh; South Newington; Northmoor; Oxford (Christ Church Cathedral); Shorthampton; Stanton Harcourt *; North Stoke; Widford; Wood Eaton.

RUTLAND. Stoke Dry.

SALOP. Alveley; Edstaston; Hughley *; Quatt.*

SOMERSET. Glastonbury (Abbey) *; Sutton Bingham; Wells (Cathedral); Wells (College of the Vicars Choral).

STAFFS. Alton; Clifton Campville; Colton *; Elford; Lichfield (the Bishop's Palace) *; Tettenhall.

SUFFOLK. Alpheton; Bardwell; Barton Mills; Belton; Great Berkhampstead *; Bures; Bury St. Edmunds (Abbey) *; Great Cornard; North Cove; Dalham; Fritton; Honington; Hoxne; Ickworth; Kentford; Lakenheath; Great Livermere; Newton *; Risby; Stansfield; Thornham Parva; Troston; Uggeshall *; Great Wenham †; Little Wenham.

SURREY. Albury †; Byfleet; Charlwood; Oakwood *; Ockham; Sanderstead; Shere.†

SUSSEX. Amberley; Arundel; Boxgrove (Priory); Coombes; Harting; Horsham *; Preston *; Rotherfield; Trotton; Winchelsea; Worth.†

WARWICK. Birmingham (St. Martin) *; Coventry (Cathedral); Shotteswell; Solihull †; Wooton Wawen.

WILTS. Avebury *; Great Bedwyn; Imber †; Inglesham; Malmesbury (Abbey); Oaksey; Purton; Salisbury (Subchantry House).*

WORCS. Halesowen *; Kyre Magna, Kyre Wyard, or Great Kyre; Lindridge †; Martley-with-Hillhampton; Worcester (Cathedral); Worcester (The Guesten Hall).

YORKS. Bedale; Wensley; York (Cathedral).

WALES

PEMBROKE. St. David's (Cathedral).

SCOTLAND

BERWICK. Legerwood.

MORAY. Pluscardine (Priory).*

F. ICONOGRAPHIC LIST

COELUM

Christ in Majesty
Eggington, Beds †; ? Headington, Oxon *; ? Lakenheath, Suffolk (or in Judgement); Northmoor, Oxon; Norwich, Cathedral, Ante-Reliquary Chapel; Oving, Bucks.†

Christ in Majesty, with Symbols of the Evangelists
Winchester Cathedral, Reliquary chest; Worcester, Guesten Hall.*

CHRIST IN MAJESTY, DISPLAYING THE WOUNDS, and surrounded by Angels holding Instruments of the Passion, and Cherubim representing Christian Virtues.
Westminster, Chapter House.

DOOM
Becklay, Oxon; ? Bishopsbourne, Kent; Bradwell, Essex; Chalgrove, Oxon; North Cove, Suffolk; Exeter Cathedral, tomb of Bishop Stapledon, Christ in Judgement; Flamstead, Herts; Houghton Conquest, Beds; Hoxne, Suffolk; ? Lakenheath, Suffolk †; Lilbourne, Northants; Madley, Hereford; Little Missenden, Bucks; Newington, Kent; South Newington, Oxon; Pickworth, Lincs; Quatt, Salop *; Rainham, Kent; Rotherfield, Sussex; Shudy Camps, Cambs; West Somerton, Norfolk; Troston, Suffolk; Trotton, Sussex; Westminster Abbey, cloisters.*

Christ in Judgement, supported by Angels
Little Missenden, Bucks (2); Pickworth, Lincs; South Newington, Oxon; Shudy Camps, Cambs.

Angels with Instruments of the Passion
? Bedale, Yorks; Bradwell, Essex; North Cove, Suffolk; Flamstead, Herts; Houghton Conquest, Beds; Hoxne, Suffolk; Newington, Kent; Westminster, Chapter House; Widford, Herts.

Cherubim and Seraphim
Westminster, Chapter House.

The Blessed Virgin in Intercession
Barton, Cambs; Chalgrove, Oxon; Kempley, Glos ‡; Lenham, Kent ‡; Nassington, Northants ‡; Newington, Kent; Pickworth, Lincs (in Doom and also in Weighing of Souls ‡); Preston, Sussex *; Shudy Camps, Cambs; Slapton, Northants ‡; West Somerton, Norfolk.

St. John the Evangelist in Intercession
Newington, Kent; Shudy Camps, Cambs; West Somerton, Norfolk.

St. John the Baptist in Intercession
Pickworth, Lincs.

The Twelve Apostles as Assessors
Hoxne, Suffolk; Pickworth, Lincs.

Angels Sounding the Last Trump
North Cove, Suffolk; Newington, Kent; West Somerton, Norfolk.

Angels Escorting Souls to Judgement
Trotton, Sussex.

Souls Rising from their Graves
Becklay, Oxon; Chalgrove, Oxon; Colton, Staffs *; North Cove, Suffolk; Hoxne, Suffolk; Lilbourne, Northants; Newington, Kent; South Newington, Oxon; Pickworth, Lincs; Quatt, Salop; Rainham, Kent; West Somerton, Norfolk; North Stoke, Oxon; Wiggenhall St. Mary Magdalen, Norfolk.

St. Michael Weighing Souls
Barton, Cambs †; Bishopsbourne, Kent †; Catherington, Hants †; Chesham, Bucks †*; Horley, Oxon †*; Hoxne, Suffolk; Jersey, St. Brelade's, Fishermen's Chapel †*; Kempley, Glos †; Lenham, Kent †; Nassington, Northants †; South Newington, Oxon; Pickworth, Lincs †; Preston, Sussex †*; Rotherfield, Sussex; Slapton, Northants †; Tarrant Crawford, Dorset.†

Separation of the Blessed and the Lost
North Cove, Suffolk; Hoxne, Suffolk.

The Just Ascending to Heaven
Becklay, Oxon; Newington, Kent.

St. Peter Receiving the Blessed
Amney St. Mary, Glos; Newington, Kent; Shudy Camps, Cambs; North Stoke, Oxon (attended by a deacon).

The Heavenly City; and the Entry into Heaven
Bedale, Yorks; Flamstead, Herts; Newington, Kent; Shudy Camps, Cambs.

Moses, with the Tables of the Law
Trotton, Sussex.

Torments of the Damned
Becklay, Oxon; Bedale, Yorks; South Newington, Oxon.

Entry into Hell
Becklay, Oxon; Bishopsbourne, Kent.

Jaws of Leviathan
Becklay, Oxon; Brooke, Norfolk ★, (engulfing separate representations of the Seven Deadly Sins); Flamstead, Herts; Little Missenden, Bucks; Newington, Kent; Wiggenhall St. Mary Magdalen, Norfolk.

Souls Taken to Heaven by Angels
St. David's, Pembroke (Cathedral); Dodford, Northants; Northmoor, Oxon; Silchester, Hants ★; Starston, Norfolk ★; Winchelsea, Sussex.

The Christ of the Apocalypse
Westminster, Chapter House; Widford, Herts (with Angels bearing Instruments of the Passion).

THE LIFE OF CHRIST
The Holy Infancy
The Annunciation
Abingdon, Berks (St. Helen, flanking a Lily Crucifix); Alveley, Salop; Amney or Ampney Crucis, Glos †; Barton, Cambs †; Brinsop, Hereford; ? Carlby, Lincs; Chalgrave, Beds †; Chalgrove, Oxon; Croughton, Northants †; Dorney, Bucks †; Enborne, Berks †; Faversham, Kent; Fring, Norfolk †; Harbledown, Kent †; Horley, Oxon ? †; Jersey, St. Brelade's, The Fishermen's Chapel; Martin, Hants ★ †; Martley-with-Hillhampton, Worcs †; Little Melton, Norfolk †; South Newington, Oxon †; Rainham, Kent †; Rochester, Kent, Cathedral (Lady Chapel †); Rotherfield, Sussex †; Sarratt, Herts; Slapton, Northants; Stanley St. Leonard, Glos †; ? North Stoke, Oxon †; Tarrant Crawford, Dorset †; Westminster, the Sedilia †; Wooton Wawen, Warwick; Worcester, the Guesten Hall. ★

The Visitation
Alveley, Salop; Amberley, Sussex †; Brinsop, Hereford; Colton, Staffs ★; Croughton, Northants; Faversham, Kent; Newton, Suffolk †; Oakwood, Surrey. ★ †

The Nativity
Baulking, Berks; Chalgrove, Oxon; Croughton, Northants; Faversham, Kent; Headington, Oxon ★; Hornton, Oxon ★ ?; Longthorpe Tower, Northants †; Newington, Kent †; Sarratt, Herts; Westminster Abbey, cloisters. ★

The Annunciation to the Shepherds
Croughton, Northants; Fairstead, Essex; Faversham, Kent; Headington, Oxon ★ ?; Orleton, Hereford; Sarratt, Herts; Westminster, St. Stephen's Chapel. ★

The Adoration of the Shepherds
? Preston, Sussex ★; Westminster, St. Stephen's Chapel.

The Journey of the Magi
Headington, Oxford ★ ?

The Magi Before Herod
Croughton, Northants.

The Adoration of the Magi
Canterbury, St. Alphege ★; Castleacre Priory, Norfolk; Chalgrove, Oxon; Croughton, Northants; Faversham, Kent; Gloucester, St. Mary-le-Crypt ★; Martley-with-Hillhampton, Worcs †; Musée de Cluny, Paris; Preston, Sussex (the Magi holding their gifts ★); Rowner, Hants ★; Westminster, St. Stephen's Chapel ★; Worcester, the Guesten Hall. ★

The Flight into Egypt
? Berkhampstead, Herts ★; Croughton, Northants; Headington, Oxon. ★

Herod Commanding the Massacre of the Innocents
Headington, Oxon ★; ? Potter Heigham, Norfolk.

The Massacre of the Innocents
Berkhampstead, Herts ★; Chalgrove, Oxon; Croughton, Northants; Headington, Oxon ★; Potter Heigham, Norfolk.

The Presentation in the Temple
Chalgrove, Oxon; Cowley, Oxon ★; Croughton, Northants; Faversham, Kent; ? Gloucester, St. Mary-le-Crypt ★; ? Stanton, Glos; Westminster, St. Stephen's Chapel. ★

The Ministry
The Baptism of Christ
? Barton, Cambs; ? Staveley, Derby ★; Wooton Wawen, Warwick.

The Marriage at Cana
Westminster, St. Stephen's Chapel. ★

The Miraculous Draught of Fishes
? Stanley St. Leonard, Glos. ★

The Parable of the Prodigal
? Brooke, Norfolk (in association with the Seven Deadly Sins). ★

The Passion
St. Mary Magdalen Washing the Feet of Christ
Notgrove, Glos.

The Entry into Jerusalem
North Cove, Suffolk; Crostwight, Norfolk; Croughton, Northants; East Hanningfield, Essex ★; Headington, Oxon ★; West Somerton, Norfolk.

The Last Supper
Barton, Cambs; North Cove, Suffolk *; Crostwight, Norfolk; Croughton, Northants; Flamstead, Herts; Peakirk, Northants; Preston, Sussex *; ? Sarratt, Herts; Stanton Harcourt, Oxon *; North Stoke, Oxon.

Christ Washing the Feet of the Disciples
Crostwight, Norfolk; Peakirk, Northants; Stanton Harcourt, Oxon.*

The Agony in the Garden
Crostwight, Norfolk; ? Lakenheath, Suffolk.

The Betrayal
Chalgrove, Oxon; Croughton, Northants; Ducklington, Oxon *; North Stoke, Oxon; ? Peakirk, Northants.

Christ Before the High Priest
Croughton, Northants.

Christ Before Pilate
Chalgrove, Oxon; Crostwight, Norfolk; Flamstead, Herts; North Stoke, Oxon.

Christ Before Herod
Jersey, St. Brelade's, The Fishermen's Chapel.

The Binding of Christ
Jersey, St. Brelade's, The Fishermen's Chapel.

Christ Crowned with Thorns
Crostwight, Norfolk.

The Mocking of Christ
Chalgrove, Oxon; ? Croughton, Northants; Flamstead, Herts; Horsham, Sussex.*

The Flagellation
Chalgrove, Oxon; North Cove, Suffolk; ? Crostwight, Norfolk; Croughton, Northants; Jersey, St. Brelade's, The Fishermen's Chapel *; Melbourne, Derbyshire *; Norwich, Cathedral, Retable; ? Peakirk, Northants; West Somerton, Norfolk; North Stoke, Oxon.

The Carrying of the Cross
Chalgrove, Oxon; Crostwight, Norfolk; Croughton, Northants; Horsham, Sussex *; Jersey, St. Brelade's, The Fishermen's Chapel *; Lakenheath, Suffolk; Norwich, Cathedral, Retable; Peakirk, Northants; North Stoke, Oxon.

The Nailing to the Cross
North Cove, Suffolk.

The Crucifixion.
Abingdon, Berks, Lily Crucifix, with Jesse Tree; Ashampstead, Berks †; Great Bedwyn, Wilts †*; Bishop's Cleeve, Glos †; Brinsop, Hereford †; Broughton, Oxon; Chalfont St. Giles, Bucks; Chalgrove, Oxon; North Cove, Suffolk *; Crostwight, Norfolk; St. David's Cathedral, Pembroke †; Dorchester, Oxon †; Faversham, Kent; Flamstead, Herts; Hatfield Peverel, Essex; Horsham, Sussex *; Lakenheath, Suffolk; Melbourne, Derbyshire; Milton Regis, Kent †; Norwich Cathedral, Retable; Norwich, St. Michael at Plea; Notgrove, Glos *; Peakirk, Northants; Purton, Wilts †; Snodland, Kent †; Starston, Norfolk * (in funeral scene); North Stoke, Oxon †; Sutton Bingham, Somerset †; Tarrant Crawford, Dorset †; Thornham Parva, Suffolk †, Retable; Turvey, Beds †; Westminster Abbey, Cloisters †*; Wimborne Minster, Dorset †; Winchester Cathedral, Hants, reliquary chest.

The Deposition
Chalgrove, Oxon; North Cove, Suffolk; Cowley, Oxon *; Croughton, Northants; Peakirk, Northants; Stanton Harcourt, Oxon.*

The Entombment
Chalgrove, Oxon; Crostwight, Norfolk; Croughton, Northants; Flamstead, Herts; Peakirk, Northants; Stanton Harcourt, Oxon.*

The Harrowing of Hell
Chalgrove, Oxon; North Cove, Suffolk; Croughton, Northants; Lakenheath, Suffolk; Stanton Harcourt, Oxon; Wooton Wawen, Warwick.

The Resurrection
Chalfont St. Giles, Bucks; Chalgrove, Oxon; Croughton, Northants; Flamstead, Herts; Gloucester, St. Mary le Crypt, Easter Sepulchre; Holcot, Northants; Norwich Cathedral, Retable; Peakirk, Northants; Rothwell, Northants; Sarratt, Herts; West Somerton, Norfolk; ? Staveley, Derby *; North Stoke, Oxon; Tewkesbury Abbey, Glos, Trinity Chantry; ? Yaxley, Hunts.

Noli Me Tangere
Preston, Sussex *; Risby, Suffolk †; Sarratt, Herts; Yaxley, Hunts.

The Angel at the Sepulchre
Faversham, Kent; Lakenheath, Suffolk.

The Holy Women at the Sepulchre
Faversham, Kent; Gloucester, St. Mary le Crypt, Easter Sepulchre *; ? Lakenheath, Suffolk; Wooton Wawen, Warwick.

The Supper at Emmaus
? Sarratt, Herts; Yaxley, Hunts.

The Incredulity of St. Thomas
Bradwell, Essex †; Holcot, Northants ?; Lolworth Cambs †; Preston, Sussex †*; Yaxley, Hunts.

The Risen Christ
Bradwell, Essex; Yaxley, Hunts.

The Ascension
Chalgrove, Oxon; North Cove, Suffolk; Crostwight, Norfolk; Holcot, Northants; Norwich Cathedral, Retable; Pickworth, Lincs; Rowner,

Hants; Sarratt, Herts; Wooton Wawen, Warwick.

The Descent of the Holy Ghost
Holcot, Northants.

Head of Christ
Barton, Cambs; ? Bradwell, Essex; Coventry Cathedral *; Kingston Lisle, Berks.

The Holy Child, within a chalice, on an altar; Preston, Sussex.*

The Agnus Dei
Bradwell, Essex; Norwich Cathedral, Presbytery Aisle; Thornham Parva Retable (background 'prints').

Figure of Christ
Horsham, Sussex * (? with St. Peter and St. Paul); Lakenheath, Suffolk; Moulton, Norfolk (in association with Works of Mercy); Pluscardine Priory, Moray *; Wickhampton, Norfolk (in association with Works of Mercy).

Christ as Creator
Cowley, Oxon.*

The Trinity
Bradwell, Essex; Canterbury Cathedral (tester over tomb of the Black Prince); Catherington, Hants; Cowley, Oxon *; Ducklington, Oxon; Gorleston, Norfolk *; Little Kimble, Bucks; Tewkesbury Abbey, Glos (Trinity Chantry).

Scenes from the Life of Christ, unidentified
Amney or Ampney Crucis, Glos; Westminster, St. Stephen's Chapel.*

Emblems of the Passion
Smarden, Kent. (See also under Doom.)

Articles of the Creed
Smarden, Kent.

The Cross
Dorchester, Oxon.

Tau Cross
Croughton, Northants (in Passion series); Westminster, St. Stephen's Chapel (in History of Tobias).

THE LIFE OF THE BLESSED VIRGIN

The Rejection of St. Joachim's Offering
Croughton, Northants; Wooton Wawen, Warwick.

The Appearance of the Angel to St. Joachim
? Potter Heigham, Norfolk.

The Appearance of the Angel to St. Anne
? Croughton, Northants.

The Meeting of St. Joachim and St. Anne at the Golden Gate
Croughton, Northants; ? Potter Heigham, Norfolk; Wooton Wawen, Warwick.

The Birth of the Virgin
Croughton, Northants; Wooton Wawen, Warwick.

St. Anne Teaching the Virgin
? Chalfont St. Giles, Bucks †; Corby, Lincs; Cowley, Oxon *; Croughton, Northants (with Annunciation) †; Gorleston, Norfolk *†; Headington, Oxon *†(? with Annunciation); Hereford Cathedral (tomb recess *); Musée de Cluny, Paris, altar panel; Slapton, Northants † (with Annunciation); Soberton, Hants.†

The Presentation of the Virgin
Croughton, Northants; ? Potter Heigham, Norfolk.

The Departure of the Virgin from Home
Croughton, Northants; ? Potter Heigham, Norfolk.

The Espousals of St. Mary and St. Joseph
Croughton, Northants.

The Death of the Blessed Virgin

The Virgin Prays to be Preserved from the Sight of the Evil One
Chalgrove, Oxon.

The Angel Gives the Palm to the Virgin
Broughton, Oxon; Chalgrove, Oxon; Croughton, Northants.

The Virgin gives the Palm to St. John
Croughton, Northants.

The Assembling of the Apostles
? Broughton, Oxon; Chalgrove, Oxon; Croughton, Northants; ? Wimborne Minster, Dorset.

The Assembling of the Neighbours
Chalgrove, Oxon.

The Death of the Virgin
Broughton, Oxon; Chalgrove, Oxon; Croughton, Northants; Musée de Cluny, Paris, altar panel; Purton, Wilts; Sutton Bingham, Somerset.

The Funeral of the Virgin, and the Miracle of the Jews
Chalgrove, Oxon; Croughton, Northants; Wimborne Minster, Dorset.

The Blinded Cured by the Heavenly Palm
Chalgrove, Oxon.

The Burial of the Virgin
Broughton, Oxon; Croughton, Northants.

St. Thomas Receives the Girdle
Chalgrove, Oxon.

The Apostles see the Girdle
Chalgrove, Oxon.

The Assumption
Broughton, Oxon; Chalgrove, Oxon; Croughton, Northants.

The Coronation of the Virgin
Broughton, Oxon; ? Canterbury Cathedral,

Chapter House, Prior's Seat †; Chalgrove, Oxon; Clifton Campville, Staffs (tomb recess) †; Fingringhoe, Essex †; Lower Halstow, Kent †; Northmoor, Oxon † (tomb recess); Sutton Bingham, Somerset †; Tewkesbury Abbey, Glos (Trinity Chantry †); Westminster (tester over tomb of Richard II); Winchester Cathedral (reliquary chest); Wooten Wawen, Warwick.†

The Virgin and Child
Amberley, Sussex; Barton, Cambs; Becklay, Oxon; Belchamp Walter, Essex; Buriton, Hants; Coventry Cathedral; Cowley, Oxon *; Little Kimble, Bucks; South Newington, Oxon; Norwich Cathedral Ante-Reliquary Chapel; Northmoor, Oxon; Waltham St. Lawrence, Berks; Little Wenham, Suffolk; Weston Beggard, Hereford *; Winchester Cathedral (reliquary chest).

The Tree of Jesse
Abingdon, Berks (St. Helen, roof); Chalfont St. Giles, Bucks; Chalgrove, Oxon; Corby, Lincs; Weston Longville, Norfolk.

The Blessed Virgin
Hereford Cathedral (tomb of Joanna de Bohun) *; Norwich Cathedral, Retable (in Ascension); Pickworth, Lincs (in Ascension); Pluscardine Priory Chapel, Moray *; Thornton Abbey, Leics.*

Head of the Blessed Virgin
Cowley, Oxon * (perhaps originally part of a Virgin and Child).

Miracles of the Blessed Virgin
Chalfont St. Giles, Bucks.

St. Mary in Attendance on the Crucifixion, with St. John
See under Crucifixion.

ANGELS
Arundel Sussex (with Wheel of the Works of Mercy); Becklay, Oxon (in semi-defaced subject); Bradwell, Essex; Chalgrave, Beds; Chedgrave, Norfolk *; Dalham, Suffolk (with the Works of Mercy); Gorleston, Norfolk *; Landbeach, Cambs; Pluscardine Priory Chapel, Moray *; Quatt, Salop *; Shudy Camps, Cambs.

Censing Angels
Catherington, Hants; Cowley, Oxon *; Eggington, Beds *; Fingringhoe, Essex; Flamstead, Herts; Gorleston, Norfolk *; Hayles, or Hailes, Glos; Inglesham, Wilts; Little Missenden, Bucks; Oxford, Christ Church Cathedral, Lady Chapel; Rochester Cathedral, Lady Chapel; Tewkesbury Abbey, Glos (Trinity Chantry); Weston Beggard, Hereford *; Winchester Cathedral (reliquary chest).

Angels Holding Drapery
Westminster, Chapter House (Majesty); St. Stephen's Chapel.*

Flying Angels
Amney St. Mary, Glos; Landbeach, Cambs.

Adoring Angels
Ashwell, Herts; Lakenheath, Suffolk; Oxford Christ Church (south choir aisle).

Angels Bearing Shields
Durham Cathedral (tomb of Bishop Hatfield); Westminster (tester over tomb of Richard II).

Angels Attendant on the Crucifixion
See under Crucifixion.

Angels Revolving Wheel of the Works of Mercy
Kingston, Cambs; ? Nassington, Northants.

Angels Enthroned
Lakenheath, Suffolk.

Dancing Angels
Oxford, Christ Church Cathedral.

Angels with Musical Instruments
Amney St. Mary, Glos; Catherington, Hants; Westminster, Chapter House.

Angels Bearing Emblems of the Passion
Winchester Cathedral, Hants (reliquary chest). See also under Doom.

Angels bearing a Soul to Heaven
St. David's Cathedral, Pembroke; Northmoor, Oxon; Silchester, Hants; Starston, Norfolk *; Winchelsea, Sussex.

Angels Bearing Scrolls
Gloucester, St. Mary-le-Crypt; Headington, Oxon * (probably part of an Annunciation); Ickworth, Suffolk (probably part of an Annunciation); Trotton, Sussex; Stanley St. Leonard, Glos (probably part of an Annunciation).

Angel Bearing Incense Boat
Idsworth, Hants.

Angels Bearing the Seven Sacraments, or the Seven Virtues
Kentford, Suffolk.

SAINTS: AND THEIR 'HISTORIES'
The Four Evangelists
See under Saints.

The Signs of the Four Evangelists
Canterbury Cathedral (tester over tomb of Black Prince); St. David's Cathedral, Pembroke; ? Horley, Oxon; Longthorpe Tower, Northants; Whaddon, Bucks; Winchester Cathedral, Reliquary Chest.

Apostles
See under Doom, and under individual Saints.

Apostles, unidentified
Chalgrave, Beds; Hayles or Hailes, Glos; Holcot, Northants; Longthorpe Tower, Northants.

The Twelve Apostles
Longthorpe Tower, Northants; Norwich Cathedral, Ante-Reliquary Chapel.

St. Alphege
Canterbury Cathedral, ? history.*

St. Andrew
Brisley, Norfolk; Holcot, Northants; Longthorpe Tower, Northants; Marholme, Northants; Newington, Kent; Norwich Cathedral, Ante-Reliquary Chapel; Selling, Kent; Lower Halstow, Kent (miracle of); Stoke Dry, Leics and Rutland (Martyrdom).

St. Anne
Harting, Sussex; see also under the Life of the Blessed Virgin.

St. Anthony Abbot
Barton, Cambs; Braybrooke, Northants *; Kempley, Glos; Potter Heigham, Norfolk; North Rauceby, Lincs.*

St. Bartholomew
Brisley, Norfolk; Chalgrove, Oxon; Holcot, Northants; Selling, Kent.

St. Catherine of Alexandria
? Gorleston, Norfolk *; East Hanningfield, Essex; Marholme, Northants; Norwich Cathedral, Ante-Reliquary Chapel; Preston, Sussex *; Rochester Cathedral, Lady Chapel; Soberton, Hants; ? Tarrant Crawford, Dorset; Thornham Parva, Suffolk, retable; Little Wenham, Suffolk; Westminster, tomb of King Sebert; Old Weston, Hunts.

'History'
Bardwell, Suffolk; Bengeo, Herts ; Burton Latimer, Northants; Castor, Northants; Eynsham, Oxon; Holcot, Northants; Little Kimble, Bucks; Padbury, Bucks; Sporle, Norfolk; ? Stoke Dry, Leics and Rutland; North Stoke, Oxon; Wooton Wawen, Warwick.

St. Christopher
Alpheton, Suffolk; ? Ashwell, Herts; Babingley, Norfolk; Barby, Northants; Barton, Cambs; Belton, Suffolk; Brisley, Norfolk; Burlingham St. Edmund or South Burlingham, Norfolk; ? Colton, Staffs; Coombes, Sussex; Corby, Lincs; Cranbourne, Dorset; Crostwight, Norfolk; Edingthorpe, Norfolk; Fairstead, Essex; Fring, Norfolk; Fritton, Suffolk; Haddiscoe, Norfolk; Hales, Norfolk; Hardwick, Norfolk; Headington, Oxon *; Hoxne, Suffolk; Ingatestone, Essex *; Kentford, Suffolk; Little Kimble, Bucks; ? Kimpton, Herts; Kingston, Cambs; Little Melton,

Norfolk; Milton Regis, Kent; Moulton, Norfolk; Paston, Norfolk; Peakirk, Northants; South Pickenham, Norfolk; Pickworth, Lincs; Potter Heigham, Norfolk; Rochester Cathedral, nave; Sedgeford, Norfolk; Seething, Norfolk; Shotteswell, Warwick; West Somerton, Norfolk; Stoke Dry, Leics and Rutland; Tarrant Crawford, Dorset; Troston, Suffolk; Little Wenham, Suffolk; Wickhampton, Norfolk; Willingham, Cambs; Wood Eaton, Oxon.

St. Demetrius
Westminster, St. Stephen's Chapel.*

St. Dominic
Thornham Parva, Suffolk, Retable.

St. Dunstan
Stifford, Essex * (and the Devil).

St. Edmund of Canterbury
Sanderstead, Surrey; Whaddon, Bucks.

St. Edmund, King and Martyr
Lakenheath, Suffolk; ? Norwich Cathedral, Ante-Reliquary Chapel; Sanderstead, Surrey; Thornham Parva, Suffolk, Retable; Whaddon, Bucks. '*History*'; ? Bishopsbourne, Kent; Thornham Parva, Suffolk, Retable; *Martyrdom*. Charlwood, Surrey; Stoke Dry, Leics and Rutland; Stow Bardolph, Norfolk; Troston, Suffolk; ? Widford, Oxon.

St. Edward the Confessor
Norwich Cathedral, south aisle.*

St. Edward the Confessor and the Pilgrim
Faversham, Kent *; Forthampton Court, Glos, panel; Westminster, Sedilia.

St. Etheldreda
? Gorleston, Norfolk.

St. Eloy
Slapton, Northants.

St. Eustace
? Stanion, Northants; Westminster, St. Stephen's Chapel, 'history'.*

St. Francis
Preaching to the Birds: Little Kimble, Bucks.
Stilling the Singing Birds. ? Longthorpe Tower, Northants.

St. George
Amney St. Mary, Glos; Barton, Cambs (in a Weighing of Souls); Great Bedwyn, Wilts; Little Kimble, Bucks; Westminster, St. Stephen's Chapel *; Winchester Cathedral, reliquary chest.

St. George and the Dragon
Amney St. Mary, Glos; Boxgrove, Sussex; Kingston, Cambs; Silk Willoughby, Lincs *; Troston, Suffolk; Willingham, Cambs.

St. Hubert
? Stanion, Northants (or St. Eustace).

St. Helena
Amney Crucis, Glos; Chalgrove, Oxon; Harting, Sussex.*

St. James the Great
Amney Crucis, Glos; Bradwell, Essex; Hales, Norfolk; Little Kimble, Bucks; South Newington, Oxon; Selling, Kent; Winchester Cathedral, reliquary chest.

St. John the Baptist
Barton, Cambs; Great Bedwyn, Wilts; Bishop's Cleeve, Glos; Chalgrove, Oxon; Eaton, Norfolk; Heacham, Norfolk; South Newington, Oxon; ? Seething, Norfolk; North Stoke, Oxon; Thornham Parva, Suffolk, Retable; Winchester Cathedral, reliquary chest.
'*History*'
Cerne Abbas, Dorset; Chalfont St. Giles, Bucks; Elsing, Norfolk *; Idsworth, Hants; Kingston Lisle, Berks; Stifford, Essex *; Wooton Wawen, Warwick.

St. John the Evangelist
Chalgrove, Oxon; Eaton, Norfolk *; ? Holcot, Northants; Newington, Kent; Norwich Cathedral, Retable (in Ascension); Pluscardine Priory Chapel, Moray *; Selling, Kent; Westminster, Chapter House (Apocalypse).
With St. Mary, in attendance on the Crucifixion, see under Crucifixion.

St. Joseph
Abingdon, Berks, St. Helen (in Jesse Tree). See under Life of Christ, Nativity etc.

St. Kenelm, King and Martyr
'*History*'; Halesowen, Worcs.*

St. Lawrence
Abbots Langley, Herts; Chalgrove, Oxon; Harting, Sussex *; Little Kimble, Bucks; ? Norwich Cathedral, Ante-Reliquary Chapel; ? Sidbury, Devon.
Martyrdom; Rotherfield, Sussex *; Widford, Oxon.

St. Leonard
? Bengeo, Herts; ? Sidbury, Devon.

St. Margaret of Antioch
Newington, Kent; South Newington, Oxon; Norwich Cathedral, Ante-Reliquary Chapel; Preston, Sussex *; Rochester Cathedral, Lady Chapel; Soberton, Hants; Little Wenham, Suffolk; Old Weston, Hunts; Thornham Parva, Suffolk, Retable; Winchester Cathedral, reliquary chest.
'*History*'. Ashby St. Legers, Northants; Charlwood, Surrey; Little Kimble, Bucks; Limpenhoe, Norfolk *; ? Stoke Dry, Leics and Rutland; Tarrant Crawford, Dorset; Wendens Ambo, Essex.

St. Martin of Tours
Martley-with-Hillhampton, Worcs; Norwich Cathedral, Ante-Reliquary Chapel.
'*History*'; Birmingham, St. Martin *; Nassington, Northants.

St. Mary Magdalen
? Chalgrove, Oxon; Little Wenham, Suffolk; Westminster, Tomb of Cardinal Langham.*
'*History*'; ? Rochester Cathedral, crypt.

St. Mercurius
Westminster, St. Stephen's Chapel.*

St. Nicholas
Norwich Cathedral, Ante-Reliquary Chapel.

Restoration to Life of the Three Boys
Bishopsbourne, Kent; Charlwood, Surrey; Colton, Staffs *; Potter Heigham, Norfolk.
'*History*'; ? Birmingham, St. Martin *; Halesowen, Worcs *; Honington, Suffolk; Inworth, Essex.

St. Osyth
Horley, Oxon.

St. Paul
Becklay, Oxon; Brill, Bucks; Chalgrave, Beds; Chalgrove, Oxon; Headington, Oxon *; ? Horsham, Sussex; Idsworth, Hants; Kingston Lisle, Berks; Longthorpe Tower, Northants; Newington, Kent; Norwich Cathedral, Ante-Reliquary Chapel; Selling, Kent; ? Swanscombe, Kent; Thornham Parva, Stuffolk, Retable; Winchester Cathedral, reliquary chest.

St. Peter
Amney St. Mary, Glos; Becklay, Oxon; Brill, Bucks; ? Chalgrave, Beds; Chalgrove, Oxon; Headington, Oxon *; Horsham, Sussex ? * Idsworth, Hants; Kingston Lisle, Berks; Longthorpe Tower, Northants; Newington, Kent; Norwich Cathedral, Ante-Reliquary Chapel; Pickworth, Lincs (in Ascension); Selling, Kent; ? Swanscombe, Kent *; Thornham Parva, Suffolk, Retable; Winchester Cathedral, reliquary chest.

St. Peter Martyr
Thornham Parva, Suffolk, Retable.

St. Richard of Chichester
Norwich Cathedral, Ante-Reliquary Chapel.

St. Stephen
? Norwich Cathedral, Ante-Reliquary Chapel; ? Sidbury, Devon.
'*History*'; North Stoke, Oxon.

St. Thomas the Apostle
Preston, Sussex.*
See under Passion, and Death of the Blessed Virgin.

St. Thomas of Cantelupe
Barton, Cambs.

St. Thomas of Canterbury
Abbots Langley, Herts; Fritton, Suffolk; ? Norwich Cathedral, Ante-Reliquary Chapel.

Martyrdom
Burlingham St. Edmund or South Burlingham, Norfolk; Eaton, Norfolk *; Faversham, Kent *; Holcot, Northants *; Honington, Suffolk; South Newington, Oxon; Preston, Sussex *; North Stoke, Oxon; Whaddon, Bucks. 'History', ? Tewkesbury Abbey, Fitz-Hamon Chantry.

St. William of York
St. Albans Cathedral.

St. Wulstan
Ely Cathedral, choir *; Norwich Cathedral, south aisle (receiving crozier from St. Edward the Confessor).*

Saints, unidentified
Amberley, Sussex; Amney Crucis, Glos; Ashley, Hants; Great Bedwyn, Wilts; Canterbury, St. Dominic; Colton, Staffs *; Corby, Lincs; Cowley, Oxon *; Crostwight, Norfolk; Dorney, Bucks; Fring, Norfolk; Lower Halstow, Kent; Holcot, Northants; Inglesham, Wilts; Little Kimble, Bucks; Kentford, Suffolk; Kingston, Cambs; Kyre Magna, Worcs; Landbeach, Cambs *; Westminster, Chapter House, Majesty; Narholme, Northants; Milton Regis, Kent; Nassington, Northants; Norwich Cathedral, Bauchun Chapel; Notgrove, Glos *; Rochester Cathedral, Lady Chapel; Smarden, Kent; Soberton, Hants; Stanford Rivers, Essex; Stanley St. Leonard, Glos; Sutton Bingham, Somerset; Widford, Herts; Winchester Cathedral, reliquary chest; Winterbourne, Glos; Wooton Wawen, Warwick; Worcester Cathedral, crypt.*

Legends of Saints, unidentified
? Castle Eaton, Wilts; Rochester Cathedral, crypt.

Blessed Thomas of Lancaster
South Newington, Oxon.

Consecration Crosses
Amberley, Sussex; Arundel, Sussex; Barningham Winter, Norfolk; Barton Mills, Suffolk; Beighton, Norfolk; Bures, Suffolk; Byfleet, Surrey; Cerne Abbas, Dorset; Charlton-on-Otmoor, Oxon; Chesham, Bucks; Colton, Norfolk; Crostwight, Norfolk; Eaton, Norfolk; Edstaston, Salop; Fingringhoe, Essex; Gloucester, St. Mary-le-Crypt; Haddiscoe, Norfolk; Lower Halstow, Kent; Heckfield, Hants *; Hughley, Salop *; Inglesham, Wilts; Kempley, Glos; Kingston, Cambs; Meon Stoke, Hants; West Mersey, Essex; ? Moulton,

Norfolk; Norwich, St. Saviour *; Padbury, Bucks; Pluscardine Priory Chapel, Moray; Potter Heigham, Norfolk; Preston, Sussex *; Rainham, Kent; North Scarle, Lincs; Seething, Norfolk; Sheering, Essex; Stansfield, Suffolk; Stow Bardolph, Norfolk *; Sutton Bingham, Somerset; Thornham Parva, Suffolk; Uggeshall, Suffolk; Wendens Ambo, Essex; Wickhampton, Norfolk; Willingham, Cambs; Wood Eaton, Oxon.

The Church and the Synagogue
York, Chapter House roof (the Church destroyed).

The Old Testament
The Temptation
Chalfont St. Giles, Bucks; Colton, Staffs *; Elford, Staffs.*

The Fall of Man
Alveley, Salop; Elford, Staffs.*

The Expulsion from Eden
Chalfont St. Giles, Bucks; Colton, Staffs.*

The Condemnation of Adam to Labour and Toil
Bedlow, Bucks; East Hanningfield, Essex.

Cain and Abel
East Hanningfield, Essex.

'History' of Job
Westminster, St. Stephen's Chapel; mainly destroyed, but some subjects preserved in the British Museum.

'History' of Tobias
As above.

Scriptural Scenes, unidentified
Barby, Northants; ? Castle Eaton, Wilts.

Kings
See under Jesse Tree.

King David with a Harp
Longthorpe Tower, Northants; and see under Jesse Tree.

Prophets
See under Jesse Tree.

Moses
Trotton, Sussex; and see under Jesse Tree.

ALLEGORIES AND MORALITIES
Christ Surrounded by Instruments of Toil
Amney St. Mary, Glos.

Instruments of Toil
Chesham, Bucks.

Labours of the Months
Longthorpe Tower, Northants.

The Seven Ages of Man
? Hoxne, Suffolk; Longthorpe Tower, Northants.

The Seven Corporal Works of Mercy
Arundel, Sussex; Chesterton, Cambs *; Cran-

bourne, Dorset; Dalham, Suffolk; Edingthorpe, Norfolk; Hoxne, Suffolk; Kentford, Suffolk; Kimpton, Herts; Kingston, Cambs; Moulton, Norfolk; ? Nassington, Northants; Potter Heigham, Norfolk; Quatt, Salop*; Trotton, Sussex; Wickhampton, Norfolk.

The Seven Deadly Sins

Alveley, Salop; Arundel, Sussex; Bardwell, Suffolk; Brooke, Norfolk*; Broughton, Bucks; Cranbourne, Dorset; Crostwight, Norfolk; Dalham, Suffolk; Felstead, Essex*; Great Hampden, Bucks ?; Hoxne, Suffolk; Hurstbourne Tarrant, Hants; Ingatestone, Essex*; Kentford, Suffolk; ? Kingston, Cambs; South Leigh, Oxon; Padbury, Bucks; ? Peakirk, Northants; Quatt, Salop*; Trotton, Sussex; Wooton Wawen, Warwick.

Sacrilege

The Black Mass; Witchcraft

Melbourne, Derbyshire; Stokesby, Norfolk.

Blasphemy

Broughton, Bucks.

'Jangling'

Colton, Norfolk; Great Cornard, Suffolk (or witchcraft); Little Melton, Norfolk; Seething, Norfolk.

Sabbat

? Crostwight, Norfolk.

The Three Living and the Three Dead

Alton, Staffs; Bardwell, Suffolk; Barnstaple, Devon; Belton, Suffolk; Charlwood, Surrey; Cranbourne, Dorset; ? Edworth, Beds; Gorleston, Norfolk*; Guernsey, Ste. Marie du Chastel; Haddiscoe, Norfolk; Hurstbourne Tarrant, Hants; Kentford, Suffolk; Limpenhoe, Norfolk*; Longthorpe Tower, Northants; Lutterworth, Leics; Paston, Norfolk; Peakirk, Northants; Pickworth, Lincs; Seething, Norfolk; Slapton, Northants; North Stoke, Oxon; Tarrant Crawford, Dorset; Tettenhall, Staffs*; Wensley, Yorks; Whaddon, Bucks; Wickhampton, Norfolk; Widford, Oxon; Wymondham, Norfolk.*

Wheel of the Five Senses

Longthorpe Tower, Northants.

Wheel of Fortune

Belchamp Walter, Essex; Old Weston, Hunts.

Wheels

Stoke Orchard, Glos; Thornham Parva, Suffolk; Legerwood, Berwick (pattern).

VARIOUS SUBJECTS

Abbots, unidentified

? Castleacre Priory, Norfolk; Westminster, Sedilia (or Bishop).

Archbishops, unidentified

Amney Crucis, Glos; Chalgrave, Beds; Kempley, Glos; York, Chapter House.*

Bishops, unidentified

Adderbury, Oxon*; Amney Crucis, Glos; Bengeo, Herts; ? Castleacre Priory, Norfolk; ? Castle Hedingham, Essex; Chesham, Bucks; Colton, Staffs*; Coombes, Sussex; Ely, Prior's House; Ely Cathedral, choir*; Lower Halstow, Kent; Headington, Oxon*; Hornton, Oxon*; Little Kimble, Bucks; Norwich Cathedral, south aisle*; Preston, Sussex*; Risby, Suffolk; Rochester Cathedral*; Stanley St. Leonard, Glos*; Old Weston, Hunts; Westminster, Sedilia (or Archbishop); Widford, Herts; Worcester Cathedral; York Cathedral, Chapter House.*

Ecclesiastics, unidentified

Amberley, Sussex; Barby, Northants; Canterbury Cathedral, Our Lady Undercroft; Shorthampton, Oxon; Stoke Dry, Leics and Rutland.

Kings, identified

? Henry III, Westminster, Sedilia; ? Edward I, Westminster, Sedilia and Coronation Chair; Coronation, Marriage, wars and Funeral of Edward I, Lichfield, Bishop's Palace*; Edward III and five sons, St. Stephen's Chapel, Westminster.*

Kings, or crowned Saints, unidentified

Bengeo, Herts; Bishop's Cleeve, Glos (in attendance on Crucifixion); Byfleet, Surrey; Castle Hedingham, Essex; Ely Cathedral; Glastonbury Abbey*; Longthorpe Tower, Northants; Lydd, Kent; Sotby, Lincs*; Yately, Hants*; Yorks, Chapter House.*

Queens, identified

Queen Philippa, and four daughters, St. Stephen's, Chapel, Westminster.

Queens, or crowned Saints, unidentified

Lower Halstow, Kent; Headington, Oxon*; York, Chapter House.*

Knights, unidentified

Barrow-upon-Trent, Derby; Braybrooke, Northants*; Nunney, Somerset*; Upchurch, Kent (in combat); Winterbourne, Glos.

Donors and Benefactors

Amberley, Sussex; Barnstaple, Devon; Barton, Cambs; ? Becklay, Oxon; Bishop's Cleeve, Glos; Broughton, Oxon; Clifton Campville, Staffs; Corby, Lincs; Cowley, Oxon*; Cranbourne, Dorset; Faversham, Kent*; Glastonbury Abbey*; Gloucester, St. Mary-le-Crypt*; Hereford Cathedral, tomb of Joanna de Bohun*; Martin, Hants; Martley-with-Hillhampton, Worcs; Nassington, Northants; South Newington, Oxon; Northmoor,

Oxon; Peakirk, Northants; Rochester Cathedral; Sidbury, Devon; ? Stoke Dry, Leics and Rutland; Tewkesbury Abbey; Westminster, St. Stephen's Chapel (see above); Winchester Cathedral, reliquary chest.

Figures, unidentified

Lakenheath, Suffolk (in adoration); Stanford Rivers, Essex; Stanion, Northants; Stretton Grandison, Hereford.

Funeral Scene

Starston, Norfolk.★

Pilgrims to a Shrine

? Canterbury Cathedral.★

Man holding Triptych (? St. Luke)

Little Kimble, Bucks.

Musicians

Longthorpe Tower, Northants; Oxford, Christ Church Cathedral.

Ships

Durley, Hants; Lower Halstow, Kent; Luddesdown Court, Kent.

Animals and Birds; the Bestiary

Amney Crucis, Glos; Barton, Cambs; Bradwell, Essex; Chedgrave, Norfolk★; Crantock Rural, Cornwall★; Dalham, Suffolk; St. David's Cathedral, Pembroke; Exeter Cathedral; Hayles or Hailes, Glos; Longthorpe Tower, Northants; Martley-with-Hillhampton, Worcs; Milton Regis, Kent; Rochester Cathedral; Salisbury, Sub-Chantry House★; Stanley St. Leonard, Glos★; Willingham, Cambs; Wymondham, Norfolk★; Yately, Hants; York, Chapter House.★ See also under St. Christopher.

Decorative Motifs with Symbolic Significance

Crown of Thorns Surrounding the Sacred Monogram

Monks Horton, Kent.

Diaper of Crosses

Malmesbury Abbey, Wilts; Chalfont St. Giles, Bucks.

Diaper of Drops of Blood, or Tears

Westminster, Chapel of Our Lady of the Pew.

Diaper of Letter J, Crowned

Canterbury Cathedral, crypt.

Diaper of Letter M, Crowned

Canterbury Cathedral, crypt; Cranford, Middlesex; Harbledown, Kent.

Diaper of the Sacred Monogram

Broughton, Beds; Canterbury Cathedral, tester over tomb of Black Prince; Chedgrave, Norfolk★; Harbledown, Kent; Wareham, Dorset.

Diaper of Suns

Canterbury Cathedral, tester over tomb of Black Prince.

Grotesques

Christ Church Priory, Hants; St. David's Cathedral, Pembroke; Fairstead, Essex; Hailes, Glos; Westminster, Abbey, Coronation Chair, and St. Stephen's Chapel★; York, Chapter House and vestibule.★

Hangings, painted representations of

Canterbury Cathedral, St. Andrew's Chapel; ? Castleacre Priory, Norfolk; Dorchester, Oxon; Exeter Cathedral, Sedilia; Headington, Oxon★; Horley, Oxon; Kingston, Cambs; Lakenheath, Suffolk; Martley-with-Hillhampton, Worcs; Little Melton, Norfolk; Newington, Kent; ? Potter Heigham, Norfolk; Slapton, Northants; Wareham, Dorset.

Heraldry

St. Albans Cathedral, feretory, nave, Abbot's door; Amney Crucis, Glos; Anstey, Herts★; Bedale, Yorks; Canterbury Cathedral, crypt; Canterbury, St. Dominic; Castleacre Priory, Norfolk; Chalgrave, Beds; Clifton Campville, Staffs; Dodford, Northants; Exeter, Bishop's Palace; Gorleston, Norfolk; Hayles or Hailes, Glos; Hereford Cathedral, tombs; Horley, Oxon; Houghton Conquest, Beds; Ingham Old Hall, Norfolk; Little Kimble, Bucks; Longthorpe Tower, Northants; Martley-with-Hillhampton, Worcs; South Newington, Oxon; Northmoor, Oxon; Norwich Cathedral, Retable; Norwich, St. Helens Hospital Chapel; Oxford, Christ Church Cathedral, tomb of Lady Montacute; Rochester Cathedral, choir, Lady Chapel and crypt; Little Shelford, Cambs; Stamford Rivers, Essex; Swinstead, Lincs; Tettenhall, Staffs; Tower of London; Trotton, Sussex; Warblington, Hants; Wells Cathedral, de Drokensford tomb, and Chapter House; Westminster Abbey, Abbot's Hall, tomb of Aymer de Valence, Chapel of Our Lady of the Pew, Sedilia, tombs of Richard II and Philippa of Hainault, north and south aisles, Muniment Room; Westminster Palace, St. Stephen's Chapel★; Willingham, Cambs; Winchester Cathedral, reliquary chest; Winterbourne, Glos; Worcester Cathedral, crypt★; Worcester, the Guesten Hall★; Great Yarmouth, Norfolk, St. Nicholas; York Cathedral, Chapter House, vestibule.

Inscriptions

Abingdon, Berks, St. Helen's; Adderbury, Oxon★; St. Albans Cathedral, feretory; Amney St. Mary, Glos; Ayot St. Lawrence, Herts★; Bardwell, Suffolk; Barnstaple, Devon★; Barton, Cambs; Becklay, Oxon; Berkeley Castle, Glos; Broughton, Oxon; Chalgrave, Beds; Chedgrave,

Norfolk *; Clifton Campville, Staffs; Corby, Lincs; Crostwight, Norfolk; Ducklington, Oxon *; Eaton, Norfolk; Edingthorpe, Norfolk; Edstaston, Salop; Faversham, Kent *; Horley, Oxon; Hoxne, Suffolk; Little Kimble, Bucks; South Leigh, Oxon *; Lenham, Kent *; Longthorpe Tower, Northants; Martin, Hants; Melbourne, Derbyshire; Milton Regis, Kent; Moulton, Norfolk; South Newington, Oxon; Norwich Cathedral, Ante-Reliquary Chapel, Bauchun Chapel *, south aisle *, Retable; Norwich, St. Saviour *; Padbury, Bucks; Potter Heigham, Norfolk; Rochester Cathedral, Sedilia *; Rowner, Hants *; Sanderstead, Surrey; Sedgeford, Norfolk; Seething, Norfolk; Little Shelford, Cambs; Slapton, Northants; Smarden, Kent; Stanley St. Leonard, Glos; Stanton Harcourt, Oxon *; Starston, Norfolk *; Trotton, Sussex; Wensley, Yorks; Westhide, Hereford; Westminster Abbey, portrait of Richard II (crowned Rs), south aisle, Chapter House, Majesty and Apocalypse; Westminster Palace, St. Stephen's Chapel*; Old Weston, Hunts; Weston Longville, Norfolk; Whaddon, Bucks; Wickhampton, Norfolk; Winchester Cathedral, reliquary chest; Wood Eaton, Oxon.

G. LIST OF DRAWINGS BY E. W. TRISTRAM IN THE VICTORIA AND ALBERT MUSEUM FROM WALL-PAINTINGS OF THE FOURTEENTH CENTURY

St. Albans Cathedral, Herts. E. 503. 1915: E. 691. 1930: E. 3426. 1931.

Ampney Crucis, Glos. E. 2802. 2803. 1923: E. 696. 697. 1928: E. 1332. 1333. 1924.

Ampney St. Mary, Glos. E. 2797–2801. 1923: E. 698–701. 1928.

Ashby St. Leger, Northants. E. 703. 1928.

Bardwell, Suffolk. E. 711. 1928: E. 609. 1930.

Barton, Cambs. E. 3369–3376. 1931.

Bishop's Cleeve, Glos. E. 715. 1928.

Brooke, Norfolk. E. 717. 1928.

Canterbury Cathedral. E. 516. 1930: E. 521. 522. 1930: E. 621–625. 1930.

Catherington, Hants. E. 734. 735. 1928.

Cerne Abbas, Dorset. E. 6. 1927.

Chalfont St. Giles, Bucks. E. 530–540. 1930.

Chalgrove, Oxon, E. 1536–1540. 1922.

Charlwood, Surrey. E. 736. 1928.

Chesterton, Cambs. E. 402. 1915.

Crostwight. Norfolk. E. 756. 1928.

Croughton, Northants. E. 43. 1925: E. 198–220. 1925.

East Hanningfield, Essex. E. 3596–3598. 1931.

Ely Cathedral, Cambs. E. 758. 759. 1928.

Faversham, Kent. E. 648–650. 1930.

Gloucester, St. Mary le Crypt. E. 3392. 1931.

Hailes, Glos. E. 448. 1915: E. 450–453. 1915: E. 455. 1915: E. 662–664. 1930.

Halstow, Kent. E. 1050. 1925: E. 779. 780. 1928.

Harty, I. of Sheppey. E. 11. 1927.

Headington, Oxon. E. 666. 1930.

Horsham, Sussex, E. 201. 1926.

Hoxne, Suffolk. E. 13–17. 1927.

Icklesham, Sussex. E. 3403, 3404. 1931.

Kentford, Suffolk. E. 1907. 1927: E. 782. 783. 1928.

Little Kimble. Bucks. E. 1541–1545. 1922.

Lolworth, Cambs. E. 784. 1928.

London, St. Stephen's Chapel. E. 20. 1927.

London, Westminster Abbey. E. 513–515. 1915: E. 194. 1926: E. 511–512. E. 516. 517. 1915: E. 540–544. 1915: E. 678. 1930: E. 22. 1927: E. 523–538. 1915.

Malmesbury, Wilts. E. 682. 1930.

Melbourne, Derby. E. 785. 1928.

Meon Stoke, Hants. E. 2804. 1923.

Newington, Kent. E. 23. 1927: E. 684. 685. 1930: E. 1340. 1341. 1924.

Norwich Cathedral. E. 470. 471. 1915: E. 482. 483. 1915: E. 789–790. 1928.

Oxford, Christchurch Cathedral. E. 795–799. 1928: E. 811–814. 1928.

Preston, Kent. E. 687. 1930.

Raunds, Northants. E. 819. 1928.

Rochester Cathedral, Kent. E. 1342–1343. 1924: E. 1350–1351. 1924: E. 1059–1063. 1925: E. 489. 1915: E. 181–188. 1926: E. 820. 1928.

Sarratt, Herts. E. 550–552. 1930: E. 700–702. 1930.

Shudy Camps, Cambs. E. 703. 1930.

Soberton, Hants. E. 1064. 1925.

South Newington, Oxon. E. 3429–3437. 1931.

Trotton, Sussex. E. 825–832. 1928.

Wells Cathedral. E. 715. 716. 1930.

West Chiltington, Sussex. E. 415. 423. 425. 1915: E. 834. 1928.

Wimborne Minster, Dorset, E. 730. 1930.

Winchester Cathedral, Hants. E. 555. 557. 558. 1930: E. 576–588. 1930. E. 732. 757. 758. 1930.

Wood Eaton, Oxon. E. 3456–3458. 1931.

York Minster. E. 835. 1928: E. 559–561. 1915.

DRAWINGS BY MONICA BARDSWELL IN THE VICTORIA AND ALBERT MUSEUM

Limpenhoe, Norfolk. Copy of painting by Winter. E. 119–121. 1932.

South Burlingham, Norfolk. E. 2256. 1924.

INDEX TO CHAPTERS I–V

PLATES

1. The Destruction of Job's Children. The Messengers of Misfortune. St. Stephen's Chapel, Westminster.

2. The Adoration of the Magi; St. George, and Edward III with his sons: St. Stephen's Chapel, Westminster.

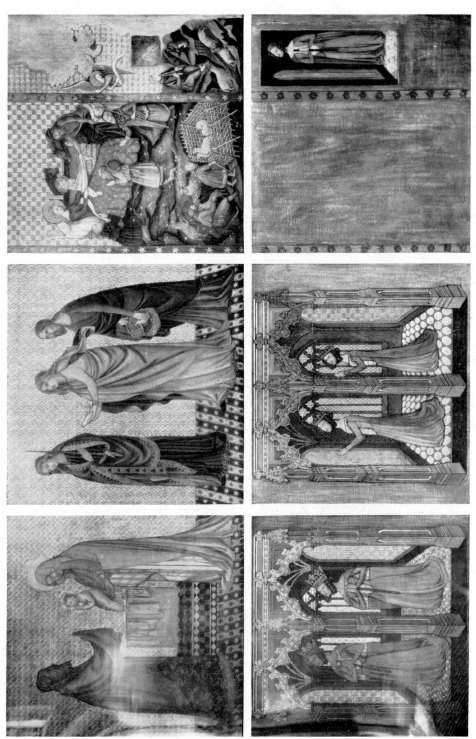

3. The Presentation in the Temple and other subjects; Queen Philippa and her daughters; St. Stephen's Chapel, Westminster.

4. King and Attendants; detail from the Adoration of the Magi; St. Stephen's Chapel, Westminster.

5. St. George, Edward III and his sons; St. Stephen's Chapel, Westminster.

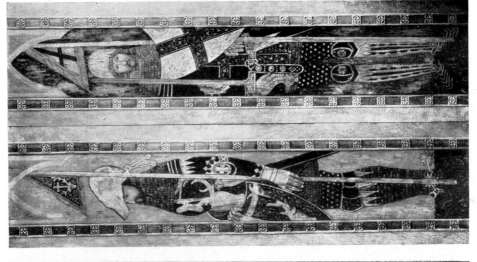

(b)

(a)

6. *(a)* Two of the Daughters of Queen Philippa. *(b)* Two Warrior Saints, St. Stephen's Chapel, Westminster.

(a)

(b)

7. (a) ? Henry III: (b) ? Edward Ist: paintings on the Sedilia, Westminster Abbey.

(a)

(b)

8. (a) Head of a Seraph, from the Majesty in the Chapter House, Westminster Abbey:
(b) The Blessed Virgin, from a painting in the Tower of London.

(a)

(b)

9. (a) Head of the Blessed Virgin; (b) Head of St. Michael the Archangel; from a painting in the Tower of London.

10. St. Michael the Archangel (part of figure); from a painting in the Tower of London.

(a)   (b)

11. (a) Apostle, Ante-Reliquary Chapel, Norwich Cathedral;
(b) St. William of York, Presbytery, St. Alban's Cathedral.

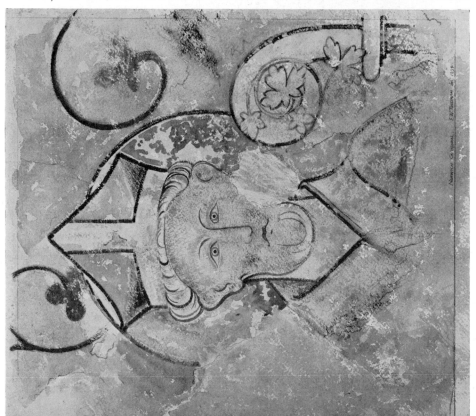

12. (a) Head of St. Nicholas: (b) Head of St. Richard of Chichester: Ante-Reliquary Chapel, Norwich Cathedral.

13. Tester over the Tomb of the Black Prince, Canterbury Cathedral.

14. One of the Signs of the Evangelists, from the Tester over the Tomb of the Black Prince, Canterbury, Cathedral.

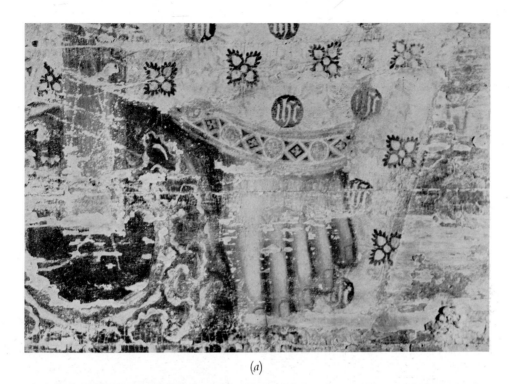

(a)

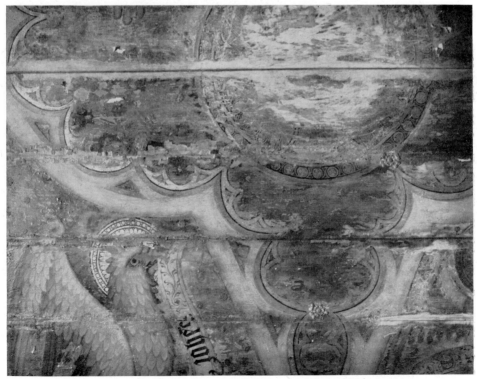

(b)

15. (a) and (b) Details from the Tester over the Tomb of the Black Prince, Canterbury Cathedral.

(a)　　　　　　　　　　　　　　　　(b)

16. South Newington, Oxfordshire; (a) The Blessed Virgin and Child; (b) St. Margaret of Antioch.

17. South Newington, Oxfordshire: Martyrdom of St. Thomas of Canterbury.

18. South Newington, Oxfordshire; Execution of Blessed Thomas Earl of Lancaster.

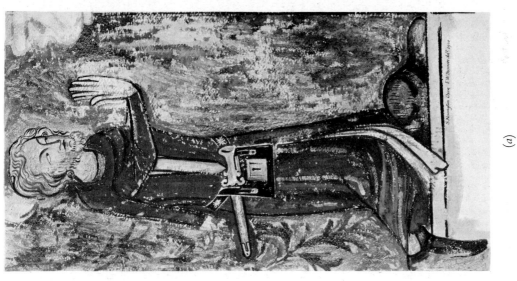

(a)

(b)

19. South Newington, Oxfordshire; (a) Figure of Donor; (b) Head of St. Thomas of Canterbury.

20. South Newington, Oxfordshire; The Annunciation.

21. Croughton, Northamptonshire: The Massacre of the Innocents and the Flight into Egypt.

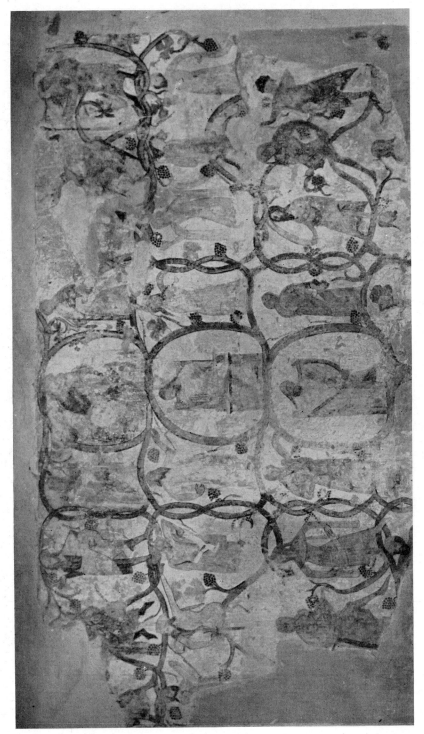

22. Weston Longville, Norfolk: The Jesse Tree.

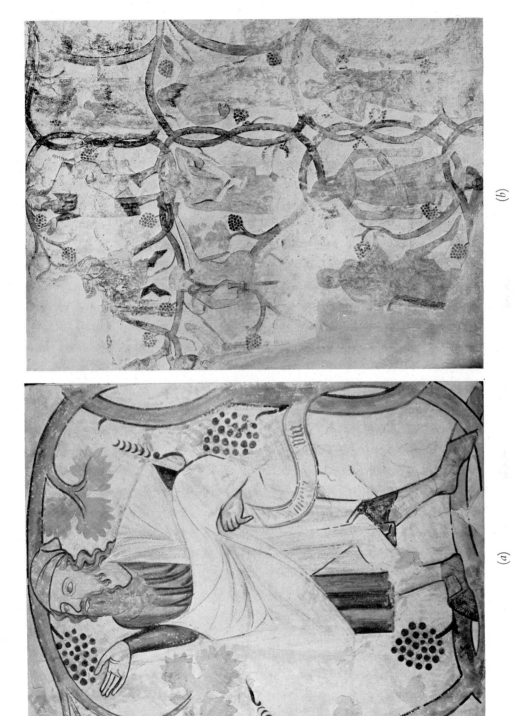

(b)

(a)

23. Weston Longville, Norfolk: (a) A Prophet, from the Jesse Tree; (b) Section of Jesse Tree.

24. Weston Longville, Norfolk; A King, from the Jesse Tree.

25. Forthampton Court, near Tewkesbury: St. Edward and the Pilgrim.

26. Christ Church, Oxford: decoration on the vaulting of the south choir aisle.

(b)

(a)

27. (a) and (b) Christ Church, Oxford; Dancing Angels.

28. Exeter Cathedral: painted hanging on the Sedilia.

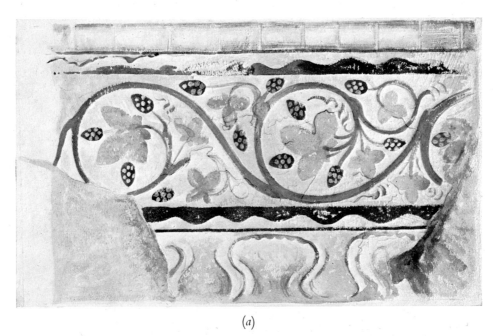

(a)

(b)

29. (a) Ornament, Norwich Cathedral: (b) Moulton, Norfolk: The Works of Mercy.

30. Chalgrove, Oxfordshire: north wall of chancel.

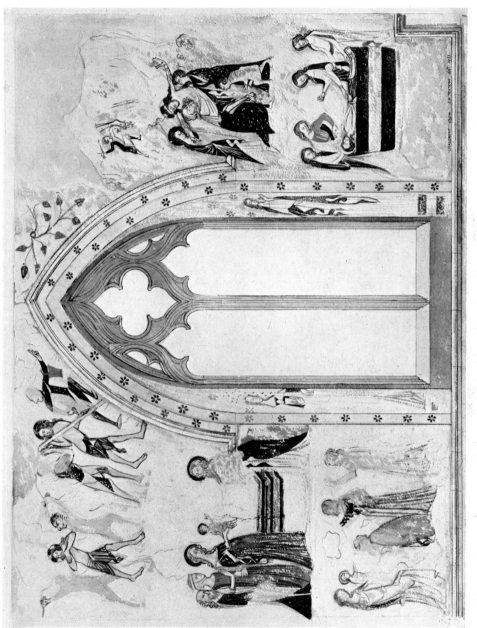

31. Chalgrove, Oxfordshire; north wall, eastern section.

32. Chalgrove, Oxfordshire; east wall of chancel.

33. Chalgrove, Oxfordshire; The Descent from the Cross.

34. Chalgrove, Oxfordshire; The Ascension.

35. Chalgrove, Oxfordshire; The Gathering of the Apostles and the Neighbours.

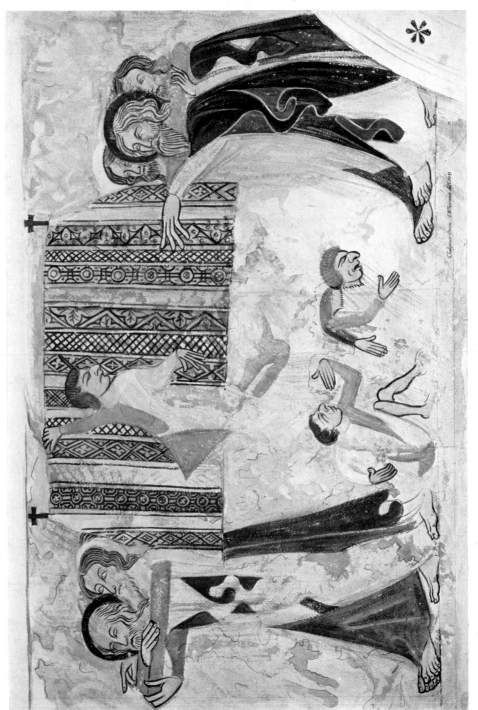

36. Chalgrove, Oxfordshire; The Funeral of the Blessed Virgin.

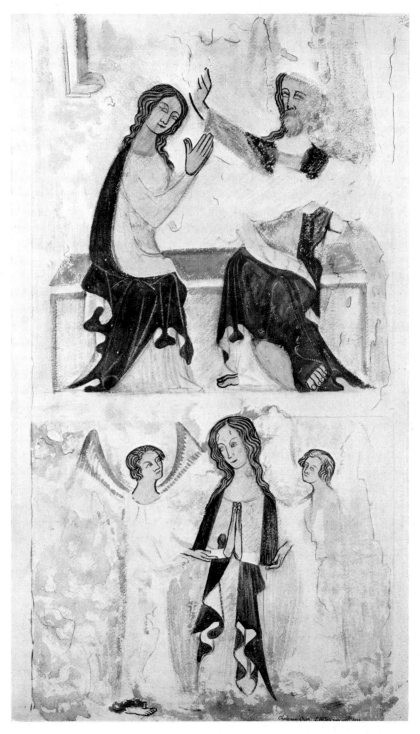

37. Chalgrove, Oxfordshire; The Assumption of the Blessed Virgin, and
her Coronation.

38. Chalgrove, Oxfordshire; The Reception of the Girdle by the Apostles.

(b)

(a)

39. Chalgrove, Oxfordshire; (a) The Figure of Christ, from the Resurrection; (b) Detail from the Assumption of the Blessed Virgin.

(b)

(a)

40. Chalgrove, Oxfordshire; (a) Head of an Angel, from the Assumption of the Blessed Virgin; (b) The Kiss of Judas, from the Betrayal.

(a)

(b)

41. Longthorpe Tower, near Peterborough, Northamptonshire:
(a) ? St. Francis Silencing the Singing Birds;
(b) Apostles with Scrolls Bearing Sentences from the Creed.

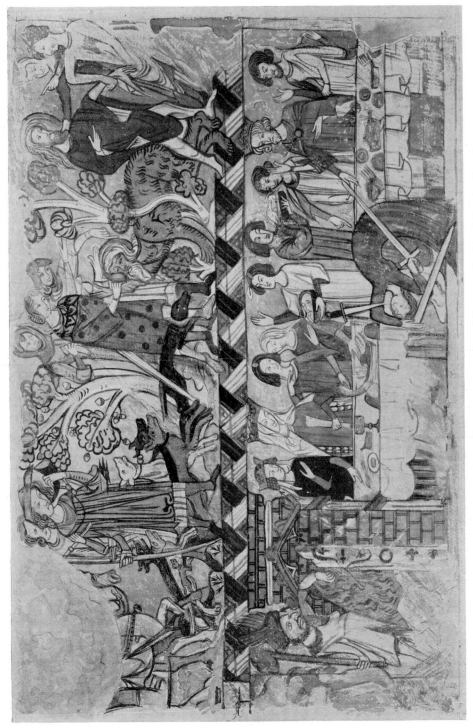

42. Idsworth, Hampshire: "Hunting Scene" and "History" of St. John the Baptist.

43. Idsworth, Hampshire; Detail of Hunting Scene.

44. Idsworth, Hampshire; Detail of Hunting Scene.

45. Idsworth, Hampshire; Herodias and Attendants.

46. Idsworth, Hampshire; St. Peter and St. Paul.

47. Burton Latimer, Northamptonshire: the Martyrdom of St. Catherine of Alexandria.

48. Burton Latimer, Northamptonshire; Figure of Maxentius.

49. Wendens Ambo, Essex: St. Margaret of Antioch Approached by Olybrius.

(b)

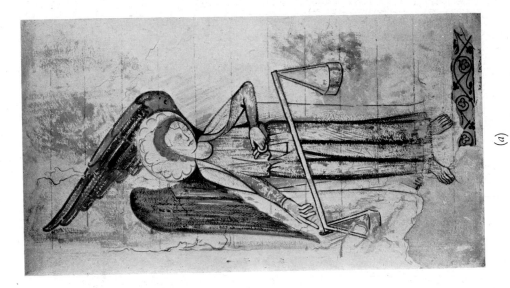

(a)

50. Rotherfield, Sussex: (a) The Weighing of Souls; (b) Wendens Ambo, Essex: St. Margaret of Antioch Taught by
her Nurse.

(a)   (b)

51. Selling, Kent; (<i>a</i>) St. Peter: (<i>b</i>) St. John the Evangelist.</div>

(a)   (b)

52   (a) Christ Church, Oxford: musician, on vaulting of the south choir aisle:
(b) Selling, Kent: St. Bartholomew.

(a)

(b)

53. Selling, Kent: (a) Head of St. John the Evangelist: (b) Head of St. Paul.

(b)

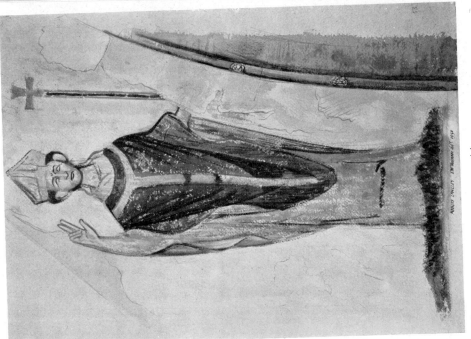

(a)

54. Abbots Langley, Hertfordshire: (a) St. Thomas of Canterbury: (b) St. Laurence.

(a)   (b)

55. Sanderstead, Surrey: (a) St. Edmund, King and Martyr;
Heacham, Norfolk: (b) St. John the Baptist.

(b)   (c)

(a)

56. (a) Starston, Norfolk: Burial Scene. (b) and (c) Consecration Crosses.

57. Clifton Campville, Staffordshire: Majesty, with donors.

58. Ducklington, Oxfordshire: The Trinity.

(a)

(b)

(c)

(d)

59. Chalgrave, Bedfordshire: (a-c,) heraldic and other decoration;
Inglesham, Wiltshire: (d) ornament.

(a)

(b)

(c)

60. (a) Inglesham, Wiltshire: drapery;
(b) and (c) Broughton, Buckinghamshire: stencilled pattern; painted hanging.

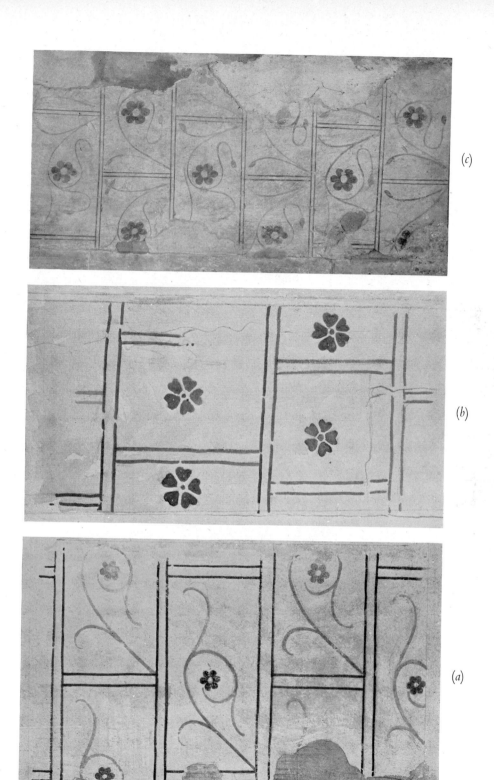

61. Inglesham, Wiltshire: (*a*) Masonry Pattern. Chalgrave, Bedfordshire:
(*b*) Masonry Pattern. Selling, Kent: (*c*) Masonry Pattern.

62. Paston, Norfolk: St. Christopher.